Spanish/English Contrasts
A Course in Spanish Linguistics

Second edition

M. Stanley Whitley

Georgetown Universit
Washington, D.(

Georgetown University Press, Washington, D.C.

Printed in the United States of America

10 9 8 7 6 5 4 3 2 1 2002

This volume is printed on acid-free offset book paper.

Library of Congress Cataloging-in-Publication Data

Whitley, Melvin Stanley, 1948-
Spanish/English contrasts : a course in Spanish linguistics / M. Stanley Whitney.—2nd ed.
p. cm.
Includes bibliographical references and index.
ISBN 0-87840-381-7 (pkb. :alk. paper)
1. Spanish language—Grammar, Comparative—English. 2. English language—Grammar, Comparative—Spanish. I. Title.

PC4099 .W45 2002
465—dc21 2002022868

To Mary Jo, Steven, and Philip—
my wife, my sons, my love.

Contents

Preface to the second edition

It was gratifying to receive the invitation from the Georgetown University Press to prepare a new edition of *Spanish/English Contrasts*. The challenge was to update the book without altering its fundamental and, I believe, unique scope: a scholarly description of the Spanish language and its differences from English, with an emphasis on applied linguistics. The years since the first edition have seen an explosion of work in all of the areas addressed by this book, from phonology, grammar, and semantics to pragmatics, sociolinguistics, and second language acquisition. At the same time, the theories and research paradigms in each area have grown so diverse and complex that it is a greater challenge now to integrate their findings in a one-volume work aimed at both a general audience and students of Spanish linguistics.

This edition therefore incorporates insights from recent research, some new exercises, and additional topics (especially in chapter 16). The overall descriptive framework, however, is still based on a standard theory broadened to accommodate other areas and other data. Obviously, that theory does not represent the way that many of us "do linguistics" now in publications directed to fellow specialists in the field; in the same way, an introduction to astronomy differs from current astrophysical research. For example, this book depicts *e*-epenthesis (*spray* → *espray*), the passive, and pronominalization as rules, respectively phonological, transformational, and pragmatic. There are other ways to account for them given richer theories of constraints, lexical specifications, and discourse strategies; indeed, approaches such as Optimality Theory have dispensed with rules as formal devices. Instructors with more advanced students may wish to point out alternative treatments and encourage discussion of them. But for the many Structure of Spanish students who are more versed in literature than in linguistics, who are primarily interested in teaching, translation, and other practical applications, and who expect a general overview of the language from pronunciation to discourse rather than concentration on one theory or research area, it is my experience that rules are still an effective, intuitive means of quickly encapsulating important processes and relationships to promote discussion and further exploration. Other introductory surveys such as Fromkin and Rodman 1998 and O'Grady et al. 2001 do likewise, using a modified standard theory to present the basics and to integrate other areas. If this book sometimes seems to overemphasize those basics, it is because of my abiding concern over the gulf between what linguists have long known and now take for granted, and what authors of Spanish language teaching materials keep writing.

Users of the first edition will find that although some discussions have been condensed to make room for new material, the overall structure of the chapters has been retained and the exercises continue to balance application, analysis, discussion, and exploration. For students with little prior study of linguistics, special terms and formalisms are explained as they come up, and the introduction and chapters 1, 5, and 14 introduce fundamental notions that can be expanded on as needed. Also as in the first edition, in-text references such as **(v. 12.1.2)** = 'see (*vide, véase*) section 12.1.2' tell readers where a point has been reentered from, or where it will be treated more fully later; alternatively, they can always consult the indexes in the back. For economy, grammatical terminology is often abbreviated (a common practice in linguistics), but readers will find abbreviations and symbols identified in the indexes. One change in notation is that this edition adheres closely to IPA usage. Some users may have different preferences, but it is best to avoid misunderstanding caused by idiosyncratic symbols—which unfortunately has happened in Spanish linguistics (see discussion in Whitley 1995b). Instructors and students who need an IPA computer font for their work with this book may download one (still gratis, at this writing) from SIL International at http://www.sil.org/.

While some users suggested a new edition in Spanish, most of the responses that the Press and I received favored the continued use of English. The reason is that many students are fluent in Spanish but still find the complex metalanguage of tense, aspect, mood, discourse functions, and so forth more transparent through English—and after all, making the fruits of linguistic research on Spanish more accessible to the public is a major goal of this book. My own policy with *Spanish/English Contrasts* has been to assign the material for out-of-class preparation and then to discuss and apply it during class in Spanish, referring students to the glossary in appendix 1 for terminology. This bilingual approach has worked well, meeting the needs of both English-dominant and Spanish-dominant students in the class.

I again acknowledge here my debt to the work of others, from oft-quoted pioneers in the field to contemporary researchers. I have tried to show some of the ways in which the latter continue to build on the former so that readers understand how scholarly views have evolved. But even with additions I found particularly useful, space limitations made it impossible to do justice to all citations, and the list of references at the end is still far from a bibliography of Spanish linguistics. Given the diversification of the field today, students should be urged to pursue topics of special interest to them by means of the Modern Language Association's bibliography, although today an increasing number of monographs can be found on the Web too.

Special thanks are due to colleagues in the field for their encouragement and suggestions, and to Gail Grella and Deborah Weiner of the Georgetown University Press for their support and assistance with this edition. And as in the first edition, I acknowledge my students, whose problems, questions, and advances in language acquisition continue to stimulate my own work as a Spanish teacher and linguist.

Chapter 0

General introduction: Language and interlanguage

0.1 Language, lects, and linguistics. Language can be thought of as a communication system of a specifically human type that conveys meaning by a medium such as sound. It consists of at least six interdependent subsystems: PHONOLOGY, the speech sounds and rules governing them; MORPHOLOGY, the inflection and derivation of words; SYNTAX, the principles of word order and of phrase and sentence construction; the LEXICON or vocabulary; SEMANTICS, word and sentence meaning; and PRAGMATICS, the background sociocultural conventions for adapting the output of the other components appropriately to the context or situation. For many languages, there is also an ORTHOGRAPHY, an alternative output system using written marks instead of sound.

The past century has witnessed a variety of proposals as to how these components function. The model shown in figure 0.1 synthesizes many of these proposals, showing (with arrows) their interaction with each other as we use them to speak, read, write, and listen. It greatly oversimplifies by omitting many internal mechanisms, by glossing over issues that have been controversial, and by neglecting the multitude of links to other kinds of human knowledge and behavior, but it should suffice for our purposes in this book.

Ordinarily, we treat a given language as a general system shared by all members of its speech community; otherwise, notions such as "Spanish language" or "Spanish-speaking" make no sense. Yet the system is not homogeneous; each component (e.g., phonology, syntax, lexicon) varies with the DIALECTS (or GEOLECTS) of particular regions, the SOCIOLECTS of different social groups or classes, and the sexual differences that make up GENDERLECTS. In fact, each individual has his or her own IDIOLECT, subtly unique in its typical modes of expression. Such variations in LECTS (a neutral term for all varieties) inevitably turn up when we compare two world languages such as Spanish and English, each with some 400 million speakers and still growing.

Figure 0.1. A model of component systems of language

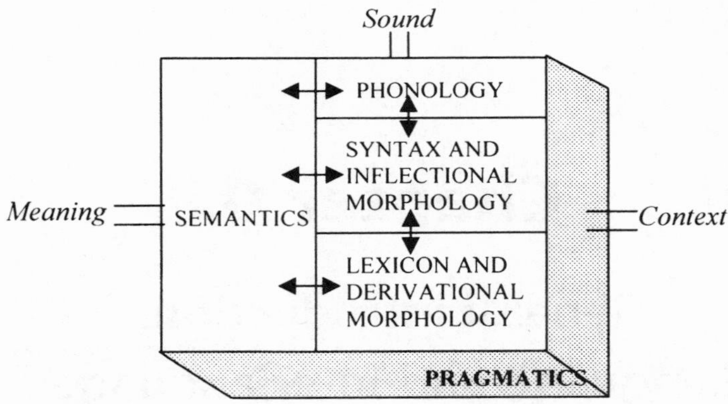

Linguistics, the scientific study of language, has several branches. THEORETICAL LINGUISTICS focuses on the nature of the components in figure 0.1 against a general background of language and cognition. DESCRIPTIVE LINGUISTICS studies how one or more of the components operates in particular languages and lects; it may take a SYNCHRONIC approach by describing the existing patterns of the language as revealed through analysis of data from speakers or writers, or a DIACHRONIC approach by studying how the system has changed over time (as in the history of English or Spanish). APPLIED LINGUISTICS takes the insights of theoretical and descriptive linguistics and applies them to such areas as translation, speech pathology, literary analysis, computer technology, sociopolitical issues, and language instruction, or SECOND LANGUAGE ACQUISITION (SLA). This last area is of special interest in this book.

0.2 Comparing and contrasting languages. One tool of applied linguistics is CONTRASTIVE ANALYSIS, which compares and contrasts two language systems (DiPietro 1971; James 1980; Selinker 1992). For there to be any meaningful comparison at all, it is assumed that languages share the same basic architectural blueprint and features: similar components, types of rules, units, constraints on these units, functions of the system, and cognitive bases. What differs is not the overall design (figure 0.1) but details of layout and furnishings. Contrastive analysis carries out parallel descriptions of language A and language B, notes similarities and differences, and predicts possible problems that A-speakers will have when they study B and vice versa, or that translators and interpreters may have in rendering A-messages in B and vice versa. Contrastive analysis is thus two-way, at least ideally; in practice, though, most such work in the United States has understandably taken English as the SOURCE LANGUAGE (i.e., the students' native or primary language, abbreviated as L1) and some other language as the TARGET LANGUAGE (the foreign or secondarily acquired language, L2). This book follows this orientation since we are interested in information that might help Spanish teachers and translators in a predominantly English-speaking country. For our purposes, then, English is the source language and Spanish the target language. Occasionally, however, it is helpful to reverse these roles; teachers who wonder why their students persist in confusing *ser* and *estar* can obtain a fresh perspective on the problem by imagining how they would go about explaining to Spanish-speaking students of English the similarly perplexing distinction of *make* vs. *do.*

0.2.1 Correspondences between languages. Contrastive analysis discerns three general categories of correspondences between two languages.

1. Language A has a feature (unit, distinction, pattern) *x* matched closely by an *x* in language B. Such a convergence arises in several ways. First, *x* may be a UNIVERSAL OF LANGUAGE: all languages have verbs, pronouns for 'I' and 'you', a syntactic unit definable as 'sentence', procedures for negating and conjoining, and numerous constraints on possible grammatical operations. Linguists take special interest in such universals because of what they indicate about the UNIVERSAL GRAMMAR of human language in general, apart from the PARTICULAR GRAMMAR of each language. Second, *x* may be shared because A and B are linguistic relatives that inherited *x* from their common ancestor. This is why Spanish, English, and other descendants of Proto-Indo-European (circa 4000–3000 B.C.) have irregular paradigms for *be*, relative pronouns, similar number and tense systems, a pervasive gender distinction, words for 'mother' beginning with *m-*, and much else in common. Third, *x* may be shared because of later linguistic and cultural cross-fertilization: English and Spanish have directly exchanged some words and share article systems, perfect tenses, and a sociolinguistic ritual involving *thanks/gracias* because of their West European upbringing. And fourth, the sharing of *x* may be a coincidence: English and Spanish both have a *ch* sound (/tʃ/) for no special reason at all.
2. Language A has a feature *x* that resembles B's *x* to some extent but differs in details of form, function, frequency, distribution, or conditions on usage. Examples here are legion for Spanish and English: their use of stress, their assignment of the roles of subject and object (cf. *gustar* and *like*), their formation and use of passives, their pronunciation of the vowel /u/ in *tú* and *too*, and so forth.
3. Language A has a feature *x,* which B lacks or which is rendered in terms of B's *y*, which operates quite differently. Thus, Spanish (but not English) distinguishes *ser/estar, tú/usted,* and the sounds *r/rr*; English (but not Spanish) distinguishes *make/do, his/her/their,* and the sounds *b/v.* Spanish has a conditional tense (*hablaría*) that partly corresponds in meaning to English *would*, but the latter is an auxiliary verb that carries other meanings as well and is subject to different grammatical restrictions.

0.2.2 Implications of the correspondences. Lado (1957) endorsed contrastive analysis for anticipating problems when students transfer their L1 rules, structures, and strategies to

L2. He defined this TRANSFER as follows before proceeding to study correspondences of the types we have just illustrated:

> Individuals tend to transfer the forms and meanings, and the distributions of forms and meanings, of their native language and culture to the foreign language and culture—both productively when attempting to speak the language and to act in the culture, and receptively when attempting to grasp and understand the language and the culture as practiced by natives. (p. 2)

This definition has since been critiqued (particularly the vagueness of "tend to") and refined, but Lado's point otherwise seems clear. Returning to our L1–L2 correspondences, we may predict that features of Category 1 have POSITIVE TRANSFER value in that they can be carried over with little modification, that is, with little comment from text or teacher. Features found to belong to Categories 2 and 3, however, have NEGATIVE TRANSFER value and may cause interference in students' use of L2. None of this is really new; teachers have traditionally recognized the difference by giving more attention to the pronunciation of *r/rr* and to the meaning of *tú/usted* (Category 3) than to the pronunciation of *ch* or to the meaning of *yo* (Category 1), and they already are quite aware of L1 interference in the "Spanglish" they deal with daily. Where contrastive analysis has more to offer is in areas such as the following.

Predicting degrees of difficulty. If, within Category 3 above, A has an *x/y* distinction that B merges into its *z*, then generally it should be easier for A-speakers to learn to use B's *z* for both *x* and *y* than for speakers of B to master an *x/y* contrast that they have never conceived of. More concretely, English distinguishes comparative/superlative and Spanish does not (*más* = both 'more' and 'most', v. 13.4.1); Spanish distinguishes pre- and postposed adjectives and English does not (*altos precios, precios altos = high prices,* v. 11.3.2). Learning both *más* and adjective position takes effort, but one predicts that English speakers will need more help with the latter than with the former.

Identifying specific problems. Every grammatical description is incomplete, and foreign language students must flesh out such descriptions by deducing consequences for specific cases, by inducing further principles from input and feedback, and by testing their tentative hypotheses about how the language works in further communicative experience. Given the severely limited contact time available to students in class situations, contrastive analysis can help to focus better on the relevant correspondences of Categories 2 and 3. That is, the entire language need not be (and cannot be) covered, and one should concentrate on those specific points identified as posing special problems, given the students' L1.

For example, French-speaking students of Spanish can pass lightly over *saber/conocer* since their *savoir/connaître* matches this distinction well enough (Terrell and Salgués 1979, 8), but Spanish *he hablado/hablé* is merged by their *j'ai parlé,* and the contrast between present perfect and preterite must receive considerable attention in the course syllabus for French speakers. For English-speaking students, however, the relative status of these two cases is exactly reversed. The contrast between *he hablado* and *hablé* is obvious to users of *I've spoken* and *I spoke,* but not the contrast between two kinds of knowing. Consequently, Spanish teachers in France and their counterparts in the United States do not present the same "grammar" of Spanish; nor should they, since their students come from different backgrounds.

In this regard, we should mention the case in which source equals target, that is, materials about *castellano* for native Spanish speakers. These materials are designed for an audience that mastered the language during childhood but needs guidance on certain standard usages: ambiguous cases of agreement, the plural of *frenesí* or *memorándum,* forms of uncommon verbs, subtleties of punctuation and syllabication, where to write *h* and accent marks, literary tense usages, and so forth. Such books tend to be silent on matters that natives get right intuitively but nonnatives are baffled by. Consequently, applied linguistics in the United States often relies on studies about Spanish by English-speaking teachers and linguists, who have posed and researched questions that may not occur to native speakers (García 1975, 275). To return to an earlier example, *ser/estar* is taken for granted by most native Spanish speakers, and the authoritative Real Academia (i.e., the Real Academia Española de la Lengua, or RAE) has little to say about it; but English-speaking linguists have revealed a great deal of information about these two verbs and their stages of acquisition. In contrast, a Costa Rican linguist who investigates *make/do* might visualize the problem better, and shed more light on it, than English-speaking grammarians.

Determining how a unit works in its own system. Linguists since Saussure ([1915] 1959) have stressed that the "value" or function of a unit must be defined in terms of the role it plays within its own system; units from different languages cannot be equated just because they look alike. In short, an apparent correspondence of Category 1 may turn out to be of Category 2 or even 3. For instance, English and Spanish have progressive verb forms that are formed similarly, and a situation described by *está lloviendo* can usually be described by *it's raining* also. Most textbooks therefore equate them and assume that students who learn the formation of *está lloviendo* can use it accurately. But contrastive analysis shows that these progressives fit into their respective systems quite differently (v. 7.2.2): *¿llueve?* can express the same situation as *¿está lloviendo?*, whereas *does it rain?* and *is it raining?* mean very different things. Hence, especially in the early part of a course, the progressive is not as essential in Spanish as it is in English; and when it is eventually taken up, it should be presented in terms of what it contributes within the Spanish tense system, not the differently operating system of English.

Assigning priorities on the basis of functional load. Some distinctions have a larger communicative weight or FUNCTIONAL LOAD than others; they are more fundamental, more frequent, even indispensable. Although two languages may share a distinction (Category 1), they may assign it different functional loads. For example, mood contrasts are possible in both languages (v. 7.3), but the functional load of the English subjunctive is vanishingly low, whereas the Spanish subjunctive contrasts sharply and frequently with the indicative and cannot be avoided. Although all textbooks devote attention to mood, one could argue that this topic deserves an earlier position in the syllabus (course sequence) than is usual.

Dealing with variation. Some grammarians treat variants by imposing a ruling for "correct" usage: use *x* here, *y* there, but never *z* because it is improper. Rather than *prescribing* such a *ruling*, linguists prefer to *describe* the actual *rules* that native speakers apply to their communication. For instance, many books give an elaborate account of where to use each relative pronoun in Spanish, and despite its complexity, students should try to master that account if it reflects native usage. But linguistic analysis of current spoken and written Spanish has shown that it does not; as one native-speaking teacher once said of such a lesson, "¡No decimos esto!" In some cases, two or more of the supposedly distinct forms are used interchangeably (v. 13.3), while in other cases a trend has emerged that is not reflected by the traditional canon of rules passed down from one book to the next. Contrastive analysis can suggest improved ways to present Spanish usage to English speakers (whose relative forms vary too) so as to avoid the transfer we hear in **la mujer quien lo hizo = the woman who did it.* (The asterisk means 'ungrammatical, wrong' in linguistics.)

Understanding errors. Foreign-language teachers have abundant experience with diagnosing their own students' problems, but as a research area, ERROR ANALYSIS (Corder 1967; Richards 1974) more systematically gathers data from groups of learners (or from single learners in some longitudinal studies) and analyzes those data for apparent sources of error, with the goal of understanding the processes in L2 acquisition. Error analysis has also stimulated research into native speakers' reactions to different kinds of learner errors (Omaggio 1993, 270–76; James 1998, 204–34). It relies on contrastive analysis to pinpoint errors due to interference from L1 (and from previously studied L2s as well), although as we will see in the next section, that is not the only source of student problems.

0.3 Interlanguage and sources of problems. There is more to what happens in the classroom than the imparting and receiving of new words, new endings, new sounds, and new structures. Students adopt a continually changing INTERLANGUAGE (Selinker 1972, 1992) that lies between the source language and target language and draws on both; but it also reflects the varying ways in which individuals are internalizing, sorting out, and applying what they take in from the input they receive, and not everything can be attributed to transfer from L1.

Among the problems that a contrastive analysis cannot account for are the following (see Van Els et al. 1984). First, different learners show different degrees and types of transfer. One invents a verb **expectar* or **involvar* and others do not; some try an -'*s* possessive on Spanish nouns while most accept *de* (supported by positive transfer of another English pattern using *of*); many say **yo veo tú* with English grammar while others make the adjustment to *te veo*. Second, many errors have an INTRALINGUAL origin (within L2) rather than an INTERLINGUAL one (transfer from L1). Thus, when students confuse *sentir* and *sentar* or overgeneralize their *sient-* (**sientía* **sientaba*), the problem is not due to L1 (except insofar as English *feel* and *sit* are dissimilar and give no help with *ie* stem changes). Third, instead of projecting L1 patterns onto L2, students may just avoid alien L2 items. For example, to the frustration of the teacher who sets up an exercise to practice Spanish pronouns, English speakers may repeat the teacher's phrase (a tactic called CUE-COPYING) rather than risking errors with tricky un-English pronouns: "¿Terminaste la tarea que asigné ayer?" "Sí, terminé la tarea que asigné ayer." Fourth, there is MISLEARNING, as when students merge *si* + present indicative (*Si estudias . . .*) and *si* + past subjunctive (*Si estudiaras . . .*) as *si* + present subjunctive (**Si estudies . . .*)—contrary to all of their input in either language. Finally, learners from all language backgrounds show certain similarities in DEVELOPMENTAL STAGES they pass through in acquiring a given item. One such stage is a tendency to simplify expression by omitting grammatical words (FUNCTORS) such as articles, prepositions, and auxiliaries, even when their L1 uses equivalents.

It has been recognized for some time (e.g., Liceras 1993, 30; Silva-Corvalán 1995, 5) that in this combination of transfer with other processes, learners' interlanguage resembles any other contact language. A CONTACT LANGUAGE is one that shows effects from, or mixture with, another language in bilingual situations. For example, in San Antonio Spanish (García 1995) there are intralingual extensions of Spanish patterns (*la problema, pidir, juegar*) as well as apparent English influence (*taxas* 'taxes', *en los sábados* 'on Saturdays'). Nevertheless, SLA in the last decades of the twentieth century focused increasingly on alternative (nontransfer) sources of error, culminating in the "L2=L1 Hypothesis" of Dulay and Burt (1974): L2 is acquired in the same way as L1 and errors can be regarded as developmental and intralingual. Originally extrapolated from their interpretation of data from children in ESL (English as a second language), their hypothesis was soon generalized and asserted as a professional "belief": "Learners' first languages are no longer believed to interfere with their attempts to acquire second language grammar" (Dulay, Burt, and Krashen 1982, 5). This development "bewildered" foreign language teachers (Rivers 1981, 82), who witness L1 interference daily in their students' speech and writing. It was also generally rejected by linguists such as those represented in Gass and Selinker 1983, who confirmed transfer of various types as they wrestled with a more adequate theory for it. Further interlanguage research has continued to reveal the impact of L1 on all subsystems of L2 and the value of contrastive analysis in understanding it (Selinker 1992; Sheen 1996).

While some continue in their belief that grammar, at least, shows "few demonstrable first-language transfers" (Lipski 1998, 250), the SLA mainstream has backed off from the Dulay-Burt position, recognizing transfer as one of several influences on interlanguage; VanPatten (1987, 163 fn.) even traced error patterns to dialect differences in students' L1. As Anderson (1983, 177) summed up this swing of the pendulum, "although we tried to make it go away, transfer kept coming back." He noted that it is the apparent similarities between languages (our Category 2), rather than the starkest differences, that seem to invite the most transfer, and in rearticulating Lado's definition, he developed a "Transfer to Somewhere" hypothesis (v. 16.3.2) that recognizes mutual interaction between L1 transfer and developmental processes.

0.4 The limits of linguistics in language teaching. Contrastive analysis, error analysis, and SLA theory are obviously intended not for student consumption but for teachers who wish to understand what happens in language learning and why. Consequently, although some of the facts revealed by linguistics can be directly applied to improved presentations, activities, syllabi, and remediation, others will be more useful to teachers as background information for the decisions they must make about selection and emphases; such is the case, for example, with much of the dialect variation surveyed in chapter 3. But the issues in foreign language education are multifaceted, and linguists do not presume to answer all the teacher's questions. They have had a great deal to say about models of language, the processes and stages of language learning, the facts of language and language usage, the sources of errors, and the principles of language testing and practice but have had less to contribute on issues such as theories of education and methods for stimulating student interest. They are among the first to admit that improved knowledge of *ser* vs. *estar,* for instance, does not by itself ensure the ability to teach and practice this distinction successfully in the classroom. The methodology of foreign language teaching is complemented by linguistics, not replaced by it, and while the two are often coupled in works addressed to teachers (e.g., Rivers, Azevedo, and Heflin 1988), they are generally recognized as distinct disciplines with their own contributions to teacher preparation and training. (See the selected bibliographies in Lipski 1998; Long 1999; and Lafford 2000.)

But what value linguistics does have in pedagogy—or in translation, computer science, literary analysis, or any other application—is predicated on the assumption that correct information about language (in general) and the languages at hand (in particular) is a necessary, if not sufficient, condition for success. It is up to the users of that information to make professional decisions about how to apply it most effectively to their own work with language.

PART ONE

PHONOLOGY

Chapter 1

Introduction to phonology

1.0 Phonology vs. orthography. Human messages are sent by sound, gesture, written marks, body movement, and electronic impulses, but the usual channels are speech and writing. Some people confuse the two by taking speech to be an imperfect reflection of the "real" language, the written one. But although writing is important, phonology is a distinct system, and the more fundamental one through which we acquire the rest of language as children. Writing is learned later, if at all—billions of people around the world use their languages without the benefit of written marks. Moreover, writing is only a partial rendition of language, ignoring aspects such as intonation (the inflection of the voice) and stress (as in the difference between the noun *object* and the verb *object*). We should also note that the rules of language are generally based on pronunciation rather than orthography. For example, Spanish *y* 'and' is said to change to *e* before the vowel *i*. What is actually meant is the sound [i], not the letter *i*, since the change also occurs before *hi*: *hijos e hijas*. But it would still be wrong to state the change as occurring before the spellings *i* and *hi*, for it does not apply in *agua y hielo* (where *hi* represents a sound that is not the vowel [i] at all).

As Moulton (1970, 117) explained to teachers and students of foreign languages:

> No ordinary writing system was ever designed to meet the needs of people who are *learning* the language; it was designed only for those who already *know* the language. No one can hope to achieve much success by looking at black marks on paper (the writing) and then trying to make appropriate noises (the language). Instead, he must first learn some of the language and then note how what he has learned happens to be symbolized in writing. Writing is not a set of directions telling us how a language should be pronounced; it is a method of reminding us on paper of things that we already know how to say.

For this reason, linguists focus primarily on phonology rather than orthography as the basic signaling system of language.

1.1 Review of phonetics. The description of speech sounds, or PHONES, is called PHONETICS, and a representation of pronunciation in terms of those phones is called a PHONETIC REPRESENTATION (or TRANSCRIPTION). Bypassing the inconsistencies of language-specific orthographies, linguists adopt precisely defined phonetic symbols and enclose them in square brackets ([ ]) for a phonetic representation. The most widespread transcriptional system is that of the International Phonetic Alphabet (IPA), which is adopted with minor additions in this book. Whenever possible, the IPA's symbols reflect their usual values in the Roman alphabet; thus, for the sound spelled *b* in English *bat* (French *bas,* German *böse,* Spanish *bajo,* and so on), there was early consensus on the representation [b]. But for many of the phones we will take up, the IPA arrived at symbols that seem unusual in terms of English or Spanish orthography: [j], for example, is neither the Spanish *jota* nor the English *j* of *jot* but the semivowel spelled *i* in Spanish *pie* and *y* in English *yet.*

It is not enough merely to symbolize phones; their articulation must also be described. For example, [b] is a consonant made by stopping the airstream with both lips while the vocal cords are vibrating, a description that is summarized by the label *voiced bilabial stop*. The next sections will review the descriptive terms found in most introductory courses in linguistics.

1.1.1 Classes of sounds. The three major classes of phones are vowels (V), glides (G), and consonants (C). VOWELS typically function as the peaks of syllables (v. 2.3) and include sounds such as the [i] of English *see/sea* and Spanish *si* and *y*, and the [u] of English *Sue* and Spanish *su*. GLIDES (or SEMIVOWELS) include sounds such as the [j] beginning English *you* (and occurring after the *f* of *few*, [fju]), and the [w] of English *we*. To get a better feel for glides, one can pronounce a two-vowel sequence like [i-a] or [u-a] and then squeeze it into a single syllable, producing [ja], [wa]. The key difference between [i] and [j], and between [u] and [w], is therefore the syllabicity of the vowel, and another way to transcribe [j] and [w] is as [i̯] and [u̯] (equally IPA-approved), the underarch meaning 'nonsyllabic'.

CONSONANTS are articulated with a greater constriction in the vocal tract than for glides, and they occur around vowels in the formation of syllables. Consonants are divided into three subclasses. NASALS (symbolized as a group by N) include the [m] and [n] of English *man* and Spanish *mano* and are characterized by nasal resonance, as the name implies. In LIQUIDS (L), there is some kind of [l] or [r] articulation with a sound that is vowel- and consonant-like. In OBSTRUENTS (O), the airstream is obstructed, either completely as with the [t] of English *stew* and Spanish *tú*, or just to the extent that frictionlike noise results, as in the [s] of English *see* and Spanish *si.*

1.1.2 Voicing. There are two muscle folds inside the larynx known as the vocal cords, which in normal breathing are spread apart, leaving an opening called the GLOTTIS. But they can be pulled together to vibrate as air from the lungs passes up between them. This vibration, called VOICE, can be felt by touching one's Adam's apple (the front of the larynx) while saying a sound such as [u]. Sounds that have voice are called VOICED;

Figure 1.1. The vocal tract

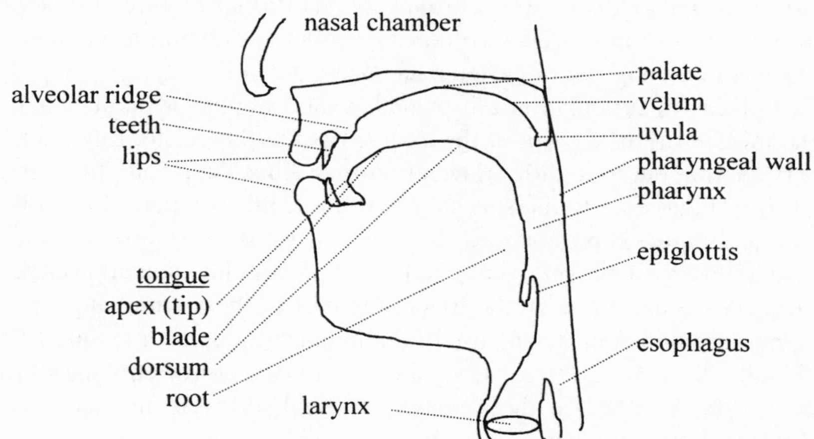

sounds in which the vocal cords are spread apart instead of vibrating are VOICELESS. V, G, N, and L are generally voiced and are heard as resonance resulting from the passage of a voiced airstream through the nasal or oral cavities. Because of this resonance, they are grouped together as SONORANTS. Obstruents, on the other hand, may be voiced or voiceless, and many languages have pairs of them contrasting in voicing: the [f] and [s] of English *fat* and *race* are voiceless, as opposed to the [v] and [z] of *vat* and *raise,* which are voiced.

The rate and energy of the vibration can be modulated for additional effects. When the vocal cords vibrate faster, the pitch rises, as in the question *Do you see?*; when they vibrate more strongly, their sound is louder and is perceived as STRESS. Stress is transcribed by an accent on the louder vowel (*óbject, objéct*) or by a vertical stroke before its syllable (*ˈobject obˈject*); lack of stress is usually left unmarked but can be shown by a breve if desired (*objéct* = *ŏbjéct*).

1.1.3 Place and manner of articulation. Consonants and glides are described in terms of two other characteristics: where they are made (place or point of articulation) and how they are made (manner of articulation). The PLACE of articulation is taken to be the point in the vocal tract where the constriction occurs (see figure 1.1). For sounds such as the [p] of *pat* and the [f] of *fat,* this is LABIAL (made with the lips), specifically BILABIAL ('both lips') for [p] and LABIODENTAL ('lip plus teeth') for [f]. For sounds such as the [t] of *tin,* the [θ] spelled by *th* in *thin,* and the [ʃ] spelled by the *sh* of *shin,* the articulation is CORONAL, meaning that the forward part of the tongue approaches or contacts some point in the area between the teeth and palate. Within this coronal zone, finer points of articulation are distinguished: DENTAL when there is contact with the upper teeth (as in [θ]), ALVEOLAR when there is contact with the gum ridge or alveolae behind the upper teeth (as in English [t]), and ALVEOPALATAL or POSTALVEOLAR when there is contact with both the gum ridge and the forward part of the palate (as in [ʃ]). Coronal sounds further require at times the specification of which part of the tongue—tip (apex) or blade—is being used, and whether the tongue surface is relatively flat or curled back (RETROFLEX).

Five other places of articulation are palatal, velar, labiovelar, uvular, and glottal. In PALATALS, the middle (never the tip) of the tongue rises to the palate; English has only one palatal, the [j] of *you*, but as a glide [j] never quite reaches the palate. In VELARS, the back (dorsum) of the tongue rises to the soft palate (velum); this is where [k] (spelled *c* or *k* as in *cook* and *q* as in *quit*) is pronounced. In LABIOVELARS, there is simultaneous labial and velar constriction; [w] is labiovelar, but like [j] it is only a glide that approaches a point of articulation. UVULARS are made on the uvula, the part of the velum hanging down in the back of the mouth. English makes no use of the uvula, although some Spanish dialects do (v. 3.1.8). Finally, in GLOTTAL articulations there is no oral constriction at all; instead, the vocal cords modify the sound without voicing it. English [h] as in *hat* is often termed a glottal or laryngeal fricative since it is just the aspiration or rushing of air through the open larynx and vocal tract.

MANNERS of articulation are named for the degree of constriction. In STOPS (or plosives) such as [p] and [t], there is a complete blockage of the airstream; in FRICATIVES (or spirants) such as [f] and [s], the airstream continues through with noisy turbulence due to a constriction that narrows the passage without stopping the flow. Thus, while stops and fricatives are both obstruents, they are analyzed as differing in their "continuance." Many subtypes are distinguished: the stop can be imploded or exploded, released or unreleased, pronounced with or without an [h]-like puff of air, and so on. Fricatives are of two main subtypes, SIBILANT (hissy), as with [s] and [ʃ], and nonsibilant, as with [f] and [θ]. Finally, it is possible to articulate a stop released as a fricative, a manner of articulation called AFFRICATE. The consonant spelled *ch* in English *chat* and Spanish *chato* is an affricate, symbolized in the IPA as a stop-fricative combination [tʃ].

There are various manners of sonorant articulation. In NASALS, the airstream is deflected through the nasal cavity; this results from a slight dropping of the velum, which otherwise (i.e., in nonnasal or ORAL sounds) is raised to shut off the nasal chamber. With LATERALS such as the [l] of English *lay* or Spanish *le*, the tongue contacts a point of articulation (the alveolar ridge in this case), but unlike stops, laterals allow the airstream to continue over the side(s) of the tongue. The other type of liquids, *r*-sounds, includes several manners of articulation that will be described later in a fuller comparison of English and Spanish (v. 2.1.3).

1.1.4 Vowels. Vowels are described in terms of tongue and lip position. For the vowel called "schwa," [ə],which occurs in the last syllable of English *data* or *circus,* the tongue is in its rest position (for English): it is MID (neither raised nor lowered) and CENTRAL (neither advanced nor retracted). The terms FRONT, BACK, HIGH, and LOW describe vowel articulations in which the tongue respectively moves forward, pulls back, is raised, or is

Figure 1.2. The vowels [i u æ ɑ] and the diphthong [aj]

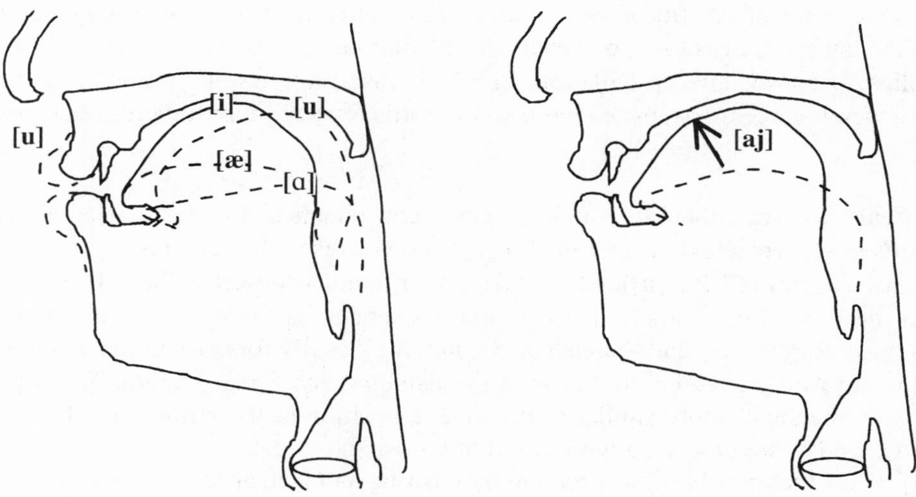

lowered from this mid central [ə] position. Alternatively, since raising and lowering the tongue may be accompanied by the raising and lowering of the jaw, high and low vowels are sometimes called CLOSE and OPEN vowels, respectively. In addition, the lips may be pursed out (ROUNDED) or spread (UNROUNDED) for any tongue position. Four vowels shared by English and Spanish (aside from details to be explained later) can be described as follows (see figure 1.2):

[i] (English *see, tea*, Spanish *si, ti*): high front unrounded
[e] (English *they, day,* Spanish *de*): mid front unrounded
[o] (English *toe, tow, though,* Spanish *todo*): mid back rounded
[u] (English *Sue, zoo, do,* Spanish *su*): high back rounded

In the tongue's low position, English distinguishes a front [æ] (*sack*) from a back [ɑ] (*sock, car*); Spanish [a] (*saca*) is between these two, roughly central or front-central.

A MONOPHTHONG is a simple vowel like [a] with a relatively steady tongue position. A DIPHTHONG is a complex vowel in which the tongue begins in one position and then glides toward another. For instance, the vowel of English *night* or Spanish *hay* begins at about [a] and then moves up into a higher position approaching palatal [j]. Some linguists transcribe a diphthong with two vowel symbols representing the beginning and ending of the movement: [ai]. Others use a vowel symbol for the beginning tongue position followed by a glide symbol for the direction of movement: [aj]. The latter practice is followed in this book (the IPA permits both).

English furthermore distinguishes TENSE and LAX vowels. In the vowels [i] of *beat,* the [e] of *bait,* the [o] of *coat,* and the [u] of *Luke*, the tongue is tensed up; in the corresponding lax vowels [ɪ] of *bit,* [ɛ] of *bet,* [ɔ] of *caught,* and [ʊ] of *look*, the tongue is more relaxed, leaving a slightly more open channel. [ə], of course, is also lax. Tense and lax are also applied to consonantal articulation, in which case they may be termed FORTIS and LENIS: in general, voiceless stops tend to be more fortis (tenser, more forceful) than voiced ones.

1.1.5 Features. Traditional terminology leaves consonants and glides labeled with one set of terms (e.g., "voiceless velar stop" for [k]) and vowels with a different set ("rounded tense high back vowel" for [u]). This makes it difficult to describe the effects of one group on the other. For example, [k] commonly changes its place of articulation when before [i] as in English *key* and Spanish *quiso,* moving slightly forward on the velum (IPA [k̟]), but it stays fully back before [u] as in English *cool* and Spanish *culto*. The [k] thus ASSIMILATES or becomes more similar to the tongue position of the vowel, and this fact is lost when C and V are described with different terms.

Phonological theory solves this problem by positing a universal set of underlying properties called FEATURES for specifying all phones in the same way. Features are shown in square brackets (e.g., [back]), and as implied by positive/negative contrasts such as "voiced/unvoiced" or "rounded/unrounded," they tend to be BINARY or two-valued: either present (+) in the sound or absent (-). Thus, [u] is indicated by the feature specifications [+back, +high, +rounded, +tense] as opposed to [i], which is [-back, +high, -rounded, +tense]. Returning to [k], then, we can describe its assimilation as a process that changes its normal [+back] specification to [-back] before a vowel such as [i] that is also [-back].

In this book, we will normally forgo feature notation in order to simplify description. However, it will be implicit in our presentation of pronunciation, and a reference list of features is given at the end of appendix 2 for more advanced readers to use in reformulating the distinctions and processes we take up.

1.2 Phonemes, allophones, and rules. Although we refer to phones in describing pronunciation, the units of phonology are more abstract entities called PHONEMES. Phonemes are shown by phonetic symbols in diagonals: /i/, /tʃ/, /t/,and so on, as are the PHONEMIC REPRESENTATIONS of words, for example, /titʃ/ for *teach*. Every language has a limited set of phonemes, about seventeen to fifty or so, which are used for contrasting its words. On the surface, speakers produce far more phones than that in their speech, but they interpret these as variants of the underlying phonemes of their language, ignoring differences that do not count in listening for word differences. For example, English speakers often round their lips in saying the /r/ of *rack,* devoice (make voiceless) the /r/ of *track,* and neither round nor devoice the /r/ of *car.* In a phonetic transcription, the three sounds could be shown, respectively, as [rʷ], [r̥], and [r]. But English speakers take these to be variants or ALLOPHONES of the same phoneme, /r/; without training, they do not hear the differences and are unaware of making them. English /r/ can become rounded [rʷ] or voiceless [r̥]

Figure 1.3. Contrastive and complementary distribution

English		Spanish	
[d]	[ð]	[d]	[ð]
• in initial position • in final position • between vowels	• in initial position • in final position • between vowels	• in initial position • after /n/ or l	• after vowels and other consonants
∴contrastive distribution		∴complementary distribution	

without any confusion with other phonemes that signal different words. Yet if the /r/ were to slide into a more lateral articulation, English speakers would readily perceive the change because /r/ and /l/ are used to contrast MINIMAL PAIRS, that is, words whose distinction depends solely on the phonetic difference: *rack* and *lack, berry* and *belly, fry* and *fly.* Thus, [rʷ] and [r] are not separate phonemes but allophones of one, whereas /r/ and /l/ are distinct English phonemes. In Japanese, on the other hand, lateralness is as nondistinctive as rounding, so its speakers perceive [r] and [l] as one phoneme, hearing no more difference between them than English speakers do between [r] and [rʷ]. While phonological structure is not entirely different from one language to the next, what is phonemically contrastive in one language may be allophonic in another.

As another example, consider the minimal pairs *den/then* and *ride/writhe.* These contrasts demonstrate a distinction between /d/ and /ð/ as English phonemes. Since these occur in CONTRASTIVE DISTRIBUTION, that is, in the same positions so as to contrast words, English speakers will be alert to the difference between, say, *She's riding* and *She's writhing.* Spanish speakers, however, do not readily sense the difference, since their language organizes [d] and [ð] as allophones of one phoneme, /d/: the voiced stop [d] occurs in one set of environments (at the beginning of an utterance and after [n] or [l]), while the voiced fricative [ð] occurs in a different set of environments (after vowels and other consonants; v. 3.1.6). With this setup, called COMPLEMENTARY DISTRIBUTION (figure 1.3), Spanish does not have and cannot have minimal pairs such as /rajd/ (*ride*) vs. /rajð/ (*writhe*). In fact, the same word is pronounced with either phone depending on its environment: *dónde* is [dónde] in *¿Dónde está?* (utterance-initial) but becomes [ðónde] in *¿De dónde es?* (after the vowel of *de*), and Spanish speakers are generally unaware of the change of articulation. Note that this is not because they have learned to *spell* [d] and [ð] with the same letter *d*; one acquires phonemes and their allophones in early childhood, well before writing. On the other hand, Spanish makes a phonemic distinction between the velar stop /k/ and the corresponding velar fricative /x/ (spelled *jota*), as in the minimal pair *carro/jarro.* English does not make this distinction, and although English speakers may unwittingly say a [x] sound in a relaxed articulation of the medial /k/ of *recognize,* they hear it as English /k/, not as a distinct phoneme.

In order to account for the difference between the underlying phonemic representation of a word and its phonetic realization (including allophones), linguists recognize PHONO-

LOGICAL RULES. For example, we can state as a general process for Spanish that /d/ changes to [ð] after V and most C, as in /dónde/ → [ðónde] in *de dónde,* /déxes/ → [ðéxes] in *¡No lo dejes!*, and /adjós/ → [aðjós] in *adiós.* The allophones of English /r/ are similarly described as resulting from the application of phonological rules. English lacks a /d/ → [ð] rule, these being distinct phonemes in its system, and Spanish lacks an /r/-rounding rule. Consequently, students who transfer their English rules to Spanish may have a non-native "accent" or may even obliterate Spanish distinctions, making word recognition difficult. Moreover, by failing to acquire the phonological rules that are particular to Spanish, learners may again have an accent or may misunderstand Spanish phonemes when these appear in their altered phonetic guises. Such interference between L1 and L2 phonologies will be our focus in the next three chapters.

1.3 Phonemes and examples. The following list shows the phonemes we assume for standard Spanish and English (figures 1.4 and 1.5). Those that are followed by a double-shafted arrow (⇒) are lacking in some dialects and are replaced by other phonemes as shown. It will be helpful to practice saying the examples out loud to associate sounds and spellings with symbols. Additional symbols will be introduced in succeeding chapters for major allophones (see appendix 2 for a fuller list).

Figure 1.4. Examples of Spanish phonemes

Spanish phonemes	
VOWELS	/l/ cola, paralelo, el
/a/ casa, álgebra	/m/ campo, cama, invierno
/e/ pesebre	/n/ canto, cana, van, nieto
/i/ piscina, y, mí	/ɲ/ caña
/o/ pozo, hipopótamo	/p/ pozo, pues, papá
/u/ tuyo, húmedo, su	/r/ caro, carta, parar, trato
	/r̄/ carro, honrado, rosa
CONSONANTS, GLIDES	/s/ sastre, casa (caza), éxito = /éksito/
/b/ baso = vaso, cave = cabe, wagón	/t/ tonto, tú
/d/ dónde, pedid	/tʃ/ chato, muchacha
/f/ fuego, filósofo	/w/ cuerno, ruego, ahuecar, causa
/g/ paga, pague, guitarra, gato, guapo	/x/ juego, página, escojo, escoge, México
/j/ comió, pie, hierro, cayó (calló)	/ʎ/⇒/j/ calló, llama
/k/ quito, casa, kilo, acción, taxi=/taksi/	/θ/⇒/s/ lápiz, lápices, cierra, caza

Figure 1.5. Examples of English phonemes

English phonemes (North American)

VOWELS

/ɑ/ far, father, pot, heart, tomorrow
/æ/ fat, laugh, ham
/ɛ/ red, head, said
/e/ made=maid, rein=rain, they, great, day
/ɪ/ hit, women, hear=here, myth
/i/ police, lily, he, meet=meat, key, grief
/ɔ/⇒/ɑ/ fall, law, daughter, ought, broad
/o/ so=sow=sew, hoe, boat, rope, though
/ʊ/ put, bull, woman, would=wood
/u/ rule, do, through=threw, mood, bruise
/ʌ/ bug, cover, blood, tough, does
/ə/ sofa, elephant, melody, circus, nervous
/ər/ herd=heard, fir=fur, word, bird, girl
/aj/ by=buy, die=dye, sight=site, sign
/ɔj/ noise, boy
/aw/ about, brown

CONSONANTS, GLIDES

/b/ bit, cab, rubber
/d/ did, sudden, stunned
/dʒ/ jet, gem, judge, age, region, strange
/f/ fat, offer, philosophy, tough
/g/ gag, baggy, guest, ghost
/h/ hot, whole=hole
/j/ yet, opinion, cute /kjut/, use /juz/
/k/ clock, kit, quit, ache, accident, ax /æks/
/l/ meal, yellow, lap
/m/ drum, drummer, dumb
/n/ fun, funny
/ŋ/ sink, sing, finger, anxious
/p/ pit, happy, nap
/r/ rare, worry, rhyme, wreath
/s/ so, boss, science, accident, box /bɑks/
/ʃ/ shut, sugar, facial, mission, nation
/t/ tatter, missed=mist
/tʃ/ church, ditch, nature
/v/ love, vet, of
/w/ wit, quit, which = /hwɪtʃ/
/z/ zoo, fizz, days=daze, easy, scissors
/ʒ/ vision, measure, rouge, usual, azure
/θ/ thin, thought, ether, bath, mouth
/ð/ then, though, either, bathe, mother

Chapter 2

Phonemes

2.0 Comparing systems. This chapter first compares the consonant and vowel systems of Spanish with those of English. Next, it discusses the different ways in which the two languages join phonemes to form syllables and words. Finally, since pedagogy usually takes up Spanish phonemes in terms of their orthography, spelling conventions are described and distinguished from phonological processes. The methods of contrastive analysis (v. 0.2.1) have been particularly successful in the arena of phonology, because a comparison of phonemic systems readily reveals cases of shared elements (e.g., Spanish /m/ = English /m/), of similar elements with different form or function (e.g., /t/ and /r/ in the two languages), and of wholly different elements or patterns (e.g., the Spanish *eñe* /ɲ/ and *erre* /r̄/ sounds, which English lacks).

2.1 Consonants. English and Spanish share many of the same consonants and spell them similarly. The main problems center on shared phonemes with different articulations or allophones, Spanish phonemes that are absent from the English system, and dialect variation at two major points in the Spanish system.

2.1.1 General comparison of consonant systems. Figures 2.1 and 2.2 display the consonant systems of Spanish and English. (Remember that these are *phonemes* and that their allophones can vary.) The two systems are constructed similarly: both make voiceless/voiced distinctions in their stops (/p t k/ vs. /b d g/), both distinguish two glides (/j w/) and three nasals, and there is direct overlap in that /f m l s tʃ n g/ and other phonemes occur in both. In learning the consonant phonemes of Spanish, therefore, the English speaker need not start from scratch, and this fact is commonly exploited by pedagogical instructions such as "Spanish *f* is pronounced like the *f* of English *find*."

2.1.2 Consonants with different articulations: /t d/. One must be careful in equating phonemes by their symbols alone. Both languages have two phonemes conventionally symbolized /t/ and /d/, but this does not mean that they are identical. One difference is

Figure 2.1. Spanish consonant phonemes (phonemes in parentheses do not occur in all dialects)

		bilabial	labio-dental	dental	alveolar	alveo-palatal	palatal	velar	labio-velar
STOP	voiceless	p		t		tʃ		k	
	voiced	b		d				g	
FRICATIVE	voiceless		f	(θ)	s			x	
NASAL	voiced	m			n		ɲ		
LATERAL	voiced				l		(ʎ)		
FLAP	voiced				r				
TRILL	voiced				r̄				
GLIDE	voiced						j		w

articulatory: these stops are dental in Spanish but alveolar in English. That is, the Spanish speaker pronounces them with the apex (tip of the tongue) against the edges of the inner surfaces of the upper front teeth, an articulation symbolized as [t̪ d̪] in a more detailed (or NARROW) phonetic transcription. The English speaker, on the other hand, articulates them with the apex on the alveolar ridge just above and behind the upper teeth, as shown in figure 2.3. Another difference is distributional: Spanish /t d/ readily occur before the glide /j/ as in *tierno* and *diente* /tjérno djénte/, but English /t d/ usually do not;[1] this is a difference of PHONOTACTICS or arrangements of phonemes (v. 2.3). Still other differences are introduced by phonological rules, whereby Spanish /d/ often weakens to a fricative [ð] (v. 3.1.6), while English /t/ in various positions is aspirated, flapped, or preglottalized (v. 3.2.1–3.2.3).

Transferring an alveolar /t d/ to one's Spanish produces a slight nonnative accent but no serious misunderstanding. Whatever their phonetic realizations, the phonemes /t d/ are

Figure 2.2. English consonant phonemes

		bilabial	labio-dental	dental	alveolar	retro-flex	alveo-palatal	palatal	velar	labio-velar	glottal
STOP	voiceless	p			t		tʃ		k		
	voiced	b			d		dʒ		g		
FRICATIVE	voiceless		f	θ	s		ʃ				h
	voiced		v	ð	z		ʒ				
NASAL	voiced	m			n				ŋ		
LATERAL	voiced				l						
APPROXIMANT OR GLIDE	voiced					r		j		w	

Figure 2.3. Alveolar (left) and dental (right) /t d/

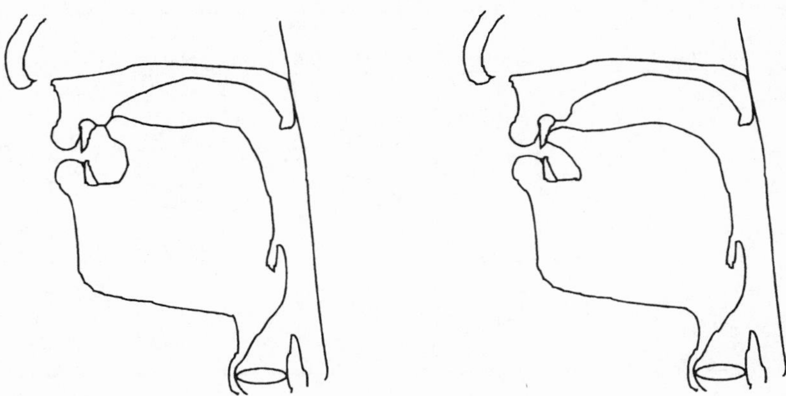

present in both languages and have similar roles: they contrast in numerous minimal pairs (*tía/día, tie/die*) and occupy comparable positions in their respective systems. More problematic are those phonemes that are present in one system but not in the other, and these receive more pedagogical attention.

2.1.3 Unshared consonants. A comparison of the two systems in figures 2.1 and 2.2 reveals that the consonants /v ð z ʒ ʃ dʒ h ŋ/ are present in English but not in Spanish. As is shown in chapter 3, many of these consonants do occur phonetically in Spanish as allophones of other phonemes: [ŋ] occurs for the /n/ of *cinco* and [ð] for the /d/ of *cada.* But in Spanish they do not contrast with other phonemes and therefore do not form minimal pairs like English /n/ vs. /ŋ/ in *run/rung* or /d/ vs. /ð/ in *dough/though.* Thus one might forget about these un-Spanish English phonemes in pedagogy and dispense with seemingly lame statements such as "the English *v* sound does not occur in Spanish." Yet they do cause interference in at least two ways. First, orthography may cue the use of an English phoneme that the student has never heard in Spanish input; for instance, Spanish has no /v/, but the spelling of *conversar* and *invitar* (pronounced /kombersár imbitár/) suggests one. Second, several Spanish phones may be equated with English phonemes because of a perceived acoustic resemblance. Thus, many students hear the fricative allophone [β] (v. 3.1.6) of /b/ in *saber* or *nueve* not as a new sound to be acquired but as a kind of English /v/, and they so pronounce it.

2.1.3.1 The *eñe* /ɲ/. The Spanish phonemes or phonemic distinctions lacking English counterparts are /ɲ/, /x/, /r/ vs. /r̄/, and the *elle* of some dialects (v. 2.1.4.1). /ɲ/ is a palatal nasal, spelled *ñ*. Contrary to the descriptions of most textbooks, it is *not* the English *ni* or *ny* of *onion* or *canyon* but rather a single nasal sound made by pressing the middle of the tongue firmly against the palate while the apex is tucked down behind the lower teeth.

Figure 2.4. Palatal nasal (left) vs. alveolar nasal + palatal glide (right)

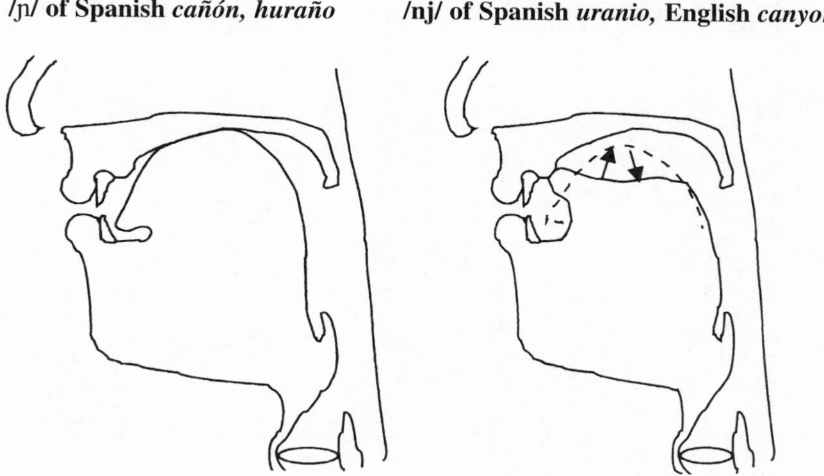

English *ni* or *ny* spells a sequence of two sounds, the /n/ of *can* followed by the /j/ of *you*: the apex contacts the alveolar ridge and then pulls away as the middle of the tongue briefly glides up toward the palate and then back down, never touching it. There is some acoustic similarity between the sound /ɲ/ and the sequence /nj/, but they are distinct, as illustrated in figure 2.4, and Spanish contrasts them in minimal pairs: *uñón* vs. *unión, huraño* vs. *uranio*.

2.1.3.2 The *jota* /x/. The symbol *x* in phonetics represents a voiceless velar fricative, never the /ks/ of English *box* or Spanish *éxito,* and it transcribes the *jota* (and *g* before *e* or *i*) of most Spanish speakers. /x/ is the fricative counterpart of the stop /k/; with /k/, the back of the tongue (dorsum) presses firmly against the velum so as to stop the airstream there, while for /x/ it comes just close enough to the velum (or for some speakers, the uvula) to constrict the airstream there and cause rough turbulence (see figure 2.5). The two contrast in numerous minimal pairs: *carro* vs. *jarro, coco* vs. *cojo, quema* vs. *gema, cura* vs. *jura,* and so on. English speakers may miss the contrast and perceive /x/ as some kind of /k/, just as they usually hear and reproduce the same sound in the German name *Bach* as English /k/. If the friction of the /x/ is weaker, they may interpret it as a kind of /h/. In fact, in southern Andalusia, the Caribbean, and much of Central America and Colombia, Spanish /x/ does weaken to the glottal fricative or aspiration [h].[2] This allophone will obviously be easier than [x] for English speakers, but it is not the stronger *jota* of most Spanish speakers.

2.1.3.3 The flap and trill /r r̄/. English has only one *r*-phoneme, and although it is symbolized /r/, it is not a Spanish /r/. In American English, /r/ is articulatorily a RETROFLEX

Figure 2.5. Voiceless velar stop /k/ vs. voiceless velar fricative /x/

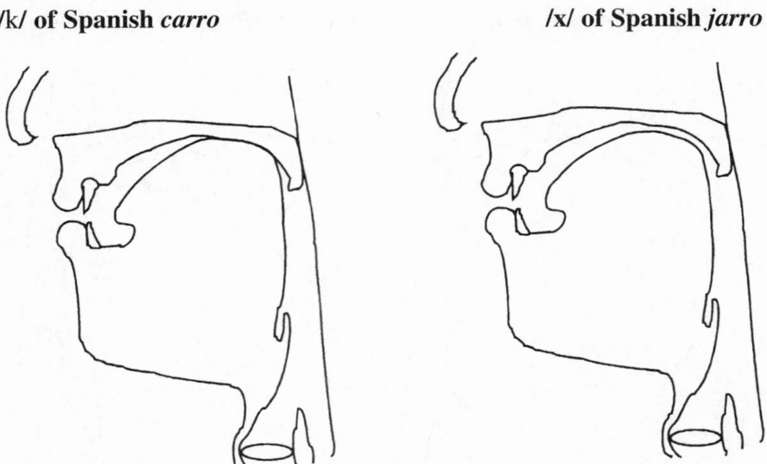

APPROXIMANT. It is retroflex in that the apex curls up and back (or, for some speakers, the tongue bunches up) and approximant in that the tongue vaguely "approaches" the roof of the mouth without making contact; it is really more like a glide (like /j w/) than a true consonant. In a narrow transcription, approximant *r* is shown as [ɹ] (or for a specifically retroflex one, [ɻ]). Moreover, it is reinforced by lip rounding before a stressed vowel, as in *rack* or *around*; since lip rounding is indicated by a raised *w*, this phone can be shown as [ɹʷ]. The two are allophones of one English phoneme, /r/.

Spanish distinguishes two *r* phonemes, neither of them rounded, retroflex, or approximant. With /r/ as in *caro,* the apex weakly hits the alveolar ridge, too briefly to form a stop there: this is an alveolar FLAP (or TAP, or *vibrante simple*), symbolized in a narrow transcription by [ɾ]. With /r̄/ as in *carro,*[3] the apex flutters rapidly against the alveolar ridge; this is the alveolar TRILL (*vibrante múltiple*). For lovers of detail, Navarro Tomás (1967, 122) determined that the trill normally has two vibrations after /n/ (*honra* /ónr̄a/), three initially or before a stressed vowel (*roca* /r̄óka/, *corremos* /kor̄émos/), and four after a stressed vowel (*carro* /kár̄o/, *corre* /kór̄e/). Nevertheless, what matters is not the exact number of vibrations in the trill, but only that it have perceptibly more than the one of /r/.

No other Spanish phonemes cause so many Anglophone students to balk right away. The flap [ɾ] should not be articulatorily difficult for Americans and Canadians since they have the same sound for their intervocalic /t/ or /d/ in *Betty, water, latter=ladder, seating=seeding* (v. 3.2.3). The problem with [ɾ] is instead phonemic and orthographic: students can and do use it, but they resolutely regard it as a /t/ or /d/ according to the laws of English phonology and spelling, not as an /r/. But the trill is the more formidable of the two, and many students have a ready response when they are introduced to it: "I can't do that!" It is pointless to instruct them to imitate motors, since those who cannot trill even for motors will only give an earnest "[ɹɹɹ]" instead of "[r̄r̄r̄]," and those who can imitate motors with a trill do not view onomatopoeic sound effects as likely consonants combinable with other phonemes to form words, any more than they would accept hiccups and cockadoodledoos in their speech. To perceive their difficulty, one can trill the lips as for *brrr!* or click the tongue as for *tch-tch* and try using these as consonants in fluently articulated words; both are so used in some languages, but they seem bizarre as phonemes to Spanish and English speakers alike.

The pronunciation of /r̄/ requires the following articulatory steps:

1. The apex rises to the alveolar ridge exactly as for the Spanish and English flap [ɾ]. Seen from above, the tongue would look concave (Navarro Tomás 1967, 122), with the tip up and the rest down. The whole tongue is relaxed, for it is not its musculature that initiates the trilling effect.
2. A well-timed voiced airstream must rush through at high velocity, under increased pressure from the lungs. The apex, instead of banging once on the alveolar ridge as in a normal airstream, will then vibrate against it like the fluttering of a flag in a stiff wind. Without this additional air pressure, there will be no trill but only a flap or series of flaps, [ɾəɾəɾə].

Most defects in students' attempts at /r̄/ come from a lack of one or both of the above components. The apex may be wrongly placed, the body of the tongue may be raised too high, the vocal cords may be spread (yielding a voiceless version), airflow may be too weak, or the tongue may be too tensed in anticipation of the legendary *bête noire* of Spanish phonology. Students can usually master /r̄/ if they know precisely what to do (with far more precision than most textbooks offer), truly wish to do it, practice doing it, and fine-tune it with guidance from a teacher who can diagnose problems and who expects mastery.

Of the two *vibrantes*, only /r̄/ occurs word-initially (*roca, rato*) and after /n s l/ (*honra, Israel, alrededor*), despite the orthographic *ere*. After other consonants (*cobra, creo, otro*), only /r/=[ɾ] appears. Word-finally or before a consonant (*armar, servir, arder*)—i.e. syllable-finally—the flap is usual, but for emphasis it can be strengthened to [r̄]; the contrast being NEUTRALIZED[4] or canceled out there, the substitution of a trill for the flap does not disrupt intelligibility. Intervocalically, though, the two contrast in numerous minimal pairs: *caro/carro, pero/perro, coro/corro, vara/barra, quería/querría, enterado/enterrado, mira/mirra,* and so on.

2.1.4 Dialect variations. In English, vowels show a great deal of dialect variation, while consonants are fairly stable and uniform; in Spanish, it is the consonants that vary more. Those variations that result from phonological rules will be taken up in the next chapter, but there are two points at which the set of Spanish phonemes varies: (1) presence vs. absence of a /ʎ j/ distinction (*calló/cayó, valla/vaya, halla/haya, arrollo/arroyo,* *llena/hiena*) and (2) presence vs. absence of a /θ s/ distinction (*caza/casa, vez/ves, cierra/sierra, bazo/baso*). According to most textbooks, both distinctions are maintained in Spain but are merged in the New World; yet the actual situation is not so straightforward.[5]

2.1.4.1 *Lleísmo* vs. *yeísmo*. The symbol ʎ represents a palatal lateral for what is spelled with *ll* in *millón,* and this sound is often equated with the *li* (/lj/) of English *million.* As with the similar mismatching of /ɲ/ with English /nj/, this is inaccurate. /lj/ in *million* is a sequence of two sounds, an alveolar lateral as in *mill* followed by a separate palatal glide beginning the next syllable; /ʎ/ is one sound, articulated (like /ɲ/) with the apex down and the middle of the tongue pressed against the palate. There are minimal pairs in Spanish that show the difference between /lj/ and /ʎ/: *polio/pollo, aliar/hallar.*

Dialects that still distinguish /ʎ/ in *calló* from /j/ in *cayó* are called *lleísta* and include parts of northern Spain and of the Andean highlands from Ecuador through Bolivia. Other dialects are *yeísta,* merging /ʎ/ with /j/ so that *calló* is pronounced like *cayó.* Even in northern Spain, *yeísmo* is normal in urban lects and is radiating outward into the countryside. Hence, *lleísmo* is a recessive feature in modern Spanish, even in Spain itself.

2.1.4.2 *Distinción, seseo, ceceo, ceseo*: /s θ/. One of the best-known features of Peninsular Spanish is the use of the voiceless dental fricative /θ/ (as in English <u>th</u>*ick*) for the sound spelled by *z* or (before *e* or *i*) *c*: *cierra* /θjéra̅/ and *vez* /beθ/ thus form minimal pairs with *sierra* /sjéra̅/ and *ves* /bes/. /θ/ is not distinguished from /s/ in any part of Spanish America, and there *cierra* and *sierra, vez* and *ves,* and so on are homonyms (homophones): /sjéra̅ bes/. This merger of /θ/ with /s/ is called *seseo*; maintenance of the distinction is called simply *distinción* (not *ceceo,* which refers to a different situation discussed below).[6]

Crosscutting this dialect difference in *distinción* vs. merger of *cierra* and *sierra* is a second one involving the articulation of /s/. Spanish speakers make a variety of fricatives in the coronal area. The three main types are described below and are pictured in figure 2.6.[7]

- Laminoalveolar. This is the /s/ that English speakers typically use. The blade (lamina) of the tongue makes light contact with the alveolar ridge while its surface forms a back-to-front groove. The airstream is directed along this groove at the inner teeth surfaces, resulting in a hiss (sibilance) that is markedly noisy and high-pitched. In Spanish, this laminoalveolar /s/ (traditionally called *s predorsal*) is found in most of Spanish America, central Andalusia, and among some Castilians too. This type is shown in a narrow transcription with a small box (the IPA diacritic for 'laminal') under the symbol, [s̻].
- Apicoalveolar. In this articulation, the apex alone rises to the alveolar ridge and forms a groove there; the blade and middle of the tongue are not used, but are sunken, yielding a concave, hollowed tongue shape. Its sibilance is lower-pitched, reminding English speakers of their /ʃ/ in *shut* (which, however, is made very

Figure 2.6. Three main fricative types used in *cierra* and/or *sierra*

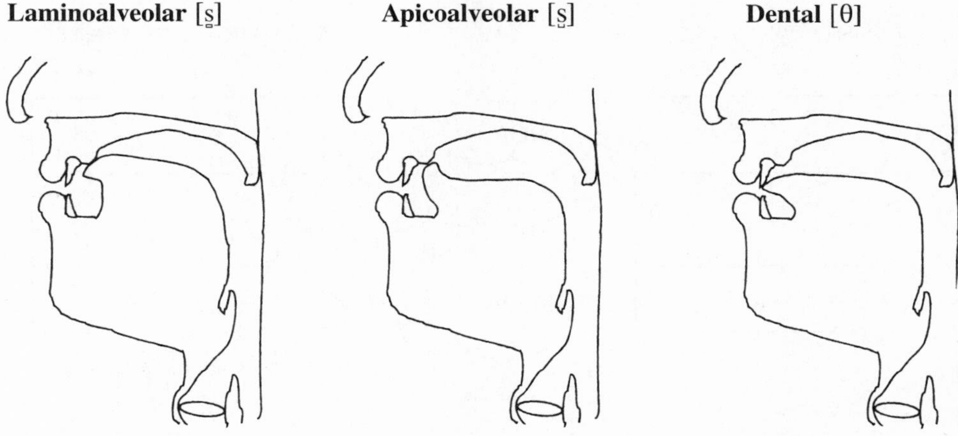

differently). Apical /s/ is shown in the IPA as [s̺] (with an inverted dental marker), although some Hispanic linguists use an accent, [ś]. It goes by several names: *ese apical, ese espesa, ese cóncava, ese castellana.* It is the /s/ used by most northern Spaniards, but it is also found in scattered areas of the Andean highlands. Despite the latter distribution, most non-users associate it with Castile, whence *ese castellana.*

- DENTAL. In this articulation, represented by [θ], the apex touches the upper teeth. Unlike both of the preceding sounds, it is not a sibilant, there being no hiss-making groove down the middle of the tongue. The apex may either protrude through the teeth (INTERDENTAL) or just touch the teeth edges without protruding (APICODENTAL), but there is not much acoustic difference between the two.

As opposed to *distinción, seseo* means the use of either type of sibilant /s/ for both *cierra* and *sierra,* usually the laminoalveolar one; and *ceceo* ('lisping') means the use of dental /θ/ for both—or of a dental [s̪], which has the blade at the alveolar ridge and the apex at the teeth and sounds like a simultaneous [θ] and [s]. Dialect surveys have shown Andalusia to contain three west-to-east bands in this regard. The northern one, northern Huelva province arching over to Almería, is like Castile in its *distinción* of /θ/ vs. some kind of /s/ (*cierra* /θjér̄a/, *sierra* /sjér̄a/); the central one, around Córdoba and Sevilla, has *seseo* (*cierra=sierra* /sjér̄a/); and the southernmost one, Cádiz to Granada, has *ceceo* (*cierra=sierra* /θjér̄a/). Yet Dalbor (1980, 14) found the Andalusian situation more variable, with a single speaker alternating among *distinción, seseo, ceceo,* and aspiration (v. 3.1.5), so that *luz* is [luθ lus luh]. This variation may be explained differently (González Bueno 1993), but at least as an informal label for it, Obaid (1973, 63) suggested the term *ceseo.*

Figure 2.7. Spanish and English vowel phonemes

SPANISH VOWELS

FRONT CENTRAL BACK

i u

e o

a

HIGH { TENSE / LAX }

MID { TENSE / LAX }

LOW

ENGLISH VOWELS (STRESSED)

FRONT CENTRAL BACK

i u

ɪ ʊ

e o

ɛ ʌ ɔ

æ ɑ

DIPHTHONGS /aj/, /ɔj/, /aw/

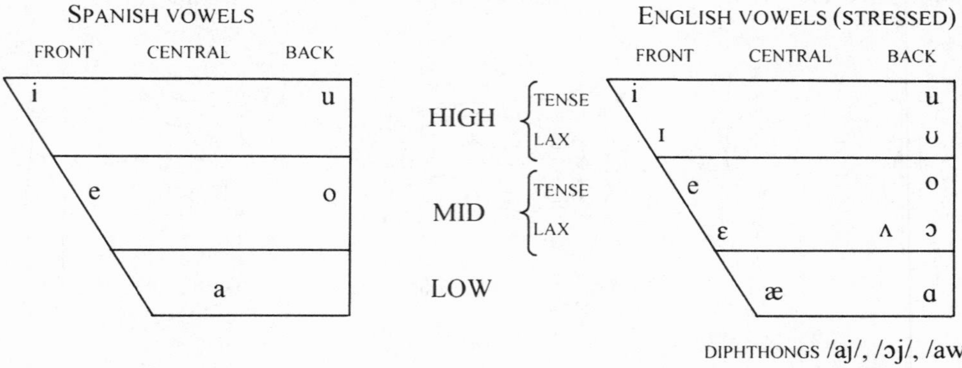

2.2 Vowels and diphthongs. The (stressed) vowel phonemes of the two languages are compared in figure 2.7. The English system is visibly the more complex one, making more vocalic distinctions than Spanish. It is also more variable due to dialect differences (Kurath and McDavid 1961; Wells 1982). Some Americans and Canadians no longer distinguish /ɔ/ from /ɑ/; their *caught, hawk, chalk, naughty, dawn* merge with *cot, hock, chock, knotty, Don.* Figure 2.7 also does not reflect the effects of syllable-final "r-dropping" in certain areas (most of England, Australia, New Zealand, New York City, and parts of New England and of the American South). Three of those effects were (1) /ɪr/ → /ɪə/ (*beer*) and /ɛr/ → /ɛə/ (*bear*), (2) merger of /ɑr/ with /ɑ/ (*spar=spa*) and of /ɔr/ with /ɔ/ (*court=caught*), and (3) the distinction of *cart* and *cot* as /kɑt/ vs. /kɒt/ (/ɒ/ = rounded /ɑ/) instead of /kɑrt/ vs. /kɑt/ as in most of North America.

English has two other vowels not shown in figure 2.7. The first is schwa, /ə/, which is a short, very lax, mid central vowel occurring in the unstressed syllables of ***a**bout, b**e**lieve, it**e**m, gall**o**p, vir**u**s, s**u**ppose,* and so on. It resembles the /ʌ/ of *dull,* which occurs in stressed syllables and is more open, longer, and more backed than the muffled schwa. Some phonologists have treated [ə] and [ʌ] as allophones of one phoneme, but schwa is more often treated today as an allophone of almost all English vowel phonemes, since they tend to reduce to [ə] when unstressed (v. 3.2.7): *phon*[ɑ́]*logy* but *phon*[ə]*lógical.* The other additional vowel is /ər/, the "er" vowel of *her, fir = fur, word, murder, were.* Phonetically, /ər/ is a single sound: in most parts of North America, a schwa with the curled-back apex of /r/ (narrow transcription: [ɚ]) or, in "r-dropping" dialects, a tenser type of schwa (narrow transcription: [ɜ]). Both /ə/ and /ər/ (whether as [ɚ] or as [ɜ]) stand out conspicuously when transferred to Spanish words such as *virus, perturbar, interpersonal, libertad*, because Spanish makes absolutely no use of the mid central zone for its vowels.

2.2.1 Two vowel systems. A glance at the two vowel systems in figure 2.7 suggests that it might be easier for English speakers to learn Spanish vowel distinctions than vice versa. On a phonemic level, this is generally true. For the Spanish student of English, the contrasts between *beat* and *bit* (/i ɪ/), *pool* and *pull* (/u ʊ/), *boat* and *bought* (/o ɔ/), and *cat* and *cot* and *cut* (/æ ɑ ʌ /) are notoriously difficult, primarily because of a tense/lax contrast not used in Spanish (where all vowels tend to be tense). English speakers, however, easily perceive the Spanish contrasts in *piso/peso/paso/pozo/puso,* and if they use their English /i e ɑ o u/ in Spanish, they should be understood as long as they avoid reducing unstressed vowels to [ə].

But a direct transfer of English vowels causes at least a perceptible accent since the Spanish vowels are not quite the same articulatorily. Spanish /a/ is equated with the English /ɑ/ in *father, cot* in most textbooks, but it is pronounced more in the front of the mouth and it will seem between most English speakers' /æ/ and /ɑ/—in other words, *saca* will sound like a cross between *sack* and *sock.*[8] Also, /i e o u/ are pure vowels (monophthongs) in Spanish, pronounced with a steady tongue position, but they are usually pronounced as diphthongs in English, with the tongue (and lip) position changing during their articulation (v. 3.2.6). In English /i e o/, the tongue usually starts near Spanish /i e o/ and glides upward toward the palatal [j] position for /i e/ and back toward [w] for /o/: phonetically, then, they are commonly [ij ej ow]. English /u/ is diphthongized like /o/ but its beginning is not as well rounded or fully backed as Spanish /u/; it is more central, as shown by the symbol [ʉ] in the narrow phonetic transcription [ʉw]. Especially in British English, diphthongized /o/ may also have a central beginning, yielding [əw].

If transferred to Spanish, English diphthongal /u o/ sound strange but are recognizable. This is because Spanish has no diphthongs [uw ow] (except in *bou)* that might contrast in minimal pairs with /u o/. But Spanish does distinguish /e/ from /ej/ and /i/ from /ij/, and English speakers who diphthongize in *reno, pena, ves, creó, amaría, brío* may be misunderstood as saying *reino, peina, veis, creyó, amarilla, brillo.*

2.2.2 Diphthongs. In addition to its diphthongized /e i o u/ = [ej ij ow ʉw], English has the three diphthongs /aj/ (*buy=by, lie=lye, hi=high, eye=I*), /ɔj/ (*boy, noise*), and /aw/ (*now, loud*). In all three, one begins with a vowel sound and then glides off toward a higher tongue position, whence the transcription of vowel plus glide, VG. But it is also possible to make a diphthong the other way around, starting with a glide and sliding down into a more open vowel; this is essentially what English speakers do in the /ju/ of *music* /mjúzɪk/, *cute, beauty*. The first kind of diphthong, VG, is RISING (or upgliding), and the second, GV, is FALLING (or downgliding).

Although Spanish has only five simple vowel phonemes, it abounds in diphthongs of both kinds:

VG	GV
/aj/: *hay, naipe, traigo, caimán*	/ja/: *piano, Asia, copia, diablo, lidiar*
/ej/: *reina, rey, ley, seis, peinar*	/je/: *pie, siete, fiel, pierdo, serie*

/oj/: *soy, oigo, prohibir*
/jo/: *odio, idioma, acción, Dios, comió*
/ju/: *diurno, ciudad, triunfo*
/aw/: *auto, auge, cauteloso*
/wa/: *cuajar, mutua, suave, actual*
/ew/: *Europa, deuda, reunir*
/we/: *puedo, juez, sueño, averigüé*
/wi/: *muy, fui, cuidado, ruina, Suiza*
/ow/: *bou*
/wo/: *cuota, arduo, continuo, averiguo*

Old Spanish also had /uj/ and /iw/, which some dialects retain today in *muy* and *ciudad,* respectively, but most dialects (including the standard) replaced them with /wi/ and /ju/. There are even TRIPHTHONGS of GVG in *buey* /bwej/, *Uruguay* /urugwáj/, and *vosotros* verb forms such as *averiguáis* /-wajs/, *averigüéis* /-wejs/, *estudiáis* /-jajs/.

Even with shared diphthongs—/aj/, /aw/, [ej]—there is an articulatory difference: the upgliding is faster and more definite in Spanish than in English. In English *eye,* the tongue dwells on the [a] and glides up a short way toward an indistinct position; in Spanish *hay,* this movement is quicker and reaches a high position. For the phonologist, though, the main problem is that the glides of Spanish diphthongs are not always glides, as shown in the next section.

2.2.3 Hiatus, syneresis, and the analysis of glides. Adjacent vowels in Spanish may count as two separate syllables or may blend into a diphthong as one of them loses its syllabicity and becomes a glide. The former condition, VV, is traditionally called HIATUS, and the latter, GV or VG, is called SYNERESIS. The rule laid down in many textbooks is as follows:

1. *a e o* are "strong" vowels, and *i u* are "weak";
2. two adjacent strongs form separate syllables, that is, stand in HIATUS: *ca-e, pro-a*;
3. strong + weak or weak + strong form one syllable, the weak becoming a glide (*cai-go, grue-so*);
4. . . . unless the weak one carries a written accent mark: *ca-í, grú-a.*

This analysis is unclear because it is letter-based. The Strong-Weak rule supposedly changes the vowel (letter) *i* to a glide ([j]) in *caigo*, making *ai* a diphthong instead of two syllabic vowels. Yet *ai* in *caigo* spells exactly the same sound as *ay* in *hay*, namely /aj/, and neither can *ever* be pronounced [a-i]. *Caigo* does not start as /ká-i-go/ and become [káj-go]; it is /kájgo/ phonemically and undergoes no *ai* → [aj] rule at all in phonology. Likewise, the [we] of *grueso* does not come from a rule that changes two individual vowels, /u/ and /e/, to a diphthong; *grueso* is always pronounced [grwé-so] and it is phonemically /grwéso/ too. *Ai* = /aj/ and *ue* = /we/ are merely letter-pronouncing instructions, like *x* = /ks/ and *qu* = /k/.

Nevertheless, there are other cases in which the [j w] of Spanish diphthongs can be analyzed as allophones of the vowel phonemes /i u/, with a phonological rule that—like the Strong-Weak rule—changes unstressed high vowels to glides when next to another vowel. In one common analysis (Harris 1969, 20–36), glides are regarded as phonemically /j w/ if they are always pronounced as glides or consonants but as allophones of /i u/ if they do appear as full, syllabic vowels in some morphological or stylistic versions of the word. The following examples may clarify the application of this criterion.

1. Always [j w], hence phonemically /j w/:
   - *caigo, naipe, hay*: always [aj], therefore phonemically /kájgo nájpe aj/.
   - *peinar, causar, cuajar, copia*: always [ej aw wa ja], therefore /pejnár kawsár kwaxár kópja/.
   - *estudiar, averiguar*: throughout the forms of these verbs, stem-final *i* and *u* always spell glides and are never pronounced [i u]; therefore /estudj- aberigw-/.

2. Alternating with high vowels, hence phonemically /i u/:
   - *aislar, aullar, prohibir*: [aj aw oj] in these forms and others with unstressed stems, but [aí aú oí] in *aíslo, aúllo, prohibo* and other forms with stressed stems; therefore /aislár aujár proibír/.
   - *enviar, continuar*: [ja wa] in these forms and others with unstressed stems, but [ío úo] in *envío, continúo,* and others with stressed stems; therefore their stems end phonologically in vowels, /embi- kontinu-/.
   - *espiritual, melodioso*: [wa jo] here, but corresponding to the glides [w j] are the vowels [u i] in *espíritu, melodía*; therefore /espiritu+al melodi+oso/.

Even granting that the Strong-Weak rule is an imperfect orthographic version of a phonological Gliding rule (v. 3.1.10) in Spanish, there are three sets of data it cannot handle. First, adjacent strongs also fuse: the expected hiatus is maintained in slow speech, but in faster styles we hear *oasis* → [wásis], *teatro* → [tjátro], *te amo* → [tjámo], *qué hubo* → [kjúβo] (v. 3.1.10). This fusion is called SYNERESIS, or SYNALEPHA when between words as in *te amo*, and is commonly shown in poetry and music with a subscript tie-bar: *te‿atro, te‿amo*.

Second, adjacent identical vowels also tend to merge, whether strong or weak: *alcohol* /alkól/. According to Quilis and Fernández (1975, 149), pairs such as *corte/cohorte, pasé/paseé,* and *azar/azahar* are distinguished only in "un lenguaje muy cuidado o enfático" and otherwise are homonyms (v. 3.1.10). Third, some authorities insist on hiatus in a few words for which the Strong-Weak rule yields syneresis. Navarro Tomás (1967, 155–67) gives *cru-el, fi-ar, su-ave, di-ario, vi-aje, bri-oso, tri-ángulo, avi-ón, jesu-ita, hu-ir* (and other *-uir* verbs), and the word *hi-ato* itself. Quilis and Fernández (1975, 71) add others (e.g., *bi-óxido, cu-ota, di-edro*) and the Real Academia (RAE 1979, 48 ff.) quite outdoes itself in hiatomania. If these hiatuses are actually observed in normal speech, then they throw a monkey wrench into the Gliding rule as well as the Strong-Weak rule, both of which predict diphthongs in all of these. But in fact, modern speakers tend to ignore these prescribed hiatuses,[9] and the prescribers disagree anyhow; Quilis and Fernández insist on *ruido* and *ruina* with [wi] while Navarro Tomás insists on [u-i].

2.2.4 Linking (liaison, *enlace*). Even with hiatus of adjacent vowels, one must link them smoothly in Spanish. Especially in slower styles (oral reading, emphatic or cautious speech, dictation), English speakers often separate the following sequences with a catch in the voice, that is, a glottal stop ([ʔ]):

1. the final vowel of one word and the initial one of the next: *two* [ʔ]*eggs*
2. the final consonant of one word and the initial vowel of the next: *ten* [ʔ]*eggs, these* [ʔ]*eggs, an* [ʔ]*aim (≠ a name).*

Outside these slower styles, glottal stop insertion is rarer and *an aim* then converges with *a name.* But as teachers are well aware, the speech style of foreign language students is typically slow, especially at first; consequently, glottal stop insertion may appear more often in their Spanish than in their English. By contrast, most varieties of Spanish[10] require full linking (LIAISON, *enlace)* among all consonants and vowels in a phrase. Thus, *tu éxito, ten éxito, un ama* will differ from *two eggs, ten eggs,* and *an aim* in their lack of glottal stop insertion.

2.3 The combining of phonemes into syllables and words. Traditional authorities such as the RAE (1979, 44–63) have devoted much attention to syllabication, the rules for dividing words into their syllables and determining syllable boundaries. The syllable boundaries are variously symbolized with periods (standard in IPA), hyphens, or dollar signs (for "$yllable"). On the basis of phonological representation (orthographically, the procedure is more difficult), Spanish syllabication proceeds as follows, with V = a true vowel, C = consonant (including O= obstruent, L = liquid, and G = glide unless specified otherwise), and + = boundary between prefix and stem.

1. VV → V.V: *leo* /lé.o/, *leían* /le.í.an/.
2. VCV → V.CV: *techo* /té.tʃo/, *carro* /ká.r̄o/, *huyen* /ú.jen/, *quiénes* /kjé.nes/.
3. VCCV → VC.CV: *bastante* /bas.tán.te/, *objeto* /ob.xé.to/, *éxito* /ék.si.to/, *euro* /éw.ro/
    a. but L goes with preceding O, → V.OLV: *abril* /a.bríl/, *hable* /á.ble/, *cabra* /ká.bra/
    b. and G goes with preceding C, → V.CGV: *apio* /á.pjo/, *hoyuelo* /o.jwé.lo/, *desierto* /de.sjér.to/
    c. **unless** + intervenes, VC+CV → VC.CV: *subrayar* /sub.r̄a.jár/, *sublunar* /sub.lu.nár/, *deshielo* /des.jé.lo/, *abyecto* /ab.jék.to/
4. VCCCV, VCCCCV: work back from the last medial (word-internal) consonant in applying the previous rules: *agrio* /á.grjo/, *constar* /kons.tár/, *extra* /éks.tra/, *acción* /ak.sjón/.

Figure 2.8. Syllable structure of *transporte*

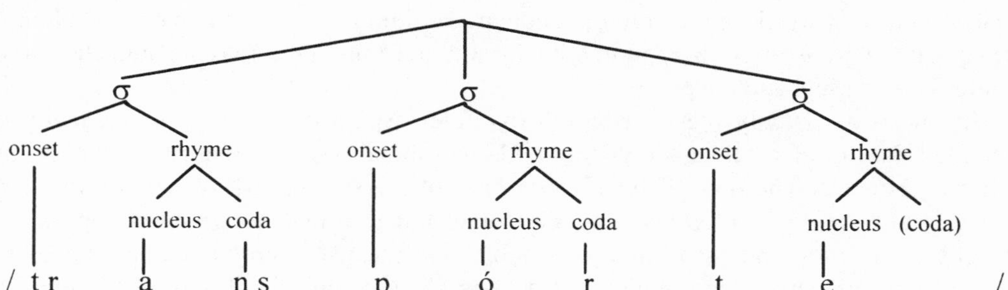

Thus, *trans-* forms one syllable in *transporte* /trans.pór.te/ but is broken up in *transeúnte* /tran.se.ún.te/.

The syllable has also received attention in phonology, not only as a unit demarcated by boundaries but as a phonological constituent with an internal structure. The central, most resonant part of the syllable is its NUCLEUS; what follows this nucleus (if anything) and completes the syllable is the CODA, and the nucleus and coda together comprise the RHYME, this being the portion that words share when they "rhyme," as with the /-ajm/ of *rhyme, time, climb.* The initial part of the syllable that precedes the rhyme (if anything) is the ONSET (*cabeza*), and it may contain several phonemes forming a CLUSTER. The only required constituent is the nucleus, which is always a vowel in Spanish; the onset and coda are optional, and they are a consonant, glide, or cluster thereof. A syllable that ends in a coda (e.g., *más, tren, miel, ir, red*) is called CLOSED; one that lacks a coda (e.g., *sí, no, pie, vio, da*) is OPEN.

This constituent analysis of the syllable is shown by a treelike branching diagram, similar to diagrams for grammatical structure (v. 5.1–2). As illustrated by *transporte* in figure 2.8, each syllable, represented by the Greek sigma, σ, consists of onset and a rhyme, and the rhyme, in turn, branches into its parts, nucleus and (if present) coda. (See Hooper 1976; Harris 1983; Hualde 1989; and Gil Fernández 2000 for further analyses of Spanish syllable structure.)

English syllables are similarly constructed, and in fact, the onset + rhyme structure is universal; languages differ primarily in the phonemes they allocate to each part. But syllable boundaries are not as clear in English as in Spanish. A dictionary may syllabify *very* and *any* as /vɛ́r.i/ and /ɛ́n.i/, but intervocalic consonants in English often belong to both syllables, as simultaneously the coda of one and the onset of the next. Indeed, a spectrographic analysis shows the retroflexion of the /r/ and the nasality of the /n/ smearing into both syllables. The term AMBISYLLABIC ('both syllables') is applied to such fence straddlers.

Syllable structure is related to PHONOTACTICS, the constraints on how phonemes combine to form words. Syllable structure and phonotactics are not quite identical; for one thing, Spanish liaison is so strong that words in a phrase are RESYLLABIFIED (Harris

1983, 43) as if the word boundaries of phonotactics did not exist: *Las hijas irán en el auto* thus becomes /la.sí.xa.si.rá.ne.ne.láw.to/. Consequently, it is difficult to study the phonemic structure of words apart from the phonemic combinations of syllables, and phonotactic generalizations about how words begin and end must take into account the possible patterns for onsets and codas.

In one way, namely the distribution of glides, Spanish is less phonotactically constrained than English. Spanish has more GV combinations, and these occur more freely after consonants. The /pw/ of *puerta,* the /trw/ of *trueco,* the /trj/ of *triunfo,* the /plj/ of *pliego,* and the /mw/ of *muero* are phonemic clusters that are rare or impossible in English, and they can give students trouble not because their phonemes are odd but because pronouncing them together in an onset is un-English. The /mw/ of *muero* thus becomes [mu-] or [muw-] in adaptation to English phonotactics. (Compare, however, students' ease in pronouncing the English-like /kw/ of *cuero.*)

On the other hand, there are at least three ways in which Spanish is more phonotactically restricted than English. First, the only consonants that commonly end a word are the coronals /d s n r l θ/. Others are rare in final position, as with the /x/ of *reloj* or the /b g k t f tʃ p/ of the borrowings *club, zigzag, coñac, complot, rosbif, sandwich, jeep (yip).* In fact, many of these words are commonly pronounced without their final C, and words spelled with final *m* (*álbum, referéndum*) are pronounced with /n/. Spanish spelling sometimes adjusts to these pronunciations: *compló, coñá.* Medially, too, codas such as /b g k t f tʃ p/ are unusual in Spanish, existing primarily in learned words borrowed from Greek and Latin. When these consonants meet with others medially, they form clusters called *grupos cultos* that sit astride the syllable boundary: /b.s/ (*absoluto*), /k.s/ (*éxito*), /k.t/ (*pacto*), /p.s/ (*cápsula*), /t.n/ (*étnico*). Outside of a fairly *culta* pronunciation, the coda C of the cluster tends to weaken to a fricative or glide, or to be dropped entirely,[11] and this results in a simplified and more normal syllable structure: *extraño* /eks.trá.ɲo/ → [es.trá.ɲo]. Again, spelling may recognize the cluster simplification: *se(p)tiembre, su(b)scripción, su(b)stituir.*

Second, clusters of two or more C at the end of the word are frequent in English up to a maximum of four (*sixths* /sɪksθs/, *glimpsed* /glɪmpst/); but these are absolutely forbidden in Spanish phonotactics and quite rare as syllable codas as well. Loanwords conform to this constraint in pronunciation (and eventually in orthography too) by losing all but one consonant or by adding a protective vowel to create another syllable:

record → /r̄ékor/	*tank* → /tán.ke/	*zinc*→ /θin, sin/
trust→ /trús.te/	*fax*→ /fas/	*film* → /fíl.me/

Third, initial clusters of /sC/ are common in English but again forbidden in Spanish. Since Roman times, the Iberian solution has been the addition (EPENTHESIS) of an initial /e/. The Real Academia adopts the *e-* in the official orthography once the word is felt to be naturalized.

station = estación	Slav = eslavo	spray = espray	slogan = eslogan
spy = espía	stress = estrés	sphere = esfera	ski = esquí
spasm = espasmo	spaghetti = espaguetis	snob = esnob	status = /estátus/

But Spanish and English phonotactics are not entirely different. For example, in neither language are double (GEMINATE) consonant sounds commonly used. What is spelled as a double consonant is either phonemically one:

funny /fʌ́ni/	*committing* /kəmítɪŋ/	*carro* /kár̄o/
borrow /bɑ́ro/	*assured* /əʃʊ́rd/	*cuello* /kwéjo/

or corresponds to two separately pronounced phonemes in different syllables:

suggest /səg.dʒɛ́st/ *acción* /ak.sjón, ak.θjón /

The only instances of true, phonemically geminate consonants are found where a stem or prefix ending in a consonant joins with a stem beginning with the same one. For example, English has /kk/ in *bookcase* and /ss/ in *misstate,* and at least in slower speech Spanish has /nn/ in *innumerable* and /bb/ in *obvio* and *subversivo.*

2.4 Phonemic vs. orthographic representation. Just as the basic units of the phonological system are phonemes, the basic units of a writing system (letters, punctuation marks, numerals . . .) are called GRAPHEMES. Although the two systems are distinct, in alphabetic writing the graphemes are at least partially based on the phonemes. Thus, the spelling of English *fat* is close to its phonemic representation /fæt/, and the spelling of Spanish *paso* is even closer to the IPA symbols used for its phonemic representation, /páso/. There is a greater PHONEMIC FIT or phoneme-grapheme match in Spanish orthography, and perhaps this transparency is why the language is chosen by some students as a supposedly easy foreign language—a false impression, as they soon discover. Like English, Spanish orthography has silent letters (*h*), two-letter combinations or DIGRAPHS for one sound (*ch, qu),* useless letters (*x* = *cs),* two or more letters for the same phoneme (*b* and *v* = /b/), and two or more phonemes rendered by the same grapheme (/x/ and /g/ = *g*). Even where Spanish is internally consistent, as in *ñ* = /ɲ/, its conventions may not match those of English. For illustration, figure 2.9 contrasts orthographic and phonemic representations for selected Spanish and English words. (See Teschner 2000a for more on Spanish phonemic/graphemic correspondences.)

Both languages have orthographic rules that alter spelling in regular ways. In English, for example, a final *y* becomes *i(e)* before a suffix (*ie* before a consonant, *i* before a vowel) but stays *y* before *i-*: *carry, carries, carried, carrier, carrying, bury, buried, burial, burying.* The main Spanish rules are as follows:

Figure 2.9. Orthographic vs. phonemic representations of selected words

(a) Spanish	
araña /aráɲa/	horario /orárjo/
aunque /áwnke/	huérfano /wérfano/
bautizar /bawtisár/, /bawtiθár/	idioma /idjóma/
cañería /kaɲería/	joyero /xojéro/
cenizas /senísas/, /θeníθas/	juguete /xugéte/
chorro /tʃór̄o/	lleváis /jebájs/, /ʎebájs/
desagüe /deságwe/	Marruecos /mar̄wékos/
Enrique /enr̄íke/	quién /kjen/
fuego /fwégo/	quincuagésimo /kinkwaxésimo/
giroscopio /xiroskópjo/	rayaba /r̄ajába/
guardia /gwárdja/	suave /swábe/
hollín /ojín/, /oʎín/	viraje /biráje/
hielo /jélo/	yunque /júnke/

(b) English	
above /əbʌ́v/	musician /mjuzíʃən/
abroad /əbrɔ́d/	natural /nǽtʃərəl/
bathing /béðɪŋ/	phase, faze /fez/
cartoon /kɑrtún/	quart /kwɔrt/
channel /tʃǽnəl/	roughly /rʌ́fli/
clock /klɑk/	shroud /ʃrawd/
crumbs /krʌmz/	strangely /stréndʒli/
equality /ikwɑ́ləti/	though /ðo/
fusion /fjúʒən/	thought /θɔt/
gesture /dʒɛ́stʃər/	treasures /trɛ́ʒərz/
hanger /hǽŋər/	use /juz/ (verb), /jus/ (noun)
huge /hjudʒ/	usually /júʒuəli/
idea /ajdíə/	whether /(h)wɛ́ðər/
kitchen /kítʃən/	would, wood /wʊd/
live /lɪv/ (verb), /lajv/ (adj.)	youth /juθ/

1. *i* (when spelling /j/) → *y* after a vowel or word-initially: *com-ió* but *ca-yó*; *durm-iendo* but *yendo, ca-yendo*; *cerrar (ie), cierro* but *errar (ie), yerro.*
2. *r* for /r̄/ word-initially → *rr* intervocalically: *romano* but *prerromano*; *regla* but *arreglar*; *revolución* but *antirrevolucionario.*
3. *g* for /x/ → *j* before *a, o, u*: *corregir, corrijo, corrija.*
4. /k/ is *qu* before *e, i* but *c* elsewhere: *chico, chiquito; rico, riqueza; marcar, marqué.*
5. /θ/ (= /s/ in *seseo)* is *c* before *e, i* but *z* elsewhere: *lápiz, lápices*; *empezar, empecé.*

6. /g/ is *gu* before *e, i* but *g* elsewhere: *lago, laguito*; *pago, pague.*
7. /gw/ is *gü* before *e, i* but *gu* elsewhere: *averiguo, averigüe*; *lengua, lengüita.*

These rules are not phonological rules and do not affect pronunciation in any way. If anything, they are an awkward way of maintaining a record of pronunciation in a system in which one grapheme has more than one value. Since *ga ge gi go gu* are /ga xe xi go gu/, the syllables /ge gi / are spelled *gue gui*; and since this preempts *gu* for /g/ before *e, i, gü* is needed for /gw/ before those vowels. Both teachers and students must also keep in mind that changes such as *pag(o) → pagu(é)* are not verb irregularities; they are quite regular, and they occur with other parts of speech as well. Students who find orthographic changes strange might recall their own language, in which *bury* is a regular verb, and its *y→ i(e)* change is just a spelling adaptation; it remains /bɛ́ri/ regardless of what suffix is added. Moreover, the same change occurs in adjectives (*sloppy, sloppier, sloppily*) and nouns (*party, parties*). Rules that change pronunciation are wholly different, as is shown in chapter 3.

Even after students show basic mastery of the phonemes and orthography of a second language, regressions are frequent in cognates. Cognates may be "free" as lexical items with carried-over meanings (v. 15.2), but they are deceptive phonologically. Many students show more accuracy with a new word like *oreja* than with a familiar friend such as *general* or *rosa.* The following are noteworthy examples whose similarity of spelling is belied by different phonemic representations (for others, see Stockwell and Bowen 1965).

radio = *radio* but /r̄ádjo/ ≠ /rédio/
usual = *usual* but /uswál/ ≠ /júʒuəl/
acción = *action* but /aksjón/ ≠ /ǽkʃən/
conversación = *conversation* but /kombersasjón/ ≠ /kɑ̀nvərséʃən/
automático = *automatic* but /awtomátiko/ ≠ /ɔ̀təmǽtɪk/
hospital = *hospital* but /ospitál/ ≠ /hɑ́spɪ̀təl/
Europa = *Europe* but /ewrópa/ ≠ /jʊ́rəp/, /jə́rəp/
ángel = *angel* but /ánxel/ ≠ /éndʒəl/

Notes for chapter 2

1. Some U.S. and most British and Australian speakers do use /tj- dj-/, but only before /u/ in *tune, duty,* and so on.

2. Many of these aspirated jota dialects retain Old Spanish /h/ (now silent in standard lects) in *harto, heno, hembra, hilo, hediondo, huir,* and a few other words. Thus, a word such as *halar* 'pull' is pronounced [halár] there and often spelled *jalar* since /x/ has merged with the [h] (Boyd-Bowman 1960, 65–68).

3. The official IPA symbol for the alveolar trill is simply [r], which causes confusion with the general convention (also accepted by the IPA) of using *r* for *r*-sounds in general. Following the usual practice in Hispanic linguistics, we add a macron, *r̄* to single out the trill specifically.

4. Neutralization is the merger or canceling out of a contrast maintained elsewhere. An English example is that the vowels of *beat* vs. *bit* are abundantly distinguished in most environments but not before /r/ (*beer*) or /ŋ/ (*Bing*); here, speakers use the /i/ of *beat* or the /ɪ/ of *bit* or a vowel in between them without differentiation. Neutralization will be encountered in other parts of language structure also.

5. For more information on the geographical distribution of the dialect variants discussed here, see Resnick 1975; Canfield 1981; Zamora Vicente 1967; Lipski 1994; Navarro Tomás 1967 and 1975; and the *Atlas lingüístico de la Península Ibérica.*

6. By saying that /θ/ is "merged" with /s/ in *seseo,* we do not mean that *seseantes* historically had a /θ/ that they changed to /s/. Actually, the Old Spanish distinction was four-way: two affricates, /ts/ in *caça* (>*caza*) vs. /dz/ in *hazer* (>*hacer*), and two fricatives, /s/ in *passa* (> *pasa*) vs. /z/ in *casa*; there was no /θ/ at all. But at the time that Spaniards began to colonize the New World, /dz/ and /z/ had merged with /ts/ and /s/, respectively, and /ts/ kept evolving. The merger of /ts/ with /s/, for example, *caza* with *casa,* won out in Andalusia and America, but in northern Spain the /t/ of /ts/ dentalized the /s/ before dropping, yielding /θ/ in *caza* and *hacer* (Alonso 1967, 84–122).

7. There are other subtypes that Navarro Tomás (1975) confirmed with detailed palatography (a technique that records where the speaker's tongue makes contact). The reader can appreciate this variety by bearing in mind that the tongue can be grooved or ungrooved; that the tip, blade, or both can be used; that the tongue shape can be convex, concave, or flat; and that contact can be anywhere from the teeth to the postalveolar area just behind the gums.

8. In northern England, eastern New England, and the Great Lakes area, however, many speakers have a fronted version of /ɑ/ that is closer to Spanish /a/.

9. None of the native speakers I have consulted pronounce most of these words with hiatus, even in careful oral reading. For a fuller study of the variability of Spanish hiatus, see Whitley 1995b.

10. The Spanish of Paraguay (Lipski 1994, 209) and the Yucatán (Lope Blanch 1992, 317) is exceptional in separating vowels of adjacent words with a glottal stop, presumably because of Guaraní and Mayan influence, respectively.

11. Syllable-final consonants are often called *implosivas* in Spanish, although "implosive" technically means a different kind of sound in phonetics. See Fernández Sevilla 2000 for a detailed account of the contemporary weakening and loss of such consonants in various dialects and styles of Spanish.

Exercises for chapter 2

1. Which Spanish phonemes have no equivalents in English? Indicate the strategies you might use in teaching their articulation to students unable to master them from modeling alone. (Note: phonetic terminology and explanations are means to the end of establishing fluent but accurate speech. Students are studying Spanish, not general phonetics, so as a teacher you should use explanations that are precise, concise, and understandable to students.)

2. Give a minimal pair in Spanish for each of the following phonemic distinctions (in the case of (k–l), just for dialects that have those contrasts). Example: /p b/ *pez, vez.*
   (a) /t tʃ/ (b) /r r̄/ (c) /k x/ (d) /p f/ (e) /n ɲ/ (f) /k g/ (g) /j w/ (h) /o u/ (i) /e i/ (j) /a o/, unstressed (k) /l ʎ/ (l) /s θ/

3. What differences exist in the Spanish and English articulations of /t/, /d/, and /r/? Where should these differences be presented in an introductory course, and how much emphasis should be given to each of them? Why?

4. According to the analysis presented in this chapter, what criterion determines whether Spanish [j w] are phonemically /j w/ or /i u/? Applying this criterion, how would you analyze the indicated glides of the following words? Why?
   (a) de[w]da (b) antig[w]o (c) act[w]ar (d) pa[j]sano (e) camb[j]ar (f) polic[j]al (g) jag[w]ar (h) ba[w]lero (i) re[j]naba (j) s[w]egro (k) resfr[j]ar (l) arg[w]ir (m) ad[j]ós (n) grad[w]ado (o) conf[j]ado (p) amá[j]s (q) ma[j]zal (r) farmac[j]a (s) anunc[j]ado (t) re[w]nir

5. The following words are in Spanish phonemic representation for a dialect that lacks /θ/ and /ʎ/. Pronounce them, and then identify them by re-writing them in their normal orthography.
   (a) /kostíja/ (b) /xwísjo/ (c) /r̄ixjéron/ (d) /jábe/ (e) /tʃantáxe/ (f) /exérse/ (g) /kombídan/ (h) /bírxen/ (i) /wélga/ (j) /tʃéke/ (k) /paɲwélo/ (l) /bóses/ (m) /kor̄jénte/ (n) /umijár/ (o) /xenxíbre/ (p) /bergwénsa/ (q) /asjénda/ (r) /wéko/ (s) /jwébe/ (t) /aberigwé/ (u) /kitamántʃas/ (v) /kawdíjo/ (w) /jér̄o/ (x) /ɲoɲés/

6. An American TV announcer has asked you for help with the pronunciation of a list of Mexican place-names. Give her a phonemic transcription (/ /) of each word using IPA, which many announcers learn in broadcasting schools. Include an indication of stress.
   (a) Palenque (b) Saucillo (c) Coahuila (d) Río Yaqui (e) Villahermosa (f) Guanajuato (g) Jalisco (h) Ciudad Juárez (i) Chichén Itzá (j) Chiapas (k) Oaxaca (l) Guerrero (m) Querétaro (n) Cuernavaca (o) Veracruz (p) Tlaxcala

7. You now advise a Mexican TV announcer on the English pronunciation of certain U.S. and Canadian place-names, again using a phonemic transcription with an indication of stress.
   (a) Phoenix (b) Milwaukee (c) Halifax (d) Charlotte (e) Dubuque (f) Ottawa (g) Duluth (h) Sioux Falls (i) Houston (j) Birmingham (k) Indianapolis (l) Worcester

8. Assuming at least a general phonemic accuracy, how will English speakers tend to pronounce the following differently from native Spanish speakers?
   (a) Él está en este hospital.
   (b) ¿Qué es un artista?
   (c) Me he enterado de ello.
   (d) Los han oído.

9. Although we are focusing on the problems that English speakers have with Spanish, sometimes the reverse approach can provide insight into the Spanish system. Explain why Spanish-speaking students of English might have trouble with the following contrasts.
   (a) bowel, vowel
   (b) peat, pit
   (c) fool, full
   (d) set, sat, sot
   (e) cheat, sheet
   (f) boat, bought, butt
   (g) yet, jet
   (h) esteem, steam
   (i) band, ban

10. One of the difficulties for students of ESL (English as a second language) is the presence of HOMOGRAPHS, words that are pronounced differently but spelled the same. Explain to a Spanish-speaker the differences in the homographs *wound, use, lead, primer, row, dove, live, bass, tear, bow,* and *advocate*, following this model.
    Model: *read*: 1. /rid/ 'leer, leo', el presente o infinitivo del verbo.
    2. /rɛd/ 'leí, leyó, leímos', etc., el pretérito (o pasado) del verbo.

11. As a shortcut to instant L2, phrase books dispense with phonetics and give a FIGURED PRONUNCIATION, rendering L2 in L1 orthography. The following examples come from one such book for speaking with (Castilian) Spanish speakers. First, identify the likely errors that English readers will make by depending on these renditions; then, at a more general level, explain the mistaken assumptions of figured pronunciation.
    (a) siete: "see-AY-tay"
    (b) diez: "dee-YETH"
    (c) todo "TAW-doh"
    (d) jabón "ha-BON"
    (e) cerveza "ther-BEH-tha"
    (f) ballet "ball-YET"

12. Find derivatives (using a dictionary if necessary) of the following nouns and adjectives that show the same spelling changes as in verbs. For example: *vago, va**gu**edad,* just as in *pagar, pa**gu**é.*
    (a) raza
    (b) agua
    (c) antiguo
    (d) poco
    (e) pez
    (f) rico
    (g) trigo
    (h) perspicaz

13. Using a phonemic transcription, predict how unwary students might mispronounce the following Spanish cognates if English pronunciation is transferred.
    (a) oxígeno
    (b) unión
    (c) anual
    (d) higiene
    (e) residuo
    (f) musical
    (g) presente
    (h) equilibrio
    (i) millón
    (j) hotel
    (k) digestión
    (l) series
    (m) autor
    (n) biología
    (o) quieto
    (p) visitar

14. A U.S. ship with a Spanish name, the *Pueblo,* was pronounced by newscasters in this country "the [puwéblow]." Also, a tire named *Tiempo* was advertised as "[tijémpow]." Why did Spanish /pwéblo/, /tjémpo/ come out in this way?

15. At least for the phonemicization of Spanish words in slow speech, one might wish to distinguish single and geminate phonemes, as in the following cases:
    (a) /unómbre/ *un hombre,* /unnómbre/ *un nombre*
    (b) /elóro/ *el oro,* /ellóro/ *el loro*
    (c) /lasálas/ *las alas,* /lassálas/ *las salas*
    (d) /labenída/ *la venida,* /laabenída/ *la avenida*
    (e) /desúso/ *desuso,* /desuúso/ *de su uso*

    As pointed out earlier, however, double vowels are merged in faster styles, and Quilis and Fernández (1975, 149) noted the same for double consonants. Have a native speaker pronounce these examples (and any others you might wish to add) and determine whether the speaker uses geminates. Instead of using directly contrastive pairs—which might induce an atypically careful pronunciation—embed the cues in sentences and mix them up.

16. We noted that Spanish allows glides in clusters (/trw/, /plj/, etc.) that are absent from English. List as many such Spanish clusters of consonant + /l r j w/ as you can think of (there are about four dozen of them), and circle those that English speakers might have trouble with.

17. Each of the following shows dialect variation in Spanish. Which variant would you select for your classroom, and why?
    (a) articulation of /s/
    (b) distinction of /θ/ and /s/
    (c) articulation of /x/
    (d) distinction of /ʎ/ and /j/

18. In section 2.3 we reviewed the traditional Spanish rules for syllabication. Current phonological theory emphasizes syllable construction according to universal principles, three of which can be expressed as follows:
    Rule 1: Above each phonemic V (=nucleus) in a word, construct the rhyme of a σ.
    Rule 2: Then scan the consonants to the left of each V: assign to the onset of its σ as many of those consonants as the language's phonotactics allows to begin a word.
    Rule 3: Finally, assign any remaining C to the coda of the preceding σ.
    How do English and Spanish, using these same rules, end up with different syllabications of *transcribe* and *transcribir*?

19. Syllabify the following words (using a phonemic notation):
    (a) perspicaz
    (b) cuádruplo
    (c) carruaje
    (d) reunión
    (e) adquieren
    (f) saldréis
    (g) pañuelos
    (h) vainilla
    (i) bronquio
    (j) abstracto
    (k) alguien
    (l) corrección

Chapter 3

Phonological rules

3.0 Types of rules: Categorical and variable, general and dialectal. The pronunciation of phonemes changes in a fairly regular fashion that depends on the phonetic environment. For example, in both English and Spanish any vowel (V) becomes somewhat nasalized (Ṽ) when a nasal consonant (N) follows, as in *moon* and *mundo.* Thus, /múndo/ → [mú̃ndo]. The general way to formulate such a process or rule is to use an arrow for 'becomes', a slash for 'when in the environment of', and a blank that specifies the position where the change occurs. Thus, 'a vowel becomes nasalized when preceding a nasal' may be written as follows:

V → Ṽ / ___N

Alternatively, feature notation (v. 1.1.5) could be adopted as shown in figure 3.1, either in the more traditional format as in (a) or in the autosegmental representation as in (b), which portrays the reassociation of the vowel with its neighbor's feature [±nasal] operating here on a separate (autonomous) tier.[1]

The arrow-slash-blank notation is also used for the insertion or deletion of sounds. As noted in the preceding chapter (v. 2.3), Spanish inserts /e/ in front of an initial sC (cluster of *s* plus consonant) so that the /s/ forms the coda of a new syllable: *ski* → *esquí* /es.kí/. This EPENTHESIS rule can be stated as follows: 'where there was nothing (Ø) preceding sC, insert /e/':

Ø → e / ___ sC

Yet this is too general as it stands, for it will insert /e/ before every sC cluster, giving not only *ski* → *esquí* but also *chispa* → **chiespa* and *asco* → **aesco*. (Recall that the asterisk means 'wrong', v. 0.2.2.) The rule must be confined or constrained so as to apply just

Figure 3.1. Showing phonological rules with feature notation

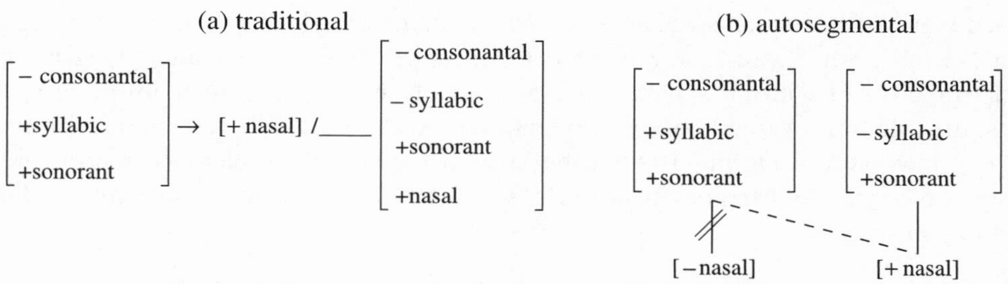

when the sC is word-initial, that is, when it follows a word boundary. The symbol for word boundary is #. Hence,

$$\emptyset \rightarrow e \ / \ \#\_\_\_ \ sC$$

To express another rule taken up in chapter 2, namely the simplification of a final CC in Spanish (*record* → /r̄ékor/), we state that a C deletes or drops (becomes zero, Ø) when it follows another C and is word-final (i.e., precedes #):

$$C \rightarrow \emptyset \ / \ C \ \_\_\_ \ \#$$

The # is not the only boundary that plays a role in phonology. A plus, +, represents a morpheme boundary, the grammatical stitch or juncture between stems and affixes within a word. A double vertical bar, ||, stands for a phrase boundary, the slight gap between breath-groups or the longer one at the end of a sentence. Rules are also sensitive to syllable boundaries (represented by **.** or $). Finally, curly braces { }, meaning 'or', are used to group changes that occur in the same environment, or environments that trigger the same change.

Some phonological rules are general throughout all (or almost all) varieties of a language, while others are limited to specific lects. Crosscutting this classification is another one, *categorical* vs. *variable*. A CATEGORICAL rule applies across the board, so that whenever it can apply, it regularly does apply; Vowel Nasalization and E-Epenthesis are categorical in this sense. A VARIABLE rule applies some of the time, with its frequency increasing or decreasing according to factors such as social class, sex, style, and age. A well-known example from English is "G-Dropping," whereby words such as *nothing, playing, singing* become *nothin', playin', singin'*; more precisely, final /ŋ/ becomes [n] when following an unstressed vowel ($\breve{V}$):

$$\eta \rightarrow n \ / \ \breve{V} \ \_\_\_\#$$

Thus, *nothing* /nʌ́θɪŋ/ → [nʌ́θɪn].

Many English speakers regard G-Dropping as substandard or indicative of slovenly articulation, and they may deny ever doing it themselves. In fact, variable rules that have become salient to a society are often dismissed in this way, acquiring a strong attitudinal component and status as social markers. Yet careful studies of actual speech have confirmed that native English speakers everywhere alternate [ŋ] ~ [n] (the ~ means 'varying with'), with lower classes using more [n] than upper classes, with men using more [n] than women, and with all speakers using relatively more [n] in their informal speech. Thus, the rule has a variable output depending on class, sex, and style. Variable rules are of great interest to sociolinguists, but because of the attitudinal element, reports are not always objective. As Medina Rivera (1999) put this point for a variable rule in Puerto Rican Spanish:

> La mayoría de los hablantes cree que no produce estas variantes no estándar; sin embargo, a la hora de ser entrevistados y grabados, los resultados muestran lo contrario. (533)

Thus, some sources on dialect variation may deny with vigor that their group (class, country, stratum, etc.) ever uses a certain *vulgarismo* when in fact, at least informally, they do.

3.1 Spanish rules. Sections 3.1.1 through 3.1.8 describe rules that apply to Spanish consonants and glides. Sections 3.1.9 and 3.1.10 focus on vowel variations. To the extent that published studies permit, the application of each rule will be identified as general or dialectal and as categorical or variable.[2]

3.1.1 Glide strengthening.

(a) becoming fricatives:

w → ɣw
j → ʝ ~ ʒ } / {$, #} ___

(b) becoming stops:

w → gw
j → ɟ ~ dʒ } / {|| ___ V, N + ___}

(almost general, some variability in output)

English /w j/ are always weak semivowels or glides; Spanish /w j/ are also glides when in diphthongs, as in word-final position (*rey, hoy*) or next to a consonant (*naipe* /nájpe/, *pie* /pjé/, *causa* /káwsa/, *aduana* /adwána/). But when beginning a syllable (={$, #} ___), Spanish glides are pronounced with greater articulatory tension and friction in most regions. In particular:

- between vowels or another glide: *Chi**hu**a**hu**a*, *a**hu**ecar*, *ho**y**o*, *va**y**a*, *a**y**udar*, *re**y**es*, *ho**y**uelo* (and *ca**ll**e*, *cue**ll**o* in *yeísta* zones)
- word-initially: ***hu**eso*, ***hu**evo*, ***hu**arache*, ***y**erno*, ***y**a*, ***hi**erro*, ***hi**edra*, ***y**ugo* (***ll**amar*, ***ll**evar*)
- beginning a stem after a prefix's consonant in a separate syllable: *ab**y**ecto*, *des**hi**elo*.[3]

/w/ is labiovelar; when strengthened, it takes on velar friction, [ɣw], or in some dialects, bilabial: /wéso/ → [ɣwéso] ~ [βwéso]. By case (b) of the rule, the constriction of initial /w/ may even become a velar stop after a pause (i.e., utterance-initially, ‖ ___V) or a nasal (as in *un hueso*). In rendering this velar friction or stopping, some dialect writers respell *huevo, hueso* as *güevo, güeso*; indeed, since /g/ becomes a fricative (v. 3.1.6), there is usually no difference between the /gw/ of *agua* and the /w/ of *Chihuahua.*

When palatal /j/ is strengthened, the middle of the tongue rises closer to the palate, yielding a voiced palatal fricative that the IPA symbolizes as [j̞] (see figure 3.6). Thus, *yerno leyes* /jérno léjes/ → [j̞érno léj̞es], while *pierna* and *ley* /pjérna lej/ keep their frictionless glides. [j̞] strikes English speakers as between their /j/ of *you* and /ʒ/ of *vision,* which it is. Again, by case (b) of the rule, the tensing results in a palatal stop, [ɟ], when /j/ is utterance-initial (*¡Ya verás!*) or when it begins a stem after a nasal (*in**y**ección, un **y**erno*), so an emphatic *¡Yo!* reminds an English speaker of *Joe.*

This friction or *rehilamiento* in /j/ varies from light to heavy. A few dialects have none; their /j/ is a weak glide in all positions as in English and may even drop when next to /i/ as in *gallina* → [gaína]; by compensation, speakers then hypercorrect, *María* → [maɾíja] (Lipski 1994, 290). In other dialects (e.g., southwest Spain and most of Argentina), the friction is enhanced with an alveopalatal articulation: thus, instead of the relatively dry-sounding [j̞] and [ɟ] (palatal, apex down) of most regions, these dialects, called *žeísta* (Zamora Vicente 1967, 79), use the juicier [ʒ] and [dʒ] (alveopalatal sibilants, apex up, grooved tongue). In Buenos Aires, this [ʒ] variably devoices to [ʃ]. As a result, perhaps no other Spanish phoneme varies today as much as /j/: a word such as *yo* can be heard as [jo j̞o ɟo ʒo dʒo ʃo] with ever greater *rehilamiento*. Saciuk (1980), who managed to distinguish nine degrees of friction for /j/, suggested that the process is a variable rule, but in general his data corroborate the tendencies summarized in figure 3.2.

Most phonological rules of Spanish apply across word boundaries in fast speech. Glide Strengthening, in that case, may depend on the dialect. For a phrase such as *voy a morir*,

Figure 3.2. Degrees of rehilamiento of /j/

	next to consonants (*comió, desierto, Dios, caigo...*) and word-finally (*hay, ley*)	syllable-initially after vowel (*leyes, cayó, hoyo, hoyuelo*) or a prefix (*deshielo*)	utterance-initially (*¡Yo!*) or syllable-initially after a nasal nasal (*inyección*)
Central America and northernmost Mexico	j (glide)	j (glide)	j (glide)
Most varieties in Spain and the Americas	j (glide)	j̞ (palatal fricative)	ɟ (palatal stop)
Andalusia, Argentina, Uruguay, Paraguay	j (glide)	ʒ (alveopalatal fricative)	dʒ (alveopalatal affricated stop)

Navarro Tomás (1967, 151) regarded both [bójamorír] (with a glide) and [bóɟamorír] as normal in Castilian. This seems less true of the Americas; Harris (1983, 61) noted that in Buenos Aires, Strengthening does not occur over the word boundary #: *ley* is [lej] and *leyes* is [léʒes], but *la ley es* is [laléjes].

3.1.2 Nasal assimilation.

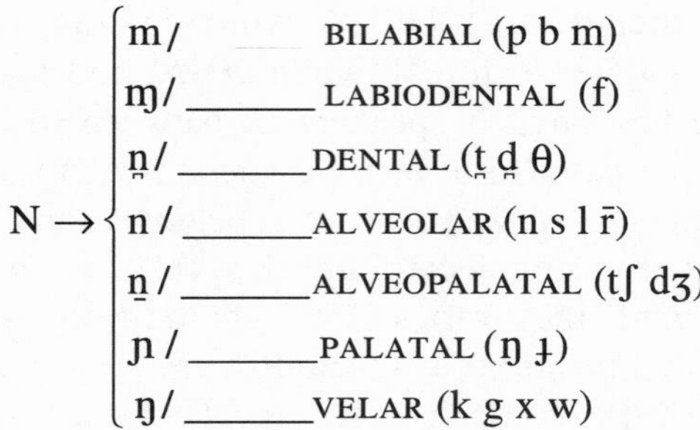

(general; categorical inside words, variable across word boundaries)

In this formulation, which spells out each possible result, the rule looks more complicated than it really is. Expressed simply, nasals ASSIMILATE to, or are pronounced in the same place as, a following consonant: bilabial ([m]) before bilabials, dental ([n̪]) before dentals, and so forth. Assimilation always occurs inside a word; across word boundaries, the rule applies in normal speech but may be blocked in slower, more deliberate styles (Harris 1969, 8–16). In the following examples, note in particular the varying pronunciations of words like *en, con, son, un*:

- bilabial [m]: *a**m**bos, e**n**viar, co**n**versar; **en** Perú, **en** Venezuela, co**n** Manuel, **un** mapa*
- labiodental [ɱ]: *é**n**fasis, triu**n**fo; **en** Francia, co**n** Fernando, so**n** fuertes, **un** fuego*
- dental [n̪]: *ca**n**ta, a**n**da**n**do, co**n**cepto* (in dialects with /θ/); ***en** Turquía, co**n** David, so**n** dos, **un** tío*
- alveolar [n]: *co**n**sta, ho**n**ra; **en** Suiza, co**n** nosotros, **un** lado*
- alveopalatal [n̠]:[4] *co**n**cha; **en** Chile, co**n** Chávez*
- palatal [ɲ]: ***in**yección, có**n**yuge, co**n**lleva; **un** yeso, co**n** llamas*
- velar [ŋ]: *mo**n**ja, co**n**quista, ho**n**go; **en** Cuba, **en** Japón, co**n** Jaime, so**n** gusanos, **un** hueco*

The phonological effect of Nasal Assimilation is to cancel (NEUTRALIZE) the nasal distinctions in coda position. The phonemes /m n ɲ/ contrast in *cama/cana/caña,* but preconsonantally no contrast is possible, since the nasal is pronounced with the consonant.

3.1.3 Lateral assimilation.

$$l \rightarrow \begin{cases} /\text{l̪}/ \_\_\_\_\_ \text{DENTAL} \\ /\text{ʎ}/ \_\_\_\_\_ \text{PALATAL} \end{cases}$$

(general; categorical in words, variable across word boundaries)

Like /n/, Spanish /l/ assimilates to a following C, but here only if the consonant is pronounced with the front or middle of the tongue. Thus, *alto* /álto/ → [ál̪t̪o], but in *palco* /pálko/ the /l/ stays alveolar since /k/ is velar (pronounced with the back of the tongue). The actual acoustic effect of this assimilation, though, is fairly negligible.

3.1.4 S-Voicing.

s → z / ___Ç̬

(regarded as general and categorical, but details are disputed)

By this rule, /s/ is voiced to [z] when a voiced consonant (Ç̬) follows—including strengthened /j w/. In dialects with apical [s̺] (v. 2.1.4.2), the voicing yields apical [z̺]; see figure 3.6. Thus, *chisme* /tʃísme/ → [tʃízme], *isla* /ísla/ → [ízla], *deshielo* /des+jélo/ (with an internal boundary meaning that /j/ starts a stem) → [dezɟélo]. Like the two preceding rules, this is an assimilation rule, but in the feature [±voice] rather than place of articulation. S-Voicing occurs within a word (as in *isla, asno, desde, rasgar, chisme, esbelto*) and across # in normal fast speech (as in *las vacas, las gafas, los maestros, los huecos, las yeguas, es duro*). On the other hand, Torreblanca (1978, 498) concluded from his data that the rule is variable rather than categorical, depending more on articulatory tension than on the nature of the following consonant: more [s] when the speaker uses a tenser articulation, and more [z] when articulation is relaxed. But whatever the distribution may be, Spanish [s] and [z] are always allophones of one phoneme, and contrasts such as English *Sue/zoo, face/phase* are not possible.

3.1.5 S-Aspiration.

s → h → Ø / ____ {C, #} (or more simply: / ___$)

(variable and dialectal, but widespread)

By the S-Aspiration rule, when /s/ is syllable-final (i.e., precedes another consonant or is word-final), it does not voice to [z] but instead weakens to a light aspiration, [h], which may then drop (→ Ø) entirely. Thus, /las tʃíspas/ → [la(h)tʃí(h)pa(h)]. In one environment, namely C = /r̄/, /s/ is aspirated in most dialects: *Israel* and (across #) *los reyes*. In the following areas, however, S-Aspiration occurs before any consonant as well as word-

Figure 3.3. Aspiration of /s/ among Miami Cubans: phonological variables

	/ __‖	/ __#	/ __C
/s/ → [h]	22%	43%	70%
/s/ → [h] → Ø	74%	54%	20%

finally: the Caribbean region, all of Hispanic South America except the highlands from Bolivia to Colombia, and southern Spain and the Canaries. In the peninsula, it has spread northward during the last century from Andalusia and Extremadura to Madrid itself (Navarro Tomás 1975, 187–90).

Given the frequency of /s/ in Spanish, S-Aspiration greatly alters the way the language sounds, especially to nonnatives. For some speakers the rule seems virtually categorical, especially in the environment / __C, but the typical situation is a variable rule. For example, Obaid (1973, 62) estimated that S-Aspiration occurs in Madrid speech about 50 percent of the time, and Hammond (1980) more precisely gave the statistics in figure 3.3 for Miami Cuban speech according to phonological environment.

Fontanella de Weinberg (1974) explored in more detail the social variables in Buenos Aires. Experiments with *porteños* revealed that both sexes and all classes aspirate, but men do so more than women, lower classes more than upper classes, and everyone more in their informal speech. A comparison adapted from her results is given in figure 3.4.

Social variables combine with geographical ones: areas such as Nicaragua and Chile tend to retain the [h] stage for /s/ while other areas (Caribbean islands and eastern Andalusia) proceed more often to outright deletion, Ø (Lipski 1994). Aspiration also

Figure 3.4. Aspiration of /s/ in Buenos Aires: Stylistic and social variables

	Style A (informal spontaneous conversation)	**Style B** (storytelling to interviewer)	**Style C** (oral reading of a written passage)	**Style D** (oral reading of individual words)
Class 4: high-level executives and professionals	14.0%	6.0%	1.5%	0% (none)
Class 3: technicians, university-trained personnel	18.5%	4.5%	5.0%	2.0%
Class 2: shop owners, self-employed business persons	41.5%	27.5%	17.0%	1.5%
Class 1: domestics, blue-collar workers	66.0%	40.0%	39.0%	16.0%

Figure 3.5. Effects of /s/ aspiration on adjacent phonemes

On the preceding vowel	On the following consonant
/as/ → [æ(h)]: *más, vas, las*	[sβ] → [hβ] → [ɸɸ]: *las* ***b****otas, des****v****án*
/es/ → [ɛ(h)]: *mes, les, ves*	[sð] → [hð] → [θθ]: *los* ***d****ientes,* ***d****esde*
/is/ → [ɪ(h)]: *mis, perdiz*	[sɣ] → [hɣ] → [xx]: *des****g****arro, las* ***g****arras*
/os/ → [ɔ(h)]: *tos, voz, arroz*	[sp] → [hp] → [pp]: *obis****p****o, los* ***p****asos*
/us/ → [ʊ(h)]: *sus, luz*	[st] → [ht] → [tt]: *es****t****e, los* ***t****renes*
	[sk] → [hk] → [kk]: *tos****c****o, las* ***c****asas*
	[sn] → [hn] → [nn]: *as****n****o, los* ***n****ombres*

depends on phonetic environment, word length, and structure (Cepeda 1995): it is more common when *-s* is lexical (part of the word, as in *más*) than when it is an inflectional suffix (as in *vas* or *camas*). According to Poplack (1980), yet another factor is the functional importance of the /s/. According to her data, it is deleted most often when it is redundant, that is, does not uniquely signal a grammatical category. In *las matas se mueren,* plurality is conveyed by two instances of final /s/ and one of final /n/. Not all of these are really needed, but if all are deleted the message changes to *la mata se muere.* She found a tendency to delete any number of the markers so long as at least one remains. Uber (1989) agreed, but other investigators (Lafford 1989; Ranson 1993) have challenged whether this "functional" restriction on /s/ aspiration and deletion really applies.

Aspiration before V is less common and less accepted even in aspirating dialects. Yet it is well attested, especially in common words such as *si* [hi], *señor, siempre, ser, casa,* and *nosotros* (Alonso 1967, 285; Obaid 1973, 63; Hammond 1980, 12; Canfield 1981, 54).

Aspiration strongly affects neighboring phonemes, and if the [h] drops entirely, these perturbations are the only traces of the underlying /s/. In eastern Andalusia (Alonso 1950; Penny 2000, 192), the [h] opens up a preceding vowel and assimilates to a following consonant, as shown in figure 3.5. This V opening may then trigger a matching opening of the vowels in other syllables: *monótonos* → [mɔnɔ́tɔnɔ], *leches* → [lɛ́tʃɛ]. Phonetically, then, the difference between singulars and plurals in such dialects may be signaled by close (tense) vs. open (lax) vowels and by simple vs. geminated consonants: *la vaca* [laβáka], *las vacas* [læɸɸǽkæ] (where [ɸ] is the voiceless version of [β]).

In Cuban Spanish, on the other hand, the main effect of [h]-dropping is vowel lengthening, with the [Vː] occupying about the same length in milliseconds as the /Vs/ sequence it replaces (Hammond 1989). This yields minimal pairs for length at the phonetic level (Núñez Cedeño and Morales Front 1999, 64): *buque* vs. *busque* [búːke], *patilla* vs. *pastilla* [paːtíʝa], *pecado* vs. *pescado* [peːká(ð)o].

3.1.6 Spirantization of /b d g/.

b d g → β ð ɣ *except/* {
|| / ______
N / ______
<l/ ______ =*for* /d/ *only* >

(general and categorical, but with minor dialectal variation)

The Spanish phonemes /b d g/ have two allophones each, stop and fricative (spirant). The stop allophones [b d g] are like their English counterparts, except that [d] is dental ([d̪]) rather than alveolar (v. 2.1.2). In most types of Spanish, these stops occur in three positions: after a pause (i.e., phrase-initially, or word-initially if the word is spoken in isolation), after nasals, and—only in the case of /d/—after /l/ too (which has in common with the nasal case the fact that /l/ assimilates to the /d/, v. 3.1.3). Otherwise, /b d g/ become fricatives, and since this "otherwise" includes most cases (between V, before C, after most C, word-finally), Spanish /b d g/ are really fricatives more often than stops. Thus, *abogado* /abogádo/ → [aβoɣáðo], *admiraba* /admirába/ → [aðmiráβa], *averiguad* /aberigwád/ → [aβeriɣwáð]. Indeed, Danesi (1982) suggested that they are phonemically fricatives, becoming stops just in the designated environments.

The articulation of the three fricative allophones [β ð ɣ] may give trouble to English speakers (see figure 3.6). [ð] differs from English /ð/ in *then, mother, bathe* only in being slightly weaker. [β] is a [b] in which the lips do not close enough to form a full stop, but close just enough to compress the airstream for light friction. It resembles English /v/ but is made with the lips alone, not with the upper teeth on the lower lip. [ɣ] is a [g] that likewise does not quite stop the airstream; [ɣ] is to [g] as [x] is to [k], though its friction is typically weak.

In normal fluent pronunciation, Spirantization is categorical inside the word, and it applies across word boundaries too, although stops may be retained in a slow, deliberate speech style (Harris 1969, 38–40).[5] Examples of /b d g/ as stops and as fricatives are given below:

Word-internal:
[b d g]: *ambos, conversar*; *andando, toldo, humilde*; *angustia, merengue*
[β ð ɣ]: *Cuba, huevo, calvo, atisbo, hablaba, árbol, abdomen, club, abre*; *podido, admira, tarde, caudal, adquirido, usted, ardid*; *hago, pegue, rasgo, algo, carga, agrio*

At the beginning of an utterance (after a pause or silence):
[b d g]: *¿Vas. . . ?, ¡Basta!, ¿Dónde. . . ?, Dos y tres son. . . , ¡Gatito!; Pues, Guillermo . . .*

Across word boundaries in connected speech:
[b d g]: *en Venecia*; *con Diego, el día*; *en Grecia, con Guillermo, son grandes*
[β ð ɣ]: *el buey, los bueyes, te vas a Bolivia, no ven*; *los días, le doy, es de ella, hay dos dientes*; *el gato, los gatos, de Grecia, a Guillermo, es grande.*

A few dialects extend the stop allophones to other places. To the basic set of environments for stops, / ‖__, N__, and (for /d/) / l__ ,

(a) some speakers in highland Ecuador, southern Mexico, and western Bolivia add /s__, as in *atisbo* ([atízbo] instead of [atízβo]), *desde, rasgo*;
(b) some speakers in Cuba, Jalisco, and Costa Rica add liquids (/r l/), that is, /L ___ (for all three phonemes, not just /d/): *tarde* ([tárde] instead of [tárðe]), *calvo, árbol, algo*;
(c) some speakers in Colombia, eastern Bolivia, and Central America between Yucatán and Nicaragua add /L___, /s____, /G____ (i.e., after liquids, /s/, and glides)—leaving the fricatives mainly just in postvocalic position: *caudal* [kawdál] instead of [kawðál].

Despite this variation, all lects of the language vary between stops and fricatives for /b d g/ and all have a version of the Spirantization rule, and in no native variety is there a phonemic distinction comparable to English *bat* vs. *vat* or *den* vs. *then.*[6]

3.1.7 D-Deletion (or Fricative deletion).

ð → Ø / V ____ {V, #}

(widespread but variable)

Except in isolated areas (Resnick 1975, 82–85), the [ð] produced by Spirantization is so weakly articulated that it variably drops. Several factors affect the rate of deletion (Navarro Tomás 1967, 99–103): phonetic environment (more deletion when /V́__V), word type (more in common everyday words), style (more in casual speech), speed of articulation (more if faster), and speaker's class and education (more if lower). It is commonest in the suffix *-ado* (*hablado* /abládo/ → [aβláðo] → [aβláo]) and in final position; indeed, *usted* and *Madrid* are generally pronounced without their *-d* today: [u(s)té], [maðrí].

Fricative Deletion affects /b g/ too in some Andean dialects. In Chile, for example, Oroz (1966) found [β] deletion in *anduve* [andúe], *cabeza, jabón, joven* and [ɣ] deletion in *aguja* [aúxa], *jugar, lagarto, laguna, seguro.* He also noted a tendency in popular Chilean speech to weaken preconsonantal [β ð ɣ] to glides (133–41):

/b/ → [β] → [w]: ***ab**domen, **ab**ril, dia**b**lo*
/d/ → [ð] → [j]: *pa**d**re, la**d**rillo, a**d**rede, po**d**rir*
/g/ → [ɣ] → [w] ~ [j]: ***ag**ricultor, di**g**no, vina**g**re, lá**g**rima*

Figure 3.6. Fricative articulations

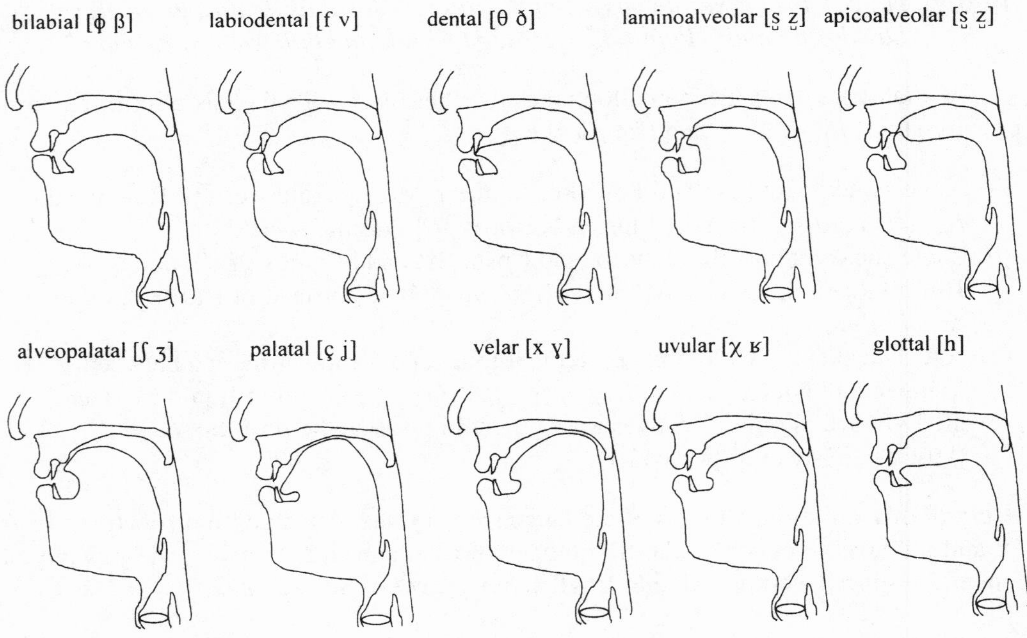

3.1.8 Other consonantal processes: /x n l r r̄ tʃ f/. We have already noted (v. 2.1.3.2) that /x/ as in *ajo* or *auge* is velar in most varieties on both sides of the Atlantic, but in parts of northern Spain it is articulated a bit further back, uvular [χ]. In Chile, Peru, Bolivia, and Uruguay (Lipski 1994), velar /x/ is fronted to a palatal position, [ç] (figure 3.6), when it precedes a front vowel or /j/: *gente* /xénte/ → [çénte], *tejió* /texjó/ → [teçjó]. This yields alternations such as *hija* [íxa] ~ *hijita* [içíta]. On the other hand, in the Caribbean, most of Andalusia, and the Canaries, /x/ is aspirated to the weaker glottal fricative [h]; as shown by Marrero (1990), both this [h] and the [h] resulting from S-Aspiration in these zones may be voiced (IPA [ɦ]) or pharyngeal (IPA [ħ]), the latter produced by pulling the root of the tongue back for friction in the throat.

In southern and northwestern Spain, in Caribbean dialects, and in Peru and Bolivia (Lipski 1994), /n/ is velarized to [ŋ] word-finally, as in *son, pan, cien, hablan, sin* (which sounds like English *sing*). In relaxed speech, this [ŋ] may drop, leaving behind a nasal vowel: *van* /ban/ → [baŋ] → [bã]. N-Velarization therefore creates alternations in words: *marrón* is [mar̄ṍ(ŋ)] but *marrones* is [mar̄ónes]. It has also been reported preconsonantally, where it then may override Nasal Assimilation to the consonant (v. 3.1.2) as in *en Panamá* [eŋpanamá]. An oft-cited pair in dialects with N-Velarization is *enaguas* [enáɣwas] vs. *en aguas* [eŋáɣwas], the latter having [ŋ] because of the word-final /n/.

The two vibrants /r r̄/ are often pronounced with friction faintly resembling that of the sibilants /s z ʃ ʒ/ and are then described as ASSIBILATED. This term is misleading, since the resulting fricatives generally lack the grooved tongue surface (and therefore fuller hiss) of true sibilants. For the assibilated version of the flap /r/, symbolized as [ř], the apex approaches the alveolar ridge for [ɾ], but contact is incomplete, yielding light turbulence as the airstream continues through. Its use in Chile has been widely observed, notably in the group /tr/ (with *otro* sounding a bit like *ocho*), but it can also be heard in other parts of the Americas and in northeastern Spain (Alonso 1967, 123–58; Navarro Tomás 1967, 117). It is especially common at the end of a syllable: *ir* [iɹ̌], *dar, por, cortar.*[7] The assibilated version of the trill /r̄/, symbolized as [ř̄], is just as widespread. It can be described as a lengthened [ɹ̌ː] or as a trill with [ʒ]-like friction between the vibrations: *corro* /kór̄o/ → [kóř̄o]. Both vibrants—whether clear or assibilated— are furthermore devoiced in some lects, the flap in final position and the trill in any position: *ir* [iɾ̥] ~ [iɹ̥̌], *rojo* [r̥̄óxo] ~ [ř̥̄óxo].

In Puerto Rico, /r̄/ has migrated to the back of the mouth in addition to fricativizing and devoicing. The results vary (Medina Rivera 1999): *corro* can have an alveolar trill [r̄], a French uvular trill [ʀ] or uvular fricative [ʁ], or a voiceless fricative, uvular [χ] or velar [x]; Canfield (1981) even found a hybrid [xr̄]. The use of [x] for /r̄/ does not result in confusion of *erre* with *jota,* since the latter is aspirated ([h]) in the Caribbean (v. 2.1.3.2); *corro* is [kóxo] and *cojo* is [kóho]. Although some Puerto Ricans regard velarized /r̄/ as rustic and nonstandard, others increasingly adopt it as a sign of local pride (Lipski 1994, 334).

A common fate of /r/ is merger (neutralization, *igualación*) with /l/ in syllable-final position, /__$ (i.e., when / __C, ___‖). This Liquid Leveling rule variously yields some kind of *r, l,* or intermediate sound for both: flap [ɾ], assibilated [ɹ̌], lateral [l], lateral flap [ɺ], glide [j], or even aspirated [h], which may then drop or assimilate just like the [h] of the S-Aspiration rule. In concrete terms, the student who has learned [káɾne] for *carne* may actually hear [káɾne káɹ̌ne kálne káɺne kájne káhne kánne].

Liquid Leveling occurs chiefly in the Caribbean region (including Panama and Venezuela) and in Andalusia—where all of the above variants coexist (Quilis-Sanz 1998). It creates homonyms (*arma = alma, mal = mar = más*) and also morphological alternations: *sol* and *olor* may end in the same consonant, but their /l/ and /r/ reemerge in *soles* and *olores.* Likewise, *el* will be [el] in *el ojo* (intervocalic) but [eɾ] or [ej] in *el cielo* (Zamora Vicente 1967, 315). Liquid Leveling tends to coincide geographically with S-Aspiration, N-Velarization, and frequent D-Deletion, giving rise to the term "weak consonantism" for characterizing such dialects' phonology in general (Canfield 1981, 36).

In Puerto Rico, Panama, northern Chile, and Andalusia, the affricate /tʃ/ is losing its stop onset, becoming a mere fricative [ʃ], especially in medial position: *muchacho* /mutʃátʃo/ → [muʃáʃo]. The phoneme /f/ is very widely pronounced as a bilabial fricative, [ɸ], on both sides of the Atlantic: *fuego* /fwégo/ →[ɸwéɣo]. While [f] is made with the upper teeth against the lower lip (=labiodental), [ɸ] is made just with the lips (=bilabial), and the two differ in exactly the same way as [v] and [β] (see figure 3.6).

Many such local phonetic processes are variable rules. In Panama, /tʃ/ → [ʃ] correlates to age group, the young applying it more than their elders (Canfield 1981, 67). Liquid Leveling varies according to sex and style in the Caribbean (Jorge Morel 1974, 77; Medina Rivera 1999), the nonstandard variants appearing more in men's speech than in women's and more in informal situations and discourse types than in formal ones. Variable rules often indicate changes in progress, and it is quite possible that articulations now viewed as "local," "informal," or "nonstandard" will become the norm in a few more decades.

3.1.9 Vowel weakening.

V̆ → V̥ / (C̥) ___ (C̥)

Under close scrutiny, Spanish vowels turn out to have several allophones. In general, they are somewhat more open when followed by CC, C#, /x/, or /r̄/ than in other environments; consequently, the /e/ and /o/ of *costa, ves, lejos, perra* are not exactly identical to those of *bota, ve, lleno, pesa.* Moreover, Navarro Tomás (1967, 44 ff.) noted that in rapid speech, the five vowels, when they are unstressed, are more relaxed and a bit less precise in their articulation. Yet these variations are subliminal to the nonlinguist and usually ignored in pedagogy. The two /e/ of *este* or *eje* seldom differ as much as the English /e/ of *mate* and /ɛ/ of *met,* and unstressed Spanish vowels never relax to the mid central zone of English schwa (v. 3.2.8). Navarro Tomás, in fact, advised foreign teachers to ignore the slightly weakened allophones of Spanish /a e i o u/ lest their English-, French-, or German-speaking students equate them with their schwas.

In Mexico (Lope Blanch 1963) and parts of the Andean highlands (Canfield 1981), however, unstressed vowels weaken more noticeably. The results are still not schwas but rather a variable laxing (shown by a strikethrough, e.g. [e̸]) and devoicing (shown by an under-ring, e.g., [e̥]). As Perissinotto (1975, 26–33) noted, an adjacent voiceless consonant (as in *machete* [matʃéte̸], *chiquito, plática*) favors the process and sometimes causes devoicing ([matʃéte̥]), but it is an adjacent /s/ that promotes the most devoicing: *visitas* /bisítas/ → [bi̥sítḁs]. The most drastic stage, full deletion, is rare except in a handful of frequent words such as *pues, entonces, gracias* [ps entóns grɑ́ss], and Perissinotto believed that non-Mexicans who have reported more rampant deletion misheard one of the other degrees. He noted that this, too, is a variable rule, occurring most often in lower classes and in casual styles.

3.1.10 Vowel gliding.

VV → V, VG, GV (two vowels merge into one, or a diphthong)

(general, and almost categorical when one V= an unstressed high vowel)

Any analysis of Spanish phonology requires a Gliding rule in order to account for alternations between the full vowels [i u] and the glides [j w] (v. 2.2.3). For example, *con-*

tinuar, continuamos, continuó have [kontinw-] while *continúo, continúan, continúe* have [kontinú-]; likewise, *ira* is [íra] while the derived *airado* is [ajráðo]. The key to Gliding is, of course, stress: if the high vowels /i u/ are unstressed and adjacent to another vowel, they form a diphthong with it by becoming glides (in feature terms, [-syllabic]), but if stressed, they remain full vowels (i.e., stay [+syllabic]). Like most other phonological rules in the language, Gliding occurs across # (word boundaries) in fast speech; note its effects on the conjunctions *y* and *u*:

dos o tres [dósotrés], *siete u ocho* [sjétewótʃo]
dos y tres [dósitrés], *dos y ocho* [dósjótʃo], *ocho y nueve* [ótʃojnwéβe][8]

In fast speech, gliding occurs in nonhigh ("strong") vowels too. As articulation speeds up, syneresis (v. 2.2.3) applies, and the less open or less stressed vowel loses its syllabicity and ends up crushed against its neighbor. Some observers perceive an intermediate stage between /e.a/ in *teatro* with hiatus and [ja] with syneresis and gliding. In this middle stage, shown as [e̯a] (where the under-arch means 'nonsyllabic'), the /e/ is merged into the same syllable as /a/ but is still more open than the palatal glide [j] of *viaje* [bjáxe]. Yet Boyd-Bowman (1960, 48) and Oroz (1966, 69) found full gliding more common in normal speech: *te hago* [tjáɣo], *lo hace* [lwáse]. Perissinotto (1975, 34) similarly recorded the following glidings in Mexican speech:

/ea/ → [ja]: *teatro, pasear, real, empleado, pelear, le habló*
/oa/ → [wa]: *toalla, Joaquín, Oaxaca, mexicano adorable*
/ae/ → [aj]: *cae, trae, mala espina*
/eo/ → [jo]: *peor, petróleo, vine hoy*
/éo/ → [ew]: *feo, peleo*
/oe/ → [we]: *cohete, héroe, soez*

Stress is one advantage to the victor in these vowel battles, but at times the more open vowel overrides, and steals, its neighbor's stress: *océano* [é.a] → [e̯á] → [já], *país* [a.í] → [ái̯] → [aj], *período* [í.o] → [i̯ó]→ [jó].

As an alternative to gliding, one of the two vowels may get deleted, usually the first one (Perissinotto 1975, 37; Dalbor 1997, 170; Boyd-Bowman 1960, 153): *la orquesta* → [loɾkésta], *la unión* → [lunjón], *me imagino* → [mimaxíno], *tengo uno* → [téŋgúno], *lo insultó* → [linsultó]. For double (geminate) vowels, this loss is quite general in normal fluent styles (*cohorte = corte, aprehender = aprender*), although careful speech may preserve them if one is stressed and an affix boundary separates them (Navarro Tomás 1967, 153; Dalbor 1997, chap. 18), as in *cre-éncia, cre-ér, cré-e*.

Pedagogy tends to recognize syneresis and gliding only when the orthography shows them, as in the contractions *a el → al, de el → del*. Nevertheless, these processes are common in speech throughout the Hispanic world; they increasingly affect even the most formal styles (Navarro Tomás accepts [já] in *cardíaco* and [jó] in *período* as standard now, despite the accent marks), and in poetry and song they are often required for the meter.

3.2 English rules. Sections 3.2.1 through 3.2.5 describe processes applying to English consonants; sections 3.2.6 through 3.2.8 describe those applying to its vowels. We omit most rules that are limited to local dialects; see Wells 1982 for a much fuller account.

3.2.1 Aspiration.

$$\underset{\text{(voiceless stops)}}{\text{p t tʃ k}} \rightarrow \underset{\text{(aspirated)}}{\text{p}^{\text{h}}\ \text{t}^{\text{h}}\ \text{tʃ}^{\text{h}}\ \text{k}^{\text{h}}} \ / \ \{\#\_\_\_\_,\ \_\_\_\_(\text{L, G})\acute{\text{V}}\ \}$$

(categorical and general)

Voiceless stops in English are exploded with a [h]-like puff of air in certain positions and are then called ASPIRATED. This process occurs basically in syllable-initial position, specifically (1) word-initially (*pick, prick, tick, trick, chick, kick, click, quick* /kwɪk/ → [k^{h}wɪk]), and (2) before a stressed vowel, even across an intervening liquid or glide (*appéar, appláud, retáin, retráin, achíeve, acquíre, acróss, accúse*). Elsewhere, /p t tʃ k/ are less aspirated, and especially after /s/ (*spy, stay, score, skill, square*) they are like their Spanish counterparts. Thus, *pie tag quints* [p^{h}aj t^{h}æg k^{h}wɪnts] but *spy stag squints* [spaj stæg skwɪnts].

The "puff of air" can be felt by placing one's hand about one inch in front of the lips while saying *pie*, as opposed to *spy*. To understand exactly where it comes from—and therefore what students must avoid in their Spanish—it is useful to study stop articulation in more detail:

- [p] in *spy*, unaspirated: After the /s/, the lips close to make the voiceless stop, holding back the airstream. They separate, release the stop cleanly, and simultaneously the vocal cords begin to vibrate for the vowel.
- [p^{h}] in *pie*, aspirated: The lips close to form the voiceless stop. They separate, releasing the stop, and the vocal tract assumes the position for the following vowel. But voicing turns on with a delay of about 50 milliseconds, not simultaneously with the release, so that unused air rushes through the glottis between the stop's release and the onset of voicing for the vowel. The puff of air is thus a voiceless beginning of the vowel, but it is perceived as a release feature of the /p/.[9]

For the English speaker, it is as natural to aspirate /p/ word-initially as it is for the Spanish speaker to fricativize /b/ between vowels; neither is aware of using different allophones according to the position, and neither can suppress the relevant rule without training and practice. Aspiration is automatic, and the English speaker identifies the [p^{h}] of *pie* with the [p] of *spy* as the "same" sound, in opposition to the /b/ of *buy,* which—as a separate phoneme—is perceived as distinct. Yet it must be recognized that aspiration reinforces the voicing contrast of *pie* vs. *buy*: if that clue is missing, as in the Spanish /p/ vs. /b/ contrast, then students may not perceive the difference in voicing. In fact, on a dictation test with unfamiliar words, some beginners will write *bata* for a native Spanish rendition of *pata.*

English /t tʃ k/ are aspirated in the same way as /p/. Aspiration of /tʃ/ makes it more fricative-sounding than Spanish /tʃ/ (Stockwell and Bowen 1965, 66). And, of course, English /t/ is furthermore alveolar, whereas Spanish /t/ is dental (v. 2.1.2).

3.2.2 Preglottalization.

p t tʃ k → ʔp ʔ(t) ʔtʃ ʔk / ___ $ (= __ ‖, __ O, __N)

(general, but with some dialectal variation in application)

Instead of being aspirated, English voiceless stops are typically PREGLOTTALIZED in syllable-final position, particularly before a pause, another obstruent, or a nasal. The voicing of the preceding vowel is cut off abruptly by a slamming shut of the vocal cords, which produces a glottal stop [ʔ] as the lips or tongue move into position for /p t tʃ k/. Thus, *top tot stock* /tɑp tɑt stɑk/ → [tʰɑʔp tʰɑʔt stɑʔk]. As Ladefoged (1982, 85) observed, some speakers do this more than others, but Preglottalization is at least a general tendency and a distinctive trait of English articulation. Many speakers proceed to drop [t] after inserting [ʔ], and the [ʔ] is then considered as standing for the /t/ as its allophone: *satin* [sǽʔn̩], *what kind* [hwɑ̀ʔkʰájnd]. In many urban British dialects (notably Cockney), this process occurs intervocalically too: *butter* [bʌ́ʔə].

Transferred to Spanish, Preglottalization in syllable-final position yields a perceptible accent because it acoustically sharpens the stop quality of /p t tʃ k/, as opposed to their weakening in that position in Spanish (v. 2.3). As Navarro Tomás (1967, 87–140) observed, syllable-final voiceless stops in Spanish tend to become weak voiced fricatives or to drop entirely. Note the contrasts in a relaxed, casual pronunciation between English *atmosphere* [ǽʔməsfɪɹ], *atlas* [ǽʔləs], *technique* [tʰɛ̀ʔkníʔk], *option* [ɑ́ʔpʃn̩] on the one hand and Spanish *atmósfera* [aðmósfeɾa], *atlas* [áðlas], *técnica* [téɣnika], *opción* [oβsjón] on the other.

3.2.3 Flapping.

t, d → ɾ / V́ (r)___(#) V̆

(general in the United States, Canada, and Australia; some stylistic variability)

By this rule, alveolar stops weaken to a flap in certain environments in many varieties of English, with the notable exception of standard Received Pronunciation in England. Flapping is almost categorical in normal fast pronunciation and leads to homonyms: *latter* = *ladder, wetting* = *wedding, patted* = *padded* ([lǽɾɚ wɛ́ɾɪŋ pʰǽɾəd]). In slower styles it is more variable and may be overridden for clarification: "I said *wai*[tʰ]*ed*, not *wa*[d]*ed*!" The [ɾ] is virtually identical to the flap /r/ of Spanish and can be used as a basis for acquiring it: *pot o' tea* → *para ti.*[10]

Flapping is most common between a stressed vowel and an unstressed one (V́__V̆): *atom* = *Adam* [ǽɾəm], but *atómic has* [tʰ]. As the rule shows, it also occurs (1) even if /r/

precedes (*hearty* = *hardy*) and (2) across #: *córd of (wóod)* = *cóurt of (láw), I lét it* = *I léd it, I húrt it* = *I héard it.* Note that English /d/-Flapping overlaps with Spanish /d/-Spirantization in /V__V and /V(r) __V; especially for beginning students, this creates both expressive and perceptual problems. They may not recognize *todo* in "[tóðo]," wondering what is meant by what sounds like "toe-though"; and in the other direction, their flapped [tʰówɾow] may be heard not as *todo* but as *toro* by Spanish speakers. Two familiar sounds of English, [ð] and [ɾ], will no longer stand for /ð/ and /d/ but must be relearned as /d/ and /r/, respectively.

3.2.4 Palatalization before Yod.

tj dj sj zj → tʃ dʒ ʃ ʒ / V́(n) __V

(general, but with some stylistic variation)

By this process, an alveolar obstruent merges with a following /j/ to become alveopalatal. The alveopalatal has become the norm in some words and would be shown phonemically in them: *issue, nature, pleasure* /ɪ́ʃu nétʃər plɛ́ʒər/ < earlier /ɪsju netjər plɛzjər/. In others, the two pronunciations are still vying with each other: *educate* /ɛ́dʒəkèt/ ~ /ɛ́djəkèt/, *controversial* /kɑ̀ntrəvə́rsjəl/ ~ /kɑ̀ntrəvə́rʃəl/. Across word boundaries the situation conforms to a more straightforward variable rule, depending on style and speed of speech: *this year* /sj ~ ʃ/, *please you* /zj ~ ʒ/, *did you* /dj ~ dʒ/, *eat yet* /tj ~ tʃ/.

Palatalization causes special interference in Spanish cognates with unstressed *tu, du, su.* Students often equate the *u* here with the underlying /ju/ or /jə/ of their English versions, and this /j/ then triggers palatalization of the /t d s/ in Spanish *mutual, educar, usual.* Students may also apply Palatalization to medial /tj dj sj/ in words such as *Asia, gracias, acción, cordial, televisión.* This is why [gradʒuaʃón kʰaʒuál naʃonál] are often heard for *graduación, casual, nacional.*

3.2.5 L-Velarization.

l → ɫ / (__$)

(general, but the environment varies by dialect)

The /l/ of Spanish *mil, col, tal* is an alveolar lateral, as is the /l/ of English *meal, coal, tall*: in both languages, the tip of the tongue makes contact with the alveolar ridge and the voiced airstream spills over the side(s) of the tongue. But in Spanish *col*, the body of the tongue is fairly high in the mouth, whence a light, clear resonance like that of the high vowel /i/; in English *coal,* the middle of the tongue is sunken and the dorsum (back) tugs back toward the velum, producing a dark and somber resonance reminiscent of /u ʊ w/. Phonemically, the symbol /l/ is used for both types of alveolar lateral, but to show detail the "clear *l*" of Spanish can be transcribed [l̥] while the "dark /l/" of English is shown as [ɫ]: Spanish [kol̥], English [kʰowɫ]. Though the difference (figure 3.7) may seem subtle,

Figure 3.7. "Clear" and "dark" /l/

Sp. [l̪] (clear) in *col, mil, tal*

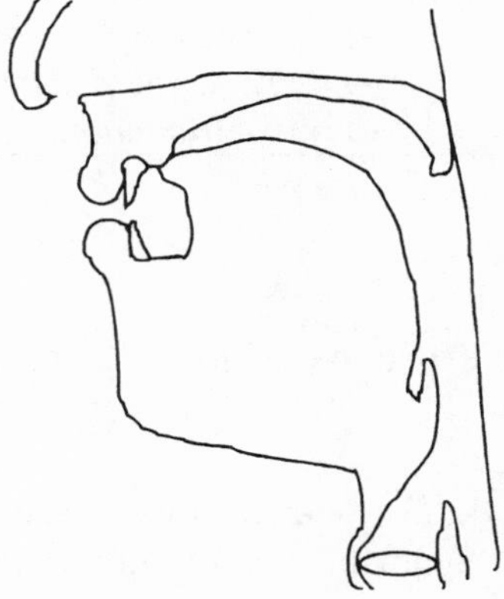

Eng. [ɫ] (dark, velarized) in *coal, meal, tall*

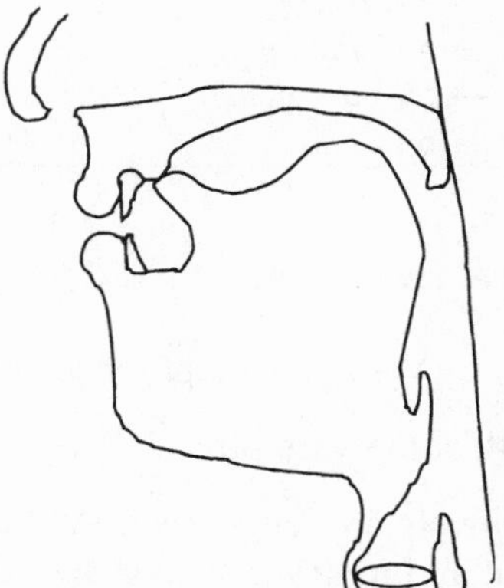

acoustically it is quite striking, and if darkening—or VELARIZATION, to use the technical term—is carried over into Spanish, *alto* and *calzar* sound like *auto* and *causar.*

Where Velarization occurs depends on the dialect or even idiolect. For some English speakers, it is strong at the end of a syllable, but otherwise /l/ is clear and Spanish-like. Others apparently velarize syllable-finally and before any back vowel; still others, including this writer, use "dark /1/" everywhere in their English.

3.2.6 Diphthongization.

i e o u → ij ej ow ʉw

(fairly general but not all dialects; some variability)

The tense vowels of English tend to be diphthongal, veering off into a palatal glide in the case of the front vowels /i e/ and a labiovelar one in the case of the back vowels /o u/ — which may centralize as well, [ʉw] (v. 2.2.1). It is necessary to say "tend" because of two sets of exceptions. First, in a few areas of North America and the British Isles, rather pure, Spanish-like articulations are used for some or all tense vowels.[11] Second, many speakers who do diphthongize stressed vowels have little or no gliding in vowels that are unstressed but not quite reduced (see the next rule). For example, in *obey* one may hear a slow, deliberate [owbéj] or a faster, more casual [əbéj], but in between there is [obéj], with a fairly pure /o/ resembling that of Spanish *obedece.* Nevertheless, Diphthongization is so general and so marked in contrast with Spanish vowels that for pedagogical purposes it can be considered a categorical rule capable of causing major interference. Thus, *puso* /púso/ comes out as [pʰʉ́wsow], and *ves* and *veis* are merged as [bejs] (or worse, [vejs]).

Figure 3.8. Vowel reduction in English

æ *(**á**tom)*	→ ə *(**a**tómic)*	aj	*(inv**í**te)*	→ ə *(ìnv**i**tátion)*
ɛ *(rep**é**titive)*	→ ə *(rèp**e**títion)*	u	*(Did y**óu**?)*	→ ə *(Dìd **you** sée it?)*
ɪ *(or**í**ginal)*	→ ə *(ór**i**gin)*	i	*(TH**É** movie to see!)*	→ ə *(th**e** móvie)*
e *(f**á**mous)*	→ ə *(ínf**a**mous)*	o	*(inv**ó**ke)*	→ ə *(ìnv**o**cátion)*
ɑ *(bi**ó**logy)*	→ ə *(bì**o**lógical)*	ʊ	*(you w**óu**ld?)*	→ ə *(Théy w**ou**ld knów it.)*
ɔ *(fact**ó**rial)*	→ ə *(fáct**o**r)*	ʌ	*(confr**ó**nt)*	→ ə *(cònfr**o**ntátion)*

3.2.7 Vowel reduction.

$$\breve{V} \rightarrow ə \text{ (except tense vowels in final or prevocalic position)}$$

(general, with some variability)

English vowels are lengthened [V:] when stressed (v. 4.1.3), whereas unstressed ones are shortened and muffled, losing their distinctiveness. In Spanish, such perturbations are negligible, but in English they are so marked that unstressed vowels sink into the mid central zone and reduce to schwa.[12] Reduction applies regularly in fluent speech, causing alternations in which a given vowel appears as a full vowel when stressed but as [ə] when unstressed (see figure 3.8). But it does not apply to tense vowels that are before another vowel (as with /i/ in *various* or /e/ in *chaotic*) or word-final (the /i/ of (*beauty*—but compare its reduction in *beautiful*). There is also variation in the pronunciation of initial syllables of fancier vocabulary: thus, the word *elaborate* may keep its initial /i/, and *gastronomy* is likelier to have /æ/ (rather than [ə]) in its initial syllable than *astronomy* (Fidelholz 1975). On the other hand, unstressed articles, helping verbs, forms of *be*, pronouns, and short conjunctions reduce so much that they lose their vowels and a consonant or two to boot: *I **can** go* [kən ~ kŋ]; *see **them*** [ðəm ~ əm]; *Harry **would** go* [wəd ~ əd ~ d], *a bag **of** groceries* [əv ~ ə]. These changes in speech are only partly reflected by written contractions: *what'd (what did) you do?* → [(h)wɑ́dʒə dʉ́w].

For teaching, we can generalize as follows. When students say a Spanish word slowly and deliberately (as in reading a word from a list or repeating it after a teacher), they may apply Reduction relatively little, but as their articulatory speed picks up in fuller discourse, they become more likely to reduce the unstressed vowels into some kind of central *uh* vowel. This can be extremely disruptive, since Spanish preserves a five-way contrast regardless of stress:

pesado ≠ pisado	pasaron ≠ posaron	maleta ≠ muleta	mercado ≠ marcado
retina ≠ rutina	piñita ≠ peñita	calor ≠ color	sociedad ≠ suciedad

Yet the worst casualty will be the inflectional system, which depends crucially on differentiating *-o* and *-a, -os* and *-as, -an* and *-on, -a* and *-e*, and so on. Thus, *buenos* and *buenas* will be fudged as [bwéjnəs] and *cantaron* and *cantaran* as [kʰəntárən].

3.2.8 Schwa deletion.

əm ən əl ər → m̩ n̩ ɫ̩ ɚ / (C) ___

(general, but stylistically variable)

By this rule, what might be pronounced as schwa plus a liquid or nasal in slow (but still reduced) styles becomes a single sound in faster, more fluent speech. In the case of /m n l/, the result is a vowelless but syllabic [m̩ n̩ ɫ̩], as shown by the vertical tick under the symbols;[13] in the case of /r/, the schwa fuses with the /r/ to yield a special vowel, either retroflex [ɚ] (which might also be considered syllabic [ɹ̩]) or British [ɜ] or [ə]. Examples:

/əm/ → [m̩]: *prism, chasm, fathom, some more, leave 'em*
/ən/ → [n̩]: *risen, mountain, ocean, ordinal, connect, scenario*
/əl/ → [ɫ̩]: *cradle, castle, label, calamity, fatally, channel, cologne*
/ər/ → [ɚ]: *murder, labor, peroxide, nurture, first, worse*

Schwa Deletion often appears in students' rendition of Spanish cognates:

túnel → [tʰúnɫ̩]	*garaje* → [gɚáhej]
excelente → [ɛ̀ksɫ̩éntej]	*oportunidad* → [àpɚtʰùnədád]

But it is well attested in their pronunciation of noncognates too, as in *derecha* → [dɚéjtʃə], *sonaba* → [sn̩ábə].

3.3 Order of difficulty: Ranking phonological problems. We have not attempted to describe all the phonological rules of English, only those that can produce relatively serious mispronunciations when transferred to Spanish. But how serious is serious? To present and practice all the features of Spanish phonology and to drum out all English interference would leave little time for getting on with communication and culture and the supporting grammar and vocabulary. Clearly, there are some phonological points that are so important that they must be mentioned early; others can be delayed a bit, and still others may not need to be touched upon at all. It is a matter of priorities, and the teacher and textbook writer will implicitly or explicitly use some kind of decision-making procedure in arranging difficulties in a hierarchy.

One such hierarchy was proposed by Stockwell and Bowen (1965, 9–18). Their ranking, from hardest to easiest, has eight "orders" of problems arranged in three overall "magnitudes" of difficulty. These are as follows, with examples that have been covered in chapters 2 and 3.[14]

Magnitude 1:

1. An obligatory feature (rule, pattern) of Spanish, lacking in English: Spirantization of /b/.

2. A phoneme or phonemic distinction of Spanish, lacking in English: *r*-sounds and /k/ vs. /x/.
3. An obligatory feature of Spanish that merges an English distinction: Spirantization of /d/, which means that [d] and [ð] must be treated as allophones, not as separate phonemes.

Magnitude 2:

4. Units that are distinguished in Spanish are obligatorily merged in English: Reduction, which merges into a schwa unstressed vowels that Spanish continues to contrast.
5. An obligatory pattern of English that Spanish lacks: Flapping, which changes /t/ and /d/ into a flap, whereas Spanish distinguishes all three in *mito, mido, miro.*
6. An English distinction that has no Spanish counterpart: *sock* with /ɑ/ vs. *sack* with /æ/, with the Spanish /a/ in between.

Magnitude 3:

7. Shared distinctions: both languages contrast /p b t d m n s f . . . / word-initially.
8. Shared rules and patterns: both languages permit the cluster /sw-/ with a vowel afterward.

As a first approximation to the problem, this hierarchy seems a principled explanation of actual pedagogical practice. The *r*-sounds and Spirantization receive considerable attention, and fairly early; the need to avoid Reduction is generally pointed out in textbooks; and the fact that Spanish contrasts /p/ and /b/ word-initially is simply taken for granted without comment. There is also some empirical support: Stockwell and Bowen predicted that for English speakers Spirantization of /d/ would be a different kind of challenge (order 3) from Spirantization of /b/ (order 1), even though these are the same rule, and Zampini (1994) confirmed that students indeed have different problems with /d/ → [ð]. Using this approach, we could proceed to fill in cases such as Spanish Glide Strengthening, English Aspiration, and so on at the proper levels.

Yet Stockwell and Bowen admitted that the hierarchy alone is insufficient, because other criteria must be applied too. Two of them are POTENTIAL MISHEARING and FUNCTIONAL LOAD. With regard to the former, we should promote the avoidance of English Aspiration to the upper orders of difficulty inasmuch as Spanish [p t k] can be misheard as [b d g] by students who still depend on aspiration. As for functional load (v. 0.2.2), this term refers to the relative weight a distinction carries in contrasting minimal pairs: /r/ vs. /r̄/ in Spanish distinguishes many words, but /ɲ/ vs. /nj/ very few; and although the student who substitutes /nj/ for /ɲ/ will have an accent, it will not wreak nearly as much havoc as the substitution of /r/ for /r̄/. Consequently, the /ɲ/ vs. /nj/ distinction might be demoted from its predicted ranking of 2. A third criterion might be called REPRESENTATIVENESS; S-Aspiration in Spanish is difficult to rank in the hierarchy and seems dialectal anyhow, but it is so widespread that it deserves more attention than it usually receives in pedagogy if only to practice listening to its effects. Finally, matters of stress and intonation do not fit well in the hierarchy, yet the authors rightly rank them high on their agenda as both difficult and important for pronunciation. These will be taken up in the next chapter.

Notes for chapter 3

1. As a third approach, the nasal vowel might be described in Optimality Theory as the best output of a VN sequence in a language that lacks nasal vowel contrasts. As explained in section 1.1.5, we adopt a more simplified notation in this book; see Núñez Cedeño and Morales Front 1999 for the application of recent theories to selected problems of Spanish phonology.

2. For geographical distributions, this chapter relies especially on Zamora Vicente 1967, Navarro Tomás 1967 and 1975, Resnick 1975, and Canfield 1981 for Spanish; and on Kurath and McDavid 1961 and Wells 1982 for English. For details, the best source is dialect atlases, which record on base maps the responses elicited from representative informants by teams of dialectologists. For Spanish, these include *Atlas lingüístico de la Península Ibérica, Atlas lingüístico-etnográfico de Andalucía* (Alvar, Llorente, and Salvador 1964), Navarro Tomás 1948 (for Puerto Rico), and several surveys currently underway in Spanish America (Lipski 1994, 155–59).

3. In the following pairs, the first member has a /j/ or /w/ strengthened because it begins a stem and its own syllable, while the second has a weak glide, though it follows the same consonant: *abyecto/abierto, deshielo/desierto, inyección/vinieron, subyuga/subió, deshueso/desuello, cónyuge/circonio.* This picture of near-minimal pairs for [j̝] and [j] and for [ɣw] and [w] led to spirited debates, for example, Bowen and Stockwell 1955 vs. Saporta 1956; see Whitley 1995b for a detailed comparison and evaluation of analyses of Spanish /j/.

4. The IPA provides no symbol for an alveopalatal nasal except [n̠] (the under-minus just means a less forward [n]); some linguists have used [ň] as typographically parallel to [š ž] (IPA [ʃ ʒ]).

5. English-speaking students learn to spirantize /b d g/ word-internally before extending the rule across word boundaries (Zampini 1998). But Torreblanca (1980) and Jorge Morel (1974, 67) believed that in native Spanish the stops and fricatives tend to pattern as shown with crossovers in both directions. After a careful examination, Amastae (1995) concluded that Spirantization is actually a variable rule.

6. In some sectors of the Hispanic world, teachers have tried to make children distinguish *be de burro* and *ve de vaca* by using a labiodental [v] for the latter, unaware that this sound (and the /b v/ distinction) disappeared from the language six centuries ago. According to Boyd-Bowman (1960, 54), [v]-loving teachers in Mexican literacy campaigns only succeeded in adding [v] as a third allophone of /b/—there is still no /b v/ distinction in Spanish.

7. In Costa Rica (Lipski 1994, 222), the friction of assibilated [ɹ̌] drops out in this end-of-syllable-position, yielding an English-type approximant, alveolar [ɹ] or retroflex [ɻ].

8. Whether a glided *y* /i/ in intervocalic or initial position, as in *cuatro y ocho* and *¿Y esto?*, can then feed into Glide Strengthening to become a palatal fricative or even a stop is a matter of dispute, or perhaps of different idiolects. Oroz (1966, 58) and Navarro Tomás (1967, 151) perceived variable *rehilamiento* of glided *y* in these positions, but Bowen and Stockwell (1955) and Quilis and Fernández (1975) found no evidence for it.

9. The IPA has no diacritic for 'unaspirated', but the approved Extensions to the IPA endorses a raised equals sign for that purpose: [p⁼] (IPA 1999). The difference between aspirated and unaspirated is technically known as VOICE ONSET TIME, or VOT. There is also a difference of voice

timing for the voiced stops /b d g/ in the two languages: while Spanish uses voicing throughout these segments, English begins voicing about midway through an initial voiced stop (/bɑr/ *bar*) and turns it off midway through a final one (/rɑb/ *rob*). As a result, an English speaker's semidevoiced *boca* sounds like *poca* to Spanish speakers (González Bueno 1997).

10. This approach to Spanish /r/ was suggested by Stockwell and Bowen (1965, 124): *photo → foro, motor → moro, meadow → mero, solder → Sara*. Yet [ɾ] for English speakers is phonemically /t/ or /d/ (v. 2.1.3.3), and this fact can interfere with the attempt to reidentify it as an /r/ for Spanish. There are three other environments for English Flapping too. In /V́n__V (*winter, plenty*), /t/ is flapped or dropped but /d/ (*sandy, bandage*) usually is not. In /V̆n__V̆ (*irritable, variety*), a flap appears more variably. And in / V__#V́ (*at eight, let out, get up, that orange*), Flapping is quite common, even though it seems the wrong place for it (note the stress on the *second* vowel in this case).

11. See Kurath and McDavid 1961 and Wells 1982 for details. One teacher who hailed from a nondiphthongizing dialect caused confusion in his class on modeling the difference between English *lay, bay, may, say* and Spanish *le, ve, me, se*. His students heard no difference, for there was none in his speech. Such dialects are in the minority in the Anglophone world.

12. For some English speakers, a few vowels reduce instead to a kind of centralized /ɪ/, [ɨ], which is like [ə] but a bit higher: business [bíznɨs] ~ [bíznəs].

13. There are certain details we omit from this Syllabification rule, for example, the effect of a preceding C: /əl/ undergoes this rule after /n/ (*channel*), yet /ən/ does not undergo it after /l/ (*fallen*).

14. Stockwell and Bowen's examples have been retained except for order 4, where they used an example limited to one dialect of English. The distinction between this order and order 5 is unclear, but from their examples it seems that order 4 has rules yielding an un-Spanish phone, whereas order 5 has rules yielding a phone that Spanish does have, but with a different status or function.

In SLA literature, this attempt to predict degrees of difficulty was misleadingly called the "Contrastive Analysis Hypothesis"; for a modification of it, see Eckman 1977, and for a critique, MacDonald 1989. For a different view of the phonological difficulties of Spanish as well as pedagogical techniques for working on them, see Terrell 1989.

Exercises for chapter 3

1. What are the allophones of each of the Spanish phonemes /j/, /b/, /r̄/, and /s/, and where (in which environments) does each allophone occur?

2. Using symbols or articulatory labels, indicate the place of articulation of each nasal.

(a) e*n*vidia
(b) i*n*fa*n*te
(c) ga*n*so
(d) a*n*hela*n*
(e) co*n*quista
(f) i*n*yecció*n*
(g) *m*a*n*go
(h) ba*ñ*a*n*do
(i) fra*n*ja
(j) e*n* Pa*n*a*m*á
(k) e*n* Huelva
(l) e*n* Vale*n*cia

3. Determine whether each italicized occurrence of /b d g/ is normally pronounced as a stop or as a fricative.

(a) om*b*ligo (d) en*v*ol*v*er (g) in*d*i*g*na*d*a (j) a*b*sur*d*o
(b) fe*d*eral (e) cur*v*a*d*o (h) no*v*iaz*g*o (k) nin*g*uno
(c) *d*es*v*án (f) fá*b*rica (i) o*b*ten*g*a (l) igual*d*a*d*

4. Repeat the above instructions for the following phrases. Assume that each capital begins a breath-group.

(a) Un *g*rifo (b) El *g*rifo (c) Faltan *g*rifos
(d) *D*ámelo (e) Me lo *d*a (f) Él *d*a poco (g) Él nos *d*a poco
(h) *V*einte (i) Hay *v*einte (j) Con *v*einte (k) Los *v*einte

5. Summarize how the English and Spanish articulations of the following differ.

(a) /l/ (b) /e/ (c) /t/ (d) /w/

6. English speakers sometimes confuse the pronunciations of the words in each of the following sets. Explain why, and also how Spanish distinguishes them.

(a) *codo, coro, corro* (b) *creó* and *creyó* (or *brío* and *brillo*)

7. Following is a synopsis of Perissinotto's data (1975, 100–115) on F-Bilabialization and R-Assibilation in Mexico City. Comment on the variables you see and compare their effects.

- /f/ → [ɸ]: males 70.6 percent of the time, females 57 percent; lower, middle, upper classes 78.3 percent, 60.3 percent, 53.77 percent, respectively.
- /r/ → [ɹ̌]: males 39 percent, females 89 percent; lower, middle, upper 54 percent, 81 percent, 60 percent, respectively; youth 73.5 percent, middle-aged 64.5 percent, older 31 percent.
- /r̄/ → [ř]: males 21 percent, females 38.5 percent; lower, middle, upper 18 percent, 40 percent, 30 percent respectively; youth 36 percent, middle-aged 34.5 percent, older never.

8. List some other variable rules of Spanish and identify the overall pattern of variation. Which of these, in your experience with native speakers, tend to be stigmatized, despite their actual extent? Which ones tend to be widely used by all social strata?

9. Using phonetic transcriptions, indicate the probable pronunciations by monolingual English speakers of the Hispanic names *Teresa, Diego, Pedro, Geraldo, Alicia,* and *Lidia.*

10. Take the following Spanish words (given in phonemic transcription) and retranscribe them phonetically in two ways. First, show how they will be pronounced by native speakers, and then show how an English speaker might render them with L1 interference. Example: *cada* /káda/, (ntv.) [káða] ~ [ká]; English [kʰɑ́ɾə].

(a) enfermas /enférmas/ (f) verdad /berdád/
(b) yunque /júnke/ (g) selva /sélba/
(c) televisión /telebisjón/ (h) pertenece /pertenése, -θe/
(d) rasgo /r̄ásgo/ (i) casualidad /kaswálidad/
(e) música /músika/ (j) inflado /infládo/

11. Using information from this chapter and the preceding one, identify where each of the following pronunciations might be heard. (*¡Ojo!* The answer will be "general" for pronunciations not limited to one or even several dialects; others may occur in a few fairly specific areas; still others have more than one identifying characteristic that allows you to pinpoint them.)

(a) gesto [çéht̪o]
(b) van [baŋ]
(c) pollo [póʃo]
(d) desde [d̪ézd̪e]
(e) chiquitos [tʃi̥kít̪o̥s]
(f) Madrid [maðɾí]
(g) falla [ɸáʝa]
(h) jarro [xářo]
(i) jarro [háxo]
(j) hablado [aβláw]
(k) desmayo [d̪ehmáʒo]
(l) huésped [ɣwɛ́ppe]
(m) charco [ʃálko]
(n) sencillo [s̪en̪θíʎo]

12. The following data are from Andalusian Spanish (Zamora Vicente 1967, 291). Explain in terms of rules why the singular is so different from the plural.

'net': sg. [r̄e], pl. [r̄ɛ́ðɛ]
'carnation': sg. [klaβé], pl. [klaβɛ́lɛ]
'bread': sg. [paŋ], pl. [pánɛ]
'kiss': sg. [béso], pl. [bɛ́sɔ]

13. Classify each of the following changes according to whether it seems to be "NG" (native and general), "ND" (native but dialectal), or "EI" (English interference).

(a) /r/ in *pardo* → [ɻ]
(b) /r/ in *pardo* → [l]
(c) /d/ in *padre* → [ð]
(d) /j/ in *mayo* → [ʒ]
(e) /n/ in *van* → [ŋ]
(f) /sj/ in *nacional* → [ʃ]
(g) /d/ in *médico* → [ɾ]
(h) /f/ in *fuego* → [ɸ]
(i) /e/ in *fuego* → [ej]
(j) /k/ in *exterior* /eks-/ → ∅

14. Pronunciation practice can be combined with form-focused activities in a two-birds-with-one-stone approach. For example, the teacher can give commands such as the following, with the instruction that students negate each one while paying attention to /b d g/ → [β ð ɣ]: *bébalo* (→ "*No, no lo* [βéβa]"), *dígalo, dúchese, guárdelo,* and so on. Create a similar exercise that practices an important grammar point along with one of the phonological rules in this chapter.

15. As noted in section 3.3, not every feature of Spanish phonology can be commented on in the classroom, so there must be prioritization. For each of the following processes, indicate (a) whether the introductory course should cover it (suitably explained in beginners' terms), (b) to what extent (i.e., what "successful mastery" would constitute at this level), and (c) which version (for rules with social or dialectal variation). Does Stockwell and Bowen's hierarchy match your priorities?

(a) Glide Strengthening
(b) Nasal Assimilation
(c) Lateral Assimilation
(d) S-Voicing
(e) S-Aspiration
(f) Spirantization
(g) D-Deletion
(h) Assibilation
(i) Vowel Gliding

Next, indicate which of the following *English* rules should also receive attention, and why.

(j) Aspiration
(k) Flapping
(l) Preglottalization
(m) Vowel Diphthongization
(n) Schwa Deletion
(o) Vowel Reduction

16. FIGURED PRONUNCIATION (v. question 11 at the end of chapter 2) attempts to render L2's pronunciation in terms of L1's writing system without benefit of phonetics. Following are examples from a dictionary in Spain that tried to indicate how to pronounce certain English terms. Use a dual phonetic transcription to show the distance between (a) the likely Spanish rendition and (b) a native English pronunciation; then explain (c) the apparent reasons why the Hispanized version differs from the English original.

Example: *jockey*: **yoke** (a) → [ɟóke], (b) [dʒɑ́ki], (c) English vowel graphemes were interpreted with Spanish values, and Spanish substituted /j/ (allophone [ɟ]) as the closest equivalent to English /dʒ/.

(a) *all right*: ol rait
(b) *goodbye*: gudbai
(c) *whiskey*: uiski
(d) *flirt*: flert
(e) *manager*: máneyer
(f) *Shaker*: chéker
(g) *jogging*: yoguin
(h) *smoking (jacket)*: esmoquin

Chapter 4

Stress and intonation

4.0 Suprasegmentals. Consonants and vowels are called SEGMENTS because they follow from a segmentation of a stretch of speech into discrete phonetic slices. But there is more to the speech signal than just these segments. By vibrating the vocal cords faster or slower, one changes the pitch of a voiced sound, respectively raising or lowering it. By making the vibration more forceful and energetic, one increases its loudness (volume, intensity). These variations in pitch and loudness are termed SUPRASEGMENTALS since they are perceived in addition to, and organized "on top of," the segments. They are also called by their classical name, PROSODIES.

4.1 Stress. A vowel or the syllable around it that is pronounced more loudly than its neighbors is STRESSED; one that is not especially loud is UNSTRESSED. Stress is indicated by an accent mark on the vowel or (the IPA's preference) in front of the syllable: *rejéct*, *reˈject*. Unstressed vowels are left unmarked in transcription, although a breve (˘) can be used over them if necessary to draw attention to their lack of stress.

English and Spanish make similar use of stress, as noted in the following section, but there are two differences in its phonetic realization. First, Spanish stress equates to greater loudness, whereas English speakers often reinforce loudness with higher pitch. Carried over into Spanish, this coupling of stress with pitch can disrupt Spanish intonational patterns, which are generally flatter than those of English (v. 4.2). Second, stressed and unstressed vowels in Spanish do not significantly differ in length (quantity) or articulation (quality); lengthening is exceptional and signals strong emphasis (Bull 1965, 78; Navarro Tomás 1967, 200–207). In English, however, stressed vowels are normally lengthened (Vː) while unstressed syllables are correspondingly shortened and reduced to schwa (v. 3.2.7). Transferred to Spanish, this stretching/shortening effect makes *paró, paré* sound like *p'róóóu, p'rééėi* and is a well-known trait of many English and German speakers' pronunciation of Spanish (Navarro Tomás 1967).

4.1.1 Stress position. Depending on the language, the position of stress can be fixed (predictable) or free (unpredictable). In French, for example, it is always the last full vowel of a word that receives the stress; in Czech, it is the first vowel; in Polish, it is the penultimate (next to last) one. In Spanish and English, however, stress position is freer and can therefore be used to contrast (distinguish) different words or different forms of words, as illustrated below. (The accent mark is used here to indicate stress regardless of whether orthography requires it.)

Spanish:	English:
sábana, sabána	súbject, subjéct
término, termíno, terminó	Áugust, augúst
éstas, estás	récord, recórd
ábra, habrá	ínvalid, inválid
amáran, amarán	rébel, rebél
pápa, papá	cónquer, concúr

But stress position is partly predictable. In Spanish, most preterites and all futures (*terminó, habrá*) are stressed on the ending; otherwise, verb stress is largely penultimate (*termíno, ábra*). In English, stress depends to some extent on part of speech: noun *súbject,* verb *subjéct*; in fact, it is hard to find minimal pairs for English stress that do not involve different parts of speech. Moreover, certain patterns dominate in each language. In native English words (nonnative ones are more complicated), there is a strong tendency to stress the first stem vowel: *móther, mótherly, mótherless, mótherlessness.* In Spanish, stress can occur only on one of the last three vowels of a word (excluding suffixed pronouns as in *dígamelo*), which limits the possibilities to just three:

(-V . . . V) . . . V́: OXYTONE (*agudo*): *Panamá, papá, tabú, alemán, españól, honór, bondád*
(-V) . . . V́ . . . V: PAROXYTONE (*llano*): *sabána, pápa, democrácia, consonánte, césped, jóven*
-V́ . . . V . . . V: PROPAROXYTONE (*esdrújulo*): *sábana, teléfono, helicóptero, análisis, régimen.*

Note that this important constraint applies to vowel *phonemes,* not vowel letters. The stress in *ventrílocuo* and *dinosaurio* is on the fourth vowel letter from the end but on the third and second vowel phonemes, respectively: /bentrílokwo/, /dinosáwrjo/.

Spanish words ending in a vowel are mostly paroxytonic (*híjo, tríbu, paciéncia*) and those ending in a consonant other than inflectional /s/ or /n/ are mostly oxytonic (*imán, olór, tribál, ustéd, cortés*). Statistically less common are the proparoxytones (*teléfono, análisis, régimen*), followed by oxytones ending in a vowel (*papá, Perú*) and paroxytones ending in a noninflectional consonant (*lápiz, césped, portátil, jóven*).[1] This scale of frequency is recognized in the restriction of the orthographical accent to the less common cases.

As in other components of language, there is variation in stress position. English speakers are aware of nonstandard stressings such as *guítar, hótel, úmbrella, pérfume,* and with *address, preferable, irrefutable,* and *harass* there is variation even among the educated. In Spanish, one similarly hears restressings such as *centígramo, méndigo, síncero, váyamos, fríjol, sútil, cólega* (Flórez 1951, 306–17; RAE 1979, 84), and the educated vary between *políglota* and *poliglóta, medúla* and *médula* (Navarro Tomás 1967, 194). The case of stress shift in syneresis, as in *océano período país ~ oceáno periódo páis,* has already been discussed (v. 3.1.10). On the whole, though, stress placement is remarkably stable in both languages.

In both languages, the stress of a word can be increased to emphasize it, and for clarification even an unstressed syllable can be highlighted: *they ímport more than they éxport, estoy refiriéndome a la ímportación, no a la éxportación* (Quilis and Fernández 1975, 160). In general, however, this seems more common in English than in Spanish. Moreover, in both languages certain words are almost never stressed: articles, object pronouns, short prepositions and conjunctions, forms of *be/ser,* relative pronouns, etc. These are phonological CLITICS, words that attach themselves in pronunciation to their stressed neighbors. *Que me lo dé* is therefore a single PHONOLOGICAL WORD, [kemeloðé], just like *contaminé* [kontaminé].

4.1.2 Degrees of stress. In many languages that use stress, a word can have several stressed vowels. Often, though, these will differ in their relative intensity or loudness, so that one stress is subordinated to the other. Standard Spanish has just one regular formation with more than one stress, adverbs in *-mente.*[2] When this suffix is added to an adjective, it receives the main or PRIMARY word stress, while the adjective's own stress drops to SECONDARY—a degree of loudness less than primary but still greater than that of the unstressed vowels. For this secondary stress, linguists commonly use a grave accent (`), reserving the acute for primary:

formál, formàlménte	nítida, nìtidaménte
alégre, alègreménte	común, comùnménte

In IPA transcriptions, a lowered vertical tick is preferred for secondaries: /forˈmal for͵malˈmente/.

In English, secondary stress is more thoroughly exploited, and it contrasts with unstressed syllables: *gráduàte* (verb), *gráduăte* (noun). In long polysyllables, there is a tendency toward alternating among the three degrees:[3]

` ˘ ´	kàngaróo, sùperséde, rèprodúce
` ˘ ´ ˘	rèferéndum, àutomátic, còmprehénsive
˘ ` ˘ ´ ˘	appèndicítis, invèstigátion
´ ˘ `	réfugèe, álcohòl, récognìze
´ ˘ ` ˘	álligàtor, sécretàry, cárburètor

˘ ´ ˘ ` ˘ refrígeràtor, extérminàting
` ˘ ` ˘ ´ ˘ rèconcìliátion, prèstidìgitátion, ànti-ìntelléctual
` ˘ ´ ˘ ` chòlinésteràse

This pattern of alternation is so entrenched that students try to impose secondaries in long Spanish sequences of unstressed syllables, as in *otorrinolaringólogo* → * *òto-rrìnolàringólogo*, and to separate adjacent stresses in *-mente* adverbs, as in *formàlménte* → *fòrmalménte* (Bull 1965, 80).

In both languages, the addition of a derivational suffix frequently alters the stress pattern. Thus, in Spanish, *biólogo biológico biología, órgano orgánico organizár organización*. Especially in Greco-Latin vocabulary, English is even more complicated, thanks to its alternating stresses: *biólogy bìológical, cómpensàte compénsatòry còmpensátion, cátegòry càtegórical, phótogràph photógraphy phòtográphic, sólid, solídify, solìdificátion*. One of the commonest derivational patterns exploited by English (but not by Spanish) is a stress contrast between compounds with ´ ` and phrases with ` ´:

a hót-dòg 'sandwich con salchicha'	a hòt dóg 'perro que tiene calor'
a Spánish tèacher 'profesor de español'	a Spànish téacher 'profesor venido de España'
the mákeùp 'composición; maquillaje'	to màke úp 'componer; reconciliarse'

The student's first task with Spanish stress is to recognize its usual position in oxytone and paroxytone patterns and the use of an orthographical accent to mark other patterns. The varying stress position (*término termíno terminó*) should not be a surprise, since English also has this, but the accents of European languages are generally regarded as mere decorations by speakers of a language that dispenses with diacritics. Many students who have mastered these conventions nevertheless make errors in cognates whose Spanish stress pattern, though transparent in the orthography, contradicts that of English:

indícan → *índican	comuníca → *comúnica
inglés → *íngles 'groins'	circúlan → *círculan
mamá → *máma 'breastfeeds'	difícil → *díficil

Moreover, students have to learn to avoid imposing secondary stresses, a problem that is again especially acute in cognates:

refrigeradór → *refrìgeradór	diagnóstico → *dìagnóstico
circulación → *cìrculàción	oportunidád → *òportùnidád

The effect of such distortions is magnified when students then lengthen the stressed vowels as in English, yielding Spanish words hammered into the mold of English rhythm.

4.1.3 Stress and rhythm. Languages are commonly regarded as falling into two main rhythmic types. One type, called SYLLABLE-TIMED, has a rhythm ticked off by relatively even syllables, each syllable (whether stressed or unstressed) receiving one quick beat called a mora. The general acoustic effect is a distinctive staccato *dot-dot-dot-dot-dot*. The other type, stress-timed, has a rhythm based on the regularly recurring stresses of groups of syllables called feet. Each foot leads off with one strongly stressed syllable followed by lesser stressed satellites. Instead of each syllable taking one mora, each foot occupies about the same measure of time regardless of its number of syllables, and to equalize the feet requires that stressed syllables be held out while unstressed syllables are correspondingly shortened and squeezed in around the stressed ones. This yields a strikingly galloping effect, *di - D U M - di - di - D U M - di - D U M*.

English, like other Germanic languages, is stress-timed; Spanish, like most other Romance languages, is syllable-timed. Native speakers readily hear the difference, though they may not be able to identify precisely what is happening. Spanish strikes the English speaker as fast and machine gun–like; English, to the Spanish speaker, can sound jerky, with alternate drawling and obliteration of syllables. To be sure, some speakers in both languages speak more rapidly than others, and everyone varies speed according to situation, emotional state, emphasis, and rhetorical effect, but such variations in rate are overridden by the more pervasive difference in the rhythmic organization of syllables.[4] Spanish sounds fast because its stressed syllables—which an English speaker expects to be held out—seem to zip past as quickly as the unstressed ones; English sounds uneven because its stressed syllables are lengthened at the expense of the unstressed ones. Spanish speakers chant their language in terms of groups of fairly even morae, one per syllable; English speakers pace their speech in metrical feet, one main stress per foot.

Consider, for example, the sentence *Lárge dógs wánt méat*: here, each word = syllable is stressed and constitutes a foot by itself, *DUM DUM DUM DUM*. Adding unstressed syllables to this sequence will not add more feet: *The lárger dógs are wánting some méat, diDUMdi DUMdi DUMdi di DUM*. The examples in figure 4.1 further illustrate this principle. For those who read music, a rough musical notation is provided to suggest the basic rhythm.[5] As can be seen, increasing the number of unstressed syllables complicates the feet (measures), although it does not greatly extend them, but adding another primary-stressed syllable, for example *nów* in the seventh sentence, creates a new foot. The overall effect is jazzlike, and one teacher of English as a second language, Graham (1978), proved how "jazz chants" can be used as a vehicle for English acquisition by speakers of syllable-timed languages.

In Spanish, stressed syllables are louder than unstressed ones but not significantly longer. Since each syllable is about even, increasing the number of syllables (stressed or unstressed) in a sentence proportionally lengthens the time needed for saying it (Quilis and Fernández 1975, 161; Toledo 1988). The only noticeable squeezing of syllables is syneresis, sometimes represented by arcs under the affected vowels: *Han ido al teatro* /a.ní.do͜al.te͜á.tro/ (v. 2.2.3, 3.1.10). Otherwise, a two-syllable sequence will be *dot-dot* (♪♪) and a six-syllable one will be *dot-dot-dot-dot-dot-dot* (♪♪♪♪♪♪), occasionally peaking in word stresses and intonational dips and rises, but still rhythmically even.

Figure 4.1. English stress-timing as measured feet

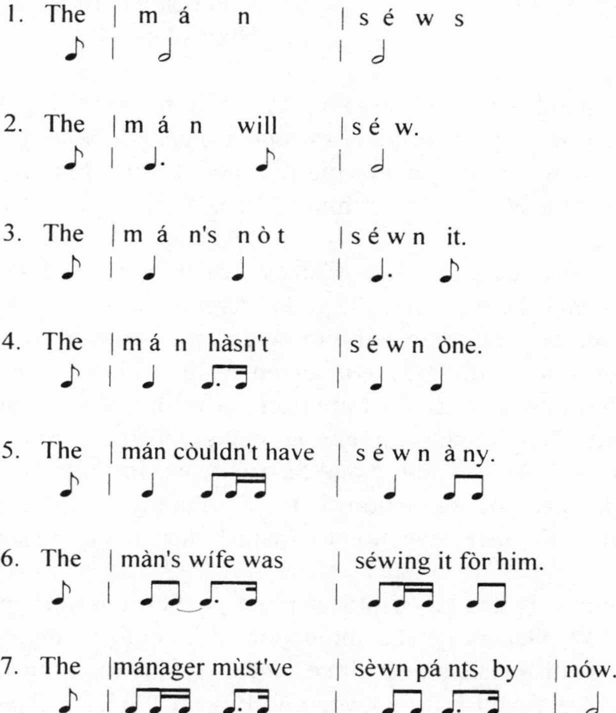

The difference between the two types is so marked that using the wrong rhythm in a normal, fluent tempo hinders the hearer's comprehension and processing of the material being transmitted (Bond and Fokes 1985). The rhythmic difference also impinges on the aesthetic side of language. In their traditional forms, Hispanic music and English music are dominated by rhythms that sprint or lurch like their respective languages. Many songs are thus distorted in translation: the words may faithfully reflect the original, but they feel out of kilter with the beat and note values. In poetry, too, the two cultures are accustomed to distinct metrical conventions based on their languages. At least in traditional schemes, lines of Spanish poetry have a determined number of syllables with parallel stress positions, whereas lines of English poetry are organized into symmetrical feet. The difference was brought out by Dalbor (1997, 82), who contrasted a Manrique poem with its translation by Longfellow, shown below. To appreciate the effect, the reader should read each version aloud with the appropriate rhythm of its language.

Recuerde el alma dormida,	O, let the soul her slumbers break,
Avive el seso y despierte	Let thought be quickened, and awake;

Contemplando	Awake to see
Cómo se pasa la vida,	How soon this life is past and gone,
Cómo se viene la muerte	And death comes softly stealing on,
Tan callando.	How silently!

The translation is a good one, even retaining the same number of syllables per line, but something has been lost from the original by a poet-translator who had to conform to his native rhythmic conventions. By saying the two poems with the *opposite* rhythms, the reader will appreciate the effect of a rhythmic "accent" in a foreign language.

4.2 Intonation. In languages such as Chinese, each syllable of a word is assigned a certain pitch (TONE), and the pitch scheme is an integral part of the word. In English and Spanish, however, pitches are organized into overall melodies or INTONATIONS that add to the neutral meaning of a word, phrase, or sentence. *Yes* and *sí* alone denote affirmation. When coupled with a falling pitch, they are declarative; but with a rising pitch, the affirmation is questioned. These pitch meanings are not an inherent part of *yes* or *sí,* since the same results obtain with *Mary's going* and *María se va*. In many respects, the two languages make similar uses of intonation, but the similarity can be deceptive. As with rhythm, the transfer of English intonation to Spanish does not quite sound right, and vice versa.

One major difference is that English uses more pitches and more pitch variation than Spanish (Kelm 1995). Generally, the intonations of English range over four pitches, whereas those of Spanish range over three, and the four of English are more widely spaced than the three of Spanish (Stockwell and Bowen 1965, 25; Alarcos Llorach 1999, 63).[6] These pitches cannot be transcribed by musical notes, since in speech "high pitch," "low pitch," and so on are relative to each individual's voice range and mood. Instead of notes for absolute pitch, many linguists prefer numbers for relative pitch. Thus, pitch **2** is one's middle speaking pitch, **1** and **3** are slightly lower and higher, respectively, and **4** is higher still. For the ideal bilingual, **2** will be about the same in the two languages, **1** and **3** might be a bit closer to **2** in Spanish than in English, and **4** will normally occur just in English.[7]

In addition, the description of intonation requires an indication of whether the voice falls, rises, or stays steady in completing the intonational contour. One way to transcribe these TERMINALS, as they are called, is with arrows: thus, **223↓** means 'middle-middle-higher, then fall', and **231↑** means 'middle-higher-low, then rise'. Both languages use these two terminals, but a terminal fall (*cadencia*) or rise (*anticadencia*) tends to be sharp and abrupt in Spanish, more gradual and trailing off in English (Terrell and Salgués 1979, 32). At the other end of the melody, both languages tend to start with pitch **1** on an unstressed syllable or stretch of unstressed syllables, rising to **2** on the first stressed syllable.

Many scholars have described the basic repertoire of intonations in one or both languages, including Dalbor (1997), Quilis and Fernández (1975), Navarro Tomás (1967), and Alarcos Llorach (1999). The list in figure 4.2 summarizes the most important and

Figure 4.2. Basic intonations of Spanish and English

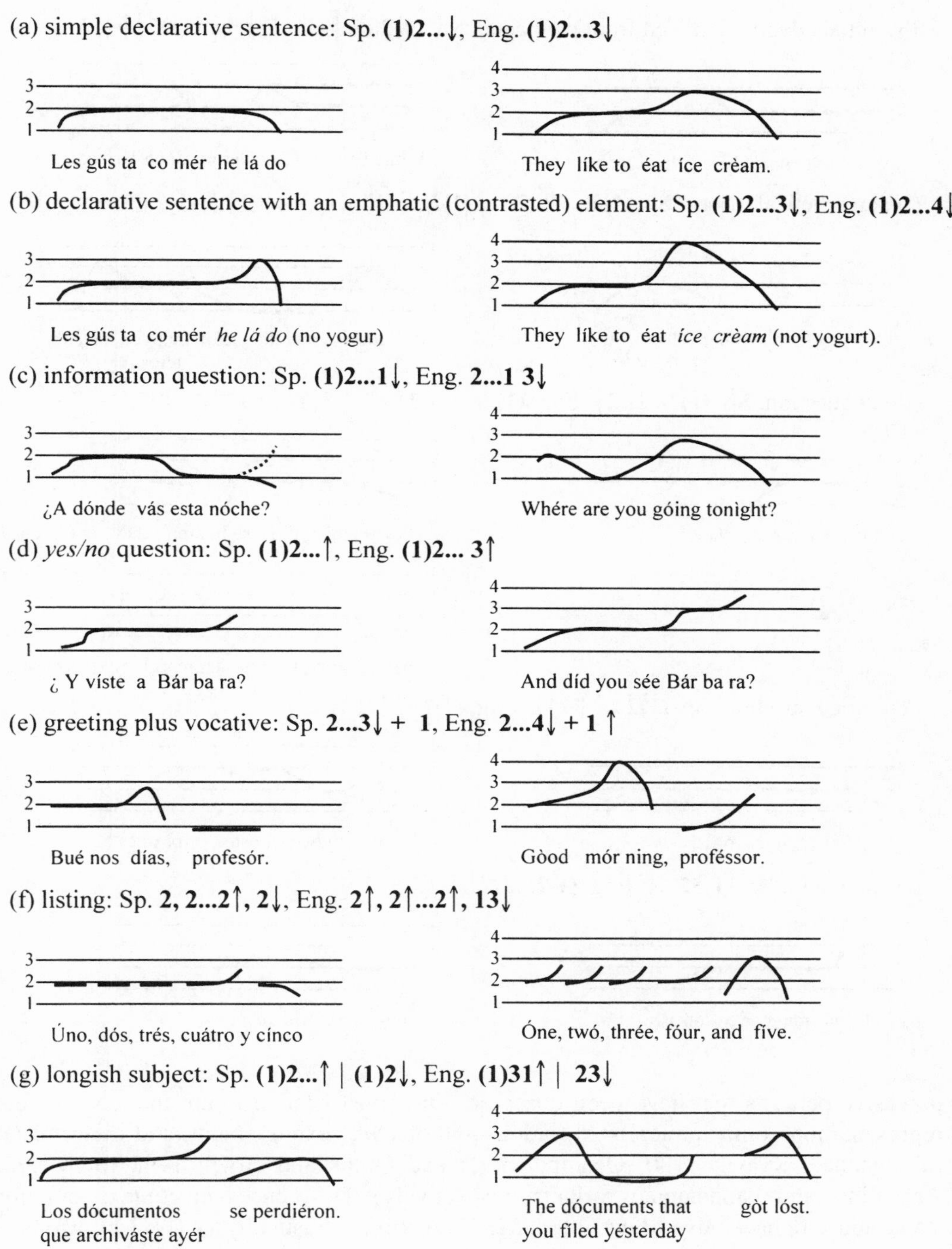

(a) simple declarative sentence: Sp. (1)2...↓, Eng. (1)2...3↓
Les gús ta co mér he lá do
They líke to éat íce crèam.
(b) declarative sentence with an emphatic (contrasted) element: Sp. (1)2...3↓, Eng. (1)2...4↓
Les gús ta co mér he lá do (no yogur)
They líke to éat íce crèam (not yogurt).
(c) information question: Sp. (1)2...1↓, Eng. 2...1 3↓
¿A dónde vás esta nóche?
Whére are you góing tonight?
(d) yes/no question: Sp. (1)2...↑, Eng. (1)2... 3↑
¿ Y víste a Bár ba ra?
And díd you sée Bár ba ra?
(e) greeting plus vocative: Sp. 2...3↓ + 1, Eng. 2...4↓ + 1 ↑
Bué nos días, profesór.
Gòod mór ning, proféssor.
(f) listing: Sp. 2, 2...2↑, 2↓, Eng. 2↑, 2↑...2↑, 13↓
Úno, dós, trés, cuátro y cínco
Óne, twó, thrée, fóur, and fíve.
(g) longish subject: Sp. (1)2...↑ | (1)2↓, Eng. (1)31↑ | 23↓
Los dócumentos que archiváste ayér
se perdiéron.
The dócuments that you fíled yésterdày
gòt lóst.

Figure 4.2. Basic intonations of Spanish and English (continued)

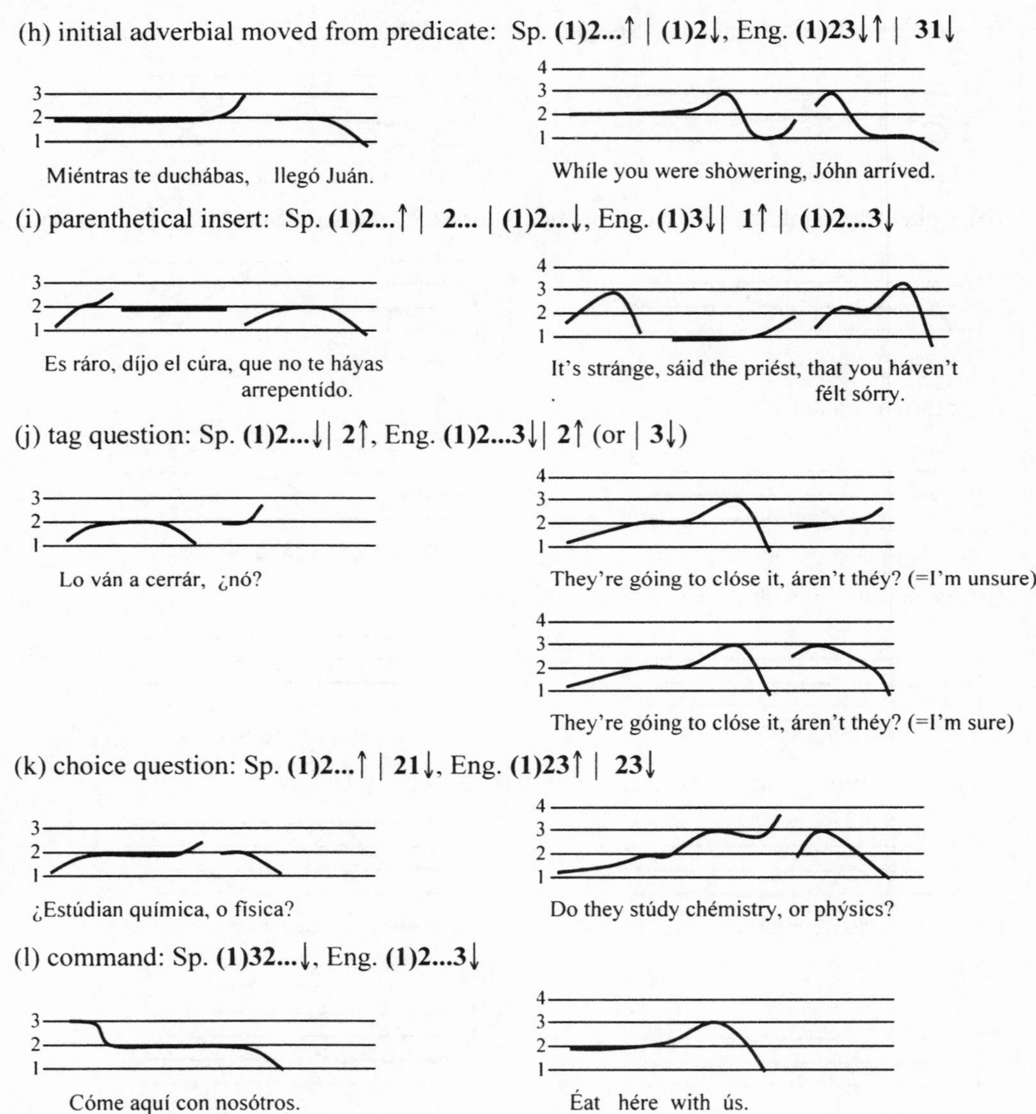
(h) initial adverbial moved from predicate: Sp. **(1)2...↑ | (1)2↓**, Eng. **(1)23↓↑ | 31↓**
Miéntras te duchábas, llegó Juán.
Whíle you were shòwering, Jóhn arríved.
(i) parenthetical insert: Sp. **(1)2...↑ | 2... | (1)2...↓**, Eng. **(1)3↓| 1↑ | (1)2...3↓**
Es ráro, díjo el cúra, que no te háyas arrepentído.
It's stránge, sáid the priést, that you háven't félt sórry.
(j) tag question: Sp. **(1)2...↓| 2↑**, Eng. **(1)2...3↓| 2↑** (or | **3↓**)
Lo ván a cerrár, ¿nó?
They're góing to clóse it, áren't théy? (=I'm unsure)
They're góing to clóse it, áren't théy? (=I'm sure)
(k) choice question: Sp. **(1)2...↑ | 21↓**, Eng. **(1)23↑ | 23↓**
¿Estúdian química, o física?
Do they stúdy chémistry, or phýsics?
(l) command: Sp. **(1)32...↓**, Eng. **(1)2...3↓**
Cóme aquí con nosótros.
Éat hére with ús.

pervasive patterns that have been observed. One must bear in mind, though, that these representations omit numerous variations—idiolectal, sexual, social, and dialectal (see, for instance, Kvavik 1980; Ocampo 1991; and Quilis and Graell 1992 for Mexican, Argentine, and Panamanian variants, respectively). Differences in context, emotional state, and emphasis also affect intonation, sometimes drastically (v. 11.3.1). Moreover, minor dips and rises are conventionally ironed out in intonational analysis, particularly the higher pitches that highlight stressed syllables in English (v. 4.1). Consequently, a **222↓** in Spanish remains relatively level until dropping with a terminal on the last stressed syllable, whereas a **222↓** in English actually contains the linguistic equivalents of a singer's appoggiaturas and mordents and a more gradual terminal. Thus, the examples in figure 4.2 show just the basic melodic lines, without the additional improvisations of dialects and idiolects.

A cursory examination of these examples reveals that both languages tend to reserve their highest pitch (**4** in English, **3** in Spanish) for emphasis and contrast, and to limit rising terminals to yes/no questions. Also, in the most common sentence type, simple declarative (a), both languages use a more or less sustained middle pitch, although Spanish descends to **1** on the last stressed syllable while English rises to **3** before descending. The differences increase with information questions (c), greetings (e), and parenthetical inserts (i), and major contrasts emerge with vocatives (e),[8] listing (f), longish subject (g), initial adverbial (h), tag questions (j), and commands (l). In these, English uses intonational twists that are unmatched in Spanish.

The risk of transferring L1 intonation to L2 is not simply one of sounding funny. While the above patterns capture regularities of "neutral" speech, it should be recalled that intonation is altered by one's emotional state or affect. As Bull noted (1965, 85), in addition to signaling sentence type, intonation can convey "insistence, annoyance, lack of interest, boredom, disgust, urgency, courteousness or curtness, servileness, in short the whole gamut of the speaker's emotional or psychological reaction to what is under consideration or to the person with whom he is speaking." If really excited, Spanish speakers may resort to a pitch **4**, so that the *normal* **4** of an English speaker's emphatic/contrastive intonation, if transferred to Spanish, can suggest a strong affective element (anger, indignation, enthusiasm) that was not intended. Likewise, English speakers sometimes flatten their general **(1)2 . . . 3↓** pattern (e.g., simple declarative (a)) to a near-monotone **2 . . . 2↓** when they feel bored, sleepy, or uninterested; thus, the Spanish speaker's normal **(1)2 . . . ↓** may convey the same characteristics to them. As another example, consider the greeting and vocative patterns in (e): in English, this combination yields **2 . . . 4↓ + 1↑** but in Spanish, **231↓ + 1**. To speakers of English, this Spanish intonation can sound abruptly unfriendly or officious, while to speakers of Spanish, the English pattern can sound ingratiating or overly friendly (Bull 1965, 86; Dalbor 1997, 233).

It is hard to delineate the boundary between purely linguistic intonations (those signaling syntactic structures) and the more subtle affective inflections that veer off into nonverbal communication. But it seems clear that students who transfer some of their English intonations may unwittingly convey rudeness or superciliousness, causing Spanish speakers to react to them in ways they did not intend. Most textbooks are silent on intonation, however, as they are on rhythm and many other aspects of pronunciation; teachers who agree with recent SLA researchers such as Benrabah (1997) and Pennington (1998) that better pronunciation training is called for may have to devise their own supplemental resources for the classroom.

Notes for chapter 4

1. The statistics cited by Núñez Cedeño and Morales Front (1999, 211) are as follows: for vowel-final words, 88 percent *llanas*, 11.1 percent *esdrújulas*, 0.87 percent *agudas*; for consonant-final words, 97.8 percent *agudas*, 2.03 percent *llanas*, 0.05 percent *esdrújulas*. There was no indication of whether their corpus was dictionary forms or whether it included inflected forms (in which case preterites and futures like *hablé hablaré* would increase the number of *agudas*).

2. But Navarro Tomás (1967, 195) and Harris (1983) also perceived minor secondary stresses in certain styles of Spanish. Boyd-Bowman (1960, 93) heard them on some speakers' postposed clitics: *¡vámonòs! ¡apúratè!*

3. When there are two or more secondaries per word, some perceive further degrees of stress: "tertiary" stress, "quaternary" stress, and so on. For expository simplification, we do not distinguish these here.

4. While this distinction in rhythmic type has a strong perceptual basis and has been widely accepted (see Dalbor 1997 and Barrutia and Schwegler 1994), the experimental evidence for it, as summarized by Toledo (1988, 1989) is more complex. Toledo's own careful measurements demonstrated that Argentine Spanish does show some lengthening of stressed syllables, especially in final position, from which he concluded that rhythmic types do not form a dichotomy but fall along a continuum. According to his data, the real rhythmic differences between English and Spanish are that the syllable lengthening/shortening is less in Spanish than in English, and that English feet tend to be regular in duration, as opposed to Spanish stress groups, which lengthen in proportion to the number of syllables they contain. These differences probably underlie the English speaker's impression that Spanish syllables sound more even than they actually are.

5. Figure 4.1 reflects my own rendition of these sentences; the exact note values of the unstressed syllables would vary from speaker to speaker, and sometimes alternative metrical groupings of the syllables are possible.

6. This analysis of Spanish intonation applies to normal speech. In both languages, certain interjections are a case apart. For instance, Boyd-Bowman (1960, 204) noted that Mexican *¿mande?* (for repetition of a previous utterance) and *¿bueno?* or *¿diga?* (for answering the telephone) are spoken "elevando casi una octava el tono de la última silaba." Otherwise, in neither language does intonation normally range over a whole octave in this way.

7. There are several transcriptional systems for speaking pitch. The IPA allows (a) numbers, (b) accents, (c) slanted arrows (↘ ↗) for overall intonations, and (d) "tone-letters" consisting of a vertical bar with a line extending from the left side (our **1**, **2**, **3**, **4**, ↓, ↑ would be ˩ ˧ ˦ ˥ ˥˩ ˩˥, respectively).

8. VOCATIVES are names or titles used for calling out to others to get their attention; they are tacked onto the sentence but are not syntactically a part of it. The same intonation tends to be used on tags such as *por favor* and *please*.

Exercises for chapter 4

1. The phonemic representation /komputo/ (without an indication of stress) corresponds to three different Spanish words. Show the difference in meaning according to stress.

2. Students who have not mastered Spanish stress mispronounce verb forms in three ways. First, they may stress the endings (sometimes producing a different tense): *trabajó, trabajás, trabajá*. Second, they may stress the first stem vowel, as in *trábajo, trábajas, trábaja*. Third, they may say *tràbajár, tràbajámos, trabàjarémos*. Explain as precisely as possible the apparent source of each error pattern.

3. With regard to the foregoing errors, give a comprehensive statement of where stress does occur in Spanish verb morphology.

4. A Mexican professor gave a speech in fluent, scholarly English, but in some cases she used un-English stress. Following are twelve examples of her stress patterns:

catégory	figúrative	Méxican	orthódoxy
cathédral	páinting	dominàted	próbably
aggréssively	univérsity	savágery	expláin

(a) Place an asterisk in front of each error and show the correct English accentuation.
(b) Compare her errors and her successes, looking for a pattern. Why is the pattern due to a general trait of Spanish rather than to direct transfer of the stresses of cognate Spanish words?
(c) In both Spanish and English, most nouns keep the same stress position when a plural suffix is added: *ánimal ánimals, cártridge cártridges, abúse abúses*; Spanish *animál animáles, catálogo catálogos, ceréza cerézas.* But Spanish *espécimen*, *régimen,* and *ínterin* change in the plural: *especímenes, regímenes*, *intérines*. (Compare the lack of change in *exámen exámenes*, *crímen crímenes*.) What does this have to do with the Mexican professor's English stress patterns?

5. Spanish has a writing system that marks stress when it does not conform to the usual rules; English, on the other hand, gets by without accents. Yet both languages have minimal pairs that contrast stress position. Why are the two cases different? (Hint: consider why *sábana/sabana* or *término/termino/terminó* would be confusing without their accents, but not *subject* or *invalid*.)

6. At least for the variety of Spanish presented in this chapter, how does intonation distinguish the three meanings of the sequence /sáka los bolétos tempráno/ (i.e., declarative, question, and command)?

7. Compare English and Spanish stress according to the following considerations:
(a) Is it just more force or loudness?
(b) Is it distinctive, or fully predictable?
(c) How many degrees of stress are used?
(d) What constraints exist on where it can occur?
(e) What effect does it have on the pronunciation of vowels?
(f) What effect does it have on rhythm?

8. Develop a lesson segment on rhythm for a first- or second-year course in Spanish. How would you present (describe and practice) Spanish rhythm to English speakers?

9. Stress-timing emphasizes stressed syllables and crushes unstressed ones; syllable-timing works best with even syllables of a regular, simple structure. Review the phonological and phonotactic rules of the two languages (chapters 2–3). Which rules seem to follow from the rhythm of each language? How does an abundance of contractions fit in with English rhythm?

10. Morphemes (stems and affixes) are sometimes classified according to whether they are CONTENT MORPHEMES or FUNCTION MORPHEMES. The former (e.g., *bird, run, -scope)* contain most or all of the semantic substance (meaning) of a word, while function morphemes (e.g., articles, short prepositions, derivational endings, tense and number endings) have grammatical meaning but not much conceptual meaning in themselves.

Take a fairly long English sentence with both content and function morphemes. Indicate with an accent all syllables with stress. Recall that these are lengthened while unstressed ones are shortened. Which morphemes—content or function—are thus more phonologically prominent and easier to process auditorily? Repeat this experiment with a Spanish sentence, perhaps a translation of the English one. Again, which kind of morphemes tends to receive stress somewhere? Given that stressed syllables are not lengthened in Spanish, comment on the ramifications of rhythm for English speakers' impressions of the speed of Spanish, and on their difficulties in processing long Spanish sentences.

11. Comment specifically on the intonational differences shown in figure 4.2. Can you add any other differences you have observed? In your opinion, how could the most important intonational contrasts between the two languages be presented and practiced in the classroom?

12. Transcribe the following Spanish-English cognates phonologically (i.e., in terms of phonemes / /, not allophones), focusing especially on differences in stress:

(a) tendencia, tendency
(b) revelación, revelation
(c) cuestión, question
(d) homogeneidad, homogeneity
(e) nacionalidad, nationality
(f) uniforme, uniform
(g) teléfono, telephone
(h) sinónimo, synonym
(i) arquitectura, architecture
(j) animal, animal
(k) democracia, democracy
(l) inventor, inventor
(m) violín, violin
(n) unanimidad, unanimity

13. One pedagogical technique for promoting auditory discrimination is "¿Cuál dije?", in which students see a list of pairs focusing on a key difference and indicate which member of each pair they hear from the teacher. (They then do the exercise with each other to promote *making* an audible distinction.) This exercise can be interlingual for English/Spanish differences, or in Spanish for Spanish phonemic or suprasegmental contrasts. Examples:

(a) English diphthongized /o/ (→[ow]) vs. Spanish /o/: *dose dos, solo solo, coal col, dough do,* and so on

(b) Spanish /k/ vs. /x/: *coco cojo, rico rijo, marquen margen, caja jaca,* and so on. Create an exercise of each kind for a class, using different phonological items.

14. Language teaching methods used to emphasize memorization of long dialogs to develop good pronunciation "habits" and to introduce new grammar and vocabulary. Such dialogs were

rightly criticized as inauthentic and not leading to the desired proficiency for creating one's own speech in the language. (In normal interactions, we do not speak in memorized conversations.) On the other hand, there *are* some authentic utterances that one *does* learn as wholes—for example, proverbs. What other examples of memorized speech occur to you? In what way could memorization of such passages benefit overall fluency?

15. Listen to a native speaker of English at the beginning or intermediate level of Spanish study and make a recording of his/her speech, preferably in two tasks to obtain different styles, for example, spontaneous conversation vs. oral reading. Then, carry out an error analysis of this student's pronunciation by describing each problem and its apparent source (cause). Distinguish between sporadic errors and fairly consistent ones. You will be drawing on information from all four chapters in this part of the book, and you may wish to sort errors and causes out as follows:

(a) basic articulatory errors with Spanish phonemes
(b) failure to master rules of Spanish or to use proper allophones
(c) transfer of English phonological patterns or rules onto Spanish phonemes
(d) errors with stress and rhythm
(e) problems with intonation
(f) false generalizations within Spanish

PART TWO

GRAMMAR

Chapter 5

Basic notions of grammatical description

5.0 The grammar of language. The term GRAMMAR has been used in many ways: for the study of letters (the original Greek sense), for morphology and syntax, for a description or reference work of morphology and syntax, for the entire structural framework of language (thus embracing phonology and semantics as well), and for the proprieties of cultivated usage, as in "Watch your grammar." In this book, it will be used mainly in the second sense, morphology and syntax (or MORPHOSYNTAX), that is, the structure of words, phrases, and sentences.

5.1 Morphology: Morphemes, allomorphs, and rules. For morphology, linguists use notions similar to those of phonology (v. 1.2). Just as the basic unit of phonology is the phoneme, that of morphology is the MORPHEME. A morpheme is any minimal form (word or part of a word) with its own meaning, function, and combinatory potential, whether stem (root) or affix (prefix or suffix). Because morphemes are the building blocks of word and phrase formation, they are also called FORMATIVES. Affixed morphemes that express syntactic properties such as person, number, tense, and case are INFLECTIONAL; those that derive a new word from another one are DERIVATIONAL. On the basis of these notions, the morphology of the word *prehistórico* can be described as follows, or as in the tree diagram in figure 5.1 (see Varela 1990).

pre+histór+ic+o: four morphemes (+ = morpheme boundary):
pre-: derivational prefix meaning 'before' forming *prehistoria* from *historia*
histor(ia): stem

Figure 5.1. Morphological structure of *prehistórico*

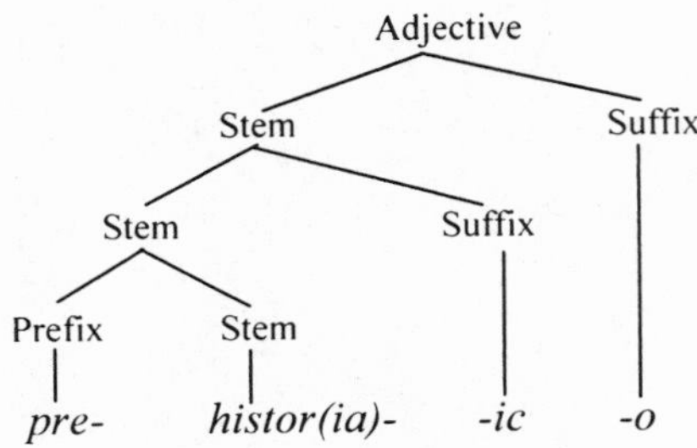

-ic-: derivational suffix forming an adjective from a noun
-o: inflectional suffix for masculine gender (contrasting with *-a*)

The stem *histor-* is a version or ALLOMORPH of *historia.* Special rules generally known as MORPHOPHONEMIC rules produce allomorphs in specific environments by altering the phonemic makeup of a morpheme. In this case, /istorja+iko/ is adjusted to /istor+iko/) by a rule that drops a final /j/ plus vowel of a stem when the /i/ of a suffix follows:

$$\text{jV} \rightarrow \emptyset \;/\; \_\_\_ + \text{i}$$

The same rule accounts for *copia+ista → copista* and *sucio+ísimo → sucísimo.*

Another example of ALLOMORPHY (presence of allomorphs instead of one invariant form) is the alternation between the sounds written as *l* and *ll* in the following: *él ~ ell-os, aquel ~ aquell-a, caballo ~ cabal-gar, bello ~ bel-dad, valle ~ Val-derrobles.* The consonant, traditionally /ʎ/, becomes /l/ word-finally or before a consonant (Harris 1983, 50):

$$\text{ʎ} \rightarrow \text{l} \;/\; \_\_\_ \; \{\text{C}, \#\}$$

5.2 Syntax: Word order, constituency, and function. Traditional grammar has focused mainly on the forms and usage of the various parts of speech or SYNTACTIC CATEGORIES: nouns, pronouns, verbs, and so on. For convenience, we will begin our study of Spanish and English grammar in the same way: verbs are discussed in chapters 6 and 7, nouns and their modifiers in chapter 8, pronominal forms and usage in chapter 9, and adverbs, prepositions, and conjunctions in chapter 10. An analysis of categories alone is insufficient, however; a full account of syntax requires a description of how these parts are combined to form the possible sentence structures of a language, and that will be the focus of chapters 11 through 13.

Many approaches have arisen in the attempt to characterize syntax. Perhaps the simplest is to represent a sentence as a left-to-right chain of categories. Letting N stand for nouns, V for verbs, Adv for adverbs, Aux for auxiliary (helping) verbs, Quant for quantifiers (e.g., numbers), D for demonstratives (or determiners, as they will be called later), and S for a sentence, we can arrive at formulas such as the following:

Emilia corrió.	S = N + V
Aquella niña corrió.	S = D + N + V
Aquella niña ha corrido.	S = D + N + Aux + V
Dos niñas corrieron temprano.	S = Quant + N + V + Adv
Aquellas dos niñas han corrido temprano.	S = D + Quant + N + Aux + V + Adv

But this procedure is atomistic: every language is a potentially infinite set of sentences, so we could list such sequences forever without obtaining many generalizations. The formulas show only one useful syntactic fact so far, namely, word order; for example, Spanish apparently prefers Aux + V over V + Aux. But the formulas say little about two other points of interest, sentence structure and the functions of the parts. With regard to structure, we note that the units joined together in each sentence sort out into two main parts or CONSTITUENTS: N with its companions D and Quant (if present), and V with its companions Aux and Adv (if present). The former constituent is a NOUN PHRASE, NP, and the latter is a VERB PHRASE, VP. Thus, for all these sentences (and infinitely more), we can state the generalization that S consists of two constituents, NP and VP, and that NP and VP in turn consist of N and V with their optional companions. The functions of the parts must also be defined: the NP functions as the SUBJECT of V, and on that fact rests the difference between *corrió* and *corrieron* and between *ha* and *han*. Function also determines the semantic interpretation or meaning of the sentence: the NP construed as the subject of the V *correr* is taken to be the runner, not the location of the running.

Many European linguists such as Tesnière (1959) have concentrated on the relationship between syntactic categories and their phrasal companions. In general, these linguists show this relationship as a DEPENDENCY and use diagrams in which the companions (D, Quant, Aux, Adv) hang down from the "head" elements, N and V, on which they depend. This approach is still found in the writings of some Spanish grammarians, for example, García Miguel (1995). On the other hand, linguists in CASE GRAMMAR (e.g., Fillmore 1968) have focused more on function. A sentence is represented as a "proposition" consisting of a verb combined with its ARGUMENTS, that is, units having a "Case" relationship with it: Agent, Patient, Instrument, Experiencer, and so on. Thus, all the sentences we examined earlier would be variants of the proposition "*correr* + Agent." Several other approaches, such as tagmemics (Pike 1954–1960; Cook 1969), have also arisen in attempts to combine these perspectives of structure and function.

The dominant approach to syntax, however, has been GENERATIVE GRAMMAR. Originating with Chomsky 1957, this theory represents the structured groupings of constituents in terms of branching diagrams called PHRASE MARKERS (since they demarcate phrases), also known as "trees." The phrase marker for the sentence *Aquella niña ha corrido temprano* is given in figure 5.2; compare the parallel representation of morphological structure in figure 5.1. This phrase marker states that S consists of NP + VP; that the NP in turn has

Figure 5.2. Syntactic structure in generative grammar

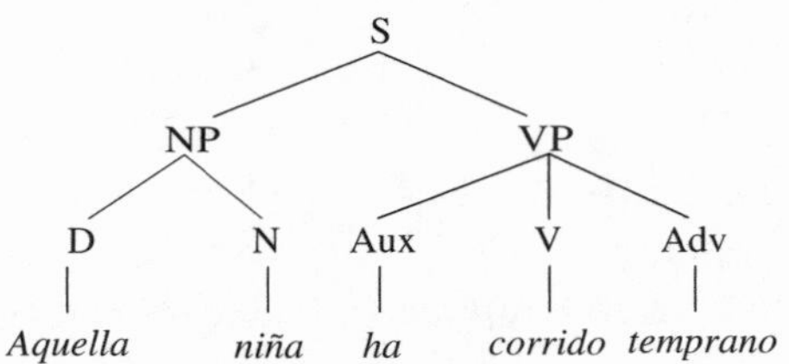

as its constituents D and N; and that the VP consists of Aux + V + Adv.

Generative grammar defines the syntactic function of each constituent by the configuration: the subject is the NP that is DOMINATED by S (i.e., has S above it as the next highest node in the tree). The *semantic* function of an NP—what Fillmore called "Case" and today is called a THEMATIC RELATION or θ (theta)-ROLE—is determined by the verb. In this case, *correr* assigns the θ-role "Agent" to its subject; *dormir*, on the other hand, assigns the inactive θ-role of "Patient."

Unlike other approaches, generative grammar treats sentence structure at two distinct levels, DEEP STRUCTURE (also called "underlying structure" or "logical form") and SURFACE STRUCTURE. These are comparable to the phonemic and phonetic levels of phonology. The Spanish word *yodo* is [ɉóðo] phonetically (on the surface, so to speak), but /jódo/ phonemically: [ɉ] and [ð] are respectively allophones of /j/ and /d/ generated by two phonological rules (v. 3.1). Likewise, the two sentence patterns *Aquella niña ha corrido temprano* (NP + VP) and *Ha corrido temprano aquella niña* (VP + NP) could be regarded as "allosentences," or more properly, as surface structures of the same deep structure. Like the phonological rules that change /j/ and /d/ to [ɉ] and [ð], Spanish has the following syntactic rule, called a TRANSFORMATION, for changing one pattern to the other. (The arrow here means 'may change to'.)

$$\text{NP VP} \rightarrow \text{VP NP}$$

Like the features of phonology (v. 1.1.5), generative grammar recognizes GRAMMATICAL FEATURES in morphology and syntax. The noun *niña* is [+feminine], and the inflectional suffix *-s* adds the feature [+plural]. Constituents such as NP (and then S) that dominate this N inherit the same specifications. By an agreement transformation, D, Adj, and V change form according to N's features: (*aquel- niñas* [+feminine, +plural] *ha corrido*) → *aquel**las** niñas **han** corrido*.

Transformations account for different surface structures of the same deep structure. Another kind of rule, the PHRASE STRUCTURE RULE (PSR), specifies the options available to a speaker in constructing the deep structure. For the examples examined so far, the PSRs of Spanish (and of English too) specify that S consists of NP joined with VP; that NP contains D, Quant, and N (D and Quant being optional); and that VP is made up of Aux, V, and Adv (Aux and Adv being optional). These PSRs are conventionally formulated as follows. (The arrows in this case mean 'consists of, has as its constituents' and the parentheses mean 'optionally'.)

S → NP VP
NP → (D) (Quant) N
VP → (Aux) V (Adv)

These three rules summarize a great deal of information on the possible sentence structures available to speakers of Spanish or English. They furthermore account for word order in stipulating D + Quant + N, Aux + V + Adv, and NP + VP; other sequences are blocked unless transformations explicitly bring these about. Consequently, generative grammar is a powerful tool for describing the key facts of syntax—order, constituency, function, and relationships between "allosentences"—and it is the approach that we adopt in this book.

Discovering the rules of languages is a first step, and the one we focus on in comparing Spanish and English. But linguistics has another goal too: to explain those rules in a theory of universal grammar (v. 0.2.1). After describing the PSRs of numerous languages, linguists found that all of them essentially conform to one general instruction: for any category X (= N, V, etc.), construct around that X an X-phrase, XP, subject to the local parameters of the language. A PARAMETER is a kind of linguistic thermostat allowing a certain range of settings. The parameter for the head's position in its phrase (N in NP, V in VP, etc.) is set close to "phrase-medial" in Spanish and English, but at "phrase-final" in Japanese, where all modifiers of N and V precede them. Likewise, there is a Null Subject parameter (Jaeggli and Safir 1989) that, in Spanish and Japanese, is set to allow not only subject dropping but the complete absence of subjects in sentences like *Llovió ayer*. In languages such as English and French, this parameter has the opposite setting, so that some subject must be inserted even when there is no logical one, as in ***It** rained yesterday*. For transformations, too, there are cross-language universals: thus, many word-order changes we will discuss individually for Spanish and English are seen (from a bird's-eye view) as manifestations of a single overall principle called "Move α," that is, Move *alpha* (= any designated constituent) subject to conditions imposed by the particular language.

5.3 Grammaticality. Another contribution of generative grammar is to establish that it is just as useful to consider ungrammatical or impossible formations as it is to investigate the grammatical ones; otherwise, one might generalize a syntactic description beyond the real limits of the language. Ideally, not only should a grammar account for all sentences that can be generated in a language, but it should be so constrained as to exclude the generation of ungrammatical ones. For example, as will be shown later (v. 11.2.3), the transformations that yield *Ha corrido temprano aquella niña* from *Aquella niña ha corrido temprano* can produce other word orders too, so why not broaden "Move α" to something like "Scramble constituents in any way you wish"? But this will go beyond the limits of the language, yielding the following:

*Ha temprano corrido aquella niña.
*Corrido ha niña aquella temprano.
*Temprano aquella niña corrido ha.

The asterisk (or "star") means 'does not conform to the language', that is, 'is ungrammatical'. As Chomsky and others have pointed out, native speakers not only know what is possible in their language but also can recognize what is not possible. Occasionally, grammaticality depends on the dialect or even idiolect: *¿Qué tú dices?* is used in the Caribbean, but it would bear an asterisk in most other lects. Grammaticality also depends on meaning: Spanish judges accepted a nonnative's *Como termino de trabajar, vamos a Italia*, not realizing that it was an Italian transfer and ungrammatical for the intended meaning, *En cuanto termine de trabajar* . . . (García Gutiérrez 1993, 108). But essentially, Chomsky is correct in noting that speakers have the ability to distinguish those sentences that conform to their language from those that do not. Certainly, teachers have had abundant practice at this, and they may wonder what is wrong with a textbook rule when students follow it and still produce something that is quite un-Spanish and deserving of an asterisk.

Chapter 6

Verb morphology

6.0 Verb forms and their nomenclature. For English speakers, the foremost challenge in Spanish morphology is the verb. While the Spanish noun has only two inflectional categories, singular and plural (gender being regarded as derivational for nouns), the verb has forty-eight distinct simple inflectional forms. ("Inflectional" excludes derived forms in *-ble, -dor,* etc.; "simple" excludes compound forms such as *he hecho*; and "distinct" precludes counting identical forms such as *(yo) hacía = (él) hacía* twice.) The PARADIGM (full set of forms) of the Spanish verb thus contrasts starkly with the inflectional options of English verbs, which range from one to eight:

one form: *must*	four forms: *walk, walks, walked, walking*
two forms: *can, could*	five forms: *sing, sings, sang, sung, singing*
three forms: *put, puts, putting*	eight forms: *be, am, is, are, was, were, been, being*

Spanish verbs have more forms because they are conjugated for more tense and mood categories and for more person and number distinctions. The latter seem redundant to English speakers until they understand that Spanish speakers often rely on the verb to indicate the subject; that is, the *-s* of *hablas* is not just a sign of agreement as suggested by fill-in-the-blanks such as *Tú* (*hablar*_____), but the usual marker of an unexpressed *tú*.

Linguists and teachers in the United States largely agree on what to call tense and mood categories: *drank* is "past," *bebí* and *bebía* are respectively "preterite" and "imperfect." In Hispanic countries, however, there is less consensus: some scholars retain traditional Latin terminology while others have substituted new terms deemed more appropriate for Spanish. Figure 6.1 summarizes the major differences (see Resnick 1984 for fuller discussion). *He dicho,* for example, has been called "presente perfecto" and "presente compuesto," both of which describe its morphology, the present of *haber* compounded with the "perfect" participle (v. 6.3.2). But it is also called "pretérito perfecto"

Figure 6.1. Nomenclatures for Spanish verb forms

B: Bello [1847] 1958
RA: Real Academia 1924
GG: Gili Gaya 1973
R: Ramsey [1894] 1956
SBM: Stockwell, Bowen and Martin 1965
US: usual U.S. pedagogical term

1. **infinitas/nonfinites:**
   decir: B, RA, GG infinitivo; SBM, R, US infinitive
   diciendo: B, RA, GG gerundio; R present participle; SBM imperfective participle; US gerund
   diciente: B, GG participio presente (others omit this category)
   dicho: B participio pasivo; RA and GG participio; SBM perfective participle; R, US past participle

2. **modo indicativo/indicative mood:**
   digo: (all systems) presente/present
   decía: B copretérito; RA, GG pretérito imperfecto; R, SBM, US imperfect
   dije: B pretérito; RA pretérito indefinido; GG pretérito perfecto absoluto; R, SBM, US preterite
   diré: B futuro; RA futuro imperfecto; GG futuro absoluto; R, SBM, US future
   diría: B pospretérito; RA modo potencial; GG futuro hipotético; R, SBM, US conditional
   he dicho: B antepresente; RA pretérito perfecto (compuesto); GG pretérito perfecto actual; R perfect or past indefinite; SBM present anterior; US present perfect
   había dicho: B antecopretérito; RA pretérito pluscuamperfecto; GG pluscuamperfecto; R pluperfect; SBM imperfect anterior; US past perfect, pluperfect.
   hube dicho: B, GG antepretérito; RA pretérito anterior; SBM preterite anterior; R, US preterite perfect.
   habré dicho: B, GG antefuturo; RA futuro perfecto; R, US future perfect; SBM future anterior
   habría dicho: B antepospretérito; RA modo potencial compuesto; GG antefuturo hipotético; R, US conditional perfect; SBM conditional anterior

3. **modo imperativo/imperative mood:**
   di, decid

4. **modo subjuntivo/subjunctive mood:**
   diga: (all systems) presente/present
   dijera, dijese: B pretérito; RA, GG pretérito imperfecto; R imperfect; SBM, US past
   dijere: B futuro; RA futuro imperfecto; GG futuro hipotético; R future; (SBM, US omit)
   haya dicho: B antepresente; RA, GG pretérito perfecto; R perfect; SBM present anterior; US present perfect
   hubiera dicho: B antepretérito; RA pretérito pluscuamperfecto; GG pluscuamperfecto; R pluperfect; SBM past anterior; US past (or plu-)perfect
   hubiere dicho: B hipotético; RA futuro perfecto; GG antefuturo hipotético; (others omit)

because the action began in the past (*pretérito*), a meaning Bello decided would be even better conveyed by "antepresente." Bello also called *diría* "pospretérito," *decía* "copretérito," and *habré dicho* "antefuturo," again appropriately in terms of their meanings (v. 7.1 ff.). In this book, we will retain the prevailing U.S. terms because they are more likely to be familiar to the reader and because other nomenclatures can cause confusion (e.g., *pretérito perfecto* for present perfect, not the preterite perfect *hube dicho).* Nevertheless, it is a good idea to familiarize oneself with the other terms, since these may appear in other works.

6.1 Spanish finite verb forms. In the verb form *hablar, habl-* is the STEM, *-r* is the infinitive suffix, and the connecting *-a-* is the THEME (or class) vowel, which identifies the conjugational class—namely, "*-ar* verb" or first conjugation, as opposed to the *-e-* of "*-er* verbs" or second conjugation and to the *-i-* of "*-ir* verbs" or third conjugation. The first conjugation has the largest membership and also absorbs most new verbs today; in Teschner's corpus (2000b, 109), there were 8,650 *-ar* verbs vs. 672 *-er* and 684 *-ir* verbs.

In inflecting a verb through its morphological categories, one adds to the *stem + theme* base the appropriate tense, mood, and person/number suffixes.[1] For the 3pl. (third person plural) preterite form of *hablar,* for example, *-ron* is added to the stem and theme vowel: *habl+a+ron.* The same formation is visible in the corresponding form of third conjugation *pedir*: stem plus theme vowel plus *-ron*: *ped+i+ron. Ped+i+ron,* however, is only the underlying formation; morphophonemic rules apply both to the stem and to the suffixes, raising the /e/ in the stem to /i/ and diphthongizing the theme vowel /i/ to /je/: *ped+**i**+ron* → *p**i**d+**ie**+ron.* To explain such changes requires further analysis of the suffixes and stems.

6.1.1 Endings as slots for morphemes. A verb form can be analyzed as morphemes allocated to specific positional slots. The English verb has just two slots, one for the stem and one for a single suffix or "zero" (Ø, no suffix): *walk+Ø, walk+s, walk+ed.* A Spanish verb form such as *hablaban,* however, consists of four morphemes in distinct slots:

STEM	THEME	IMPERFECT	PERSON/NUMBER
habl	*+a*	*+ba*	*+n*

If, in the fourth slot, *-n* is replaced by *-s,* a new form results, *habl+a+ba+s,* which is otherwise the same but for the change to 2sg. If, in the third slot, *ba* is replaced in turn by *ra, ía,* and Ø, three other forms are created: *habl+a+ra+n, habl+a+ría+n, habl+a+Ø+n.*

Note that what is often taught as one ending, *-aban,* actually contains three morphemes. The theme vowel *-a-* identifies the conjugational class (as well as present tense if the next slot has Ø); *-ba-* signals imperfect; *-n* is the marker for 3pl. These morphemes, and the whole Spanish setup, are inherited from Latin. But even in Latin the neat sequence of morphemes was disrupted by irregularities and mergers, and the evolution of Spanish resulted in further disruptions.

1. Verbs in *-er* and *-ir* largely converge on the same theme vowel, *-e* (but → *ie* in *-ie+ndo, -ie+ron*). Their theme vowels are distinct only in the infinitive, *vosotros* commands, and *nosotros* and *vosotros* present indicatives. In some nonstandard dialects, even this much difference disappears, and the two conjugations merge entirely (Sánchez 1982, 28).
2. Theme vowels indicate a mood change if switched. Thus, in the present subjunctive the characteristic *a* of an *-ar* verb becomes *e* and the *e* of an *-er* (or *-ir*) verb becomes *a*. The present indicatives of *sentir creer vender parir* therefore overlap with the present subjunctives of *sentar crear vendar parar,* and vice versa.
3. In the preterite, the usual set of person/number suffixes changes (except *nosotros*):[2]
   1sg. *-o* → Ø   1pl. *-mos* = *-mos*
   2sg. *-s* → *-ste*   2pl. *-is* → *-steis*
   3sg. Ø→ *-ó*   3pl. *-n* → *-ron*
4. The suffixes of adjacent slots interact at many points in the verb paradigm. Even in Latin, the *-o* ending canceled out the preceding theme vowel in the first conjugation, so that the sequence *am+a+o* was just *amo,* and still is in Spanish. Fusion of adjacent suffixes occurred on a grand scale in the development of Spanish preterites such as *amó,* whose *-ó* merges three originally distinct morphemes: /am+á+wi+t/ (stem + theme + past + 3sg.) → /am+á+w+t/ → /am+áw/ → /am+ów/ → /am+ó/. Similarly, English *drank* fuses *drink+ed* into one form (technically called a PORTMANTEAU) whose underlying morphological stitches are invisible.

It is not necessary to survey each form in detail. All teachers know that the inflections are not just a matter of "every ending for itself," for there are certain general principles that govern formation. Past subjunctives are best described on the basis of *ellos* preterites; most imperatives are present subjunctives; the future is the entire infinitive used as a base combined with the present indicative of *haber* (*am+a+r* + *he* → *amaré, am+a+r* + *has* → *amarás,* etc.). The real pedagogical challenge is the infamous irregular verb.

6.1.2 Stem changes: Regular or irregular? Some verbs change a phoneme or two in their stems as they are inflected. English *do* /du/, for example, becomes /dʌ/ before *-s* and *-ne* and /dɪ/ before *-d*. Others switch to a wholly different stem, as when *go* becomes *wen-* before *-t* (the same *-t* as in *kept*). Both cases involve stem allomorphs, but the latter is so drastic that it receives the special name of SUPPLETION. Comparable cases in Spanish are *ven- vien- vin-* for *venir* versus the suppletive *s- er- fu-* for *ser* (*s+oy, er+a, fu+i*).

What makes a verb regular or irregular? These labels are used very loosely in textbooks; some call a verb irregular if it undergoes any kind of change, whether orthographic, morphophonemic, or totally suppletive. Technically, though, REGULAR means 'rule-governed' (Latin *regula,* Spanish *regla*) and IRREGULAR 'not rule-governed'. If we adhere to these definitions, then regular verbs should include all those whose allomorphy conforms at least in part to general rules. This makes morphological description analytically and pedagogically neater, and in fact brings hundreds of so-called irregular verbs within the pale of normalcy.

The following sections review the main types of stem and ending changes in Spanish, and the rules governing them. Most of these rules have pedagogical relevance in that the student who learns a single rule covering the changes in fifty verbs is better equipped than one who must memorize each form of each verb paradigm individually. On the other hand, it is obvious that when a rule affects only one or two verbs, it is easier just to commit their quirks to memory.

6.1.2.1 Orthographic changes.

1. *tocar, toqué* — *averiguar, averigüé*
   pagar, pagué — *escoger, escojo, escoja*
   rezar, rece — *distinguir, distingo, distinga*
   vencer, venzo, venza — *delinquir, delinco, delinca*

These are called "orthographic changing" verbs, and the spelling changes are their only oddity. In terms of their pronunciation, there is *no stem change at all*: /pag+á+r/, /pag+é/, and so on. What would indeed be irregular would be to have *pagar pagé* with the change of /pag/ to /pax/. Hence, even the greatest aficionados of irregularities distinguish spelling changes from other types.

Unfortunately, no matter how much the teacher or textbook writer emphasizes the regularity and predictability of spelling changes, students tend to see them as anomalous. Part of the problem is that many classes fail to digest Spanish spelling conventions (v. 2.4) sufficiently before the preterite or present subjunctive is encountered. Students thus perceive the *g* → *gu* change in *pagué* as a preterite peculiarity of *pagar* rather than an automatic spelling convention that is language-wide. Moreover, they have learned to depend on the written word, taking that as primary over pronunciation (v. 1.0); what they think should be conjugated is the visual sequence *PAG* (*pago, page*), not the phonemic sequence /pag/.

2. *leer, leyendo* — *creer, creyó, creyeron*

The change of *i* to *y* here is likewise orthographic, though not always recognized as such. Phonetically, the *y* of *-yó* in *creyó* is more fricative ([j]) than the *i* of *-ió* in *comió* ([j]) (v. 3.1.1), but the two phones are allophones of the same phoneme, which Spanish spells with *i* after a consonant but with *y* after a vowel or word-initially. However spelled, *-ió -ieron -iera -iendo,* or *-yó -yeron -yera -yendo,* these endings are phonemically /jó jéron jéra jéndo/. Since the spelling change is predictable, *leer* and *creer* ought to be pulled out of the irregular verb listings.

3. *variar, varía, varíe* *continuar, continúo, continúa*

There are about forty such verbs, and their problem is a conflict between phonology and orthography. Phonologically, the stems of these verbs end in a high vowel, /i/ or /u/, and when the stems are stressed, that last stem vowel receives the stress as usual: /barío barías baría kontinúo kontinúas kontinúa . . . /. When the stress is on a suffix vowel, however, the high vowel becomes a glide by the Gliding rule (v. 2.2.3, 3.1.10): /bariár kontinué/ → [barjár kontinwé]. In contrast, the stems of *estudiar* and *averiguar* end in glides /j w/ throughout their paradigms, so these are /estudj/ and /aberigw/; when the stress falls on the last stem vowel of /estudj/, as in *estudio* /estudj+o/, the form must be /estúdj+o/, as opposed to *varío* /barí+o/. Yet orthographically, there is nothing about the infinitives of *variar* and *estudiar* to suggest different behavior. The change does not seem to be an underlying /i/ becoming a glide [j], but a /j/ somehow becoming [í] as signaled by an accent mark appearing out of nowhere.

6.1.2.2 Morphophonemic changes. Unlike orthographic changes, morphophonemic changes (v. 5.1) alter the phonemes themselves, not merely their spelling. Spanish verbs show numerous types of morphophonemic changes, described below after representative examples.

1. *pensar, pienso, piense* *llover, llueve*
   contar, cuéntelo *pedir, piden, pida*

The changes here are Diphthongization in the case of *e* → *ie* /je/ and o → *ue* /we/ and Raising in that of *e*→ *i*. Diphthongization also applies to /i/ and /u/ in *adquirir* and *jugar* (*jogar* in Old Spanish). These changes are not predictable from the spelling or phonemic representation of the infinitive: *apostar* 'bet' and *apostar* 'station (troops)' have identical infinitives, but the former diphthongizes and the latter does not; *defender* and *tentar* diphthongize but the related *ofender* and *intentar* do not; *sentir* takes Diphthongization while *rendir* takes Raising. Textbooks therefore signal these changes with the cues *(ue), (ie), (i)* in vocabularies, and students should learn these with the infinitives, just as they learn articles with nouns, as keys to morphology.[3]

The reason why the infinitive alone is a poor guide to Diphthongization and Raising is that the stem is then unstressed, whereas these changes occur *just under stress*:

$$\left.\begin{array}{l} \text{o} \rightarrow \textit{ue} \text{ (/we/)} \\ \text{e} \rightarrow \textit{ie} \text{ (/je/) or /i/} \end{array}\right\} \text{/ whenever stressed}$$

Hence, /pénso/ → [pjénso], but the rule will not apply in *pensar* /pensár/, *pensamos, pensando*. This simple rule suffices for all four dozen forms of well over a hundred such verbs. To apply it, though, requires mastery of the correct stress position in Spanish; students who persist in singing out the traditional oxytonic Conjugational Chant of *haBLÓ, haBLÁS, haBLÁ* are not using standard forms of *hablar* and will be unequipped for mastering stress-cued stem changes.[4]

As with orthographic changes, students must learn that the *e ~ ie* and *o ~ ue* alternations are not quirks of verbs but are found throughout the language (v. 15.1.4). The following examples show the same stress-based alternations outside of verb paradigms; some of them (*nueve noventa, siete setenta)* occur early enough in most courses to reinforce the same changes in verbs.

nuéve, novénta
Venezuéla, venezoláno
cuéllo, collár
muérte, mortál
diénte, dentísta
fiésta, festívo
valiénte, valentía

buéno, bondád
nuéstro, nosótros
vergüénza, vergonzóso
puérto, portéño
tiérra, aterrizár
pimiénto, pimentál
ciégo, ceguéra

puéblo, población
cuérpo, corpúdo
fuérza, forzóso
huésped, hospedár
siéte, seténta, seteciéntos
ciélo, celestiál
viéjo, vejéz

2. *sentir, sintió, sintamos* *dormir, durmieron, durmiendo*

This is a different kind of raising (*e* → *i, o* → *u*) from the type just discussed: it occurs when an *unstressed* stem precedes either a stressed /a/ (*sintamos, durmamos*) or a diphthong beginning with /j/ (*sintió, durmiendo*). Unstressed Raising is a strange morphophonemic rule whose rationale lies buried in ancient sound changes. Two generalizations are useful, however. First, Unstressed Raising applies just to the third conjugation (exception: the *pudiendo* of *poder*). Second, virtually all third conjugation verbs whose last stem vowel is /e/ or /o/ (and there are about four dozen of them) undergo both this rule and the preceding one. A student who knows this can predict with some certainty that a new verb, say *embestir,* will have *embistamos, embistió* by Unstressed Raising and either *embiesto* or *embisto* (the latter, as it turns out) by Stressed Diphthongization/Raising. The only exceptions worth mentioning are *sumergir, divergir,* and *convergir,* and the last is currently leaving the third conjugation (→ *converger*).

3. *conocer, conozco, conozca* *traducir, traduzco, traduzca*
venir, vengo, venga *salir, salgo, salgamos*
caer, caigo, caiga *oír, oigo, oigan*

All such verbs have in common the addition of a stem extension containing a velar whenever a back vowel follows:

$$\left.\begin{array}{l} V\theta \rightarrow V\theta k \\ V \rightarrow Vjg \\ l,\ n \rightarrow lg\ ng \end{array}\right\} / \underline{\quad\quad} + \{a, o\}$$

In this Velar Extension rule, the first change (orthographically *c*→ *zc*[5]) is, like Unstressed Raising, fairly predictable, since virtually all the dozens of verbs ending in a vowel plus *-cer* or *-cir* undergo it, from the *conocer* and *traducir* of first-year courses to *ennoblecer* and *pacer* at higher levels. The only exceptions are (1) *hacer* and *decir,* which have their own morphological itineraries, and (2) *mecer* and *cocer* (*mezo, cuezo*), in which even some native speakers use *zc* (Boyd-Bowman 1960, 170). The *ig* /jg/ addition is general for verbs in -vowel+*er*/*ir,* but there are only five candidates for it: *caer, traer, raer, roer, oír.*[6] The *g* addition is automatic for high-frequency verbs in *–n*/*l*+*e*/*ir* (*salir, venir, tener, poner, valer*), but verbs such as *pulir* bypass it.

4. *construir, construyo, construya, construye*
   argüir, arguyo, arguyamos, arguyes

Without exception, all the thirty or so verbs in *-uir* (when pronounced /uir/, which excludes (*con*)*seguir*, *distinguir*, etc.) undergo a Yod Extension rule that adds "yod" (the palatal glide /j/ spelled *y*) to the stem whenever a mid or low vowel follows—i.e., whenever *i* does *not* follow:

u → *uy* (/uj/) / ___ {a, o, e}

Hence, *construy-a construy-o construy-e* but *constru-ir constru-ía constru-imos.* The change is absolutely regular.

5. *teñir, tiñó, tiñendo* — *bullir, bulló, bulleron*
   reír, rió, rieron — *henchir, hinchó*

Here we see a rule of Yod Absorption. When a stem ends in a palatal or alveopalatal phoneme (/ʎ ɲ j tʃ/), any /j/ beginning the ending is absorbed. Thus, /teɲ+jó/ → (Unstressed Raising) [tiɲ+jó] → (Yod Absorption) [tiɲó]. Again, this Yod Absorption is not a verb peculiarity; the adjective formation *amarill(o)+iento* becomes *amarill-ento* just as the verb *bull-iendo* /buj+jendo/ becomes *bull-endo.* The /j/ is also absorbed when the stem ends in /i/ from Raising of /e/: hence, in *reír* and *freír,* /r̄e+ír fre+ír/ → *ri-yó fri-yó* → *rió frió.* Despite its generality, though, Yod Absorption only has a few verbs to which it can apply.

6. *poder, podré* — *poner, pondré*
   salir, saldría — *decir, diría*

Such futures and conditionals are called "syncopated" because of the dropping or SYNCOPE of the expected theme vowel in the infinitival base. When this Syncope rule leaves the clusters /nr/ and /lr/, a [d] is inserted: *pondré, saldré.* The changes *deciré haceré* → *dir-é har-é* are considered syncopations too. Old Spanish extended Syncope to several other verbs, but it was retained only in a handful of high-frequency verbs of the second and third conjugations.

7.	*saber, supe*	*conducir, conduje*	*hacer, hizo*
	estar, estuvimos	*tener, tuviste*	*venir, vinieron*

In Germanic linguistics, a verb that changes its stem vowel in the past tense (*take took, drink drank, drive drove, get got*) is called STRONG. This label has also been applied to Spanish verbs that have any of the following changes throughout their preterite paradigm:

Vowel change: *hacer hice, poder pude, venir vine*
Consonant change: *traducir traduje, traer traje*
Both: *saber supe, tener tuve, decir dije, querer quise, estar estuve, poner puse*

Old Spanish had far more strong preterites, now regularized: for example, *destruir destruxe, meter mise, creer crove, prender prise, ver vide, conocer conuve*. As can be seen, the general trend in strong preterites is toward a high vowel in the stem; in fact, *traer* conformed to this pattern too in Old Spanish *truxe*, retained as *truje* in some modern dialects.

It cannot be predicted from the infinitive whether a given verb will be strong or not: *traer, hacer, andar* are strong, while the similar *caer, nacer, mandar* are not. Yet these verbs are not altogether lawless, for if one knows that a verb is strong, three facts follow. First, it will preserve that strong stem throughout the preterite, unlike verbs such as *dormir* or *seguir* that undergo Unstressed Raising in specific forms. Second, stress will always be penultimate, yielding *hice hizo* as opposed to *nací, nació*. Third, the suffixes will be those of *-er/-ir* verbs, but with *-e -o* instead of *-í -ió* and—just for strong stems in /x/ *(dij-, traj-, traduj-)*—with *-eron* instead of *-ieron*. (This last quirk came from Yod Absorption, but it does not apply to "weak" preterites such as *rigieron*.) Finally, the past subjunctive will use exactly the same strong stem.

6.1.2.3 Other changes. Other changes are partly predictable, but analysis of them brings increasingly smaller returns with less pedagogical usefulness. *Dar* has preterites that would be unremarkable if only its infinitive were *der* or *dir.* The imperatives *haz, sal, pon, ten, ven, val* have in common the use of naked infinitival stems. There is an interesting pattern in the addition of *-y* to monosyllabic *yo* forms: *soy, voy, doy, estoy.*[7] But with *veo, sé, he hay, quepo,* and most forms of *ser* and *ir,* there is little to do but *llamar al pan, pan*: these are truly irregular, just like English *brought, went, was,* and *made.* Languages, after all, are not quite as systematic as we might like, and although some irregularities are ironed out over time by analogy to regular formations, high-frequency verbs tend to retain their idiosyncrasies.

A verb can satisfy the conditions for two or more changes. Sometimes the rules do not conflict since they apply to different domains (one to stressed stems, the other to unstressed ones); other times, they clash and the more irregular change then seems to win out. Examples:

- *reñir*: both kinds of Raising, plus Yod Absorption: *reñ-ió* → *riñ-ió* → *riñ-ó*
- *seguir*: both kinds of Raising, with regular spelling changes: *sigo, sigamos*
- *decir*: has *dig-* where *salir* and *conocer* add a velar; obeys both Raisings (*dices, diciendo*); strong preterite (*dije*)
- *tener, venir*: strong preterites; Diphthongization except with Velar Extension, which blocks it (*tengo, vengo*—although *tiengo* and *viengo* do exist in nonstandard dialects)
- *oír*: Yod Extension like verbs in *-uir,* except when satisfying the conditions for Velar Extension: thus, *oye* like *construye,* but *oigo oiga* like *caigo caiga*
- *yacer*: never settled down (*yago* ~ *yazgo*) and ended up on epitaphs

The derivational offspring of stem-changing verbs tend to follow their parents' conjugation: *detener detengo detuve.* This is obvious to teachers but as Champion (1979, 317) pointed out, students often fail to see *tener* in *detener, mantener, obtener,* or if they do see it, they may conjugate inconsistently (thus, *detengo* but **detenieron*). Perhaps the morphological or etymological relationship is not always obvious to native speakers either, given that some derivatives have been partly regularized. *Bendecir, predecir, maldecir* retain some quirks of *decir* but are regular in the imperative, participle, and (for some speakers) the future. English behaves similarly; *understand, forgo, forget, overthrow, withdraw, become* follow *stand, go, get, throw, draw, come,* but the past tense of *broadcast* for many is *broadcasted,* unlike *cast* for *cast.*

6.2 English finite verb forms and modals. In contrast with the Spanish verb, English verb morphology is paltry. In fact, if the term *tense* is limited to purely inflectional possibilities, a verb such as *give* has only two real tenses: present *give(s)* and past *gave* (*given* being a participle, not a tense). English has no true future or conditional tenses because *will* and *would* are modal auxiliaries,[8] patterning like *can* and *may* rather than like tense endings. Thus, whereas Spanish permits contrasts among five simple tenses (not counting compound ones) for a main verb in the indicative (*Ella me lo da/dará/dio/daba/daría*), in English there are only two options morphologically (*She gives/gave it to me*), supplemented by a few more possibilities from the modal system (*She will/would/could/might give it to me*).

But however its system is analyzed, it is clear that in all categories the English verb is less inflected for person and number than its Spanish counterpart. *Be* has the most differentiation (present *am/is/are,* past *was/were*); all other verbs have pasts unmarked for person and number, and a special person form in the present just in 3sg. (*give-s*). In nonstandard English, even this much differentiation breaks down (*I says, he don't*). The teacher may direct students' attention to person-number inflection in their native language, but English offers a poor point of departure for taking up Spanish verb forms. In fact, transfer can be negative, since English *-s* represents 3sg. while Spanish *-s* represents informal 2sg.. And although English likewise has strong verbs, irregular verbs, and stem-changing verbs, their morphophonemics is too different to give much help with Spanish.

6.3 Nonfinites and compound forms. Many European languages have a set of verb forms called NONFINITES. Unlike the FINITE forms, which serve as the main verb of a sentence and which are conjugated or *de-**fined*** for tense, person, number, and mood, nonfinites function like nouns, adjectives, or adverbs and do not show these inflectional categories. Their terminology is borrowed (like much else) from Latin, and the Latin verb had a host of nonfinites: two infinitives, three participles, four gerunds, a gerundive, and two oddities called supines. Since Spanish and English have a smaller set of nonfinites, retention of the Latin terminology may cause confusion: one grammar will call *amando* a gerund, another a participle. Although we retain here the prevailing traditional terms, it is with the proviso that they are relative to the system; a Spanish gerund does not necessarily match an English or Latin one.

6.3.1 Infinitives. One nonfinite is the INFINITIVE, which is the conventional CITATION FORM of the verb (i.e., how it appears in dictionaries and the form by which the whole paradigm is represented). In Spanish, it is signaled by the suffix *-r* after the theme vowel. In English, it consists of a bare verb stem with no suffixes. (*To* is not part of the infinitive; whether this preposition appears depends on syntax, not on morphology; compare *want to go* but *should Ø go*.) In both languages, the infinitive form equips the verb for specific functions, primarily nounlike (nominal) ones, and it patterns like subordinate clauses (v. 13.0.2–13.3.4). The infinitive is also the usual form taken by a verb constructed with a preceding verb (v. 6.4): *debe ir, should go.*

6.3.2 Gerunds and participles. Spanish has two other nonfinites. The GERUND ends in *-ndo*: *amando* /am+á+ndo/, *comiendo* /kom+é+ndo/ → /kom+jé+ndo/. It has an adverbial function in describing the manner, circumstances, or means by which an event took place. While it usually refers back to the subject of the main verb, it is not adjectival (Keniston 1937, 239):

Salió riéndose.
Los sábados nos divertíamos jugando al tenis.

The PARTICIPLE ends in *-do*: *amado* /am+á+do/, *comido* /kom+é+do/→ /kom+í+do/. Exceptions to this pattern are a handful of irregulars inherited from Latin: *abierto, cubierto, dicho, escrito, frito, hecho, impreso, muerto, puesto, roto, resuelto, visto, vuelto.*[9] Unlike the gerund, the participle has an adjectival function, generally with an implied past and/or passive value. Thus, in *Las empobrecidas clases bajas se sentían excluidas de la sociedad, empobrecidas* suggests prior reduction to poverty and *excluidas* suggests 'eran excluidas por alguien' (v. 12.3). But for the English speaker, at least, two groups of *-do* forms take on special meanings, as illustrated in figure 6.2. The forms in group A imply no passiveness at all and may be considered independent adjectives. Those in group B seem anomalous in being translated with *-ing* forms in English: *está dormida, she's sleeping*. Yet *-ing* and *-ed* cannot always be equated with *-ndo* and *-do*; in this case, such verbs are intransitive in English and the state is expressed with the progressive, while they are reflexive in Spanish and the state is expressed as the result of a change upon oneself (v. 9.3.5).

Some grammarians include a fourth Spanish nonfinite in *-nte.* In Latin, this was a present active participle, contrasting with the past (or perfect) passive one that Spanish inherited as its *-do* form. It is true that a great many Spanish verbs accept *-nte*: *amante, influyente, importante, hablante, oyente, flotante, siguiente, conveniente, creciente, preocupante,* and so on. But most verbs do not (**trabajante, *lloviente, *divirtiente, *ordeñante*); some *-nte* forms have moved on to become nouns (*estudiante, dirigente, sirviente*) or prepositions (*durante, mediante*); and many retain little connection with their original verbs (*poniente, ocurrente, teniente, corriente, estante*). Such facts suggest that the *-nte* form now lies outside the verb paradigm and that *-nte* is derivational, like *-dor, -dero, -tivo* (v. 15.1.1). Given this exclusion (implicit in U.S. pedagogy), the Spanish *-do* form can be called simply *the* participle.

English has a gerund ending in *-ing,* and like the Spanish one it can be used adverbially:

He went out laughing.
On Saturdays we enjoyed ourselves playing tennis.

but also as a noun (i.e., as subject or object; v. 13.1.1–13.2.1):

Building a house is hard.
Before building a house, save up a lot of money.

and as an adjective, in which case it is considered a present participle:

I have a surprising answer.
The couple building this house is wealthy.

In these last two functions, *-ing* causes considerable interference: **una respuesta sorprendiendo, *la pareja construyendo esta casa, *mujeres trabajando* (or worse, **mujeres trabajandas*). The usual reason is that textbooks hastily equate *-ing* with *-ndo* in order to introduce the progressive (*está lloviendo = it's raining,* v. 6.3.4) and fail to clarify and practice the Spanish gerund's strictly adverbial functions. For nounlike functions, Spanish uses the infinitive (*construir una casa es difícil, antes de construir una casa*); for adjective-like functions, it uses a corresponding adjective if one exists (*una respuesta sorprendente, mujeres trabajadoras*) or a relative clause (*las mujeres que trabajan, la pareja que construye esta casa*).

The other English nonfinite is a past (or passive) participle that ends in *-ed* or *-t* and is then homophonous with the past tense form, although most strong verbs have a distinct form with *-en* and/or a vowel change: *driven, given, eaten, sung, begun, broken, forgot-*

Figure 6.2. Some -do forms with special meanings

A. nonpassive, nonpast	B. translated by English *-ing*
agradecido 'thankful'	aburrido 'boring'
atrevido 'bold'	acostado 'lying down'
concurrido 'busy, crowded'	agachado 'stooping, squatting'
considerado 'considerate'	arrodillado 'kneeling'
desconfiado 'distrustful'	divertido 'entertaining, fun'
descreído 'unbelieving'	dormido 'sleeping'
descuidado 'careless'	escondido 'hiding, hidden'
entendido 'in the know'	exagerado 'exaggerating, prone to exaggerating'
necesitado 'needy'	inclinado 'leaning, bending over'
ocupado 'busy'	parado 'standing'
parecido 'similar'	sacrificado 'self-sacrificing'
pesado 'heavy'	sentado 'sitting, seated'
porfiado 'stubborn'	tumbado 'lying down'
presumido 'presumptuous'	
sabido 'smart'	

ten, and so on. To distinguish participial *-ed* from past *-ed*, many linguists call the former the *-en* suffix, even for the *-ed* allomorph. This *-en* has a rather consistent past or passive force in contrast with the active or present force of *-ing*; a murdering man is carrying out murder while a murdered man is the victim; a falling tree is descending now while a fallen tree has already hit the ground.

Despite the many differences in use of nonfinites, there are four constructions in which the two languages converge nicely: absolutes, perfects, progressives, and passives.

6.3.3 "Absolutes." This term is another borrowing from Latin grammar. It describes a gerund or participle that presents background information for the main clause and is set off from it. Its subject is normally expressed only if different from that of the main clause (v. 13.2.3):

Rompiendo la ventana, logró entrarse. (Breaking the window, . . .)
Estando en huelga los obreros, el jefe los sustituyó. (With the workers being on strike, . . .)

As illustrated, *with* often accompanies English absolutes and it makes possible the deletion of *being*: *with the workers on strike* . . . But while both languages form gerund absolutes, participle absolutes are more common in Spanish than in English, which prefers a gerund or *with*:

Llegado el dichoso día, . . .	The happy day *having* arrived . . .
Decidida la ruta . . .	The route *having been* decided, . . .
	(*With* the route *decided* . . .)

6.3.4 Perfects, progressives, passives. "Compound" tenses are compounded from a helping verb and a gerund or participle. Two sets of them, perfect[10] and progressive, are usually included in traditional paradigms. The PERFECT consists of *haber/have* + (past) participle and the PROGRESSIVE of *estar/be* + gerund.

Lo ha bebido.	He has drunk it.
Lo está bebiendo.	He's (He is) drinking it.

They can be combined as long as the perfect precedes the progressive:

Lo ha estado bebiendo.	He has been drinking it.
*Lo está habiendo bebido.	*He is having drunk it.

At beginning levels, Spanish compound tenses tend to be equated with their English counterparts. But their meanings within their respective systems can differ (v. 7.2.2), and the compound forms act more like an integral unit in Spanish, especially the perfects:[11]

¿Lo *han recibido* los hijos?	*Have* the kids *gotten* it?
(*¿Lo *han* los hijos *recibido*?)	
Nunca se *ha detenido.*	She *has* never *stopped.*
(*Se *ha* nunca *detenido.*)	

Then, too, constructions with *hacer* and *llevar* cover some of the ground conveyed by the English perfect:

Hace doce años que vive ahí.	She's been living there (for) twelve years.
Lleva dos días preparándose.	She's been getting ready (for) two days.

Some observers, such as Butt and Benjamin (1988, 209), discern another perfect construction with *tener* in sentences like *Tengo plegadas las sábanas.* But unlike the true perfect with *haber*, this construction is possible only with a direct object, and the participle agrees with it. Semantically, *las tengo plegadas* may imply *las he plegado* but not necessarily (someone else could have folded them for me), like English *I've got them folded*, and it refers not to the previous action but to the resulting state, like *están plegadas*. Actually, *tener* + participle belongs to the pattern *tener/mantener* + adjective: *Tengo listas (plegadas) las sábanas, Mantengo limpia (cerrada) la puerta*. In short, *tener* does not form perfect tenses at all.

As for the passive, which consists of the copula *ser/be* + (past) participle, this has sometimes been analyzed as a transformation, and will be so treated later (v. 12.3).

6.4 Verb + verb and auxiliaries. The endings on verbs serve mainly to convey tense and mood. But the available sets can express only a subset of the huge number of possible characterizations of an event. For additional distinctions outside the inflectional system, many languages resort to verb + verb combinations. For example, instead of adopting an affix to express potentiality or obligation as some languages do, English and Spanish deploy a helping verb (AUXILIARY, Aux): *can/should speak, puede/debe hablar.*[12] To emphasize the fact that verb + verb (V + V) is a kind of secondary conjugation of the verb, Spanish grammarians use the term *perífrasis* or *conjugación perifrástica.* In fact, the compound forms described above (v. 6.3.4) are also *perífrasis,* though they are traditionally included in the verb paradigm proper.

In verb + verb, both languages inflect just the first verb; the second stays in one nonfinite form, typically the infinitive (V-inf, as in *puede hablar*) but sometimes the gerund (V-ger, as in *sigue hablando*) or participle (V-pcp, as in *ha hablado*). Therefore, students who know that *hablar* is an infinitive and *poder* is 'can' are presumed to know enough to generate *puedo hablar, puedes hablar, puede hablar*. Yet often students overgeneralize a pattern beyond the limits of either L1 or L2, and in this case the constant dictum "conjugate those verbs!" leads to **puedes hablas, *quieres hablas, *quería hablaba.* As speakers of English, they would never say **she wants to speaks* or **she wanted to spoke,* and once this is pointed out to them and they are reminded that Spanish acts the same way, such errors should diminish.

A more difficult problem is the question of which nonfinite form is required, and which relator, if any, is needed for joining the two verbs. To assist the student, almost any reference grammar will present a taxonomy such as the following:

V + V-inf:
deber, hacer, mandar, saber, intentar, querer, desear, preferir, necesitar, anhelar, esperar, pensar, lograr, conseguir, poder, soler, acostumbrar, decidir, rehusar, oír, ver, sentir . . .

V + relator + V-inf:
= *a*: *ir, comenzar, empezar, echar, ponerse, aprender, enseñar, llegar, venir, volver, acostumbrarse, atreverse, tender, obligar, pasar, negarse, invitar . . .*
= *de*: *terminar, acabar, dejar, haber, deber, gozar, olvidarse, tratar, guardarse . . .*
= *en*: *convenir, vacilar/dudar, insistir, consentir, quedar, tardar . . .*
= *por*: *acabar, hacer, impacientarse, luchar . . .*
= *que*: *tener, haber*

V + V-ger:
estar, ir, venir, andar, seguir, continuar . . .

English has the same types and occasionally agrees with Spanish in how it classifies a verb: *deber* and *should* both take V-inf, *tender* and *tend* both take *a/to* + V-inf. More often, the two languages disagree: *saber* requires no relator but *know* takes *how to*; *tener* requires *que* but *must* takes Ø and *have* takes *to*; *terminar* takes *de* + V-inf while *finish* takes V-ger, and so on. Some verbs allow two or more options for different meanings: *pienso hacerlo ≠ pienso en hacerlo, voy a estudiar ≠ voy estudiando, he renunciado ≠ he de renunciar, acabo de afeitarme ≠ acabo por afeitarme.* The use of relators in V + V is thus hard to explain, just as it is in V + object (v. 9.4.1, 10.3.3.2). Teachers can point out that verbs of ending take *de* and those of learning or beginning take *a*, but this takes students just a short way into a setup that is ultimately arbitrary and verb-specific. In learning that *tratar* takes *de* but its synonym *intentar* does not, while English *try* can take either *to* + V-inf or Ø + V-ger, students can only memorize what takes which.

With V + V, we cross a boundary between the inflectional patterns of verb morphology and the combinatory patterns of syntax. *Intentar, invitar a, decidir, querer, esperar, ver,* and so on can be followed by an infinitive or by a *que*-clause, and many linguists have explained *quiero envolverlo* as derived from a deep structure such as *quiero que lo envuelva.* This connection will be explored later in chapter 13.

Notes for chapter 6

1. Both languages have verb prefixes too, but for derivation, not tense inflection: *oír desoír, tener retener, tell foretell, go undergo.*

2. Outside the standard, there are variants in the person-number suffixes: *-nos* for *-mos* (*amábanos*), *-stes* or *-tes* for *-ste* (*amastes, amates),* and a migrating *-n* (*márchesen* for *márchense*). There are also special suffixes for *vos* (v. 9.2).

3. In nonstandard varieties, the diphthongized or raised vowel is often extended throughout the paradigm: *aciertar, quiebrar, güeler (=oler), siguir, dicir, pidir* (Boyd-Bowman 1960, 168; Sánchez 1982, 28). Likewise, some verbs have jumped to or from Diphthongization and Raising: *escuendo* for *escondo, apriendo* for *aprendo, apreto* for *aprieto, colgo* for *cuelgo, frego* for *friego, escrebir* for *escribir* (Oroz 1966, 312; Jorge Morel 1974, 107).

4. Some textbooks call (*ie, ue, i*) verbs "boot verbs" because a boot could be drawn around the *yo, tú, él, ellos* forms that undergo these changes. There is nothing wrong with a mnemonic device for otherwise inexplicable cases, but this one misses the real explanation, it requires arbitrary footwear shapes for each tense, it is useless for the same changes in other parts of speech, and it is wholly unnecessary.

5. Those who rely on the written form instead of pronunciation may see this change as the insertion of a *z* in the stem *cono-c-*. But the *z* is a respelling of *c* for /θ/=/s/ when *e* or *i* does not follow; phonologically, the change is /konoθ-/ → /konoθk-/.

6. There are only five candidates, that is, if the next group in *-uir* is excluded from this vowel *-er/ir* case. But at least in Santo Domingo (Jorge Morel 1974, 108), the *-uir* group has been assimilated to it: many speakers say *huigo, distribuigo* for standard *huyo, distribuyo.*

7. *Estar* acts as if monosyllabic (whence the stress in *estás, estés,* etc.) and is generally analyzed as underlyingly /star/, with an /e/ that is automatically added by Epenthesis, as in *esnob* (v. 3.0).

8. Modals are a special class of moodlike English auxiliaries with a limited syntactic distribution: *can, could, will, would, shall, should, must, may, might.*

9. Spanish regularized many Latin participles or relegated them to nooks outside the verb system. Thus, today *tinto, confuso, distinto, maldito, incluso* are words in their own right, differen-

tiated from *(he) teñido, confundido, distinguido, maldecido, incluido.* Outside the standard, there is more regularization: *ponido* for *puesto, abrido* for *abierto,* and so on (Boyd-Bowman 1960, 169). Derivatives generally retain the irregularities of their primaries—*descrito* like *escrito, compuesto* like *puesto, descubierto* like *cubierto*—but *bendecir* and *corromper* diverge from *decir* and *romper* in having regular participles, and although *imprimir* has *impreso, comprimir* has *comprimido.*

10. Perfect forms are so called not for lack of imperfections but because in Latin (to which one constantly returns in such matters) the *perfectum* depicted an event as already carried out or "perfected"; compare the Spanish *imperfecto,* which still conveys unperfected aspect (v. 7.1.3).

11. An object pronoun (clitic) can break up the combination of auxiliary + participle when the former is infinitivized: *haberse arrepentido.* In Old Spanish, object pronouns were freer in their position than they are today: *se había arrepentido, habíase arrepentido, había arrepentídose.*

12. For now, no rigorous distinction is made in V + V between an auxiliary + main verb and a main verb + dependent verb; v. 13.1.2.7 for one criterion for the difference.

Exercises for chapter 6

1. The citation form of a verb is the infinitive. Why is this a rather unrevealing form for stem changes? What is the minimum information a text or dictionary-maker could add to this citation form to key the remainder of the conjugation in Spanish? Why?

2. One can address the particular problems of students by diagnosing the sources. Carry out an error analysis (v. 0.2.2–0.3) of each of the following, focusing especially on the apparent cause: an incorrect analogy from within the Spanish system, transfer of an English pattern, or some other reason.

(a) *comaban
(b) *yo dijo, yo habló
(c) *ella sabes
(d) *venzco, *venco (*for* venzo)
(e) *estaron
(f) *¿has tú comido?
(g) *trato a hacerlo
(h) *tienes a escucharme
(i) *abiertaste, *abiertaron
(j) *piensaba
(k) *vivemos
(l) *está dormiendo
(m) *van trabajar
(n) *su pasatiempo está bailando
(o) *lo conseguye (*for* consigue)
(p) * habló, hablás . . . (*orally, for present*)
(q) *deben terminan
(r) *dijó, hizó, estuvó

3. Name the specific rule(s) that account for the changes in each of the following verbs:

advertir	esquiar	regir	convencer
colgar	diluir	escocer	valer

4. Some students will render any English *-ed* form with the imperfect, then later with the preterite, still later with the participle, according to whichever of these is being focused on in the course at a given moment. What mistaken generalization is being made?

5. *Divertir* has the stem allomorphs *divert- diviert- divirt-*; *divergir* keeps *diverg-* (respelled *diverj-*) throughout. How is it possible to argue that both are "regular"?

6. It was pointed out (v. 6.1.2.2.) that Diphthongization is not limited to verbs but is found that throughout Spanish (v. 6.1.2.2). Find more examples by giving related or derived forms of the following, in which the diphthong reverts to *e* or *o* when unstressed. (Use your dictionary if necessary.)

Buenos Aires	hierro	nieve	tierno	cuerno
niebla	sueño	fuerte	rueda	invierno
hierba	gobierno	viento	fuente	huevo
estiércol	cien (to)	serpiente	nuevo	diestro

7. What value do you see in getting students to see that the endings *-an, -aban, -aron* actually consist of several morphemes (slots, pieces, parts, or whatever) rather than one? Why?

8. How is the mastery of *conjugación perifrástica* somewhat easier for the student than the normal inflectional conjugation? More difficult?

9. Olbertz (1998, 550) calculated the average frequency of auxiliaries in *perífrasis* per 10,000 words in both oral and written Spanish text. (She omitted verbs such as *querer* that are not true auxiliaries.) Her data yield the following ranking in descending order: *ir a* + inf. (16.63), *estar* + ger. (16.04), *tener que* + inf. (15.65), *poder* + inf. (9.78), *ir* + ger. (4.58), *deber* + inf. (3.72), *volver a* + inf. (2.77), *acabar de* + inf. (1.71), *llegar a* + inf. (1.61), *seguir* + ger. (1.32), *dejar de* + inf. (1.25), *pensar* + inf. (0.92), *soler* + inf. (0.86), *empezar a* + inf. (0.82), *acabar* + ger. (0.56), *comenzar a* + inf. (0.40), *venir a* + inf. (0.36), *continuar* + inf. (0.26), *quedar(se)* + ger. (0.20). (Fewer than 0.20 occurrences per 10,000 words: *acabar por* +inf., *cesar de* +inf., *estar por* +inf., *pasar a* +inf., *terminar de* +inf., *andar* +ger.) To judge from frequency in the language, which V+V combinations receive adequate attention in Spanish teaching? Which ones receive too much attention, or too little?

10. Following are some more typical student errors with Spanish:

ibamos for *íbamos*	*sabo* for *sé*	*detenieron* for *detuvieron*
jugo for *juego*	*creíba* for *creía*	*saliremos* for *saldremos*
cubrido for *cubierto*	*andé* for *anduve*	*habemos* for *hemos*
volvido for *vuelto*	*producí* for *produje*	*sale* for *sal*

As it turns out, every one of these is also found among native Spanish speakers who have spoken the language all their lives (Boyd-Bowman 1960, 168). This fact does not mean that such forms are acceptable to the Real Academia or on the final exams of Introductory Spanish, but it does teach one something about the acquisition of the Spanish verb system. Not all student errors are committed by native speakers; why would both groups produce forms such as those above?

11. Why, in general, does the Spanish verb give trouble to English speakers? In what ways is its inflection different in its extent and function from the English system?

12. Traditionally, verb morphology has been treated in terms of ITEM-AND-PARADIGM. In this approach, one takes an "item" (an infinitive) and shows each form through the entire paradigm in the sequence *yo, tú, él, nosotros, vosotros, ellos,* person by person, tense by tense, and mood by mood. Some textbooks still present paradigms in this way for memorization by the student. Other textbooks emphasize an ITEM-AND-PROCESS approach, whereby students are given general rules on

how to carry out stem changes in producing forms. In your opinion, which specific changes best lend themselves to the latter approach, and why? Which ones might best be learned by rote memorization, à la item-and-paradigm, and why?

13. Studies of morphophonemic alternations distinguish three types of changes. In PHONOLOGICAL CONDITIONING, the change depends on neighboring phonemes and features such as stress; no other information is needed to apply the rule. In GRAMMATICAL CONDITIONING, the change depends at least in part on grammatical features: the rule for the change must make reference to stipulations such as "in the present tense," "just in the third person," or "only in verbs." In LEXICAL CONDITIONING, the change cannot be stated generally because phonological and grammatical information alone do not suffice to define where and when the change takes place: speakers can only memorize which words do and do not undergo the rule.

Review the rules in this chapter for stem changes and ending changes, and classify each one as to whether it is phonologically, grammatically, and/or lexically conditioned.

Chapter 7

Tense and mood

7.0 Approaches to tense and mood. There have been many treatments of tense and mood, but two main trends can be discerned. On one side are analysts who see a category as a constellation of distinct uses and who try to itemize all of them. The lists vary according to the listmaker. For the Spanish present indicative, the RAE (1924, 289) found three uses, Michalson and Aires (1981, 47) four, Sallese and Fernández de la Vega (1968, 118) five, and Garcés (1997) six. DaSilva and Lovett (1965, 4) gave four uses for the imperfect and two for the preterite, while the RAE (1979, 466–69) perceived five and three, respectively.

On the other side is a long line of scholars—Bello ([1847] 1958), Ramsey ([1894] 1956), Bull (1965), Gili Gaya (1973), and most since them—who have sought a unified description of each category, that is, one basic, general concept underlying the surface uses. This concept is defined on the basis of how the category contrasts with others in the same system, because the meaning of 'present' in a two-tense system may cover more ground than in a five-tense one. Thus, in order to understand such theories, it is first necessary to examine the overall system.

7.1 The tense system of Spanish and English. One of the most coherent theories of tense is that of Bull (1965, 149–71), who distinguished SYSTEMIC from NONSYSTEMIC meaning. The former is the meaning each category has within the overall system, and in general Spanish and English concur here. The latter includes specialized functions it has acquired outside that system by way of extension, and the two languages diverge more in this case.

7.1.1 Systemic meanings. Bull first noted that the tense one chooses for portraying a situation depends on his/her orientation or perspective: 'right now', for example, vs. 'back then'. Each such orientation is an axis or timeline along which the event being described is located in one of three ways: as ANTERIOR to the orientation the speaker adopts, as SIMULTANEOUS with it, or as POSTERIOR to it. The different tenses in the system

Figure 7.1. The tenses that are oriented toward the present point (PP)

ANTERIOR	SIMULTANEOUS	POSTERIOR
	PP	
present perfect	**present**	**future**
Lo han vendido	Lo venden.	Lo venderán
They've sold it.	*They sell it.*	*They will sell it.*

express these three "ordered relations" (as Bull called them) according to different perspectives. The difference of perspective is crucial in Bull's theory: linguistic tenses are not all located on the same line as points in real time must be.

7.1.1.1 Present perfect, present, future. In using these three, the speaker views matters from his/her current perspective, the present: these are oriented toward the PRESENT POINT ('now'), which Bull symbolizes as PP. Events (actions, processes, states) that are concurrent or simultaneous with PP appear in the present tense. Events that have begun before PP are anterior to PP, and they are expressed by the present perfect. Those events that are viewed from PP as posterior may be expressed by the future tense. These three tenses therefore constitute the "present system," and their relationship to PP is depicted by Bull as in figure 7.1. (For now, we hold off on the difference between simple and progressive forms.)

7.1.1.2 Past perfect, past, conditional. When narrating in the past, the speaker usually switches perspective from PP to some RECALLED POINT, RP, a strategy Bull called BACKSHIFTING. Tenses oriented toward RP indicate how matters stood 'back then' instead of 'right now'. Anteriority is again depicted by a perfect tense, the past perfect, for it expresses what had already happened before RP. Simultaneity with respect to RP is expressed by the past tense in English and by the preterite or imperfect in Spanish (v. 7.1.3). Finally, posteriority with respect to RP represents what was foreseen or predicted to happen subsequently, that is, what would happen, and it is expressed by the conditional. Figure 7.2 portrays how Bull summarized RP relationships.

Figure 7.2. The tenses that are oriented toward the recalled point (RP)

ANTERIOR	SIMULTANEOUS	POSTERIOR
	RP	
past perfect	**past (pret./imperf.)**	**conditional**
Lo habían vendido	Lo vendieron/vendían.	Lo venderían
They had sold it.	*They sold it.*	*They would sell it.*

Figure 7.3. Backshifting to a narrative point of view

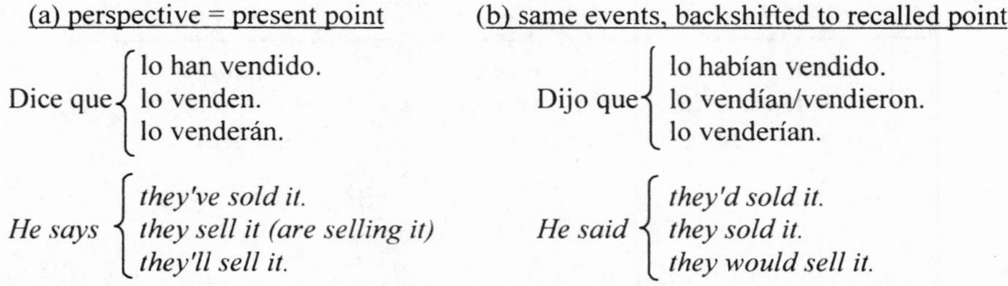

(a) perspective = present point
Dice que lo han vendido.
lo venden.
lo venderán.
He says they've sold it.
they sell it (are selling it)
they'll sell it.
(b) same events, backshifted to recalled point
Dijo que lo habían vendido.
lo vendían/vendieron.
lo venderían.
He said they'd sold it.
they sold it.
they would sell it.

As can be seen by a comparison of figures 7.1 and 7.2, the two sets of tenses—present system and past system—are parallel, which is Bull's point. Present perfect and past perfect express anteriority; present and past (imperfect or preterite) indicate simultaneity with a given perspective point; and future and conditional both indicate posteriority. The only difference between the present and past systems is the speaker's point of view, as shown in figure 7.3: with backshifting from PP to RP, the tense forms in A systemically shift to those in B. (The *dice/dijo* and *he says/said* are used here to bring out PP and RP, respectively, as reference points.)

7.1.1.3 Future perfect and conditional perfect. These two tenses are less frequent than the others because they deal with a more specialized outlook from PP and RP. Both tenses project forward onto some surmised, expected plane and speculate about anteriority on that axis, that is, what may have transpired prior to some ANTICIPATED POINT, AP. For the future perfect (*lo habrán vendido*), AP is projected from PP; for the conditional perfect, AP is surmised from the RP point of view. Consequently, both of the following sets of sentences strongly imply a 'by then, by that time' AP, and both express anteriority with respect to that AP.

<u>AP from PP perspective</u>	<u>AP from RP perspective</u>
Dice que lo habrán vendido.	Dijo que lo habrían vendido.
He says they will have sold it.	*He said they would've sold it.*

7.1.1.4 Summary of the tense system. Figure 7.4 depicts the overall system defining the eight basic tenses that Bull investigated. There are four axes, two major ones (those of PP and RP) and two minor ones (those of AP projected from the other two). Note that it is the system that determines the tense distinctions: a present perfect such as *lo han vendido* means little in itself except in reference to a perspective (PP) and in contrast with other relationships (anteriority vs. simultaneity or posteriority, and anteriority to PP vs. anteriority to RP or AP). Moreover, Bull's analysis postulates that tense categories correspond to a speaker's discourse strategies: in adopting conditional as opposed to future,

Figure 7.4. The overall tense system in Bull's analysis

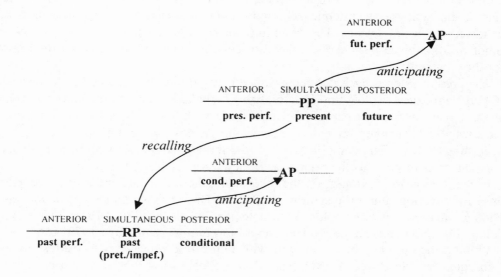

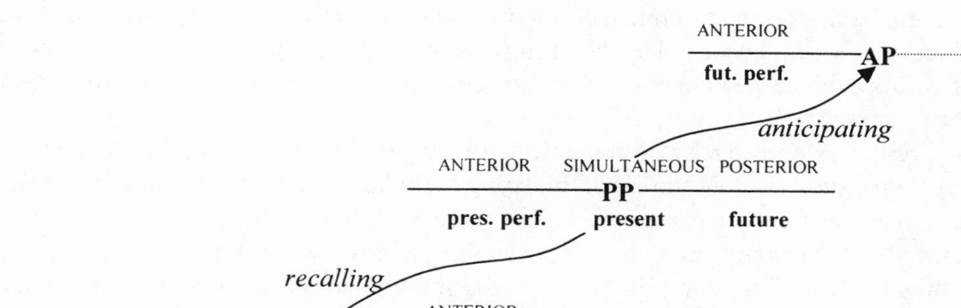

one shifts back to another plane, and in adopting conditional perfect one shifts beyond to some hypothesized plane.

Tense, then, is a matter of what speakers wish to say, how they choose to express it, and the point of view they select; it is not equatable with real-world time. As Bull put it,

> A system based on four axes of orientations (with three ordered relations to each) cannot be synchronized with the three notions of calendar time: past, present, and future or yesterday, today, and tomorrow. The traditional approach that the tense system is a time construct has led textbook writers (and teachers) to believe that the functions of tense systems can be defined by relating them to adverbs of time. The preterite, for example, is associated with *ayer* (*lo vendimos ayer*), the present with *hoy* (*lo vendemos hoy*), and the future with *mañana* (*lo venderemos mañana*). This association . . . can only lead to confusion and contradictions in a pedagogical explanation of the functions of tense systems. (p. 157)

In fact, with *hoy* we can say *vendemos* or *hemos vendido* or *vendimos* or *vendíamos* or *venderemos* or *venderíamos* or *habíamos vendido,* depending on our perspective; and with *mañana,* we could say *vendemos, venderemos, venderíamos, habremos vendido.* As Gili Gaya (1973, 157) added, it is even possible to use the preterite for an event that is chronologically still in the future, as when a traveler whose train is approaching the station says *Ya llegué* before actually getting there. Time is beyond human control, but tense is adapted to human viewpoints and is set up for manipulation by humans in humanly edited discourse.

7.1.2 Nonsystemic extensions: Present, future, conditional. Language stretches to conform to its users' needs, and just as the literal denotation of a word expands to cover figurative meanings, the systemic or basic meaning of a tense can spread to express other characterizations of events. The resulting nonsystemic meanings are not necessarily minor in importance but are less related to contrasts among the primary ordering relationships on Bull's four axes.

The present extends back into the past and forward into the yet-to-come, and speakers of both languages exploit this lack of fixed boundaries. For the so-called HISTORICAL PRESENT, one interrupts a narrative in past tense with a switch to the present, and RP becomes PP: "Dábamos un paseo y de súbito se nos *acerca* un tipo que *dice* . . ." According to Silva-Corvalán (1983, 778), who researched this strategy in Spanish narratives, the speaker presents the events "as if they were occurring before us."

In the ANTICIPATORY PRESENT, on the other hand, there is a forward shift of the present tense for covering future time: *salimos mañana*. This shift is variously explained as (1) lending "more vivacity and color to the statement" (Ramsey [1894] 1956, 337), (2) indicating "intención presente de realizar una acción futura" (Gili Gaya 1973, 156), and (3) combining the currency of the present with future reference so as to express intended "subsequence" (Stockwell, Bowen, and Martin 1965, 148 ff.). Yet it is not always clear whether *salimos mañana* is intended as different from *saldremos mañana* or, for that matter, from the periphrastic *vamos a salir mañana*. Some observers (e.g., Kany 1951, 152) believe that in many dialects the inflectional future (*futuro sintético*) is disappearing in favor of the anticipatory present and the *ir a* construction (*futuro perifrástico*).[1] Silva-Corvalán and Terrell (1989) confirmed this trend in Caribbean Spanish but noted that the inflectional future remains common there for expressing probability.

With *Ya serán las dos y todos estarán en casa,* the speaker intends simultaneity at PP, not posteriority. The same is true of *Ya serían las dos y todos estarían en casa* when the perspective has been backshifted to RP. Systemically, the future and conditional make a conjecture about the future, and nonsystemically that conjecture is applied to situations concurrent with PP and RP as well. English tends to adopt an adverb of probability (*surely, probably, allegedly*) or a main verb of supposition or speculation (*I guess, suppose, reckon,* or in questions, *Do you think. . . ?*), but it is not true that English never uses this FUTURE OF PROBABILITY. After a knock on the door, we can say *Who will that be?* (like Spanish *¿Quién será?*), and on seeing an approaching vehicle, we may say *That'll be our bus now* (*Será nuestro autobús*). The difference between the two languages is not grammatical but pragmatic (v. 16.0): English speakers do not exploit this communicative strategy as much as Spanish speakers do.

In its systemic meaning, the conditional is the backshift of the future; it expresses posteriority with respect to RP, that is, what the future looked like in the past. But in both languages, the distance between RP and PP can be psychological rather than temporal, and by extension the conditional has come to be used for posteriority with respect to some hypothetical situation—what consequences might ensue if a certain RP existed or, with anteriority highlighted, if it had existed:

¿Se comportaría así?
Would she behave that way?

¿Se habría comportado así?
Would she have behaved that way?

If the hypothetical condition (PROTASIS) is stated, its verb is in the past subjunctive.[2]

¿Se comportaría así *si tuviera la oportunidad*?
Would she behave that way *if she had the chance*?

This conditional construction is traditionally called CONTRARY TO FACT. It is essentially atemporal, and for that reason some Hispanic grammarians have regarded the conditional as another mood (*el modo potencial*) rather than a tense.

In both languages, the conditional and past subjunctive have been adapted for another function, the softening (MITIGATION) of a request or suggestion. The rationale seems to be that speakers are suggesting what might be the case *if* they were to ask more directly:

Querría/Quisiera un poco más.
I would like some more.

¿Podría Ud. ayudarme?
Could you help me?

The *could* here stands for **would could* 'would be able': since English modals do not combine, the conditional of *can* is not distinct from its past. Modals have their own non-systemic functions (v. 7.2.1), and these can cause interference when students take up the Spanish tense system.

7.1.3 Aspect and tense: Preterite and imperfect. With the exception of the subjunctive, no topic in Spanish morphology has aroused more debate than the preterite/imperfect distinction. Perhaps no single analysis has captured it in a way that covers all cases, accounts for native speakers' intuitions, and also satisfies the needs of floundering students. Yet it is true that some treatments have been less successful than others. The following illustrates a popular but particularly unsatisfactory one.[3]

IMPERFECT

(1) tells what was happening
(2) recalls what used to happen
(3) describes a physical, mental, or emotional state in the past
(4) tells time in the past
(5) describes the background and sets the stage upon which another action occurred.

PRETERITE

(1) records, reports, narrates
(2) with certain verbs, causes a change in meaning

The defects here are numerous. First, this treatment represents the two categories as arbitrary lists of independent uses—five separate imperfects, two different preterites—and the fact that "recording" ends up as preterite rather than imperfect seems as capricious as the classification of tomatoes as vegetables instead of fruits. Second, it visually suggests that the preterite is the less used of the two, so that the imperfect looks like the safer bet; actually, the preterite is much more frequent. Third, it is impossible to apply because its vagueness in specific contexts robs it of criterial value. If students wish to convey *I slept all day,* should they opt for "what was happening," "describes physical state," "describes background," or "records, reports"? All of these seem applicable and therefore useless; yet their teacher insists on *Dormí todo el día*, not *Dormía todo el día.*

Fourth, it is wrong even when it is clear, for counterexamples are easy to find:

Llovió a cántaros ayer ("what was happening," but preterite)
Viví allí hasta mudarme ("used to," but preterite)
Estuvimos cansados ("physical and mental state," but preterite)
Se me cayó la copa y entró horrorizada Mamá ("background" for her entry, but preterite)
Esta foto no está bien porque Abuelita masticaba chicle y Jorge bostezaba y Papá se sonaba la nariz ("recording, reporting, narrating," but imperfect)

One understands the zeal of writers to streamline difficult grammar: reducing a point to "use X here, Y there" avoids complicated explanations, makes the point at least look manageable, and allows the class to move on to the featured *lectura* on Machu Picchu. But in this case, shortcuts are doomed to failure. Students may try to memorize seven uses sorted into two neat piles, but their best efforts keep colliding with actual usage. In their confusion, they guess randomly or merge the two categories into one, even melding the forms into a conjugation such as *yo vendí, tú vendías,* and the hybrid **él vendío.* The facts that this approach has repeatedly failed with numerous generations of students and that it must recognize some verbs (the "meaning-changers") as beyond the pale suggest that it is fundamentally wrong.

With the preterite/imperfect distinction, we must begin with two important facts. First, these are not separate tenses, despite the convenience of calling them that, but categories that represent different ASPECTS of the same past tense. From this follows the second fact: both can be used in the same RP context, with a contrast in meaning:

A las siete miraron/miraban la luna.
Hernando siempre asistió/asistía a sus clases.
Ese coche costó/costaba $15.00.

"Recording, reporting, narrating, backgrounding" and so on are not aspects but communicative FUNCTIONS of language; in carrying out *any* of these, the Spanish speaker can choose between preterite and imperfect and even combine them for different characterizations of the situation:

María rió cuando Pablo salió.
María reía cuando Pablo salió.
María rió cuando Pablo salía.
María reía cuando Pablo salía.

ASPECT refers to (1) the nature of the event being described (e.g., instantaneous and pointlike vs. enduring or recurring) and (2) which part of the event is being depicted at RP (e.g., ongoing or ended). The first type is called LEXICAL ASPECT since it is held to be a lexical property of the verb itself; the second type is called DISCOURSE ASPECT or VIEWPOINT ASPECT (Salaberry 1999, 167) since it is a function of how the speaker is choosing to present the event during a story. English does not consistently make such distinctions, and it may be useful for students to reflect first on what they mean in English when they narrate.[4] As an example, consider the form *rained* in English. In *It rained yesterday,* we confine an event of some duration to a limited period, assigning it a beginning and an end; in *The clouds gathered and suddenly it rained,* we now focus on the beginning (= 'it began to rain'); in *As it rained, I noticed some leaking,* we recall a moment in the middle of the downpour; and in *Where I grew up it rained every day,* we describe a recurrent, indefinitely repeated event, a series of rainings. All these different events can be expressed by *rained,* but in Spanish the first two will be *llovió* and the second two *llovía.*

The consensus of scholars since Ramsey ([1894] 1956, 317–28) and the RAE (1924, 291) has been that with the imperfect, a narrator brings listeners or readers to some recalled point in the *middle* of an event or a series of events that, at RP, was fairly open-ended and continuing. For a single event, as in *A las ocho, me bañaba*, being 'in the middle' can be visualized as in (1) in figure 7.5; for being in the middle of a series of recurring or habitual events, for example, *De niño, me bañaba cada noche*, the situation is as in (2).

The preterite, on the other hand, can express an occurrence from the viewpoint of either RP or PP, and it handles *any aspect but middleness*. At a recalled point, it can indicate that the event ended (concluded, culminated) then, as shown by (3) *A las ocho, me caí* in figure 7.5, or that it began (broke out, came into existence) then, as in (4) *A las ocho, llovió a cántaros*. On the other hand, with respect to the present point, the preterite can indicate that the event simply happened and is now over and done with, as in (5a); it may have lasted for a long interval (5b) and even recurred repeatedly (5c); but, unlike the imperfect in cases (1) and (2), the preterite depicts that interval as now discontinued from the later viewpoint, and the listener or reader is *not* going to be taken back to some moment in the middle of it.

Bull (1965, 152–70) and Gili Gaya (1973, 157–62) agreed that 'beginning' vs. 'end' for the preterite depends on the nature of the event, the verb's own lexical aspect. Some verbs inherently represent the onset of a state of affairs that is understood as continuing indefinitely unless expressly terminated. Thus, *ver* is to catch sight of (= beginning) and to keep on seeing (=continuing state); *pensar* is to take thought and to continue in reflection; *caminar* and *correr* are to commence putting one foot in front of the other and to continue this process. Such verbs were called NONCYCLIC by Bull, *imperfectivos* by Gili Gaya. Other verbs express an event that culminates (is "perfected") and cannot then continue unless one repeats a cycle by starting over. For example, *caerse* is to lose balance and hit the ground; falling thereupon ends, and that is the moment to which *se cayó* refers. Unlike seeing, thinking, or walking, to continue falling requires going through the

Figure 7.5. Ways of visualizing past events

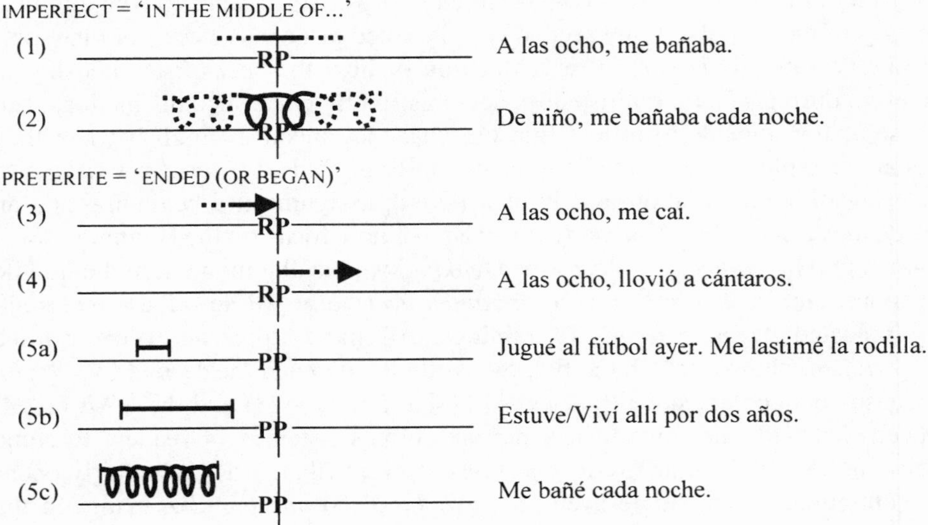
IMPERFECT = 'IN THE MIDDLE OF...'
(1)
RP
A las ocho, me bañaba.
(2)
RP
De niño, me bañaba cada noche.
PRETERITE = 'ENDED (OR BEGAN)'
(3)
RP
A las ocho, me caí.
(4)
RP
A las ocho, llovió a cántaros.
(5a)
PP
Jugué al fútbol ayer. Me lastimé la rodilla.
(5b)
PP
Estuve/Viví allí por dos años.
(5c)
PP
Me bañé cada noche.

cycle of getting back up and falling again. Verbs like *caerse* were therefore called CYCLIC by Bull, *perfectivos* by Gili Gaya. In this theory, as illustrated by the diagram and examples in figure 7.6, the preterite expresses at RP the beginning of noncyclic (imperfective) verbs but the end of cyclic (perfective) ones. And of course, the imperfect of any kind of verb depicts the middle.

Guitart (1978), however, argued that the meaning of the preterite does not always reduce so neatly to beginning vs. end for a given verb, nor are all verbs either cyclic or noncyclic. He expanded the classification as follows.

A. Cyclic events: *pasar*
En ese momento pasó (vs. pasaba) un coche.

The preterite here means 'occurred before PP', and "that is all it means" in contrast with the imperfect (p.137). If one infers that the car's passing did terminate, the tense ending alone does not necessarily imply this.

B. Noncyclic events: *hablar, caminar, correr*
El presidente habló (vs. hablaba) por televisión.
El hombre corrió (vs. corría) hacia el avión.

Again, the event took place before PP, but this event could have gone on indefinitely, or it may have ended. The preterite of a noncyclic verb, by itself, does not really say which was the case.

Figure 7.6. Imperfect as middle aspect, and preterite as beginning or end

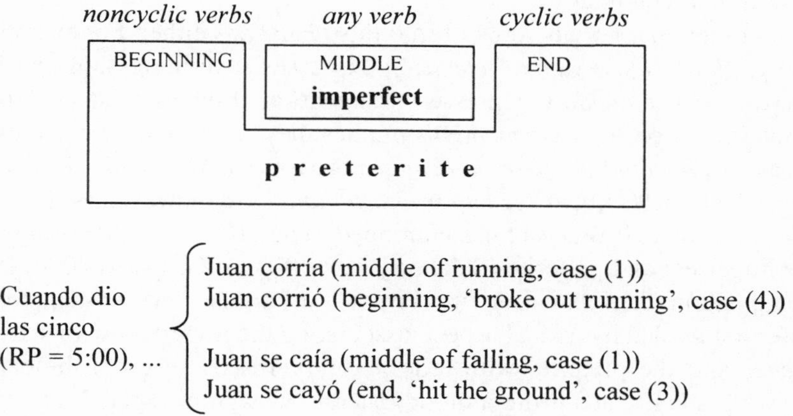

C. States: *ser, estar*
Pedro fue (vs. era) comunista.

The preterite here suggests that Pedro used to be a communist (at some RP) but no longer is (at PP). For noncyclic verbs such as (B) above, this is not necessarily true.

D. State-egressives: *costar, tener que*
El libro costó (vs. costaba) $40.00
Tuve (vs. Tenía) que ir al aeropuerto.

By "state-egressive," Guitart meant situations that can continue in effect or come climactically to an end (i.e., "egress"). *Costaba $40.00* expresses a state of potential, 'the book was for sale for $40.00', whereas *Costó $40.00* has a dynamic, completive meaning, 'it was bought for $40.00'. *Tenía que ir al aeropuerto* describes a sense of pending obligation, while *Tuve que ir al aeropuerto* means that the state of obligation ended or egressed with my actually going there.

E. State-ingressives: *gustar*
Me gustó (vs. gustaba) el lugar.

Guitart's state-ingressives signify in the preterite that a state came into effect (ingressed rather than egressed); unlike noncyclic verbs (B), with which Bull grouped these, state-ingressives are understood as continuing once begun. In some contexts, *ser* and *estar* belong to this category rather than to (C); for example, in *Fue una experiencia inolvid-*

able, the speaker focuses on the coming-into-effect of his/her perception that the experience was unforgettable *and still is* unforgettable at PP; *Fue comunista* in (C), however, implies 'not true anymore at PP'.

Guitart admitted that not all verbs fit into this reanalysis either. For example, *quedarse* in *Irma se quedó dormida viendo televisión* expresses state-ingression, but in *La puerta estaba abierta y así se quedó* it expresses continuation of the same state. Adverbials may also alter interpretation: *Fueron enemigos* implies they are no longer enemies, hence case (C), whereas *Desde aquel día fueron enemigos* is case (E). *Me gustó ese cuadro* is ingressive, hence case (E); *Me gustó ese cuadro hasta aquel día,* however, is (D).

Classification by lexical aspect has continued in an effort to explain stages of acquisition of the imperfect and preterite (Salaberry 1999; Liskin-Gasparro 2000; López Ortega 2000). One position, the LEXICAL ASPECT HYPOTHESIS, argues that in attempting to narrate, students are first guided by lexical aspect, associating the imperfect with stative verbs like *ser* and *tener* and the preterite with telic verbs (verbs of accomplishment, essentially cyclic) before gradually acquiring a more general "viewpoint aspect" that is extended to any verb type according to the narrative situation. The opposing DISCOURSE HYPOTHESIS, on the other hand, surmises that students initially focus on viewpoint aspect, interpreting it in terms of discourse functions: the imperfect for backgrounding (in the middle of a situation) and the preterite for events that are completed in the narrative foreground. This debate is difficult to resolve, given the long, complex process of developing true proficiency in narration[5]—not to mention the conflicting pedagogical treatments to which the students being tested have been exposed.

Whatever their theory of verb classification, scholars agree on two important points. First, while the exact aspectual meaning of the preterite depends on verb type and narrative context, the imperfect always conveys 'middleness', suggesting—as Guitart put it—that in the middle of one event "some other situation took place or was taking place" (p. 154). So strong is this implication that one seldom says just *El hombre corría hacia el avión* in isolation, but goes on to mention "at least one other experience or situation that took place or was taking place over the same stretch of time" (p. 141). Guitart therefore approved of Bello's term for the imperfect, *copretérito* (v. 6.0), which so clearly brings out this notion of accompaniment.

Second, there is general agreement that "meaning-changing" verbs do *not* change meaning at all (see Studerus 1989). Most such verbs are noncyclic states, egressive (like *costar*) or ingressive (like *gustar*). Therefore *sabía, conocía, tenía* express the middle of continuing states already begun and in effect at RP; *supe, conocí, tuve* generally refer to the beginning or "ingression" of these states—the start of knowledge, familiarity, possession. *Podía* and *quería* indicate the middle of the state of ability or desire, a latent potentiality or attraction; *pude* and *quise* express culmination (state-egression), with the latent state being put to the test and fulfilled. English sometimes changes verbs to convey the same senses, but not necessarily; contrary to the dictum that *sabía* is 'knew' and *supe* is 'found out', one good translation of *Después de pensarlo bien, supe el motivo* would be 'after thinking it through, I *knew* the motive'. At any rate, translation equivalents in other languages have absolutely no bearing on the Spanish grammatical system and its regularity; by the same reasoning, *hijo* would be an irregular meaning-changing noun because its English translation in the feminine changes from 'son' to 'daughter'.

7.2 The contributions of auxiliaries. As noted in the previous chapter (v. 6.2–6.4), many tenselike meanings are expressed by auxiliary verbs (Aux). Hence, in addition to choosing from inflectional possibilities of the type V+tns (verb with a tense ending), speakers have at their disposal a rich PERIPHRASTIC system of Aux + V. One criterion for which combinations are truly Aux + V will be discussed later (v. 13.1.2.7); for now, we can accept the common view that the following, at least, are to be classified as Aux rather than as main verbs in their own right.

English: modals (*can, may, will, shall, must, perhaps, ought to,* and *used to* and their morphological pasts), *have* (in the perfect), *be* (in the progressive)
Spanish: *poder, soler, deber, haber* (in the perfect), *estar* (and other progressive Aux)

7.2.1 Meanings of modals. One problem in mastering the Spanish equivalents of English modals is that the former are fully conjugated in the same categories as other verbs. English modals, however, are defective: uncombinable in the standard variety (**she should can do it* for *debe poder hacerlo*), uninflected for person (*she may,* not **she mays*), and severely limited in tense options. *Must* has no past form at all, and the morphological pasts of the others—(*can*) *could,* (*may*) *might,* (*will*) *would,* (*shall*) *should*—are often not semantically past or related to Bull's RP (compare *Tomorrow he could/should/might change his mind*). Also, because modals do not combine, there is no direct way to convey 'posteriority' (future and conditional)—**will can go, *would may* go. Consequently, the Spanish tense distinctions for verbs such as *deber* cannot be grasped through English *should, ought to,* or *must* (Keniston 1937, 199 ff.):

Debes/Deberás/Debías/Debiste/Deberías probarlo.

The difficulty is compounded by the fact that English speakers remedy modal defectiveness by borrowing from the perfect for backshifting to RP: *you should have tried it* corresponding to *debiste probarlo.* Thus, in pedagogy a lesson or two might well be devoted to directing students' attention to modals and to the finer distinctions exploited by Spanish speakers.

Some English modals are pedagogically matched not with a Spanish Aux but with a tense category. Thus, *shall go* and *will go* are described as "future tense" corresponding to *iré,* and *should go* and *would go* are described as "conditional tense" corresponding to *iría*. Strictly speaking, the modals are Aux, not tenses, but it is true that they supply tense-like information. The problem is that English modals have additional nonsystemic meanings that are ignored when they are paired up with Spanish tenses. Systemically, *will* and *would* occupy positions on Bull's axes corresponding, respectively, to the Spanish future (PP posteriority) and conditional (RP posteriority). Nonsystemically, however, they also convey willingness (*Will/Would you shut the door?*) or habitual occurrence at PP and RP (*Every day he will/would come in here to show he's just one of the guys*). Willingness is conveyed in Spanish by *querer,* and since habitual occurrence is simultaneity, it is expressed by the present (PP) or imperfect (RP) of Spanish, not by its future and conditional. *Shall* and *should* are a case apart; in American English (standard British differs on this point), neither one represents true posteriority in Bull's sense at all. For Americans, there is a sharp contrast between *Shall we sit down?* and *Will we sit down?* and between *Should they sit down?* and *Would they sit down? Should* expresses mild obligation and matches *deber* rather than the Spanish conditional; *shall* indicates prescribed procedures in constitutional language (*Each person shall have one vote*) or first-person offers (*Shall I tell it to you?*). This second *shall* corresponds to the simple present in Spanish (*¿Te lo cuento?*). Hence, textbook writers should be careful in explaining the future and conditional in terms of *will* and *would* and should avoid confusing students by tossing in *shall* and *should.*

In passing, we note that the imperative, which is typically used in response to offers such as *Shall I tell it to you?* and *¿Te lo cuento?,* does not fit readily into the basic tense system. For want of a better pigeonhole, most grammarians call it a mood; others describe it in terms of an imperative transformation, a precedent we will follow later (v. 12.4).

7.2.2 "Secondary" modifications: Perfect and progressive. According to Bull, *he hablado* contrasts with *hablo* as anterior to PP vs. simultaneous with PP, and with the preterite as anterior to PP vs. simultaneous with PP. Stockwell, Bowen, and Martin (1965, 157) described the present perfect as showing "relevant anteriority," emphasizing that an event began in the relatively recent past and continues to be in effect or to impinge in some way on PP. For past perfect and future perfect, one adjusts PP to RP and AP accordingly. In both languages, this "relevance" depends on the nature of the verb. It can represent a state that began in the past and continues into the present:

Hemos estado muy contentos en esta casa.

or a series of events that has continued right up through the present (= 'so far'):

Ya te lo he dicho mil veces.

or one event that ended but with abiding repercussions in the present:

El huracán ha destruido su casa.

(See Zagona 1991 and Mackenzie 1995 for fuller analyses of perfect tenses.)

As for the progressive, both languages use this to characterize events as ongoing, in progress (whence the name). But they relate this shared meaning to those of the simple tenses quite differently. In Spanish, the simple present can convey at least four verb aspects:

1. occurring now at PP (middle): *¡Mamá! El bebé llora.*
2. recurring generally, though not necessarily at PP: *El sol sale a las siete. Juana se lava con Jabondelux. Trabajo en una oficina. Truena mucho en las montañas.*
3. about to happen (anticipatory present, v. 7.1.2): *Se van mañana a las ocho.*
4. occurs and is completed during observation (= end): (witness describing a scene as it unfolds) *El tren entra en la estación; se detiene; salen los pasajeros; se les revisa el equipaje.*

With so many aspects for one tense, Spanish resorts to its progressive to highlight the first one. The progressive is thus optional in Spanish: *El bebé está llorando* can refer to the same event as *El bebé llora,* but it excludes interpretations (2), (3), and (4) and can be reserved for an event "unfolding before the speaker's eyes" (King and Suñer 1980). Backshifted, the imperfect progressive *estaba llorando* has the same relationship with the imperfect *lloraba,* but as Gonzales (1995) proved in an analysis of oral narratives, it serves as a special "framing device" for a subsequent event, vividly setting the stage for it.

In English too, the simple present potentially has all four meanings, but normally the first—'occurring at PP'—only applies to stative verbs such as *be* or *know.* For a process or action verb such as *die* or *fall,* the simple present is *not* used for meaning (1) at all; the progressive must be used instead. Thus, for meaning (1) the English speaker says *I know it* (state) but *I'm dying* (process), not **I'm knowing it* or **I die,* and the equivalent of the first Spanish example is *The baby's crying,* not *The baby cries* (= meaning (2), maybe (4)). Also unlike the Spanish setup, English allows meaning (3) to be expressed by either the simple present or the progressive: *They leave tomorrow at eight, They're leaving tomorrow at eight.*

Thus, Spanish restricts its progressive as a special alternative for meaning (1), whereas English uses its progressive as an alternative for meaning (4) and as a form *contrasting* with the simple present for meanings (1) vs. (2). This can be depicted as in figure 7.7.

The (partial) optionality of the Spanish progressive is to some extent true of the perfect also, which is why Stockwell, Bowen, and Martin called both of them "secondary modifications" (1965, 139). That is, just as Spanish *está llorando* can also be handled by *llora* and English *he's leaving tomorrow* by *he leaves tomorrow,* the perfect lends precision but need not be used when "relevant anteriority" is already clear from context (e.g., because of adverbs and relators), as illustrated in:

Antes que hubieran cenado = Antes que cenaran
Before they'd eaten supper = Before they ate supper

Figure 7.7. The progressive in relation to the simple present

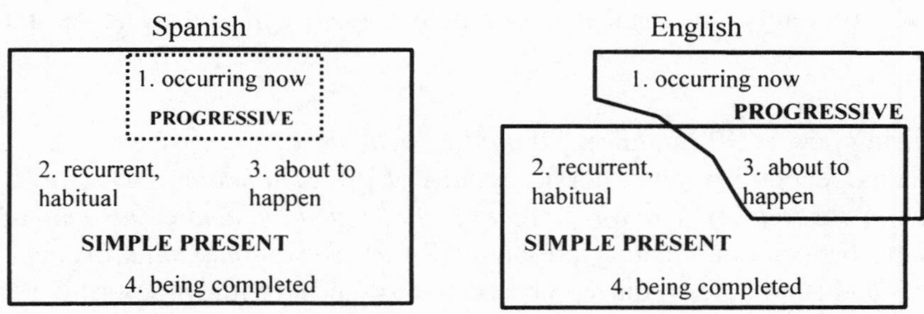

When secondary modifications are used, there are as many of them available as there are corresponding simple tenses; in other words, Spanish has more perfects and progressives than English, thanks to its richer tense and aspect system. Thus, contrasting with the imperfect progressive *estaba estudiando*, which recalls being in the middle of an event that was underway, there is *estuve estudiando toda la bendita mañana*, which terminates that duration. In fact, there are numerous other Spanish progressives that are in frequent contemporary use but are almost never mentioned in textbooks that merely match Spanish progressives with the English one:

ir (*iba/fui estudiando*): gradual development of the activity
venir (*venía/vine estudiando*): gradual progress toward a goal
andar (*andaba/anduve repasando*): aimless activity without progress
seguir (*seguía/seguí repasando*): continuation (with preterite, resumption)

7.3 Mood: Indicative vs. subjunctive. Most of our references to tense so far have applied to the indicative system. It often dismays students to learn, after what seems to be the light at the end of the tunnel in a long succession of Spanish tense forms, that there is a second system of tenses. Their textbook then names the tenses covered up to that point as "indicatives," the new set as "subjunctives," and both as "modes" or "moods." All these terms are quite mystifying, as are other terms inherited from ancient grammar. On taking up the study of Spanish, most students have heard of and can identify "present tense" and perhaps "infinitives"; the subjunctive, however, is generally new to them, and this category is not easily explained.

Some books point out to students the English subjunctive; for example,

It's urgent that she *come* (*comes) / that she *be* on time (*is on time).

The English subjunctive may also contrast with indicative forms:

I insist that she drive/drives very carefully.
I suggest that she sign up/is signing up today.
If Frank was/were guilty . . .

These subjunctives and their meanings compare well to certain Spanish usages, but they are nevertheless a poor pedagogical point of departure. They are relics and of little help to students who seldom use them today and are unsure of them when they hear or read them. The English subjunctive is moribund, and current usage relies more on modals and infinitival constructions (v. 13.1.2) to convey the nuances expressed by the Spanish subjunctive:

Sugiero que se esfuerza más.	I suggest that she's trying harder.
Sugiero que se esfuerce más.	I suggest for her to try/that she should try harder.

Consequently, students must approach the Spanish subjunctive on its own terms as a new category for which there is essentially no equivalent in English grammar.

7.3.1 The tense system in the subjunctive. The subjunctive is a second tense system, or better, the same system as in the indicative but shifted to another mode or kind of perspective, from the "creo que . . ." to the "dudo que . . ." of human judgment. Any proposition that is believed can also be doubted, so that for every indicative form there should be a corresponding subjunctive. Yet the subjunctive system is simpler thanks to two neutralizations. First, posteriority (future for PP, conditional for RP) is not distinguished from simultaneity (present for PP, past for RP): the *vienen* and *vendrán* of *Creo que vienen* vs. *Creo que vendrán* both become *vengan* in *Dudo que vengan.* Old Spanish had a future subjunctive in *-are, -iere* that has largely fallen into disuse; normally today, the present subjunctive handles both posteriority and simultaneity. Second, Spanish has never distinguished aspect (preterite/imperfect) in its subjunctive; there are two sets of past subjunctives (*-ra, -se*), but these do not stand for any tense or aspect distinction.[6] Since a form such as *viniera* (*viniese*) neutralizes the distinction between *venía* and *vino* and the distinction between these and *vendría* as well, the term "imperfect subjunctive" for it is definitely imperfect; "past subjunctive" is descriptively correct. Hence, the ten systemic categories of the indicative are reduced to only four in the subjunctive, as shown in figure 7.8.

In imitation of Latin grammar, some Spanish scholars handed down a principle of "sequence" or "agreement" of tenses—*concordantia tempōrum* in Latin—whereby a main verb on Bull's present (PP) axis may introduce any tense in the subordinate clause, but one on the recalled (RP) axis requires that the subordinated verb's tense be of its own system; that is, past takes past. In the list given in figure 7.8, *Creo que* . . . could introduce options (1a)–(4c) in the indicative, and *Dudo que* . . . could introduce (1)–(4) in the subjunctive, but *Creía (Creí, Creería) que* . . . would be limited to taking (3a)–(4c) in the indicative, and *Dudaba (Dudó, Dudaría) que* . . . would be limited to (3)–(4) in the sub-

Figure 7.8. Correspondence of tenses between the indicative and the subjunctive

Tenses	Indicative	Subjunctive
present	(1a) *vienen*	(1) *vengan*
future	(1b) *vendrán*	
present perfect	(2a) *han venido*	(2) *hayan venido*
future perfect	(2b) *habrán venido*	
imperfect	(3a) *venían*	(3) *vinieran (viniesen)*
preterite	(3b) *vinieron*	
conditional	(3c) *vendrían*	
past perfect (imperf.)	(4a) *habían venido*	(4) *hubieran (hubiesen) venido*
past perfect (pret.)	(4b) *hubieron venido*	
conditional perfect	(4c) *habrían venido*	

junctive. But in reality, modern speakers select the appropriate tense according to the meaning they wish to convey, not according to strict tense-matching. Gili Gaya (1973, 175, 290–93) conceded that the battle for *concordantia* is lost in the indicative but tried to retain it for the subjunctive; yet Studerus (1979, 333–35) quoted convincing examples of nonagreement in the subjunctive as well, for example, *Propuso que se fabrique heno en la parte norte de Puerto Rico,* meaning (as opposed to *se fabricara*) that the speaker sees the event as still unrealized at PP and the unfulfilled proposal as still pending. Since such sentences are common on both sides of the Atlantic, teachers might spare their students a foray into *concordantia tempōrum* and focus on the more important question of the meaning of mood.

7.3.2 The meaning of mood: Theories and approaches. As with treatments of tense and aspect, two approaches to mood can be distinguished. Some scholars itemize all discernible uses of the subjunctive and correlate each use to the choice of verb or conjunction in the main clause. In this approach, the subjunctive carries little meaning in and of itself since it is determined by the sentential context. Others seek in mood contrasts one or two common denominators that subsume the various surface uses, and they maintain that the selection of mood depends on the meaning one wishes to convey, not on main clause cues.

7.3.2.1 The subjunctive as a set of uses. Ramsey ([1894] 1956, 415–57) observed that the use of the Spanish subjunctive is governed by verbs and conjunctions that sort out into the following classes:[7]

command	emotion, feeling	exception
demand, request	impersonal expression	concession
proposal, suggestion	denial, doubt	temporal clause of futurity
desire	indefinite relative	permission

negative result	imperative	approval, preference
supposition	exclamatory wishes	prohibition, hindrance
proviso	conditions of implied negation	

Bergen (1978a) brought together all such taxonomies he could find and arrived at a total of thirty-four separate rules for the Spanish subjunctive.

Aside from the psychological question of whether a learner (native or nonnative) could internalize and then apply thirty-four separate rules for one mood, and the philosophical question of why such a catch-all category would develop in an otherwise systematic language, this approach is objectionable because it misleads students into thinking that mood selection is dictated by the type of main verb or conjunction; if they learn enough cases of "*pedir* and *para que* take subjunctive," "*saber* and *porque* take indicative," and so on, they will be ready for the fill-in-the-blanks. However, (1) there are too many subjunctive-takers to commit to memory, (2) subjunctive-takers need not take the subjunctive (*Ordenó que hicieran cola, Ordenó que tenían que hacer cola*), and (3) a huge number of contexts allow either mood with a contrast in meaning (*Gritó que saltaban/saltaran*). This approach persists in some quarters today, and the doubt and uncertainty it engenders in students last well into the advanced levels of language study.

7.3.2.2 The subjunctive as a marker of meaning. Gili Gaya (1973, 131 ff.) focused on mood in noun clauses, as in *Niego que sean honrados.* Although he began with the traditional canon of cataloged uses, eventually he arrived at the generalization that most uses reflect just two types: the (classical) *subjuntivo* of doubt and uncertainty and the *optativo* of necessity and desire. Then he generalized one step further: both suggest UNREALITY in contrast with the indicative, which expresses reality. That is, both *dudo que* and *deseo que* introduce propositions whose reality at PP is unguaranteed and unrealized. But there is another kind of subjunctive that does not conform to the real/unreal principle: its use with emotional reactions such as *temo, me alegro, me gusta, espero,* and *es sorprendente,* regardless of whether the situation is real or unreal. For example, in *Temo que nos vean* the speaker fears a situation that may or may not come to pass, whereas in *Siento que estés descontenta* he/she reacts to a situation acknowledged as real. For Gili Gaya, the subjunctive of emotional reaction is a special case that overrides the normal contrast; he speculated that it arose in analogy to the reaction-to-something-uncertain case (*Temo que nos vean*) or, alternatively, that it follows from the fact that emotion is a subjective state that has "realidad interna pero no fuera de nosotros" (p.137)—that is, emotions are not really real.

Bull (1972, 174–97) agreed with Gili Gaya that mood usage is based on a limited number of principles, and that emotional reaction ("psychological response") is one of them. But he pointed out that some verbs can be used either to express psychological responses (with the subjunctive) or to make reasonable predictions (with the indicative). For example, *temer* with the indicative as in *Temo que ha llegado* does not express fear, but politely implies 'creo que . . .'. Clearly, then, it is futile for students to commit to memory classifications such as the one in 7.3.2.1; verbs such as *temer* do not "take" the subjunctive, but are used with or without it according to whether the speaker intends to express emotional reactions.

Bull's second principle for the subjunctive is similar to Gili Gaya's reality/unreality distinction. The indicative suggests that an event or entity has been experienced and found to be real, whereas the subjunctive suggests that it is unexperienced (anticipated but uncertain, yet to be encountered, unproven). This principle underlies mood contrasts in many noun clauses (*Sé que saldrá* vs. *Dudo que salga*), relative clauses (*Busco un gato que no tiene/tenga pulgas*), and adverbial clauses (*Vamos después que regresan/regresen*). When some expressions (*sin que, para que*) always introduce subjunctives, it is not because of grammatical requirements but because of their meaning, which is 'as yet unexperienced'; others (*cuando, hasta que, mientras*) may introduce experienced or unexperienced events; with still others, some speakers have generalized one mood while others preserve a contrast. An example of this last case is *Se sentaron antes que (llegó/llegara) Jorge,* in which many speakers assume that at RP George's pending arrival was not a certainty and should be expressed by *llegara*; others accept *llegó* if George is known (at PP) to have arrived eventually, but they would prefer *llegara* otherwise.

In developing his third principle, Bull noted that one key to the subjunctive is that it SUBJOINS one event to another in a causal way. Cause-and-effect is expressed equally well in *Se abre el grifo y sale el agua* and *Se abre el grifo para que salga el agua,* but the former just joins cause and effect while the latter subjoins (subordinates) effect to cause so that one depends on the other. When a verb of communicating introduces a subjoined verb, the indicative will report an event while the subjunctive will be used for the special cause-and-effect of trying to influence behavior. Thus, *Oigo que te vas* merely reports; *Mando que te vayas* aims at the effect of getting the addressee to do something. Verbs such as *decir* can introduce either situation, and Bull notes a progression from the quoting of a direct command to the subjoining of an indirect one:[8]

Reporting an event:	Relaying a command:
(1) Papá: ¡Se va!	(1) Papá: ¡Váyase!
(2) Papá dice—¡Se va!	(2) Papá dice—¡Váyase!
(3) Papá dice que se va.	(3) Papá dice que se vaya.

Yet the principle of influencing behavior is not entirely distinct from that of unreality and nonexperience. At the moment that an attempt is made to influence someone's actions, the implied command is as yet unfulfilled, with no certainty that it will be carried out. The noun clause of *Mando que regresen* or of *Dice que se vaya* thus expresses a proposition that, for now (at PP), is as unreal as that of *Dudan que regresen* or *Me escondo para que se vaya.*[9]

Jelinski (1977) modified Bull's theory by conflating psychological response with influencing behavior as one type, CAUSE-AND-EFFECT. But Zlotchew (1977) disagreed and pointed out how emotional reactions are both structurally and semantically distinct from cause-and-effect patterns. Stockwell, Bowen, and Martin (1965, 241 ff.) had much the same theory as

Bull but distinguished four cases for pedagogy: uncertainty (*dudo que . . .*), necessity (*es necesario que. . . , quiero que . . .*), unidentifiable antecedents (*busco un gato que . . .*), and adverbial clauses with events yet to occur or be confirmed *(para que. . . , antes que . . .*).

The pages of the journal *Hispania* were the forum for a lively debate that sharpened mood analysis. It began with Lozano (1972), who elaborated on Gili Gaya by positing two grammatical features governing mood, [+optative] and [+dubitative]. Optative expressions, exemplified by *querer,* include any implicit or explicit command; in fact, for Lozano emotional reactions such as *es importante que . . .* and *me gusta que . . .* are optative too in expressing a speaker's wishes. Dubitative expressions are epitomized by *dudar* but include any expression of doubt, from strong *negar* to weak *quizás.* Lozano further marked as [+dubitative] relative and adverbial clauses of unexperienced entities and events, as well as contrary-to-fact conditional sentences with *si.* He denied that optative and dubitative can be merged, inasmuch as a negated [+optative] still takes subjunctive (*no quiero que . . .*) whereas a negated [+dubitative] cues a switch to the indicative (*no dudo que . . .*); hence, there are two subjunctives. He then proceeded to illustrate how mood selection in syntax follows from the choice of features, for example, *Llámalo antes que* [+dubitative] *yo* EMPEZAR → *Llámalo antes que yo* ***empiece*** (Lozano 1972, 84).

Bolinger (1974) replied that Lozano split asunder what is regarded as a single mood. If optative and dubitative expressions were really distinct, then combining them with one subjunctive clause should be a ZEUGMA, a joining that makes no sense, but Bolinger combined a dubitative, optative, and, for good measure, an emotional reaction: *Es posible, tal vez necesario, pero sin embargo deplorable, que él sea nuestro representante.* He pointed out expressions that introduce the subjunctive without clearly belonging to either of Lozano's categories: *es interesante que. . . , es típicamente profesorial que. . . , no tiene ninguna importancia que. . . .* Bolinger therefore advocated a return to the "traditional" view that the subjunctive is a single mood with a consistent meaning in its contrast with the indicative. Selection of one over the other is controlled not by some feature in the main clause but by the speaker, who uses the indicative for expressing "intelligence" (straightforward information) and the subjunctive for expressing "attitude" toward information. Even in those cases where one mood seems required, as in Lozano's negated dubitatives, Bolinger found freedom of choice, including affirmative *creo que*:

> Creo, señor Gordon, que la prensa de su país no esté bien informada correctamente respecto al Dr. Fidel Castro.

This freedom of choice does not make pedagogy easy, but Bolinger suggested an English clue: if a "performative" expression such as *I'm afraid, I assure you, I'm sorry,* or *it's probable* can be added after a clause, then the Spanish equivalent will have the indicative; if not, then the clause will have a subjunctive:

He's coming, I think.	Creo que *viene.*
*He's coming, I don't think.	No creo que *venga.*

You've broken it, I fear.	Temo que lo *has* roto.
*You've broken it, I'm sorry.	Siento que lo *hayas* roto.

Lozano (1975) countered by noting that Bolinger's theory was not "traditional" at all, and he proceeded to explicate dubitative/optative more fully and to sort out troublesome cases into a finer classification. As for the speaker's freedom of choice, there is certainly little freedom after *mandar* and *para que,* and certain syntactic constraints limit one's choice even further. In rebuttal, Bolinger (1976) repeated that dubitative and optative are just manifestations of speaker attitude, and that knowledge of mood selection is more than knowledge of Lozano's classifications. For example, how would the latter (or a speaker using them) anticipate a novel but perfectly normal subjunctive in *Yace en la mente de Dios que el hombre* ***obedezca*** *a Sus mandamientos* (p. 44)? Also, Bolinger continued finding counterexamples with subjunctives after affirmative *parece que, estoy seguro que, supongo que,* revealing some degree of choice. If some choices are less frequent or unlikely (e.g., the combination of a main verb of commanding with a clause conveying the reporting of intelligence, **Mando que te vas*), this is because of semantic incompatibility, not some syntactic feature that compels speakers to follow up with the right mood after selecting a main verb. "A grammar that creeps along a sentence from left to right and attempts to determine everything on one side from what has already occurred on the other is a fun thing to make up as an exercise in guesswork, but is not true to life" (p. 48).[10]

What Bolinger called "speaker attitude" is analyzed today in terms of PRESUPPOSITION. Whenever we make a statement, we assert some information but presuppose or assume as givens other facts. For example, in both *The teacher criticized Jan for cheating* and *The teacher accused Jan of cheating,* we assert that the teacher blamed Jan for having cheated, but the presuppositions differ: with *criticized,* we evaluate the proposition and assume that Jan did indeed cheat, whereas with *accused* we leave the question open. Such presuppositional differences underlie mood selection too: as Keniston (1937, 163) observed, the subjunctive introduces "an approach toward the action or state as an assumption rather than as a fact." That mood contrasts occur almost exclusively in "subjoined" clauses is significant: by placing a proposition in a subordinate clause, speakers set up a syntactic environment in which they can hold it up for comment, appraisal, and inference in the main clause.

Goldin (1974) perceived two patterns in the presuppositional thrust of the subjunctive. First, this mood accompanies expressions of emotional reaction because the speaker is then EVALUATING an proposition rather than asserting it. The point of *Me alegro de que vengas* is not that the hearer is coming, which is presupposed, but that the speaker finds this news satisfying. Goldin noted that emotion is not the key, for one can also evaluate something unemotionally, as in *Es lógico que tengan la culpa.* Second, the subjunctive portrays shadings of truth value. Goldin considered three stances in this regard: POSITIVE PRESUPPOSITION is the assumption that the proposition is true, has happened, is certain; NEGATIVE PRESUPPOSITION is the opposite, ranging from denial to hedged reservation; and

INDEFINITE PRESUPPOSITION is a suspension of belief one way or the other (the proposition is perhaps false, perhaps true). The indicative, then, conveys positive presupposition (*Es verdad que se van*), while the subjunctive conveys negative (*Es dudoso que se vayan*) or indefinite (*Es posible que se vayan*) presupposition. But with *si*-clauses the system shifts: here, the indicative shows both positive (*Esquiamos si nieva*) and indefinite presupposition (*Esquiaremos si nieva*), so that the subjunctive is reserved for the negative presupposition of contrary-to-fact (*Esquiaríamos si nevara*).

Not surprisingly, Goldin believed that it is pedagogically feckless, and linguistically unrealistic, to force mood selection into either/or decisions based on sentential context alone, as in fill-in-the-blank exercises. Like Bolinger, he held that native speakers do not select mood solely on the basis of conjunctions or main verbs. The speaker's presuppositions may not be clear from the rest of the sentence, so that to choose between moods students should begin with how they, as speakers of a sentence, wish their assumptions to be understood.

Terrell and Hooper (1974) similarly argued that to assert something is to introduce it as confirmed, believed, or inferred, whether strongly (*it's certain that. . . , I know that . . .*) or weakly (*it seems that. . . , I gather that . . .*). To presuppose something is to take it for granted and proceed to comment on it. The proposition *She dances* is asserted in *It's obvious that she dances,* presupposed in *It's great that she dances,* and neither asserted nor presupposed in *It's not certain that she dances.* As shown in the following classification, Terrell and Hooper discerned two subcases in each of these three, giving six approaches a speaker can take to a proposition:

1. Asserted: (1a) by the speaker: *me parece que, sé que, es cierto que*
   (1b) by others: *cuentan que, contesta que, se cree que*
2. Presupposed: (2a) in the learning of a proposition: *se da cuenta de que, aprende que*
   (2b) for commentary: *me alegro de que, es lástima que, es interesante que*
3. Neither: (3a) it's doubted: *duda que, niega que, no creo que*
   (3b) it's willed: *manda que, quiere que, pido que*

The indicative covers the first three cases (1a–2a), and the subjunctive the last three (2b–3b).[11]

Like others, Terrell and Hooper sought evidence in contrasts. *Dice que viene,* for instance, reports another person's assertion (1b), while *Dice que venga* relays a command (3b), which neither asserts nor presupposes that anyone is necessarily coming. And like Goldin, they advocated abandoning the practice of filling in blanks according to cues in the main clause—which, in numerous cases like *Dice que (viene/venga)*, is impossible anyhow. Instead, students should practice manipulating presupposition by being invited to react to a clause such as *Mañana nos visitarán* by doubting it, commenting on it, asserting it, wishing it, and so on.

Bergen (1978a, 211) strove to reduce all rules, categories, features, and uses of the subjunctive to just one principle: "whereas the indicative denotes that the speaker (or actor) of the higher clause regards his proposition . . . as an objective fact, the subjunctive expresses a subjective reservation on the part of the speaker (or actor) concerning the reality of that proposition." Others (recall Gili Gaya) saw this principle as underlying most mood contrasts, but Bergen perceived SPEAKER RESERVATION in all subjunctives and proceeded to apply it to a host of interesting examples. But Bell (1980) disagreed, insisting that there are four applications of the subjunctive, all of which are rooted in presupposition but not really combinable. These are (1) commenting on a fact, with the presupposition that the hearer may already know the fact but expects a reaction to it, (2) subjective reservations (doubt, noncommitment) about truth value, (3) unrealized or unexperienced entities and events (à la Bull), and (4) indirect commands.

The debate continued: Takagaki (1984) disputed Bell and returned to the position that each mood has one general sense. The indicative denotes "independency": its proposition is "affirmatively evaluated" and stated as a proposition in its own right. The subjunctive shows "subordinance": information that is subordinated to the speaker's main point (as expressed in the main clause), and that either (a) is not affirmed as such or (b) if it *is* affirmed, "it does not come to be stated" (p. 251). As Takagaki noted, "independency" can just as well be expressed in an independent clause, while "subordinance" characterizes information that is both syntactically and informationally subordinated to the main proposition. (Compare Bull's notion of "subjoining.") Thus, in the following sentences,

(1) No creo que Paco venga.
(2) No creo que Paco viene.
(3) Creo que Paco viene.

Sentence (1) does not affirm Paco's coming or not coming; what it *states* is the speaker's disbelief. The last two sentences, however, state Paco's coming (as someone else's belief in (2), as the speaker's in (3)) and represent loose joinings of what Takagaki takes as independent assertions:

(2a) Paco viene, pero no lo creo.
(3a) Yo lo creo: Paco viene.

Bolinger's (1974, 253) comparison with English *He's coming, I think* is therefore apt.

7.3.3 Summary of mood usage. Most of the participants in the Great Mood Debate have claimed pedagogical value for their theories, in that the principles they posit reflect the factors and options that native speakers take into account for mood selection—and that students need to master if they are to use mood in a nativelike way. The decision making in five of these theories can be represented in terms of flowcharts such as those in

Figure 7.9. Five theories interpreted as decisions speakers make in using mood

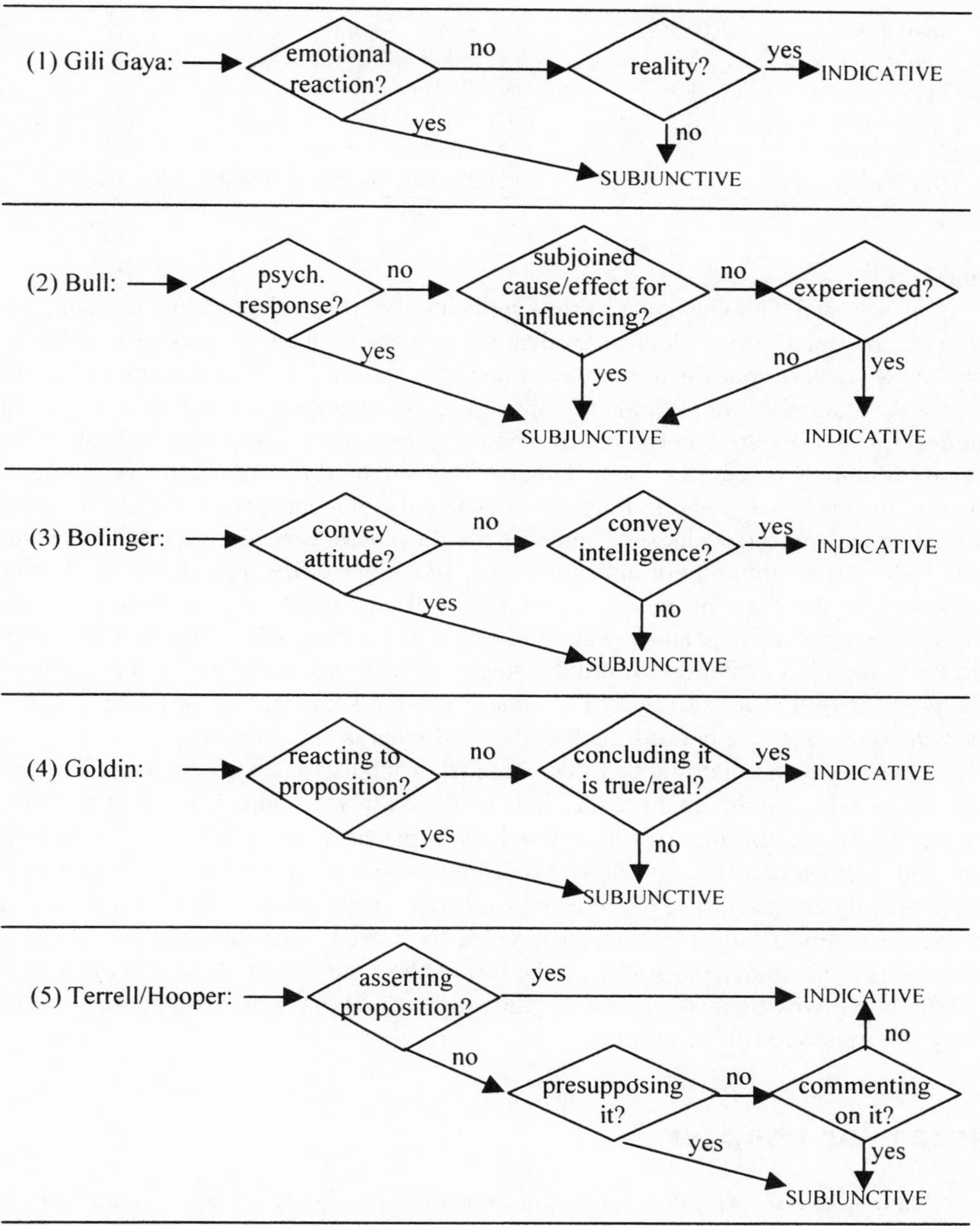

Figure 7.10. Puerto Ricans' use of the indicative after selected main-clause cues (Lantolf 1978)

(1) *Piden que ...*	10%	(7) *Es posible que ...*	14%
(2) *Sugiero que ...*	7%	(8) *¡Qué bueno que ...*	54%
(3) *Quiero que ...*	1%	(9) *Es bueno que ...*	15%
(4) *Es necesario que ...*	0%	(10) *Se sorprendió de que ...*	34%
(5) *Espero que ...*	1%	(11) *Se alegró de que ...*	38%
(6) *¡Qué ridículo que ...*	7%	(12) *Siempre me sorprende el hecho de que...*	18%

figure 7.9.[12]

As we saw with Gili Gaya, the hardest application of the subjunctive to account for is its use with emotional (psychological, evaluative) reactions, given the pervasive reality/unreality (or whatever) contrast found elsewhere; this special status shows up in "reaction," "response," "attitude," or "comment" appearing as separate decisions in the flowcharts. Interestingly, its oddity is borne out by contemporary usage. Lantolf (1978) asked Puerto Ricans to complete sentences with either of two verb forms, indicative or subjunctive. Some of his results are cited in figure 7.10, where the percentages show the use of indicatives after the indicated phrase. (Compare similar mood variation revealed by Studerus 1995.) There is a sprinkling of indicatives after *piden que* or *quiero que,* but these are negligible next to the surge of indicatives after cues of emotional reaction such as *qué bueno que, se sorprendió de que,* and *se alegró de que.* For Goldin (1974, 300), such data suggest that the system is gravitating toward the single contrast of positive vs. negative presupposition—or as Bull (1965, 192) put the same point, the subjunctive is no longer automatic after *alegrarse* or *temer* but reflects the reality of what is being reacted to.

Perhaps the most important fact to emerge from scholarly debates on the subjunctive is that mood selection in Spanish has less to do with automatic triggers than with the speaker's attitude toward a proposition he/she places in a clause. Consequently, the common practice of filling in blanks according to sentential context is as unrealistic for understanding and acquiring mood as it is for past tenses; students must learn that native speakers actively exploit the contrast in order to convey different meanings. As long as selection is made to depend solely on the rest of the sentence, students cannot be blamed for wondering why Spanish has such apparently useless machinery when the context can always be rigged to suffice entirely.

Notes for chapter 7

1. Many scholars have offered their impressions of the "overuse" or "underuse" of certain tenses, but for a precise, data-based approach to this question, see the study by Moreno de Alba (1978), who calculated the statistical frequency of each tense (including nonsystemic applications) in a sampling of Mexican Spanish.

2. Historically, the English verb forms in the protasis of conditionals are past subjunctives as in Spanish, but these have generally been merged with the past indicative. Some speakers still distinguish them in *If she were a thief, she'd tell us* (= contrary-to-fact) vs. *If she was a thief, she'll tell us* (= granting a possible fact), but most speakers have generalized *was* in both. In Spanish, too, many speakers generalize one form for both parts of conditional sentences (Kany 1951, 159; Gili Gaya 1973, 321): *Si yo lo tuviera, se lo daría.* → *Si yo lo tenía, se lo daba*, or *Si yo lo tuviera, se lo diera.*

3. This listing comes from DaSilva and Lovett (1965, 4–6). They eventually proceeded to a generalization, but this itemization of uses is representative of what many students recall as the kind of explanation they received.

4. This, in fact, was the strategy adopted by LaMadrid, Bull, and Briscoe (1974a), who spent parts of three lessons on "the nature of events" in storytelling before finally introducing preterite/imperfect.

5. Salaberry (1999) had students at various levels retell the plot of a movie segment in Spanish, and his data brought out a complex mixture of strategies (overgeneralization of a "default" preterite, lapses into the present, overreliance on progressives, assignment of the imperfect on the basis of lexical aspect, use of viewpoint aspect) that continually shifts over years of study.

6. De Mello (1993) confirmed that although *-se* has special currency in Spain and Puerto Rico, the *-ra* form is more frequent everywhere. The original past subjunctive was with *-se*; the *-ra* form was a past perfect indicative displaced by *había* + participle. As Kany (1951, 170 ff.) noted, the *-ra* form survives as a past perfect in cultivated usage. He also noted the lingering use of the future subjunctive in some regions (p. 185), and Jorge Morel (1974, 131) confirmed it among upper-class Dominicans: *Si **fuere** necesario, lo visitaré.* But for Mexico, Boyd-Bowman (1960, 227) found the more typical situation of *-re* just "en el estilo literario o retórico, en oraciones, proclamaciones y casos parecidos; sentido como arcaísmo, el futuro de subjuntivo sirve para prestar al lenguaje burocrático un tono de solemnidad."

7. Yet Ramsey ([1894] 1956, 465 ff.) concluded with generalizations that still compare favorably. Bello ([1847] 1958) took the same approach, starting with a list of subjunctive takers before arriving at a general meaning (p. 220). Writers who have followed these giants of Spanish grammar have not always picked up on their eventual generalizations.

8. Note that it is in indirect discourse, whether reported at PP (*Papá dice que se va/vaya*) or narrated from RP (*Papá dijo que se iba/fue/fuera*), where the entire point of tense, mood, and aspect distinctions really emerges. For a course that programmatically applies indirect discourse and backshifting (v. 7.1.1.2) to the development of narrative skills in Spanish, see Whitley and González 2000.

9. Bull (1965, 184) had problems in applying his theory to *si* clauses: the conditional clause of *Deberás usar botas si llueve* seems just as "subjoined" as the one in *Deberás usar botas con tal que llueva,* but the two differ in mood.

10. For an update on this strand of the Great Mood Debate, see Lozano 1995.

11. Yet Smead (1994) showed that syntactic features of [±affirming] and [±presupposed] could not explain Mexican mood usage. Mejías Bikandi (1994) also found problems with [±presupposed] for several verbs and, in a reanalysis of the Terrell-Hooper theory, pointed out that their type (2a) is actually assertion, so [±asserting] alone suffices. See also his more pragmatically based theory in Mejías Bikandi 1998.

12. In summarizing the theories in this way, I have borrowed an idea from Margarita Suñer.

Exercises for chapter 7

1. In each of the following, indicate what other simple tense and mood forms could occur in the same context as the italicized one, and explain the change of meaning.
   (a) Es muy dudoso que *viniera* Amanda.
   (b) Hoy se *cierran* las escuelas.
   (c) Ayer a las ocho *ponían* la tele.
   (d) Sugirió que María *comprara* tallarines.
   (e) Si llueve, *pasaremos* el tiempo jugando a los naipes.
   (f) Salen de modo que no *llegan* tarde.
   (g) Dijo que te *callarías.*

2. To what extent can the student get along without progressives and perfects in Spanish? Why? What priority would you assign them in the sequencing of materials in a first-year book?

3. It was pointed out that when a Spanish auxiliary verb such as *deber* corresponds to an English modal, the tense distinctions of the former may be difficult to understand. Take the forms *puedo/podré/podía/pude/podría/he podido* and contrast them with those of *can* and *be able to.* How would you explain them to English speakers?

4. To what extent is the either/or approach of fill-in-the-blanks possible in cases such as preterite vs. imperfect and indicative vs. subjunctive? To what extent does it lead to active control over these distinctions? Suggest alternative activities and testing procedures that might focus on more expressive ability in more communicative activities.

5. Take a passage from a written or recorded oral narrative in Spanish and analyze the distribution of preterite and imperfect (and present, if it appears), explaining the writer's or speaker's apparent point in selecting each.

6. Hernán (1994) reported on success in using video to help students visualize the difference between preterite and imperfect. Assume that you have a production team for creating such a video for your classes, and describe how you would portray the two aspects (a) in contrasting representations of the same events and (b) in a short naturalistic narrative.

7. The following examples come from the Spanish newspaper *El País Internacional.* Explain the italicized subjunctives.
   (a) (From an interview with President Siles Zuazo of Bolivia, 13 Feb. 1984, 7):
   Pregunta: ¿Qué le parece que España *haya* firmado esa declaración?
   Respuesta: Creo que la presencia de España es una evolución . . . muy positiva.
   (b) (Comment on the Guatemalan regime's decision to hold elections, 9 July 1984, 2):
   No hay que pensar que el Ejército se ha vuelto demócrata porque el Espíritu Santo le *haya* pasado por encima. Ha tomado una decisión estratégica . . . reversible.

8. Summarize the uses of the Spanish conditional and future. Which ones are systemic? Which nonsystemic ones might be interpreted as extensions of the basic meaning? To what extent do these tenses match the English modals *will, would, shall, should*?

9. What mergers of indicative categories occur in passing to the subjunctive? What advantage is there in calling the "imperfect" subjunctive simply "past"?

10. Which uses (applications, principles) of the subjunctive do English speakers seem to have the most trouble with? The least? Which ones are prescribed in some grammars but not consistently adopted by native speakers in current usage?

11. In your experience as student or teacher, what tense and aspect errors do beginning and intermediate students of Spanish tend to make? Which categories do they overuse, and which do they underuse? Which errors reflect a transfer of the English system? (Alternatively, you might turn this into a research project and carry out an error analysis of a recorded sample of a student's Spanish.)

12. Draw up a plan for an "ideal" textbook by indicating the sequence in which Spanish verb categories (tenses, aspects, moods, *perífrasis*) ought to be taken up. Then compare your results with those of your classmates. To guide your thoughts, consider these factors:

(a) relative order of difficulty in both morphology and usage
(b) systemic vs. nonsystemic functions (from most to least basic)
(c) relative communicative need for the functions
(d) interrelatedness of morphology (e.g., preterites before past subjunctives), meaning. (e.g., conditionals and past subjunctives with *si*), and structures (e.g., subjunctives and *que*-clauses).

13. Bull (1947, 58) carried out a tense frequency study for written Spanish, obtaining the following averages across several genres—short stories, novels, dramas, essays, poetry.

(1)	present indicative	34.496%	(11)	conditional perfect	1.600%
(2)	infinitive	19.623%	(12)	conditional	1.535%
(3)	preterite indicative	14.310%	(13)	past perfect indicative	1.091%
(4)	imperfect indicative	11.303%	(14)	past perfect subjunctive	0.406%
(5)	gerund	4.110%	(15)	perfect infinitive	0.284%
(6)	present subjunctive	3.554%	(16)	present perfect subjunctive	0.154%
(7)	present perfect indicative	2.606%	(17)	future perfect indicative	0.098%
(8)	future indicative	2.268%	(18)	preterite perfect	0.005%
(9)	imperative	2.220%	(19)	future subjunctive	0.003%
(10)	past subjunctive	1.965%			

Additional statistics for specific works showed variation, for example, an increase of past-tense forms in a novel (preterite 22.417%, imperfect 15.673%, past subjunctive 2.816%). Bull proceeded to make a strong argument about the consequences of his study for Spanish language courses. Discuss the impact that these statistics might have on your "ideal syllabus" (question 12). As with the past tenses in narration, which forms tend to be associated with which communicative functions?

14. This chapter has treated mood in depth in order to present a variety ideas on explaining it to students. Apply this information now by studying the following examples of the two moods and addressing the following points:

(1) To what extent do the textbook explanations you are most familiar with cover these?
(2) How well do the theories discussed in this chapter account for them?

Whether by synthesizing others' theories or by developing your own, describe how you would explain mood contrasts to students. Compare your ideas with those of your classmates.

I. Some contexts admitting indicative only (or usually):
(a) El sol sale a las seis.
(b) (Recuerdo, Sé, Me doy cuenta de) que no sabes mi número.
(c) (Consta, Es verdad, Es obvio, Es evidente, Es cierto, Estoy seguro de) que se muere.
(d) (Ven, Oyen, Observan, Notan, Se dan cuenta, Comprenden) que es algo difícil.
(e) (Declaro, Afirmo, Supongo, Parece) que no se lo merecen.
(f) (Salimos, Saldremos) si hace buen tiempo.
(g) (Ésta es la mujer que) denunció el robo.
(h) (Volvieron porque, ya que, puesto que) les dolían los pies.
(i) (Volviste después que, cuando, en cuanto) surgieron problemas.

II. Some contexts admitting subjunctive only (or usually):
(a) (Puede, Es (im)posible, Es (im)probable, Es (in)concebible) que jueguen.
(b) (Rechazo, Dudo, Es dudoso, No es cierto, No es evidente, No es) que la paguen.
(c) (Prohíbo, Impido, Me opongo a, No es lícito) que Ud. lo estacione aquí.
(d) (Mando, Exijo, Ruego, Pido, Quiero, Prefiero, Se permite) que lo hagas así.
(e) (Necesito, Es necesario, Es importante, Conviene, Es regla general) que asistan.
(f) (Me gusta, Nos sorprende, Me alegro, Celebro, Estoy contento de) que os caséis.
(g) (Es un milagro/una barbaridad, Es triste/típico) que se hayan escapado.
(h) (Cruzan la calle antes que, con tal que, a menos que, para que) los vea el policía.
(i) (Saldrían si, Salían como si) hiciera buen tiempo.
(j) Ojalá que no llueva/lloviera.

III. Both, in contrast:
(a) (Dijo, Escribió, Murmuró, Hizo señas de) que firmaban/firmaran el contrato.
(b) (Insisto, Advierto, Sugiero, Pretendo) que no comen/coman productos lácteos.
(c) (Sospecho, Temo, Siento) que se van/vayan.
(d) (El ateísta no cree, no sabe, no está convencido de) que hay/haya un ser supremo.
(e) (Confío en, No es dudoso, Es lógico) que se ha/haya resuelto el problema.
(f) Se trata de que todos son/sean respetados.
(g) (Te dejaré el libro que, cuando, como, donde) quieres/quieras.
(h) (Vienen aunque, siempre que) nieva/nieve.
(i) No fracasas porque eres/seas incapaz (sino por pereza).
(j) (Dijo que vendrían en cuanto, después que, cuando) se acabó/acabara la fiesta.
(k) Por muy difícil que parece/parezca el asunto, vamos a solucionarlo.
(l) Esteban va cortando los árboles de modo que caen/caigan lindamente.
(m) Quizás tiene/tenga razón.
(Feel free to add examples of other instances.)

Chapter 8

Noun phrase syntax and morphology

8.0 Nouns and noun phrases. A noun with its adjacent modifiers, if any, constitutes a NOUN PHRASE, NP. Since pronouns (v. 9.0) and noun clauses (v. 13.0.1–13.1.3) occur in the same positions and with the same functions, many linguists generalize and call these NPs too. NPs are conspicuous in grammar because of their interaction with verbs and because of phenomena such as agreement holding inside them.

8.1 Functions of noun phrases with verbs. NPs have five main functions in the syntax of both Spanish and English: SUBJECT (Subj), DIRECT OBJECT (DO), INDIRECT OBJECT (IO), PREDICATE ATTRIBUTE (PA), and OBJECT OF A PREPOSITION (Obj of Prep, or OP). These are illustrated in figure 8.1.

Of the five, PA (the traditional "predicate nominative," v. 11.1.2) and OP (v. 10.2.2) are rather straightforward; PA follows a copula (verb of being) and OP is governed by a preposition. The other functions are more elusive and harder to define. Students with prior grammatical training in English or other languages may have a kind of feel for them that can help when they study Spanish. But many students today lack such a background, and when the textbook fails to explain Subj, DO, and IO clearly and accurately, the burden falls on the Spanish teacher. Describing these notions of general grammar inevitably takes valuable class time from practice with Spanish grammar in particular; yet simplistic definitions offered in the interest of brevity may leave students even more confused.

8.1.1 Subject and direct object. Suppose that we follow traditional grammar and tell students that Subj is the doer or agent, the entity that acts upon the verb and carries out the event. This works for most verbs of action, as in *Benjamín saltó* or *Benjamín me abrazó,* but what is to be done with the following?

Benjamín	padece una enfermedad grave.
	recibe cartas.

está sin empleo.
se parece a mi primo.
huele a cebolla.

In these sentences, Ben does nothing, carries out nothing, acts upon nothing; he is, in fact, quite passive. Technically (v. 5.2), the Subj here has the thematic role of "Patient," not "Agent." If we analogize from actors and actions and use "Agent" for explicating subjecthood in general, it is only as an approximation.

As for DO, the traditional definition that this is the NP that "receives" the action is literally in trouble with the receiving Subj of *recibir* and runs aground elsewhere too:

Luisa oyó a Ricky.
admiró
comprendió
grabó
recordó

Here, Ricky received nothing from Louise, was not acted upon in any clear sense, and may never have been directly affected by Louise's behavior. *A Ricky* merely completes directly (whence the apt Spanish term *complemento directo*), in a purely syntactic sense, the grammatical constituent beginning with the verb, that is, the verb phrase (VP) of the sentence.

As a second approach, we might appeal to syntactic characteristics, telling students that (1) Subj precedes the verb and DO follows it, (2) Subj is the NP a verb *must* have while DO is optional, and (3) Subj is the NP the verb agrees with. Of these, only (3) is reliable, but it is also circular since verbs agree with Subj NPs because these are Subj. The other two work fairly well in English but not in Spanish. In English, Subj usually precedes the verb, but Spanish syntax is freer (v. 11.2.2), and an English processing of word order will lead to the wrong results in *A Sergio lo odian todos sus vecinos.* As for optionality, it is true that English permits *John ate the custard* and *John ate,* but not just **Ate* or **Ate the custard,* so Subj is the required NP and DO is the optional one. But Spanish surface structure requires neither: *Juan comió el flan, Juan comió, Comió, Comió el flan.* Of course, the last two sentences have an "understood" or underlying Subj—*Juan*, or *él*—that is deleted after leaving its trace on the verb ending. But meteorological *hacer*

Figure 8.1. Five syntactic functions of NPs

Subj:	*El caballo* comenzó a correr.	*The horse* started to run.
DO:	Ayer vimos *el caballo.*	Yesterday we saw *the horse.*
IO:	(Le) di heno *al caballo.*	I gave *the horse* hay.
PA:	El animal más bello es *el caballo.*	The most beautiful animal is *the horse.*
OP:	Está encima de*l caballo.*	It's on *the horse.*

(*hace calor*) and existential *haber* (*hay un problema*) take DO but not Subj (v. 11.1.1), and *llover* and *tronar* normally take neither. In these cases, Spanish uses its 3sg. verb form not out of agreement with an underlying Subj but because this is the unmarked, neutral form (Suñer 1982, 182); *-o, -s, -mos, -n* carry more specific person and number information. Hence, Subj is optional in Spanish; English, on the other hand, requires Subj even in these cases, adopting an *it* with no reference and no meaning: *It's hot, It rained, It thundered* (v. 9.1.2).

Subj and DO are real notions of grammar that determine agreement, pronominalization, use of "personal" *a*, and word order. The verb agrees with Subj and is subcategorized according to whether it can take DO (TRANSITIVE verb, e.g., *comer*) or not (INTRANSITIVE verb, e.g., *morir*)—a crucial difference that dictionaries mark as *v.tr.* vs. *v.intr.*[1] Yet Subj and DO do not convey single meanings consistent with all verbs. More precisely, they are syntactic functions that do not match up with semantic functions or thematic roles (Dowty 1991). Fortunately, the Subj and Obj specifications of most Spanish verbs resemble those of their English counterparts, so that if students know that the Subj of *sow* is not the seed or the field but the sower, they can transfer this same knowledge to how *sembrar* is constructed. That, in fact, is implicit every time that *sembrar* or any other verb is given in a vocabulary list with an English gloss and no further instruction on usage. In the next three sections, however, we see less agreement between the two languages.

8.1.2 Indirect object: The involved entity. The IO in English is any entity to which or for which the Subj "verbs" the DO. This entity need not be a person: *I gave my attention to John/to the puppy/to the dahlias/to philosophy/to the issue at hand.* One English test for it is a transformation called DATIVE SHIFT, whereby the *to* or *for* is deleted and the IO flips over the DO: *I gave John (the puppy, the dahlias, philosophy, the issue at hand) my fullest attention.* By this test, the last NP in *I mailed the letter to Tanzania* is not IO (**I mailed Tanzania the letter*), but the one in *I mailed the letter to Tanya* is (*I mailed Tanya the letter*).[2]

English criteria again fail us in Spanish, however. *A* accompanies DO (v. 11.2.3) as well as IO, so the presence of a 'to' in front of NP does not uniquely identify a Spanish IO. There is no Dative Shift: the change *(le) di la cerveza a Juan →*(le) di Juan la cerveza* occurs in student interlanguage but is not Spanish. Yet the main difference is that the IO is used much more broadly in Spanish, not being restricted just to giving-to or doing-for. It represents a generalized involvement in or effect from the Subj + V (DO) event or relationship. Consequently, Bull (1965, 258) renamed it the INVOLVED ENTITY. The specific role of that involvement depends on the nature of the event—that is, on the verb—as illustrated by the following examples. (For others, see Goldin 1972; Davis 1969; RAE 1979, 205; and Butt and Benjamin 1988, 110).

Elena le	dio/mandó/escribió/mostró una carta *a José*.	'. . . to Joe'
	hizo/cocinó/compró la comida *a José*.	'. . . for Joe'
	quitó/exigió/escondió/robó la llave *a José*.	'. . . from Joe'

puso/echó/tendió otra sábana *a José*. '. . . on Joe'
notó/observó cierto desdén *a José*. '. . . in Joe'
apuntó/cambió/revisó el número *a José*. '. . . of Joe, Joe's'

Most textbooks fail to prepare students for this meaning of generalized involvement and for understanding and using the un-English IOs of *Le queda muy ajustado a José, Le quieren algo a José, Le fue bien a José, Le regañé el error a Juan*. Nor do they point out the systematic pattern of an IO that is *syntactically* "involved" with expressions that already have the DO position filled:

Elena le tiene miedo (toma el pelo, saca provecho, hace caso, hace frente) *a José*.
Elena le da cuerda (da media vuelta, echa un vistazo, echa la culpa) *al reloj*.

or the contrasts resulting from deletion of that DO (here, *dar/pegar un golpe, disparar un tiro*):

Elena le dio/pegó/disparó. 'Helen hit/beat/shot him.'
Elena lo dio/pegó/disparó. 'Helen gave/stuck/fired him.'

Some textbooks do, however, note the corollary case of involvement as possessor:

Elena le lavó el pelo *a José*. 'washed Joe's hair'
Elena le amarró los pies *a José*. 'bound Joe's feet'
Elena le admiró la estrategia *a José*. 'admired Joe's strategy'

That such IOs are nevertheless not equivalent to possessive *de* phrases was brought out by Kliffer (1979), who, like Bull, insisted that casting an NP as IO rather than as object of *de, para,* or *por* more strongly involves the entity in the event.[3]

With such broadness of meaning and multiplicity of specific roles, the Spanish IO is occasionally ambiguous: *Elena le compró la moto a José* can express a purchase from Joe or for his benefit. Fortunately, the ambiguity is more potential than real in most contexts.

8.1.3 Variation between direct and indirect objects. In Spanish, both kinds of Obj can be marked by *a*, and the distinction is observed in pronouns only in the third person non-reflexive, and is shaky even there (v. 9.1.3, 9.2, 9.4.1). Hence, DO and IO contrast most distinctly when both simultaneously accompany the same verb, as in the following VPs:

aconsejar(les) la buena conducta a los niños
enseñar(les) biología a los alumnos
reñir(le) el descuido a la secretaria

Cuervo (1948, 338) noted that when these verbs are used with only the *a*-phrases (i.e., for the meanings 'advise the children', 'teach the pupils', 'fuss at the secretary'), it is unclear whether *a* + NP stays IO or becomes DO. In fact, one hears both *aconsejarlos, enseñarlos, reñirla* and *aconsejarles, enseñarles, reñirle.* To these variable-object verbs can be added many others: for example, *ayudar, cansar, llamar, honrar, aventajar, escuchar, obligar, estorbar, convencer, obedecer, entender, hacer* + V (*hacer sufrir a alguien,* v. 13.1.2.5), *ver* + V (*ver salir a alguien*), as well as most PSYCH VERBS of psychological or emotional experience (*sorprender, preocupar, inquietar, distraer, molestar, alegrar*). Is this a kind of free variation—either Obj is permissible with no semantic difference—or does a Spanish speaker mean something different in choosing *aconsejarlos* over *aconsejarles* and *ayudarlo* over *ayudarle?*

García and Otheguy (1977) insisted that there is a difference. Returning to a case where objects contrast, *(Yo) le di una carta a Juan,* they postulated that Subj is the most active and potent participant, DO is the least, and IO falls in between, being less active than Subj but more potent than DO. When there is one Obj, there is the same contrast: the speaker's strategy is to use *verlo, ayudarlo, aconsejarlo* for a relatively inactive Obj, *verle, ayudarle, aconsejarle* for a more active or potent one. To test this hypothesis, they gave native speakers from six countries a questionnaire in which *le, lo,* or *la* was to be placed in blanks next to forms of *ayudar, llamar, distraer,* and *ver salir.* They found that the incidence of *le* rose when Subj was inanimate and less potent; that is, *le distrajo* was more likely for the Subj *el ruido* than for the Subj *Luisa.* The incidence of *le* also rose when the referent was male, a finding that required special explanation.[4]

In another experiment, Hurst (1951) limited the objects to feminine humans (to bypass the *leísmo* problem, v. 9.2.2). She found that choices between IO and DO were affected by two main factors. First, the more forceful, physical, or dynamic the event, the greater the preference was for DO with single-Obj verbs; thus, the incidence of DO rose higher with *irritar* 'physically irritate (e.g., the skin)' and *sorprender* 'show up unexpectedly' than for the same items as psych verbs for 'irk' and 'amaze'. Second, the incidence of IO shot up when the Subj was nonhuman. Both findings mesh with the García-Otheguy theory, but Hurst stated them as tendencies, not rules. That is, potency scales affect the role selection of NPs but do not dictate it. As we saw earlier, Subj is not necessarily active or potent, and IO—though always expressing some kind of involvement in Bull's sense—can be passive, remote, and impotent (Keniston 1937, 62). This is particularly evident with *gustar,* a verb that takes IO, never DO, regardless of how actively or passively one likes something, and its Subj is typically inactive. The García-Otheguy principle is to some extent constrained by another basic fact: NP roles are determined by the verb.

8.1.4 Different construction, "reverse" construction. English and Spanish do not always agree on how to cast the NPs accompanying their verbs (i.e., on the verb's construction with NPs, or *régimen,* as it is called in Spanish grammar):

wait *for the bus* (OP)	esperar *el autobús* (DO)
look *for a book* (OP)	buscar *un libro* (DO)
look *at the tower* (OP)	mirar *la torre* (DO)

ask/pay *Dad* (DO)	preguntar*le*/pagar*le a papá* (IO)
ask *a friend* (DO) *for money* (OP)	pedir*le dinero* (DO) *a un amigo* (IO)

Part of the problem is that certain verbs in both languages require prepositions in order to join up with an Obj NP (v. 10.4.2). But more generally, each verb seems to impose its own special *régimen.* Searching and waiting do not require OP in English because of their meaning, for alongside *wait for* and *look for* there are the synonyms *await* and *seek,* which take DO. And in giving, the presenter and the beneficiary are not irrevocably Subj and IO, since alongside *Fulano le da algo a Zutano* we can say *Zutano recibe algo de Fulano* for the same event.

All textbooks take up this problem in REVERSE CONSTRUCTION, by which is meant any case in which English and Spanish verbs have opposite *régimen.* The prototype is *like/gustar,* and in dealing with *Mary* (Subj) *likes oranges* (DO) vs. *A María le* (IO) *gustan las naranjas* (Subj), writers have proposed various strategies. One of the least conventional is that of LaMadrid, Bull, and Briscoe (1974a, 350 ff.), who introduce *gustar* only after preparing a cognitive grounding for it. First, they have students consider their English verb *disgust,* with which the displeased person appears as Obj and the unpleasant entity as Subj: *Mangos disgust Mary.* Spanish *disgustar* is similar, though the Obj is IO: *Los mangos le disgustan a María. Dis-* is a negative prefix, as in *displease, distrust, disobey*; hence the opposite of *disgust* should be *gust.* Of course, English has no such verb (aside from *gusting winds*), but one can get used to thinking in terms of it with a little imagination: *Mangos disgust Mary but oranges "gust" her a lot.* Spanish has "gust," it takes IO like *disgustar,* and students are now ready for *Las naranjas le gustan a María,* or with inversion (v. 11.2.3, 11.3.1), *A María le gustan las naranjas.*

Unfortunately, there are numerous other reverse construction verbs, as illustrated in figure 8.2, so inventing a one-time crutch for *gustar* takes the student no farther than this verb alone. The real problem here is not a lexical gap where *gust* should be in English, but the fact that *gustar* and its kinfolk in Spanish tend to be intransitive; a DO is therefore impossible and even the IO is not required: *Las pizzas siempre gustan.* As illustrated in figure 8.2, English actually permits several patterns. One option corresponding to *gustar, please,* is much closer to it syntactically than *like,* so if students must use an English crutch for *gustar*, *Oranges are pleasing to me* is more on target than *Oranges gust me.* Similarly, although *¿Qué te parece? No me importa* can be rendered as *What do you think of it? I don't care about it,* a syntactically closer equivalent is *How does it seem to you? It doesn't matter to me.*

Nor is a language that can recast *dar* as *recibir* limited to reverse construction: *A Juana le faltan recursos = Juana carece de recursos, A Juana le hace falta un curso avanzado = Juana necesita un curso avanzado, A Juana le da miedo = Juana lo teme.* Many psych verbs are especially versatile since they can be reflexivized (v. 9.3.7) for a different construction: *A Juana le aburre el arte = Juana se aburre del arte, A Juana le interesa el comercio = Juana se interesa en/por el comercio, A Juana le enfadó su novio = Juana se enfadó con su novio.* As shown by Whitley (1995a), these twin options are not always

Figure 8.2. Some reverse-construction verbs and their English equivalents

Spanish	English
aburrir: Le aburre la política.	He's bored with politics. Politics bores him.
bastar: Le basta harina.	She has enough flour. There's enough flour for her.
caer bien: Te cae bien.	It looks good on you. You look good in it.
costar: Eso me costó mucho.	I had a lot of trouble with that. That was really hard for me.
doler: Le duelen las encías.	His gums hurt (him), are hurting (him). He has sore gums.
encantar: Nos encanta la isla.	We love the island. The island delights us.
faltar: Te falta un botón.	You lack/are missing a button. A button's missing on your...'
gustar: Les gusta el queso	They like cheese. Cheese pleases/is pleasing to them.
importar: Me importas, hijo.	I care about you, son. You matter (you're important) to me, son.
interesar: Le interesa el arte.	She's interested in art. Art is interesting to her.
molestar: Les molesta el humo.	Smoke bothers them. They find smoke bothersome.
parecer: ¿Qué te parece?	What do you think of it? How does it seem to you?
quedar: Nos queda sólo uno.	We've only got one left. Only one is left for us (remains to us).
venir bien: Le viene bien.	She approves of it. It suits her, seems fine to her.

synonymous, but grammatically one does have some choice in verb construction for the casting of NPs.

Nevertheless, it is true that the psych verbs of English and Spanish have gravitated toward the patterns epitomized respectively by *I like it* vs. (*Eso*) *me gusta,* with the thematic role (v. 5.2) of Experiencer assigned to Subj in English but to Obj (especially IO) in Spanish. Whitley (1999) demonstrated this trend in a historical study of a large corpus of psych verbs in the two languages, from the earliest attestations to recent coinages such as *obsess* and *obsesionar*: compare *She obsesses over this* (Experiencer as Subj) vs. *Eso le obsesiona* (Experiencer as IO). Indeed, the prototypes themselves exemplified this evolution and crossed paths: *like* used to be like *gustar* (*it liketh me*) while *gustar* began with a *like*-like construction (*gusto de eso*) before crossing over into its present niche.

8.2 Noun morphology. The head of NP is the noun (N), and it shows two properties or grammatical features with which inflected modifiers agree: number and gender. Both are fundamental in morphology, and both tie in with how humans perceive and organize nature.

8.2.1 Number and the count/mass distinction. In most European languages, the noun is inflected for number. The ancestor of many of these languages, Proto-Indo-European, made a three-way distinction among SINGULAR (one of something), DUAL (a pair), and PLURAL (three or more). Some of its daughter languages retained this setup, but in the historical processes leading to Spanish (and other Romance languages) and to English (and other Germanic languages), it was reduced to just two terms, SINGULAR (one of something) and PLURAL (two or more).

It is a universal tendency in languages with a number distinction that the UNMARKED (plain) form serves for the singular while the MARKED one (the one with something added) represents the plural (Greenberg 1963, 94). Thus, in both Spanish and English, the singular ending is Ø (nothing) and the plural is a suffix—or suffixes, for the plural morpheme has allomorphs:

Spanish		English	
-es / {C, G} ____	(color-*es*, ley-*es*)	-[əz][5] / sibilant_______	(bush-*es*)
-s / V _________	(taza-*s*)	-[s] / voiceless ______	(hat-*s*, cup-*s*)
		-[z] / voiced ________	(dog-*s*, row-*s*, pin-*s*)

This case illustrates a recurrent theme in contrastive analysis: superficially, there is a convergence that could facilitate the student's task, but on closer scrutiny, major differences emerge. Here, both languages use alveolar sibilants to represent the plural and sometimes insert a vowel in front of them, resemblances that are reinforced by the same spelling for the sibilants (*s*) and for the inserted vowel (*e*). Yet the sibilant is phonetically [s] in Spanish but most often [z] in English; the inserted vowels ([e] and [ə]) are different; and the insertion occurs in a different place (after sibilants /s z ʃ ʒ tʃ dʒ/ in English, after all consonants and glides in Spanish); hence, English *color*[z], *ray*[z] but Spanish *color*[es], *rey*[es]. Many if not most Spanish speakers also extend the *-es* case to nouns ending in a stressed high vowel: *colibrí-es, tabú-es.*

In at least four other particulars, the pluralization patterns of the two languages seem more alike than they really are. First, a few nouns have a Ø plural suffix (i.e., the sibilant ending is dropped), so that the singular and plural are homophones. In English these are unpredictable from the sound or spelling: *these sheepØ* (vs. *these heaps*), *these deerØ* (vs. *these steers*). But in Spanish the deletion is predictable: /s/ drops as an ending after any unstressed vowel plus *s*:

$$s \rightarrow \emptyset / \ldots \breve{V}s+ \_\_\_$$

Hence, *el/los lunes, el/los análisis, el/los atlas, la/las caries, el/los paraguas, el/los virus* (but because of the final stress, *el compás, los compases*). The deletion also occurs after -V̆t (*el/los déficit*) and with family names (*los Montano*), not counting royalty (*los Habsburgos*).

Second, some words have not settled into normal patterns. In English, these include a few irregular Germanic plurals (*man men, foot feet*) and Latin or Greek loanwords that variably retain their classical plurals (*antennae ~ antennas, cacti ~ cactuses, curricula ~ curriculums,* etc.) The loanwords that vary in Spanish are Anglicisms ending in a consonant: *clubs ~ clubes, zigzags ~ zigzagues, gánsters ~ gánsteres.* Third, in both languages some nouns are always plural, and in this regard *scissors* and *tongs* agree with *tijeras* and *tenazas.* But *pliers* and *pants* are plural whereas Spanish has *un alicate* vs. *dos alicates* and (for many speakers) *un pantalón* vs. *dos pantalones. Clothes* is plural, *ropa* is singu-

Figure 8.3. Grammatical differences between count and mass nouns

	COUNT NOUN (*car, carro*)	MASS NOUN (*air, aire*)
1. can be pluralized? counted?	yes	no
2. occur with *a(n), un(a)*?	yes	no
3. occur with *some* [sm̩], *much, un poco de*?	no	yes
4. occur as a "naked noun" (no modifier: *I have__, tengo __*)	no	yes

lar; *vacation* and *funeral* contrast with *vacations* and *funerals* while Spanish generalizes the plurals *vacaciones* and *funerales.* The number for nouns in *-ics (acoustics, genetics, politics)* is unsettled in English but *-ica* is singular in Spanish. *People* has no plural suffix but is grammatically plural (*these people are*), but *gente* is singular, with *gentes* for subgroups. Other English collective nouns (*family, faculty,* and, in British, *the government*) vary between singular because of form and plural because of meaning; in Spanish, grammatical number takes precedence over semantic plurality.

Fourth, in both languages some nouns are ordinarily not pluralized at all because they are mass nouns. In our environment, some entities occur as individual units with physical boundaries delineating them from the rest of the world: *carrot, car, pen, island, animal, planet.* These are COUNT NOUNS, because their referents are discrete and stable enough to be counted in quantity: *one carrot, two cars, three pens.* Other entities, however, occur not as self-contained things that can be counted but as shapeless substance or abstraction: *water, soil, peace, air, gravitation.* These are treated as MASS NOUNS, which contrast with count nouns as shown in figure 8.3.

Yet one can count mass nouns indirectly by imposing form or measure on them, as in *a cup of water, two cubic meters of air, three bars of soap.* Expressions such as *a bar of* are called COUNTERS and they contrast interlingually: *three bars of soap, tres panes de jabón* (see Stockwell, Bowen, and Martin 1965, 82 ff., for other examples). Also, one can pluralize mass nouns to indicate not exemplars of a count entity but servings (*two* ***milks****, please*) or types (*sugars* and *salts* in chemistry) of the substance. More limited is a third practice of pluralizing mass nouns for metaphorical senses: *take the waters, hacer las paces.*

The count/mass distinction is less obvious when extended to things that are not readily classifiable as either discrete units or shapeless substance. *Egg* is a count noun when the egg is bounded by a shell or emptied into a puddle, but smeared or scrambled it becomes a mass noun, as in *You've got egg (*an egg) on your chin. Rock* and *stone* are mass as a material, count as a chunk that can be lifted and thrown. And when looking at rice, does one see a mass of white substance (like flour) or a pile of small things (like peas)? The grammatical solutions to such quandaries can be arbitrary, so two languages may not arrive at the same classification. English and Spanish happen to agree that *egg/huevo* and *stone/piedra* can be count or mass, and that *rice/arroz* is mass, but there are cases where they differ, as shown in figure 8.4 (see also Prado 1989). If there is a tendency here, it is

Figure 8.4. Differences in mass/count classification

(a) English mass noun vs. Spanish count noun	
(a piece of) furniture	un mueble, unos muebles
(a slice of) toast	un tostado, unos tostados
(a bolt of) lightning	un rayo (relámpago), unos rayos (relámpagos)
(an item of) news	una noticia, unas noticias
(a piece of) candy	un dulce (bombón), unos dulces (bombones)
(a bit/piece of) advice	un consejo, unos consejos
(a piece of) junk	una porquería, unas porquerías

(b) English mass noun vs. Spanish mass or count noun	
(an item of) information, business	información(es), negocio(s)
(a piece of) luggage	equipaje(s)
(a stick of) chalk, gum	tiza(s), chicle(s)
(a bout of) diarrhea	diarrea(s)
(a round of) applause	aplauso(s)

that Spanish more readily "countifies" than English (Stockwell, Bowen, and Martin 1965). Thus, English speakers may resist pluralizing a Spanish noun that, from their perspective, should be mass; and since dictionaries seldom identify countness, there is little help there. But with gender, our next topic, dictionaries are much more informative.

8.2.2 Gender. The rationale for a gender distinction resembles that for count/mass, but it tends to be more salient to biological language users. Just as in nature there are many entities that are easily classifiable as count or mass, many entities are clearly of either male or female sex. This natural distinction is the origin of the masculine/feminine distinction in Spanish (*el muchacho, la muchacha*) and in English (*the boy . . . he, the girl . . . she*)—or, more generally, in Indo-European. But like count/mass, gender becomes blurred when extended to the large realm of sexless things. In Proto-Indo-European, the distinction became grammaticalized and all nouns—sexed or sexless—came to be classified as MASCULINE, FEMININE, or NEUTER (Latin for 'neither'), often arbitrarily. Latin inherited this setup, but as it passed on to Spanish, the neuter fell out ("neuter" *lo, esto,* etc., evolving in another direction; v. 8.4.2). This was just as well, since the Latin neuter included some obviously sexed creatures and its masculine and feminine already swarmed with sexless things and abstractions. English went a step further by dropping the gender distinction entirely except for sexed referents; something that is sexually neither a *he* nor a *she* is an *it*.

In Spanish one rarely uses a noun without marking its gender, thanks to the required agreement of modifiers. Spanish speakers therefore get abundant practice with gender from infancy onward and the decision to say *la sal es blanca* instead of **el sal es blanco* takes no more effort than for an adult English speaker to say *she thought* instead of **she thinked.* But masculine and feminine seem unfathomable to English speakers, especially

Figure 8.5. Bull's statistics on gender classification according to noun ending

-n (excluding *-ción, -sión*): 96.3% M	**-a**: 98.9% F
-o: 99.7% M	**-d**: 97% F
-r: 99.2% M	**-ción, -sión**: 100% F
-s: (excluding *-tis, -sis*): 92.7% M	**-sis, -tis**: 99.2% F
-e: 89.2% M	
-l: 96.6% M	

for things. Why is *idioma* masculine but its synonym *lengua* feminine? Is it *el* or *la mar, el* or *la fin*?[6]

Fortunately, gender is partly predictable. One clue is orthographic/phonemic, namely, how the noun ends. Expanding on the traditional rule that *-o* signals masculines (usually) and *-a* feminines (usually), Bull (1965, 109) offered the statistics in figure 8.5 for the gender of nouns. Nouns in *-z* "show no significant statistical pattern" (p. 108) and are as likely to be feminine as masculine, and although he also supplied data for *-b, -c, -ch, -i, -m, -t, -y,* and so on, such nouns are too few to justify pedagogical rules for them. One can therefore memorize an acronym such as *NORSEL* (LaMadrid, Bull, and Briscoe 1974a, 104) or *LONERS* (Briscoe and LaMadrid 1978, 2) for masculines. Other linguists, such as Bergen (1978b) and Teschner (2000b, 186 ff.), have extended this treatment with statistical refinements from further data.

A head count does not take word frequency into account, however. About 99 percent of Spanish nouns in *-o* and *-a* are respectively masculine and feminine, but the 1 percent of misbehavers in each class includes everyday words that are encountered early by the student. *Día* and *mano* come to mind immediately; figure 8.6 lists other common exceptions to a *NORSEL* rule. Obviously, students who guess that their first 100 nouns ending in *-l* will be 96.6 percent masculine will not make 3.4 and only 3.4 mistakes, for their sampling in vocabulary lists is not that of the lexicographer. They will also run across homonymous pairs with different genders, as illustrated in figure 8.7.

The other criterion for gender is meaning. To be sure, there are many masculine/feminine pairs with no consistent semantic underpinnings, as in *el mango/la manga* and the

Figure 8.6. Common exceptions to the *NORSEL* rule

-n = F:	imagen, opinión, región, religión, razón, sartén, virgen
-o = F:	mano, moto, foto, polio
-r = F:	flor, labor, mujer
-s = F:	diabetes, res, sintaxis, tos, caries
-e = F:	calle, carne, clase, costumbre, fuente, leche, llave, muerte, noche, nube, sangre, tarde
-l = F:	cárcel, col, piel, sal, señal, vocal
-a = M:	clima, día, drama, mapa, planeta, poema, problema, programa, síntoma, sistema, tema
-d = M:	ardid, ataúd, césped

Figure 8.7. Examples of masculine/feminine homonyms

el canal 'canal, channel'	la canal 'gutter'
el capital 'money'	la capital 'capital city'
el cólera 'cholera'	la cólera 'anger, rage'
el coma 'coma'	la coma 'comma'
el cometa 'comet'	la cometa 'kite'
el corte 'cut'	la corte 'court'
el cura 'priest'	la cura 'cure'
el frente 'front'	la frente 'forehead'
el orden 'order, arrangement'	la orden 'order, command'
el papa 'pope'	la papa 'potato'
el parte 'communiqué'	la parte 'part'
el pendiente 'pendant'	la pendiente 'slope, grade'

others shown in figure 8.8 (see also Batchelor and Pountain 1992, 46–52), but meaning can help nonetheless. Names of rivers, trees, ships, days, and months are masculine, as if referring to *río, árbol, barco, día, mes*; especially noteworthy is the pattern of *el árbol/la fruta* in *naranjo/naranja, avellano/avellana, peral/pera, manzano/manzana*. And of course, nouns referring to persons tend toward sex gender, and at this point the Spanish system comes into sharp focus by matching masculine/feminine with male/female. There are four main morphological patterns:

1. different roots: *el padre/la madre, el hombre/la mujer, el yerno/la nuera*
2. common roots with idiosyncratic derivational suffixes: *el actor/la actriz, el rey/la reina, el poeta/la poetisa, el héroe/la heroína*
3. same word, with gender assigned according to sex: *el/la idiota, el/la homicida, el/la hincha, el/la atleta, el/la artista, el/la testigo, el/la joven, el/la mártir, el/la modelo, el/la cantante, el/la reo, el/la estudiante* (but always *la gente, la persona, la víctima, la criatura*)
4. same stem, with a femininizing *-a* added to the masculine and replacing its *-e* or *-o* if present: *el abuelo/la abuela, el hijo/la hija, el viudo/la viuda, el monje/la monja, el señor/la señora, el español/la española, el profesor/la profesora, el huésped/la huéspeda, el autor/la autora*

In ranks or roles that women have entered only fairly recently, there is some uncertainty about which pattern to apply (De Mello 1990). Some speakers follow pattern (3) and say *la jefe, la presidente, la médico*; others opt for pattern (4) and say *la jefa, la presidenta, la médica.* Part of the problem comes from competing patterns in which the masculine represents a person (traditionally male) and the feminine is preempted for something else (Bergen 1980): the field or profession (*el físico/la física, el matemático/la matemática, el gramático/la gramática*) or a collective group (*el policía/la policía, el*

Figure 8.8. Some pairs in *-o/-a* differing idiosyncratically in meaning

el barco 'ship'	la barca 'small boat'
el brazo 'arm'	la braza 'breast stroke, fathom'
el cargo 'position, job, responsibility'	la carga 'cargo, load, charge'
el cuchillo 'knife'	la cuchilla 'cleaver'
el fruto 'fruit (metaphorical)'	la fruta 'fruit (food)'
el huerto 'vegetable garden'	la huerta 'large farming area'
el huevo 'egg'	la hueva 'roe, spawn'
el hoyo 'hole, dent'	la hoya 'pit'
el leño 'log'	la leña 'firewood'
el mango 'handle; mango'	la manga 'sleeve; hose'
el marco 'framework'	la marca 'mark, brand'
el partido 'party; match, game'	la partida 'departure; certificate'
el puerto 'port'	la puerta 'door'
el velo 'veil'	la vela 'sail; candle'

escolta/la escolta). So one may well hesitate to call a female musician *la música* 'the music' or a female chemist *la química* 'the chemistry'.

Similar to the ambiguous area between count and mass is EPICENE gender: human nouns and pronouns that refer to neither sex in particular but to either or both. In English, there have been four main treatments of epicenes (Whitley 1978): words such as *parent, driver, child, who, anyone,* and *nobody* are referred to by *he* (traditionally prescribed), by *he or she* or *he/she* (current but awkward), by *s/he* (succinct but unpronounceable), and by singular *they* (nonstandard but widespread, convenient, and longstanding). In Spanish, the student must realize, whatever his, his/her, s/his, or their stance on sexism in language, that it is the masculine gender that generally handles epicenes. In *Necesito otro consejero* or *¿Hay profesores arriba?*, the speaker may be referring to males only or to males plus females or to anyone regardless of sex; the same applies to *los padres, los hijos, los españoles,* and pronouns such as *nosotros* and *ellos*. From one point of view, then, the Spanish "masculine" gender ([+masculine]) should be renamed "nonfeminine' ([-feminine]) to indicate that this category means 'not exclusively females'.[7]

Spanish differentiates the sexes of the higher or more familiar animals according to human patterns, as does English to some extent: *gato/gata, perro/perra, vaca/toro, carnero/oveja, zorro/zorra, león/leona, tigre/tigresa, mono/mona, ganso/gansa*; compare English *lion/lioness, fox/vixen, stallion/mare*. In both languages, the epicene treatment M + F = M prevails for the species: *lion + lioness = lions, león + leona = leones*. In some cases, the species name is distinct: *buck + doe = deer, stallion + mare = horses, gallo + gallina = pollos, toro + vaca = reses*; or it may be the feminine term: *drake + duck = ducks, carnero + oveja = ovejas*. Wilder animals arbitrarily end up in one gender or the other in Spanish: *el chimpancé, el rinoceronte, el canguro, el tiburón, la jirafa, la liebre, la cebra, la ballena, la comadreja*. If the sexes must be distinguished, *macho* and *hembra* are added, yielding a pattern of misagreement: *el chimpancé hembra, la jirafa macho.* Lower animals and plants are undifferentiated, as though—aside from biologists and gardeners—no one cared about the sex of these (compare English *it* here): *el mosquito, la mosca, el sapo, la rana, el gusano, la culebra, la abeja, el lagarto, el acebo.*

One complication of the gender system is what could be called the "transvestite" *el,* which is *la* in disguise. *La* becomes *el* when directly preceding a noun beginning with /á-/, although the noun stays feminine. Textbooks bring this out for *el agua,* but the pattern is general: *el álgebra, aula, acta, hacha, ala, ave, hambre, alma,* and so on. Historically, this *el* is not the masculine article at all but a relic of the earlier feminine article *ela,* which contracted to *el'* in these cases but to *'la* in all others, including nouns with initial unstressed /a/, as in *la acera (habilidad, atmósfera). Una* became *un'* in the same environment (*un aula, ala, arma*). But students are confused because they learn articles as markers of gender: *el agua* should be masculine, like *el día.* Native speakers are sometimes confused, too, to judge from the fact that *el arte* wound up as masculine in the singular; compare *las artes.* The rule is now a strange one, since it does not apply before an adjective beginning with /á-/ (*el agua agria, la agria agua*), nor to names of letters (*la a, la hache*).

8.3 Modifiers in the noun phrase. As defined earlier, NP is a noun plus any modifiers accompanying it, or any constituents that can substitute for it or occur in the same syntactic slots. In the following sections, the system of constituents that can make up NP is investigated in terms of English and Spanish phrase structure rules (v. 5.2); subsequently, the morphology and usage of the inflected noun modifiers in NP are discussed.

8.3.1 Noun phrase constituents. The phrase structure rules given in figure 8.9 present the main options available for the construction of NP in English and Spanish. These formulas summarize a great deal of information. In each one, the first line indicates that NP can consist of a sequence of the following elements: an optional determiner, D (= articles, demonstratives, preposed possessives); an optional quantifier, Quant *(= two, five, many, few,* etc.); any number of adjectives, Adj (the raised ^{n} = choosable any ***n***umber of times); the head noun, N; and optional prepositional phrases, PP. Only N is required in this lineup (but v. 8.4); the other constituents are optional and arranged in the order shown if any of them appear. The second line states that the NP can alternatively consist of an NP conjoined with any number of other NPs by conjunctions (Conj). The third line represents an NP with a relative clause (. . . *who voted,* . . . *que votaron*), which is a sentence S that modifies D + N, D + Adj + N, or whatever (v. 13.3.1 for relative clause formation). The fourth line is for pronouns, and the fifth is for embedded sentences that act like NP, the traditional "noun clauses"—for example, ***That you work so hard*** *surprises me* (v. 13.1).

As shown, the Spanish PSR (phrase structure rule) is similar to the English one.[8] At this level, the only apparent difference is that the Spanish NP has two normal positions for its Adj (the postposed one being repeatable), a fact that will be taken up later in the discussion of word order (v. 11.3.2). There are other differences as well that cannot be

Figure 8.9. Options for noun phrase structure

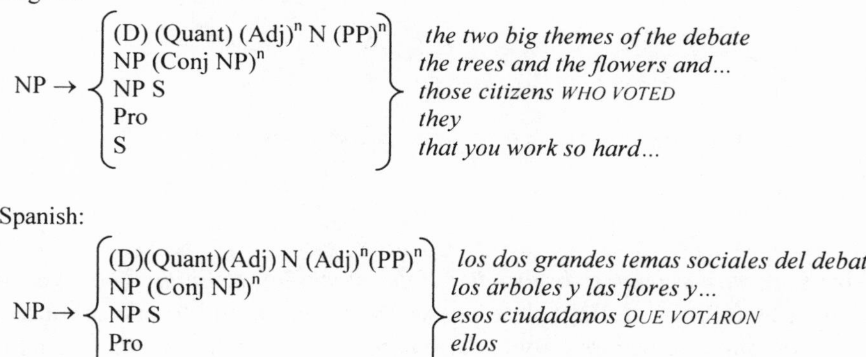

shown in these generalized formulas, and the following sections concentrate on three of them: possessives, articles and demonstratives, and agreement.

8.3.2 Possession and other noun-to-noun relationships. English speakers have two means of expressing possession inside NP: with a possessive NP in the determiner (D) slot, and with a postposed NP introduced by *of* in the PP slot. These are illustrated in figure 8.10 by means of phrase markers based on the PSR for NP given in the preceding section.

Spanish has the former option (preposed, in D) only when the possessor is pronominal, in which case *yo* → *mi, tú* → *tu, nosotros/-as* → *nuestro,* and so on. Since English pronouns also form possessive determiners (*I* → *my, we* → *our,* and so on), these forms give little trouble for the most part. In the third person, however, the male/female and singular/plural distinctions of the corresponding pronouns are neutralized in Spanish: *él ella ellos ellas usted ustedes* → *su.* Many students are slow to accept this neutralization, for their English experience demands at least a distinction between *su* for the singular possessors *él ella usted* and *sus* for the plural ones. Instead of using the PP alternatives (e.g., *de él, de usted, de ellos*) for clarification as Spanish speakers do, they adopt *su casa, *su casas* for 'his, her, your house(s)' and **sus casa, sus casas* for 'their, your house(s)'. This error is persistent even for students who have otherwise mastered agreement. (For the long-form possessives *mío tuyo suyo*, v. 8.4.1 and 11.3.2.)

When the possessor is a noun or noun-based NP instead of a pronoun, Spanish puts it in the PP: *las acciones de la empresa.* Beginning students understand this pattern because it is an option in English too, but in active performance they occasionally forget that it is the only option in Spanish in this case. Fortunately, errors such as **la empresas acciones* need not be corrected too many times before students get the point. Another difference is that Spanish optionally uses the postposed pattern even for pronominal possessors, con-

Figure 8.10. Two ways of expressing possession

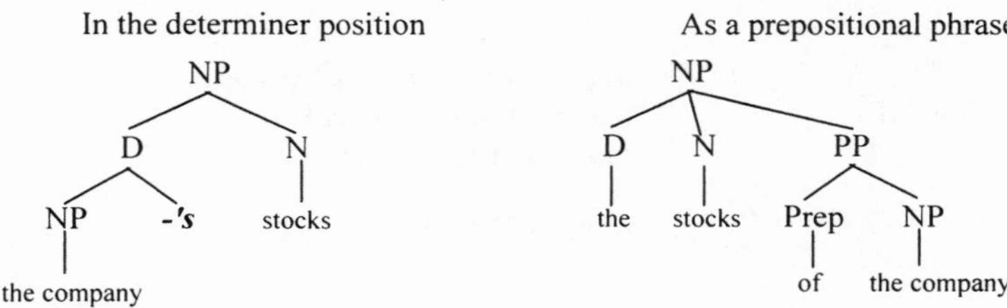

trary to English usage: *las acciones de usted/él, *the stocks of you/him.* The two languages thus contrast as follows: in English, a possessive noun-based NP can occur as D or as PP but a pronominal one occurs only as D, whereas in Spanish a possessive noun-based NP occurs as PP but a pronominal one as either D or PP.[9]

When leading off a PP after the head noun, *of* and *de* indicate not only possession but, more broadly, modification of the head noun by a second NP. Specific relationships are expressed by more specific prepositions in English, where Spanish tends toward *de* with any NP that identifies the head noun:

the girl *with* the green eyes	la chica *de* los ojos verdes
the woman *from* Denmark	la mujer *de* Dinamarca
the statue *in* the park	la estatua *de*l parque
the best hotel *in* Malaga	el mejor hotel *de* Málaga

For locative relationships with some other preposition, Spanish tends to switch to a relative clause, which is an alternative in English too:

the guest (who's) at the door	el invitado que está a la puerta
the book (that's) under the table	el libro que está debajo de la mesa

But Spanish does allow other NP-to-N connectors besides *de*. *Con* and *sin* appear when accompaniment and its lack are meant literally: *arroz con pollo, café con/sin leche, frascos con/sin fecha. Para* appears when the PP indicates purpose: *cartas para ti, cajas para cigarros, ropa para caballeros.* Abstract nouns are constructed with special prepositions: *interés en la política, afición a los deportes, enojo con su novia, repudio a drogadictos, invitación a una fiesta, habilidad en los idiomas, su fe en Cristo, semejanza a la poesía, derecho a libertad de cultos, remedio contra amibas*. To a certain extent, such NPs recreate VP structure: *Dios ama al hombre* → *el amor de Dios al hombre.*[10] A French-like *a* for manner has also entered the language: *un juguete a pilas, asesinato a patadas.* Prepositional usage is difficult to pin down, descriptively or pedagogically, and it often enters the realm of idiom (v.10.4).

A major source of interference in learning Spanish is the fact that nonpossessive N_1 *of* N_2 relationships in English may be changed to N_2 N_1; the stress pattern is usually the compounding Ń Ǹ but sometimes the phrasal Ǹ Ń (v. 4.1.2):[11]

the bottom of the lake → the láke bòttom
a leg of a chair → a cháir lèg
a watch of gold → a gòld wátch
the economy of the world → the wòrld ecónomy

There is no theoretical limit to how many English nouns can be piled up in this way: the following example shows four.

a manufacturer of screws of furniture of metal → a metal furniture screw manufacturer

This pattern is highly productive in English (v. 15.1.2) but severely limited in Spanish. Even when N + N occurs, it is the second noun that modifies the first, the reverse of English usage: *esposa modelo (model wife), caso límite (borderline case), lengua madre (mother tongue).* Otherwise, English N_2 + N_1 generally corresponds to N_1 Prep N_2 in Spanish:

bookshelf, estante para libros
teacup, taza para té
gold watch, reloj de oro
bus station, estación de autobuses
data banks, bancos de datos
noodle soup, sopa de fideos
tomato seeds, semillas de tomate
color TV, televisión en colores
six-cylinder engine, motor de seis cilindros
winter clothes, ropa de invierno
orange juice, jugo de naranja
physics book, libro de física
sodium chloride, cloruro de sodio
history files, archivos de historia

The same difference appears when the modifying N is a nominalized verb, which will be a gerund in English but an infinitive in Spanish (v. 6.3.2):

sewing machine	máquina de coser
writing table	mesa de escribir

Alternatively, Spanish switches to an adjective:

world problems	problemas del mundo = problemas mundiales

For this purpose, the language has a more productive derivational morphology (v. 15.1.1) than English:

problemas de impuestos /de petróleo /de automóviles / de universidades / de la frontera
→ problemas impositivos / petroleros / automovilísticos / universitarios / fronterizos

8.3.3 Articles, demonstratives, and other determiners. Following classical grammar, words such as *a(n)* and *the* were classified as ARTICLES, *this* and *that* as DEMONSTRATIVES, and *my your their* as possessive adjectives, and modifiers like *such* and *no* were left in limbo. The syntax of both English and Spanish treats all these as subclasses of one category "determining" the noun's reference, and it assigns them to the same syntactic slot. To capture this generalization, linguists call them DETERMINERS.[12]

The nonpossessive determiners match up fairly well in the two languages except for the difference in inflection: *the = el, la, los, las*; *a(n), some = un, -a, -os, -as*; *no, (not . . .) any = ningún(o), -a*; *this, these = este, -a, -os, -as*; *that, those = ese, -a, -os, -as (aquel, -lla, -llos, -llas*), and so on. The agreement on these determiners is much closer than between either language and, say, Russian. Nevertheless, students must revise their English system of spatial orientation for 'that'. They have little trouble grasping that *ese* (with *ahí*) refers to something at an intermediate distance, often near the addressee, while *aquel* (with *allí, allá*) refers to something more remote from speaker and addressee, 'over there, over yonder'; *yonder,* in fact, is a relic of a similar distinction English once had. In active practice, though, students sometimes confuse *ese* with *aquel* because of English *that*, or with *este* because they differ in a mere /t/.

The articles of both languages have two main functions. First, the indefinite article is used for introducing a singular count noun into conversation or discourse for the first time: *I saw a horse.* This article is related to *one*—obviously so in Spanish, but etymologically *a(n)* was once an unstressed allomorph of *one* in English too—and it selects one member out of a class for comment. *Vi un caballo afuera* means 'of all horses I might discuss, I am selecting one I saw outside and proceeding to tell you about it'. After this introduction, the speaker switches to definite reference (a definite pronoun or definite determiner) to maintain what Bull (1965, 216) called "common focus" or what Alonso (1974, 158) called "lo consabido en la esfera de atención." Hence, *Vi* ***un*** *caballo afuera.* ***El*** *caballo se comía tus petunias, mami.* If the speaker instead proceeds to say *Un caballo se comía tus petunias, mami,* the listener infers that there was another horse or that the speaker is confused. But for objects that are already identifiable in the context, speakers take shortcuts to definite reference; just as our planet has one sun, which is *el sol* (and need not be introduced first as *un sol*), one often strikes up a conversation about *el presidente, el bebé, la escalera, el tren, la sala, el partido,* or *el inodoro,* and the referents of these NPs will be clear on first mention to those who share the same situation or cultural niche.

The second main function of articles is to indicate GENERIC REFERENCE, all members of a group in general: *A/The cat has four legs, Un/el gato tiene cuatro patas.* These signify that cats in general, any and all of them, have four legs—not this cat, that cat, or a particular cat I am focusing on to discuss as an individual, but the entire set of domestic felines.

Spanish and English mainly differ on how these shared meanings are applied to four specific contexts where one language uses an article and the other dispenses with it.

1. With titles and names:
   Vi al señor/general/profesor López en la Calle Kennedy.
   I saw (*the) Mister/General/Professor Lopez on (*the) Kennedy Street.

Both languages use a definite article for established reference in *Vi al general en la calle, I saw the general on the street,* but when the name of the person or street is added, English drops the article. In vocatives, however, in which one addresses people instead of referring to them, both languages omit the article: *¡General López!*

2. With nonspecific dates:

Lo terminarán el lunes.	They'll finish it (on) Monday.

Both languages use the definite article for specific dates that are modified: *Lo terminarán el último lunes del mes, They'll finish it (on) the last Monday of the month.* English drops it otherwise, and also when the modifier is *next* or *last* with reference to the present point: *next Monday* (but in a narrative, *on the next Monday*). Spanish, though, retains the article for all such dates, as well as in time-telling (*son las tres, a las tres*).

3. In generic references:

Me gustan las papas.	I like potatoes.
El hombre es mortal.	Man is mortal.
Los seres humanos son mortales.	Human beings are mortal.

As noted earlier, both languages express genericity with articles. In English, however, a competing pattern with Ø (no determiner) has won out with plurals and certain singulars (Quirk et al. 1972, 147). The Spanish construction is consistent, and the English speaker has only to learn that generic reference regularly requires the article in Spanish. The Spanish-speaking student of English encounters an apparent grammatical anarchy:

The tiger *has four legs* = generic or particular	***The man*** *has two legs* = particular only
Tiger *has four legs* = proper name	***Man*** *has two legs* = generic

4. In nonparticular references:

Jorge salió sin abrigo.	George left without a coat.
¿Tiene hijo tu prima?	Does your cousin have a child?
Nora suele llevar sombrero.	Nora generally wears a hat.
Mauricio es arquitecto.	Maurice is an architect.

Here it is Spanish that, to the student, is oddly omitting articles. But *un* retains its value of 'one', and in these cases the speaker is not selecting one and only one entity from a group, but referring to unquantified membership in the group denoted by the "naked" noun. Omission of *un* signifies that the noun is being used for its sense alone, without reference to an individual (Suñer 1982, 219). The real force of *sin abrigo* is 'coatlessness', that of *tiene hijo* is 'parenthood', that of *es arquitecto* is 'membership in the architectural profession'. Spanish may show a contrast between Ø and *un*: *¿Sabes que Nora ha comprado automóvil?* implies the status of car ownership, while *¿Sabes que Nora ha comprado un automóvil?* introduces a particular car, and just one, into the conversation (Alonso 1974, 136). If there is any reason why English does use *a(n)* here despite the lack of individualization, it is because its nongeneric singular count nouns are not used without some kind of D: **George left without coat, *Nora has bought car.*

In short, speakers of the two languages agree on the functions of articles but differ in fairly circumscribed omissions for the NAKED NOUN construction Ø + N. The problem becomes more confused than it really is only when students are led to adjust Spanish grammar to English through the addition of ad hoc amendment rules to English ("Do use the article here, *don't* use it there"). As Bull (1965, 221) expressed it, "the student . . . is taught to project English patterns onto Spanish except when he is told not to. He operates, consequently, with a set of exceptions to his English intuition rather than with a clear understanding of how the Spaniard organizes reality. Moreover, the number of rules needed to define the Spanish exceptions to English patterns exceeds the number needed to describe the entire Spanish system." In the usual textbook lists of "uses of the articles," it is easy to lose sight of the forest in focusing on each tree.

8.3.4 Adjectives and agreement. Within the NP, the head noun's grammatical features of gender and number spread to its inflected modifiers (v. 5.2). Bull (1965, 105) described this as a process of "matching": one says *la otra hija morena* because the modifiers take on the *-a* of the noun, matching its form. But "matching" is unhelpful in *aquel pobre país destruido*, and little is gained by the change in terminology. The traditional term AGREEMENT remains as good as any other.

The difference between English and Spanish is not in absence versus presence of agreement, but in its extent. In English, only a few determiners agree, and then just in number: *this nail/these nails, a nail/some nails*. In Spanish, agreement in number and gender is carried out over everything in the NP except PP (figure 8.11), and is also extended to a PA inside VP.

Ideally, a modifier will have four forms corresponding to the N's four values for the features [gender] and [number]: masc. sg., masc. pl., fem. sg., fem. pl. This parallelism is exact for an adjective like *alto, -os, -a, -as* (like *abuelo, -os, abuela, -as*) or *hablador, -es, -a, -as* (like *profesor, -es, profesora, -as*). It breaks down in four cases, however.

1. The masc. sg. of articles and demonstratives is irregular: *el, los, la, las*;[13] *este, -os, -a, -as*; *ese, -os, -a, -as*; *aquel, -llos, -lla, -llas.* The expected "matching" forms in *-o, lo esto eso aquello,* are preempted for the neuter (v. 8.4.2).
2. Most numerical quantifiers—cardinal numbers in particular—agree semantically with plural nouns without showing the agreement morphologically: *cuatro*

Figure 8.11. Agreement inside NP

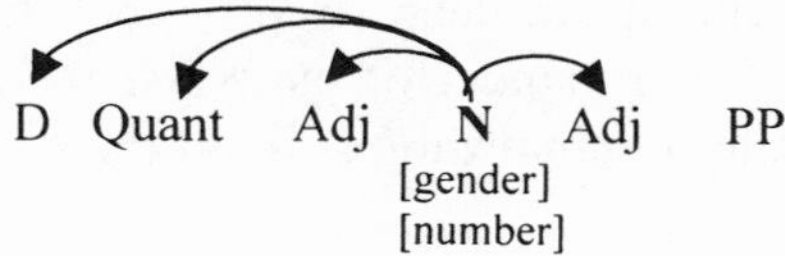

(*cuatras) cuerdas.* Only *uno* and *-cientos* forms (including *quinientos*) have overt gender and number agreement.

3. Adjectives, and the possessive determiners (*mi, nuestro*) and noncardinal quantifiers (*segundo, mucho*) that act like them morphologically, sort out into two distinct groups: FOUR-FORM and TWO-FORM. They have four forms if their masc. sg. ends in *-o*: *alto, nuestro, mucho -a, -os, -as.* They have only two (singular/plural, with no gender marking) if their masc. sg. ends in *any other way*, as illustrated below:

mi, mis	común, comunes	cortés, corteses	indígena, indígenas
su, sus	verde, verdes	mejor, mejores	agrícola, agrícolas
cursi, cursis	feliz, felices	joven, jóvenes	realista, realistas

There are two sets of exceptions. First, adjectives that should have two forms since they end in "any other way" are given four forms if they denote nationality, ethnicity, religious affiliation, or a similar concept and end in a consonant (*español, francés, musulmán, andaluz -es, -a, -as*), or if they end in *-dor, -ón, -ote, -án* (*conservador, trabajador, chillón, holgazán, -es, -a, -as*). Second, an adjective has only one form if it ends in -V̆s (*gratis, isósceles* like *atlas, caries*), or if it is still regarded as a noun or a foreign word (*camisas lila/naranja/rosa/café/beige/sexy*).

4. A few adjectives and quantifiers shorten or APOCOPATE before a masculine singular N: *un* (and *veintiún*), *primer, tercer, ningún, buen, mal, algún, postrer.* Two-form modifiers are gender-blind in apocopation: *gran, cualquier.* Formerly, *ciento ~ cien* was explained in the same way—*hay ciento* but *cien árboles*; but *cien* is now generalized (*hay cien*), with the form *ciento* being more restricted to numbers 101–99 (*cien, ciento uno, ciento dos . . . ciento noventa y nueve*).

8.4 NP without N. The PSRs in section 8.3.1 provide for optional modifiers with an obligatory noun. Thus, as the DO of *ver,* we could say *Veo unos cerdos, Veo aquellos cerdos hambrientos, Veo los cinco cerdos gordos de Ramón,* or simply *Veo cerdos.* D, Adj, Quant, and PP are grammatically optional elements arranged around the head N *cerdos.* Yet there are two cases in which the modifiers appear with no head, as discussed in the following sections.

8.4.1 Nominalization and pronominalization. Sometimes the missing noun is understood from the context, and modifiers show agreement with it. The usual treatment is to assume that the N is present in deep structure but deleted in surface structure for communicative economy. The remainder of the NP is then said to be NOMINALIZED. The following sentences illustrate nominalizations, with the deleted head nouns indicated in parentheses.

I bought *eight bottles* and John bought *six* (bottles), so now there're *too many* (bottles).
Yo compré *ocho botellas* y Juan compró *seis* (botellas), de modo que ahora hay *demasiadas* (botellas).

As shown, with most Quant the rest of the NP stays intact. Otherwise, nominalization can be complicated, especially in English, when the lineup is one of the following.

1. Article + N. In this case, nominalization is pronominalization, inasmuch as a definite article is replaced by a third-person pronoun when the noun is dropped:

   I fixed *the* (washer) → I fixed *it*. Arreglé *la* (lavadora) → *La* arreglé.

   The connection between definite articles and third-person pronouns is obvious in Spanish (*la* = *la*), and Bull (1965, 248) believed that there is still pedagogical value in presenting pronominalization as noun deletion and pronouns as article "residuals" of NP. On the other hand, when the deleted N is singular indefinite, English changes *a(n)* to its original form *one*; Spanish similarly changes apocopated masculines (*un, ningún,* etc.) back to their full form:

   I saw *a* (meteor) → I saw *one*. Vi *un* (meteoro) → Vi *uno*.
   I have *some* (letters) → I have *some*. Tengo *algunas* (cartas) → Tengo *algunas*.

2. Possessive + N. Likewise, possessive D revert to their long forms in nominalization:

   My (house) is small. → Mine is small. *Mi* (casa) es chica. (= *la* casa *mía*) → *La mía* es chica.

   When the possessor is not a personal pronoun, both languages just drop the N, but the difference between a preposed possessor in English and a postposed one in Spanish (v. 8.3.2) yields strikingly different patterns, despite the shared rule of noun deletion:

   Paula's (house) is beige. → *Paula's* is beige.
   La (casa) *de Paula* es beige. → *La de Paula* es beige.

Nominalization with a postposed possessor is impossible in English unless *one(s)* is inserted, but a Spanish-like pattern exists with *that* or *those*:

The (stocks) of the company → **The* of the company → *The ones* (*Those*) of the company
Las (acciones) de la empresa. → *Las* de la empresa.

3. Demonstrative + N. Here, Spanish again just drops the noun, leaving a bare demonstrative on which an accent is often written (although it has not been required since 1959). English follows suit for plurals but inserts *one* for singulars (and plurals, too, in some dialects):

this (tool) → *this one*	*esta* (herramienta) → *esta (ésta)*
these (tools) → *these*	*estas* (herramientas) → *estas (éstas)*

4. Other NPs: D + Adj + N, D + N + PP, D + N + S. When the noun is modified by an adjective, prepositional phrase, or relative clause, Spanish again just deletes the N:

the red (birds) → *the red ones*	*los* (pájaros) *rojos* → *los rojos*
the (statue) *in the park* → *the one in the park*	*la* (estatua) *del parque* → *la del parque*
the (cop) *who saw me* → *the one who saw me*	*el* (poli) *que me vio* → *el que me vio*

However, Spanish has a seldom-recognized hitch with PP: nominalization is generally possible only when the preposition is *de*: *el balde de plástico* → *el de plástico*, but not *el balde para agua* → **el para agua* or *el balde con agua* → **el con agua*. English again replaces the N with *one(s)*, although there are Spanish-like nominalizations for some adjectives: *the rich, the poor, the former, the latter, the powerful*.

One more case is what happens when the dropped N is NAKED (no D, no modifiers). Spanish, as usual, just drops the deemphasized noun. This yields a puzzling construction for English speakers, whose language requires some marking of the vacated NP:

(1)	A: ¿Venden Uds. carburadores? B: No, no vendemos.	A: Do you sell carburetors? B: No, *we don't sell. (→ . . . sell any/them/those)
(2)	A: ¿Tienes harina? B: Sí, tengo.	A: Have you got flour? B: *Yes, I've got. (→ I've got some/it/that.)

In surface structures such as *No vendemos* and *Sí, tengo*, nothing remains of the NP to call "nominalized"; yet the same Spanish rule of N deletion is occurring here as in the other cases. For this and other reasons, Agard (1984, 111) preferred to call the process "noun throw-away."

8.4.2 The Spanish neuter. The neuter is a second case in which NP modifiers surface without N. The forms *ello lo esto eso aquello* are described as neuter because they derive from Latin neuters, not because they agree with neuter nouns or refer to sexless inanimates.[14] Simply put, these forms are used when there is no gender-determining noun, explicit or implicit, with which they might agree. They have come to represent general concepts, preceding ideas, unnamed qualities or events, and indefinite extents. English lacks such a form, so equivalents vary:

Lo mismo les sucedió a ellos.
The same (thing) happened to them.

Hay que tomar *lo bueno* con *lo malo.*
You have to take *the good (part, aspect, point)* with *the bad.*

¿Has oído *eso* del instituto?
Have you heard *that matter (stuff, news)* about the institute?

Neuters therefore contrast with nominalized modifiers that refer to a deleted noun with gender:

Lo mío no es *lo tuyo.* (*La mía = mi bicicleta, casa, filosofía . . .*)
Esto me molesta. (*Este = este tipo, aparato, curso . . .*)
¿Qué es *eso*? (¿Qué es *esa*? = 'name or define that kind of *comida, falda, moneda . . .*')
Lo de Alejandro nos fascina. (*La de Alejandro* = la novia, la madre, la obra . . .)
Lo que mencionaste me extraña. (*El que mencionaste* = el cuento, el libro, el criterio . . .)

Otheguy (1978, 241–57) suggested that this contrast between *el* ~ *la* and *lo* involves DISCRETENESS. With *el* ~ *la*, speakers assign clearly delineated boundaries ("delineated" by a noun they have in mind), whereas *lo* suggests nondiscreteness. Thus in the following sentences, *lo que* remains open-ended and is interpreted as 'what *serendipity* means', whereas the gender of *la que* limits reference to a feminine noun, which in context is inferred to be *la palabra*:

Alcánzame ese diccionario. A ver, aquí está **lo que** quiere decir *serendipity.*
Alcánzame ese diccionario. A ver, aquí está **la que** quiere decir *serendipity.*

The fact that the first case might be rendered as 'what' and the second one as 'the one that' hints that English implicitly has the same distinction, as does the contrast between *this/that* (neuterlike) vs. *this/that one* (nominalized):

This is impossible. (*This one* is impossible. = this step, recipe, exercise . . .)

Because of the nebulousness or "nondiscreteness" of *lo,* it has expanded to express extent or degree of modification. The *lo* remains nounless, yet its adjective agrees with a later noun:

No sabes *lo torpes* que son esos tipos. (. . . *lo bien* que hablan alemán)

This *lo* + Adj/Adv + *que* corresponds to English *how* + Adj/Adv + clause, at least functionally, but the agreement of the adjective (but not *lo*) with a noun strikes students as decidedly odd.

The neuter equivalents of the pronouns *él/ella* and *lo/la* are *ello lo*, which often refer back to a whole preceding idea:

A: ¡Manuel se ha casado! B: No *lo* sabía. Pero no hablemos de *ello*.

English *it* can be used here in the same way, but Spanish *lo* is also used as a pronoun for a predicate attribute (González and Whitley 1999; Alarcos Llorach 1999, 374), while English has no regular PA pronoun:

A: Estas sandías no están maduras. B: No, no *lo* están. (No *lo* parecen.)
A: ¡Esto es una barbaridad! ¡Un escándalo! B: Sí, *lo* es.
A: La novia de Alfonso no es muy linda. B: Sí, pero él cree que *lo* es.

(Compare English *Yes, but he thinks that she is Ø*.)

With nominalizations and neuters, we cross an unclear boundary between nouns and pronouns. The latter will be discussed in the next chapter.

Notes for chapter 8

1. Despite the importance of transitivity for sentence construction, Teschner and Flemming (1996) observed that textbooks devote scarce attention to it and that even Spanish dictionaries disagree on the *tr./intr.* classification of numerous verbs. For a much richer resource on verb construction based on carefully researched literary attestations, see Cuervo [1886–93], 1953.

2. Dative Shift is an option in cases like *Mary lent twenty dollars* (DO) *to John* (IO) → *Mary lent John twenty dollars* and *Mary made some paella* (DO) *for us* (IO) → *Mary made us some paella*. For some verbs, however, it is obligatory (**The car cost $7,000 to Ed* → *The car cost Ed $7,000*), while for others it is oddly blocked: compare *tell* and its near-synonym *say* in *He told that lie to Ed* → *He told Ed that lie* vs. *He said that lie to Ed* → **He said Ed that lie*. Such quirks are stumbling blocks to Spanish students of English, who overgeneralize the rule to verbs that do not allow it: **Explain me that, please*.

3. Of special interest in Kliffer's analysis are contrasts like *levanto la mano* vs. *me lavo la mano*: the former implies doing something with the hand while the latter (with its *me* contrasting

with *te, le,* and other possible IOs) suggests doing it to one's hand. *Me levanto la mano* combines both meanings, as if forcing one's hand up. For other analyses of the IO of possession, see García 1975 and Kempchinsky 1992.

4. "A male is generally viewed as stronger, more active, and socially higher than a woman would be. He is thus at least potentially more active than a woman would be" (García and Otheguy 1977, 75)—a claim whose verification lies outside the bounds of linguistics.

5. The [əz] allomorph (*bushes, buses, watches*) is pronounced by some with a higher vowel, front [ɪ] or mid [ɨ].

6. The answer here is "both." Nouns such as *margen, fin, cutis, análisis* have vacillated in gender and still vary dialectally. Jorge Morel (1974) found variation in Santo Domingo on the gender of *azúcar, calambre, calor, hambre, mar, radio, reuma, sartén,* as did Cárdenas (1967, 71–75) in Jalisco, Mexico.

7. In technical terms, the so-called masculine is grammatically UNMARKED and the feminine is MARKED. Prado (1982) developed this point more fully, noting that it is the masculine that handles unclear assignments by default, not only epicenes but also loanwords (*el bar*), infinitives (*el atardecer*), compounds (*el cuentagotas*), nominalized adverbials and interjections (*el sí, el más allá*), and nonagreeing participles (*ha comprado*). Moreover, the augmentatives of feminines become masculines, except in speaking of females: *la sala → el salón, la silla → el sillón*, but *la mujer → la mujerona*. But even if the masculine form is unmarked and therefore traditional for epicenes, Spanish editorial style sheets and guidelines have begun to reflect concern about sexism (Stewart 1999, 31). Thus, *los profesores* may now be corrected to *las profesoras y los profesores,* and one sees phraseology such as *Si es separado/a o divorciado/a . . . o está casado(a) con un(a) español(a) . . .*

8. There are other options and combinations that we omit for simplicity, for example, Quant Quant (*two more stamps, dos timbres más*), Quant D (*all the pages, todas las páginas*), partitives with *of/de* (*most of the people, la mayoría de la gente*), appositives (*General Gómez,* v. 11.1.3), and the fact that "Adj" should actually be "AdjP" (adjective phrase) since the adjective may have its own modifiers. See Hadlich (1971), Stockwell, Bowen, and Martin (1965), and Stiehm (1978, 413) for a fuller NP schema for Spanish.

9. In some regions a possessive pronominal NP may occur as D and PP at the same time: Andean dialects have *su amiga de Juan* 'John's friend', *su casa de mi papá* 'my dad's house'. See De Granda (1998) for an evaluation of Quechua influence on this *doble posesivo*.

10. In earlier generative grammar, this similarity was accounted for by means of a transformation converting VPs to NPs; in more recent theory, the solution has been to assign the two phrase types parallel structures.

11. Note that in N + N such as *world problems*, the first N is not a true adjective (cf. *very serious problems* but not **very world problems*), and that not all N *of* N combinations can change to it (*a man of courage, *a courage man; the island of Cuba, *the Cuba island; a glass of water ≠ a water glass*). This unpredictability can be very frustrating to students of English.

12. In Old Spanish, possessives had not yet joined the D category, so combinations with articles were possible: *el mío Cid*. Modern Guatemalan and Salvadoran dialects still permit the indefinite article with a possessive (Lipski 1994, 259): *una mi amiga* (= *una amiga mía* in other dialects).

13. In nonstandard lects, *el* and *la* are both pronounced *l'* before a vowel: *l'amigo, l'amiga* (cf. French *l'ami, l'amie*). Sánchez (1982, 32) noted this as the usual practice in Chicano speech.

14. Latin had three genders, as in *iste leō* (M), *ista mulier* (F), *istud nōmen* (N). All neuters

were reassigned to masculine or feminine in Spanish (neuter *nōmen* thus became masculine *nombre*), whence modern *este león* (M), *esta mujer* (F), *este nombre* (M). The neuter form *istud* > *esto* was displaced from the system to occupy a new niche in which it never modifies any noun.

Exercises for chapter 8

1. Error analysis: account for the apparent source of each student error:
   (a) *los animals
   (b) *los atlases
   (c) *esto cuchillo
   (d) *la arroz
   (e) *hay un otro razón
   (f) *la gente lo quieren
   (g) *me gusto legumbres
   (h) *carros francesos
   (i) *los unos que oí
   (j) *busco por mi libro
   (k) *es mi biología libro
   (l) *no tengo ningunos clases los fin de semanas
   (m) *trabaja en su padres oficina
   (n) *ciencia nos ayudará
   (o) *conocí a señora Pardo en Hotel Ritz
   (p) *el sofá es un pedazo de mueble

2. Pilleux and Urrutia (1982, 78) defined the Spanish IO as follows: "aquellas FN [frases nominales, NP] que nombran a los seres . . . en que se cumple o termina la acción del verbo transitivo ejercida ya sobre el complemento directo." Identify the IOs in the following sentences; to what extent do they conform to this definition? Why might they give trouble to students?
   (a) ¿Te examino la oreja?
   (b) A ese autor no le estoy de acuerdo con las opiniones.
   (c) Le han robado la muñeca a mi hija.
   (d) Le hacía ruido el estómago y le picaba la nariz.
   (e) Nos comienzan las clases mañana.
   (f) Le impusiste demasiados deberes a la alumna.
   (g) ¡No me saques la lengua!
   (h) La criada le pasó el dedo a la mesa.
   (i) Al gerente le bastará el surtido actual.
   (j) A Raúl le salió bien el informe.

3. It was pointed out in section 8.1.4 that English and Spanish do not agree on the roles in which NPs are cast with *ask/pedir.* The following verbs also differ; identify their difference in construction. Example: *X asks Y for Z, X le pide Z a Y.*
   (a) wait; esperar
   (b) thank; agradecer
   (c) look; buscar, mirar
   (d) ask; preguntar
   (e) hold; caber
   (f) replace; sustituir
   (g) pay; pagar
   (h) listen; escuchar
   (i) marry; casar(se)
   (j) have enough; bastar
   (k) hit; golpear, pegar, dar
   (l) hurt; doler
   (m) need; hacer falta
   (n) provide, supply; proporcionar, suministrar

   Can you add to this list of verbs with different *regímenes*?

4. How would you explain the different constructions taken by the following verbs?
   (a) Quedan dos problemas más. ¿Dónde queda el estadio? La chaqueta me queda ajustada. Me quedo aquí. Me quedo con este. Me queda poco tiempo. Quedé cojo después del accidente.
   (b) Esto le extraña. Te extraño mucho. Se extrañó de mi conducta.
   (c) Le parece bien. Se parece a su tía.
   (d) Le faltan las palabras. Él faltó a su palabra (porque faltó a clase).

5. How predictable is the gender of each of the following nouns?

(a) barril	(e) virtud	(i) cometa	(m) unión
(b) honor	(f) profeta	(j) cliente	(n) Amazonas
(c) calle	(g) apendicitis	(k) sucursal	(o) calambre
(d) nariz	(h) víctima	(l) alarma	(p) examen

6. The gender of trees, days, and some fruits can be explained in terms of apposition to an understood noun such as *árbol, día, fruta.* What are the understood appositives for the following (or are there any understood ones)? Do you think that the connection would be pedagogically useful?

(a) la consonante, la fricativa	(e) el jerez
(b) la catedral	(f) la capital (e.g., Madrid, Buenos Aires)
(c) el dos, el tres	(g) la central (e.g., del sindicato)
(d) la diagonal, la divisoria	(h) la efe, la eñe, la equis

7. Variation has been reported among native speakers for the following forms. Regardless of which form you use yourself or regard as standard, explain why this particular variation might arise on the basis of competing patterns, tendencies, or rules in Spanish. (By extending this list, you might also create a questionnaire to submit to native speakers on their usage.)
   (a) fem. of *marrón*: *una chaqueta marrona* ~ *marrón*
   (b) fem. of *presidente*: *la presidente* ~ *la presidenta*
   (c) pl. of *rubí*: *rubís* ~ *rubíes* ~ *rubises*
   (d) fem. of *ninguno*: *no hay ninguna águila* ~ *no hay ningún águila*
   (e) gender of *radio* 'radio'(*la* ~ *el radio*) and of *cutis* (*el* ~ *la cutis*)
   (f) plural of *club*: *clubs* ~ *clubes*
   (g) singular of *alicates*: *alicates* ~ *alicate*
   (h) agreement with two nouns: *nuevos estrategias y trucos* ~ *nuevas estrategias y trucos.*

8. In what ways do Spanish and English agree, and disagree, on the following points?
   (a) the expression of possession within the NP
   (b) their use of ∅ + N, that is, of naked nouns
   (c) the constituents of NP
   (d) count/mass noun classification
   (e) the casting of NPs as Subj and Obj (particularly with psych verbs).

9. PARTITIVES are quantifiers that mean 'part of' and use *de*/*of* to connect with a following N or NP. Here are examples of partitives in Spanish:

un millón de usuarios	*el 35 por ciento de* los votantes	*un sinfín de* quehaceres
un poco de azúcar	*un par de* señoras	*una cantidad de* gente
dos litros de agua	*algunos de* los muebles	*tres quintos de* la población.

(a) Add at least five more examples of the same pattern.

(b) Try to incorporate this structure into the PSR for a Spanish NP. In your opinion, are the italicized expressions unit items that modify the noun, or do they subordinate the noun so that the latter is in a PP following a head N such as *millón, par, poco*? Consider syntactic evidence such as verb agreement with such complex phrases (does *un millón de usuarios* take a singular or plural verb?). Dialect evidence may also be relevant: Boyd-Bowman (1960, 157) and Kany (1951, 148) found *un poco de pan* vs. *una poca de agua* in some regions.

10. N + N combinations in Spanish have begun to appear more often in journalistic and technical writing: *avión espía, fecha límite, misiles mar-tierra, coche-bomba, ciudad dormitorio, punto clave, padre-dios, casa-refugio.* As shown, hyphenation varies; pluralization does too, as witnessed in one newspaper that discussed *buques-hospital* but *coches-bombas.* Examine samples of current Hispanic writing, and see how many such N + N combinations you find and whether there is any pattern in punctuation and pluralization.

11. In most textbooks, demonstrative pronouns, possessive pronouns, relative pronouns such as *el que,* and nominalized adjectives are presented separately. What reason is there for treating all of them—perhaps together with the neuters—in a single lesson on nominalization? How would you explain them to English-speaking students?

12. Consider the following premodifiers (preposed elements of the NP) and determine which sequences of them in NPs are grammatical and which ones are ungrammatical. Do you find any sequences whose English equivalents differ? Next, try to develop an improved phrase structure rule for NP to reflect more precisely the co-occurrence options. Do not hesitate to subdivide the categories of D, Quant, and so on if your analysis requires finer distinctions.

mucho(s)	primero(s)	propio(s)	demás	alguno(s)
cierto(s)	sendos	el, los	otro(s)	tal(es)
cada	un(os)	todo(s)	diez	bastante(s)

13. According to Wonder (1981), Spanish seems to show two kinds or degrees of nominalization in D + Adj, as shown by the following pairs. Specify, as clearly as possible, what the difference is.

(a) Juan es el verdadero rico. Juan es el verdaderamente rico.
(b) Aquel eterno quejumbroso nos molesta. Aquel eternamente quejumbroso nos molesta.
(c) Entre los convidados se contaban dos autores españoles y un americano. Entre los convidados se contaban dos autores españoles y uno americano.
(d) Fue hecho por algún descuidado. Fue hecho por alguno descuidado.

Chapter 9

Pronouns

9.0 Pronouns as proforms. A PRONOUN is a word that takes the place of an NP, especially a previously mentioned one,[1] and is so called because in classical grammar it was regarded as standing 'for a noun' (Latin *prō nōmine*). There are also PRO-VERBS (the *do* in *They eat more than I do*), PROADVERBS (the *allí* in *Fui al armario pero no vi nada allí*), and PROADJECTIVES (the *lo* in *¿Es rico? Sí, lo es*; v. 8.4.2), and all of these are sometimes called PROFORMS. The main proforms, though, are pronouns, and they are traditionally classified as follows:

personal, which show person (1, 2, 3) and are definite (like *el, este*): *I, she*; *yo, ella*
indefinite, which do not distinguish person: *someone, nothing*; *alguien, nada*
interrogative, for questioning NPs: *who, what*; *quién, qué*
possessive: *mine, ours*; *mío, nuestro*
demonstrative, which are deictic (pointing) words: *this, those*; *éste, ésos*
relative, which introduce relative clauses: *that, who*; *que*
quantifying: *few, some, several*; *pocos, algunos, varios*

Many of these are just nominalizations (v. 8.4.1): *ese aparato → ése, mi casa → la mía, algunos maestros → algunos.* Others are best treated with the syntactic processes in which they play a role: interrogatives with questioning (v. 12.1.2), relatives with relativization (v. 13.3.1). This chapter focuses on reflexive and nonreflexive personal pronouns, which form their own systems.

9.1 Nonreflexive pronouns. As can be seen in figure 9.1, the English and Spanish systems of personal pronouns are based on the same categories of number, gender, person, and case (distinction of forms for Subj, DO, etc.). Nevertheless, they differ in so many particulars that Spanish pronouns offer as big a challenge to English speakers as Spanish verbs, especially when textbooks move quickly from one set (e.g., DO forms) to the next (IO and OP forms) with insufficient time to digest each set, develop skill with it, and keep it distinct from the others.

Figure 9.1. Nonreflexive personal pronouns

<table>
<tr><th colspan="2">English (standard system)</th><th rowspan="2">Person/number</th><th colspan="4">Spanish (maximal system)</th></tr>
<tr><th>Subj</th><th>Obj (OP, IO, DO)</th><th>Subj</th><th>OP</th><th>IO</th><th>DO</th></tr>
<tr><td>I</td><td>me</td><td>1sg.</td><td>yo</td><td>mí</td><td colspan="2">me</td></tr>
<tr><td colspan="2" rowspan="2">you</td><td rowspan="2">2sg.</td><td>tú</td><td>ti</td><td colspan="2">te</td></tr>
<tr><td colspan="2">usted</td><td rowspan="2">le</td><td rowspan="2">lo/la</td></tr>
<tr><td>he/she/it</td><td>him/her/it</td><td>3sg.</td><td colspan="2">él, ella (ello)</td></tr>
<tr><td>we</td><td>us</td><td>1.pl.</td><td colspan="2">nosotros, -as</td><td colspan="2">nos</td></tr>
<tr><td colspan="2" rowspan="2">you</td><td rowspan="2">2.pl.</td><td colspan="2">vosotros, -as</td><td colspan="2">os</td></tr>
<tr><td colspan="2">ustedes</td><td rowspan="2">les</td><td rowspan="2">los/las</td></tr>
<tr><td>they</td><td>them</td><td>3.pl.</td><td colspan="2">ellos, -as</td></tr>
</table>

9.1.1 Person. In Spanish, the three persons are not strictly speaker/addressee/all others, because the second-person *usted* has grammatically third-person forms. The reason is its etymology from the phrase *vuestra merced* (v. 9.2). English pronouns are not person-ambiguous, with the exception of personal vs. impersonal *you* (v. 9.3.9), and many students have difficulty accepting that *lo, la,* and *le* can refer to the addressee as well as to third persons.

9.1.2 Gender. Both languages distinguish masculine from feminine in 3sg. forms, but otherwise English lacks gender distinctions in pronouns, while Spanish is inconsistent. The form *nosotros* is distinct from *nosotras,* but the DO/IO form *nos* applies to both genders; the form *ustedes* does not distinguish gender but its DO form does (*los* vs. *las*); and *yo* and *tú* show no gender distinction at all, nor does any pronoun in the IO form.

Contrasting with *he* and *she,* English has an *it*, or actually several *its*. First, there is the dummy pronoun inserted into Subj position because English requires some kind of Subj, not because this *it* stands for anything (v. 11.1.1). Spanish grammar has no such requirement (v. 5.2):

It's 68 degrees outside.	Hace veinte grados afuera.
It's obvious it'll snow.	Está claro que va a nevar.

Next is the *it* that is "neuter" in the Spanish sense of referring to an unnamed concept (v. 8.4.2). Here Spanish has Subj/OP *ello* and DO *lo*, though *ello* is rare as a Subj, especially in Spanish America (Cárdenas 1967, 139).

He snores; does *it* bother you?	Él ronca; ¿te molesta (ello)?
Yes, but I don't complain about it.	Sí, pero no me quejo de ello.

Third is the *it* referring back to an inanimate noun, which is neuter = 'thing' in English but not neuter = 'no noun' in Spanish. Depending on the gender of the noun, one chooses between *lo* and *la* for DO and between *él* and *ella* for OP, but for Subj this *it* is ordinarily not expressed.

I need my pencil; where is *it* (Subj)? Do you have *it* (DO)?
Are you writing with *it* (OP)?
Necesito mi lápiz; ¿dónde está? ¿*Lo* tienes tú? ¿Estás escribiendo con *él*?

Thus, a good rule of thumb for students is "Don't express *it* as a subject in Spanish."

9.1.3 Case. CASE refers to a distinction of forms according to their functions. Hispanic grammarians retain the Latin case names *nominativo, dativo, acusativo* for the forms serving respectively as *sujeto, complemento indirecto,* and *complemento directo.* Yet neither language distinguishes Subj, DO, IO, and OP throughout. English, in fact, merges the last three into one all-purpose Obj form, but this form is consistently distinguished from the Subj form (except for *you*). Spanish distinguishes DO and IO in the third person but not otherwise, and merges OP with the Subj forms except for the special OP forms *mí, ti,* and reflexive *sí* (allomorphs *-migo, -tigo, -sigo* after *con*). Spanish DO/IO distinctions such as *lo sirvo* 'I serve up some masculine thing' vs. *le sirvo* 'I serve him (something)' will pose problems to speakers whose language makes no DO/IO contrast morphologically, and who in fact see no IO in *I serve him.* Moreover, there are certain Spanish prepositions that take Subj, not OP, forms: *según tú, excepto tú, como yo, entre tú y yo.* Neither language provides for a fifth function, a personal PA (v. 8.1, 11.1.2): in this case, all but the most formal styles of English use Obj forms with a nonagreeing *be*, whereas Spanish adopts the Subj forms with an agreeing *ser*: *it's me, it's them* vs. *soy yo, son ellos.*

Because of such differences, any translation-based approach will just short-circuit mastery. For *her* there are six equivalents (*la, le, se, ella, su, sus*) and for *you* there are seventeen, eight of which (*lo, la, le*, etc.) represent other pronouns too. Students who persist in matching L2 with L1 soon confuse *nos* with *nosotros, lo* with *le* and *él, me* with *mí* and *yo*. Others who do manage to stay afloat in distinguishing *él, ella, lo, la, le* from each other and from reflexive *se* often sink below the waves once they are introduced to the *le(s)* → *se* merger (v. 9.3.1) and to variations of the types described below.

9.2 Variation in the pronoun system. Old English had a number distinction in the second person: sg. *thou*, pl. *ye.* This later shifted to sg. *thou* for an intimate or talking-down relationship vs. *you* for both polite singular address and all plural address, like the distinction in French *tu* vs. *vous.* Eventually, *you* won out, leaving a neutralization of singular/plural in a language that otherwise makes consistent number distinctions. As a solution, the folk have developed their own local plurals: *y'all (you-all), y'uns (you-ones), you guys,* and *youse.*

Spanish second-person pronouns likewise show dialect variation that originated in the past. Old Spanish had a distinction like that of French *tu/vous* and English *thou/you,* namely *tú* for singular intimate address and *vos* for singular polite or plural. Then *-otros* was added to *vos* to mark plurality, like the *all* of Southern U.S. *y(ou)all*; this addition spread to *nos* as well for a parallel *nosotros*. Gradually, the politeness of singular *vos* and plural *vosotros* wore down and they joined *tú* in expressing intimate relationships (v. 16.1.1 for the social basis of this). As a new polite second-person expression, the elegant substitute *vuestra merced(es)* 'your grace(s)' arose and then contracted to *usted(es)*. It still betrays its etymology in its third-person verb and pronoun forms (like English *your honor/grace has, is, does* vs. *you have, are, do*).

These changes left the following variations in the modern language:

1. *Vosotros* fell out of use in America and most of Andalusia. In these areas it is now literary or biblical, like English *thou* and *ye*, and *ustedes* serves as the plural of both *tú* and *usted.*
2. As *vosotros* waned, the *vuestra* of *vuestra merced* was replaced by *su. Sumercé(d)* survives in some places (Carricaburo 1997), and at least for Colombians, it suggests greater familiarity than *tú*, especially in the family, but its use is declining (Uber 1985, 390).
3. When *vos* descended to the level of *tú,* it displaced it in some areas. *Voseo* (use of *vos*) is especially common today in Argentina, Paraguay, Uruguay, and Central America (except Panama). Its morphology is a hybrid of *tú* and *vos(otros)*: Subj and OP *vos,* IO and DO *te*, possessives *tu, tuyo*. So are its verb forms, which come in three sets as summarized in figure 9.2. (Regional affiliations are only approximate since the sets often coexist in the same area, giving rise to conflicting reports; see Carricaburo 1997 for details of form and distribution.)

Following Bello ([1847] 1958, 89), who regarded *vos* as improper, teachers in Spanish America have promoted *tú* in the schools. The *tú* campaign has succeeded in displacing *vos* in Chile but not in Argentina, while in areas such as El Salvador (Lipski 1994, 259) it only led to a three-term system in which *tú* is intermediate between *vos* and *usted* in its degree of personal closeness.

The Spanish system varies in the third person too. There is not much difference in how Spanish marks IOs and DOs (v. 8.1.3), and in the pronoun system the distinction is not shown in most forms: *me, nos, te, os, se* = IO or DO. Given such SYNCRETISM or coales-

Figure 9.2. Verb forms in three types of *voseo*

western Argentina, Chile, southern Peru, Zulia (Venezuela)	vos *habláis, coméis ~ comís, pedís, sois*
most of Argentina, Uruguay, Paraguay, western Colombia, most of Central America, Arequipa (Peru)	vos *hablás, comés, pedís, sos*
areas of Bolivia, highland Ecuador, Áncash (Peru)	vos *hablas, comes, pides, eres*

cence in form, great pressure is exerted on the sole point where a distinction was inherited between *dativo* (IO) and *acusativo* (DO), namely, *le(s)* vs. *lo(s)* and *la(s)*. Already by the sixteenth century, this lone contrast was eroding among Castilians, who were using *le(s)* for DO (Kany 1951, 102). The eventual compromise in peninsular usage was to reserve *la(s)* for feminine DO and *lo(s)* for masculine inanimate DO, and to allow *le(s)* for masculine human DO and all IO. This practice is known as *leísmo*, as opposed to what is called "distinción etimológica" of *lo(s)* for all masculine DO (human or not) vs. *le(s)* for IO only, as retained in the Americas.

As with *seseo* and *yeísmo* (v. 2.1.4), however, it is incorrect to portray the difference as Spain vs. America. The Real Academia Española (1979, 205) accepts both usages as standard, and actually prefers *distinción etimológica* because of its greater "order and clarity," recommending it for cultivated usage (Alarcos Llorach 1999, 250). Meanwhile, at the colloquial level in the peninsula, fluctuations have yielded five distinct *pronombrismos,* as Gili Gaya (1973) called them. These are shown in figure 9.3. System 1 is *distinción etimológica,* dominant in America but still practiced in Spain too outside of Castile and León; System 2 is *leísmo,* System 3 is *laísmo,* System 4 is called *loísmo,* and System 5 reserves *lo* for neuter *ello* only. (See Fernández-Ordóñez 1994 for further details of use and geographical distribution.)

Except in a few *leísta* spots such as Ecuador and Paraguay (Lipski 1994, 310), Spanish America retains the original setup, System 1. Yet usage varies between *dativo* and *acusativo* for verbs that take one Obj (e.g., *ayudar, asustar*), and Kany (1951) quoted from writers who alternated between *le* and *lo* with the same verb in the same paragraph. Perhaps the contrast between DO and IO is neutralized with single-Obj verbs, so that the two are then interchangeable; or perhaps the variation is due to imitative flourishes of Castilian *leísmo*; or perhaps *le ayudo* and *lo ayudo* imply different degrees of involvement or potency, as García and Otheguy believed (1977; v. 8.1.3).[2] For whatever reason, the situation is not neat.

There is more variation. On both sides of the Atlantic (Alarcos Llorach 1999, 119) the *de* of compound prepositions may fuse with a pronoun Obj to yield a pseudopossessive: *delante de mí → delante mío, alrededor de ella → alrededor suyo*. Likewise, throughout

Figure 9.3. Five *pronombrismos* in Spain

		System: 1	2	3	4	5
For DO:						
masc. human:	(Al hombre) ___veo.	lo	le	le	lo	le
masc. inanimate:	(El coche) ___veo.	lo	lo	lo	lo	le
feminine	(A la mujer) ___ veo.	la	la	la	la	la
For IO:						
masculine	(Al hombre) ___ daré uno.	le	le	le	lo	le
feminine	(A la mujer) ___daré uno.	le	le	la	la	la

the Spanish-speaking world one hears the replacement of special OP forms *mí, ti, sí* by the Subj pattern: *para yo, por tú, a él (mismo)* like *para nosotros, por ustedes. Nosotras* is not used in some areas (Boyd-Bowman 1960, 154), and *le* colloquially replaces *les,* as in *le viene natural a los niños* (Butt and Benjamin 1988, 133). When we go on to recognize other variants (Kany 1951, 92–127) and to open the ebullient cauldron of reflexives (v. 9.3), the Spanish pronoun system swells with formidable complexity. Yet in the classroom Spanish synthesized for U.S. consumption, most of this variation is ignored in favor of the system shown in figure 9.1. There is little practical alternative, because that system is a big enough challenge as it is. If students master it, they will be able to communicate adequately and to understand the pronouns of native speakers—of most of them, that is, and most of the time.

9.3 Reflexives. In English, reflexive pronouns end in *-self* or *-selves,* so that for each Obj pronoun there is a contrasting reflexive counterpart: *me* vs. *myself, you* vs. *yourself (-ves), her* vs. *herself, them* vs. *themselves,* and so on. In Spanish, the contrast is marked only in the third person (including *Ud.* and *Uds.*): *le(s) lo(s) la(s)* vs. *se,* and in the standard language, *a él (ella Ud. ellos Uds.)* vs. *a sí (consigo).* Reflexive morphology, at least, is clear in the two languages.

The meaning of the reflexive is more elusive, however. Reflexive is etymologically 'bending back', and in its most literal sense it describes a case in which the Obj refers back to the Subj: *(Jenny saw Jenny)* → *Jenny saw herself.* Here, Subj and DO are the same person: Jenny verbs Jenny and not someone else. Yet the reflexive has spread out to other patterns with other meanings, not just in Spanish but in other languages too. For example, in all of the following the Subj is not literally acting upon itself, despite the italicized reflexive morpheme:

Spanish: *Se* construyó un puente. 'A bridge was built.' (lit. 'a bridge built itself')
French: Ça *se* voit. 'That's apparent.' (lit. 'that sees itself')
German: Die Tür öffnete *sich.* 'The door opened.' (lit. 'the door opened itself')
Russian: Kak pishet*sya* éto? 'How is that written?' (lit. 'how writes-self that?')
Latin: It*ur*. 'One goes' (lit. 'goes-self')
English: No opportunity presented *itself.*

Bull (1965, 265–73) believed that these evolutions are natural. If we can say, by way of contrast,

Yo no vestí a Manuel; él *se* vistió.

then why not

Yo no paré el motor; *se* paró.

and one step further,

Yo no rompí ese vaso; *se* rompió.

and finally, a long way from where we started,

Yo no pude esquiar bien allí, pero otros dicen que *se* esquía sin problema alguno.

In other words, regardless of whether a Subj can logically act upon itself or not, the reflexive has become a marker that, in varying degrees, deemphasizes personal agency from without. The various usages of *se,* according to Bull, thus lie on a continuum.[3]

Other analysts have been more taxonomic, sorting out distinct uses of *se* as in the following classification. But the reader should keep in mind that not everyone would distinguish all these categories, since some (if not all) can be grouped around one central principle.

9.3.1 Pseudo-reflexive or "spurious" *se.*

Les di la llave (→ *Les la di) → Se la di.

Le and *les* change to *se* when followed by another pronoun beginning with *l*-. This rule is strange, and misinformed writers have explained it as a "cambio eufónico" so as to avoid the "cacofonía" of two successive occurrences of /l/. Yet no one regards the same sequence as cacophonous in *paralelo, aleluya, darle lo mejor, vale la pena, Lola le lastimó,* nor has the language ever tried to purge itself of it. In reality, this *se* comes from a medieval *ge* /ʒe/ with the same Latin origin as *le.* When /ʒ/ began to evolve into modern /x/, /ʒe/ crossed paths with /se/ and got confused with it. In short, pseudo-reflexive *se* is a historical accident that has nothing to do with the reflexive. Nevertheless, it causes problems when students overgeneralize the *le* → *se* rule to produce **se gusta, *se duele la cabeza, *se di una llave.*

9.3.2 True reflexive *se.*

Ella se vio en el espejo.	She saw herself in the mirror.
El gerente se criticó.	The manager criticized himself.
Olga se compró una blusa.	Olga bought herself a blouse.

Here the reflexive has its original meaning, namely that the DO or IO is the same entity as the Subj. In both languages, it contrasts with nonreflexives:

Ella la vio en el espejo.	She saw her (someone else) in the mirror.
El gerente lo criticó.	The manager criticized him (someone else).
Olga le compró una blusa.	Olga bought her/him (someone else) a blouse.

The two languages thus correspond rather well here. Of course, since the concept of IO is broader in Spanish (v. 8.1.2), Spanish may use a reflexive IO where English does not: hence, corresponding to nonreflexive *Mamá le lavó la cara a su hija* and *Tomás le puso/quitó una chaqueta a su hija,* Spanish has

Mami se lavó la cara.	Mom washed her (own) face.
Tomás se puso/quitó una chaqueta.	Tom put on/took off his/a jacket.

In equating the two languages' patterns, what many textbooks fail to point out is that English often dispenses with its reflexive marker (see Haiman 1983, 803), so students may not perceive reflexivity in Spanish.

Spanish	Assumed English equivalent	More common usage
Pedro se lavó.	Peter washed himself.	Peter *washed (up)*
Pedro se vistió.	Peter dressed himself.	Peter *got dressed.*
Pedro se afeitó.	Peter shaved himself.	Peter *shaved.*
Pedro se bañó.	Peter bathed himself.	Peter *took a bath.*

Spanish thus contrasts *se lavó* with *lo lavó,* while English contrasts *washed Ø* (no Obj pronoun, implicit reflexive) with *washed him* (someone else). The option *lavó Ø* in Spanish could be construed as meaning that Peter took in laundry to wash.

A criterion for the true reflexive in Spanish is the possibility of emphasis with *a sí mismo* (*a mí mismo,* etc.). For example, one can say *ella se vio (se lavó) a sí misma* but not **ella se atrevió a sí misma,* indicating that *verse* and *lavarse* are true reflexives (whether or not English uses *-self*), while *atreverse* must belong to some other category (v. 9.3.4).[4]

9.3.3 Reciprocal *se*.

Lucía y Joaquín se miraron.	Lucy and Joaquin looked at each other.

When the referents of a plural Subj carry out something on each other, the construction is called RECIPROCAL. English uses *each other* or *one another*, but like the reflexive *-self* forms, these cues are not reliable since they are often omitted: *they agreed (with each other), they fought (one another), we hugged (each other), you got married (to each other).* Spanish applies its reflexive system to the reciprocal, but the reciprocal emphasizer is not *a sí mismo* but *uno a otro,* whose *a* represents IO or DO. (If the verb requires a different preposition, *a* is replaced accordingly: *se alejaron uno de otro.*) Colloquially, *entre ellos* is also used (Roldán 1973, 203). Without emphasizers, a plural reflexive can be ambiguous: *todos se miraron* could be 'everyone looked at himself/herself' or 'everyone looked at each other'. To judge from students' overuse of *uno a otro*, they believe that the ambiguity is greater than it actually is in context.

9.3.4 Lexical or inherent *se*.

Ella se quejó de la sopa (*a sí misma). She complained (*herself) about the soup.

Quejarse is inherently reflexive in that a speaker who selects *quejar* automatically adds a reflexive morpheme. The *se* agrees with the Subj (*yo me quejo, tú te quejas,* etc.), but because *a sí mismo* is impossible with it, it is not a true reflexive; it is simply part of the verb, meaningless in itself since it contrasts neither with Ø (no Obj) nor with *lo(s), la(s), le(s),* or some other Obj. Other such verbs include *arrepentirse, resentirse, percatarse, abstenerse, atreverse, jactarse,* and *atenerse*, but they are fewer than most vocabulary lists imply; most of the reflexive verbs that are included with them (e.g., *acercarse*, v. 9.3.6) are not inherent reflexives at all. English parallels exist but are even rarer: *avail oneself, pride oneself, perjure oneself.*

9.3.5 Meaning-changing and/or inchoative *se*.

Ella bebió el café.	She drank the coffee.
Ella se bebió el café.	She drank down (up) the coffee.
Ellos durmieron.	They slept.
Ellos se durmieron.	They fell asleep.

The verbs of this category (1) contrast with nonreflexive versions (unlike lexical reflexives), (2) fail the *a sí mismo* test for true reflexivity (**ella se bebió el café a sí misma*), and (3) show a special shift of meaning. In *reírse, olvidarse, temerse, entrarse, merecerse, beberse, comerse, se* intensifies the action like the English particles *up, down, out, away* (v. 10.5). For Bello ([1847] 1958, 246) and Ramsey ([1894] 1956, 380), what is intensified is the involvement or affect of the Subj as simultaneous IO. Bello's glossings are illustrative:

me temo: 'el interés de la persona que habla'
se lo bebió: 'la buena disposición, el apetito, la decidida voluntad'
te lo sabes: 'la presunción de saberlo todo'
te entraste: 'cierto conato o fuerza con que se vence algún estorbo'

According to García (1975, 4, 155), at least some such cases of *se* concentrate a focus on the Subj by blocking external agency: *Olga murió* could be the result of homicide while *Olga se murió* suggests a natural demise; *Juan quedó solo* could result from an external event (e.g., loss of his family) while *Juan se quedó solo* suggests a decision on his part not to join others.

On the other hand, the idea of subject involvement or focus makes little sense with *dormirse*, and for this kind of verb Roldán (1971b) explained the *se* as marking INCHOATIVE ASPECT, that is, the initiation of a process whereby the Subj enters a new state. She pointed out an important property of such inchoatives, namely, that their state—once entered—is expressed by *estar* + participle:

Process:	State:
Se durmió. 'She fell asleep'	Está dormida. 'She's asleep, sleeping'
Se murió. 'She died'	Está muerta. 'She's dead'
Se casó. 'She got married'	Está casada. 'She's married'
Se calló. 'She shut up'	Está callada. 'She's quiet'

But Roldán noted that by this test many other reflexives are inchoative too:

Se arrepintió. 'She repented, felt sorry'	Está arrepentida. 'She's sorry, regretful'
Se enojó. 'She got angry'	Está enojada. 'She's angry'
Se cerró. 'It closed'	Está cerrada. 'It's closed'
Se resintió de eso. 'She resented that'	Está resentida. 'She's resentful'

Pedagogically, her observation is useful in explaining why the participle is used with *estar* instead of the gerund as in English: *she's sitting* = *está sentada* (≠ *está sentándose*).

As illustrated by the following list, however, there remain many verbs whose reflexives convey other meanings in other structures: *le quedan dos* (*el vestido le queda mal, la estación queda a 2 km. de aquí*) vs. *se queda en su casa* and *se quedó con el vestido.* There is no inchoativity here (**está quedada*), and the only common denominator is a semantic change that seems idiomatic.

quedar 'be left, be'; quedarse 'stay, remain'	salir 'go out, leave'; salirse 'leak, overflow'
ir 'go'; irse 'go away, leave'	saltar 'jump'; saltarse 'skip (something)'
sonar 'sound'; sonarse 'blow one's nose'	fijar 'attach, drive in'; fijarse 'notice'
llevar 'carry'; llevarse con 'get along with'	pasar 'pass, spend'; pasarse 'go bad, spoil'

9.3.6 Intransitivizing *se*.

Ella se detuvo en el andén.	She stopped on the platform.
El aluminio se ha fundido.	The aluminum has melted.
Los vasos se rompen.	Glasses break.
El barco se hundirá.	The boat will sink.
El conejito se movió.	The bunny moved.
Las fronteras se extienden al mar.	The boundaries extend to the sea.

Many English verbs can be used transitively (with DO) or intransitively (without DO) with the special semantic contrast of 'X caused Y to verb' vs. 'Y verbed by itself': *Joe stopped her* 'caused her to stop' vs. *She stopped.* The Spanish counterparts to such verbs generally take *se* for the intransitive sense.[5] Thus the preceding examples show the intransitive meaning in contrast to the following transitives, in which there is an external agent:

José la detuvo en el andén.	Joe stopped her on the platform.
El incendio ha fundido el aluminio.	The fire has melted (down) the aluminum.
Emilia rompe los vasos.	Emily breaks glasses.
El pirata hundirá el barco.	The pirate will sink the boat.
La niña movió el conejito.	The girl moved the bunny.
El rey extiende las fronteras al mar.	The king extends the boundaries to the sea.

At first glance, this intransitive/transitive contrast resembles that between *se lavó* 'he washed (himself)' and *la lavó* 'he washed her': Spanish seems to use a reflexive when the Subj acts upon itself while English optionally deletes its reflexive. But the analogy collapses: in English there is no reflexive optionally deleted from *the aluminum has melted (*itself)*, nor can *a sí mismo* be added to *se ha fundido.* (*Por sí mismo* can be used, but for the quite different meaning of 'all by itself'.) Note the following additional examples of the nonreflexivity of intransitivizing *se*; each verb could also be nonreflexive with an external agent.

Guillermo se arrodilló (se inclinó, se acostó, se enfermó) **a sí mismo.*
Las cajas se rompieron (se empaparon, se aplastaron, se agotaron) **a sí mismas.*

On the other hand, certain verbs with *se* show a dual potential here: (1) they can be intransitivized, in which case the event happened by itself without an agent (and *a sí mismo* is blocked), or (2) they can be true reflexives, in which case the Subj caused the event to happen to itself (and a *sí mismo* can be added). As one informant put it, "depende de la intención."

El perro se mojó.	The dog got wet.
El perro se mojó (a sí mismo).	The dog wetted himself.
Pilar se lastimó.	Pilar got hurt/injured.
Pilar se lastimó (a sí misma).	Pilar hurt herself.
Él se llama Zorro.	His name is Fox.
Él se llama Zorro (a sí mismo).	He calls himself Fox.

As Ramsey ([1894] 1956, 377 ff.) noted, the pedagogical generalization is that Spanish adds *se* to a transitive verb where English intransitivizes it by omitting a DO. Consequently, dictionaries and vocabularies should avoid one-word glosses like 'stop' and 'move' and more clearly distinguish *detenerse* and *detener, moverse* and *mover* as 'stop' vs. 'stop someone', 'move' vs. 'move something'. But like all generalizations, Ramsey's equation of Spanish V vs. V + *se* with English transitive vs. intransitive has holes in it (as he himself quickly pointed out). One is that English often adopts distinct verbs for the contrast:

apagar (tr), apagarse (intr)	turn off/out (tr), go off/out (intr)
acostar (tr), acostarse (intr)	put to bed (tr), go to bed (intr)
encargar (tr), encargarse (intr)	put in charge (tr), take charge (intr)
criar (tr), criarse (intr)	bring up, rear (tr), grow up, be raised (intr)
acercar (tr), acercarse (intr)	bring closer, pull up (tr), approach (intr)
sentar (tr), sentarse (intr)	seat (tr), sit down (intr)
reunir (tr), reunirse (intr)	bring together (tr), meet (intr)
desatar (tr), desatarse (intr)	untie (tr), come untied (intr)
disculpar (tr), disculparse (intr)	excuse (tr), apologize (intr)

Verbs of becoming (which Roldán would call inchoative) fall into the same pattern:

El café me pone nervioso. (tr)	Coffee *makes* me nervous.
Yo me pongo nervioso. (intr)	I *get* nervous.
La hicieron ejecutiva. (tr)	They *made* her an executive.
Se hizo ejecutiva. (intr)	She *became* an executive.
Lo convertí en un garaje. (tr)	I *converted* it into a garage.
Se convirtió en un garaje. (intr)	It *turned into/became* a garage.
La pastilla la enfermó. (tr)	The pill *made* her sick.
Ella se enfermó. (intr)	She *got* sick.

The other problem is that not all Spanish transitive verbs require *se* for intransitivity. Given the relationship between *lo acabé* (tr.) and *se acabó* (intr.), one would expect *lo terminé* vs. *se terminó,* but Spanish does not require *se* for the intransitive of *terminar*: *el curso terminó.* Other verbs that can be transitive or intransitive without *se* include *parar* 'stop', *mejorar* 'improve', *cambiar* 'change', *empezar* and *comenzar* 'start', *engordar* 'make/get fat'. Especially interesting are verbs such as *bajar, subir,* and *volver,* which can function either as intransitive verbs of motion, or as transitive actions that then add intransitivizing *se* as usual:

intransitive	transitive	intransitivized
Él subió al tercer piso.	Él subió la maleta.	Él *se* subió a la mesa.
Ella volvió a su puesto.	Ella volvió la página.	Ella *se* volvió.

The distinction is hard to appreciate via English: *went up, took up, got up on*; *went back, turned, turned around.*

9.3.7 Reflexive *se* of emotional reaction.

Se alegra mucho de esto.	She's very happy about this.

The psych verbs (v. 8.1.3) in this group form a large, important set, as illustrated here:

aburrir(se)	deprimir(se)	entusiasmar(se)
alegrar(se)	desesperar(se)	extrañar(se)
animar(se)	desilusionar(se)	inquietar(se)
asombrar(se)	divertir(se)	interesar(se)
asustar(se)	enfadar(se)	molestar(se)
calmar(se)	enojar(se)	ofender(se)
confundir(se)	enfurecer(se)	preocupar(se)
conmover(se)	entristecer(se)	sorprender(se)

When nonreflexive, the cause of the emotional reaction is cast as the verb's Subj, and the experiencer is cast as Obj (generally IO as with *gustar*, v. 8.1.3):

Esto les aburre/sorprende.	This bores/surprises them.
Tú me enojaste.	You made me mad.

When reflexive, such verbs cast the experiencer as Subj and the cause of the reaction as an optional PP (v. 10.4.2, 13.2.1):

Ellos se aburrieron (de la tele).	They got bored (with TV).
Ella se sorprendió (de que vinieras).	She was surprised (that you were coming).
Me enojé (del programa).	I got mad (at the program).

Syntactically, this category could be analyzed either as inchoative *se* (cf. *se preocupó* vs. *está preocupado* like *se durmió* vs. *está dormido*) or as intransitivizing *se* (*él me alegró, yo me alegré, *me alegré a mí mismo*). Babcock (1970), though, placed such verbs in their own category more because of their semantic properties as psych verbs.

9.3.8 Causative *se*.

Juan se operó anoche.	John had an operation last night.

The verbs in this group are few: *operarse, bautizarse, retratarse, vacunarse, cortarse (el pelo),* and some others. *Se* here indicates that the Subj causes something to be done for or upon himself/herself. Since these verbs are transitive, they can also occur nonreflexively: *el médico operó a Juan.* They may or may not be ambiguous between reflexive and causative senses: in a culture in which self-baptism is not recognized, *Juanito se bauti-*

zará is clear ('will be baptized'), but in *la enfermera se vacunará* the nurse may vaccinate herself or have herself vaccinated.

9.3.9 Passive and impersonal *se*.

Se cierra la puerta a la una.	The door is closed at 1:00; one closes the door at 1:00.
Se habla español.	Spanish is spoken; one speaks/you speak Spanish.

This category is likewise hard to separate from the intransitivizing *se*. Whereas English *close* can be transitive or intransitive (*I close the door, the door closes*), in Spanish one does not say *la puerta cierra* but *la puerta se cierra* or *se cierra la puerta,* with an intransitive ('it closes'), passive ('it is/gets closed'), or impersonal sense ('one closes/you close it')—or even a true reflexive sense when said of automatic doors. Perhaps *se cierra* has just one meaning, 'no external causer' underlying all these senses, as Bull's theory predicted. But given the equivalence in many contexts of *la puerta se cierra* and *la puerta es cerrada (por Juan, por el viento),* "passive/impersonal" *se* is commonly treated as a distinct category.

Or as two: Perlmutter (1971), Contreras (1974), Alarcos Llorach (1999), and others have shown that passive *se* differs from impersonal *se* in several ways. First, many speakers see *se cerró la puerta* as so passive in its force that they add an agent phrase as in true passives: *se cerró la puerta por el guarda = la puerta fue cerrada por el guarda.* This agent phrase is impossible when the sentence is meant impersonally (**se habla español por el guarda*). Second, impersonal *se* is distinct from passives because it can be used in true passives: *se es juzgado por la posteridad* 'one is judged by posterity'. Third, passive *se* only accompanies transitive verbs (intransitives cannot be passivized: **fui venido),* in which case it converges with intransitive *se*:

Se cerraron las puertas.	The doors were closed, The doors closed, The doors got closed.

Impersonal *se,* in contrast, accompanies either kind of verb, transitive or intransitive, provided that a human subject is implied (**se llueve* is odd for the same reason as **ella llueve*):

Se está muy cómodo aquí.	One is very comfortable here.
Se vivía bien en aquel entonces.	One/They lived well back then.
¿Se puede entrar?	Can one enter?
Se caminó todo el día.	People walked all day.
Como se vive, se muere.	One dies as one lives, You die as you live.

Fourth, with passive *se* the NP is the subject. The verb agrees with it, and this Subj precedes or follows the verb like any other Subj or is dropped when deemphasized (compare *Silvia comió ~ Comió Silvia ~ Comió*):

Las fiestas se organizarán así.	The festivals will be organized this way.
= Se organizarán *las fiestas* así.	
Ø Se organizarán así.	They'll be organized this way.

With impersonal *se*, however, the verb is always 3sg. and the NP occupies a DO position after the verb and (when deemphasized) changes to a DO pronoun (compare *Silvia comió las nueces* ~ *Silvia las comió*):

Se organizar*á* *las fiestas* así.	One/you/they will organize the festivals this way.
Se *las* organizará así.	One will organize them this way.

Nevertheless, granting the syntactic differences between, say, *¿Cómo se define?* (passive *se*) and *¿Cómo se la define?* (impersonal *se*), often there is little difference in meaning (García 1975, 237). In English, too, there is more structural than semantic difference between *How is this defined?* and *How does one define this?* since both downplay the personal identity of an agent.

In pedagogy, the more immediate problem is the lack of a single handy English equivalent for impersonal/passive *se*. Formal English uses *one* whereas colloquial usage favors *you* or *they*, which are also possible in Spanish. English speakers unconsciously distinguish personal and impersonal *you* in context, as in knowing whether to respond to *How do you get good grades?* with *I study a lot* (*you* = personal) or with *You study a lot* (*you* = impersonal), but they are generally unaware of these functions or of their subtle aspectual restrictions. *One* and *you* are normally limited to habitual events, as in *one checks/you check the tires every day* for *se revisa las llantas cada día*; for single, one-time events, English switches to a passive, as in *the tires were/got checked* for *se revisó las llantas*. *People* and *a person* are also a general English strategy for expressing impersonality, whence students' overuse of *las personas* and *una persona* in their Spanish.

As an alternative to impersonal *se*, Spanish likewise uses *uno*: *es que no se tiene suficiente cuidado* = *es que uno no tiene suficiente cuidado*. They seem equivalent, and *uno* is the only option when the verb is already reflexive: *Uno se baña cada día* (**Se se baña cada día*). But *se* and *uno* are not entirely interchangeable (Roldán 1971b, 26; Perlmutter 1971, 36). One difference is that a female speaker can use a feminine *una,* with agreement: *Una está satisfecha consigo misma* (compare **Se está satisfecha consigo misma*). Another is that only *se* is used when the verb's Subj is implicitly many people indefinitely; *uno* particularizes (for obvious etymological reasons), which is why **A las nueve uno empezó a llegar* sounds odd. Third, *uno* counts as a genuine NP, occurring in any NP slot, while *se* can represent only an impersonal Subj. Hence, only *uno* can be used for an impersonal Obj (IO, DO, OP): *Le deprimen a uno las noticias.*

It is again worth noting that all these types of *se* are not entirely distinct; a given reflexive verb may convey several of them depending on context. *Verse* in *los novios se ven* is a true reflexive or reciprocal; in *se ven muy cansados* it is a synonym of *parecen* and seems to be "meaning-changing"; in *se ven muchas películas extranjeras* it is passive *se*. One also relies on world knowledge in interpreting *se*: *¿Se mató la gallina?* might ask if the chicken killed itself or if the chicken was or got killed or if someone killed the chicken, but the intended meaning here is probably passive *se* since chickens do not engage in suicide. But with humans, who do unto others and do unto themselves, clarification may be needed. For example, with *matar* + *tirano* the true reflexive is distinguished from the passive/impersonal sense by employing personal *a* (v. 11.2.3) for the latter—demonstrating, once again, that the NP with impersonal *se* is the DO:

Nunca se matará el tirano.	The tyrant will never kill himself.
Nunca se matará *al* tirano.	People will never kill the tyrant.

If a female DO is pronominalized, it becomes *la*: *se critica a la reina → se la critica.* For males, grammarians have recommended *le*, although *lo* is well attested too: *se critica al tirano → se le critica ~ se lo critica* (Roldán 1971b, 25).

9.3.10 So-called "unplanned occurrences." Spanish has an IO of general involvement in an event (v. 8.1.2) and a *se* that reflexivizes, intensifies, intransitivizes, passivizes, or impersonalizes the verb. When the two are used together, sentences such as the following result:

Tomás se murió (+ a nosotros) → Tomás se nos murió.
El peine se cayó (+ a mí) → El peine se me cayó.
Se olvidó la respuesta (+ a mi) → Se me olvidó la respuesta.
Se perdieron las llaves (+ a Uds.) → Se les perdieron las llaves.
Se armó un lío (+ a ella) → Se le armó un lío.

Consequently, the addition of an IO to a reflexive construction is as unremarkable as it is in other VPs such as *es difícil (+ a mí) → me es difícil, pagan bien (+ a él) → le pagan bien, fue dado (+ a ella) → le fue dado.*

Yet *se* + IO + V has been singled out by many U.S. textbook writers as the expression of accidents, unplanned events, and escape from responsibility (e.g., Mujica 1982, 35). Interestingly, the Real Academia, Gili Gaya, and other Hispanic authorities have seen nothing of the sort in this construction, nor have they set it up as a special category. In reality, many cases could not possibly be construed thus: *se te pagó* is a deliberate compliance with responsibility, and *Tomás se nos murió* does not imply a dodging of responsibility (nor does nonreflexive *Tomás murió* necessarily imply a planned death). With *yo olvidé la respuesta* vs. *se me olvidó la respuesta,* it is true that the former spotlights the speaker as Subj and proceeds to comment on what he/she did, while the latter casts him/her as an involved entity. But subjecthood does not always entail willful agency or deliberate causation (v. 8.1.1), and with both statements the hearer can hold the speaker accountable for a faulty memory. Neither version, in itself, necessarily implies *sin querer, por casualidad,* or *con intención*. If the forgetting was intentional, that is, something that the speaker *did*, then *olvidé la respuesta* is more direct, but it would be dangerous to generalize from this unlikely case (after all, how many forgettings are planned?) to the host of other such constructions, and doing so in fact would obscure the real meaning of *se* + IO + V.

It is even more dangerous to introduce notions such as "responsibility" and "avoidance of responsibility," for these convey an ethical or moral sense more than a grammatical one. Students studying a foreign culture already have woeful stereotypes of it, and to explain the frequency of *se* + IO + V in terms of cultural mores reinforces the very misimpressions teachers are trying to combat. Indeed, one student who read his textbook's "avoidance of responsibility" presentation of this construction proceeded to explain it to his classmates in terms of the fatalism, indolence, and lack of initiative that he assumed as typical of Hispanics.

"Unplanned occurrence" is the tenth category of perceived uses of *se*. It ought to be banned, not only because of its false reasoning but because the other nine are more than sufficient.

9.3.11 Summary. The functions of *se* are varied and complex, and for that reason, many textbooks focus on its reflexive meaning (*se levanta, se ducha, se viste*) in the predictable lesson that Lozano (1997, 551) criticized as the "Waking Up Scene." The many nonreflexive senses are postponed (if taken up at all) to final chapters on passives or grammatical miscellanea. But if a textbook's organization is predicated on a syllabus based on frequency and function, the nonreflexive senses of *se* (particularly intransitivizing, impersonal, and passive) deserve more, and earlier, attention; they are difficult to avoid in communication and occur more frequently than the true passive (v. 12.3), and probably more than the true reflexive sense as well.

9.4 The syntax of pronouns. Beyond their meaning and morphology, Spanish pronouns also give problems to English speakers because of their strikingly different sentence position and combinations with each other. In fact, they may no longer be real pronouns.

9.4.1 Pronominalizing with clitics. Pronominalization is the process whereby NPs are changed into pronouns. In English, this process does not greatly affect word order, for pronouns occur in the same positions as other NPs:[6]

Mary	gave	her phone number	to	the man who asked her out.
She	gave	*it*	to	*him.*

In Spanish, though, position depends on the type of pronoun. Traditionally, two sets are distinguished, the Subj/OP forms and the DO/IO forms:

Set 1: Subj/OP: *yo, mí, tú, ti, Ud., él, ella, ello, nosotros (-as), vosotros (-as), Uds., ellos (-as), sí*

Set 2: DO and IO: *me, te, le, lo, la, nos, os, los, les, las, se* (all types)

The two sets go by various names—DISJUNCTIVE and CONJUNCTIVE, STRONG and WEAK, STRESSED and UNSTRESSED, EMPHATIC and CLITIC—but all these labels make the same point. The first set is stressed and forms constituents that can be separated (disjoined) from the verb and moved: *ellos saben, saben ellos.* The second set is unstressed and always joined phonetically to the verb, 'leaning on' (Greek *enklitikos*) it. They normally occur before the verb (PROCLITIC) but occur after it (ENCLITIC) in the case of infinitives, gerunds, and affirmative commands: proclitic *se va,* enclitic *váyase.* Following prevailing usage, we call this second set simply CLITICS.

It is very misleading to equate clitics like Spanish *me* with English pronouns like *me.* The former are no longer independent words as they are in English, but are evolving into verb prefixes or, as Alarcos Llorach (1999, 246) called them, "incrementos personales del verbo" for expressing Obj, just as the verb suffix expresses the Subj. Some of the key contrasts of Spanish clitics with English pronouns are the following (see Whitley 1990):

1. They do not occupy NP positions in surface structure: *Vi los animales. *Vi los.*
2. They cannot be used apart from a verb: *—¿A quién prefieres? —*Te.*
3. They cannot be joined by conjunctions: **Te y me vieron.* (English: *They saw you and me.*)
4. They generally do not share verbs: *Puede lavarse y vestirse, *Puede lavar y vestirse.*
5. They cannot be emphasized as separate words. For emphasis or contrast, Spanish instead adds forms from Set 1 to the basic clitic + V "nucleus" (v. 11.2):

neutral:	He introduced her to you.	Te la presentó.
emphatic Subj:	*HE* introduced her to you.	**Él** te la presentó. ~ Te la presentó **él**.
emphatic Obj:	He introduced her to *YOU*.	Te la presentó **a ti**. ~ **A ti** te la presentó.

6. Even when the Obj is "spelled out" as a specific pronoun or when the IO is named by a full NP, the clitic still accompanies the verb, a phenomenon called CLITIC DOUBLING:

   *(Lo) vi a usted.
   Aquellos tipos *(lo) tratan a uno como inferior.
   A Sonia *(le) gustan las plantas.
   *(Nos) lo dieron a mí y a mi hermana.
   *(Le) di los dulces a mi amigo.

   (The asterisk-parenthesis notation means 'ungrammatical if missing'.) While some speakers still accept the version *Di los dulces a mi amigo,* for many if not most speakers today, this version is awkward or even ungrammatical, and clitic doubling (***Le** di los dulces a mi amigo*) has become the norm for IO expression—and has started spreading to DOs as well.[7] Weissenrieder (1995) therefore urged that this *le* be regarded as a prefix of verb agreement with the IO, just as the verb ending agrees with the Subj.

An *a*-phrase is also used to emphasize a DO clitic: *¿Me escogiste* ***a mí****? ¿Lo quieres* ***a él****?* Consequently, *a* + NP may represent DO, IO, or a PP that is not an Obj of the verb at all, and its pronominalization is not obvious from form alone. Compare the following examples:

1. DO: atender *a Clara* → atenderla; visitar *a Clara* → visitarla
2. IO: hablar *a Clara* → hablarle; servir *a Clara* → servirle
3. PP: regresar *a Clara,* regresar *a ella*; referirse *a Clara* → referirse *a ella*

The DO can be ascertained by passivization (v. 12.3): we can say *Clara fue atendida* but not **Clara fue hablada* or **Clara fue regresada,* so *a Clara* is a DO in case (1). This leaves us with the problem of distinguishing cases (2) and (3), which is not as straightforward. There are sentences in which the *a*+ NP seems to have a locative adverbial force suggesting PP as in (3), and yet Spanish allows these to be treated as IO.

Clara se acercó *a nosotros* → Clara se *nos* (IO) acercó.
El artículo se antepone *al sustantivo.* → El artículo se *le* (IO) antepone.
La fama vino *al general* muy temprano → La fama *le* (IO) vino muy temprano.

9.4.2 Sequences of clitics. When pronominalization yields two or more clitics with one verb, they form a phonetically melded clump with it. If they are clitics of the second verb in V + V, they optionally move to the first verb by a transformation called Clitic Promotion or Clitic Climbing (v. 13.1.2.8), although if they move, they must be promoted together (Suñer 1974): *querían mostrármelo* → *me lo querían mostrar* (not **lo querían mostrarme*).

What determines which of two clitics precedes the other in this "clump"? The traditional pedagogical rule is "IO before DO": *me* (IO) *lo* (DO) *dan*, not **lo me dan*. It works often enough in textbook examples for its credentials to seem impeccable, but they are peccable nonetheless. Aside from the students' problem in keeping IO and DO straight (no mean task in Spanish, as we have seen), scholars of the language have repeatedly shown that the IO–DO rule does not work. A century and a half ago, Bello ([1847] 1958, 293) pointed out that regardless of function, *te* and *os* precede *me* and *nos,* and that the latter precede *le(s), lo(s), la(s)*: *me le humillé, te les aficionaste, te me recomendaron, te me acerqué, te nos rendiste*—all of which contradict IO–DO order. More succinctly, the RAE (1924, 218; 1979, 427) has given the lineup as *se* + second person + first + third, with no comments on an IO precedence over DO.

Nevertheless, the IO–DO rule enjoyed such favor in the United States that Holton (1960) felt compelled to demonstrate its inadequacies anew. He observed that in *nos le reunimos* 'we joined her', the reflexive DO precedes the IO and that the predicted ordering **le nos reunimos* is flatly wrong. Furthermore, the pedagogical rule cannot handle what happens with *two* IOs, which is quite possible: *¡no me (IO) le (IO) calientes la oreja a la muchacha!* (compare **no le me . . .*).

In order to account for the permissible sequences and to exclude the ungrammatical ones, Perlmutter (1971, 45) posited a SURFACE-STRUCTURE CONSTRAINT (SSC), shown in figure 9.4, that acts like a filter in allowing only certain combinations of clitics to surface from deep structure. This SSC was not at all revolutionary, since it merely reformulated the RAE's earlier analysis of *se* + 2 + 1 + 3.

Note that only one slot or box is available for all clitics beginning with *l-*. If pronominalization yields two of these (*le lo, les la,* etc.), the *le(s)* travels to the *se* box—a descriptively neat way of handling "pseudo-*se*." Moreover, there is only one box for *se*, regardless of whether it is reflexive, pseudo (for *le* or *les*), intransitivizing, impersonal, inherent, or whatever; if the syntax generates two *se*'s, the SSC runs out of room and the sentence cannot pass. Thus, the SSC correctly blocks the following as ungrammatical.[8]

> **Se se arrepiente pronto* for 'one is soon sorry'
> **Se se lo puso* for 'he put it on (himself) for her' or 'someone put it on him'
> **Se se los dio* for 'they were given to him'

Hence, the SSC has considerable pedagogical value; it covers more ground than the IO–DO rule, it is more accurate, and students can memorize and apply it with relative ease.

However, although each individual DO and IO has grammatical permission to become a clitic in accordance with the SSC, processing them grows harder as they stack up (García 1975, 411–89); ambiguity increases as well, as indicated by the question marks on the following examples:

> Me presentó.
> (?) *Te me* presentó.
> (??) *Te me le* presentó.
> (???) *Se te me le* presentó.

Spanish speakers find longer clitic clumps awkward and may avoid them. According to Suñer (1974), three clitics are the limit: thus, for the meaning 'someone (impersonal) sent

Figure 9.4. The SSC (surface-structure constraint) on clitic lineup

se	te os	me nos	l-

flowers to you', the result is *se te mandó flores*, and if *flores* is also pronominalized, *se te las mandó*. But if we now try to express 'someone sent them to you for me', the result **se te me las mandó* fails.[9]

Why? Further refinements of the SSC require more data, and unfortunately (for linguistic analysis), Spanish speakers just do not go around saying things like **se te me las mandó,* whether because of grammar, stylistics, semantics, situational need, or cognitive complexity. Instead, at this point they switch to a clearer structure such as PP: *se te las mandó* ***para mí***. Prepositions, after all, are syntactic devices that allow more precision than can be handled by the morphology of even a richly endowed language like Spanish, and we turn to them in the next chapter.

Notes for chapter 9

1. This traditional definition is actually true only of ANAPHORIC pronouns, those that refer back to a preceding N in the discourse. DEICTIC pronouns such as *yo* and *tú* point directly to someone in the speech situation.

2. García and Otheguy (1977) admitted that there was more *leísmo* in Spain than in America. The overall incidences of *le* usage with single-object verbs in their study were 73 percent for the Spaniards, 41 percent for the Ecuadorians, 38 percent for the Mexicans, 29 percent for the Colombians, 27 percent and 22 percent for Cubans (two groups), and 13 percent for the Argentines.

3. Babcock (1970) also saw reflexives as interconnected. For her, *se* indicates what was called "middle voice" in classical grammar ("middle" between active and passive and between transitive and intransitive). In particular, *se* incorporates the Subj into the verb and identifies it with some element therein, downplaying external agency. García (1975) agreed that all types of *se* are connected, but posited that their connection is based on the meaning 'low deixis' that depends on inference from the sentential context. For an argument in favor of separate types of *se*, see Lozano 1975. The fact that one can play on the senses, as in the following joke (Azevedo 1992, 266), suggests that speakers perceive a distinction:

—¿Cómo se llama usted?

—Yo no me llamo, los que me llaman son los demás.

4. As a matter of terminology, the reader should bear in mind that *reflexivo* tends to be reserved in Spanish for true reflexives. Verbs like *atreverse, irse,* and *referirse,* which are merely conjugated with a reflexive pronoun (whether inherent, intransitivizing, or meaning-changing), are *verbos pronominales*.

5. Aid (1973, 80–108) argued for DECAUSATIVE for this *se*. In pairs such as *Rosa apagó el cigarrillo* vs. *El cigarrillo se apagó,* and *La serpiente asustó a Eva* vs. *Eva se asustó,* Aid saw *se* as a kind of verb inflection signifying 'removal of external cause'. She was able to accommodate meaning-changing and passive *se* into the same account.

6. The exception is a pronominalization such as *Mary gave John her number → She gave him it,* which some speakers accept and may use, while others find it awkward or even ungrammatical.

7. Clitic doubling for DO (*Lo conozco a Juan, No lo encuentro a mi hijo*) is still dialectal; according to Lipski (1994), it is found in Argentina, Paraguay, Peru, and a few other areas. It is, however, the next logical step in the evolution of Obj inflection on the Spanish verb.

8. Note that this restriction against *se se* is not a global one against two instances of *se* in the same sentence; as long as they stay in different clitic blocks, there can be two of them, as in *Hoy día se* (impersonal*) prefiere bañarse* (reflexive) *por la mañana.* (But with Clitic Promotion, **Hoy día se se prefiere bañar . . .*)

9. Other amendments proposed for the SSC may be a matter of idiolect rather than general grammar. For example:

(a) Many speakers balk at "clumps" that are ambiguous between DO and IO interpretations, for example, *María te me recomendó* = you to me? me to you? (Perlmutter, 1971). Following Bello's suggestion ([1847] 1958, 293), such speakers prefer *María te recomendó a mí* for 'Mary recommended you to me'. Bello, however, cited abundant literary attestation for *te me* and admitted that it is well established.

(b) Some speakers favor keeping reflexive clitics (not just *se*) before nonreflexive ones. For 'I exerted myself for your sake', they find **me te esforcé* (blocked by the SSC) ungrammatical but also feel an awkwardness with *te me esforcé* (Szabo 1974).

Exercises for chapter 9

1. Error analysis:

(a) *Se gusta.
(b) *Me gusto.
(c) *Dio me $20.00.
(d) *Escribí a le.
(e) *Les la ofreció.
(f) *Nos tenemos dos.
(g) *Lo hice como te.
(h) *Tú lo me di.
(i) *Se lavas.
(j) *Es yo. *Es mí.
(k) *Da la familia satisfacción.
(l) *Vio su mismo.

2. One common error in first-year classes is exemplified by **Lo está aquí, *Lo parece gris, *Se lo gusta.* What is the problem here, and how can teachers obviate it?

3. Many teachers have firm opinions on whether *vosotros* should be included in class work. Textbook writers therefore find themelves in the quandary of damned if they do present and use it, and damned if they do not. Moreover, in questions directed to the student some writers alternate between *tú* and *usted,* presumably to practice both equally. Almost none introduces *vos*, despite its widespread use. What policy do you think writers should adopt toward *tú, vosotros, usted(es),* and *vos?* As a teacher, what ground rules would you establish in the classroom for address (a) between students and yourself and (b) among students? Why?

4. In what ways is the Spanish system portrayed in figure 9.1 incomplete or unrepresentative? As a teacher, what would your policy be toward adhering to it, and why?

5. If you were designing, writing, and teaching from your own "ideal" text, how would you take up and present the Spanish IO? Address the following points and outline your presentation and sequencing. (For some of these points you might wish to review 8.0–8.1.4.)

(a) meanings and functions of IO
(b) IO pronoun forms
(c) time between the presentation of DO and IO forms, and between these and "double object" combinations (*se lo, me las,* etc.)

(d) emphasis with *a él, a mí,* and so on
(e) the clitic doubling construction, for example, ***le** escribí a Miguel*
(f) reverse-construction verbs and others taking IO rather than DO

6. In teaching reflexives, one sometimes tells students that *acostarse* is really 'put oneself to bed', *llamarse* 'call oneself', *sentarse* 'seat oneself', *detenerse* 'stop oneself', and so on. Why is this misleading, in terms of both the Spanish system and the English one? Are these true reflexives? What test can be used for them?

7. *Enojarse, acercarse, alegrarse, vestirse* are usually introduced as reflexive verbs in vocabularies along with *quejarse.* Why is this treatment misleading? What can teachers and textbook writers do in order to ensure that students perceive reflexive/nonreflexive contrasts? What relationship do such verbs have with the *estar* + participle pattern?

8. Classify each of the following reflexives according to the taxonomy presented in section 9.3. Writing sentences with them may help, but assume that none is being used impersonally, passively, or with "pseudo-*se*," since these are separate options. What criteria do you apply in classifying them? Where is the classification unclear or ambiguous?

agotarse	despedirse	equivocarse	negarse
apoyarse	desquitarse	fiarse	oponerse
arrepentirse	divertirse	imaginarse	parecerse
avergonzarse	emborracharse	imponerse	peinarse
burlarse	empeñarse	llamarse	refugiarse
calmarse	encontrarse	mantenerse	resquebrajarse
darse cuenta	enderezarse	meterse	reunirse
deshacerse	enemistarse	mudarse	vengarse

9. What meaning (if any) does the third-person clitic *las* have in *me las arreglo* 'I get by', *no le hace* 'it doesn't matter', and *ándale*? How is it similar to inherent *se*?

10. In what ways are clitics more like verb affixes than separate words, unlike their English counterparts? How does this setup cause problems for English speakers?

11. The following sentences come from the international edition of *El País* (May 28, 1984, Feb. 25, 1985). Explain the uses of the italicized occurrences of *se.*

(a) O *se* destruyen las ciudades o *se* las transforma desde sus símbolos.
(b) La ambición de no ser quien *se* es es bastante común.

12. Explain the (potential) ambiguity of each of the following:

(a) No se bebió la leche.	(d) No se lo podrá comprar.	(g) Se ha mojado.
(b) Se mataron las reses	(e) Se cerrará la taquilla.	(h) Ellos se aburrieron.
(c) Los herejes se mataron.	(f) Se lo pondrá después.	(i) Te nos presentó.

13. Explain the differences in meaning within each of the following sets of sentences.
   (a) Se lavó a Emiliano. Se lavó Emiliano. Lo lavó Emiliano.
   (b) Se engañará a la maestra. Se engañará la maestra.
   (c) Se ve en el espejo. Se ve muy linda hoy. Se ve una diferencia.
   (d) Se hizo unos medicamentos. Se hicieron unos medicamentos. Se hicieron médicos. Se los/les hizo médicos.
   (e) Él vistió a Manolito. Él vistió su uniforme. Él se vistió.
   (f) Le quedó corto. Le queda poco. Se quedó un rato. Se quedó con el regalo.

14. The following exchanges (T = teacher, S = student) show the kinds of problems that occur once Obj pronouns have been taken up. Explain the students' difficulties.
   (a) T: ¿Qué ropa se ha puesto Ud. hoy?
       S: He puesto una camisa y un pantalón.
   (b) T: ¿A quién se lo dije?
       S: Ud. dijo lo a Juan.
   (c) T: ¿A quién se lo dije?
       S: Juan se lo dijo.
   (d) T: ¿Ud. les presta su dinero a sus amigos y a sus familiares?
       S: No, yo nunca pres-, presto uhh . . . presto mi dinero . . . a mis amigos y familiares.
   (e) T: ¿Lo quiere Ud.? ¿Se lo doy?
       S: Sí, quiero lo. Se lo dé, por favor.
   (f) T: ¿Se habla allí portugués?
       S: No, no hablo portugués.
       T: No, escuche: ¿se habla portugués en Brasil?
       S: ¡Ah! No, yo no *ME* hablo portugués en Brasil.
   (g) T: ¿Cómo se llama Ud.?
       S: Me llamo es Susana. (*or* Mi llama es Susana)

15. (a) Many textbooks and reference works give lists of verbs that take certain prepositions. Why is the syntax of verbs with *a* unclear from a mere vocabulary entry? Study the following examples in answering this question, using the tests discussed in section 9.4.1.

acceder a NP	dedicarse a NP	parecerse a NP
acercarse a NP	dirigirse a NP	pegar a NP
acostumbrarse a NP	esperar a NP	preceder a NP
adelantarse a NP	ganar a NP	referirse a NP
adorar a NP	inquietar a NP	robar a NP
añadir X a NP	llegar a NP	someterse a NP
contestar a NP	obedecer a NP	sustituirse a NP
corresponder a NP	oponerse a NP	unirse a NP

(b) Turn this exercise into a project by testing native speakers' pronominalizations of sentences containing these verbs. Note your informants' backgrounds and any cases where they admit two possibilities—interchangeably or with different meanings.

16. Pronouns and verbs are often practiced and tested by fill-in-the-blanks that tell the teacher very little about students' ability to use the forms in discourse. A more revealing and naturalistic technique emphasized by Whitley and González (2000) is to retell a passage by changing point of view, reporting first person as third or vice versa. Following is an example (p. 86, adapted). Test one or more Spanish students with this passage or with a similar one appropriate to their level (but still containing a variety of verb and pronoun types), and then carry out an error analysis on the results. What strategies do students show in their interlanguage? How accurately are they processing the forms?

> **En la aduana**. *Cambie la siguiente narración a la tercera persona.*
>
> Soy una mujer de negocios y tengo clientes internacionales. Me gusta viajar pero me preocupo cuando llego a la aduana. No sé por qué, pero los aduaneros siempre me causan problemas. Me piden el pasaporte, me comparan con la foto y dicen que no soy la misma persona. Les contesto que sí lo soy, pero los retratos no me salen bien. Luego, les abro mi equipaje y ellos me lo revisan. Me preguntan si tengo algo que declarar y contesto que no, pero desconfían de mí y se fijan en cada cosa que llevo conmigo. Me tratan como narcotraficante y en busca de mi "contrabando" revuelven mi ropa y hablan de cada artículo en voz alta. Me quejo cortésmente, pero no me hacen caso.
>
> Al final, me siento humillada pero con una sonrisa sádica me dicen "Gracias, señora, pase y perdone la molestia". Me queda poco tiempo ahora para llegar a mi destino, pero me tranquilizo, me quedo allí un ratito cerrando las maletas con calma y les replico, "No fue molestia ninguna, señores".

Chapter 10

Adverbs, prepositions, and conjunctions

10.0 The uninflected words. In describing Greek and Latin grammar, classical scholars dealt at length with those parts of speech that offered interesting inflectional paradigms: verbs, nouns, adjectives, and pronouns. Other words were consigned with little comment to three other categories. These were the class standing 'at the verb' (Latin *ad-verbium*), the class 'positioned before' others (*prae-positiō*), and the class for 'joining together' (*con-jūnctiō*). With rare exceptions, modern grammarians, linguists, and text writers have retained this focus on the "major" categories of V, N, Adj, and Pro, to the relative neglect of what are still called ADVERBS, PREPOSITIONS, and CONJUNCTIONS.

It is understandable why these last three categories have been overshadowed by the others. They are fewer in number, simpler in morphology, and apparently straightforward in their meanings and grammatical roles. Thus, aside from notes on *por/para, pero/sino,* and mood contrasts after conjunctions, these parts of speech are relegated to vocabulary lists in Spanish courses. However, errors such as the following suggest the need for more attention to them.

*¡Estás tarde!
*Paré el coche porque del tráfico.
*Mi amiga nos esperaba afuera el restaurante.
*Escuchamos a la radio mientras estudiando.
*Es difícil a romper.

Given the usual vocabulary matchings *tarde = late, porque = because, afuera = outside, mientras = while, a = to,* with no further input or explanation from book or teacher, it is natural for students to generate the foregoing sentences on the basis of how the English words are used. Corrected in piecemeal fashion, such errors will continue because the problem is as much grammatical as it is lexical. In fact, in order to master the usage of Spanish adverbs, prepositions, and conjunctions, students require at least four kinds of information about them: lexical, categorial, semantic, and grammatical.

Lexical. Spanish speakers do not say *because,* they say *porque*; they do not say *while,* they say *mientras.* Only this much is clear from vocabulary lists, and even so, important lexical relationships in both languages are obscured in a list of *palabras sueltas.* For example, Spanish *por* is to *porque* as *para* is to *para que,* but this connection is lost when all four words are presented separately in terms of English *for, because,* and *in order that.*

Categorial. The way in which words are syntactically CATEGORIZED (classified) is crucial for knowing how to use them in a sentence, but it is not obvious from meaning alone. For indicating exterior location, English uses *outside* as both adverb and preposition (and noun and adjective, for that matter), whereas Spanish requires a distinction of *(a)fuera* as adverb and *fuera de* as a preposition. Yet many students today have only a sketchy idea of parts of speech, and injunctions such as "Don't use *afuera* as a preposition" may mean little to them.

Semantic. Both *por* and *para* can translate *for,* while *a* conveys both *to* and *at*. But *por* and *para* are no more synonymous for the Spanish speaker than *to* and *at* are for the English speaker. Such words reflect conceptualizations that are relative to the semantic organization of their language, and they cannot be conveyed by one-word glosses in another language.

Grammatical. Many uses of prepositions have little to do with their primary meanings. They have become GRAMMATICALIZED or grammatically fixed in certain constructions as markers of syntactic relationships and functions (i.e., as FUNCTORS). In pedagogy as well as in linguistic analysis, such words cannot be explained apart from the constructions they mark.

The following sections explore these four kinds of information, with special emphasis on the problems that three rather neglected parts of speech keep causing in language acquisition.

10.1 Lexical relationships. It is useful to retain the tripartite division among *adverbium, praepositiō,* and *conjūnctiō,* but in reality, the three are closely related. In order to clarify the relationship, it is useful to look first at verbs and adjectives. A verb can be subcategorized according to the Obj or complement it governs. Four possibilities for a verb such as *creer* are (1) no Obj, (2) an Obj NP (containing a noun or pronoun), (3) a noun clause complement, or (4) an infinitival complement, VP-inf. Case (1) is traditionally described as intransitive and case (2) as transitive; cases (3) and (4) are variously analyzed (v. 13.1.2).

(1) V + Ø	*Ella cree.*
(2) V + Obj NP	*Ella cree nuestro cuento.*
(3) V + clause	*Ella cree que lo ha explicado bien.*
(4) V + VP-inf	*Ella cree haberlo explicado bien.*

An adjective such as *contento* has the same possibilities, although it requires a connecting *con* or *de* to form a phrase with its complement:

(1) Adj + Ø	*Está contenta.*
(2) Adj + *con* + Obj NP	*Está contenta con su regalo.*
(3) Adj + *de* + clause	*Está contenta de que todos la respeten.*
(4) Adj + *de* + VP-inf	*Está contenta de haberlo entendido.*

Now, consider the word *después,* whose category we will provisionally call "X." It occurs in exactly the same four patterns.

(1) X + Ø	*Saliste después.*
(2) X + *de* + Obj NP	*Saliste después de la primera función.*
(3) X + (*de*) + clause	*Saliste después (de) que terminaron.*
(4) X + *de* + VP-inf	*Saliste después de comer.*

Traditional grammar does not assign V or Adj to wholly distinct categories according to their transitivity or complements, but that is exactly how it has treated X-words. Used "intransitively" (no Obj), *después* is called an adverb (Adv); used with an Obj NP or infinitive, it is renamed a preposition (Prep); and used with a *que* clause, it is renamed a conjunction (Conj). Occasionally, Prep and Conj are grouped together as RELATORS, but there is syntactic and lexical justification (Aid 1973) for recognizing a higher relationship among all three as subcategories of what we will call ADVERBIALS (Advl).

The ways in which Advl relationships are reflected in the lexical setup of Spanish and English are illustrated in figure 10.1. For locatives, it can be seen that Spanish employs the base form (e.g., *delante*) as an Adv and adds *de* for the Prep (*delante de*). English sometimes behaves in the same way (*ahead, ahead of*) but often assigns one form to both functions (*behind*). With nonlocatives there is less consistency, but the general Spanish pattern is the use of the base form as Adv (*después*), adding *de* for the Prep (*después de*) and *de que,* or more often just *que,* for Conj (*después (de) que*). English may categorize one form as all three (*before*), derive Adv or Prep from Conj (*because* → *because of*), or derive Adv from the Prep/Conj (*after* → *afterward*). Both languages have a few lexical gaps filled in by phrases verging on idioms (*por eso* corresponding to *por* and *porque*) or by suppletive forms (*mientras* and *durante, while* and *during*).

The Spanish system is the neater one overall, and the triplet pattern of *X, X de, X que* for Adv, Prep, and Conj (Keniston 1937, 245) deserves more pedagogical attention. Moreover, since labels such as "adverb" may have little meaning for students, teachers may need to create activities that manipulate options such as *por eso, por el tránsito,* and *porque había mucho tránsito,* or *después, después de la fiesta, después de celebrar,* and *después que celebraron,* so that students learn which Advls stand alone and which ones introduce other elements.

10.2 Analysis and classification. There have been three approaches to a general TAXONOMY or classification of Advl types. These are classification by meaning, classification by formation, and classification by position and function.

Figure 10.1. Examples of adverbial systems

Locatives

Spanish		English	
Adv	**Prep**	**Adv**	**Prep**
debajo, abajo	debajo de	underneath, below	under, below
detrás, atrás	detrás de	behind, in back	behind, in back of
(a)dentro	dentro de	inside	inside (of)
al lado	al lado de	on/to the side	beside, next to
lejos	lejos de	far, far away	far from
cerca	cerca de	nearby, close	near, close to
más allá, allende	más allá de	beyond	beyond
encima	encima de	on top	on top of, on

Nonlocatives

Spanish			English		
Adv	**Prep**	**Conj**	**Adv**	**Prep**	**Conj**
después	después de	después de que	afterwards	after	after
antes	antes de	antes de que	before(hand)	before	before
por eso	por	porque	so, therefore	because of, for	because
hasta entonces	hasta	hasta que	until then	until	until
además	además de	además de que	besides, in addition	besides, in addition to	besides the fact that
mientras tanto	durante	mientras	meanwhile	during	while

10.2.1 Classification by meaning and formation. Adverbial expressions tend to sort out into a limited set of semantic groups, as illustrated below.

manner: (Adv) *bien, despacio, contentamente, aprisa, al azar, gratis . . .*
(Prep) *con, de, mediante, conforme a . . .*
(Conj) *de modo que, como . . .*

time: (Adv) *entonces, siempre, ayer, antes, tarde, dos veces, en seguida . . .*
(Prep) *durante, desde, antes de, por . . .*
(Conj) *cuando, hasta que, siempre que, en cuanto . . .*

place: (Adv) *allí, afuera, arriba, acá . . .*
(Prep) *en, a, detrás de, junto a . . .*
(Conj) *donde*

reason: (Adv) *adrede, por eso, por (lo) tanto . . .*
(Prep) *para, por, a causa de, a raíz de . . .*
(Conj) *así que, porque, puesto que . . .*

extent: (Adv) *tanto, más, demasiado . . .*
(Prep) *por, hasta . . .*
(Conj) *tanto que, cuanto más . . . más . . .*

A semantic taxonomy of this sort is sometimes used in reference works to bring out common denominators of meaning. It also underlies the formation of questions (v. 12.1.2), in which *cuándo* corresponds to Advls of time, *dónde* to Advls of place, *cómo* to those of manner, and so on. Another important group consists of adverbs such as *quizás, tal vez, evidentemente, seguramente*, which Otaola (1988) called "adverbiales modales" and integrated into a theory of mood based on speaker attitude (v. 7.3.2.2).

When adverbs, prepositions, and conjunctions are classified by formation, a distinction is made between SIMPLE (consisting of a single morpheme) and DERIVED (formed from other morphemes). Several formations are consistent enough to be pointed out in pedagogy, as illustrated in the following sections.

10.2.1.1 Adverbs. Spanish has a limited set of simple Advs, including *bien, nunca, siempre, ya, quizás, tarde* (Keniston 1937, 250–53). For the most part, their English equivalents tend to be simple as well: *well, never, always,* and so on.

Derived Advs are more abundant. Those formed off Adj usually have *-mente* in Spanish corresponding to *-ly* in English. The suffix *-mente* is specifically added to the feminine Adj form, betraying its origin as a feminine noun.[1] When the feminine is not morphologically distinct, as with two-form Adj (v. 8.3.4), students often overgeneralize the *-a-*: **felizamente, *alegramente.* Other Advs have arisen from the joining of Prep with Adv, Adj, or N: *aparte, abajo, apenas, ahora, despacio (de + espacio), encima.* Similarly formed but still written as separate words are the expressions discussed in 10.4.1: *de repente, a propósito, en fin, de paso, en vano,* and so on. Another pattern is a compound of N +Adv: *cuesta arriba, río abajo* (v. 15.1.2).

It is not obvious whether such combinations with Advl functions should be analyzed as phrases or as single Adv. The spaces between words in the written language are too arbitrary to be relied on as a criterion, inasmuch as both *encima* and *en seguida* (or *enseguida*) are pronounced as single words, as are *aparte* and *a propósito*, *despacio* and *de repente*. There is good reason to consider an Advl such as *a propósito* as LEXICALIZED or fixed as one lexical unit: if it were truly Prep + NP, one would expect possibilities such as *a tu propósito nuevo, a propósitos abstractos, al propósito reciente,* and so on, but these are odd because *a propósito* is a fixed combination.

10.2.1.2 Prepositions. Spanish has a limited set (about twenty) of simple Preps, including *a, con, contra, de, desde, durante, en, entre, para, por, sin, sobre.* The derived Preps, also called compound, *compuestas*, are a more open-ended class, for Spanish has several formulas for creating new expressions that link NP to the rest of a sentence.

Adv + *de* (v. 10.1): *alrededor de, cerca de, además de . . .*
Adj + *a*: *conforme a, junto a, contrario a . . .*

N + Prep: *cara a, respecto a/de, frente a, rumbo a, gracias a . . .*
Prep + N + Prep: *a causa de, a diferencia de, a pesar de, a lo largo de, al lado de, de parte de, en calidad de, de acuerdo con, en torno a, a cambio de, en vez de . . .*

English uses compound Prep too, although not always with the same formations: examples include *in place of, apart from, as to, in view of, by means of, in addition to, up through,* and *with respect to.*

10.2.1.3 Conjunctions. In their formation, conjunctions fall into four groups. The simple ones are again a limited set: *y ~ e* 'and', *o ~ u* 'or' , *ni* 'nor', *pero/sino* 'but', *como* 'as, how', *si* 'if, whether', *cuando* 'when', *mientras* 'while', *pues* 'because'. A second type, called CORRELATIVE, consists of two parts, each one preceding one of the conjoined constituents (CONJUNCTS): *cuanto más. . . , más . . .* 'the more . . . the more . . .' ; *ni . . . ni . . .* 'neither . . . nor . . .', *o . . . o . . .* 'either . . . or . . .' , *tanto . . . como . . .* 'both . . . and . . .'. A third group, like compound Prep, is formed off other words with which they retain only a tenuous semantic connection; most can be considered lexicalized units.

a medida que 'as'
a menos que 'unless'
así que 'so, thus'
aunque 'although, even if'
como si 'as if'
de modo/manera que 'so (that)'
en cuanto 'as soon as'
en tanto que 'inasmuch as'
por si 'in case'
puesto que 'as, since, because'
siempre que 'whenever; provided that'
ya que 'since, because'

The fourth group is formed specifically from Prep (simple or compound) + *que*:

a fin (de) que 'so, in order that'
a pesar (de) que 'in spite of'
antes (de) que 'before'
conque 'so'
con tal (de) que 'provided'
desde que 'ever since'
hasta que 'until'
luego (de) que 'after'
para que 'so (that), in order that'
porque 'because'
salvo que 'except that'
sin que 'without'

This Prep + *que* group is a special one in Spanish in that these relators allow their clause to reduce to VP-inf under certain conditions while other Conj do not (Whitley 1986b). For example, *antes de que vayas* can become *antes de ir,* whereas *mientras vayas, si vas, aunque vayas,* and *siempre que vayas* never permit this infinitivization: **mientras ir, *si ir, *aun(que) ir, *siempre ir.* English relators, on the other hand, more freely allow this reduction, although to gerunds, not usually infinitives: *before going,* but also *while going, if going, although going* (v. 13.2.1).

Except in this last case of Prep + *que*, classification by formation has more analytical than pedagogical importance. Both languages have these Advl subtypes and students do not need to know that *a diferencia de* is "compound" and *tanto . . . como* is "correlative" in order to use them. Problems arise mainly when one language has an Advl with no direct equivalent in the other, or when one has a multiple categorization of one Advl for which the other provides different forms. Examples of the former case include *sin que* (English *without* is Prep with no Conj equivalent) and *a pesar de que* (which must be rendered by something like 'in spite of the fact that'); examples of the latter include *until* = Prep/Conj (vs. Spanish *hasta ≠ hasta que)* and *late* = Adv/Adj (vs. Spanish *tarde*, which is Adv only—*llegué tarde* or *estaba atrasado*, not **estaba tarde*). *Según* illustrates both problems in being doubly categorized as Prep and Conj, unlike the English Prep *according to,* which lacks a Conj counterpart except something like *according to how.*

10.2.2 Classification by position and function: The adverbial phrase. Linguists define constituent types and categories by means of syntactic position and function. One definition of NP, for example, might be the class of constituents that can occur in such sentence frames as *Vi* ___ *ayer,* ___ *no me sorprende,* and *Tengo confianza en* ___ . Likewise, the D in the NP could be defined in terms of what could occur in an environment such as ___ *empleado me atendió.*

Advls are categorized in similar fashion in terms of where they can occcur in a sentence. One useful notion in this respect is what Spanish grammarians have called the *complemento circunstancial.* This constituent, like the *complemento directo* (DO) and *complemento indirecto* (IO), occurs with a V in the VP, but it expresses "el lugar, modo, tiempo, medio, causa o instrumento de la acción verbal" (Gili Gaya 1973, 70). As an analog to the constituent class NP for what serves as Subj, DO, IO, and PA (v. 8.0), the term ADVERBIAL PHRASE (AdvlP) will be used here as a syntactic characterization of *complementos circunstanciales.* A defining sentence frame for AdvlP might be the following: *Elena lo investigó* ___. Many Advs qualify for this slot—*Elena lo investigó despacio, eficazmente, bien, pronto*—and they often modify the verb in the same way that Adjs modify a noun, yielding parallel structure between NPs such as *una investigación eficaz* and VPs such as *lo investigó eficazmente.*

Not all Advs occur in such a frame as elements of AdvlP, however; some need not occur *ad verbum* 'at the verb' at all, or even in VP. One group (including *quizás, además, desgraciadamente, en cambio*) typically provides discourse linkage as transitions between sentences and/or indicates the speaker's attitude toward the proposition. Such words have been called SENTENCE ADVERBIALS (v. 16.3.1). A second group is comprised of modifiers of modifiers, serving to qualify the intensity or degree of modification. These are called DEGREE WORDS (Deg) and include *muy, más, menos, tan, algo, poco, bastante, extremadamente,* and *sumamente* in Spanish and *very, more, less, that, so, somewhat* (and colloquial *kind of, sort of*), *not very, rather, extremely,* and *highly* in English. While some of these could occur in the AdvlP slot of VP to indicate extent (*Elena lo investigó más*), they also precede and modify Adj and Adv:

Se siente muy cómoda.	She feels very comfortable.
Es algo aburrido.	It's kind of boring.

Qué serves as an exclamatory Deg, as in *¡Qué fácil/estúpido/lindo!*; the corresponding interrogative Deg (as in English *how comfortable?*) varies dialectally in Spanish (v. 12.1.2).

A third group of Advs that cannot be categorized solely as elements of AdvlP is a smallish group including *sólo* (*tan solo, solamente, nomás*) 'only, just', *hasta* (*aun, incluso*) 'even', *por lo menos* (*al menos*) 'at least', *especialmente* 'especially', *también* 'also, too', and *casi* 'almost'. These have been called "distinguishing adverbs" (Keniston 1937, 246) and "focus attractors" (Suñer 1982, 234), and they can modify virtually any constituent type. For example, *sólo* can be applied to NP (*sólo la madre*), Quant (*sólo dos*), Adv (*sólo allí*), and VP or S (*sólo escribió su nombre de pila*) and is free-floating in its position (*sólo tengo dos, tengo sólo dos*). Semantically, it does not convey Gila Gaya's "place, way, time, means" but signals the speaker's focus on information that turns out to be less than the expected.

Besides Advs, NPs are also used to present the "circumstances" of the verb event. Both languages generally require that such NPs be introduced by Prep, with which they form a PREPOSITIONAL PHRASE, PP. Since PPs freely occur in our sample sentence frame, they too can be classified as members of AdvlP: *Elena lo investigó con su hermana, por varios años, antes de su graduación, de acuerdo con nuestros criterios*. But in addition to NP, the Obj of Prep may be Adv or even another PP:

PP = Prep + NP: *desde aquel día, since that day*
PP = Prep + Adv: *desde abajo, from underneath*
PP = Prep + PP: *desde antes de la revolución, since before the revolution*

The two languages differ in the Preps they allow in this last (Prep + PP) construction: Spanish *por* forms such combinations freely (*por encima de la mesa, por detrás del taller*) while English *through* and *for* do not. Likewise, both languages permit Deg before PP, but again without much agreement: Deg + PP occurs in *Estamos muy por debajo de los demás países* and in *He went right through the chute,* but unlike Spanish *muy,* English *very* happens not to occur with PP (**We're very under the other countries, *He went very through the chute*).

Although Prep is usually needed for NP in AdvlP, it is not required with certain NPs of measurement and time, for example, *hoy, ayer, el viernes, cada mes, dos veces, todos los días, el año que viene, setenta kilos.* Their double functions as *complementos circunstanciales* and as Subj or Obj are illustrated in figure 10.2. On one notable point, the two languages diverge here: dates and days of the week take an optional Prep (*on*) in English but Ø in Spanish.

Some conjunctions link two elements of the same type with roughly equal importance, including clauses (sentences, S). These COORDINATING conjunctions include *y ~ e, o ~ u, ni, pero, sino que,* and the correlatives *ni . . . ni. . . , tanto . . . como . . .* (v. 11.1.1, 13.0):

NP Conj NP: *tanto tu cuñada como mi nieto*
VP Conj VP: *descubrió el desorden y se enfureció*
Adj Conj Adj: *difícil pero interesante*
S Conj S: *Jorge puso la mesa, e Isabel llenó los vasos.*

Figure 10.2. Adverbial and nonadverbial NPs

NP as *complemento circunstancial*	NP as subject or object
(1) No se esquía *hoy.*	*Hoy* (Subj) es lunes.
There's no skiing *today.*	*Today* (Subj) is Monday.
(2) La vimos *la semana pasada.*	*La semana pasada* (Subj) fue un horror.
We saw her *last week.*	*Last week* (Subj) was awful.
(3) Cumplirá los veinte *el jueves.*	Prefiero *el jueves* (DO).
She'll turn twenty years old (on) *Monday.*	I prefer *Monday* (DO).
(4) Pesaba *setenta kilos.*	Consumieron *setenta kilos* (DO).
He weighed *seventy kilos.*	They consumed seventy *kilos* (DO).

Other Conj introduce a clause that occurs in the AdvlP slot to provide circumstantial information (such as time, place, or reason): *Elena lo investigó cuando era candidata, puesto que le gustaba la ciencia, como si se tratara de su futuro profesional.* These adverbial Conj such as *cuando, puesto que,* and *como si* are called SUBORDINATING conjunctions (v. 13.2), and they are a larger group than coordinating conjunctions—and more valued in cultivated exposition and narration because they clarify the connection between clauses more precisely than plain *y* or *and.*

In summary, the options available to Spanish and English speakers in forming the *complemento circunstancial* of VP can be expressed by the PSRs shown in figure 10.3.[2]

10.3 Semantic problems. If asked for a definition of *pájaro*, Spanish speakers probably would not hesitate in offering something like "pues, es un animalito que tiene plumas y dos alas, que pone huevos y puede volar." Asked what *de, pero,* or *si* means, on the other hand, they might be at a loss. This is because unlike words such as *pájaro,* Advls often have abstract senses or functions that become precise only when they appear in specific constructions. When meaning is thus tied to, and relative to, the construction, interlingual glosses are highly misleading. For example, *in that* as a gloss for *por cuanto* can wrongly suggest to students the meaning 'en eso', since the Conj functions of *in that* are not apparent outside a sentential context; and *that* for *que* can wrongly suggest a demonstrative rather than any of the various grammatical functions both words have as relators. Dictionaries and vocabulary lists could offer more useful information to language learners by always illustrating relators in context.

Figure 10.3. Phrase structure rules for adverbial and prepositional phrases

$$\text{AdvlP} \rightarrow (\text{Deg}) \begin{Bmatrix} \text{Adv} \\ \text{PP} \\ \text{NP} \\ \text{Conj S} \end{Bmatrix} \qquad \text{PP} \rightarrow \text{Prep} \begin{Bmatrix} \text{Adv} \\ \text{PP} \\ \text{NP} \end{Bmatrix}$$

On the other hand, most pedagogical materials do address the problems posed by the Spanish equivalents of English *but, so, to, in, from, for*, and *by*, and these are commented on in the following sections.

10.3.1 'But'. The territory covered by *but* is divided among three distinct Spanish relators and their synonyms. *Menos* (with *salvo*) expresses exception to or subtraction from a generalization: *everyone but Martha, todos menos Marta. Pero* (with *mas*) adds an opposed consideration, 'but on the other hand, yet, however'. *Sino* (+ *que* before S) cancels what precedes and replaces it with what one regards as the true situation: 'but instead, but on the contrary'. The fact that *pero* and *sino (que)* can contrast once again undermines the value of fill-in-the-blanks:

No enseña música, *pero/sino que* toca el violín.

With *pero*, the sentence suggests that although she doesn't teach music, she does play the violin; with *sino que*, it corrects the assumption that she's a music teacher; instead, she's a violinist.

10.3.2 'So'. English *so* has several functions that can lead to confusion in Spanish.

(1) Deg: He's *so* dumb. Es *tan* bruto.
(2) proform of manner: And he *so* did it. Y *así* lo hizo.
(3) proform of PA: He's witty and *so* is she. Él es gracioso y ella *lo* es también.
(4) proform of a proposition: Is it too late? I think *so.* ¿Ya es tarde? Creo *que sí.*
(5) Conj: She ate too much, *so* she's sick. Comió demasiado, *así que* está enferma.

As a Conj (case 5), *so* and its variant *so that* express (a) logically inferred or generally experienced consequence, or (b) hoped-for consequence or purpose. Spanish distinguishes these two by mood and by Conj (although *de modo/manera que* may be used for both):

(a) She bought it, *so (that)* she doesn't have much money left.
Lo compró *así que* (*conque, de ahí que, de modo que*) no le queda mucho dinero.
(b) She bought it *so (that)* she would have it ready.
Lo compró *para que* (*a fin que, de modo que)* lo tuviera listo.

10.3.3 'To, in, from'. Compound Preps (v. 10.2.1.2) generally have more precise meanings and a lower frequency of usage than the simple ones. In fact, in view of the lengthy itemizations of discrete senses for each simple Prep that are given in some grammars and textbooks—"usos de *a*, usos de *de,* usos de *por* . . ." (RAE 1979, 438–43)—it is a valid question whether each Prep has one specifiable meaning. However, once idiomatic expressions and grammaticalized functions (v. 10.4) are set aside, many Preps can be analyzed as having at least one basic primary sense in their contrasts with others in the same system.

Figure 10.4. Nine potential spatial relationships

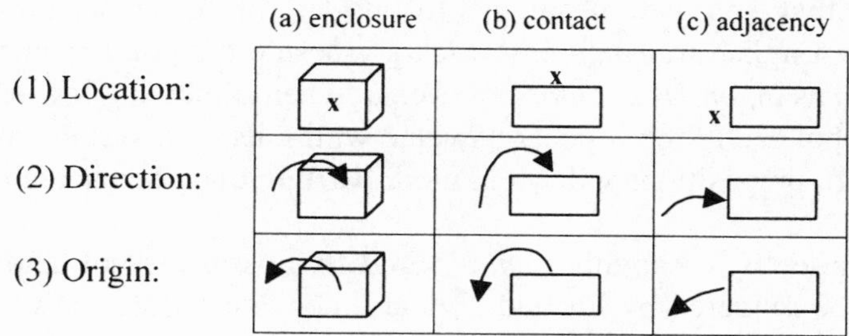

For example, *a, en,* and *de* form an interesting subsystem in Spanish that is often obscured when they are associated with English glosses. To grasp this system, we should first imagine how location might be depicted. In the top row of figure 10.4, *a* represents enclosure of object *x* within a three-dimensional space, *b* surface contact (e.g., with a two-dimensional wall or tabletop), and *c* adjacency (as opposed to enclosure or contact). We can furthermore describe object *x* as (1) already located in and staying in one of these places (static location), (2) approaching and entering that position (direction), or (3) leaving that position (origin). Three places times three modes will yield the nine possibilities of figure 10.4.

This setup in fact, is the English system, as depicted on the left in figure 10.5. The basic Spanish system, on the other hand, is less differentiated in that three simple Preps normally suffice for all nine possibilities, as shown on the right in figure 10.5. If greater precision is felt necessary, the more specific *sobre, junto a, dentro de,* and so on may be substituted.

It is hard to convey the Spanish concepts in English. *De* represents generalized origin, whether it is origin from within, from adjacent to, or from the surface of. *A* means unenclosed position at a point, while *en* broadly expresses containment, whether by a two-dimensional surface (*está en el techo/la mesa/la pared*) or by a three-dimensional space (*está en la casa/el aire*). Spanish relies on the verb for further information on location and

Figure 10.5. Basic spatial relationships: English vs. Spanish

English

	(a)	(b)	(c)
(1) Location:	*in*	*on*	*at*
(2) Direction:	*into*	*onto*	*to*
(3) Origin:	*out of*	*off(of)*	*from*

Spanish

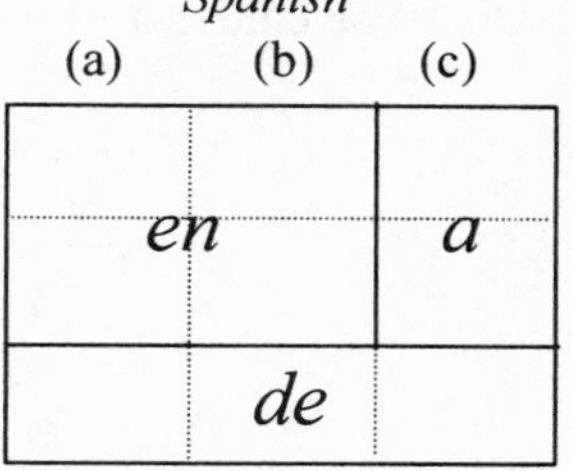

movement: *está a la puerta* ('at'), *vino a la puerta* ('to'), *lo puse en la maleta* ('on'), *lo metí en la maleta* ('in'), *lo quité de la nevera* ('off'), *lo saqué de la nevera* ('out of'). Yet it is not the case that *a* has two meanings, 'to' and 'at', or that *en* has four or *de* has three; these are merely English translations, which are beside the point. Some students find it hard to accept *en* as *in, on, into, onto,* and even *at* when something is actually *in* the space (*en la escuela*), but each Prep reflects its value within its own system, and until students grasp that system, prepositions will seem more baffling than they actually are.[3]

10.3.4 'For' and 'by'. As with *a en de,* English glosses are not helpful with *por* and *para*; both can be rendered by *for* and *by* and other translations as well. Instead of the usual lists of uses for *por* and for *para,* many linguists have sought one general underlying meaning for each, as was done above for *a en de.* In a manner of speaking, one looks for one "use-eme" behind the various superficial "allo-uses."

One of the best explanations of *por/para* is that of Bull (1965, 1972), which is paraphrased here. Again, it is helpful first to depict their basic meanings visually, as in figure 10.6 (Whitley and González 2000, 255). *Por* emphasizes passage through A, with respect to A, among the parts of A, whereas *para* indicates passage toward some goal B. These abstract meanings become more concrete (like those of other prepositions) in specific sentential contexts.

1. Location.
   El humo se extendió por/para el dormitorio.
   La familia salió por/para la plaza.
   Venga Ud. por/para acá.

   Por conveys extension or movement over area A or by a point, whether through, across, past, down, up, out, or along it. This vagueness allows a speaker to modify *aquí* ('this specific point') to *por acá* ('around here'). The movement can be through an area already defined by some other PP: *pasó por encima/delante de la estación. Para* indicates a goal (B) of the action, contrasting not only with *por* but also with *hacia* (toward B but not necessarily with B as goal), *hasta* (B as endpoint), and *a* (arrival at a position at B, not necessarily with B as endpoint or goal).

Figure 10.6. The contrast of *por vs. para*

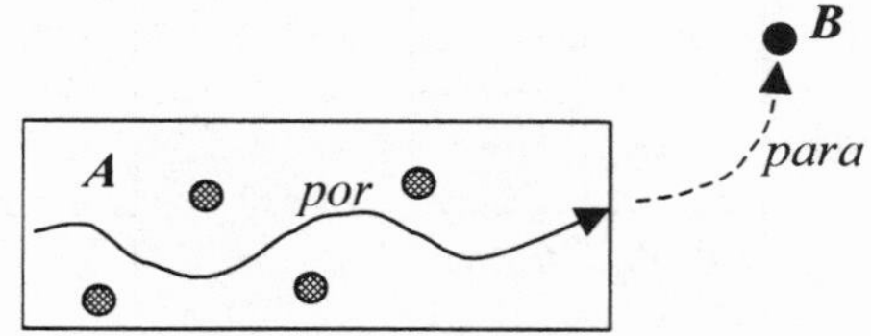

2. Time.
   Se quedaron en casa por/para la Semana Santa.
   Háganlo por/para la tarde.

   With *por*, 'passage-through' time becomes duration ('for, during'); with *para,* goal is again emphasized, whether as purpose or as deadline ('by').

3. Persons and things.
   Compré los zapatos por/para mi mujer.
   El joven trabaja por/para su papá.
   La autora quiere mucho dinero por/para su novela.

   Many textbooks explain *por* here as meaning 'reason', supposedly in contrast with 'purpose'. Unfortunately, the English word *reason* covers both the *por qué* and the *para qué* of an event or situation, and it is therefore useless as a criterion for distinguishing the two. *Para* again denotes goal; with persons and things, it specifically means purpose, the result one aims for or the benefactor one hopes to satisfy if and when the event is fulfilled. *Por* more generally covers any prior or existing reasons other than goal that have influenced the event or its agents from its conception or during its implementation. These factors can be almost anything contrasting with purpose: means, behalf, agency, request, cause, explanation, and so on. Thus, in the first example above, *para* suggests that the purchase was intended for my wife while *por* could mean in her place (she couldn't make it to the store) or on her behalf (she asked me); *por veinticinco dólares* would indicate what I exchanged in buying the shoes, *por un simple estrategema* the means I used, *por vanidad* my motive, *por estar cerca de la zapatería* the explanation, and so on. In *trabaja ___ su papá*, *por* could mean 'on behalf of' while *para* is the purpose of work (inferred as the employer). In *quiere mucho dinero ___ su novela*, *por* is 'for' in the sense of 'in exchange for', while *para* is 'for the purpose of' (e.g., a subsidy to get the work published).

4. Abstract grounds for judgment.
   Ramona cose con bastante destreza por/para su edad.

   Por here means 'given her age as a cause for reaching a judgment', that is, 'because of her age, on account of her age'. *Para* again denotes goal, but 'goal' interpreted here as standard of judgment: gauged against what one expects for someone of her age, Ramona sews skillfully.

Por is less specific in all these cases than *para,* and another way of looking at their contrast is *para* for goal and *por* for the rest. When greater precision is required, *por* can be replaced by specialized alternatives such as *durante, por medio de, en vez de, con motivo de, a causa de, a consecuencia de, a lo largo de, a través de.*

10.3.5 Abstract relationships. The meaning of a relator becomes more elusive when it is pressed into use for conveying relationships more abstract than location, time, goal, and so on. For example, the basic meaning of *con* is accompaniment (*fuimos con Maripili*), but *con* also conveys manner (*se lo expliqué con paciencia = pacientemente*). *Sobre* indicates an upper position, whether in contact ('on') or not ('over, above'), but it also expresses topicality (*habló sobre la política*). *De* denotes origin, as noted earlier, but also composition (*es de plástico*), origin of an emotion (*loco de alegría*), capacity (*trabaja de joyero*), time (*trabaja de noche*), ownership (*es de Miguel*), topicality (*habló de política*), and much else. *Por* and *con* can contrast in locative contexts, but both may express means (*los estafó con/por un simple truco*), as can *a* (*lo hice a mano*). The semantic extensions of English prepositions are just as problematic.

With sufficient abstraction, linguists can describe general senses that accommodate such extensions (Bull 1965, 275–90). With a little reflection, one can see how 'origin' becomes 'composition' and 'possession' and how 'accompaniment' evolves into 'means'. But in trying to account for why 'manner' is *a* in *a caballo (pie, gatas), con* in *con furia (cariño, los ojos abiertos), de* in *de mala gana* (*memoria, canto), por* in *por fuerza (escrito),* and *en* in *en broma (grande, voz alta),* explanation becomes a posteriori rationalization that is useless for the language learner, and we throw up our hands and cry "idiom!"

10.4 Lexically or grammatically fixed usage. One approach to the problem of "idiomatic" Advls is to determine the extent to which one has a real choice in using one relator over another. Certainly in the sentence frame *Cristina se fue ___ la plaza,* we have a choice among *para, por, a, hacia,* and several other Preps, and we select the one that best conveys the intended meaning. We have less latitude in *Cristina se fue ___ buena gana,* however, for in this case it is conventional to use *de*, and *de* only. *De buena gana* is a lexicalized unit, and the use of *de* can be described as lexically fixed in it. In the sentence *Cristina se fue llena ___ esperanza, de* is likewise the only choice but for a different reason: here, *de* is "grammatically fixed" by the grammar of Adj + complement, not by the properties of *esperanza.*

10.4.1 Relators that introduce adverbial idioms. Spanish and English concur in some of their adverbial idioms, that is, "concur" in beginning them with Preps that match elsewhere:

murió *de* hambre, died *of* hunger	cuatro *a*l menos, four *at* least
están *en* huelga, are *on* strike	*por* su cuenta, *for* his part
en efecto, *in* fact	dejarlo *en* paz, leave him *in* peace
salimos *a* las dos, we left *at* two	(manejó) *a* 100 km. por hora, *at* 100 km. per hour

But often they have lexically fixed Preps that differ, and all one can do is to arrange them in sets:

- *a*: a propósito, a la larga, al contado, a medias, a sus anchas, a continuación, a menudo, al azar, al revés, al contrario, a oscuras, a gatas, a medias . . .
- *de*: de rodillas, de vez en cuando, de repente, de nuevo, de acuerdo, de buena gana, de paso, de vuelta, de prisa, de canto, de ordinario, de continuo . . .
- *en*: en seguida, en cambio, en punto, en principio, en todo caso, en regla, en adelante, en suma, en vano, en grande . . .
- *por*: por supuesto, por lo general, por lo pronto, por tanto, por casualidad, por fin, por favor, por poco, por si acaso . . .

Hence, it is pointless to try to explain *a propósito* in a list of "uses of *a*": it is a unit, and just as in *aconsejar, agradecer,* and *atenerse*, the reason for its *a* is a matter of etymology, not grammar.

10.4.2 Relators that are functors. Prepositions are also fixed in the following cases, but this time by the grammar of the construction, not by idiomatic properties of the words:

1. Vi ____ Silvia anteayer. (= *a*)
2. El caballo me fue regalado ___ Felipe. (= por)
3. La amiga ___ Rubén pidió sopa ___ tomate. (= de, de)
4. Quiere una escalera ___ tres metros ___ alto. (= de, de)
5. El libro es difícil ___ leer porque está lleno ____ errores. (= de, de)

A, por, and *de* here are FUNCTORS, grammatical markers with little semantic substance in themselves, and they are learned as part of the construction. The "personal" *a* signals DO (v. 8.1.3, 11.2.3) and *por* identifies the agent of a passive (v. 12.3). *De* marks numerous grammatical links, notably the modification of one NP by another (v. 8.3.2), as in sentence (3)—and therefore of measurements too, as in sentence (4). It is also the default link between the complement (NP or infinitive[4]) of an Adj, as in sentence (5), unless the Adj has its own preference in this regard (*contento con, lento en, primero/último en, equivalente a, paciente con*). Sometimes English adopts similar functors, as in *was given **by** Philip* in the English counterpart to sentence (2); but it is meaningless to seek an equivalent of personal *a* in a language that has no DO marker, or the equivalent of *de* in a grammar that piles up modifiers in front of the head noun (*Reuben's friend, tomato soup, a three-meter-high ladder*) instead of stringing them out in PP as Spanish does.

Yet the hardest use of Prep to master in a foreign language is as a link between verbs and Obj NPs. In *La leyenda de don Juan influyó en la cultura europea,* the PP *en la cultura europea* is not a freely added *complemento circunstancial* (AdvlP of location) but a constituent that completes *influir* like the DO of *tener* or the IO of *gustar*. This kind of complement PP (*en* + NP for *influir*) is called an OBLIQUE OBJECT of the verb. The reason for *en* is both grammatical and lexical: being an intransitive verb in Spanish, *influir* is blocked from taking a DO; the grammar requires a Prep for a following NP, but the particular Prep is dictated by the verb. As Klein (1984, 417) noted, "the determination of which preposition is linked to a given verb is essentially arbitrary, and must be learned as a lexical fact about that verb." A good dictionary indicates that *influir* takes *en, quejarse* takes *de, interesarse* takes *en* or *por,* and so on.

There are other differences between an oblique object and a *complemento circunstancial* besides the verb-imposed Prep (Alarcos Llorach 1999, 352, 385). First, the two cannot be conjoined: *acabó con rapidez* (= *acabar* + manner adverbial), *acabó con sus ahorros* (= *acabar* + oblique object), but not **acabó con rapidez y sus ahorros*. Second, an oblique object may be an Adj, as in *las dos presumían de* ***guapas*** *(pecaron de* ***ingenuas****, se pasan de* ***listas****, se dieron por* ***vencidas****).* Third, V + Prep semantically forms an idiomatic unit in taking an oblique object: *reparamos los baches* 'we fixed the potholes' vs. *reparamos* ***en*** *los baches* 'we noticed the potholes'.

English has its own arbitrary classification of transitive and intransitive verbs, with the latter dictating special Preps exactly as in Spanish, but the classifications differ, as illustrated in figure 10.7.[5] There are hosts of such verb differences (see Batchelor and Pountain 1992, 208–28), and the resulting interference with Spanish endures right up into the advanced levels of study: **pido por agua, *depende en su opinión, *influyó la cultura europea.*

10.5 More on the verb connection: Particles and direction/manner. In Germanic languages such as English, many adverbs and prepositions have become particles that join with verbs to form TWO-WORD VERBS. Particles (Prt) are words such as *up, down, out, in, back, through,* and *over* that can move over the verb's DO (a transformation called PARTICLE MOVEMENT). As shown below, these differ from true Adv and Prep, which do not hop around in this way:

V Prt NP: She found *out* the answer. → She found the answer *out.*
V PP (= Prep NP): She flew *out* the window. → *She flew the window out.
VP NP Adv: She found the answer *fast.* → *She found fast the answer.

The difference of structure is illustrated in figure 10.8.

V + Prt is semantically a unit, usually an idiom: *find out* has nothing to do with outness but means 'discover, learn'. Spanish lacks two-word verbs and the Prt category, so these give both syntactic and semantic problems to a Spanish-speaking learner of English, especially since they also contrast with Prt used as a verb prefix: compare *look* ***over*** *the wall* (V + PP) ≠ *look* ***over*** *his work* (V + Prt + N 'check his work', → *look his work over*) ≠ ***over****look an error* ('fail to see'). English-speaking learners of Spanish must likewise remember that *look up, throw up, ring up, fill up, sign up, set up, make up, put up, take up* do not translate as V + *arriba.* In general, the Spanish counterparts are separate verbs: *find out* 'averiguar', *look over* 'revisar', *look up* 'buscar (en un diccionario)', *throw up* 'vomitar', *throw away* 'botar', and so on.

Another special linkup of V and Advl is the expression of movement and direction (Vásquez Ayora 1977, 282). English, like other Germanic languages, tends to combine a

Figure 10.7. Examples of Verb + (Prep) + NP in Spanish and English

Spanish = V + NP, English = V + Prep + NP:

anhelar; long for
aprobar; approve of
atropellar; run over
buscar; look for
cobrar; charge for
enfocar; focus on
escuchar; listen to
esperar; wait for/on
interferir; interfere with
lograr; succeed in/with
mirar; look at
operar; operate on
padecer; suffer from
pagar; pay for
pedir; ask for
presidir; preside over
solicitar; apply for
tratar; deal with

Spanish = V + Prep + NP, English = V + NP:

abogar por; advocate
abusar de; abuse, misuse
acabar con; destroy, eliminate
acordarse de: remember
asistir a; attend
cambiar de (ropa); change
coger de; grab
confiar en; trust
dar a; face
dar en; hit
desconfiar de; distrust
disponer de; have available
entrar en/a; enter
exceder de; exceed
gozar de; enjoy
influir en; influence
parecerse a; resemble
presionar sobre; pressure
renunciar a; give up, quit
reparar en; notice
salir de; leave
tirar de; pull
unirse a; join

Spanish and English = V + Prep + NP (but not necessarily with equivalent Prep):

aburrirse de; be/get bored with
acusar de; accuse of
adelantarse a; get ahead of
apostar por; bet on
basar/estribar en; base on
consistir en; consist of/in
contar con; rely on
convenir en; agree on
convertir en; change into
culpar X de Y; blame X for Y, Y on X
dar/topar con; run into
depender de; depend on
deshacerse de; get rid of
dividir entre; divide by
dudar en; hesitate in/with
empeñarse en; insist on
esforzarse por; strive for
interesarse en/por; be interested in
librarse de; get out/free of
luchar por; fight for
oler a; smell of/like
pensar en; think about
prepararse para; prepare for
servir de; serve as
soñar con; dream of
sustituir (a) X por Y; replace X with Y
tropezar con; run across
votar por; vote for

Figure 10.8. Particle vs. preposition

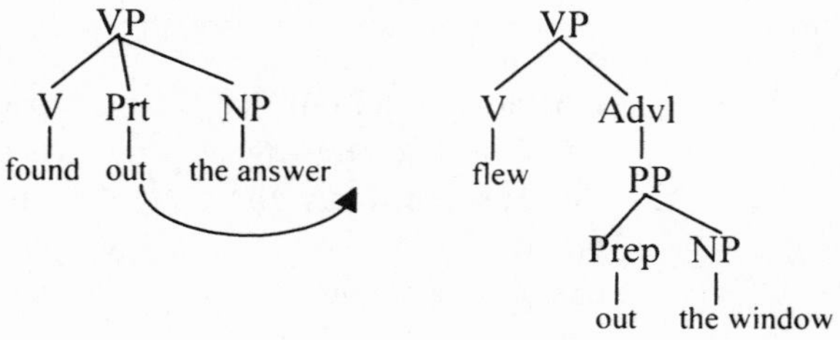

V of manner with an Advl or Prt of direction, whereas Spanish, like other Romance languages, prefers a V of direction with an Advl or gerund of manner, as illustrated below.

English: V of manner + direction		Spanish: V of direction + manner	
She sneaked	in.	Entró	a hurtadillas.
They kicked it	out.	Lo echaron	a patadas.
We elbowed our way	through.	Nos abrimos paso	a empellones.
She hopped	out.	Salió	brincando.
I rushed	down.	Bajé	de prisa.
They swam	across the lake.	Cruzaron el lago	nadando.
Everyone drove	away.	Todos se fueron	en coche.

In the same way, where English combines a V of manner with an Adj of result, Spanish prefers a V of result with an Advl of manner:

English: V of manner + result		Spanish: V of result + manner	
They shot it	dead.	Lo mataron	a tiros.
She slammed the door	shut.	Cerró la puerta	de un golpe.
I cut the boat	loose.	Solté el bote	cortando la soga.

Given the frequency with which movement, manner, and result are expressed in narration, such contrasts ought to be pointed out more often in course materials (see Whitley and González 2000, 50, 178)—if only to head off students' search through dictionaries for literal equivalents of English verbs like *sneak, slam,* and *elbow*.

Notes for chapter 10

1. The suffix *-mente* comes from *la mente* 'mind'. The Romance languages agree in pointing back to the ablative case form *mente* of Latin *mēns* 'mind' for adverbializing adjectives. Thus, the ancestor of *contentamente* would have been *mente contentā* or *contentā mente* 'with or by a contented mind'. Adj + *mente* still acts like a phrasal Adj + N combination (i.e., as NP) in that it has

a double stress (v. 4.1.2), which is rare in single words in Spanish, and when conjoined to other *-mente* forms, it becomes Adj Conj Adj N: *armoniosa y alegremente,* just like *una armoniosa y alegre melodía.*

2. Our rule for AdvlP would be disallowed in generative grammars that require a given XP to contain X (v. 5.2). The problem, though, is the retention of the traditional terminology of Adv/Prep/Conj; as noted in section 10.1, these could and should be grouped together as a single category, Advl. This step was taken by Agard (1984, 63–73), permitting a better analysis of AdvlP for the Romance languages.

3. One exception to our analysis of *en* vs. *a* appears with verbs of movement. In *Sofía fue a Venezuela,* it is not the case that she went up to the shore of Venezuela and stopped, adjacent to it without entering. *A* here supplants the expected *en,* as it does also in the Americanism *entrar a* for *entrar en.*

4. More precisely, Spanish uses Adj + *de* + V, *ese libro es difícil de leer,* in referring to a noun that is understood as the Obj of this verb; v. 13.1.1.

5. Figure 10.7 excludes cases in which the preposition is actually a PARTICLE (v. 10.5).

Exercises for chapter 10

1. Error analysis:
   - (a) *probablamente
   - (b) *antes de leyendo
   - (c) *Están al restaurante.
   - (d) *Ella está dentro la casa.
   - (e) *Este regalo es por ti.
   - (f) *El vidrio es fácil romper.
   - (g) *Saliste la habitación.
   - (h) *Buscaron para su papel.
   - (i) *Terminó sin mi ayudándolo.
   - (j) *Ambos Julio y Luis se matricularon.
   - (k) *Está dos millas lejos de aquí.
   - (l) *Ponlo debajo el escritorio.
   - (m) *A la escuela aprenden mucho.
   - (n) *Depende en otros factores.
   - (o) *Ella trabaja tan programadora tan puede ganar más dinero.

2. Review figure 10.1 and create a similar bilingual chart for correspondences to the following: *arriba, (a)fuera, enfrente, delante, así, luego, desde, sin*. Are there gaps in the pattern? How would you present and practice such distinctions in a class?

3. Why in Spanish does one say *Mamá está* ***en*** *casa/la playa/la oficina* for *Mom is* ***at*** *home/the beach/the office*?

4. Study the following reminders from teachers and then the Spanish sentences that students later encounter. Why is there an apparent contradiction (and why is it only apparent)?
   - (a) "With *mirar*, don't translate the *at* of *look at*." (*Miraron a su mamá.*)
   - (b) "With *pagar,* don't translate the *for* of *pay for*." (*Pagaron ochenta dólares por la llanta.*)
   - (c) "With *pedir,* don't translate the *for* of *ask for*." (*Les pedí un vaso para Lucía.*)
   - (d) "With days of the week, don't translate *on*." (*Insisten en el domingo próximo para el mitin.*)
   - (e) "Use *para,* never *por,* for purpose." (*Van por pan.*)

5. The following Spanish sentences differ in various ways from their English equivalents. Describe the differences and predict student problems with *sustituir* and *reemplazar.*
   (a) El vaso reemplazó/se sustituyó a la copa. The glass replaced the goblet.
   (b) Juan reemplazó/sustituyó la copa por el vaso. John replaced the goblet with the glass. John substituted the glass for the goblet.

6. Many textbooks observe that *-mente* is used less than English *-ly*. In this regard, Butt and Benjamin (1988, 319) judged the following sentence as stylistically "barbarous":

   Evidentemente, todas las lenguas evolucionan constantemente, y sería totalmente absurdo pretender detener arbitrariamente su crecimiento.

They suggested as more Spanish the following version:

   Es evidente que todas las lenguas están en constante evolución, y sería totalmente absurdo pretender detener de manera arbitraria su crecimiento.

Compare the two versions (noting that English *-ly* would be fine in translation), add other examples, and describe the alternatives to *-mente* in Spanish.

7. Explain the following contrasts beween *por* and *para*.
   (a) ¿Por/para qué está el periodista en la cárcel?
   (b) Terminé de escribir mi informe por/para la tarde.
   (c) Salieron por/para Puerto Vallarta.
   (d) Conseguí comida por/para la anciana.

8. In many areas (Kany 1951, 363; Keniston 1937, 264), *donde* and *cuando* have become Prep: *Me alojé donde el director, Se refugió donde su querida, Los edificios se arruinaron cuando las invasiones.* Why do you think these conjunctions have acquired these functions?

9. As the RAE (1979, 435) put a point made in section 10.3, prepositions "dicen muy poco a la mente del que las oye o lee, fuera de una vaga idea de relación que sólo el contexto puede precisar." What are the "ideas" of *a, de, por,* and *para,* and how do they become more precise in context? Give examples of other relators whose roles are best understood in context.

10. Adverbs may occupy Deg (degree word) slots in adjective and adverbial phrases (10.2.2). Both languages permit NPs of extent to function as Deg too: *diez veces mejor, ten times better* (NP + Adj); *veinte años después, twenty years later* (NP + Adv). But the two languages do not entirely agree on the construction of Deg + Adj or Deg + Advl when Deg = NP. Study the following examples, and comment on how Spanish would convey the same message. Try to arrive at a general description about the use of NP for Deg in Spanish.

   Deg = Adv: This table is *very* old/*quite* high/*too* long.
   Deg = NP: This table is *twenty years* old/*two feet* high/*five feet* long.

11. List all two-word verbs you can think of based on *turn,* and contrast them with Spanish equivalents (e.g., *turn in* 'entregar; acostarse'). Why do such verbs cause interference? Write a brief description of them that could be inserted into course materials with the goal of alerting students about trying to use them in Spanish.

12. The following sample of expressions with *de* and *a* is from Dowdle (1967). Classify each one as follows, using information from this chapter and your own intuitions and evidence:
I. follows from the primary (basic) meanings of *de* or *a*; not idiomatic
II. unrelated to these basic meanings, but based on some other general principle of the language
III. unpredictable, inexplicable; a fixed usage, lexicalized as an idiom.

de

(a) aprenderlo *de* memoria
(b) dejé tres dólares *de* propina
(c) se lo dieron *de* comer
(d) trabajan *de* día
(e) son *de* Bilbao
(f) había más *de* ocho
(g) no se hará *de* esta manera
(h) cinco metros *de* diámetro
(i) lo cogió/agarró *del* mango
(j) muy fácil *de* digerir
(k) lo había aprendido *de* joven
(l) una casa *de* adobe

a

(m) avanzaron *a* tientas
(n) le robaron la bolsa *a* Emilia
(o) hueles *a* vino
(p) *a*l día siguiente madrugaron
(q) lo logré *a* duras penas
(r) se acercaron *a* la puerta
(s) más vale no hacerlo *a* medias
(t) no vire/gire *a* la izquierda
(u) *a* un lado está el campeón
(v) nos lo prestó *a* largo plazo
(w) cocínelo *a* fuego lento
(x) está *a* doce pesos la docena

13. In pedagogy, a GRAMMATICAL SYLLABUS organizes the material around a sequencing of grammatical items, as in reference grammars or linguistics books like this one: a unit on nouns, then on articles and adjectives, and so on. A FUNCTIONAL SYLLABUS develops a sequence of communicative functions, such as interviewing, inviting, describing, narrating, exposition, and argumentation, and selects and organizes the grammatical and lexical tools needed for each one (Whitley and González 2000). A THEMATIC SYLLABUS is organized around subject areas or situations—the environment, banking, dealing with the doctor, and so on—and introduces functions and grammatical and lexical tools as needed according to their relevance to each such theme.

Consider the material we have studied in this chapter. What would be the reasons for studying adverbs, prepositions, and conjunctions together in a grammatical syllabus? What would be the reasons for separating them in a functional or thematic syllabus, and how? Discuss the different approaches that would result.

Chapter 11

Word order and constituency

11.0 Rules of syntax. The previous chapters have followed traditional grammar in treating each of the major parts of speech. We now turn to how these categories join to form sentences and how sentence structure is altered for different communicative effects. As explained in chapter 5, we are using a model of generative grammar that treats grammatical structure at two levels, deep and surface. One set of rules, phrase structure rules (PSRs), specify the underlying patterns of deep structure by describing the parts or CONSTITUENTS of a sentence (S), then the possible configurations of elements that make up those constituents, and so on until the phrase marker has branched into the terminal nodes onto which words are inserted according to their syntactic category (N, V, Adj, etc.). Another set of rules, transformations, may then convert these deep structures into various surface structures. Other models have different interpretations of the rules for syntax, but we will focus here on a single approach to the description of Spanish and English for applied purposes.

11.1 Phrase structure rules. The rule S → NP VP (v. 5.2) is read as 'a sentence consists of a noun phrase joined with a verb phrase', 'expand S as NP VP', or 'rewrite S as NP and VP'.[1] Through the use of parentheses for elements that are optionally present and of curly braces, { }, for 'or' (i.e., alternate "expansions" of structures of the same type), one PSR can abbreviate several options for constructing a sentence. In addition, PSRs specify a particular order: S is NP followed by VP, and the sequence VP NP for S will be disallowed (defined as ungrammatical) unless later transformations specifically produce it by rearrangement of the deep structure order.

11.1.1 Sentences. In English, a Subj NP is obligatory for S. Even when there is no "logical" or real Subj of the verb, something occupies the initial NP node of S, as with the *it* of *It snowed* (v. 9.1.2). There are some apparent counterexamples whose surface structures lack an overt Subj: for example, *Get out of here!* and *Want an apple?* Yet these have an understood Subj *you,* and they are equivalent to the fuller structures *You get out of* *here!* and *Do you want an apple?* It can be assumed that the *you* is generated in deep structure, and that transformations later delete it.[2] The generalization about an obligatory Subj for deep structure can thus be retained for English:

(1Eng) S → NP VP

In Spanish (a Null-Subject language, v. 5.2), by contrast, the initial NP is optional. In sentences such as *Vas/Van/Vamos a la playa hoy,* verb agreement indicates an understood Subj in deep structure. Therefore linguists generally treat these surface structures as derived from *Tú vas/Ellos van/Nosotros vamos a la playa hoy* (Hadlich 1971, 63–66). A Spanish transformation called Subject Pronoun Deletion, or Pro Drop, optionally drops a pronominal Subj after the verb agrees with it.[3] On the other hand, sentences such as *Llovió/Tronó/Anocheció a las ocho* have no Subj, explicit or understood, meaningful or dummy, even in deep structure; the verb is 3sg. not because of agreement but because this is the unmarked or default form (v. 8.1.1). Hence, in the PSR for Spanish, we place parentheses around the NP to show that it is not required in all cases:[4]

(1Span) S → (NP) VP

Sentences with *there is* and *hay* require comment. In standard Spanish, *haber* is a subjectless verb like *llover* and *tronar*; it does not agree with an NP, and the NP asserted as existing is its DO, as shown by pronominalization: *¿Hay tazas en la mesa? Sí, las hay* (**ellas hay*).[5] In standard English, however, *there is* agrees with the following NP, which is therefore its Subj. Linguists account for this by deriving *There are five bugs in my soup* from *Five bugs are in my soup*; after subject-verb agreement applies, the Subj flips over the form of *be* and the *There*-Insertion transformation fills in the vacated Subj node with a dummy *there* that has no real meaning (note its contrast with adverbial *there* = 'in that place' in *There're several cars there*).

Both languages also permit compound sentences, which consist of S joined with other S by coordinating conjunctions (v. 10.2.1.3, 13.0). This can be shown by the notation S (Conj S)^n, meaning that one can generate S plus any number (^{n}) of Conj S sequences: S Conj S, S Conj S Conj S, S Conj S Conj S Conj S ad infinitum. The compounding option can be incorporated into our earlier rules for S as shown in figure 11.1, with curly braces for 'or'.

11.1.2 Phrases. Additional PSRs are now needed for stating the internal structure of NP and VP and for their constituents in turn. The PSRs for NP have already been presented (v. 8.3.1) and are repeated in figure 11.1. When NP consists of NP + S (NP with a relative clause) or just S (a noun clause), special transformations adjust the structure in ways that will be described in chapter 13.

A VP has as its head a verb (V), optionally preceded by auxiliaries (Aux) and followed by the *complementos circunstanciales* described in chapter 10 as AdvlP. Independently of the AdvlPs, the V may take NP as a DO and/or a special prepositional phrase (PP). This

Figure 11.1. Phrase structure rules for S, NP, and VP

$$\text{(1Eng) S} \rightarrow \left\{ \begin{array}{l} \text{NP VP} \\ \text{S (Conj S)}^{n} \end{array} \right\} \qquad \text{(1Span) S} \rightarrow \left\{ \begin{array}{l} \text{(NP) VP} \\ \text{S (Conj S)}^{n} \end{array} \right\}$$

$$\text{(2Eng) NP} \rightarrow \left\{ \begin{array}{l} \text{(D) (Quant) (Adj)}^{n} \text{ N (PP)}^{n} \\ \text{NP (Conj NP)}^{n} \\ \text{NP S} \\ \text{Pro} \\ \text{S} \end{array} \right\}$$

$$\text{(2Span) NP} \rightarrow \left\{ \begin{array}{l} \text{(D)(Quant)(Adj) N (Adj)}^{n}\text{(PP)}^{n} \\ \text{NP (Conj NP)}^{n} \\ \text{NP S} \\ \text{Pro} \\ \text{S} \end{array} \right\}$$

$$\text{(3) VP} \rightarrow \text{(Aux)} \left\{ \begin{array}{l} \text{V - intr} \\ \text{V - tr (NP)} \\ \text{V - cop \{NP/Adj\}} \\ \text{VS} \end{array} \right\} \text{(PP) (AdvlP)}^{n}$$

PP can be an IO, as in *les gusta a los bailarines* (v. 8.1.2) or an oblique object (NP with a verb-specified preposition, v.10.4.2): *influyó **en** los bailarines, me refiero **a** los bailarines, disponemos **de** varios bailarines*. The presence of these other constituents generally depends on the verb's subcategory. Transitive verbs, V-tr, may (or must) take a DO: *comer* + NP, *destruir* + NP. Intransitive verbs, V-intr, do not take a DO: **caer* + NP, **morir* + NP. A third subcategory, linking verbs or COPULAS, V-cop, take a special NP or Adj we have called PREDICATE ATTRIBUTES, PA (v. 8.1). The following sentences illustrate copulas + PA (italicized):

Jorge fue/se hizo *ingeniero.*	George was/became *an engineer.*
Rebeca se puso/pareció/estaba *pálida.*	Rebekah got/seemed/was *pale.*
El gráfico salió/resultó *estupendo.*	The graphic ended up/turned out *great.*

The generalized PSR for VP in both languages, shown in figure 11.1, takes into account the constituents that depend on verb subcategorization. For English, it would also be necessary to add an optional (Prt) after V to accommodate the particles of two-word verbs (v. 10.5).

Rule (3) indicates that a VP may contain any number of adverbial phrases, (AdvlP)^n. The PSRs for AdvlP developed earlier (v.10.2.2) are repeated in figure 11.2. We have also noted (v. 10.1, 10.2.2) that adjectives may be preceded by a Degree word (Deg), as in *muy alto* and *very tall,* and that they may be followed by two kinds of complements: PP, as in *seguro de la verdad* and *sure of the truth,* or a clause (S), as in *seguro (de) que todo saldrá bien* and *sure that everything will turn out fine.* Hence, like the N of NP, the V of VP, and the adverbials of AdvlP, Adj can be the head of its own phrase, AdjP. This AdjP can be compound like NP and S: *una niña triste y decepcionada.* "Adj" in rules (2) and (3) should therefore be replaced by "AdjP," for which rule (6) in figure 11.2 specifies internal structure.

Rules (1) through (6) account for most of the deep structures of English and Spanish, but we would need to include many other details in a fuller analysis, either by building them into the PSRs or by describing them as transformational variants of other structures. Among them are the following.

Sentence adverbials. As noted earlier (v. 10.2.3), some Advls are not part of the VP but sentence modifiers providing discourse linkage (*sin embargo, por eso*) or an indication of the speaker's attitude (*desgraciadamente, probablemente, en realidad*). One way of providing for these adverbials would be to revise the rule for S to something like S → (AdvlP) NP VP. Both languages also provide for an Adv slot at the beginning of VP, although in a different position relative to Aux: compare *Pablo siempre/nunca ha estado contento* with *Paul has always/never been happy*.

Multiple IOs in Spanish. Both languages allow one DO per V, hence V + NP, although this NP may of course be compound (*Vi a Laura y a Sonia*). In Spanish, however, there can be more than one IO (v. 9.4.2); hence, rule (3) should be revised to allow two or more PP after V, at least in its Spanish version. Moreover, when pronominalized, the Spanish IO and DO become clitics adhering to the verb (v. 9.4), and some linguists provide for a Clitic node in the VP rule: VP → (Clitic) Aux V . . .

Figure 11.2. Phrase structure rules for Adv1P, PP, and AdjP

$$\text{(4) Adv1P} \rightarrow \text{(Deg)} \begin{Bmatrix} \text{Adv} \\ \text{PP} \\ \text{NP} \\ \text{Conj S} \end{Bmatrix} \qquad \text{(5) PP} \rightarrow \text{Prep} \begin{Bmatrix} \text{Adv} \\ \text{PP} \\ \text{NP} \end{Bmatrix}$$

$$\text{(6) AdjP} \rightarrow \begin{Bmatrix} \text{(Deg) Adj (PP) (S)} \\ \text{AdjP (Conj AdjP)}^{n} \end{Bmatrix}$$

Compound VPs. Like S, NP, and AdjP, the VP may be compound. Yet many linguists have preferred to treat sentences like *Mercedes abrió el sobre y leyó el mensaje* as derived from an underlying compound sentence, *Mercedes abrió el sobre y Mercedes leyó el mensaje*. That is, VP Conj VP is regarded as a simplification of S Conj S in deep structure.

11.1.3 NP complements and appositives. In the phrase types surveyed so far, one constituent is the main one while others are subordinated to it as modifiers, Obj, and so on. But there are certain structures that equate elements rather than subordinating them to a head. One such case is the AdjP and NP that complement a Subj or Obj at long distance like a PA (Alarcos Llorach 1999, 321, 382), as shown in the examples in figure 11.3. (See Demonte 1991 for an analysis of such structures.)

Another case is APPOSITION, in which two constituents of the same type are juxtaposed:

NP = NP: *El comandante Martínez* lo ordenó.
Adj = Adj: Fue muy *raro, extraño.*
VP = VP: Luego *endóselo, fírmelo en el dorso.*

An APPOSITIVE names, reformulates, or exemplifies its companion (Gili Gaya 1973, 210; Escandell and Leonetti 1989), functions that can be made more explicit with expressions such as *es decir, precisamente, especialmente, o sea, por ejemplo, e.g., i.e.*, and, of course, their English counterparts. As with relative clauses (v. 13.3.3), there may be a contrast between restrictive and nonrestrictive appositives:

My friend Peter helped us. ≠ My friend, Peter, helped us.

Quirk et al. (1972, 874 ff.) included in the appositive category those structures in which an abstract noun introduces a complement noun clause: *The fact that the court hasn't decided doesn't change your condition.* Spanish has a similar construction equating N with a following noun clause, but the two are normally joined by *de*: *El hecho* ***de*** *que el tribunal no se haya decidido no cambia tu condición* (likewise, *la creencia/hipótesis/noticia* ***de*** *que* . . .). The *de* distinguishes the noun clause from a relative clause: *la*

Figure 11.3. Special types of predicate attributes

Ya tenemos *terminado* el proyecto.

Ellos vivían *felices* en su nueva casa.

Consideran *un capataz* a Juan.

La eligieron *presidenta de la junta.*

Figure 11.4. A sample phrase marker and the rules that construct it

from rule 1: S → NP VP
from rule 2: NP → D N
from rule 3: VP → V NP AdvlP
from rule 2 again: NP → Quant N
from rule 5: AdvlP → PP
from rule 6: PP → Prep NP
from rule 2 again: NP → D Adj N

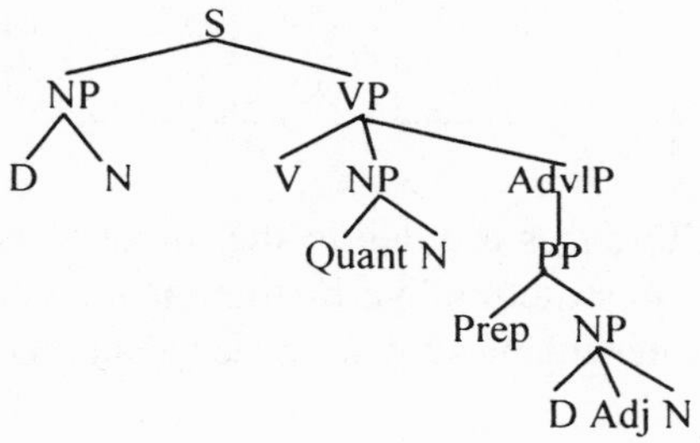

noticia que publicaste (relative) vs. *la noticia de que publicaste* (appositive), and it also appears when the appositive is an infinitive or noun: *la satisfacción de verte, el riesgo de confusión.* It differs from the *de* that introduces a PP modifying the head noun (v. 8.3.2): *la costumbre de la siesta* equates 'custom' and 'nap' appositively whereas *la costumbre de la gente* is possessive. English phrases such as *the problem of land reform, the satisfaction of seeing you, the city of Atlanta* show a similar appositional *of.* Again, there is no agreed-on analysis for these structures (but see Hadlich 1971, 145–58).

11.1.4 Summary. Although the details of some constructions have yet to be worked out fully, the PSRs established in sections 11.1.1–11.1.2 suffice to generate a multitude of different sentence patterns. For example, one can form the structure shown in figure 11.4 by following the indicated PSRs; this structure is defined as grammatical (insofar as syntax is concerned) since each branching conforms to options permitted by the PSRs, and it is the framework for both of the following sentences and for a great many others in both languages.

Ese payaso reventó doce globos con su larga aguja.
That clown burst twelve balloons with his long needle.

Not only do Spanish and English share the same pattern in these two sentences, but their phrase structures in general coincide remarkably. Perhaps this is why Spanish courses dwell far more on morphology, taking basic word order and constituency for granted. Spanish nouns, pronouns, and verbs are inflected differently from their English counterparts, but NPs and VPs largely have the same functions, positions, and constituents in the two languages. English-speaking students of Spanish are fortunate in this regard; their friends in a Japanese class encounter a VP, for example, that is (AdvlP) (NP) V (Aux), exactly the reverse of Spanish and English VPs.

Yet there are differences. Some of them lie in the PSRs themselves: unlike English, Spanish has an optional Subj in its S, two Adj positions in its NP, and no Prt in its VP.

Figure 11.5. The internal ordering of the parts of the Spanish sentential nucleus

no	se	te os	me nos	l-	**VERB STEM**	*tense/mood suffixes*	*person/number suffixes*

Other differences are due to the many constructional quirks of particular words, as with "reverse construction" verbs like *gustar* (v. 8.1.4). More differences arise when transformations alter the basic word order generated by PSRs, as shown in the following sections.

11.2 From deep to surface structure. Both languages have deep structures consisting of NP + VP, with VP in turn consisting of V and its Aux, NPs, and Advls. But in passing to the surface level, Spanish syntax undergoes transformational reorganizations with no counterparts in English. A non-emphatic pronominal Subj is deleted by "Pro Drop"; only the verb ending then signifies the underlying Subj. Pronominal Objs become clitics attached to the verb. Finally, NPs (if they are still intact in the surface structure) can be moved out of their deep structure positions and repositioned. The result is a structure consisting of nucleus and satellites.

11.2.1 The nucleus. The NUCLEUS in Spanish (Alarcos Llorach 1999, 322) consists of a verb stem (*estudi-*), its ending (*estudi-an*), and clitics (*lo estudi-an*). Only this much is obligatory in surface structure, and it is pivotal for the rest. Thus, *Yo vi a Hernán en el parque ayer a las cuatro* is a complete sentence, but so is the bare nucleus *Lo vi*; in just two syllables the Spanish speaker utters a complete sentence indicating 'I + see+past + him/it' plus information on mood and aspect. The ordering within this nucleus, shown in figure 11.5, is quite fixed (v. 9.4.2). The clitics hop over to the other side of the verb in affirmative commands and with gerunds and infinitives; if the latter nonfinites follow another V, one has a choice of positions, with clitics optionally marching leftward and upward through the phrase marker (v. 13.1.2.8): *Está intentando hacerlo → Está intentándolo hacer → Lo está intentando hacer.* Old Spanish permitted freer clitic placement, but the nucleus eventually congealed in its modern form.

For the English speaker, there are two features of the Spanish nucleus that cause special problems. First, with a deleted Subj and pronominalized Obj, the English-like order "Subj V Obj" (SVO) becomes "Obj V Subj" (OVS): the Obj is now a kind of prefix, and the Subj is incorporated into the verb suffix. Listening for Obj information before a verb stem and Subj information after it can be quite difficult for speakers of a firmly SVO language, and a nucleus like *lo abrí* is apt to be misunderstood as 'it opened' instead of 'I opened it'.

Second, a lot of information is packed into a flurry of unstressed clitics and short verb suffixes that meld further with Syneresis and Gliding (v. 2.2.3, 3.1.10): *se le olvidó →* [seljolβiðó], *no os he hecho →* [nosétʃo]. English speakers are not used to processing so much information in phonetically inconspicuous syllables; they expect distinct words for

Subj, V, and Obj but hear only a verb with assorted consonants and vowels attached to it. Hence, they often balk at even simple exchanges such as *¿Se lo doy? Sí, démelo.* To the Spanish speaker, though, these stripped-down nuclei can suffice entirely.

11.2.2 Satellites. Constituents outside the nucleus can be called SATELLITES because they are grammatically optional elements that pivot around the nucleus in surface structure. They may occur to the left, to the right, or not at all.

¿*A María* se lo han dado *los jueces*?	¿*Los jueces* se lo han dado *a María*?
¿Se lo han dado *los jueces a María?*	¿Se lo han dado?

Being stressed in their own right, satellite NPs and Advls are more audible than the incorporated elements of the nucleus, but their free-floating position contradicts the patterns English speakers rely on to process relationships in the sentence. Students hear the prominent words—NP, Advl, V—and process their meaning on the basis of English word order without paying attention to the relationships defined by the rapidly passing nucleus; consequently, *A nosotros nos ayudaron los policías* is misunderstood as 'We helped the police officers'.[6] The task ahead of the student is to learn to anticipate satellite transpositions and to grasp what these transpositions mean.

11.2.3 Transposed satellites and "personal" *a*. Languages with a strong inflectional system tend to have a relatively free word order. Latin, for instance, had five cases for its nouns, each designating a different kind of syntactic relationship to other elements in the sentence. If there was one basic, unmarked word order, it was Subj Obj V, or SOV; this was the most ordinary way to construct a sentence, and presumably the deep structure generated by Latin PSRs. But permutations were possible because the case endings clearly indexed NPs for who was doing what to whom. Thus, 'Paul saw Julia' was normally *Paulus Jūliam vīdit,* but for special effects this could be transformed to *Jūliam Paulus vīdit, Vīdit Jūliam Paulus, Vīdit Paulus Jūliam,* and so on. No matter how the words were scrambled out of their deep structure position (and Roman writers were quite adept at scrambled syntax), the *-us* of *Paulus* and the *-am* of *Jūliam* signaled Subj and DO, respectively.

English nouns, on the other hand, are inflected only for number (v. 8.2.1); the Latin-like case system of Old English has been lost. The language therefore depends on word order to indicate function, and the deep-structure configuration of SVO tends to be preserved in surface structure. One can say *Paul saw Julia,* and the so-called DISLOCATED variant *Julia, Paul saw* (with a sharp intonational setoff); otherwise, permutations will confuse Subj and Obj (*Julia saw Paul*) or yield an ungrammatical sentence (**Saw Paul Julia*).

Spanish, like English, is an SVO language—as long as we understand "V" to be the whole nucleus and "O" to be an uncliticized object NP. SVO is the usual ordering (Meyer 1972) as well as the one that best qualifies for deep structure (Suñer 1982). But even though Spanish also has lost its noun case system, its transformations can shift satellites around in surface structure, and in this respect Spanish resembles its Latin parent more than it does English.

Gili Gaya (1973, 81ff.) sorted out the possibilities into four grammatical and two ungrammatical orders, as shown below. Note that all of these are declaratives, not questions.

SVO Mi padre compró una casa.
VOS Compró una casa mi padre.
VSO Compró mi padre una casa.
OVS Una casa compró mi padre.

SOV *Mi padre una casa compró.
OSV *Una casa mi padre compró.

He believed that although poets resort to the starred orders for special effects called *hipérbaton* (English poets have aspired to similar grammar-warping rights), these are now strained or ungrammatical. He generalized to state that the V must occupy the first or second syntactic slot in the modern language (p. 88), and the RAE concurred (1979, 399).

Meyer (1972) noted details that Gili Gaya missed. First, in OVS the preposed Obj is definite and triggers the insertion of a clitic copy (clitic doubling, v. 9.4.1) in the nucleus:[7]

*Un coche se ha comprado José.
*El coche se ha comprado José. → El coche se *lo* ha comprado José.

Second, for VSO the Subj is usually indefinite (v. 11.3.1): *Se ha comido un niño la manzana.*

Third, a definite Subj NP tends to be sentence-initial, although this SVO can shift to VOS to emphasize the Subj, as in *Se ha comido la manzana* ***Eva***. Meyer's data also showed a strong tendency toward VSO in subordinated clauses, except to contrast the Subj:

Si tuviera María el libro, me lo daría.
Si *María* tuviera el libro, me lo daría.

But it is in yes/no questions that Meyer found the most variety: VSO is then most common (regardless of Subj definiteness), but SVO, VOS, and OVS also appear:

VSO ¿Se comió Eva la manzana?
VOS ¿Se comió la manzana Eva?

SVO ¿Eva se comió la manzana?
OVS ¿La manzana se la comió Eva?

Yet Meyer relied on one informant for her data and suspected that further studies would yield different native speaker judgments on what orderings are possible and under what conditions (p. 192). Such has been the case, and more recent investigators have therefore focused on general tendencies, allowing for idiolectal variation in certain details (v. 0.1).[8]

Agard (1984, 105) noted that Spanish is not the only Romance language allowing permutations of the underlying SVO order; Portuguese, Italian, and Rumanian do likewise. How to account for the permutations is debated; some linguists posit a generalized "Move

Figure 11.6. Agard's transformations for verb-satellite permutations

SVO	*Ramón recibió el premio.*	no transformations; same as deep structure
SVO→VSO	*Recibió Ramón el premio.*	Inversion (Postposing)
SVO→VOS	*Recibió el premio Ramón*	Extraposing
SVO→OVS	*El premio lo recibió Ramón.*	Preposing + Inversion

alpha" transformation (v. 5.2) in which any "alpha" or designated constituent may move anywhere in the sentence, subject to language-specific constraints. Obviously, those constraints are stricter in English than in Spanish. Other linguists describe each particular movement as a transformation, and this was Agard's approach. For Spanish, he posited three rules that are grammatically optional in that the speaker has the "option" of applying them or not. These are (1) SUBJECT POSTPOSING (SVO → VSO) or INVERSION; (2) SUBJECT EXTRAPOSING (SVO → VOS); and (3) OBJECT PREPOSING, which is normally accompanied by inversion (SVO → VSO → OVS) and clitic doubling. Figure 11.6 illustrates these transformations. We generalize his "object preposing" to just PREPOSING since Advls (*Por este acto de heroísmo recibió Ramón un premio*) and PAs (*Grande fue el premio*) can also be moved forward out of VP. A fourth transformation, sometimes called HEAVY NP SHIFT, accounts for the inversion of a long or complex DO over a shorter following IO or Advl: *Lea este informe sobre los gastos bien* → *Lea* ***bien*** *este informe sobre los gastos.*

In section 11.3 we take up the meanings of these transposings. For now, though, how is it that Spanish has more surface word orders than English when neither marks NPs for case? Despite having lost the Latin case endings, Spanish still has resources that speakers rely on in determining the underlying function of NPs. First, NP V NP is unambiguous: this deep structure sequence receives the interpretation of SVO (OVS usually requiring clitic doubling). Second, the verb ending agrees with the Subj, so that the Subj need not stay in one place that shows its subjecthood. However the sequence *Ana* + *vio* + *los árboles* is rearranged, *vio* indicates a 3sg. Subj, and of the two NPs only *Ana* qualifies. Of course, this clue fails with two NPs of the same person and number, as in *Ana* + *vio* + *el árbol* or *Los monjes* + *vieron* + *los árboles.* When these constituents are permuted, neither word order nor the verb ending is helpful, but semantics comes to the rescue, since humans see but trees do not.

In addition, Spanish has its distinctive "personal" *a*. The traditional rule for it, as the name suggests, is that *a* is inserted before human DOs—with two exceptions. First, *a* does not accompany *tener* 'have', although it may follow *tener* 'hold'; likewise (in many versions of the rule), it does not accompany *querer* 'want', but it may follow *querer* 'love'. Second, *a* may be used with nonhuman DOs if these are "personified," as in the metaphor *La Luna admiró al Sol.*

Spanish speakers do not need a Prep to remind them of which NPs represent real or adopted members of their species. Actually, *a* is used to mark the DO so that it will not be confused with the Subj in a language with movable satellites. There is no ambiguity in any permutation of *Ana* + *vio* + *el árbol*, but consider what happens when word order, verb ending, and semantics do not help, as in *Vio + Ana + Pedro* (=VSO? VOS?). Function is unclear here, since either person could see or be seen, and the Spanish solution is to insert *a* for the DO:

Ana vio a Pedro. Vio a Pedro Ana. Vio Ana a Pedro. A Pedro lo vio Ana.

Likewise, in *invitarán + los padres* it would not be clear in surface structure whether the NP is DO (with a dropped Subj *ellos* or *Uds.* conveyed by the verb ending) or a postposed Subj. *A* before the DO clarifies function, so that *Invitarán los padres* means 'the parents will do the inviting' while *Invitarán a los padres* is 'they'll invite the parents' or 'you [pl.] will invite the parents'.

Contrary to the traditional rule, *a* may be inserted before nonhuman DOs to clarify their function too. In any permutation of *El gato comerá las gallinas,* the verb ending will match *el gato* only; of course, in *Los gatos comerán las gallinas* the verb ending is unhelpful, but the constituents are in SVO order, and we know that cats normally eat chickens, not vice versa. But with dogs chasing cats, chickens seeing cows, and any two animate entities with roughly equal likelihood of acting as Subj, *a* may appear, especially once the SVO order is altered.

Los perros persiguen (a) los gatos.→ Persiguen a los gatos los perros.

Nor is *a* limited to animate beings. Ramsey ([1894] 1956, 43) gathered examples of *a* before inanimates without any personification:

El bullicio siguió al silencio. Alcanzó al vapor el yate.

And Gili Gaya (1973, 84) noted that while the following need no *a* thanks to their SVO order,

La amistad dominó el interés de todos.
El arenal desvió la corriente.

permutation might cause confusion—friendship dominating interest or vice versa, sandbar pushing aside current or vice versa—unless *a* is inserted:

Dominó la amistad al interés de todos.
Desvió a la corriente el arenal.

As for the traditional subrule for *querer* and *tener,* Fish (1967, 81) noted that the lost child wailing *¡Quiero a mi mamá!* is expressing desire, not filial affection; and Pensado (1995, 34) gave the following contrast for what she aptly called the *complemento directo preposicional*:

Almodóvar quiere a Sara Montiel para su próxima película. (= 'desea')
Almodóvar quiere locamente su profesión. (= 'ama')

Likewise, Miles and Arciniegas (1983) found numerous cases of *tener a* for 'have', not 'hold':

Tenía, a su lado, a Magda López.
Yo no tengo a nadie.
Hay varios estados que tienen al español como idioma oficial.

The problem with *a* is that it differentiates DO from Subj, yet—unlike the Latin accusative ending—it is not obligatory with all DOs. Fish's explanation (1967) is illuminating. The *a* has clearly spread to most human DOs: **vemos Patricia* is ungrammatical, even though the objecthood of *Patricia* is clear here and in any permutation. Yet it is less used with indefinite or naked nouns, even if human, and in this respect *tener* and *querer* are hardly unique:

¿Tienes hermanos?
Quiero médico.
Se busca secretaria.
Hay que escoger otro capitán.

Fish saw this omission as a downplaying of individuality, as in the following further examples:

¡Llame el chofer!
Perdimos tres hombres y una ametralladora.
No tengo padres pero sí tengo a mi hermana que me educa.

On the other hand, a nonhuman DO is distinguished by *a* when its status seems more equal to that of the Subj. This occurs when that DO is "upgraded" (in Fish's terms) as an active individual,

Ahuyentó a una mosca de su cerveza.
Ve al lobo, y abandonando sus ovejas, huye.

or when the verb expresses a relational state between NPs (even inanimate ones) that seem equal: *seguir, preceder, comparar, distinguir, unir, separar, afectar, reemplazar*. Fish gave a list of such verbs (see also Butt and Benjamin 1988, 269–75) and added examples such as the following:

El segundo surco tocaba al primero.
Cuide que la carga contrapese al agua.
Cada una de estas rectas corta a la otra.

Weissenrieder (1991) offered a simpler explanation. According to her, the common denominator for all cases of "personal" *a* is DO SALIENCY or relative prominence. Whenever the DO might compete with the Subj in saliency, it is marked with *a*, whether this is because both are human, or because both are equally active in the discourse situation, or because both are assigned the same role (as with verbs of relationship). In her most convincing minimal pair (cited below), the Subj in (1) is a clear agent, and therefore more salient in discourse, whereas in (2) the Subj and DO have equal roles in the relationship and *a* marks the DO:

1. El profesor re(e)mplaza el libro. ('replaces it, with something else')
2. El profesor re(e)mplaza al libro. ('takes the place of it')

Weissenrieder admitted that this account does not make for an easy pedagogical rule. Teachers can point out the basic tendencies for using *a*: where it is required (and why), where it is an option, and where it tends not to be used. In this respect, *a* is really no different from any other complex point of usage such as the subjunctive or the indefinite article. By contrast, the simpler traditional rule may seem more attractive, but that rule, in the words of Miles and Arciniegas (1983, 84), is a "myth": "the observant student, leaving the classroom and confronted with Spanish in the real world, must sooner or later be puzzled by usage that clearly contradicts what he has been taught."

11.3 The meaning of Spanish word order. Thus far, we have considered word order just from a grammatical point of view: there are PSRs that generate a set of basic sequences, and transformations that can rearrange these sequences. As a result, speakers have options in encoding a message: there are several places in the grammar where they may choose either X + Y or Y + X. Often the selection of one ordering over the other will signal a different way of presenting information, particularly in the case of nucleus with satellites, nouns with determiners and quantifiers, and nouns with adjectives.

11.3.1 Nucleus with satellites. What is the difference between *A María le dio el premio Juan, Juan le dio el premio a María,* and other permutations? None, grammatically; *Juan* remains the Subj, *le . . . a María* the IO, and *el premio* the DO, and these variants would be analyzed as surface structures formed off the same deep structure. However, each rearrangement alters the thrust of the sentence and the way that one is presenting the information.

In order to develop this idea further, note that we have been using SUBJECT in its grammatical sense, which is hard to define (v. 8.1.1). At least for most action verbs, the grammatical Subj is loosely the agent or doer of the verb. But SUBJECT also means theme or topic, and it is not by accident that grammarians came to use the same word for both. In *Lidia me trató con desdén,* the NP *Lidia* is both the subject = agent of the verb and the subject = topic of the statement. The VP *me trató con desdén* comments on this topic, makes a predication about it, whence the traditional term PREDICATE. Thus, on the grid of

NP + VP, one assumes an informational schema of TOPIC + COMMENT, or THEME + RHEME as they are also called. When other constituents are topicalized, the Subj NP may move out of its usual theme position to make room. Even with the more fixed word order of English, we have already seen the dislocated version OSV, as in *John, I can't stand, but Mary's okay.* Spanish likewise uses movement rules to adjust thematic structure, but on a much grander scale.

As the Real Academia (1979, 395) described unmarked SVO order, "el sujeto representa de ordinario el término conocido, la continuidad del discurso." If some other constituent is the given, familiar term being carried over from previous discourse, then it moves into this favored thematic position and the Subj moves out of it. That is, clause-initial position is reserved for singling out a topic presumably familiar to the hearer, a step Stiehm (1978) called "paradigmatic focus" because the speaker is selecting from a "paradigm" of possible themes. Normally, just one topic begins the sentence, which is why OSV and SOV are rare although not impossible. Then, the speaker proceeds to comment on this theme, presenting or "predicating" new information about it. Since intonation highlights constituents toward the end with rising or falling terminals (v. 4.2), key elements of the rheme gravitate toward that position of "syntagmatic focus." Thus, a topicalized Obj or Advl tends to move to the front, and a Subj which is not the real topic but a part of the new information in the comment will move toward the end.

The rationale for transformed word order becomes clearer when we go beyond isolated sentences and consider context. Consider a speaker who, in the course of a conversation about a dinner party and the subsequent cleanup, asks *¿Qué hicieron Samuel y Susana?* The topic is established, and the new information will be what these two did. The hearer, who knows what Susana did, answers *Pues, Susana lavó los platos*. But if the question is *¿Quién lavó los platos?*, washing the dishes becomes the topic and the point of departure for a comment, and the Subj = agent becomes the new information to be focused on; the hearer may now respond with OVS, *Pues, los platos los lavó Susana.* Alternatively, speakers may stick to SVO and highlight the subject with unusually elevated intonation and stress and slower tempo: *Pues, SUSANA lavó los platos.* This phonological highlighting is the *normal* strategy in English:

"What did Sam and Susan do?" "Well, Susan washed the plates."
"Who washed the plates?" "Well, SUSAN washed the plates"

The difference between the two languages here is therefore a tendential one: English occasionally moves an NP to reflect a different thematic structure but more often sticks to the same word order and adds phonological highlighting, whereas in Spanish the tendency is the reverse.

Suñer (1982) explored in greater depth the theme-rheme structure of Spanish sentences. The theme or topic is PRESUPPOSED as already presented or taken for granted; the rheme or comment is material that is ASSERTED about that theme, with special focus on the last constituent. Like others, Suñer posited that in the unmarked case, a neutral declara-

Figure 11.7. Grammatical structure and thematic structure

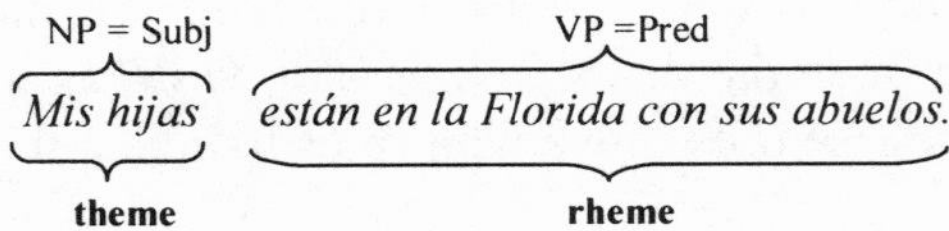

tive sentence, the Subj is the theme and the VP the rheme, as shown in figure 11.7 for *Mis hijas* (theme) *están en la Florida con sus abuelos* (rheme). But the theme is not always old information; in response to another speaker's observation *Se te ve muy cansada,* the whole sentence in figure 11.7 would be new information, whereas in response to *¿Dónde están las niñas que no las oigo?*, just the focused PPs *en la Florida* and *con sus abuelas* would be new information (Suñer 1982, 5).

Suñer noted two special conditions for thematic structure and therefore word order. First, in PRESENTATIONAL SENTENCES the speaker introduces a referent into the discourse, and this NP will be rheme (asserted), not theme (presupposed). Consequently, the presented NP moves rightward into the rheme if it is not already there in deep structure, as shown in figure 11.8 for the change *Un elefante apareció en el jardín → En el jardín apareció un elefante.* This latter presentational sentence would answer a question such as *¿Qué viste en el jardín?* because the AdvlP becomes the theme (the questioner broached *en el jardín*, so the answerer can presuppose it) while the elephant is presented in the focus position of the rheme, though it remains Subj. When the presented noun is NAKED (no modifiers, v. 8.4.1), this change is obligatory under normal intonation because the noun is being presented for the first time and cannot be presupposed. Suñer called this requirement the NAKED NOUN CONSTRAINT (p. 208 ff.):

(*Dirección* falta.) → Falta dirección.
(*Abogados* vivían allí.) → Allí vivían abogados.
(*Niños* juegan en el parque.) → En el parque juegan niños.

Presentational sentences thus favor Subject Postposing (Inversion), especially of a naked N. Alternatively, the passive (v. 12.3) can be applied for the same effect: (*Guerrilleros implantaron la bomba) → La bomba fue implantada por guerrilleros.*

Figure 11.8. Transformation for conforming to the thematic structure of presentational sentences

NP = Subj VP =Pred
Un elefante apareció en el jardín. → *En el jardín apareció un elefante.*
theme rheme

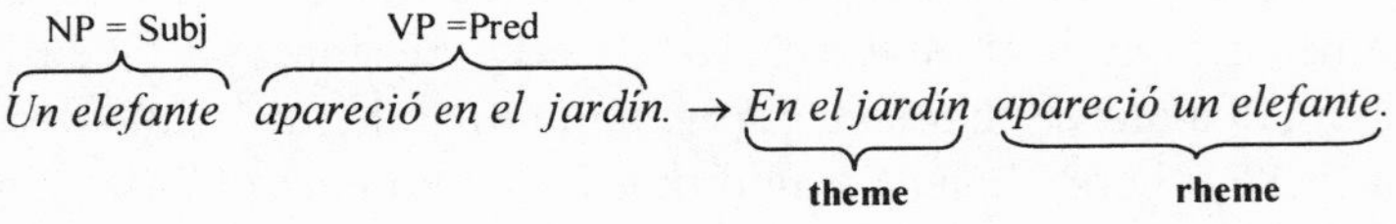

Yet the Naked Noun Constraint can be overridden and the Subj can stay in its initial position provided that it is being strongly contrasted with a previously mentioned element. Suñer illustrated the effect of contrast in exchanges such as the following (p. 229–40):

1. A: Surgió gas, ¿no? B: No, PETRÓLEO surgió.
2. A: ¿Surgió petróleo? B: PETRÓLEO no surgió pero sí agua.

Although B's responses have the naked noun *petróleo,* it is not postposed. This is because A's questions introduced 'something coming up' into the discourse; the substance that A was thinking of, though, differs from the one that B knows to be the case. Thus, in example (2), *petróleo* leads off B's response because, despite its nakedness, it is thematic, already broached by A; in example (1) *petróleo* can begin B's response because, although it is new information, it is part of the established theme of 'something coming up'. B's use of phonological heightening on *petróleo* instead of syntactic inversion emphasizes its contrast with *gas* in (1) and with *agua* in (2).

Suñer attributed NP movements to two transformations (see figure 11.6): Subject Postposing, which moves this NP into the focus of the rheme, and Topicalization (Agard's Preposing, v. 11.2.3), which moves VP elements to the front of the sentence when these are treated as the topic rather than as a part of the assertion. The two combine with her principle of contrast to yield several discourse options, as summarized in the following examples.

3. A: ¿Por qué estás tan contenta? B: El petróleo surge a carradas.
4. A: ¿Surgió petróleo? B: Petróleo no surgió.
5. A: ¿Qué pasó? B: Surgió petróleo.
6. A: ¿Surgió agua? B: No, surgió petróleo.
7. A: ¿Surgió agua? B: No, PETRÓLEO surgió.

In (3), B's *petróleo* is new information but serves as the topic for a comment. In (4), B's *petróleo* is the theme (A broached it), with a contrasting predicate. In (5), B's response is presentational; the whole sentence is a rheme or new information, so the Subj is postposed. Finally, in both (6) and (7) B's responses use *surgió* as the theme and *petróleo* as the rheme, so that *petróleo* is postposed (6) unless the speaker opts to emphasize the contrast with the theme *agua* (7).

Not all postposings serve to present new information: in *Es muy sencilla la cosa* (with intonation **131↓**), the speaker's emphasis is on *sencilla* and the extraposed but low-pitched Subj *la cosa* is like an afterthought referring to the issue at hand. Overall, however, the principles explored by Suñer have been borne out in further studies. Ocampo (1991) studied discourse and found that NPs and PPs of new information tend to occur after the V, but before it if thematic or contrastive. Liceras, Soloaga, and Carballo (1992) sampled native-speaker judgments and likewise observed the effects of *foco informativo* (resulting in postposition) vs. *foco contrastivo* (initial position with heightened intonation). Unlike Suñer, they also included topicalized Obj and PA and noted that a contrastively focused DO in OVS may dispense with the usual clitic doubling. Thus, *El pepino lo detesta Elena* (with an inserted *lo*) is normal for talking about cucumbers as a topic, but for contrasting it (e.g., with *la lechuga*), one would say *El PEPINO detesta Elena.* Consequently, as Suñer concluded, "'free' word order is not so free after all. Different word orders convey different functional perspectives: Subject-verb does not carry the same information as verb-subject" (1982, 317).

11.3.2 Nouns with determiners and quantifiers. In both languages, determiners and quantifiers normally precede a head N, but Spanish allows certain postposings:

mi casa → la casa mía
este tipo → el tipo este
cualquier obrero → un obrero cualquiera
no hay ningún motivo → no hay motivo alguno[9]

For Gili Gaya (1973, 220), postposition of a possessive merely follows from the use of *el* or *un* before the N; there being only one determiner slot, the possessive is displaced when the D node is already occupied by an article, and the postposing is grammatically automatic (Stiehm 1978, 414). However, a "grammatically automatic" postposition rule fails to explain why a speaker might choose *la casa mía* instead of *mi casa*; both are grammatical, both are definite, both have the same possessor. As for postposed demonstratives (*el tipo este*), these have sometimes been explained as disparaging or connoting contempt; yet preposed demonstratives may suggest disparagement too, and postposed ones do not always suggest it (Keniston 1937, 103).

Ramsey ([1894] 1956, 112) was on the right track in observing that postposing modifiers expresses emphasis. *Mi casa* is fairly neutral or unmarked, and although *MI casa* is possible for strong contrast, the postposed version *la casa mía* is the usual way of highlighting the possessor as the key information. Postposing *cualquier(a)* and *ningún(o)* (→ *alguno*) similarly gives them a more sweeping characterization of reference, and postposing demonstratives (*este tipo → el tipo este*) gives them a stronger deictic (pointing) force, which is not necessarily disparaging (Alarcos Llorach 1999, 110). The overall principle, then, is that such modifiers have greater strength when postposed than when they stay in their neutral position before the N.

11.3.3 Nouns with adjectives. In English the Adj regularly precedes its head N, as stipulated by the NP rules presented earlier (v. 11.1.2). But if it is actually an AdjP with a dependent PP or S, it moves over the N.

a kind woman, but *a woman kind to everyone*
an independent people, but *a people so independent that they reject help*

In the Spanish PSR for NP, however, we recognized that Adjs occur more systematically in pre-position and postposition, often with a difference in meaning.[10] This difference has often been commented upon in Spanish grammar and linguistics in a kind of running dialogue (as with aspect and mood, v. chapter 7) periodically impinging on pedagogy; indeed, if the question of word order is ever raised in a textbook, it is in the case of Adj + N vs. N + Adj.

The original explanation is that of Bello ([1847] 1958, 34 ff.), later adopted by the Real Academia (1924, 192): a preposed Adj characterizes the entire group delimited by the N and indicates some natural property of it. It is "explicativo" in just commenting on a trait regarded as implicit in the noun's own meaning. The postposed Adj restricts the noun's referential scope; it is "especificativo" in specifying some members of the group and excluding others. Thus, in Bello's oft-quoted examples, the Adj in *las mansas ovejas* brings out the inherent tameness of sheep and adds essentially nothing, but in *los animales mansos* it selects gentle animals from the group of *animales* and excludes wilder ones.

Ramsey ([1894] 1956, 665 ff.) accepted Bello's account, but in contrasting Spanish with the English of his readers he added two new insightful observations. First, postposition often corresponds to heightened stress on an English Adj: *vivos colores* 'bright cólors' vs. *colores vivos 'BRÍGHT* colors.' Second, some Adjs seem to change meaning, having one sense in Adj + N and a distinct one in N + Adj, as illustrated in figure 11.9. Some of these distinctions may be correctly stated: *cierto, nuevo, simple,* and *varios* do have a kind of determiner force when preposed like other determiners, but when postposed they add descriptive meanings to the noun or attribute characteristics to it. Yet the adjectives do not really "change meaning" since counterexamples are easy to point out:

los antiguos templos egipcios 'the ancient (*not* former) Egyptian temples'
Anhelaba la pura agua de las montañas 'she yearned for pure (*not* mere) mountain water'
El paro es el otro gran problema de la economía 'unemployment is the other big (*not necessarily* great) problem of the economy'

Even so, after Ramsey the effort to sort out Adjs into one position or the other snowballed in pedagogy. By the 1960s, DaSilva and Lovett had worked out for the student the following classification of adjectives that "regularly" follow their nouns (1965, 161):

1. Adjs of nationality and religion: *los perfumes franceses*
2. Adjs of color and shape: *una mesa blanca, una mesa redonda*
3. Adjs referring to "branches of learning, classifications, or scientific terminology": *un estudio psicológico, ácido acético*
4. Adjs modified by Adv (Deg): *una canción muy triste*
5. participles used as Adj: *una figura arrodillada*

Figure 11.9. Adjectives that are said to change meaning in Adj + N vs. N + Adj

antiguo	el antiguo rey 'the former king'	el rey antiguo 'the ancient king'
cierto	ciertas fórmulas 'certain formulas'	fórmulas ciertas 'true formulas'
grande	una gran reina 'a great queen'	una reina grande 'a large queen'
medio	media manzana 'half an apple'	la manzana media 'the average apple' la clase media 'middle class'
mismo	el mismo portavoz 'the same spokesperson'	el portavoz mismo 'the spokesperson himself'
nuevo	se puso una nueva blusa 'she put on a new (different) blouse'	se puso una blusa nueva 'she put on a brand-new blouse'
pobre	la pobre hija 'the poor (pitiful) daughter'	la hija pobre 'the poor (not rich) daughter'
puro	¡es pura agua! 'it's merely water!'	¡es agua pura! 'it's pure water!'
simple	un simple caso de confusión 'a mere case of confusion'	un caso simple de confusión 'a simple (not complex') case of confusion'
varios	hay varios solicitantes. 'there're several applicants'	hay solicitantes varios. 'there're all kinds of applicants'

Despite the wide and continuing appeal of such lists, they are quite wrong since all five groups can be preposed as well as postposed.[11] Even if they are interpreted as mere statistical projections (e.g., *psicológico* is more likely to occur after than before), there is no explanation of why this is so. And at any rate, unless the Adj clearly fits one of these five categories (and *rápido, lleno, fácil, preocupante, manso,* and most others do not), the student is at a total loss.

Bull (1965, 226 ff.) abandoned the rule-and-subrule approach and elaborated Bello's *explicativo/especificativo* distinction into a theory of the "mathematical" organization and presentation of entities. Pre-position signifies totality, the whole set, meaning (with a plural noun) the description of all the noun's referents or (with a singular noun) reference to one unique entity. Thus, *los pequeños arbustos* implies that conversation has been about a certain group of shrubs, all of which are small, and *el pequeño arbusto* suggests that conversation has been about a single shrub, which happens to be small. Postposition, on the other hand, signifies partitiveness (subset)—a group (plural) or individual (singular) that has been selected from a larger group defined by the noun. Thus, *los arbustos pequeños* and *el arbusto pequeño* select the small shrubs and one small shrub, respectively, from the shrubs being discussed. In *los blancos cabellos de don Hugo*, we presuppose that his entire head is white, while in *los cabellos blancos de don Hugo* we imply that only some hairs are white and single these out for some comment. Likewise, *su linda mujer* assumes monogamy and *su mujer linda* suggests polygamy (p. 227).

According to Bull, if only one option is open, that is because of real-world factors, not grammar: thus, we say *el famoso autor de Don Quijote* rather than *el autor famoso de*

Don Quijote since the latter implies another, less famous author. The same rationale applies to Adjs that are usually postposed: in *hombres españoles, problemas astronómicos,* and *naciones republicanas,* "all men cannot be Spanish, all problems cannot be astronomical, and all nations are not republican" (p. 227). It should be noted, however, that in Bull's "mathematical organization" the speaker need not be accurate or even honest about the portrayal of the world. "*Las hermosas mujeres de Tehuantepec* sustains a legend, but does not describe all of the facts. *Las gloriosas tradiciones de nuestra república* may well be a politician's little white lie" (p. 228).

Cressey (1969) accepted Bull's account but brought out a parallel in relative clauses. In some analyses, Adjs in the NP are explained as coming from relative clauses (v. 13.3.4): *the box which is blue* → *the blue box*. For Cressey, a postposed Adj comes from a restrictive relative, because both specify one or some entities from a group, while a preposed Adj comes from a nonrestrictive relative, because both attribute something to all members of the set. Hence, *Los hombres que son valientes* (= some men) *nunca huyen* → *Los hombres valientes nunca huyen*; *Los araucanos, que son valientes* (= all of them), *nunca huyen* → *Los valientes araucanos nunca huyen.* For the classroom, Cressey therefore proposed drills like the following:

1. T: ¿Lee Ud. *libros que son aburridos*?
   S: No, no leo *libros aburridos.*
2. T: Nuestra *banda, que es malísima,* tocará esta tarde, ¿verdad?
   S: Sí, nuestra *malísima banda* tocará esta tarde. (p. 880)

Moody (1971) agreed but pointed out a hitch: many students do not readily understand the restrictive/nonrestrictive distinction in English, so this will be difficult to apply to Spanish.

As the debate unfolded, the Bello-to-Bull theory came under criticism. Gili Gaya (1973, 216–19) observed that it works best for NPs with definite D (*el, este, su,* etc.); with undetermined or indefinite nouns, it fails. In the following, for example, there is little or no totality/partitive (explicative/specifying, nonrestrictive/restrictive) contrast in meaning:

Blancas nubes/Nubes blancas asomaban en el horizonte.
Valiosos cuadros/Cuadros valiosos adornaban el salón.
Esperamos *tiempos mejores/mejores tiempos.*

For Gili Gaya, the distinction was more aesthetic than logical. A preposed Adj suggests subjectivity, an affective quality "synthesized" with the referent, whereas a postposed one has a more objective thrust in "analyzing" or setting off a quality from the N itself. But this principle can be overridden by prosodic factors such as rhythm, melody, stress group, and word length (short Adj before longer N); fixed combinations (*idea fija, sentido común, libre albedrío*); arbitrary assignment to one position (*la mera opinión*); and differentiation of senses by position (as with Ramsey).

Fish (1961, 701), after looking at a large corpus of examples, also criticized the "persistent effort to cram all embarrassing cases into the Procrustean bed of the restrictive," but he erred in the opposite direction, a proliferation of principles for Adj position:

Postposed for
1. restrictive modification (Bello, Bull): *el gato doméstico, los ángulos adyacentes*
2. pictorial effect: *el aire claro y suave*
3. affiliation: *el espútnik ruso*
4. explanatory comment: *su Mallorca natal, el Dios poderoso*

Preposed for
1. affective comment: *la triste noticia de su fallecimiento*
2. impressionistic comment: *un ser de extrañas costumbres*
3. attitude or evaluation: *la desastrosa política del gobierno*
4. moral-aesthetic judgment: *unas bellas muchachas luciendo sus esbeltas figuras*

Fish thus ended up with multiple Adj classes, each with its own philosophy.

In another attempt to find just one general principle for Adj placement, Stockwell, Bowen, and Martin (1965) suggested the following approach to the problem:

> Another way of looking at the same distinction [pre- and postposition] might be termed the "relative informativeness" of the noun and adjective. In *un famoso héroe,* the order suggests that we expect heroes to be well known, but in *un héroe famoso* we are differentiating the hero who is famous from others who have not been acclaimed. The item in final position carries more information. (p. 89)

Bolinger (1972) interpreted this key notion of "carrying more information" as greater SEMANTIC WEIGHT. To some extent, as Ramsey ([1894] 1956) had observed, the English Adj receives greater stress to show that semantic weight: *ricos hombres* 'rich *MEN*' vs. *hombres ricos* '*RICH* men'; but Bolinger found a better parallel in the English VP, where certain Advs can be placed before or after the V. He offered the following comparisons between the Spanish NP and the English VP:

Tenía ricos ornamentos.	It was richly ornamented.
Tenía ornamentos ricos.	It was ornamented richly.
Sufrió terribles daños.	It was terribly damaged.
Sufrió daños terribles.	It was damaged terribly.

In both cases, the last element in the phrase carries more semantic weight, reflecting the speaker's center of interest and informational focus.

The reason Bolinger offered for this property is the way that modifiers combine to specify the set of entities (referents) that their N can represent. As the Spanish NP unfolds from left to right, each successive modifier narrows down the reference one step further, a process Bolinger called LINEAR MODIFICATION. Take, for example, the NP *las grandes repúblicas democráticas europeas.* Here, the D *las* leads off as usual to signal definiteness, often as a carryover of topicality from previous discourse. We then proceed to broach the greatness associated with the republics we have in mind; subsequently, we subclassify the great republics by limiting these to the democratic ones; finally, we close the linear modification by adding our most informative element, *europeas,* to indicate that the great democracies we have in mind are specifically those of Europe. A different sequencing would deliver a different organization of information and a different characterization of *repúblicas.*

Terker (1985) supported Bolinger's theory with well-documented examples and urged that it be more widely adopted in pedagogy. He noted, however, four special cases that must be borne in mind whenever one develops a Spanish NP by linear modification.

First, preposing signals more, not less, semantic weight if the Adj receives heightened intonation. Thus, *su GALLARDA contribución* is more emphatic than *su contribución gallarda.* (Recall Suñer's similar observation on contrasted nouns such as *petróleo* at the sentential level.)

Second, conjoined Adjs have equal weight regardless of order: *usos militares o civiles = usos civiles o militares.*

Third, the greater the determiner force of a modifier (as opposed to descriptive content), the earlier it appears in the NP. Thus articles, the prime determiners, always come first; and although both *único* and *posible* could precede or follow N, *único* precedes if both are preposed because of its stronger force in determining reference: *la única posible solución, *la posible única solución.* For the same reason, so-called meaning-changing Adjs precede N when they determine reference like D or Quant (*ciertas formulas,* like *unas fórmulas*) but follow it when they give important descriptive information (*fórmulas ciertas,* like *fórmulas fiables*).

Finally, complex AdjP (Adj + PP, Adj + S) must be postposed, this being a grammatical requirement overriding the constituents' relative informativeness: *las rutas difíciles de ascender* (**las difíciles de ascender rutas*). It is this complexity that matters, not mere length as claimed by Gili Gaya, which is why one could say either *una mujer distinguida* or *una distinguida mujer.*

According to Bolinger (1972, 94), the problem with the Bello-to-Bull theory was not that restrictiveness (partitiveness) plays no role, but that it is only a partial explanation that seizes on one application of the overall principle of informativeness. Thus, in the following examples,

1a. Juan es el dedicado médico de Jipijapa
1b. Juan es el médico dedicado de Jipijapa
2a. Juan es un dedicado médico
2b. Juan es un médico dedicado

Bull was correct in predicting that *el dedicado médico* in (1a) refers to one unique Jipijapa doctor, whereas *el médico dedicado* in (1b) selects one doctor, the *dedicated* one, from all

Jipijapa doctors. But as Gili Gaya noted, this "mathematical" interpretation vanishes in (2) with an indefinite determiner. After all, definite determiners, as in (1), "define" reference by singling out from a universe of possible referents the one(s) on which the speaker has focused (v. 8.3.3). A postposed and thus more informative Adj therefore proceeds further with the defining of reference begun by *el/la*; hence, *el médico dedicado* has Bull's partitive or Bello's specifying sense. A preposed Adj has less semantic weight, and therefore it will not define the reference any more than the plain D + N would; hence, both *el médico* and *el dedicado médico* indicate an individual for whom the hearer presumably requires no further specification. When reference is indefinite, as in the second pair of sentences, a postposed Adj has little defining or differentiating value for singling out the one from the many, but it continues to have more semantic weight in final position than when preposed. In other words, quite apart from the partitiveness imposed by the D, in both of the (a) sentences Adj + N highlights Juan as doctor and deemphasizes any uniqueness about his dedication, while in both of the (b) sentences N + Adj suggests that Juan, as a doctor, is a particularly dedicated one. Bello's and Bull's theory holds for one case; Bolinger's apparently covers both cases with one generalization.

11.3.4 Summary and generalization. Bolinger believed that his principle of semantic weight, as part of a strategy of linear modification, applied to other areas of Spanish syntax too. In general, whenever the syntax allows both X + Y and Y + X as grammatically equivalent options, Y will carry more information in the order X + Y than in Y + X (provided, as Suñer and Terkel pointed out, that neither element is highlighted for contrast). Adjectives conform to this principle, as already noted. Demonstratives, possessives, and quantifiers conform too, since they have a more forceful thrust when postposed. At the level of S, informativeness applies to theme + rheme structure. Both *Carmen quiere la leche* and *A Carmen le gusta la leche* use Carmen as a point of departure, that is, as a topic already established by discourse or presupposed as the center of interest; what Carmen wants or likes is then presented as the rheme. But in *La leche la quiere Carmen, Quiere la leche Carmen, La leche le gusta a Carmen,* and *Le gusta la leche a Carmen, Carmen* moves to or remains in postverbal position to occupy the sentence's stage of attention ("rhematic focus"). Here, *Carmen* is higher in informational value, asserted or presented rather than presupposed; the speaker takes 'wanting milk' or 'liking milk' as thematic and focuses on Carmen. Just like modifiers in the NP, satellites in the S move into positions reflecting the center of interest.

In their initial year or so of Spanish study, students have little sensitivity to discourse and therefore to the editing of sentence structure for a more effective delivery of information. In fact, although they constantly highlight or downplay information in their English, largely through phonological means, they have little awareness of doing so since high school grammars of English no more touch upon *rich MAN* vs. *RICH man,* or *HE came with his date* vs. *He came with HIS date,* than their Spanish textbooks explain Subj + V vs. V + Subj, or D + N vs. N + D, or (except for the supposed difference between 'great' and 'big' for *grande*) Adj + N vs. N + Adj. Moody's criticism of Cressey is therefore apt:

there *are* parallels in English, but they involve subtleties that students are not conscious of, and to adopt them as springboards for Spanish word order would require tangents on English syntax first. The teacher will have to evaluate the cost-effectiveness of such tangents, the appropriate level for them, and the degree of active mastery students should show at a given level. Few books address Spanish word order at *any* level, and according to González (1997), English speakers do not really succeed in resetting their underlying parameters for movement to Spanish values until their third or fourth year of study, or even later in the case of OVS.

At least for the "receptive skills" of reading and listening, however, the variability of Spanish word order does require early comment and practice with processing strategies (VanPatten 1997, 96) when textbooks and listening passages proceed to use normal but unexplained permutations such as *Al juez lo criticó el abogado*. Students misunderstand who did what to whom, and as they continue reading the story, their misinterpretations mount up until the plot seems so bizarre that they conclude that this language and its literature are impenetrable.

Notes for chapter 11

1. Recent syntactic models replace S with InflP or IP (inflection phrase), AgrP (agreement phrase), or CP (complementizer phrase), and also NP with DP (determiner phrase), at least for certain levels of structure. In addition, options that follow from universal grammar (e.g., that XP contains X or can consist of XP Conj XP) are now factored out of the PSRs of particular languages. We have recognized such refinements earlier (v. 5.2), but rather than pursue the special arguments for them, we retain here a simpler model for readers with limited backgrounds in linguistics.

2. Specifically, Subj *you* is deleted by the Imperative Transformation (v. 12.4) in *Get out of here!* and by Ellipsis in *Want an apple?* ELLIPSIS is the dropping of elements that are understood from context, especially in colloquial styles: *Do you want an apple?* → *You want an apple?* → *Want an apple?* → *Apple?*

3. In the Caribbean area the erosion of final consonants (*-s, -n, -r*) has led to more dependence on Subj pronouns (Lipski 1994, 335). In some Dominican dialects, the result seems to have been a resetting of the Null Subject parameter: even sentences with no logical Subj are given a dummy *ello* like English *it*: *ello es fácil llegar* 'it's easy to get there' (p. 241).

4. As a minority viewpoint, Pilleux and Urrutia (1982, 80–82) argued that the deep structure Subj of *llover, tronar,* and *anochecer* is "El Allí". The only reason they offered for an obligatory Subj is that "su presencia en la estructura profunda se da como supuesta." They gave no citation for the *suponedor* of this *supuesto*.

5. In nonstandard usage, *haber* agrees with the NP: *Habían varios restaurantes*. Jorge Morel (1974, 127–31) found this agreement widespread in Santo Domingo, even in the first-person plural: *Aquí habemos muchos enfermos* 'there are lots of sick among us'; and Kany (1951, 212–17) noted its use in other countries, including Spain. Even so, pronominalization demonstrates that the NP is Obj. Compare this situation with the reverse one in English, where agreement (*There are several restaurants*) is standard and nonagreement (*There's several restaurants*) is regarded as nonstandard, although it is widespread in colloquial styles.

6. De Miguel (1993, 186) used a grammaticality-judgment technique to check understanding of Spanish word order. Nonnative but advanced students were given a list of sentences and were asked to correct any that were ungrammatical. "Corrections" such as the following confirmed students' miscomprehension:

Guardó Juan el secreto. → "Guardó a Juan el secreto."

Telefoneó María más tarde que de costumbre. → "Telefoneó a María . . ."

Marcos (1993, 209) showed the same kind of misinterpretations in students' judgments of sentences with question inversion (v. 12.1.1–2):

¿Qué ha publicado el periódico? → "¿Qué he publicado en el periódico?", "¿Quién ha publicado el periódico?"

7. Meyer (1972) called this Obj fronting "dislocation" and punctuated it with a comma: *El coche, se lo ha comprado José.* I omit her comma because Spanish does not use it and because the slight break it is meant to convey is insignificant compared to that of the more clearly dislocated OSV of English *The cár, Joe bought.*

8. Sentences such as *Una muestra del problema la ofreció el estudioso danés* contradict Meyer's (1972) constraint against OVS with indefinite Obj. Perhaps she meant a naked-noun Obj: D'Introno (1990) offered the following minimal pair for OVS and clitic doubling:

—¿Consiguieron *agua*? (= naked N) —Sí, agua conseguimos.

—¿Consiguieron *el agua*? (= definite N) —Sí, el agua ***la*** conseguimos.

Butt and Benjamin (1988, 395) pointed out that OSV (which Gili Gaya [1973] and Meyer ruled out) is possible with clitic doubling, as in *El libro Inés lo leyó* or *Este problema el presidente lo ve como el más crítico.* The informants I questioned agreed that SVO is usual but hardly unique, and that OVS and VSO are common but OVS generally requires the clitic. On VOS they disagreed: some accepted it readily, others only when a context led up to it, but one replied "¡No! Nunca diría eso a menos que sea interrogativo." Lipski (1994) noted several dialects (e.g., in Ecuador) where clitic doubling does not apply to preposed Obj as it does in most varieties. Liceras, Soloaga, and Carballo (1992) also encountered individual variation but concentrated, as we do in this chapter, on the overall tendencies.

9. The postposing of numbers (*el día quince, Carlos cinco, el siglo veintiuno*) is regarded as converting them to ordinals, in which role they then assume the same responsibilities as postposed adjectives (Gili Gaya 1973, 220). Postposed *alguno* is an exception to the rule that negation spreads lexically to all indefinites (v. 12.2).

10. The Spanish terms *anteposición/posposición* are difficult to render in English. There is no word *anteposition*, and *preposition* is preempted for Prep. For the noun of *preposed,* I adopt the hyphenated *pre-position.*

11. For example, against the first case, in the following quote from *El País (edición internacional,* Apr. 9, 1984, 22) an adjective of nationality precedes the noun: "Siempre metido en sus oficinas de *la barcelonesa calle* Provenzal . . . desde allí maneja sus múltiples negocios."

Exercises for chapter 11

1. Consider the following sentences and determine whether "personal" *a* is impossible, possible (but optional), or required in the blank. Then generate permutations of the SVO order and repeat the procedure. To what extent does the traditional rule for *a* cover these cases?

(a) El entusiasmo vence __ la dificultad.
(b) El tren atropelló __ un camión.
(c) La casa sostenía __ el árbol.
(d) Alicia buscará __ un médico.
(e) El niño acarició __ el perrito.
(f) El complemento sigue __ el verbo.
(g) El médico tiene __ una enfermera antipática.
(h) La cocinera mató __ el gallo.
(i) Estas tribus adoran __ los misioneros.
(j) Necesitamos __ un jefe bilingüe.
(k) Los mercaderes vendían __ los esclavos.
(l) La economía afecta __ la natalidad.
(m) El pato mató __ la gallina
(n) La palabrería sustituye __ la acción.

2. How similar are Spanish and English in their basic deep structure patterns? In their surface structures?

3. In what ways are copulas different from other verbs in the constituents they take?

4. How do *there is* and *haber* differ syntactically? *Rain* and *llover*?

5. Draw tree diagrams (phrase markers) to show the deep structure constituency of each of the following. Use the PSRs described in this chapter as a guide for what is what (and a part of what). When an "understood" constituent has been deleted or the word order has been transformed, restore the sentence to its deep structure configuration.
(a) Las jóvenes acataron a sus mayores.
(b) Los veinte obreros fatigados salieron de la fábrica.
(c) Permaneceremos allí cuatro días pero visitaremos a varios amigos.
(d) Juan cantaba una canción obscena y Luisa le pegó.
(e) Entró en el cuarto una mujer de ochenta años.
(f) Puedes mostrarle ese aparato al ingeniero esta tarde.
(g) Su hija ha sido la directora de las sucursales centroamericanas.
(h) El carro ese lo compró un cliente perspicaz.
(i) Llamó a la policía la pobre víctima sueca.

6. How do the units of the Spanish nucleus differ from those of the satellites? Why do these surface constituents cause trouble to English-speaking students?

7. Explain the difference in how information is being presented in each of the following pairs. To clarify your explanation, you might give examples of questions or discourse lead-ups that might precede each version.
(a) Esta tarde salgo para Caracas. Salgo para Caracas esta tarde.
(b) Acudieron a verlo ocho turistas ingleses. Ocho turistas ingleses acudieron a verlo.
(c) La Sra. Ortiz es una magnífica representante. La Sra. Ortiz es una representante magnífica.
(d) Carlos escribió el capítulo once. El capítulo once lo escribió Carlos.
(e) Mi colección ya no sirve para nada. La colección mía ya no sirve para nada.
(f) Una jirafa grande apareció en la calle. En la calle apareció una jirafa grande.
(g) Hay que reemplazar los quebradizos ladrillos del puente viejo. Hay que reemplazar los ladrillos quebradizos del viejo puente.
(h) Estudiamos las grandes obras del Siglo de Oro. Estudiamos las obras grandes del Siglo de Oro.

8. Study the following sentences, place an asterisk before each sentence you find ungrammatical, and correct it. Then describe the overall principles for clitic doubling.

(a) direct objects	(b) indirect objects
Vi a la mujer.	Dimos un cheque a la mujer.
A la mujer vi.	A la mujer dimos un cheque.
La vi.	Le dimos un cheque a la mujer.
La vi a la mujer.	A ella dimos un cheque.
Vi a ella.	Dimos un cheque a ella.
	Lo dimos a ella.

9. Draw up a lesson on Spanish adjectival position based (to some extent) on one or more of the theories described in this chapter. Give special attention to (a) how you would explain the meaning of position, (b) how you would illustrate it, (c) and how you would practice it to develop a testable skill. Explain also the extent to which you would expect active mastery.

10. Both English and Spanish can highlight information phonologically and syntactically. How do they differ on their relative use of the two means? What is the main function of phonological highlighting in Spanish?

11. Most textbooks touch upon adjectival position in some way but otherwise bypass most questions of word order. Consider the following solutions and choose the one you prefer.

(a) Describe to students the "normal" SVO order in Spanish and assume that they will eventually pick up alternative orders on their own through exposure in listening and reading.

(b) Describe "normal" SVO order but also comment later on alternative orders and their communicative functions.

Defend the position you prefer. If you choose (a), address the question of whether the syntax of dialogues, readings, and exercises should be controlled to SVO (and if so, until what point in language study); if you choose (b), indicate when permutations should be introduced, how they should be explained, and the level of mastery expected.

12. Construct a Spanish sentence of a nucleus plus two to three satellites. Make a list of all possible permutations, including some less used ones and even some that Gili Gaya and others might exclude. Now, make a list of Spanish questions that might elicit different presentations of the material in the sentence. Scramble the two lists, and then have native speakers match questions with preferred answers. Do your "judges" agree? Are there any permutations left over that they reject totally? (As a second experiment, do the same with lower-level students of Spanish and then compare the two groups' responses.)

13. Silva-Corvalán (1982) urged more analysis of Spanish word order in large samplings of discourse. She launched such an investigation of Mexican-Americans in Los Angeles. As an interviewer, she posed stimulating questions and then recorded the free conversation as it unfolded. Subsequently, she analyzed the rates of Subj deletion (Pro-Drop) and pre- and postposition. Some of her statistics are quoted below. Discuss them, identifying the relative strength of each variable in its effect on deletion and movement. Given that the variables interact and that each represents a discourse TENDENCY rather than a categorical grammatical rule, how would you interpret the implications of her study for teaching Spanish?

Definitions of terms: SAME REFERENCE means that the Subj is the same as (is carried over from) the preceding clause; SWITCH REFERENCE is when the speaker introduces a new Subj. PERSON-AMBIGUOUS describes a verb form like *hacía* that, by itself, could be 1sg. or 3sg.; PERSON-UNAMBIGUOUS is one like *hizo,* which can only be 3sg.; CONTEXTUALLY UNAMBIGUOUS is a form like *hacía* that is clear in context (e.g., *yo* since the speaker has been talking about himself or herself). ARGUMENTS are Subj, DO, IO satellite NPs—that is, not deleted and not cliticized; *Juan vio a Alicia* has two arguments, *Juan la vio* one, *la vio* none. Silva-Corvalán excluded from analysis impersonal verbs, nonfinites, exclamations, questions, and relative clauses because these have special properties with regard to Subj.

I. Deletion of Subj

(a)	Same reference:	75% deleted
	Switch reference:	47% deleted
(b)	Person-ambiguous:	31% deleted
	Contextually unambiguous:	61% deleted
	Unambiguous:	62% deleted

II. Placement of Subj when not deleted

(a)	Same reference:	74% preverbal
	Switch reference:	53% preverbal
(b)	Person-ambiguous:	64% preverbal
	Contextually unambiguous:	79% preverbal
	Unambiguous:	54% preverbal
(c)	Subj = old information:	61% preverbal
	Subj = new information:	36% preverbal
(d)	With preposed Advl:	15% preverbal
	With postposed Advl:	64% preverbal
(e)	One argument:	46% preverbal
	Two to three arguments:	64% preverbal

(With the postverbal-subject remainder of the two-to-three argument case, she found the orders OVS, VSO, VOS almost exactly equal in occurrence.)

Chapter 12

Questions, negations, passives, and commands

12.0 Simple affirmative active declarative sentences. The sentence patterns surveyed so far have largely been "simple affirmative active declarative," which we will abbreviate as SAAD. An example of a SAAD sentence is *Los líderes de Occidente se reunirán mañana en Bruselas.* It is SIMPLE in not containing any internal clauses; there is only one verb with its associated NPs and Advls (sometimes grouped together as the verb's ARGUMENTS). It is AFFIRMATIVE as opposed to negative; and it is ACTIVE as opposed to the passive sentence *Los líderes serán reunidos por el primer ministro.* It is DECLARATIVE in asserting information, not asking a question or giving a command that overtly requires a hearer's response.

SAAD structure can be changed by transformations that rearrange, delete, and introduce elements. Though preserving the underlying relationships of the constituents as defined in deep structure by the PSRs, transformations edit their surface form and produce alternative patterns. We have already seen several processes that are treated as transformations, including nominalization (v. 8.4.1), agreement (v. 8.1.1, 11.2.1), clitic promotion (v. 9.4.1, 11.2.1), and "personal" *a* insertion and rules for preposing and postposing (v. 11.2–11.3.3). Similarly, questions, negations, passives, and commands have often been described as transformational variants (or TRANSFORMS) of the more basic SAAD types.[1] Teachers should recognize that this treatment resembles the usual pedagogical approach whereby students first learn a structure such as *Víctor admira a Mercedes* and then learn ways to change this to *¿Admira Víctor a Mercedes?*, to *Mercedes es admirada por Víctor,* and so on.

12.1 Questions. English and Spanish have several kinds of questions and form them in similar ways—but with numerous differences of detail. The three most important question types are tag questions, yes/no questions, and information (*Wh-*) questions.

12.1.1 Tag and yes/no questions. In a TAG QUESTION, a "tag" is added to the end of a declarative sentence to elicit agreement with the assertion. In English, the tag begins with a negated form of the first auxiliary (Aux) or the copula *be,* or a positive one if the sentence is negative to begin with; if there is no Aux or *be*, then a "dummy Aux" *do* is used in the tag. The Aux or *be* is then followed by a pronoun version of the Subj:

The strikers will accept it, *won't they?*	The strikers won't accept it, *will they?*
You are sick, *aren't you?*	You aren't sick, *are you?*
Ann won the match, *didn't she*?	Ann didn't win the match, *did she?*

Spanish more simply adds *¿verdad?* or, after affirmatives only, *¿no?*

Los huelguistas lo van a aceptar, *¿no/verdad?*
Los huelguistas no lo van a aceptar, *¿verdad?*

A YES/NO QUESTION requests "yes"or "no" for an answer. In English, the transformation for this type, called Question Inversion (or Verb Fronting), again depends on the kind of VP: the first Aux (if there is one) is inverted over the Subj; if there is a form of *be* but no Aux, then this *be* is inverted; if neither is present, the Aux *do* is inserted and inverted, taking with it the tense/number inflection of the main verb. In all three cases, a contracted *not* → *-n't* (v. 12.2) is carried with the fronted verb. Finally, the sentence is generally given a rising terminal intonation (v. 4.2).[2] Thus,

Mary will/won't come. → Will/Won't Mary come?
Mary was/wasn't a nurse. → Was/Wasn't Mary a nurse?
Mary left the room. (→ Mary *do*+past leave the room) → Did Mary leave the room?

Spanish can form a yes/no question similarly with inversion and rising intonation: *¿Salió María del cuarto?* But there are three key differences. First, no dummy Aux is ever inserted (**¿Hace María salir?*). Second, inversion is optional, reflecting a strategy for presenting information (v. 11.2–11.3) more than a device for creating questions. Rising intonation suffices, so that *¿María salió del cuarto?* coexists with *¿Salió María del cuarto?* English, too, can omit the inversion step, but this yields an ECHO QUESTION: *Mary left the room?* echoes, with an incredulous or 'I didn't quite catch that' tone, the same statement asserted or implied just before. Third, if inversion occurs in Spanish, it is not just the Aux that moves forward but the whole V nucleus, often with an Obj or PA in tow as well.

Hasn't Larry eaten it?	*¿No lo ha comido* Lorenzo?
Is Larry that tall?	*¿Es tan alto* Lorenzo?

Students who have not learned to treat the nucleus as one agglutinated unit may mistakenly generate **¿Ha Lorenzo lo comido?* or **¿No lo ha Lorenzo comido?*

12.1.2 Information (*Wh-*) questions. A third question type is the INFORMATION QUESTION, also called *WH*-QUESTION, because it asks for information specified by words usually beginning with *wh-* in English (*who, which, when, why . . .*). As a Spanish counterpart, Stockwell, Bowen, and Martin (1965, 221) proposed "*K/D*-question" since the phonemes /k/ and /d/ begin Spanish equivalents of *Wh*-words, or *K/D*-words, but the terms "*Qu*-question" and "*Qu*-word" (Suñer 1982, 263) have won out. We can retain the traditional INTERROGATIVES as a neutral term for both *Wh-* and *Qu*-words.

Information questions are formed in two steps: first, Subj-V inversion (Subj-Aux in English, Subj-nucleus in Spanish) applies as in yes/no-questions;[3] then, the interrogative is moved from its deep structure position (as DO, IO, Subj, or whatever) to the front of the sentence by a transformation called *WH*-MOVEMENT (*MOVIMIENTO DE QU*) as illustrated below.

John has eaten *what/where/how?* → **Has** John eaten *what/where/how?* →
 What/where/how has John eaten?
¿Juan ha comido *qué/dónde/cómo?* → ¿**Ha comido** Juan *qué/dónde/cómo?* →
 ¿Qué/dónde/cómo ha comido Juan?

Exactly the same rules—inversion and then *Wh*-movement—also apply in the formation of Spanish indirect questions and exclamations, whereas English does not invert here (Marcos 1993, 202):

No sé qué coche *compró Juan.*	I don't know which car *John bought.*
¡Qué vestido más bonito *tiene María*!	What a pretty dress *Mary has.*

Wh-movement has recently received a great deal attention in linguistics. Two of its properties are that an interrogative modifier of N takes the whole NP with it (a constraint called PIED-PIPING) and that an interrogative can be fronted even if it comes out of a subordinated noun clause deeper in the sentence:

You think (that) they stole *which* jewels?→ *Which jewels* do you think (that)
 they stole?
¿Ud. supone que robaron *qué* joyas?→ *¿Qué joyas* supone Ud. que robaron?

Yet the two languages differ in how they treat interrogatives inside PP. In English, an interrogative OP optionally carries the Prep with it to the front of the sentence:

You talked *to who(m)?*→ *Who(m)* did you talk *to?* ~ *To whom* did you talk?
You spoke *about what?* → *What* did you speak *about?* ~ *About what* did
 you speak?
He came *from where?* → *Where* did he come *from?* ~ *From where* did he come?

while in Spanish, the whole PP must be fronted because Prep can never be "stranded" or left behind:

¿Le hablaste *a quién?* → ¿*A quién* le hablaste?
¿Hablaste *de qué?* → ¿*De qué* hablaste?
¿Vino *de dónde?*→ ¿*De dónde* vino?

Whatever preconceptions teachers may have about "stranded" prepositions, this construction is prevalent in modern English and is the one that occurs to students when they form questions in Spanish: **¿Qué hablaste de?, *¿Qué mano escribes con?*

The *qué/cuál* contrast also gives problems. English allows the substitution of *what* for *which* (as in *What's your address?*) while Spanish observes a distinction between *qué es*, which asks for a definition or classification, and *cuál es*, which asks for a selection from the set of possibilities for a category:

1. —¿Qué es tu dirección? —Es donde vivo, mi domicilio.
2. —¿Cuál es tu dirección? —Es la Calle Séptima, núm. 367.

As a result, English speakers often ask questions of type (1) when they really mean type (2). Their confusion is not helped upon learning that the Spanish contrast is also neutralized before N: for the interrogative adjective or determiner, traditional usage prefers *qué* instead of *cuál*, as in *¿Qué dirección es la tuya?* But although some authorities regard *¿Cuál dirección es la tuya?* as ungrammatical (Butt and Benjamin 1988, 288), *cuál* + N is quite common and fully accepted in many Spanish American countries, as it was in Old Spanish too (Kany 1951, 48). Consequently, correcting students' *cuál* + N to *qué* + N may not have high priority when they have succeeded in mastering the more fundamental distinction between *qué* and *cuál* in other environments.

Although questioning is a vital skill that students must acquire, interrogatives are often treated as just a set of vocabulary items: *qué, quién, cuál, cómo, cuándo, cuánto, dónde* are quickly matched with *what, who, which, how, when, how much, where,* and—except for notes on *qué* vs. *cuál*—the matter is then dropped. But interrogatives represent requests for the hearer to fill in missing information in a proposition, so that in principle there is a questioning strategy for each possible constituent slot. The traditional canon of matched interrogatives does not cover all strategies and ignores how they are tied to their respective languages (Whitley 1986a). One gap in this canon is the questioning of VP, illustrated below. Note that either the full VP or an embedded VP can be questioned, and that a distinction is made in both languages between VP caused by the Subj (role: Agent) and VP noncausally undergone by Subj (role: Patient).

Subj = Agent: Lydia *decided to escape.* → Lydia *did what?*→ *What* did Lydia do?
Lydia decided *to escape.* → Lydia decided *to do what?* → *What* did Lydia decide *to do?*

Lidia *decidió escaparse.* → ¿Lidia *hizo qué?*→ *¿Qué hizo* Lidia?
Lidia decidió *escaparse.* → ¿Lidia decidió *hacer qué?* → *¿Qué* decidió *hacer* Lidia?
Subj = Patient: Mark *died.* → *What happened to* Mark?
Marcos *murió.* → *¿Qué le pasó a* Marcos?

Another gap in the traditional canon is the elicitation of adjectival information, for which there is a variety of expressions based on the formula *what* + N + *of*:

Lydia wants *a (Adj) car.* → *What kind/color/model/size . . . of car* does Lydia want?
Lidia quiere *un carro (Adj).* → *¿Qué clase/color/modelo/tamaño . . . de carro* quiere Lidia?

Continuing this probing for interrogatives, we eventually add many other overlooked expressions to the inventory: *de qué manera, cada cuánto, a cuánto, hasta qué hora, a qué hora*, and so on.

In two places, there are holes left by the obsolescence of two Spanish interrogatives. First, both languages can question a possessive PA following a copula: *This book is yours* → *Whose is this book?, Este libro es tuyo* → *¿De quién es este libro?* However, prenominal possessives (D) can be questioned in English but not directly in Spanish. Some dialects retain an older *cúyo* for this function, but in standard Spanish it is necessary to switch to a structure in which the PP *de quién* can be generated:

Your book got messed up. → *Whose* book got messed up?
Tu libro se ha estropeado. (→ ¿*Cúyo* libro se ha estropeado?) → *¿De quién es* el libro *que* se ha estropeado? ¿El libro *de quién* se ha estropeado?

Second, textbooks equate *cómo* with *how,* but this practice is misleading, even aside from the *¿cómo?* = 'what?' for failure to understand. *How* in English actually questions three constituent types. One is Advl of manner, and a second is Adj in the PA position; in both cases, *cómo* matches up well enough (though *qué tal* is used too):

How did you arrive? *¿Cómo* llegaste?
How are you/do you feel? *¿Cómo/qué tal* estás/te sientes?

But a third, and seldom mentioned, function of English *how* is to represent Deg (v. 10.2.2), which precedes Adj or Adv and expresses the extent or degree of modification. With a regular interrogative for this category, the English speaker freely creates questions with *how* + Adj and *how* + Adv: *how tall, how tired, how true, how fast, how big, how dangerous, how regularly, how well*; *how much/many* belongs to the same series. *Cuán* originally served this function in Spanish, but although it still appears in cultivated styles, in normal usage it is following *cúyo* into oblivion. In its stead (Whitley 1986a), *qué tan* prevails from Mexico to the South American cone, while *cómo de* has appeared in Spain and some parts of the Americas:

How tall is the table?
(¿*Cuán alta* es la mesa?) → ¿*Qué tan alta* es la mesa? ~ ¿*Cómo* es *de alto* la mesa?

Neither formation is used as freely as English *how*, and other questioning strategies are often adopted. When *how* + Adj/Adv broadly represents extent in time, place, or degree, Spanish may prefer adverbial *cuánto* + V or an expression indicating endpoint with *hasta*:

How far/long did she run? ¿*Cuánto* corrió?
How long did you stay? ¿*Hasta cuándo* permaneció Ud.?
How involved is he? ¿*Hasta qué punto* está *involucrado*?
How important is this? ¿*Cuánto importa* esto?
How tall is she? ¿*Cuánto mide* ella (de alto/altura)?

As shown by Whitley's survey, however, the most common solution, aside from *qué tan,* is to switch from Adj or Adv to *qué* + N, which then requires syntactic adjustments for the resulting NP:

How often does she come? ¿*Con qué frecuencia* viene?
How tall is she? ¿*Qué altura tiene*?
How fast does it go? ¿*A qué velocidad* alcanza?
How far away is the capital? ¿*A qué distancia* está la capital?
How long/wide/thick is it? ¿*Qué largo/ancho/grosor tiene*?

English allows a similar N-based strategy, but not always. Thus, *What is its height/weight/width?* matches *How tall/heavy/wide is it?,* but one seldom says *What is its difficulty/coldness/stability?* for *How hard/cold/stable is it?* The student therefore has two challenges: to switch from Deg questioning to NPs in Spanish, and to master N equivalents of Adj and Adv. Most introductory and even intermediate textbooks do not address this problem at all, even though *how* + Adj/Adv is frequent in English, causes errors in Spanish, and represents an important question type. Perhaps *qué tan* deserves attention as the simplest solution.

12.2 Negating and disagreeing. Like Question Inversion, the Negative Transformation in English depends on what is present in the VP. A sentence-negating *not* (allomorph *-n't*) is moved into S and placed to the right of the first Aux, or *be* if there is no Aux; if neither is present, the dummy Aux *do* is again inserted, taking the main verb's tense inflection:

NOT Louise should have left. → Louise should *not* have left.
NOT Louise is over there. → Louise is *not* over there.
NOT Louise knows it. → Louise *does not* know it.

Once again, Spanish lacks *do* insertion. Regardless of verb type, *no* is placed at the beginning of the entire verb nucleus:

NO Luisa lo sabe. → Luisa *no* lo sabe.

But if some other negative word is already in place before V in Spanish, or before or after it in English, the sentence-negator *not/no* does not appear:

Louise has *never* lied.	Luisa *nunca* ha mentido
Nobody knows it.	*Nadie* lo sabe.

The contrast in the conditions for omitting *not/no*—a negative *before* V in Spanish vs. one *before or after* it in English—has major consequences. Spanish negation requires one negative before the nucleus, so that the Subj postposing or inversion (v. 11.2.3) of *Nadie lo sabe* requires the *no*: ***No** lo sabe nadie.*[4] Furthermore, the negation spreads rightward to all subsequent indefinites: **No tengo algo* → *No tengo nada.* This MULTIPLE NEGATION is not unknown to English speakers since it occurs in nonstandard speech: *I don't have nothing.* It was quite proper in English until grammarians assailed it as illogical, reasoning that language must behave like algebra: $(-x)(-y) = +xy$, two negatives yield a positive. Consequently, educated speakers are programmed to avoid multiple negation by changing *some(-body, -one, -thing, -where)* to *any(-body, -one, -thing, -where),* not *no(-body, -one, -thing, -where).* That is, they are familiar with multiple negation but will have a mental block against a teacher's attempt to explain *Yo nunca le dije nada a nadie tampoco* in terms of *I never said nothing to nobody neither.*

There is much more to the subject of negation once we pass from isolated sentences to connected discourse. In a typical interaction, speaker A offers new information to B by asserting the proposition *P* or its negation *not P* (formulaically *-P*). B may then indicate agreement (+) or disagreement (-) with either kind of proposition, which yields four options: 'I agree with *P*' = *+(P),* 'I agree with *not P*' = *+(-P),* 'I disagree with *P*' = *-(P),* and 'I disagree with *not P*' = *-(-P).* Spanish and English both have all four but express them differently:

1. P → +(P)	A: Ann sells tickets.	A: Ana vende boletos.
	B: Yes, she sells them. = Yes, she does.	B: Sí, los vende.
2. P → -(P)	A: Ann sells tickets.	A: Ana vende boletos.
	B: No, she doesn't sell them. = No, she doesn't.	B: No, no los vende.

3. -P → +(-P)	A: Ann doesn't sell tickets.	A: Ana no vende boletos.
	B: No, she doesn't sell them. = No, she doesn't.	B: No, no los vende.
4. -P → -(-P)	A: Ann doesn't sell tickets.	A: Ana no vende boletos.
	B: Yes, she *dóes* sell them. = Yes, she *dóes.*	B: Sí, sí los vende.

Case (4) is mentioned in pedagogy (if at all) as merely a lexical matter; as one textbook put it in a vocabulary list, "*sí*: indeed". But *indeed* is a bad rendition here. In English, speaker B corrects A's negative proposition by reversing *do(es)n't* to its emphatic affirmative *do(es)*; Spanish does the same thing but by reversing *no* to its affirmative counterpart *sí.* This discourse function of *do* (and the rationale for *sí*) is lost when textbooks wrongly claim that a Spanish present-tense form such as *vende* "means" *sells, is selling, does sell.*

Next, consider what happens when speaker B asserts that A's proposition *P* or *-P* is also true (+) or not true (-) of himself/herself or another entity besides the one that A has in mind:

5. P → +(P)	A: Ann sells tickets.	A: Ana vende boletos.
	B: And I sell them too. = And I do too. = Me too.	B: Y yo los vendo también. = Y yo también.
6. P → -(P)	A: Ann sells tickets.	A: Ana vende boletos.
	B: But I *dón't* sell them. = But I *dón't.* = Not me.	B: Pero yo no los vendo. = Pero yo no.
7. -P → +(-P).	A: Ann doesn't sell tickets.	A: Ana no vende boletos.
	B: I don't sell them either. = I don't either. = Neither do I. = Me neither.	B: Yo no los vendo tampoco. = Yo tampoco.
8. -P → -(-P)	A: Ann doesn't sell tickets.	A: Ana no vende boletos.
	B: But I *dó* sell them. = But I *dó.*	B: Pero yo sí los vendo. = Pero yo sí.

In addition to the *do/sí* problem, here the student encounters *tampoco* for both 'either' and 'neither' and the problem of case (*I, me*). Colloquial English discards the Subj/Obj distinction when V is absent, so that both *I saw them too* and *He saw me too* reduce to the elliptical form *Me too.* Spanish maintains the distinction between *Yo también/tampoco* and *A mí también/tampoco,* but its usage here reflects the way that grammar carries across sentences in discourse and cannot be learned from *palabras sueltas* in a vocabulary list.

Another complication is the SCOPE of a negative morpheme, that is, the material it applies to. In the following sentences, both languages agree that a negative before Aux + V applies just to Aux; that is, the meaning of ***not*** *have to do it* is 'not obligated' = 'you may or may not, as you wish':

Tienes que hacerlo hoy.	You have to do it today.
No tienes que hacerlo hoy.	*You don't have to* do it today.

But now consider the negation of *haber que,* which is also an Aux of obligation and is often glossed as 'one must, has (got) to, it's necessary'. When *no* precedes *haber que* + V, it is the V (the main verb) that is negated: *no hay que* + V is thus 'it is necessary ***not to verb***'. English *must* works the same way, but *have to* does not:

No hay que llenar este espacio.	= One/You *must not* fill in this blank.
	≠ One/You *do(es)n't have to* fill in this blank.

The 'must not' meaning of *no hay que* is seldom pointed out, but it is not hard to imagine cases in which students could fatally misinterpret *no hay que* as 'it's not required, so I'll do as I like'.

12.3 Passive and related structures. In a sentence such as *Mike killed the chickens,* the NP *the chickens* occupies a sentence position indicating not only DO but also asserted information (v. 11.3.1). Suppose that we wish to preserve the respective Subj and DO roles of *Mike* and *the chickens* but highlight *Mike* in the rheme and topicalize *the chickens*. In English, it is not possible just to exchange the two NPs, because *The chickens killed Mike* puts *Mike* under the spotlight but also makes him the DO (and dead). How then can the DO be fronted (preposed) for topicalization and the Subj postposed, without altering deep structure functions?

The answer is Passivization, which yields the passive version *The chickens were killed by Mike.* Passivization is a complex rule that can be broken down into five steps, as shown in figure 12.1. The effect is to move Subj and Obj but to mark with *be, by,* and the participle morpheme the fact that the new surface Subj is not the underlying one. This rule

Figure 12.1. Formation of the passive in English

Initial string of morphemes:	Mike kill+past the chickens.
(1) Move the deep structure Subj NP to the end of the clause and give it the Prep *by*, with which it forms a PP called an AGENT PHRASE:	∅ kill+past the chickens ***by** Mike.*
(2) Front the deep structure Obj NP to the vacated Subj position:	*The chickens* kill+past by Mike.
(3) Insert the passive Aux *be* before the V, giving it the latter's tense and making it agree with the new Subj:	The chickens ***be****+past+3.pl.* kill- by Mike.
(4) Give the V the past participle (pcp) ending:	The chickens ***be****+past+3.pl.* kill-pcp by Mike.
(5) Final morphological mop-up:	The chickens ***were killed*** by Mike.

precedes Inversion, for its output can then be questioned: → *Were the chickens killed by Mike? By whom were the chickens killed?*

In addition to moving the deep structure Subj and Obj into rheme and theme positions, respectively, the English passive is used for downplaying the identity of an underlying Subj, that is, for when a speaker cannot or will not identify it. In this case, the sentence must be passivized; a subjectless S is generally impossible (but see commands, 12.4), so something must move into the Subj position. Hence, *(unidentified NP) killed the chickens* becomes *The chickens were killed,* an AGENTLESS PASSIVE.[5] An alternative passive Aux in this construction is *get* (*The chickens got killed*), although it occurs in full passives as well, especially in informal English (*The chickens got killed by a truck*). Thus, English actually has several variants of the passive.

The Spanish passive parallels the English one in figure 12.1, with the use of *ser* as the inserted Aux and *por* to introduce the agent phrase.[6] The transformation again proceeds step by step:

Miguel mata+preterite las gallinas.
→ *Las gallinas* mata+preterite ***por*** *Miguel.*
→ Las gallinas ***ser****+preterite+3pl.* mata- por Miguel.
→ Las gallinas ***ser****+preterite+3pl.* mata-pcp por Miguel.
→ Las gallinas ***fueron matadas*** por Miguel.

This transformation therefore relates the active version *Miguel mató las gallinas* to the passive *Las gallinas fueron matadas por Miguel*—although not to the output *Miguel fue matado por las gallinas* that some inattentive students produce.

But the Spanish passive is less frequent than its English counterpart because the language has less need of it (RAE 1979, 379). One reason is that the Spanish speaker can rearrange an active sentence from SVO to VSO, VOS, or OVS to highlight theme and rheme (v. chapter 11) without the gymnastics of passivization: for example, *Mató Miguel las gallinas* or *Las gallinas las mató Miguel.* Another reason is that one more commonly deemphasizes the identity of a Subj in Spanish by resorting to the impersonal/passive *se*: *Se mató las gallinas* (v. 9.3.9).

There are also differences of detail between the English and Spanish passive:

First, the English participle is invariable, but the Spanish participle is treated as an Adj in PA position. It therefore agrees with the new (passive) Subj (*el gallo fue matado, las gallinas fueron matadas*) and can be pronominalized with *lo* (*Sí, lo fueron*, v. 8.4.2).

Second, Spanish passivization operates at a level at which the Obj has not yet become a clitic or been marked with "personal" *a*—rules that English lacks. Once these rules finalize the active version of the sentence, its relationship to the passive looks less direct—which is why students often have trouble passivizing sentences such as *Miguel siguió* ***al*** *director* or *Miguel* ***lo*** *siguió.*

Third, English passivization moves "Obj" into the vacated Subj position (step 2 in figure 12.1), and this object can be direct, indirect, or even oblique (OP):

I gave *some money* (DO) *to George* (IO).
→ *Some money* was given to George by me.
or → *George* was given some money by me.
The teacher talked about (went over, delved into) *the crisis* (OP).
→ *The crisis* was talked about (gone over, delved into) by the teacher.

Moreover, certain verb idioms consisting of V + NP + Prep + NP allow either NP to be passivized:[7]

Jessica took *good* ***care*** *of the* ***cats***.
→ *Good care* was taken of the cats by Jessica.
or → *The cats* were taken good care of by Jessica.

But Spanish passivizes the DO, *only* the DO, *never* IO or OP, to the frustration of students who say **Yo no fui permitido ir* without realizing that *yo* is the IO of *permitir* in deep structure. The closest equivalent to English IO and OP passivization is the impersonal *se* construction:

Se le dio dinero a Jorge ~ *A Jorge se le dio dinero* 'George was given some money'
Se habló de la crisis 'The crisis was talked about'
No se me permitió/permitía ir 'I wasn't allowed to go'.

Both languages allow the past/passive participle (pcp) to be used adjectivally: *boiled/baked/fried potatoes* like *raw/small/dirty potatoes*; *papas cocidas/asadas/fritas* like *papas crudas/pequeñas/sucias.* Many linguists have explained these adjectival participles in the NP by deriving them from passivized relative clauses (v. 13.3): *potatoes that were fried (by . . .) → potatoes fried (by . . .) → fried potatoes.* Although this explanation may seem unnecessary for pedagogy, it does account for two facts. First, such participles tend to retain the force of a passive: *papas fritas* implies 'papas que fueron fritas por alguien' (*papas crudas* has no such implication). Second, adjectival participles can surface with dependent VP constituents, including a passivized Subj or agent phrase: *las papas fritas ayer con cuidado por tu mamá.* On the other hand, it should be borne in mind that there are many morphologically participial Adjs that have no passive thrust at all (*divertido, pesado, considerado,* etc.; v. 6.3.2).

Once the participle acquires an adjectival function, it becomes ambiguous with copulas. In English, the surface structure NP + *be* + V-pcp can be understood in two ways. For example, *The dishes were washed* can be passive, referring to an action in the past with a deemphasized Subj, or it can describe a state, meaning that the dishes were clean, not dirty, as the result of having been washed previously. The terms TRUE PASSIVE and PASSIVE OF RESULTING STATE, respectively, are sometimes used to distinguish the two interpretations. Spanish contrasts them by using *ser* as the Aux of a true passive but *estar* as the copula of a resulting state:[8]

ser + pcp = true passive: *Los platos fueron/eran lavados.*
estar + pcp = resulting state: *Los platos estaban/estuvieron lavados.*

As shown, when the *ser/estar* contrast is combined with that of preterite/imperfect, four distinct messages emerge for the Spanish speaker. For the English speaker who uses *The dishes were washed* with no awareness of finer distinctions, the Spanish options seem overdifferentiated. In fact, still other shades of meaning are possible in Spanish through the use of other copulas or intransitive verbs: *La ley es/va/queda/resulta firmada por el presidente.* But in a way, the Spanish setup is underdifferentiated. In adopting the above solution, Spanish forgoes marking a contrast between normal states vs. changed ones, that is, the usual *ser/estar* contrast with Adj (v. 15.4.2). Thus, in *Fueron casados* it is unclear whether the speaker is referring to a passivized event ('alguien los casó') or to a civil state regarded as the terminated norm for two people ('no fueron solteros sino casados'). English *They were married* is, of course, even more ambiguous.

12.4 Commands. The IMPERATIVE is considered a third mood for lack of a better pigeonhole for it (v. 7.2.1). If it is a mood, it is a defective one in that it lacks a *yo* form and overlaps morphologically with other categories (with the subjunctive in Spanish, with the infinitive in English). It is not even clear which forms should be included since there are numerous strategies for giving orders and requests (see Terrell and Salgués 1979, 176):

- direct command: *dámelo, démelo*
- question: *¿Me lo da(s)?*
- *mejor* + indicative: *Mejor me lo das.*
- *deber*: *Debe(s)/Debiera(s) dármelo.*
- wish with *que* ("indirect command"): *que me lo dé(s)*
- wish with *ojalá (que)*: *ojalá que me lo dé(s)*
- *(Hacer) el favor de*: *Hazme/Hágame el favor de dármelo, Favor de dármelo.*
- various businesslike formulas: *Se ruega/Tenga la bondad de remitírnoslo.*
- plain infinitive: *Remitir solicitud y currículum a esta dirección.*

Furthermore, for pedagogical purposes, it is important to include the questioning form used for *inviting* a command, which is usually the simple present indicative in Spanish (*¿Te lo doy? ¿Se lo damos?*) vs. *shall* in English (*Shall I give it to you? Shall we give it to her?*).

Traditional grammar, though, limits the imperative to direct commands issued to *tú, usted, vosotros, ustedes,* and *nosotros*. These forms are compared in figure 12.2. Spanish has the more complicated system. Yet aside from irregulars like *sal* for *salir* (*pon, ten, di, haz, sé*, etc.), the *tú* forms are the present indicative minus *-s* (*para, come, sigue*) and the *vosotros* form just changes the infinitive's *-r* to *-d*. The other imperatives are present subjunctives, and under negation all persons take that form: *no salgas* (*no salga, no salgamos . . .*).[9] The subjunctive connection and the *que* of the "indirect commands" (*que salga/salgan)* suggest a noun clause (v. 13.1–13.1.2.7) following an understood verb of

Figure 12.2. Spanish and English imperatives

	tú	*usted*	*vosotros*	*ustedes*	*nosotros*
Spanish	Sal	Salga	Salid	Salgan	Salgamos
English	Leave				Let's leave

wishing or ordering, and teachers and linguists alike sometimes explain imperatives in that way: *(yo mando/quiero que) salgan.*

In Spanish, what has sometimes been called the Imperative Transformation deletes the Subj unless it is emphatic, in which case it is inverted over the verb. In addition, unless there is a *no* or other negative before the nucleus, clitics are suffixed to the imperative verb, which necessitates a morphophonemic adjustment for *vosotros* reflexives: *sentad+os* → *sentaos*. In nonstandard lects, there is also an adjustment of *ustedes* reflexives in that a second *-n* is added to the end: *siéntense* → *siéntense**n*** (Kany 1951, 112). In English, on the other hand, Obj pronouns stay put, but Subj *you,* if not dropped, oddly precedes an affirmative command and follows the *don't* of a negative one. Major differences therefore emerge between the two languages:

Despiértala (tú).	(You) Wake her up.
No la despiertes (tú).	Don't (you) wake her up.

Students balk at a rule that postposes clitics with affirmatives and preposes them for negatives, especially with a change in verb form as well. Its origins lie in leveled-out variations from the older language rather than in logic or reason, and it makes as little sense today as the preposing of English Subj *you* in affirmatives and its postposing in negatives.

Nosotros commands behave syntactically like the second-person ones: *despertémosla (nosotros), no la despertemos (nosotros). Vamos* irregularly appears instead of the expected *vayamos* for both the imperative of *ir* and the *ir a* periphrasis, but only in the affirmative: *vamos a casa* (*vamos a despertarla*) but *no vayamos a casa*. Again, there is a morphophonemic adjustment in the dropping of the *-s* of *-mos* before clitics beginning with /s/ and /n/: *demos+se+la* → *démosela, demos+nos prisa* → *démonos prisa, vamos+nos* → *vámonos*. The English equivalents of these *nosotros* commands are hard to describe. The negative of *let's wake her up* is *let's not wake her up* for some speakers, *don't let's wake her up* for others, and there exists an emphatic affirmative *let's* ***us*** *wake her up,* which becomes bizarre the more that one thinks about it (**let us us wake?*).

The Imperative Transformation can apply to the output of Passivization, so that passives can be commanded too, as in *be guided by my advice* or the quaint *sé tú amado* included in the RAE's paradigms (1924, 69). But as pointed out earlier, the Spanish passive or impersonal reflexive is more frequent than the true passive, and it yields command forms too: *véase la página 3, consúltese la guía de teléfonos, échese una taza de agua.*

Notes for chapter 12

1. The deep structures of questions, negatives, and commands have been analyzed as containing morphemes such **Q** (for questioning), **Neg** (for negation), and **Imp** (for Imperative tense) that trigger changes in structure. For example, **Neg** *Juan está allí* (roughly, 'it is not the case that *Juan está allí*) → *Juan* ***no*** *está allí.* The passive has likewise been considered a transform of the active (as in pedagogy): *La policía arrestó a Juan* → *Juan fue arrestado por la policía.* After Chomsky 1981 and 1982, however, generative grammar adopted a more restricted view of transformations in order to focus on universal properties of movement and deletion rules. (See Suñer 1989 for a summary of how these proposals applied to Spanish.) As with the PSRs in chapter 11, in this chapter we continue at a simpler level of description rather than recapitulate the more complex theories that now apply to rules like *Wh*-movement or to structures like the passive.

2. A falling intonation is not unusual, though, when several yes/no questions are asked in succession (Harris 1971).

3. Spanish more regularly inverts with information questions than with yes/no questions. Yet inversion is still not obligatory: *¿Cómo los gobernadores han podido resolverlo?* When the Subj is a pronoun, most speakers do invert, but *¿Qué tú dices?* is common in Caribbean dialects (Kany 1951, 125; Jorge Morel 1974, 122).

4. In some lects, for example, those of Argentina and Paraguay, the restriction requiring one negative before the nucleus does not hold: there may be two negatives before the verb, as in *nadie no está* (Lipski 1994, 174–75).

5. Readers may note a contradiction here. We assumed earlier (v. 11.1.1) that English PSRs require a deep structure Subj, yet here we see surface structures with no *by NP* representing an underlying Subj. Linguists have proposed four solutions:

- Posit a deep-structure Subj *someone* that gets deleted: *Someone killed the chickens* → *The chickens were killed*; yet the agent of death could just as well be some*thing* (a truck, disease, lightning, contaminated feed . . .).
- Posit a kind of silent pronoun called "PRO" (v. 13.0.2) as the deep-structure Subj.
- Allow the Subj NP node to be empty in deep structure.
- Account for the Passive in some other way (rather than as a transformation).

6. The use of *de* instead of *por* in passives, as in *Es amado de todos*, has long been declining, and the rather contrived traditional rules for it are no longer valid, much less useful to students; see Suñer 1981 for a fuller critique.

7. Other examples of V + NP + Prep + NP verb idioms are *lose/keep track of, make fun of, take advantage of, keep pace with, pay attention to,* and *make use of* (Quirk et al. 1972, 848). Other syntactically parallel constructions do not allow these special passives: *They lost the labels off their luggage* → **Their luggage was lost the labels off.* Likewise, not all OPs can be passivized: *They flew through the air* → **The air was flown through by them.* Fortunately, English speakers do not need to know which OPs in Spanish undergo passivization, but simply the fact that *none* of them ever does.

8. Note that in practicing passive *ser* vs. *estar* with fill-in-the-blanks, it is wrong to use *por* + NP as a cue for *ser*; the agent phrase could just as well accompany *estar* + V-pcp for what Bull (1965, 292) called "maintenance of resulting state." In other words, either *fue* or *estaba* could occur in a context such as *El camino ___ bloqueado por las tropas.*

9. For this reason, Alarcos Llorach (1999, 190) accepted for the Real Academia *only* the affirmative *tú* and *vosotros* commands as *imperativos*; other direct commands are merely "apelativos"

that just happen to have the same syntax, function, and intonation as imperatives. While his distinction is true etymologically, it makes little sense in a synchronic analysis.

Exercises for chapter 12

1. Error analysis:
   (a) *¿Ha Juan salido?
   (b) *¿Son Vicente y su papá altos?
   (c) *Cristina no quiere algo.
   (d) *¿Cómo largo es el sofá?
   (e) *¿Qué hablaste sobre?
   (f) *¿De quién toalla usaste?
   (g) *Pedro está no caminando.
   (h) *No tú hazlo.
   (i) *¿Hace Carmina saberlo?
   (j) *No estudiantes participarían.

2. In what ways are the following student responses inappropriate or even ungrammatical? What special usages of Spanish are being misunderstood?
   (a) Teacher: ¿Qué hace Ud. por la mañana?
   Student: Hago estudiar.
   (b) Teacher: Yo prefiero las películas cómicas. ¿Y Ud.?
   Student: Mí también. ¿No? ¿Me también?
   (c) Teacher: ¿Qué tal le parece nuestro equipo este año?
   Student: Me parece un equipo de fútbol.
   (d) Teacher: ¿Qué les pasó a las víctimas del terremoto?
   Student: Les pasó, fueron llevadas al hospital.
   (e) Teacher: ¿A quién se lo dio Ud.?
   Student: Yo se lo dio. ¿No? ¿Yo se lo *di*?
   (f) Teacher: ¿Se llamó a la policía?
   Student: No, ella no se llama policía. Se llama María.

3. Command forms are complex in Spanish. Why do native Spanish-speaking children nevertheless master these forms quickly and accurately? Why do English speakers continue to have trouble with giving commands well into intermediate levels of study? In listing the reasons, distinguish between difficulties *within* Spanish and those that arise from English interference.

4. Discuss the ways in which English and Spanish differ on (a) inversion in questions, (b) formation and use of the passive, and (c) meanings of copula + participle in surface structure.

5. Why do English speakers have trouble finding suitable equivalents for *anybody, anything, anywhere, ever,* and *either* in a Spanish dictionary?

6. Draw up a lesson plan in which students practice a range of interrogatives by forming information questions to elicit designated constituents of declarative sentences. For example,
   Se lo regalé *a Beatriz.* (→ *¿A quién se lo regalaste?*)
   Mi dirección es *la Avenida K, núm. 123.* (→ *¿Cuál es tu/su dirección?*)
   Los martes *trabajo en una farmacia.* (→ *¿Qué haces los martes?*)
As part of the same lesson, how would you explain the ways in which *how* + Adj/Adv is conveyed in Spanish? Which option(s) would you emphasize for active mastery?

7. Why is the following kind of sentence (often attempted by students) ungrammatical?
*Elena fue mandada/permitida/prohibida (a) destruir los documentos.
On the other hand, why is *Elena fue obligada a destruir los documentos* okay?

8. The Spanish Passive Transformation can be used to distinguish cases of *a* + DO from *a* + IO and *a* + adverbial OP (v. 8.1.3, 9.4.1, 10.2.2). Use it to discern DOs in the following:

(a) La revolución ha reemplazado a las urnas.
(b) Las lluvias invernales siguen a la sequía.
(c) Su rango corresponde a su renta per cápita.
(d) Las ventanas dan al patio.
(e) El ejecutivo renunció al puesto.
(f) No has contestado a Jaime.
(g) No has escuchado a Dorotea.
(h) Los perros olían al reo.
(i) Los perros olían a orina.
(j) Miguel no asistió a esta clase.
(k) La moza sirvió a don Marcos.
(l) El gerente discrimina a las mujeres.

9. Passivization also distinguishes verb + DO from verb + PA or adverbial NP. Which of the following are thereby true DO in Spanish?

(a) Lupe fue *una ingeniera famosa.*
(b) Lupe midió *el perímetro.*
(c) Lupe midió *158 centímetros.*
(d) Lupe asistió *varias veces.*
(e) Lupe llamó *el perrito.*
(f) Lupe lo llamó "*Perrito*".
(g) Lupe pasó *dos semanas allí.*
(h) Lupe se quedó allí *dos semanas.*

10. One transformation that we have not discussed is "Gapping." Following are some examples of it; study them and then state informally how the rule operates. How is it similar to Nominalization (v. 8.4.1) in operation and in function?

Ella defendió a Carlos y yo defendí a Ramiro. → Ella defendió a Carlos y yo a Ramiro.
Mercedes quiere tomar vino y su novio quiere tomar cerveza. → Mercedes quiere tomar vino y su novio cerveza.

11. We examined certain differences in negation between the two languages, but there are others as well (Steel 1985, 273). In each of the following, indicate whether the italicized negation is required or optional (variable, idiolectal), give an English version, and then try to explain the presence of the negative in Spanish.

(a) Me importa más a mí que a *nadie*.
(b) Ella sabe más que *ningún* experto.
(c) Se empeñaron más que *nunca*.
(d) Antes que resuelvas *nada*, consúltalo con la almohada.
(e) Es mejor ir a pie que *no* esperar el autobús.
(f) Hasta que *no* presenten pruebas, eres inocente.

12. "Indirect commands," as in *que se calle José,* are treated as third-person imperatives, but they are not so limited: *y que te calles tú también.* Like other scholars, Carnicer (1977, 51) analyzed them as ellipses of a fuller *mando (digo, quiero . . .) que se calle/te calles*; the *que,* in other words, is not an imperative marker but the complementizer of a noun clause (v. 13.1.2) following a verb of communication. He similarly treated sentences such as the following as ellipses of fuller sentences containing something like *yo te digo* . . . or *tú me preguntas*. . . :

Que sí.	Que si quieres arroz.	¿Que ya vienen?
Que no es así.	¿Que por qué hago esto?	Que eso no se dice.

Carnicer judges *que,* from its many uses, as "este gozne fundamental del castellano." How would you characterize the effect of these *que*-fragments? What is their effect in a conversation?

13. Hurley (1995) analyzed conversations in Otavalo, Ecuador, and demonstrated the contrast between a present imperative, *ven/venga,* with the meaning of 'do it now', and a future one, *vendrá(s),* meaning 'do it later'. In this dialect, **venga mañana* is ungrammatical, and clitics are suffixed to future imperatives (*llamarásle*) just as they are to present ones. Hurley attributed the contrast to Quechua influence, since it is particularly common among Quechua/Spanish bilinguals and a similar distinction is found in Quechua. Yet it is also used by monolingual Spanish speakers of all social strata in Otavalo, and one could point out the parallel in the *Diez Mandamientos* (*No tendrás. . . , no tomarás. . . , seis días trabajarás, no matarás. . . , no hurtarás. . . , no codiciarás. . .* , Éxodo 20). How do you analyze this usage? Do you see any relationship to intralingual and interlingual influences in interlanguage (v. 0.3)?

14. Because of their connection to the Passive Transformation, past participles have been called passive participles (v. 6.3.2). Study, however, the following examples and demonstrate that they could not come from the Passive Transformation.

Los contrabandistas chilenos *huidos a Argentina* no quieren rendirse.
El dinero *salido del país* valdría unos dos millones de dólares.
El portavoz reveló un accidente *ocurrido a diez kilómetros de la capital.*
Participó mucha gente en los debates *habidos aquí sobre el aborto.*
No piensan volver los ciudadanos *recién venidos de las Islas.*
El país se ha atenido a la estrategia de un general *nacido en 1902.*

If a name helps, Bello ([1847] 1958, 152) called such participles "deponentes" after a similar Latin category. What, exactly, does Spanish allow here that English grammar generally does not?

Chapter 13

Complex sentences

13.0 Compound vs. complex sentences. At several points in the phrase structure rules examined in chapter 11, the symbol S for 'sentence' appeared inside another S or inside some constituent of another S. Thus, S may contain S, that is, sentences can be combined to form longer ones. This property is universal, although the structuring of combined sentences depends on the grammar of each language to some extent. Many languages, including Spanish and English, show two distinct types of sentence combinations, compound and complex.

A COMPOUND SENTENCE consists of two or more internal sentences (CLAUSES) joined by coordinating conjunctions (v. 11.1.1). It results from the application of the rule S → S (Conj S)^n, that is, 'S may consist of S combined with the sequence Conj + S any number of times'. An example is *[Tú saliste] y [la camarera te vio],* whose coordinated or compound S Conj S structure is shown by phrase marker (a) in figure 13.1. (Note the introduction of two common conventions here: brackets are used to enclose and highlight constituents, clauses in this case; and in the trees of figure 13.1 the triangles abbreviate irrelevant internal details of constituents.)

A COMPLEX SENTENCE also contains two or more clauses, but instead of being loosely or additively joined as in compound S, one is built into the other. The larger S is called the MAIN OR MATRIX CLAUSE; the internal one is described as EMBEDDED IN, SUBORDINATED TO, or a COMPLEMENT OF some constituent in the main clause. Whereas a coordinated clause plays no grammatical role in its compound mate, a subordinated clause carries out a syntactic function within the main clause, generally acting like a noun, adjective, or adverbial.

13.0.1 Types of embedded clauses. Some embedded clauses function like NP, as the Subj or Obj in the main clause. These are NOUN CLAUSES and are generated by the PSR NP → S, that is, 'an NP can consist of S alone'. This rule specifies the structure in tree (b) of figure 13.1 for *Yo sé [que la camarera te vio].* Note that the bracketed material in this example is itself a sentence (*la camarera* = NP, *te vio* = VP, and NP + VP = S), and that it carries out the same Obj function in the main clause as the final NP of *Yo sé los*

Figure 13.1. Types of clauses and their structures

(a) Coordinated clauses

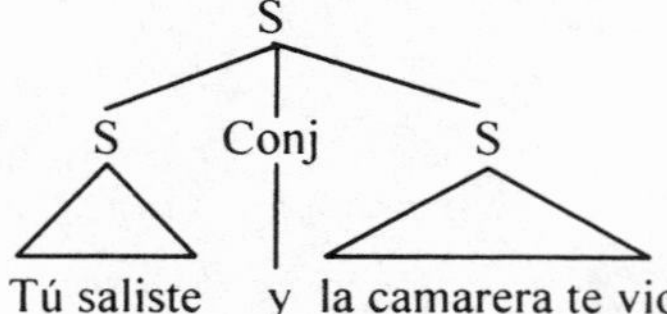

(b) Subordinated: object noun clause

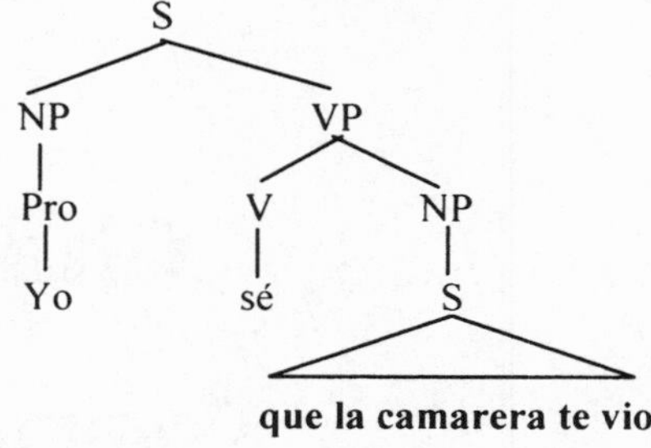

(c) Subordinated: appositive noun clause

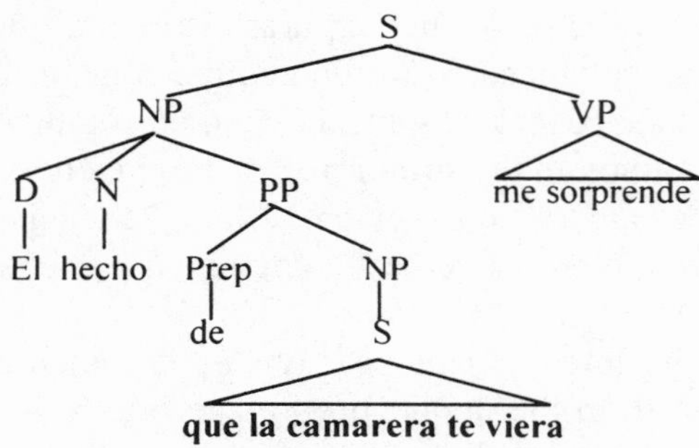

(d) Subordinated: relative clause

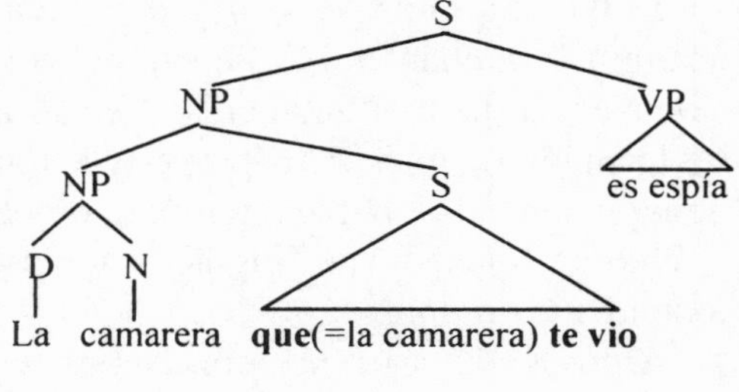

(e) Subordinated: adverbial clause

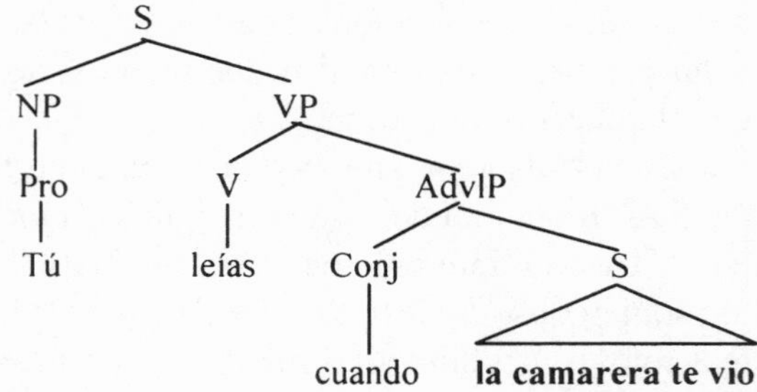

números. The *que* that introduces the noun clause *que la camarera te vio* is a functor (v. 10.4.2) whose only meaning is to fit the noun clause into the larger sentence and to mark its subordination. It is called a COMPLEMENTIZER (Comp), and in some analyses, a noun clause is in fact described as a COMPLEMENTIZER PHRASE (CP).

A noun clause may also serve as an appositive (v. 11.1.3) to some noun in the matrix. An example of an appositive noun clause is found in *El hecho de [que la camarera te viera] me sorprende,* shown in tree (c) of figure 13.1. In this case, the bracketed clause is equated with *hecho* in much the same way that *Lima* is equated with *ciudad* in *la ciudad de Lima.*

Instead of being equated with N, an embedded S can modify NP like an adjective, in which case it is called a RELATIVE (or ADJECTIVE) CLAUSE. A relative clause conforms to the rule NP → NP S, that is, 'NP may consist of some other NP (e.g., D + N) combined with a modifying S'. Tree (d) in figure 13.1 shows the structure of a sentence containing a relative clause, *La camarera [que te vio] es espía. Que te vio* identifies which *camarera* is meant, just like the Adj in *la camarera sospechosa.* The *que* that introduces a relative clause is a RELATIVE PRONOUN, not Comp, since it does not just introduce the clause but acts as its Subj and refers to someone (the head noun) as other pronouns do: *que = ella, la camarera.*

Another possibility is for the embedded clause to be governed by an adverbial (Prep or Conj) and thereby carry out an adverbial function in the matrix VP. It is then called an ADVERBIAL CLAUSE and is represented as in an AdvlP. The structure of a sentence containing an adverbial clause, *Tú leías [cuando la camarera te vio],* is given in (e) of figure 13.1. Note that the bracketed clause has the same position and function (*complemento circunstancial*) as the Adv in *Tú leías entonces* or the PP in *Tú leías durante la misa.*

Finally, as is shown later in this chapter, comparative sentences can be analyzed as complex too, although pedagogically they are usually treated as simple sentences.

13.0.2 Reduced clauses. While the clauses of compound sentences tend to preserve their own structure, subordinated clauses are more tightly integrated into the matrix and undergo processes that adjust them according to what is present in the main clause. In particular, they may REDUCE to simpler constructions in which the V is nonfinite and its Subj may be absent. For example, *La camarera afirma [que ella te ha visto]* has a shorter variant that means the same thing: *La camarera afirma [haberte visto].* Many linguists have explained this relationship with a transformation that whittles down the full clause to the infinitival phrase *haberte visto.* Other linguists treat reductions as SMALL CLAUSES that lack tense and have a kind of silent pronoun PRO as Subj.[1] Either way, infinitives are seen as a type of clause, and this perspective provides insight into a variety of patterns that textbooks often consign to lists of miscellaneous *usos del infinitivo.*

13.1 Noun clauses. Noun clauses—full or reduced—function as Subj of the matrix sentence (section 13.1.1), as the verb's DO (section 13.1.2), or as OP (section 13.2.1).

13.1.1 As subjects. Suppose we wish to comment on the proposition *John smokes cigars* by making it the Subj of the VP *bothers Henry.* The resulting sentence is *[John smokes cigars] bothers Henry,* but its embedded clause *John smokes cigars* needs a complementizer (Comp) to mark its subordination. Standard English permits three types of Comp for Subj noun clauses:

that NP VP: [*that* John smokes cigars] bothers Henry
for NP ***to*** VP: [*for* John *to* smoke cigars] bothers Henry
NP-possessive VP-***ing***: [John*'s smoking* cigars] bothers Henry

A clause with *that* or *for . . . to . . .* can be uprooted and moved to the end of the main clause, whereupon a dummy *it* is inserted into the vacated Subj position. This transformation is called EXTRAPOSITION:

[that John smokes cigars] bothers Henry → ***it*** bothers Henry [that John smokes cigars]
[for John to smoke cigars] bothers Henry → ***it*** bothers Henry [for John to smoke cigars]

On the other hand, *for . . . to . . .* and possessive + *-ing* differ from *that* in introducing clauses that exclude tense and modals (**for John to smoked, *John's woulding smoke*). In addition, their Subj can be missing, in which case *for* NP *to* VP becomes just *to* VP, and NP-possessive VP-*ing* becomes just VP-*ing*. This reduction to a subjectless infinitive or gerund occurs under two conditions. First, the Subj NP can drop when it is referentially identical to (coreferential with) some other NP in the main clause, a condition called EQUI-NP:

[for **Henry** to smoke cigars] bothers **Henry** → [Ø to smoke cigars] bothers Henry
(+ *Extraposition*) → ***it*** bothers Henry [to smoke cigars]
[**Henry**'s smoking cigars] bothers **Henry** → [Ø smoking cigars] bothers Henry

Second, no Subj NP appears in surface structure when it is referentially IMPERSONAL. This generalized subject is analyzed as an unpronounced pronoun PRO (v. 13.0.2).[2]

[for PRO to smoke cigars] is expensive → [to smoke cigars] is expensive
(+ *Extraposition*) → ***it*** is expensive [to smoke cigars]
[PRO's smoking cigars] is expensive → [smoking cigars] is expensive

Thus, English actually has the following full set of Comp options in surface structure,

full clause, tensed:	*that* NP VP (*that* Henry smokes cigars)
infinitive (untensed):	*for* NP *to* VP (*for* Henry *to* smoke cigars)
	to VP (*to* smoke cigars)
gerund (untensed):	NP-possessive VP-*ing* (Henry's smoking cigars)
	VP-*ing* (smoking cigars)

In Spanish, the usual Comp is *que*,[3] with its alternate *el que. (El) que* NP VP resembles *that* NP VP, but it allows mood contrasts according to the way the proposition is viewed or evaluated (v. 7.3.2.2). Subject noun clauses may be extraposed in Spanish as in English, although without insertion of *it*. But this is nothing special in Spanish, which allows extraposition of *any* Subj NP (v. 11.2.3–11.3.1), so the changes in (1) and (2) below are really the same transformation:

1. [que Juan fume cigarros] le molesta a Enrique → le molesta a Enrique [que Juan fume cigarros]
2. Juan viene → Viene Juan.

Like English, Spanish uses its infinitive as a second Comp. Unlike English, however, Spanish allows *el* to precede this infinitive (like its *que* clause), postposes the infinitive's Subj (if expressed),[4] and never uses any equivalent of English *for* in this construction:

[(el) fumar cigarros Juan] le molesta a Enrique

Given Equi-NP, the infinitive's own Subj drops as in English:

[(el) fumar cigarros **Enrique**] le molesta a **Enrique** → [(el) fumar cigarros Ø] le molesta a Enrique (+ *Extraposition*) → le molesta a Enrique [fumar cigarros]

Impersonal PRO, or as Gili Gaya (1973, 189) called it, "sujeto indeterminado," has the same effect:

[(el) fumar cigarros PRO] es costoso → es costoso [fumar cigarros]

Spanish has no Comp like English NP-possessive VP-*ing*, for its gerund is assigned to adverbial functions (v. 6.3.2). Thus, the Spanish Comp inventory includes the following:

full clause (tensed):	*que* NP VP (*que* Enrique fume cigarros)
	el que NP VP (*el que* Enrique fume cigarros)
infinitive (untensed):	VP-inf (fumar cigarros)
	el VP-inf (*el* fumar cigarros)
	el VP-inf NP (*el* fumar cigarros Enrique)

Although each language has multiple Comp options, these are not interchangeable. For one thing, the infinitive and gerund versions dispense with the tense and mood information of a full clause. Spann (1984) furthermore showed that the English gerund is more nounlike than other Comps in how it passes syntactic tests for noun-based NPs. Applying the same tests to Spanish data, she demonstrated that the two languages match up as shown in figure 13.2.

Given the lineup *it is Adj [to V NP]* resulting from reduction to an infinitive and then extraposition, English allows the NP to jump out of its clause and become the Subj of ___

Figure 13.2. Spann's correlations for subject noun clauses and their reductions

English	Spanish
that + tensed clause	*que* + tensed clause
[That Julia stays at home] is absurd.	[Que Julia se quede en casa] es absurdo.
subjectless infinitive	subjectless infinitive
[To stay at home] is absurd.	[Quedarse en casa] es absurdo.
NP-possessive VP-*ing* (gerund)	*el que* + tensed clause
[Julia's staying at home] is absurd.	[El que Julia se quede en casa] es absurdo.
subjectless VP-*ing* (gerund)	*el* + subjectless infinitive
[Staying at home] is absurd.	[El quedarse en casa] es absurdo.

is Adj. For example, *To play a French horn is tough → It is tough to play a French horn → A French horn is tough to play.* This transformation is called (logically enough) TOUGH MOVEMENT, and its trigger is the presence of an Adj such as *tough* that evaluates the infinitivized clause: *hard, easy, (im)possible, expensive,* and so on. The change is also possible when the NP is OP: *It is hard to play arpeggios* ***on*** *a French horn → A French horn is hard to play arpeggios* ***on***. Spanish also has *Tough* Movement, as shown by (a) in figure 13.3, but it requires insertion of *de* before the infinitive and does not allow the rule to apply to an NP governed by Prep (except "personal" *a*, which as usual does not count in the Prep restrictions of the language):

Es *difícil* (*fácil*) [tocar la trompa] → La trompa es difícil (fácil) ***de*** [tocar]
Es difícil [entender **a** esa profesora] → Esa profesora es difícil ***de*** [entender]
Es difícil [trabajar **para** esa profesora] → *Esa profesora es difícil ***de*** [trabajar para]
Es difícil [tocar arpegios **con** la trompa] → *La trompa es difícil ***de*** [tocar arpegios con]

13.1.2 As objects. When considering noun clauses used as a verb's Obj, two key facts must be kept in mind. First, in this case English allows optional deletion of *that* whereas Spanish continues requiring *que*: *I say that he'll do it → I say Ø he'll do it, Digo que lo hará, *Digo Ø lo hará.* Second, with Obj clauses, the choice of Comp is determined by the governing verb in the main clause. Consequently, generalizations of the type illustrated in figure 13.2 for noun clauses as Subj are more elusive here. We will limit ourselves to a handful of illustrations.

13.1.2.1 With *creer* vs. *believe*. *Creer* takes a *que* clause that, under Equi-NP, optionally reduces to a subjectless infinitive:

Marta cree [que Ana lo ha logrado]
Marta cree [que (**Marta**) lo ha logrado] → Marta cree [haberlo logrado]

Figure 13.3. Two clause adjustment transformations

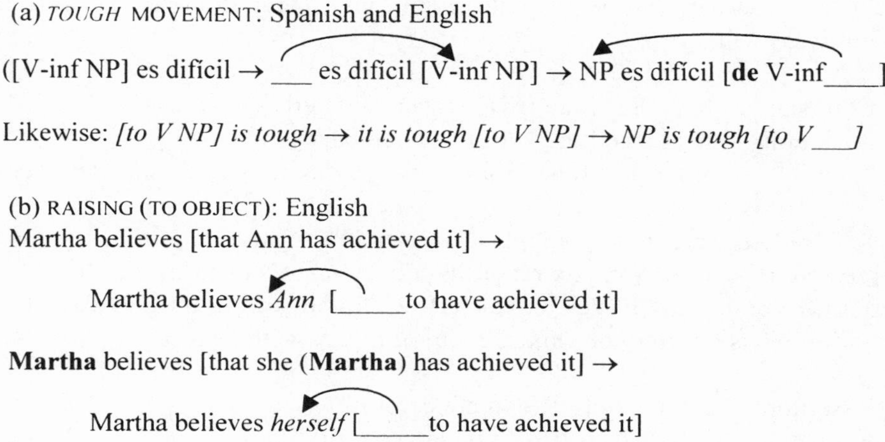

(a) TOUGH MOVEMENT: Spanish and English
([V-inf NP] es difícil → ___ es difícil [V-inf NP] → NP es difícil [**de** V-inf___]
Likewise: *[to V NP] is tough → it is tough [to V NP] → NP is tough [to V___]*
(b) RAISING (TO OBJECT): English
Martha believes [that Ann has achieved it] →
Martha believes *Ann* [_____to have achieved it]
Martha believes [that she (**Martha**) has achieved it] →
Martha believes *herself* [_____to have achieved it]

Believe also takes a *that* clause, but with a quirk that Spanish lacks: reduction to an infinitive is possible regardless of Equi-NP. As shown by (b) in figure 13.3, the infinitive's Subj moves up into the main clause by a transformation called RAISING, becoming the DO of *believe* in surface structure: *Martha believes Ann [___ to have achieved it].* That the infinitive's Subj becomes the DO of *believe* is proved by two facts. First, under Equi-NP the result is a reflexive, *herself,* as shown. Second, the raised NP can subsequently be passivized like any other Obj: *Ann is believed by Martha to have achieved it.* This is not possible in Spanish: **Marta cree a Ana haberlo logrado, *Ana es creída por Marta haberlo logrado.*

In both languages, verbs of the *believe* type also allow a transformation called NEG(ATIVE) TRANSPORT, whereby a negative *not/no* in the noun clause can move up into the main clause: *Martha believes [that Ann has **not** achieved it] → Martha **does not** believe [that Ann has achieved it].* In Spanish, though, there are apparently two results, differing in mood:

> Marta cree [que Ana no lo ha logrado] → Marta ***no*** cree [que Ana lo ***haya/ha*** logrado]

According to Reider (1990), only the subjunctive version (*haya*) is really due to Neg Transport, inasmuch as it matches the original in implying that Ann's achievement is not being affirmed (in the sense of Takagaki 1984, v. 7.3.2.2); on the contrary, it is taken as false or at best as a denial that is going unchallenged. The version *Marta no cree que Ana lo ha logrado*, on the other hand, implies Martha's own disbelief of an affirmed achievement, so its *no* originates with the main verb instead of coming from the clause by Neg Transport.

13.1.2.2 With *decir* vs. *say/tell*. *Decir* introduces a *que* clause whose verb is subjunctive if reporting a command, indicative if reporting an asserted fact (v. 7.3.2.2). Only in the latter case can the clause reduce, and only under Equi-NP, yielding a subjectless infinitive as with *creer.*

Command: Juan dice [que Uds. tengan cuidado]
Assertion: Juan dice [que Uds. tienen cuidado]
Juan dice [que (**Juan**) tiene cuidado] → Juan dice [tener cuidado][5]

Say and *tell* are more complicated. An Obj clause reporting an asserted fact is expressed as *that* NP VP; one reporting a command is expressed as *for* NP *to* VP in the case of *say* and (with *for* deleted) as NP *to* VP with *tell*. In this last case, the NP Subj of the infinitive is raised to become the Obj of *tell,* as with *believe*:

Assertion: John says [that you are careful]
John tells us [that you are careful]
Command: John says [for you to be careful]
John tells [you to be careful] → John tells *you* [to be careful]

This raised version again allows an un-Spanish passive: *You were told by John to be careful.* As for *say,* reduction to a subjectless infinitive occurs for the Impersonal PRO sense and just for commands: *John says [PRO to be careful]*. Oddly, though, the passive version of *say* NP *to* VP does express an assertion: *Mary is said to be careful.*

Decir and *say/tell* are representative of a large, frequent class of verbs of communication. English interference is common here since students assume that infinitives can convey reported commands in Spanish (*She told me to leave* → **Me dijo salir*) as in English and therefore see no need for subjunctives. What they must learn is that the difference between English *that* NP VP and (*for*) NP *to* VP corresponds in Spanish to a mood difference in a full clause.

13.1.2.3 With *preferir, querer, intentar* vs. *prefer, want, try.* In Spanish, such verbs always take a full *que*-clause (with the subjunctive) when subjects are different, but under Equi-NP they *require* reduction to a subjectless infinitive:

Prefiero [que lo haga Laura]
(Prefiero [que lo haga yo]) → Prefiero [hacerlo]
Quiero [que Daniel se vaya)
(Daniel quiere [que Daniel se vaya]) → Daniel quiere [irse]
Intento [que no lleguen tarde]
(Intento [que yo no llegue tarde]) → Intento [no llegar tarde]

Their English equivalents, on the other hand, are absolutely erratic. *Prefer* can take all three Comp types, regardless of Equi-NP. Whether or not the noun clause's own Subj is retained in reduction under Equi-NP depends on its emphasis:

I prefer [that Laura do it]	I prefer [that I do it]
I prefer [for Laura to do it]	I prefer [for *ME* to do it], I prefer [to do it]
I prefer [Laura's doing it]	I prefer [*MY* doing it], I prefer [doing it]

Prefer also allows reduction with Impersonal PRO, so that *I prefer [doing it this way]* is ambiguous. *Want,* on the other hand, only allows NP *to* VP, reduced to just *to* VP under Equi-NP; it never takes a *that* clause, and yet its synonym *desire* can:

I want [Daniel to go away]
(Daniel wants [Daniel to go away]) → Daniel wants [to go away]
I desire [that Daniel go away]

Try, like *want*, never takes a *that* clause; it requires a subjectless infinitive and Equi-NP:

*I try [(for) them not to arrive late]
(I try [me not to arrive late]) → I try [not to arrive late]

For such verbs, the Spanish side of the equation is straightforward, but because of the verb-specific preferences on the English side, problems are rampant in language acquisition in both directions. The two languages agree only in favoring or requiring reduction with Equi-NP.

13.1.2.4 With *mandar* and *impedir* vs. *order* and *prevent*. *Mandar* and *impedir* are followed by a noun clause in the subjunctive, but unlike the numerous Spanish verbs that require Equi-NP for clausal reduction, these allow reduction if the infinitive's Subj is raised to become a matrix IO (see Hadlich 1971, 167, for details of this change):

Jaime (les) mandó/impidió [que ellos derribaran el muro] → Jaime ***les*** mandó/impidió [derribar el muro] *a ellos*

Such verbs also allow reduction for an Impersonal PRO Subj of the infinitive: *Mandó derribar el muro.*

The syntax of *order* (and *command*) depends on stylistic level. In formal English, one can use a *that* clause with a relic subjunctive (*tear* instead of *tore*) but without the Spanish IO:

James ordered (*them) [that they tear down the wall]

More commonly, *order* takes the reduced version NP *to* VP, and the infinitive's Subj undergoes Raising into the main clause to become DO (as with *believe* and *tell*), not IO as in Spanish.

James ordered [them to tear down the wall] → James ordered *them* [to tear down the wall]
(+ *Passive*) → They were ordered [to tear down the wall] by James
(+ *Extraposition*) → They were ordered by James [to tear down the wall])

But the Impersonal PRO option of *mandar* is excluded: **He ordered to tear down the wall.*
While *impedir* follows *mandar* exactly,

Rita (les) impidió [que los vecinos vinieran] = Rita les impidió [venir] a los vecinos

English *prevent* and *keep* take neither a *that* clause nor an infinitive, only a gerund whose NP is raised to become DO. In this way, the two languages' surface structures could not be more different.

Rita kept/prevented [the neighbors from coming] → Rita kept/prevented *the neighbors* [from coming]
(+ *Passive*) → The neighbors were kept/prevented [from coming] by Rita

13.1.2.5 With *hacer* vs. *make, have.* These verbs join with others to form a CAUSATIVE construction, indicating that an agent causes or brings about an event. English *have* and *make* never take *that* clauses but are usually constructed with just NP VP-inf. (no *for* with the NP, no *to* with VP-inf.): *I had [the horse run], I made [the horse run].* But English also allows many verbs to be directly (i.e., lexically) transitivized without a causative V, *I made the horse trot = I **trotted** the horse*, an option that Spanish generally lacks (*hice trotar el caballo*, not **troté el caballo*).

Like *mandar, hacer* takes a *que*-clause in the subjunctive and allows optional reduction to an infinitive without Equi-NP. But the reduced version, *hacer* V-inf NP, has three special quirks: the NP is raised to become the DO of *hacer* (not IO as with *mandar*), *hacer* + V-inf. acts as a unit in surface structure, and this V-inf. can be understood as either active or passive:

Hice [que corriera *el caballo* (Subj)] → Hice correr *el caballo. Lo* hice correr.
Hice [que la casa fuera construida] → Hice construir *la casa. La* hice construir.

The passive connection is confirmed by the option of an agent phrase: *Hice construir la casa por Hernández e Hijos.* Without that phrase, there can be ambiguity: *Hice matar a Juan* could be the reduction of either *Hice que Juan matara* or *Hice que Juan fuera matado.* English distinguishes these cases: *I made/had John kill* vs. *I had John killed (by* *assassins).* The Spanish causative, then, is deceptive in its surface simplicity (see Contreras 1979 for further analysis), which is perhaps why English speakers avoid it and prefer English-like *causar*—which unfortunately does not form causatives at all (**Causé matar a Juan*).

In passing, we should note that *dejar* acts like *hacer* (D'Introno 1990):

Dejé [que el caballo corriera] → Dejé correr el caballo. Lo dejé correr.

Like *hacer*, *dejar* + V-inf. acts as a unit and takes DO, not IO (unlike *permitir*). There can also be a passive force, especially when that DO is reflexive:

Ana se dejó controlar por sus amigos. 'Ann let herself be controlled by her friends.'

13.1.2.6 With *ver* vs. *see*. Verbs of perception take as complements full clauses, infinitives, or even, in Spanish in this case, gerunds. In both languages the nonfinite complements resemble those of causatives in word order and in the fate of the subordinated clause's Subj:

Vieron [que Alicia (Subj) cantaba]
Vieron [cantar Alicia (Subj)] → Vieron [cantar] *a Alicia* (DO). *La* vieron cantar.
Vieron [cantando Alicia (Subj)] → Vieron [cantando] *a Alicia* (DO). *La* vieron cantando.
They saw [that Alice (Subj) was singing]
They saw [Alice sing] → They saw Alice (DO) [sing]. They saw *her* sing.
They saw [Alice singing] → They saw Alice (DO) [singing]. They saw *her* singing.

The three Comps are not synonymous, for there is an aspectual difference between V-inf and V-ger reminiscent of that between preterite and imperfect. *La vieron cantar* and *They saw her sing* suggest completion of the performance, whereas *La vieron cantando* and *They saw her singing* indicate that she was viewed in the middle of the activity.

The preceding comparisons have focused on the Comps of a few representative verbs but have barely scratched the surface of the descriptive, theoretical, and pedagogical issues of complex sentences. Such analysis is more useful to the teacher for understanding interference than to the student for acquiring Spanish syntax. In fact, students who proceed on the basis of verb-by-verb comparisons to (and worse, translations from) English only complicate their task. They learn that *querer* takes an infinitive for Equi-NP, otherwise a clause, but that *mandar* does allow an English-like NP *to* VP without Equi-NP. They find that *impedir* and *preferir* never take gerund complements like English *prevent* and *prefer*, but *ver* does; that *intentar* takes a clause for which *try* has no equivalent; that even safe cases like *decir* + *que* have mood contrasts, again without English counterparts; and so on until Spanish looks hopeless. What students must understand is

Figure 13.4. V + V from V + noun clause

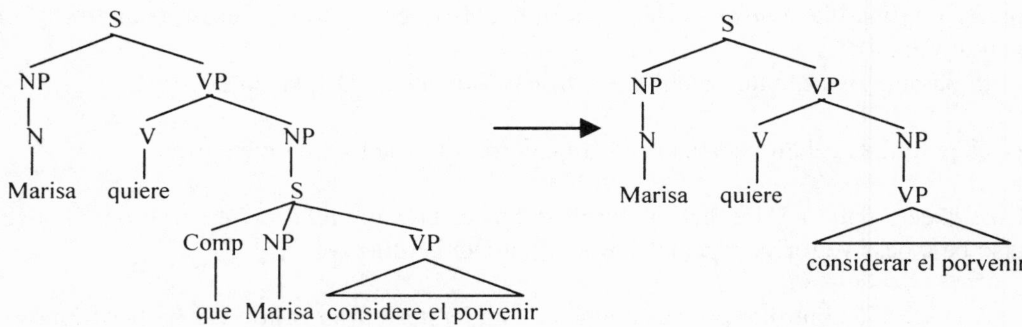

that the goal is to acquire Spanish structure on its own terms. However their English counterparts may behave, most Spanish verbs with object clauses follow the types described above, and generally along semantic lines. *Gritar* follows *decir, afirmar* and *dudar* behave like *creer, necesitar* is like *querer,* and *oír* is like *ver.* One who knows these prototypes thoroughly (and ignores English syntax) can predict the behavior of most others in the language.

13.1.2.7 *Querer* + V vs. *poder* + V. Not all sequences of V + V in surface structure are derived from V + noun clause. Hadlich (1971, 58) and Olbertz (1998) showed how *querer* and *poder* differ in this respect. One can ask *¿Qué quiere Marisa?* and get the answer *Quiere considerar el porvenir. Querer* is transitive and *qué* elicits NP; thus, *Quiere consider el porvenir* is V + NP, a fact captured by our analysis of the infinitive as a reduced noun clause, as in figure 13.4. But in *Marisa puede considerar el porvenir, poder* is intransitive and thus cannot take a DO or an Obj noun clause. Thus, the structure of *poder* + V is distinct from that of *querer* + V. Figure 13.5 shows two possible analyses, the second of which was preferred by Hadlich for a true Aux like *poder,* although the first one is a common treatment of nonauxiliaries like *tender a* that likewise take an infinitive but not an Obj noun clause (*Marisa tiende a preocuparse, *Marisa tiende a que nos preocupemos*).

Figure 13.5. V + V not derived from V + noun clause

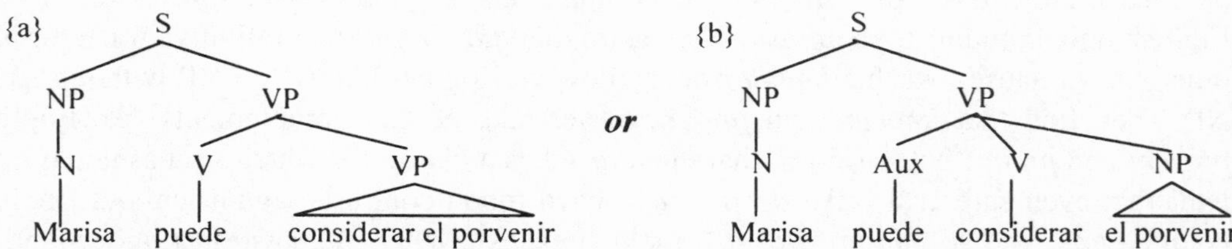

13.1.2.8 Clitic promotion. Clitics normally precede a conjugated verb but are suffixed to a gerund or infinitive. This yields two options for V + V: *tengo que dárselo* ~ *se lo tengo que dar, estoy lavándolo* ~ *lo estoy lavando.* In explaining these variants, we assume that the clitic originates next to the V whose Obj it really is in deep structure, and that it then advances to the left by an optional transformation called CLITIC PROMOTION or CLITIC CLIMBING (v. 9.4.2):

Puede haber estado haciendo***lo*** → Puede haber***lo*** estado haciendo → ***Lo*** puede haber estado haciendo

Once a noun clause reduces to an infinitive, the doors to clitic promotion are opened wide. Clitic promotion is blocked as long as *que* stands in the way and its clause is tensed. But with reduction, a clitic can climb up through the syntactic tree, carrying along with it any higher clitics it meets on the way. The process is illustrated in figure 13.6.

Several observers (e.g., Roldán 1974; Bordelois 1978; Contreras 1979; Reider 1989) have discovered subtle constraints on this verb-to-verb romp, and others (Butt and Benjamin 1988, 249; Davies 1995) have provided reference lists of verbs that do and do not permit it, but the more pressing problem in second language acquisition is a psycholinguistic one. It will be recalled (v. 11.2) that English speakers have trouble processing Obj before V: *se lo escribo* as opposed to the *I write it to him (her,* etc.) that they are accustomed to. When clitic promotion follows on the heels of clausal reduction, students' problems multiply: the Obj pronouns hop leftward and upward from branch to branch until coming to rest in front of a verb with which they have no semantic connection. Since

Figure 13.6. Clitic promotion after a noun clause reduces to an infinitival VP

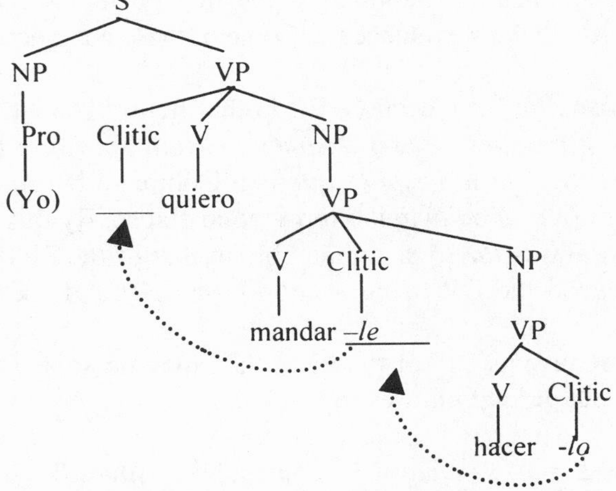

Quiero mandar*le* hacer*lo*→ Quiero mandár*selo* hacer → *Se lo* quiero mandar.

each English verb keeps its own pronouns and in the postposed Obj position, 'him it want-I order do' may elicit a blank look from someone expecting 'I want to order him to do it'.

13.1.3 Noun clauses that are questions. Interrogative noun clauses are called embedded or INDIRECT questions. In an embedded yes/no question, English adopts *whether* or *if* as the Comp, and Spanish uses *si* (or *que si*). In an information question, both languages front the interrogative to the Comp position as in direct questions (*Wh*-movement, v. 12.1.2). Unlike direct questions, indirect questions in English lack inversion and *do*-insertion:

Queremos saber [¿Llegará José?] → Queremos saber [***si*** llegará José]
Queremos saber [¿Dónde/Qué comiste?] → Queremos saber [dónde/qué comiste]
We want to know [Will Joe arrive?] → We want to know [*whether/if* Joe will arrive]
We want to know [Where/What did you eat?]) →We want to know [where/what you ate]

Like other noun clauses, indirect questions can reduce to infinitives given Equi-NP, and they then suggest a questioning of obligation: *Queremos saber si matricularnos (o no)* (= *Queremos saber si debemos matricularnos*), *Queremos saber qué hacer/cuándo regresar*. The reduced indirect question *qué hacer* must be distinguished from the *que hacer* of *hay mucho que hacer,* which is a reduced RELATIVE clause as we will see shortly (v. 13.3.4); and the Comp *si* 'whether' must be distinguished from the Conj *si* for conditional 'if' because the latter does not allow reduction, as we will also see in the following sections.

13.2 Adverbial clauses. Adverbial clauses supply locative, temporal, causal, and other circumstantial information in the matrix. Traditionally, they are treated as a subordinating Conj + S. But at least in Spanish, there is evidence that some of these conjunctions are Prep.

13.2.1 Preposition + clause. We have seen (v. 10.1) that many Spanish prepositions have conjunction counterparts: *después de* and *después (de) que, por* and *porque, para* and *para que,* and so on. Yet the *que* in *después que* is a Comp, so if *veo que llovió* is V + noun clause, then *después (de) que llovió* is Prep + noun clause. By this analysis, the structure of the PP *después (de) que llovió* is comparable to that of the PP *después de la lluvia*; it is a difference between the OP being a noun-based NP and a clausal NP, as shown in figure 13.7.

Just as noun clauses may reduce as Obj of the verb, they may do so as OP, becoming infinitive phrases in Spanish but gerund phrases in English.

Elena lee *después de [que (Elena) se acuesta]* → Elena lee *después de [acostarse]*
Helen reads *after [she (Helen) goes to bed]* → *Helen reads after [going to bed]*

Figure 13.7. Adverbial clauses as noun-clause objects of prepositions

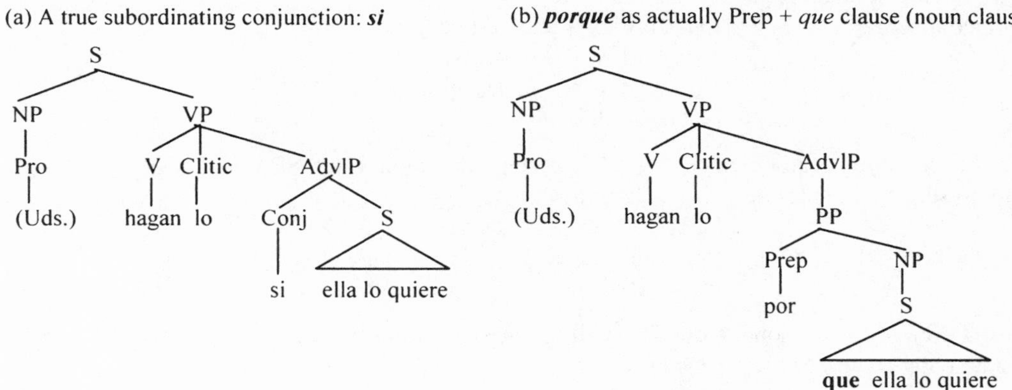

The same reduction occurs with verbs that specify Prep for oblique objects (v. 10.4.2), whether these are Ns or noun clauses: *oponerse a (que S), invitar a (que S), confiar en (que S), quejarse de (que S).* Most English Preps, on the other hand, cannot introduce either full clauses or infinitives—only gerunds. The following examples illustrate the differences that emerge:

Nos oponemos **a** . . .	las armas
	[que el gobierno venda armas]
	[vender armas]
We're opposed **to** . . .	weapons
	[the government('s) selling weapons]
	*[that the government sell weapons]
	[selling weapons]
	*[sell weapons]

The Spanish end of this comparison is also complex (Whitley 1986b, De Mello 1995b): the reduction of a *que* clause after Prep sometimes requires Equi-NP and sometimes not, as summarized in figure 13.8.[6] In other words, the prepositions of both languages impose the same conditions on the reduction of their Obj clauses as do verbs, and they fall into distinct groups in that respect, just like *decir, querer, mandar*, and so on.

13.2.2 Subordinating conjunction + clause. Other adverbial clauses are introduced by a true subordinating Conj, such as *si, cuando, como si, en cuanto* (v. 10.2.1.3, 10.2.2). These differ from the group just discussed (*después que, porque, para que* . . .) in not consisting of Prep + Comp *que*. This is a crucial difference in syntax, as shown in figure 13.7, not just a matter of etymology. Spanish permits the reduction of adverbial clauses *if*

Figure 13.8. Reduction to infinitives after prepositions

para : reduction under Equi-NP, and required:	
Los recojo para	[que José los vacíe después]
	* [vaciarlos José después]
	* [que yo los vacíe después]
	[vaciarlos después]
antes de: reduction required under Equi-NP, permitted without Equi-NP:	
Antonio se prepara antes de	*[que él salga]
	[salir]
	[que Julia salga]
	[salir Julia]
por and *después de*: optional reduction with or without Equi-NP	
Juan ha renunciado por	[que es terco]
	[ser terco]
	[que su jefe es terco]
	[ser terco su jefe]

and only if these consist of Prep + noun clause; when the adverbial clause is introduced by a true Conj, reduction is impossible even with Equi-NP (Whitley 1986b):

Háganlo . . . si pasan por acá (*si pasar por acá, *si pasando por acá)
como si lo disfrutaran (*como si disfrutarlo)
como quieran (*como querer)
cuando hayan terminado (*cuando haber terminado)
mientras se bañen (*mientras bañarse)

As a partial solution for this limitation, *al* and *de* arose as prepositional counterparts to *cuando* and *si*, respectively: *cuando terminan/terminen → al terminar, si lo hubiera sabido → de haberlo sabido*.

English, on the other hand, allows reduction to gerunds and even participles after many of its Conj—provided that Equi-NP holds.

Do it . . . if you pass this way, *if passing* this way
as if you enjoyed it, *as if enjoying* it
as you desire, *as desired*
when you've finished, *when finished*
while you bathe, *while bathing*

Several observers (Hadlich 1971, 183; Ozete 1983, 77; Garcés 1997, 131) have analyzed adverbial gerunds in the absolute construction (v. 6.3.3) as surface structure realizations of underlying clauses. Thus, the initial phrase of *[Visitando mi esposa a su madre], aproveché la ocasión* is simply an adverbial clause that, ungoverned by either Conj or Prep, obligatorily reduces to a gerund phrase in order to modify the rest of the sentence.

At the introductory level, the connection between full clauses and reduced versions will elude students who are still acquiring the structure of simple sentences. But at higher levels, they are using, hearing, and reading more complex sentences, and just as they encounter both *impide que coman* and *impide comer* but not **impide comiendo,* they must now cope with both *antes que coman* and *antes de comer*, finding their own **antes de comiendo, *mientras comiendo,* and **sin comiendo* marked wrong. The reason for what happens in adverbial clauses is the same as for what happens in a verb's noun clauses, and students might profit from an overview of the process—with far more information than their textbooks typically supply.

13.3 Relative clauses. A relative or adjective clause is a sentence embedded inside an NP, modifying that NP's head noun like an adjective. The modified head N is called the ANTECEDENT, and some NP inside the relative clause refers to it. In some theories, the deep structure assigned to a relative clause is the phrase marker shown on the left in figure 13.9. In that phrase marker, NP_1 (the antecedent) and NP_2 (inside the relative clause) match referentially: *the man = the man.* NP_2 is thereupon RELATIVIZED, that is, changed to a RELATIVE PRONOUN (such as *who(m)* or *that*), which then moves leftward to the same position as the Comp of a noun clause. In other theories, the relative pronoun begins as *who(m)* or *that* (as on the right) and then moves to the Comp position in the same way.

Relative pronouns obey the same constraints as interrogatives (v. 12.1.2) in *Wh*-movement. In particular, a Prep governing the relative pronoun must move with it in Spanish (*el hombre con quien hablé*) while in English it can be left behind (*the man with whom I spoke* ~ *the man who(m) I spoke with*).

Figure 13.9. Relative clause formation

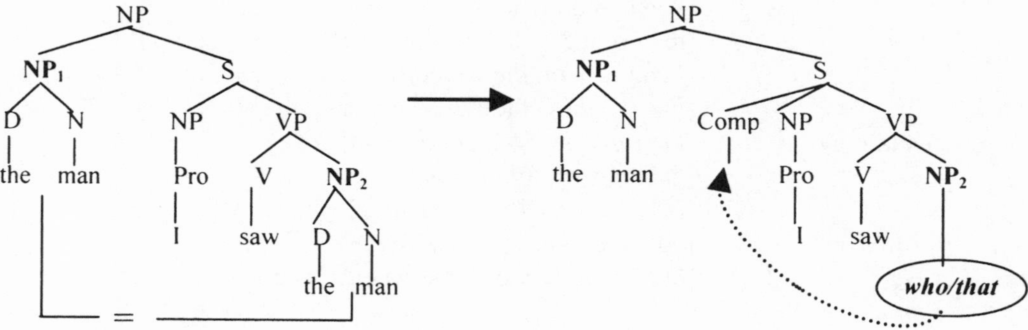

13.3.1 Relativization according to NP type. Both languages show a variety of relative clause patterns. We begin our survey of them by considering what happens when the relativized NP is a thing originating as Subj, DO, or OP in its clause:[7]

I have the book . . . [*the book* describes climate]
[Cervantes wrote *the book*]
[you kept leaves in *the book*]
Tengo el libro . . . [*el libro* describe el clima]
[Cervantes escribió *el libro*]
[guardaste hojas en *el libro*]

Relativization yields the following surface structures:

I have the book . . . [*which/that* describes climate]
[*which/that/Ø* Cervantes wrote]
[*which/that/Ø* you kept leaves in] = [in *which* you kept leaves]
Tengo el libro . . . [*que* describe el clima]
[*que* escribió Cervantes]
[en *(el) que* guardaste hojas]

Note that in English, nonhuman NPs become *which* or *that,* but only *which* occurs when a governing Prep (*in*) is fronted with the relative. Moreover, a relative *that* is often deleted (Ø) in English as long as no Prep has been fronted and it is directly followed by NP (i.e., the clausal Subj): *I have the book Ø Cervantes wrote,* but not **I have the book Ø describes climate* or **I have the book in Ø you kept leaves.* By contrast, Spanish usage is simpler: *que* is used for humans or nonhumans and is never deleted. (Compare the similar difference on the deletability of the Comp *that/que,* v. 13.1.2.) Seldom noted, though, is the Spanish tendency to invert the Subj in a relative clause: *el libro que escribió Cervantes.*

Next, consider what happens if the NP is a person:

This is the woman . . . [*the woman* wrote the speech]
[you should hear *the woman*]
[they sent $50 to *the woman*]
[I can rely on *the woman*]
[*the woman's* face has enchanted me]
Esta es la mujer . . . [*la mujer* escribió el discurso]
[deberías oír a *la mujer*]
[le mandaron $50 a *la mujer*]
[puedo contar con *la mujer*]
[la cara de *la mujer* me ha encantado]

Relativization yields many possibilities here in both languages:

This is the woman . . . [*who/that* wrote the speech]
[*who(m)/that/Ø* you should hear]
[*who(m)/that/Ø* they sent $50 to] = [to *whom* they sent $50]
[*who(m)/that/Ø* I can rely on] = [on *whom* I can rely]
[*whose* face has enchanted me]

Esta es la mujer . . . [*que* escribió el discurso]
[*que/a quien* deberías oír]
[a *quien*/a *la que* le mandaron $50]
[con *quien*/con *la que* puedo contar]
[*cuya* cara me ha encantado]

The English relative pronouns for humans are *who(m), Ø, that,* never *which.* Conditions on deletability and Prep fronting are as for nonhumans, but a complication arises with *whom,* which is inconsistently distinguished from *who* even in formal styles and is abandoned entirely in colloquial ones. In Spanish, *que* is used for clausal Subj, and alongside *a quien* for DO, but with Prep, only *quien* and the article form *el que/la que* appear for humans, not plain *que.* Both languages also have a possessive relative, *whose* and the four-form *cuyo,* which can be used for nonhuman antecedents as well: *a river whose water is polluted, un río cuya agua está contaminada.* Extraposition is possible for relative clauses, as for noun clauses (v. 13.1.2):

I saw someone [who knows you] last night → I saw someone last night [who knows you]
Vi a alguien [que te conoce bien] anoche →Vi a alguien anoche [que te conoce]

When the relativized NP is OP, Spanish grammars prescribe *que* for nonhumans and *quien* for humans after the short prepositions *a, con, de,* and *en* but *el cual* after long prepositions—and after short ones, too, if such a genderized relative removes the ambiguity of antecedents: *la hija del señor* ***a la cual*** *le escribiste.* Studies of current usage (Ozete 1981; Butler 1992), however, show that the article form *el que* is being generalized with prepositions regardless of Prep length or the antecedent's humanness.[8] This makes for a much neater rule, especially for students bewildered by their textbooks' statements:

la mujer *con la que* puedo contar
el cantante *al que* me refiero
los futbolistas *en los que* pensábamos
las llaves *con las que* se abre esta puerta

Donde is another possibility when the relative is locative:

Visitamos la casa [Bolívar había dormido *en la casa*] → Visitamos la casa [*donde*/*en la que* había dormido Bolívar]

There are other cases where the traditional rules for relatives do not reflect evolving usage (Kany 1951, 132). First, many speakers have extended the DO *que* to IO: *esa mujer que le faltan los dientes.* Second, despite condemnations from on high (Alarcos Llorach 1999, 125), *cuyo* is yielding to *que su* in the spoken language: *esa mujer que su papá se ha muerto.* Given these developments and the statistical infrequency of the prepositional case (*con la que, en los que . . .*), Suñer (2000) argued that the Spanish relative pronoun is simply becoming Comp, that is, plain *que*, and urged teachers not to complicate this pattern with the less common alternatives at lower levels of instruction.

13.3.2 Headless relatives and clefting. Some relative clauses lack an overt noun antecedent or head. A Spanish example is *[Quien no trabaja] no come,* in which *quien no trabaja* is a HEADLESS RELATIVE.[9] An alternative to *quien* here is *el que* (or *los que*), which was described earlier as a nominalization (v. 8.4.1), as in the following case:

¿Ves a aquellos dos hombres? Pues, *el que* (= el hombre que) está a la derecha es mi tío.

But there is no real nominalization in *El que no trabaja no come* when uttered with no previous mention of a masculine noun; *hombre* is not necessarily the antecedent the speaker has in mind, if any noun is. It is therefore possible to enumerate four distinct *el que* in Spanish: (1) the *el que* resulting from nominalization, (2) the *el que* equivalent to *quien* in headless relatives, (3) the *el que* allomorph of the relative *que* after Prep, and (4) the *el que* serving as a Comp (v. 13.1.1).

In English, *he who* has been prescribed in traditional grammar for headless relatives—*He who doesn't work doesn't eat*—but current usage favors *those who, anyone who, whoever, people who,* or for a true nominalization, *the one(s) who/that.*

A common but pedagogically neglected use of headless relatives in both languages is a transformation called CLEFTING. Clefting highlights information, especially a NP, with a contrastive force, often in the context of correcting a supposition (D'Introno 1990, 240):

—Ganará el concurso Miss Canadá, ¿no?	Miss Canada will win the contest, right?
—No, *la que* lo va a ganar *es* Miss Chile.	No, *the one that*'s going to win *is* Miss Chile.

As illustrated, clefting splits a sentence into two parts. The NP to be highlighted (here, *Miss Chile*) moves to prime rheme position at the end of the sentence; its original position is occupied by *el que* or *quien* (English *the one that/who*) introducing the rest of the sentence, and the two parts are finally joined by *ser/be*. Other transformations can then apply as usual, for example, extraposition:[10]

Miss Chile lo va a ganar. → Quien/La que lo va a ganar es Miss Chile. → Es Miss Chile quien/la que lo va a ganar.

On the other hand, a thing or idea (as opposed to a specified individual) is clefted with the Spanish neuter form, not with *qué* as English speakers might expect (cf. *What I made was . . .*):

Hice una torta en casa → *Lo que* hice en casa fue una torta
Me gustaría el yogur → *Lo que* me gustaría es el yogur

As usual, the two languages part company on how to treat OP. English leaves the Prep behind:

It depends *on* individual taste → What it depends *on* is individual taste
I'm referring to the ambassador → The one I'm referring *to* is the ambassador

whereas Spanish requires duplicating the Prep so that it governs *both* halves of the clefting:

Depende del gusto individual → *De lo que* depende es *del* gusto individual
Me refiero a la embajadora → *A la que* me refiero es *a* la embajadora

A further evolution of clefted relative clauses is a structure called "pleonastic" or "intensive" *ser*:

Trabajo *es* en la universidad (= *Donde* trabajo es en la universidad)
Me fijaba *era* en la luz (= *En lo que* me fijaba era en la luz)

This construction apparently originated in Colombia and has spread to neighboring countries (Lipski 1994, 215, 301). Time will determine the extent to which it catches on elsewhere.

13.3.3 Nonrestrictive relative clauses. Relative clauses restrict the reference of their antecedent and are used to define it. In *The brown shoes which/that are dirty are Veronica's,* the speaker selects from an understood set of brown shoes just those that were dirty and asserts that only those belong to Veronica. Contrast this with the following sentence, where commas indicate a slight pause and a broken off, interrupted intonation (v. 4.2): *The brown shoes, which are dirty, are Veronica's.* Here the speaker implies that all of the brown shoes under consideration are dirty; rather than restricting reference to a subset of the whole, the relative clause just makes a parenthetical observation, 'all the brown shoes are Veronica's (and they happen to be dirty)'.

This contrast between restrictive and nonrestrictive resembles that between preposed and postposed adjectives in Spanish, as in *los zapatos sucios* vs. *los sucios zapatos.* Cressey (1969) proposed that this parallel be emphasized in pedagogy (v. 11.3.2). *Los zapatos marrones que están sucios son de Verónica* implies 'los zapatos marrones sucios', whereas nonrestrictive *Los zapatos marrones, que están sucios, son de Verónica* implies 'los sucios zapatos marrones'.

In English, the nonrestrictive relative pronouns are *who(m), which,* and *whose* but never *that* or Ø: **The brown shoes, that are dirty, are Veronica's, *The brown shoes, Ø you messed up, are Veronica's.* In Spanish, there is again a difference between prescribed and actual usage; whereas some recommend *quien, el que,* and especially the elegant *el cual* for nonrestrictive clauses, many speakers use plain *que* (Ozete 1981): *La mujer alta, quien/la cual/la que/que acaba de recibirse, se va mañana.*

13.3.4 Reduced relative clauses. It should not be surprising that if noun clauses and adverbial clauses can reduce, so can relative clauses. Thus, for English, *Jane has a lot of work [that Paul should do] → Jane has a lot of work [for Paul to do].* The Subj element *for* NP drops from relative clauses under the same conditions as from noun clauses:

Equi-NP: Jane has a lot of work [*for Jane* to do] → Jane has a lot of work [to do]
Impersonal PRO: There's a lot of work [*for* PRO to do] → There's a lot of work [to do]

The connection between (*for* NP) *to* VP after a noun and full relative clauses is clinched by the occasional appearance of relative pronouns in the former structure (Quirk et al. 1972, 879):

Chez Nous is a good place [to eat (at)] ~ [at *which* to eat].

In Spanish, an infinitival relative always begins with a relative pronoun:

Juana tiene mucho trabajo [*que* hacer].
Chez Nous es un buen lugar [*donde* comer].

Infinitival relatives convey a sense of obligation, advisability, or suitability, and for that reason many grammarians and linguists (e.g., Bello [1847] 1958, 339; Ramsey [1894] 1956, 353; Klein 1984) have seen *que* VP-inf after a noun as the reduced version of a relative clause with *poder* or *deber.* (Compare the similar thrust of 'obligation' in reduced indirect questions, v. 13.1.3.) Where the two languages differ is in constraints on usage. First, the Spanish relative reduces only with Equi-NP or Impersonal PRO. For the equivalent of *Jane has a lot of work [for Paul to do],* a full relative clause has to be used:

*Juana tiene mucho trabajo [que Pablo hacer, que hacer Pablo].
Juana tiene mucho trabajo [que deberá hacer Pablo].

Second, as illustrated in figure 13.10, the antecedent in Spanish must be interpretable as DO, IO, or OP of the infinitive; Spanish otherwise requires a full clause, whereas English also allows a Subj interpretation (note the ambiguity in *You need someone to teach*).

A third difference is that in Spanish, reduced *que*-relatives may be replaced by PP (Prep + infinitive): *Juana tiene mucho trabajo que hacer, Juana tiene mucho trabajo para hacer.* Drake, Ascarza, and Preble (1982), who studied such constructions, brought out their semantic differences:[11]

En esta tienda hay muchos libros . . . *para* vender ('available for sale').
por vender ('remaining to be sold').
sin vender (nonperformance, i.e., 'unsold').

They also observed that *a* in this construction, disdained in some quarters as a Gallicism, has caught hold in Spanish and is spreading rapidly, sometimes displacing *para* or *que*: *un ejemplo a imitar, libros a consultar, mensualidades a abonar, métodos a seguir.*

Our survey of relative clauses warrants three pedagogical observations. First, the typical textbook presentation focuses very narrowly on pronoun and mood selection; it gives little information on how to form relative clauses in the first place (or reduce them) and for what purposes. Second, the elaborate rules laid down for even those selected areas tend not to reflect current usage. Third, instead of promoting active formation of relative clauses for useful communicative functions (defining, clefting, etc.), most books overemphasize the mechanical procedure of filling in blanks (*el hombre ___ vi es el director*). As a result, students learn how to insert relative pronouns into someone else's sentences but otherwise avoid the clauses in their own Spanish or rely on L1 transfer to create them. The textbook's rules, accurate or not, are quickly forgotten because relative clause formation does not become a part of the students' own competence in Spanish.

13.4 Comparative sentences. Comparative sentences establish a relationship between the degree or amount of one thing and that of another. The latter is subordinated to the former by morphemes that tend to be DISCONTINUOUS (separated) parts consisting of Deg plus Comp, for example, ***more*** *complex* ***than*** . . . or ***as*** *much* ***as***. . . .

Figure 13.10. Infinitival relatives

	ENGLISH	SPANISH
Subj	He's seeking someone [to help him]	*no reduction* (Busca a alguien [que lo ayude].)
DO	He's seeking someone [to help]	Busca a alguien [a quien/que ayudar]
IO	He's seeking someone [to write to]	Busca a alguien [a quien/al que escribir(le)]
OP	He's seeking something [to gripe about]	Busca algo [de que quejarse]
	[to fix it with]	[con el que arreglarlo]
	[to dive off of]	[desde donde lanzarse]

13.4.1 Patterns and forms. Traditionally, three kinds of comparison are distinguished: EQUALITY (*as . . . as . . .*), SUPERIORITY (*more . . . than . . .*), and INFERIORITY (*less . . . than . . .*), though the last two are often merged as INEQUALITY because of their similar formation.

Equality:	Mateo está *tan* nervioso *como Pilar*. Matt's *as* nervous *as* Pilar.
Superiority:	Mateo está *más* nervioso *que* Pilar. Matt's *more* nervous *than* Pilar.
Inferiority:	Mateo está *menos* nervioso *que* Pilar. Matt's *less* nervous *than* Pilar.

At least in these examples, the two languages agree nicely; the only problem for the student so far is that *as* is *tan* in one place, *como* in another. With one exception, *tan* precedes any Adj or Adv: *tan rápido, tan ridículo, tan silenciosamente.* That exception is *mucho(s),* for in this case the expected **tan mucho(s)* becomes *tanto(s). Tan* is sometimes presented as a shortening of *tanto,* but both etymologically and syntactically, *tan* is the basic morpheme, and in just one case this Deg fuses with its Adj or Adv.

The morphemes for inequality require comment. As we have often pointed out before, much of our grammatical terminology comes from classical grammar. Latin had three degrees of comparison called POSITIVE, COMPARATIVE, and SUPERLATIVE. English distinguishes the same three, so the inherited terminology is appropriate for its system:

Positive	Comparative (for two)	Superlative (for three or more)
beautiful	*more/less beautiful*	*most/least beautiful*

The same distinction was assumed for Spanish since it descended from Latin. The comparative is obvious: one places *más/menos* before the adjective or adverb, giving *más/menos bonito.* But *más/menos* are also 'most/least' (as in *¿Qué deportes te gustan más? ¿Menos?*), so where is the Spanish superlative?

Some point to the *-ísimo* form, since it comes from the Latin superlative suffix *-issimus.* Yet *-ísimo* no longer implies comparison, but just intensifies the Adj/Adv like *muy* and *súper* and corresponds to English *very, real(ly),* not to the usual sense of *most.* Other grammarians decided that Spanish adds the definite article to *más/menos* to form a superlative: *bonito, más bonito, el más bonito.* This is a false analysis, for the definite article merely conveys definiteness or uniqueness, and it accompanies the comparative too:

Pilar es **la** *más* bonita de las dos. Pilar is *the more* beautiful of the two.
Pilar es **la** *más* bonita de las tres. Pilar is *the most* beautiful of the three.

In short, *there is no comparative/superlative distinction* in Spanish, and the class time traditionally spent on this artifice should long ago have been redirected to weightier matters.

In addition to using comparative Deg (*more, most, less, least, más, menos*) with the Adj or Adv, both languages have inherited inflected comparatives, ending in *-er/-est* in English and in *-r/-s* in Spanish:

young, younger, youngest	(joven), menor
old, older, oldest	(viejo), mayor
good/well, better, best	bueno/bien, mejor
bad, worse, worst	mal(o), peor
much/many, more, most	mucho, más
little, less, least	poco, menos

This type is limited in Spanish and is also less fixed. *Más bueno* is fine for ethical goodness (RAE 1979, 418), as are *más joven* and *más viejo* when not speaking of ages in a set such as family. *Mayor* and *menor* actually lack a positive, for they signal relative importance, seriousness, rank, or size, not just age, and they are not always felt to be comparative in themselves to judge from phrases such as *niños de diez años y niños más mayores.* English *-er* and *-est,* on the other hand, are freely applied to short adjectives: *taller, younger, prettier* are normal, *politer* alternates with *more polite,* and *beautifuler* is replaced by *more beautiful.*

We will note in passing certain other patterns that are sometimes called comparatives, since they are built up with similar elements:

Está *tan* nerviosa *que* le tiembla la mano.	(*so . . . that*)
Es *el mismo* dependiente *que* me atendió a mí.	(*the same . . . as*)
Estos electrodomésticos son *iguales que* esos.	(*the same . . . as,* but not identical)
Estos electrodomésticos son *parecidos a* esos.	(*like, similar to*)
Estos electrodomésticos son *diferentes de/a* esos.	(*different . . . from/than*)
Cuanto más me esfuerzo, *menos* logro.	(*the more . . . the less*)
Es *demasiado* joven *como para* ayudar.	(*too . . . to*)

Yet despite their frequency in comparison, these constructions are often ignored in textbooks because they happen to have been overlooked in the traditional canon.

13.4.2 The structure of comparative sentences. At first glance, comparatives such as *Yo tengo más hijos que tú* seem simple, not complex. Yet they imply a comparison between two propositions: *Yo tengo hijos + tú tienes hijos.* In fact, full-clause alternatives are possible, if unwieldy: *Yo tengo más hijos que tú tienes (hijos).* Hence, comparatives have been analyzed as reductions of fuller sentences (Hadlich 1971, 177; RAE 1979, 545), with transformations that prune out of the comparative clause those constituents that are identical (aside from agreement) to their counterparts in the main clause. This reduction is shown in figure 13.11. Such a treatment explains the pronoun form following the Comp (*que, como*):

Ella tiene más hijos que yo tengo hijos → Ella tiene más hijos que **yo**.
Ella tiene tantos hijos como yo tengo hijos → Ella tiene tantos hijos como **yo**.
Ella te ama a ti más que me ama a mí. → Ella te ama a ti más que **a mí**.

Figure 13.11. Reduction of a full comparative structure

Yo *tengo* más *hijos* [que tú *tienes hijos*] → Yo tengo más hijos [que tú ∅ ∅]

English may neutralize this distinction to Obj forms once the comparative clause is reduced:

She has more children than I have (children). → She has more children than **me**.
She loves you more than she loves me. → She loves you more than **me**.

This *I/me* merger occurs elsewhere too (*me too,* v. 12.2), and students will not understand the Spanish distinction until they perceive the underlying syntactic structure that defines it.

There is a second type of comparative sentence in which *more than* and *less than* establish a direct relationship between two quantities instead of two clauses or propositions. Such is the case with *I have more than five children,* which is usually not construed as 'I have more (toys, clothes, etc.) than five children have'. Here, *more than five* expresses the quantity '>5', that is, 'six or more'. Spanish distinguishes two cases in this regard, *más de* when *more than* means '>' and a negated *no más que* for '=' (i.e., 'neither more than, >, nor less than, <, but exactly, only, just'):

Tengo *más de* cinco hijos. I have more than five children.
No tengo *más que* cinco hijos. I just have five children, I don't have but five.

The two can contrast (Ramsey [1894] 1956, 143): *No necesito más que dos* is 'I only need two, exactly two' while *No necesito más de dos* is 'I need not >2 but ≤2, two or fewer, two at most'.

There is another *más de* construction that does have an internal clause, but unlike the first kind of comparative (*Yo tengo más hijos que tú (tienes hijos)*), the clauses show different verbs:

Siempre *compras* más alimentos de los que *necesitas.*
You always *buy* more food than you *need.*

The Spanish version, with its *más de*, resembles the *Tengo más de cinco hijos* type. In fact, it is the *same* type: the embedded clause is actually a relative clause, as we see in the fuller version:

Siempre compras **más** alimentos **de** *los alimentos* [*que necesitas*].
You always buy more food than the food [that you need].

In pruning down this fuller deep structure, Spanish merely applies nominalization (v. 8.4): *más alimentos de los alimentos [que necesitas] → más alimentos de los Ø [que necesitas].* If there is no implied noun, the neuter is adopted as usual: *Es más cómico de **lo** que piensas.* English shifts to a different surface structure by deleting the second NP (*the food*) and the relative pronoun (*that*): *more food than the food [that you need] → more food than Ø Ø you need.* Alternatively, it replaces both with *what*: *more food than what you need.* The same structures are used where Spanish has a neuter: *He's funnier than Ø you think ~ He's funnier than **what** you think.*

As with the *than me* problem, referring to deep structure helps explain the surface differences between the two languages. Unfortunately, textbooks proceed on the basis of mere surface structures, informing students to amend *más que* to *más de* before numbers. This will not work: it cannot explain *más de los que necesitas* or *más de lo que piensas*, nor contrasts before numbers as the following pair:[12]

Coma Ud. *más de* una galleta. (Eat more than one cookie; how about a second one?)
Coma Ud. *más que* una galleta. (Eat more than a cookie; how about a sandwich?)

13.5 Complex sentences: General summary. This chapter has surveyed an area that has been a major target of linguistic research for the last forty years: complex sentences and the processes operating inside them. Unfortunately, little of this work has been applied to improving textbooks (Campos 1993 is a striking exception) so that they foster both comprehension and creation of complex sentences; most pedagogical works still seem to underestimate the hurdles that students of Spanish face once they progress beyond simple sentences to combine clauses as in English.

Subordinated clauses act like nouns, adjectives, and adverbials in a main clause or as complements to comparatives and other constituents. Their deep structures in the two languages are similar, and if all embedded propositions were expressed in their full forms, as in figure 13.1 at the beginning of this chapter, then mastery might be an easier affair. But economy and flexibility are gained when tense/mood information is dispensed with and excess structure is pruned out, and the grammar of each language provides ways to simplify clauses and to further edit their structure with processes such as clitic promotion, *Tough* Movement, raising, and extraposition. These changes differ interlingually and depend on particular verbs and relators. Thus, it will not be obvious to students why a certain lineup in L2 allows (or requires) infinitivization of V and the deletion of NP, why an analogous lineup does not, why similar-looking structures reflect distinct deep structure relationships, or why a change necessitates a morpheme (*que, a, para, de, that, to, for, of*) in one language but not the other. What we have termed "reduction" makes communication easier and more flexible for mature speakers, but at a higher price for language learners.

Notes for chapter 13

1. Generative grammar (Jacobs and Rosenbaum 1968) originally treated infinitives as noun clauses (S in NP position) that were reduced by a transformation: *Tom wants [Tom do it]* → *Tom wants to do it*. This analysis accounts for why the clause (full or reduced) satisfies the DO requirement of a transitive verb like *want*, and why *to do it* is understood as having *Tom* as its deep structure Subj. It is especially useful for Spanish, which has *Tomás quiere [que Laura lo haga],* but where one expects *Tomás quiere [que Tomás lo haga], Tomás quiere hacerlo* appears instead. Traditional grammarians likewise saw infinitives as "elipsis" (Bello [1847] 1958, 339), "oraciones incorporadas" (RAE 1979, 487), and "abridged clauses" (Curme 1947, 156), and linguists followed suit (Hadlich 1971; Contreras 1979; Pilleux and Urrutia 1982).

Yet the machinery of clause-to-infinitive reduction is not as well oiled as it should be. In recent generative grammar, *Tom wants to do it* is no longer derived directly from *Tom wants [Tom do it]* but from *Tom wants [PRO to do it],* where the reference of PRO depends on the element in the main clause that is defined as controlling it. For the mixed audiences of this book, we informally combine these perspectives (without committing solely to either of them) in order to promote comprehension of structure without further theoretical elaboration of the principles that now apply to embedded clauses and anaphors. Advanced readers may interpret "reduction" as merely a pragmatic strategy rather than an actual transformation.

2. In current analyses, PRO (see previous note) is used for both kinds of Subj. In the Equi-NP interpretation, PRO is controlled by a matrix NP; in the impersonal one, it is uncontrolled and therefore unspecified as to coreference.

3. A variant of the Comp *que* is *de que*, as in *Me dicen de que es falso* or *Es indudable de que él no tenía nada*. Although this "*dequeísmo*" is condemned as an overgeneralization of *antes (de) que. . . , el hecho de que. . .* , and so on, De Mello (1995a) found it common even in cultivated speech for imparting a sense of "independence" to a clause. In the Canaries, though, *dequeísmo* is a syntactic variable rule, applying more among the young than among the old, more among men than among women, and most in the lower middle class (Serrano 1998).

4. *El* + VP-inf + Subj NP is uncommon in the spoken language, but it appears more often in the literary language (Ramsey [1894] 1956, 345; Gili Gaya 1973, 189).

5. While sentences like *Juan dice [tener cuidado]* ('John says he's careful', not 'John says to be careful') appear in journalistic styles, some native speakers find this reduction more acceptable with a perfect infinitive, as in *Juan dice [haber tenido cuidado].*

6. In Caribbean lects and also highland Colombia, Equi-NP is suspended for clause reduction after Prep: *antes de yo salir de mi país, para yo entender eso*, and so on (Lipski 1994, 215, 233).

7. Relativization is obviously based on the grammatical feature [±human] in both languages. Animals are therefore treated like things (*the dog that/which had its pups*) unless they have a personal identity to the speaker (*the dog who had her pups*).

8. This rise of the article form with Prep is functional in distinguishing relative clauses from adverbial ones (Alarcos Llorach 1999, 135): *Se asomaba al balcón* ***desde que*** *la veía* (adverbial clause, 'since . . .'), *Se asomaba al balcón* ***desde el que*** *la veía* (relative clause, 'from which . . .').

One other candidate for relativization besides subjects and objects is the NP that follows a comparative Comp (v. 13.4.2). As pointed out by Liceras (1993, 33), this constituent can be relativized in many lects of English, but never in Spanish:

That's the woman [I'm taller than *the woman*] → That's the woman that I'm taller than.
Esa es la mujer [soy más alta que *la mujer*] → * Esa es la mujer que soy más alta que.

9. The term 'headless relative' (Suñer 1982, 43) makes sense syntactically (no head, no antecedent N) although it unfortunately suggests decapitated kinfolk.

10. Some analyses (e.g., Teschner 2000b, 283) distinguish CLEFT (*Es Miss Chile quien lo va a ganar*) from PSEUDOCLEFT (*Quien lo va a ganar es Miss Chile*), but for Spanish there is actually one cleft formation that can then undergo extraposition and pre-position like any other surface lineup of nucleus and satellites.

11. The study by Drake, Ascarza, and Preble (1982) is one of the few to have tackled infinitival relatives, but one should be careful in using it because the authors were not sensitive to structure. Some of their examples do show a relative-like Prep + VP-inf after an antecedent interpreted as Obj of the infinitive: *Quiero pizza para llevar* (= pienso llevar la pizza DO). Others arise from wholly different structures, such as *No tiene el interés para doctorarse* (which cannot mean '*se doctorará el interés') or *Salió el sol para ocultarse en seguida*, where *para* introduces an AdvlP that has absolutely no syntactic connection with the inverted Subj *el sol.*

12. This example was suggested by Michael Reider (personal communication).

Exercises for chapter 13

1. Error Analysis: identify each error, correct it, and explain its apparent source.
   (a) *Estudias más que me.
   (b) *Tan musico, Casals tenía mucho talento.
   (c) *Después de viajando me siento cansado.
   (d) *Escribiendo es difícil.
   (e) *Necesito Roberto hacerlo.
   (f) *Teresa dijo te estudiar.
   (g) *El tema que hablaste sobre nos interesó.
   (h) *La asignatura preferimos es la historia.
   (i) *Queda una cosa para nosotros a hacer.
   (j) *La chica quién vino es mi sobrina.

2. Following is a list of sentence pairs. On the basis of the analysis presented in this chapter, identify which of the listed rule(s) account(s) for the relationship in each pair.

   Clause Reduction
   Clitic Promotion
   Extraposition
   Raising (of embedded Subj to matrix Obj)
   Relativization
   Tough Movement

   (a) Es imposible ver Neptuno sin telescopio. Neptuno es imposible de ver sin telescopio.
   (b) Nos mandaron que los siguiéramos. Nos mandaron seguirlos.
   (c) Afirman que no pueden resolver la crisis. Afirman no poder resolver la crisis.
   (d) Que tengas la culpa es bien probable. Es bien probable que tengas la culpa.
   (e) Intentan ayudarme. Me intentan ayudar.
   (f) Juan es el hombre; yo conozco bien al hombre. Juan es el hombre que yo conozco bien.
   (g) Hizo que todos obedecieran. Les hizo obedecer a todos.

3. Identify each embedded clause in the following, then state whether it is a noun clause, a relative clause, or an adverbial clause with a true conjunction. If it is a noun clause, indicate its function (Subj, DO, or OP) and whether it has been moved (extraposed).
   (a) Es lógico que el general haya mentido.
   (b) Me preguntó si cabrían otras dos sillas.
   (c) Te lo preguntaré si no nos avisa Tomás.

(d) Te lo preguntaré después de que Pilar nos deje.
(e) Quieren que nos esforcemos más.
(f) Los médicos con los que nos reunimos ayer van a cambiar de idea.
(g) No llevábamos paraguas cuando empezó a llover.
(h) El que ese tipo se enamore de ti no debe influir en tu decisión.

4. Under the assumption that clausal fragments and infinitivized VPs originate as full clauses, describe the underlying syntax of the italicized constituents in the following sentences. (You may either use rough paraphrases or draw phrase markers.)
(a) El presidente dice *haber acatado la ley.*
(b) No puede encontrar una herramienta *con la que aflojar la tuerca.*
(c) Les prohibimos *salir del teatro.*
(d) Encendió la luz *para ver mejor.*
(e) Juana escribió más poemas *que nosotros.*
(f) No sé *si obedecerle o no.*
(g) *Este modelo de carro* es muy fácil de *manejar.*

5. The following sentences are ambiguous; how does Spanish distinguish the senses?
(a) She has more than three students.
(b) Visiting relatives can be boring.
(c) We need someone to help.

6. Why is it misleading to lump *cuando, mientras, así que. . .*, on the one hand, with *después que, porque, para que, hasta que,* on the other, in a vocabulary list of "conjunctions"? How are they different?

7. In section 13.1.2, we noted that some Spanish verbs can have full clauses as Obj, and that these clauses may or may not, must or must not, reduce under certain conditions. Study the behavior of each of the following and classify it in one of the five types that were presented (*creer* or *decir, preferir, mandar, hacer, ver*)—or other types, if needed. Then contrast its syntax with that of its English equivalent.

pedir	exigir	negar	conseguir
esperar	lamentar	aconsejar	rogar
evitar	oír	temer	sugerir
prohibir	animar a	decidir	instar a
acordar	aguantar	alegrarse de	pretender

8. Also in section 13.1.2 we saw that *poder* + V and *querer* + V are structurally different in that the former's infinitive is not related to a noun clause. Each of the following can also appear with an infinitive; decide whether it is more like *poder* or like *querer*, and show why.

volver a	lograr	dejar de	decidir
prometer	tender a	comenzar a	necesitar
saber	acabar de	deber	soler

9. Combine the following sentence pairs according to the model, thereby producing indirect questions in I and nominalized relative clauses in II. (Alternatively, submit this exercise to native speakers and elicit their responses.)

(I) *Model*: Les pregunté eso. [¿Cuándo iban a volver?] → Les pregunté cuándo iban a volver.

(a) Quiero saber eso. [¿Por qué trabajas tanto?]
(b) Me pregunto eso. [¿Cada cuánto se baña?]
(c) Me pregunto eso. [¿En qué insistirán?]
(d) Pienso en eso. [¿En qué insistirán?]
(e) Pienso en eso. [¿De dónde provinieron?]
(f) Se trata de eso. [¿De qué se compone esa aleación?]

(II) *Model*: Me ayudó él. [Él conducía un *Jeep*.] → Me ayudó el que conducía un *Jeep*.

(g) Se presentó él. [Él había servido de testigo.]
(h) Fíjate en ella. [Ella viste tejanos amarillos.]
(i) Se presentó ella. [Confías tanto en ella.]
(j) Depende de ella. [Te casas con ella.]
(k) Me refiero a ellos. [Confías tanto en ellos.]
(l) No hay que contar con ellos. [Trabajamos para ellos.]

What happens when there is a clash of Prep governing the clause and Prep inside (and moved to the front of) the clause? In other words, how does Spanish handle (j) 'it depends on who you're getting married to'?

10. In addition to occurring as Subj, DO, and OP (i.e., after a relator) in a main clause, noun clauses may occur in the PA (predicate attribute) slot. For example, *El problema es [que los votantes lo rechazan]*. Following the mode of argumentation used in this chapter, find or create more examples of PA clauses, both full and reduced, state the conditions for reduction, and compare your rules with what happens in comparable English examples.

11. After reviewing clitic promotion (v. 13.1.2.8), determine whether each italicized clitic can be moved to the left of the conjugated verb. Do any restrictions emerge?

(a) Tienen que hacer*lo*.
(b) La vi matar*lo*
(c) ¿Tu hija? Sí, la vi arreglar*se*.
(d) Espero poder terminar*lo*.
(e) Renuncian a hacer*lo*.
(f) Muero por ver*lo*.
(g) Le hice leer*lo*.
(h) Lo/le hice suicidar*se*.
(i) La oyeron mencionar*me*.
(j) Me oyeron mencionar*la*.
(k) Deseo volver a ver*lo*.
(l) Creo poder hacer*lo*.
(m) Ella me parece saber*lo*.
(n) Te hice pegar*lo*. ('I made you glue it')
(o) Te hice pegar*le*. ('I made you hit him')
(p) Dejó de prometer hacer*lo*.

12. How would you explain to students how Spanish expresses the following meanings?

(a) I had her (to) steal a book.
(b) I had her book stolen.
(c) I had stolen her book.
(d) I had her book to steal.
(e) I had her stolen book.
(f) I had to steal her book.

13. The following sentences begin with a type of embedded clause that receives little pedagogical attention (Whitley and González 2000, 232). How would you analyze their formation, their syntactic relation to the matrix sentence, and the obvious interlingual differences? (Add other examples to test your hypotheses.)

(a)	[Whatever happens], don't go out.	[Pase lo que pase], no salgas.
(b)	[Whoever it is], there's no more room.	[Sea quien (el que) sea], no hay más sitio.
(c)	[However you do it], finish it soon.	[Lo hagas como lo hagas], termínalo pronto.
(d)	[Whether long or short], tests are hard.	[Sean largos o cortos], los exámenes son difíciles.

14. Although the phenomena described in this chapter cause interference early on in L2 acquisition, many of them are seldom addressed in pedagogy except in "usos del infinitivo." In this respect, Klein (1984) was especially critical of textbooks that continue treating *para, a, que,* and so on as just vocabulary items (*para* = *for, a* = *to* like *árbol* = *tree*) instead of as grammatical markers of clauses and reductions. The following sentences illustrate the problem. For each, indicate the proper Spanish equivalent(s) and the probable errors students will make if they translate literally. Show, too, something of the deep structures of the sentences.

(a) *For Mark, to lie* would be incredible.
For Mark to lie would be incredible.
It would be incredible *for Mark to lie.*
It would be hard *for Mark to lie.*

(b) It is hard *to read.* ('reading is hard')
It is hard *to read.* ('that thing is hard to read')
The library is a good place *to read/for reading.*

(c) Mariluz has a strong desire *to help her friends.*
Mariluz told us *to help her friends.*
Mariluz kept us *from helping her friends.*
Mariluz came *to help her friends.*
Mariluz came *for her friends to help her.*
Mariluz is believed *to help her friends.*

The crux of the problem is that Spanish treats reduced clauses differently from English, but students do not see any embedded clauses—full or reduced—in such sentences. Few would advocate that students first be taught tree diagrams, PSRs, and transformations in order to perceive the underlying differences; what, then, would be a practical pedagogical alternative?

PART THREE

BEYOND GRAMMAR

Chapter 14

Introduction to the study of words and usage

14.0 What it means to know a word. In addition to the phonology and grammar of their language, native speakers know its vocabulary or LEXICON. They learn and store each word as an item subject to the rules and categories of their language, and each LEXICAL ENTRY contains the information needed for using the word appropriately and accurately. For many readers, "lexical entry" may suggest what is recorded in a dictionary: syntactic category and subcategory (e.g., "transitive verb"), morphological peculiarities, pronunciation, and meaning(s). But the contents of one's mental lexical entry are richer than dictionaries can portray, inasmuch as meaning and usage tie in with the wealth of experiences that people have had, individually and collectively, in using language in sociocultural contexts and in a universe that they understand in specific ways.

14.1 An example: The meaning of *compadre*. The breadth of knowledge contained by lexical entries can be illustrated by Spanish *compadre*. García-Pelayo y Gross (1983) gave it a definition that reads in part as follows:

> COMPADRE *m.* Padrino del niño respecto de los padres y la madrina de éste. (SINÓN. v. *Padrino).* || *Fam.* Amigo o conocido.

This definition is accurate, but it presupposes far more information than it states. It relies on the knowledge of what *padrino, niño, padres,* and *madrina* mean, and interpreting it requires complex linguistic and cognitive skills to pick up on points such as the following:

1. *Padre* has several senses (duly listed under PADRE), but it is assumed that the reader will consider the context of *los padres* and construe it as 'parents', not 'priests', 'ancestors', or 'fathers'. The reader must also draw on familiarity with biology and culture to fill in the connection between *padres* and *niño*.

2. Definite articles (*el niño, los padres, la madrina*) suggest that reference is already established and sufficiently defined—which it is, but by the reader who draws on his/her background knowledge structure (SCHEMA) for this situation, not by the dictionary writer.
3. *Respecto de* implies a vis-à-vis relationship between *padrino* and *padres* and between *padrino* and *madrina.* This relationship will be taken for granted by readers from a Hispanic culture, but it is not expressed by the definition itself.

To proceed further in our semantic analysis, we pick up the reference "v(éase) *Padrino*." This noun is defined in turn as follows:

> PADRINO *m.* El que asiste a otro para recibir el bautismo, en el casamiento, en un desafío, certamen, etc. . . || *Fig.* El que favorece y ayuda a otro en la vida . . . (SINÓN. Protector).

The key word here is *bautismo*, for this ceremony establishes the links between *el padrino* and *el niño* and among *el padrino, los padres,* and *la madrina.* The writer assumed a culture based on Christian—and specifically Hispanic Roman Catholic—customs. *Bautismo* and the roles it defines might be unclear to nonbaptizing societies or even to Christians who are used to a different kind of baptism. Even to North Americans who likewise practice infant baptism and recognize certain adult roles in the ceremony, the sponsor or godparent does not assume the network of responsibilities and family ties to which the *padrino* commits himself. The *compadre/padrino* has a special status in the Hispanic world, and the dictionary takes that for granted.

Other points of information that Spanish speakers would fill in include the following:

1. The referent of *compadre/padrino* is an adult. (*¡Hola compadre!* is not normally used with toddlers, even for the sense of 'amigo o conocido'.)
2. Assuming the role of *compadre* initiates a lifelong relationship named *compadrazgo,* and the two words are morphologically and semantically linked. Other associated derivatives include *compadrar, compadrear, compadraje, compadrería, compadrito* (RAE 1992).
3. The child becomes the *ahijado* of the *compadre*, and the latter commits himself to helping provide for the child. He becomes literally the 'co-parent', *compadre,* of that child and an extended family member, related to the parents as *compadre* and to the child as *padrino.*
4. The *compadre* is accompanied by a *comadre/madrina,* whose co-responsibility for the child can be just as great, although with an implicitly distinct role. The roles of *compadre* and *comadre* also have different cultural connotations, as witnessed by the secondary meanings the dictionary gives: 'friend or acquaintance' for *compadre* vs. 'gossipy woman' for *comadre.*

5. One does not become a *compadre* when standing as *padrino* in a duel or contest ("*desafío, certamen*"); indeed, modern readers might regard *padrino* in this sense as archaic, quaint, perhaps barbaric.
6. In situations the writer vaguely labels as "fam(iliar)" and "fig(urativo)," the words *compadre* and *padrino* take on senses other than those defined by baptism. But Spanish readers recognize that these secondary usages ('friend or acquaintance', 'protector') are natural extensions of the kind of relationship a *compadre* has with other adults and as *padrino* to children.

Finally, we note that the references to *sinón(imos)* imply a systematic organization of one's lexicon with mental links to other words. By synonymy, *compadre* is linked to *padrino*; by antonymy, to *ahijado*; by taxonomy (classification), to *padre, abuelo, tío,* and so on as *parientes*. Thus, the lexicon is as much a thesaurus and an encyclopedia as it is a dictionary, and knowledge of any word entered into it implies knowledge of a culture, of a society, and of a world.

14.2 The ranges of usage and meaning. As the preceding example showed, the study of words and usage is complex and open-ended. It has been addressed by scholars of LEXICOGRAPHY (dictionary compilation), SEMANTICS (word and sentence meaning), and SEMIOTICS or SEMIOLOGY (meanings of communicative symbols in general), as well as by grammarians, literary critics, philosophers, psychologists, anthropologists, and specialists in information theory, artificial intelligence, second language acquisition, speech communication, and reading. It should therefore not be surprising that there have been numerous theories on the subject, and it would be impossible here to sketch them all even briefly.

For applied linguistics, though, the approach of Stockwell, Bowen, and Martin (1965, 265–81) gives a useful point of departure. In their analysis, the use of a word is held to "range" over a set of grammatical, referential, and situational contexts, and they discern seven ranges where the words from two languages are used differently.

- SYNTACTIC RANGE, the domain of structures in which a word is used. Syntactic categorization or part of speech is one part of this range: English *down* is N, V, Adv, Prt, Prep, or even Adj (*the computer is down*), while Spanish *abajo* is Adv only. But although English *want* and Spanish *querer* are both verbs, they also differ in syntactic range in specifying distinct Comps (v. 13.1.2.3). Likewise, pairs such as *ask* and *pedir, like* and *gustar, depend* and *depender* differ in their *régimen* or construction with NPs (v. 8.1.4) and in the Prep they assign (v. 10.4.2).
- MORPHOLOGICAL RANGE, the full inflectional and derivational potential of a word. *Can* and *poder* differ in the tense distinctions they can show; *aburrir* and *bore* have different derivational patterns (*aburrido* vs. *boring, aburrimiento* vs. *boredom*). The word *compadre* examined in section 14.1 has a derivative *com-*

padrazgo where English *godfather* has a LEXICAL GAP for the relationship (no special name for it).

- GRAMMATICAL RANGE, the grammatical functions a morpheme has. In this respect, *se, a,* and *hacer* do not match *-self* (v. 9.3), *to* (v. 11.2.3), and *do* (v. 12.1–2). But since such functions are relative to the syntactic system, dictionaries cannot easily show them. As Stockwell, Bowen, and Martin (1965, 269) put it, "when the meaning of *a* or *se* is indicated in a list, it necessarily applies only to certain contexts, which are usually not specified, and is basically fallacious."
- COOCCURRENCE RANGE, the conventional expressions or COLLOCATIONS formed when a word tends to combine with others. English *take* is the verb of choice to combine with *a trip, a train, a look, a walk, an oath, a size 14,* but Spanish prefers *hacer un viaje, tomar* (or *coger*) *un tren, echar una ojeada, dar un paseo, prestar juramento, usar una talla 14.* Ignorance of such L2 collocations is often a major factor in the lack of an "idiomatic" flavor in students' output.
- DENOTATIVE RANGE, the semantic space or conceptual area(s) covered by the basic meaning of a word. Stockwell, Bowen, and Martin note that *abrigo,* though often equated with *coat,* actually denotes 'protection or shelter from', and it is this more general sense that underlies derivatives such as *abrigar, desabrigar, abrigado,* and *al abrigo de.* Since a word is usually a POLYSEME, conveying several senses, it tends to correspond to several distinct words in another language, as with *volar* = *fly* or *explode*, and *work* = *trabajo* or *obra*. Derivatives may distinguish those senses: *volar* 'fly' has the noun *vuelo* 'flight' whereas *volar* 'explode' has *voladura* 'explosion'.
- CONNOTATIVE RANGE, the secondary meanings associated with a concept. These reflect the special values and experiences of individuals with the concept within their culture. For example, one must ignore a great deal of connotative difference in equating *maid* with *criada, honest* with *honesto,* and *guts* with *entrañas.* As already shown in 14.1, *compadre* has a set of warmer and more favorable connotations in Hispanic culture than *godfather* does in English; in fact, the latter sometimes connotes a sinister character in North American culture.
- CIRCUMSTANTIAL RANGE, the special behavior a word or expression cues in a social context. *One way* matches *una manera* as a straight translation, but in the context of traffic signs it instead corresponds to *dirección única* or *sentido único.* Likewise, in offering something the English speaker says *Here you are* or *Here's (NP),* while the Spanish speaker carries out the same ritual with *Aquí tiene(s) (NP)* or a command, *Toma (Tome).*

Previous chapters have explored much of what Stockwell, Bowen, and Martin called syntactic and grammatical range, and the remaining two chapters turn to the information they might place in the other ranges. Of special concern will be two pedagogical implications. First, whenever we match English words to Spanish words, this is "only because some part of their ranges in some way or other overlaps with some part of some range of the Spanish items, but they are rarely if ever wholly equivalent" (Stockwell, Bowen, and Martin 1965, 81). Unfortunately, students are not warned of this mismatch, and each time they learn a Spanish word and proceed to use it as they have used its English equivalent, they unwittingly open seven doors to potential error. Second, since much of a word's range must be understood within the experiences, culture, and society of native speakers, L2 learners are being asked to acquire more than just new phonemes, phrase structures, and lexical labels; they are involved in a profound transmutation of their inner thought and being, and some hold back and retreat to the security of L1 while others adapt, integrate, and advance toward proficiency in L2.

Chapter 15

Words and their meanings

15.0 The lexicon. The term LEXICON is used in linguistics for the set of words a speaker knows and for the larger set available to the speech community as a whole. Strictly speaking, the two are not identical; individual speakers may have a personal vocabulary of some sixty thousand words, many of them known passively (receptively) but seldom used actively (expressively), whereas the language of the larger community, as encoded in dictionaries, has several times that number.[1]

There are several reasons for the difference, as we learn by skimming through a dictionary and comparing its lexical stock with our own. Some words are archaic, appearing only in poetry or older literature (e.g., *exir* 'salir', *maguer* 'a pesar de que', *remanir* 'permanecer'); some are restricted to certain dialects (e.g., English *brolly,* Spanish *choclo*); and still others belong to the specialized vocabulary, or ARGOT, of certain fields and subcultures (v. 16.1.3).

Lexicographers pool their experiences to record words that appear in print (words appearing in speech are hard to monitor). Despite their efforts to keep up with the communal lexicon, however, it is impossible to give an exhaustive listing because new words or NEOLOGISMS are constantly arising. Borrowing is one source of neologisms, and though purists may condemn *tipiar, sexy, el chip, chequear,* and *el lonche,* languages do not exist in a vacuum; borrowing has always been a simple, direct way of enriching vocabulary in both English and Spanish. At least in Spanish, loanwords are felt to be naturalized once their orthography is adapted and they begin spinning off derivatives: *leader* → *líder liderar liderazgo, stress* → *estrés estresar estresante, diskette* → *disquete disquetera, clone* → *clon clonar clonación, scanner* → *escáner escanear, folklore* → *folclor folclórico*. The borrowing may be masked by LOAN TRANSLATION in which each morpheme of the original is converted: *luna de miel, videocintas, baloncesto, anticuerpos, retroalimentación, interfaz,* and *bebé probeta* are based on English *honeymoon, videotapes, basketball, antibodies, feedback, interface,* and *test-tube baby*; *mercadotecnia* and *miembresía*, created to fend off *márketing* and *membership,* could be included in the same category. There is also SEMANTIC BORROWING of a meaning, as in *ignorar* 'no saber'

→ 'no hacer caso de' due to English *ignore*, or the adaptation of *servidor* to the computer sense of English *server.*

In addition, native speakers create neologisms within their language by using existing morphemes and morphological rules. Americans who refer to the *pre-Reaganite* era or Nicaraguans who speak of *neosomocistas* are utilizing the resources of their languages to create perfectly intelligible words (at least within their respective societies) that may or may not enter the dictionaries. By studying the patterns of word formation, or DERIVATIONAL MORPHOLOGY, we get a glimpse of how the lexicon continues to adapt and grow.

15.1 Derivational morphology. There are three main ways by which English and Spanish derive new words from old ones: by adding affixes to stems, by COMPOUNDING (combining stems), and by shortening. Like other Romance languages, Spanish has an abundance of derivational affixes; like its Germanic sisters, English makes frequent use of compounding; and both languages today make growing use of shortening.

15.1.1 Affixes. The affixes that derive new words are classified by their position in the word. Those that precede the stem are PREFIXES; those that follow it are SUFFIXES. The latter are more numerous in English and Spanish, and when several of them are added to one stem, they line up in an order that reflects derivational stages, with purely inflectional ones (number, tense, etc.) coming last of all. Thus, *personalidades* is morphologically *persona+al+idad+es,* that is, the inflected plural (*-es*) form of the noun *personalidad,* which is derived from the adjective *personal* formed off the noun *persona,* which here serves as the stem or base of the whole. This structure can be shown as in figure 15.1, with brackets enclosing each successive layer of derivation or, alternatively, with a tree diagram of the constituents.

A second way of classifying derivational morphemes is by their relative productivity. Some morphemes are frozen, that is, little used in new formations. The prefix *ob-,* for instance, appears in English *obscene* and Spanish *obsceno,* but in neither language is it

Figure 15.1. Two ways of showing morphological structure

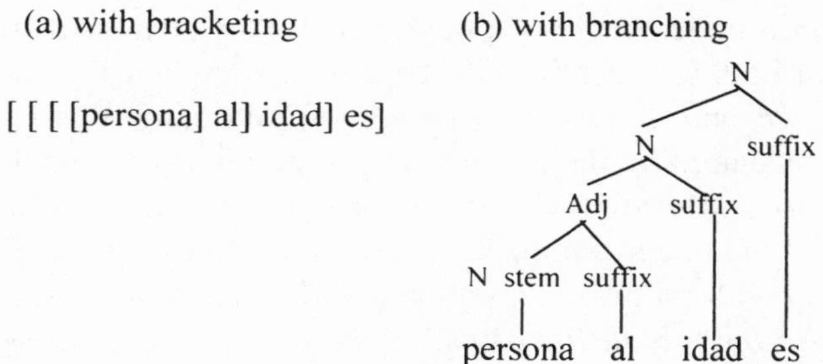

likely to be used in current neologisms. At the other extreme, Spanish *des-* and *-ero* and English *un-* and *-able* are freely used to create new words. If one describes a hammer-wielding friend as a *martillero* or a difficult nail as *unhammerable,* hearers will not have to ask what either word means in context, nor will they be especially shocked on not finding it in a dictionary. Between these extremes are various degrees of productivity, and the two languages may not always agree on the value they assign to otherwise comparable affixes: English *un-* is more productive than Spanish *in-,* but Spanish uses diminutives, singly and serially *(chico, chiquito, chiquitico . . .*), far more than English.

A third way of classifying derivational morphemes is in terms of their function. Many serve primarily to adapt a word for use in a different syntactic category:

- Adj → N: Spanish (arid)*ez,* (alt)*ura,* (alt)*eza,* (alt)*itud,* (cert)*idumbre,* (posibil)*idad* (allomorphs *-tad, -dad*); English (good)*ness*, (similar)*ity*, (wid)*th,* (likeli)*hood*
- V → N:[2] Spanish (observa)*ción* (allomorphs *-ión, -sión),* (par)*o,* (para)*da,* (cort)*e,* (corta)*dura,* (vir)*aje,* (mud)*anza,* (empuj)*ón,* (casa)*miento,* (emplea)*dor,* (emplea)*do,* (cerra)*zón,* (canta)*nte,* infinitive (*bienestar*); English (observ)*ation,* (bore)*dom,* (paint)*ing,* (pay)*ment,* (revers)*al,* (paint)*er,* (employ)*ee,* (disinfect)*ant,* (cover)*age,* Ø suffix (work)
- N → Adj: Spanish (nacion)*al,* (lluvi)*oso,* (republic)*ano,* (guerr)*ero,* (art)*ístico,* (estudiant)*il,* (esperanz)*ado,* (barb)*udo,* (mujer)*iego,* (fronter)*izo,* (di)*ario,* (telefón)*ico*; English (nation)*al,* (ruin)*ous,* (sugar)*y,* (care)*ful,* (world)*ly,* (burden)*some,* (fool)*ish,* (republic)*an,* (atom)*ic* (allomorph *-ical*), Ø suffix (as in *gold watch, student life*)
- V → Adj: Spanish (convenie)*nte,* (resbala)*dizo,* (diverti)*do,* (conta)*ble,* (trabaja)*dor,* (llor)*ón,* (articula)*torio,* (deriva)*tivo,* (hace)*dero*; English (expect)*ant,* (exclama)*tory,* (work)*ing,* (work)*able,* (tire)*d,* (deriva)*tive*
- N or Adj → V: Spanish (civil)*izar,* (traicion)*ar, a*(clar)*ar,* (humed)*ecer, en*(roj)*ecer,* (telefon)*ear,* (clas)*ificar*; English (civil)*ize,* (hard)*en,* (simpl)*ify,* Ø suffix (book)
- Adj → Adv: Spanish (rápida)*mente,* Ø suffix (*rápido*); English (rapid)*ly,* Ø suffix (*fast*)

Students cannot predict the particular morpheme combinations that have already been set up within the Spanish lexicon. They might study derivational morphology enough to perceive *cortar* in *corte* and *cortadura* (which are not synonymous), but they should not try to create **cortanza* or **cortación* on their own as they create new sentences. Spanish-speaking students of English must likewise cope with unpredictable formations like *-ment* for *pay, -al* for *reverse,* and *-ation* for *observe,* all for the same V→ N function.

Some patterns are shared by the two languages, and many textbooks exploit the similarity of *-oso* to *-ous, -ción* to *-tion, -izar* to *-ize,* and so on (v. 15.2). One option not extensively shared is the one symbolized by Ø in the preceding list. English often transforms part of speech with no overt derivational suffix. There may be a morphophonemic change (N *shelf, use* /jus/, *bath* /bæθ/ vs. V *shelve, use* /juz/, *bathe* /beð/) or a stress change (V *permít recórd convíct* → N *pérmit récord cónvict*), but not always (N *book* → V *book*, N *gold* → Adj *gold (watch)*). In Spanish, the similarity of N and Adj inflection does allow some direct crossover between these two categories (as with *hablador, médico, hueco, vacío, vecino, enemigo, santo, malentendido, realista*); otherwise, categorial changes usually require the addition of derivational suffixes.

In changing syntactic category, morphemes may also affect meaning. Thus, *-ción* and *-tion* create abstract nouns of action or countable instances thereof, *-dor* and *-er* express the verb's Subj, and *-do* and *-ee* indicate the verb's Obj. The following derivational morphemes more strongly affect meaning, with or without a change in part of speech (Devney 1992):

- opposite, negative, lack: Spanish *in*(útil, -cumplir), *des*(hacer, -empleo), *no* (violencia); English *un*(happy, -do), *dis*(honest, -assemble), (harm)*less*, *non*(violence), *de*(frost), *mis*(understand)
- feminine (v. 8.2.2): Spanish (doctor)*a*, (abad)*esa*, (act)*riz*; English (lion)*ess*, (major)*ette*
- diminutive and/or endearment:[3] Spanish (carr)*ito*, (carr)*illo*, (carr)*ico* (allomorphs *-cito, -cillo, -cico*); English (dadd)*y*, (hors)*ie*, (pig)*let*, (kitchen)*ette*
- affiliation, origin, language: Spanish (itali)*ano*, (franc)*és*, (panam)*eño*, (canad)*iense*, (marroqu)*í* (manch)*ego*, (britán) *ico*, (santander)*ino*, (crist)*iano*, (húngar)*o*; English (Puerto Ric)*an*, (Span)*ish*, (Christ)*ian*, (Chin)*ese*
- doctrine, lifestyle, adherent: Spanish (capital)*ismo*, *-ista*;[4] English (capital)*ism*, *-ist*
- fractional part or ordinal: Spanish (quinz)*avo*, (cent)*ésimo*; English (fifteen)*th*
- degree: Spanish (roj)*izo*, (blanc)*uzco*, *sub- sobre- semi*(desarrollado), (grand)*ísimo*, *re- requete*(bueno); English (redd)*ish*, *under- over- semi*(developed)

Spanish has more resources in this meaning-adapting category than English or even its sister language French (Lang 1990, 34); for example,

- augmentative, pejorative: (sill)*ón*, (libr)*ote*, (cas)*ucha*, (perr)*azo*
- area for the purpose of: (manzan)*ar*, (naranj)*al*, (desembarca)*dero*
- associated person, receptacle, outlet: (joy)*ero*, (azucar)*ero*, (gasolin)*era*, (partid)*ario*
- associated store or occupation: (zapat)*ería*
- blow to or with: (pal)*iza*, (cod)*azo*, (puñ-, nalg)*ada*
- set: (profesor)*ado*, (muebl~mobl)*aje*, (estant)*ería*, (doc)*ena*, (alam)*eda*

As a result, Spanish produces large word families with no equivalent in English, for example, *cabeza, cabezazo, cabecita, cabecear, cabecera, cabezudo* (Lang 1994), and given its stock of derivational morphemes, it has no trouble supplying new words as needed. As Stewart (1999) concluded from her survey of contemporary vocabulary expansion,

> Clearly the potential of the Spanish language for creating neologisms through the mechanisms described above is enormous and its speakers exploit them creatively. . . . It would appear that the voices which proclaim the end of the Spanish language is nigh, on the basis of the English interference they detect in some of the "CyberSpanglish" appearing on the Internet, are misjudging the current resilience of the language. (p. 95)

15.1.2 Compounding. While Spanish has more suffixes, English makes more use of compounding, as seen in the contrast *trig**al*** vs. *wheat field*. The main compounding patterns of Spanish are shown below (see Varela 1990; Lang 1990; Núñez Cedeño 1991); the first three are fairly productive for new products and relationships, but otherwise compounding is uncommon.

- N + N = N (v. 8.3.2): *aguanieve, bocacalle, grupo control, lengua madre, estado-nación, fecha tope ~ fecha límite, ciudad dormitorio, fotos tamaño carnet*
- N + Prefix-N = N: *tratamiento antidroga, una póliza multirriesgos, aparato contraincendios*
- V + N-*s* = N: *cuentagotas, lavaplatos, salvavidas, lanzacohetes, paraguas, cumpleaños*
- N-*i* + Adj = Adj: *boquiabierto, barbiesposo, pelirrojo*
- N + Adj = N: *bancarrota, hierbabuena, aguardiente*
- N + Adv = Adv: *patas arriba, cuesta abajo, río abajo*

English has many more patterns (see Quirk et al. 1972), most of them very productive. Whether written as one word or two, with a hyphen or without, they tend to have the distinctive stress pattern primary-secondary (ˊ ˋ , v. 4.1.2):

- Adj + N = N: *fathead, paleface, loudmouth, drywall, blackbird*
- Adj + N-*ed* = Adj: *thickheaded, red-faced, long-lived, three-toed*
- N + Adj = Adj: *tax-free, dust-proof, carsick, brick-red, diamond-hard*
- V + N = N: *pickpocket, scarecrow, drawbridge, dodge ball*
- N + V-*ing* = N/Adj: *air-conditioning, bookkeeping, storytelling, meat-eating*
- V-*ing* + N = N: *washing machine, chewing gum, spending money, baking soda*
- N + V-*er* = N: *biology teacher, gate-crasher, babysitter, songwriter, paper cutter*
- N + N = N: *toothache, coffeepot, book review, table leg, tax cut, applesauce, workbench*
- V + Prt = N: *makeup, setup, workout, hangover, turnout, turnover, login*
- Prt + V =N/V: *outbreak, upset, income, outcome, outgo, overhang, input*
- Prt + N = Advl/N/Adj: *uphill, downtown, indoor, throughway, outlaw, online*

As in other Germanic languages, the English compounds may in turn be compounded to produce complex pileups such as the following title of a letter from an automobile manufacturer: *Corolla airbag malfunction indicator lamp special service campaign*.

To the English-speaking student, whose personal lexicon includes hosts of compounds and a proclivity for creating more, the uncompounded Spanish equivalents for these concepts may seem maddeningly unpredictable. In working on vocabulary development, then, it is necessary for students to grasp at least enough about compounding to avoid transferring it.

15.1.3 Shortening: Clipping and acronyms. Both languages also create new terms by shortening (abbreviating) existing words. By CLIPPING, syllables are lopped off the end: *taxicab* → *taxi* (and *cab*), *microphone* → *mike, biology* → *bio*. The clipped version may then coexist with the original as a more informal synonym, but often it develops its own meaning, as in *fanatic* → (sports) *fan, caravan* → *van*. Spanish used to have relatively few clippings (*fotografía* → *foto, motocicleta* → *moto, cinematográfico* → *cine*), but today the process is accelerating in colloquial styles: *analfa(beto), mili(tar), poli(cía), bici(cleta), profe(sor), ampli(ficador),* Argentine *subte(rráneo)*. When two clippings are compounded, the result is a BLEND, as in English *mo(tor)* + *(ho)tel* → *motel,* Spanish *pe(tróleos) mex(icanos)* → *PEMEX*.

A second type of shortening is abbreviation to an ACRONYM consisting of the initial letters of a phrase. In both languages this process began slowly, picked up in the mid–twentieth century, and today has become explosive. An acronym begins as an on-the-spot pronoun for a phrasal name, as in technical and bureaucratic writing, then spreads to become the usual term. In English, some acronyms are still pronounced as letters, as in *United Nations* → *UN* /jù ɛ́n/, *deoxyribonucleic acid* → *DNA* /dí ɛ̀n é/; others come to be pronounced as words, as in *North Atlantic Treaty Organization* → *NATO* /nétò/, *acquired immune deficiency syndrome* → *AIDS* /édz/, *light amplification by stimulated emission of radiation* → *laser* /lézər/. Spanish prefers pronounceable acronyms, retaining or epenthesizing a vowel (especially /e/) if necessary. The gender is that of the head noun, plurals are sometimes shown by doubled letters, and lowercase is preferred as the word becomes more common:

objeto volador no identificado → un *ovni* /óbni/
Organización del Tratado del Atlántico del Norte → la *OTAN* /ótan/
Partido Socialista Obrero Español → el *PSOE* /pesóe/
unidad de cuidados intensivos → la *UCI* /úsi/
Juegos Olímpicos → los *JJ.OO*

Pronounced forms subsequently enter the derivational processes of the language:

síndrome de inmunodeficiencia adquirida → *SIDA, sida* /sída/ → *sidoso*
Partido Revolucionario Institucional → *PRI* /prí/ → *un priísta*
Partido Popular → *PP* /pepé/ → *un pepero*

While some prominent English acronyms have been borrowed into Spanish (*el láser, el CD-ROM* /sederón/), students must understand that this kind of technical shorthand abbreviates language- and culture-specific phrases; they cannot transfer terms like *GPA* (grade-point average) or *CPR* (cardiopulmonary resuscitation) to L2 and expect to be understood.

15.1.4 Morphophonemics: Phonology in the lexicon. Adding a derivational suffix may trigger changes in the stem's pronunciation. These MORPHOPHONEMIC changes (v. 5.1) are also found in inflection; the pairs *viejo vejez* and *nueve noventa* show the same stress-based diphthongization as the verb forms *pienso pensar* and *puedo poder* (v. 6.1.2.2). Yet processes that apply consistently in inflection weaken in derivation, and there is a gamut of types ranging from general and predictable to one-of-a-kind irregularities, as illustrated here. (For a fuller listing, see Saporta 1959.)

Predictable. Spanish Adjs in *-ble* change to *-bil-* with derivational affixes: *posible posibil+idad posibil+itar, amable amabil+ísimo amabil+idad.* Also, Ns in *-en* change to *-in-*: *origen origin+al, examen examin+ar.*

Usual. The final unstressed vowel of a Spanish word tends to drop when a vowel-initial suffix is added: *hijo hij+ito, feo afe+ar, base bás+ico, católico catolic+ismo, día di+ario.* If this leaves the sequence /-Cj+i-/, then the /j/ drops too: *copia* /kópja/ *cop+ista, sucio suc+ísimo*. But the vowel fails to drop in *golpe golpe+ar, álgebra algebra+ico, espíritu espiritu+al.*

Common, but with many exceptions or subconditions. Spanish stem-final /k/ becomes /θ/~/s/ before a derivational suffix beginning with a front vowel, /i e/: *médico medic+ina, eléctrico electric+idad, magnífico magnific+encia.* But it stays /k/ with diminutives, *-ísimo, -ero,* and *-e*: *poco poqu+ito poqu+ísimo, vaca vaqu+ero, arranc(ar) arranqu+e.* Oddly, *-ense* induces the change but its synonym *-eño* does not: *costarric+ense* but *puertorriqu+eño.* Diphthongization also shows inconsistency in derivation: *diestro* has *destr+eza* and *viejo* has *vej+ez,* just as we would expect when the stress shifts, but *a+diestr+ar, viej+ísimo, encuest+ar, presupuest+ar,* and *muestr+eo* (from *encuesta, presupuesto, muestra*) keep an unstressed diphthong. As another example of a common pattern, numerous stems with medial /d/ show /t/ in derivatives: *nadar natación, lado lateral, Ecuador ecuatoriano, estado estatal.* This alternation is due to sound changes that are now dead in the language (compare *medir medición* and *mito mítico*).

Idiosyncratic. The following Spanish pairs have the same V/N relationship as *observar observación* and *prohibir prohibición,* but they show odd allomorphs that seem wholly unpredictable:

dirigir /dirix-/, *dirección* /direk-/
construir /konstru-/, *construcción* /konstruk-/
confundir /konfund-/, *confusión* /konfus-/
conseguir /konseg-/, *consecución* /konseku-/
oír /o-/, *audición* /awdi-/
digerir /dixer-/, *digestión* /dixest-/
devolver /debolb-/, *devolu-* /debolu-/
recoger /r̄ekox-/, *recolección* /r̄ekolek-/

Similar quirks appear in the stem changes of N-Adj pairs such as *leche láct-eo, año anu-al, ley leg-al, reflejo reflex-ivo.*

Linguists have debated the extent to which native speakers exploit or even perceive morphophonemic relationships in the lexicon. For Harris (1969), *leche* and *lácteo* have a common base like *cariño* and *cariñoso, puerto* and *porteño,* and he posited rules to derive them from the same form. Other linguists acknowledge a semantic relationship between *leche* and *lácteo*[5] but see no more of a common stem in them (or the need for rules to explain the difference in pronunciation) than in *corazón* and *cardíaco, perro* and *canino, bosque* and *silvestre,* or for that matter English *milk* and *lactic.* In the classroom, of course, matters are different: it is admirable if students infer useful patterns within Spanish, but what is more often expected of them is to recognize the meaning of *lácteo* and *dirección,* not because of morphophonemic rules that derive their consonants and vowels from those of *leche* and *dirigir,* but because of their cognate resemblance to English *lactic* and *direction.*

15.2 Cognates: True friends, or false? In linguistics, the term COGNATE is used with a more specific meaning than in pedagogy. A given word W_x from Language X and a word W_y from Language Y are termed "cognates" if and only if they have been inherited from the same ancestor language of X and Y. They are *not* true cognates, in this sense, if their resemblance is a coincidence, or if X borrowed W_x from Y (or vice versa), or if both borrowed their words from a third language Z. Some examples of each case may illustrate the distinction.

INHERITANCE (Spanish < Latin < Indo-European; English < Germanic < Indo-European): *madre/mother, me/me, es/is, seis/six, mente/mind, nombre/name, yugo/yoke, diente/tooth, seguir/see, oveja/ewe, vivo/quick, estar/stand, joven/young, ver/wit, lengua/tongue*

COINCIDENCE: *haber/have, mucho/much, otro/other, o/or*

BORROWING

English → Spanish: *estándar, eslogan, boicot, sandwich, mitin, penalty, fútbol, túnel, software, test, picnic, suéter, driblar, revólver, roc(anrol)*

Spanish → English: *ranch, vista, canyon, patio, tornado, caramel, vanilla, cigar, cinch, mosquito, cockroach, intransigent*; (via Spanish from Arabic): *algebra, alcohol, guitar*; (via Spanish from Amerindian languages): *tomato, tobacco, potato, chocolate, hurricane*

Both from a third language: (both from Latin): *adjetivo/adjective, rápido/rapid, exacto/exact, actor, animal*; (both from French): *hotel, control, menú/menu, garaje/garage, silueta/silhouette, turno/turn, tren/train*; (both from Italian) *piano, soprano, banco/bank*; (both from Greek) *mapa/map, diploma, planeta/planet, bio-, auto-, fis-/phys-, -grafía/-graphy*; (Spanish inherited from

Latin, English borrowed from Latin or French) *valle/valley, razón/reason, sol/sol(ar), fiesta/feast.*

But such distinctions involve too much etymologizing for language learners. In fact, true cognates tend to be pedagogically useless because during the five thousand years since the breakup of Indo-European, meaning and pronunciation have changed too drastically (*vivo/quick*) for the relationship to be clear to the nonspecialist. It is the borrowing category, which contains no cognates at all for the linguist, that pedagogy treats as "cognates," and we will follow this usage here.

Cognates are touted as hosts of words for free, meaning that they require little effort to master (aside from pronunciation, spelling, part of speech, gender, stem changes, and so on). To a certain extent, this claim is true. Having developed in the same general region and culture, the two languages exchanged many words, borrowed from French, were flooded by Greco-Latin roots, and today participate in a kind of international trade zone for scientific and technological neologisms. Furthermore, students learn that there is a good chance that their words in *-nce, -ity, -ic(al), -ist, -ment, -tion, -ize* will be acceptable currency in Spanish if amended to *-ncia, -idad, -ico, -ista, -mento, -ción, -izar*; and with *-al, -ble,* and *-sis,* even less effort seems necessary.

Yet for several reasons, cognates are as much a bane as a boon. First, they are phonetically seductive, inviting transfer of L1 pronunciation (v. 2.4). Second, they can differ in stylistic level: *aumento, socorro, renunciar* are ordinary Spanish words that are free of the formal tones suggested by English *augment, succor, renounce* (which may even be absent from some speakers' lexicons). Vice versa, some Spanish words are rarer than their English look-alikes, and the reading passage that avoids *cómodo, exigir, unir,* and *por fin* for the English-like *confortable, demandar, conectar,* and *finalmente* may seem unnatural and inauthentic.

Third, students overextend cognate patterns and create Spanglish words that do not exist:

abortion → *aborción (aborto)
portable → *portable (portátil)
serious → *serioso (serio)
visitor →*visitor (visitante)
vaccination → *vaccinación (vacunación)
procrastinate → *procrastinar (aplazar)
protective → *protectivo (protector)
deterioration → *deterioración (deterioro)

Fourth, the two lexicons abound with items that resemble each other in spelling but not in meaning. These have been called "false friends" or "false cognates" (*false* = 'treacherous'; all of these "cognates" are *false* = 'wrong' in the linguistic sense). The classic example is *embarazada* ≠ *embarrassed*; following is a small sampling of others.

fábrica ≠ fabric
avisar ≠ advise
actual ≠ actual
lectura ≠ lecture
dormitorio ≠ dormitory
desgracia ≠ disgrace
rato ≠ rat (or rate)
largo ≠ large
colegio ≠ college

éxito ≠ exit
sensible ≠ sensible
casual(idad) ≠ casual(ty)
pinchar ≠ pinch
decepción ≠ deception
billón ≠ billion

Almost as false are those cognates whose common Spanish meanings are carried by the English words just in restricted contexts; their usual English senses, and therefore the ones that come to students' minds, do not match at all.

tabla ≠ table 'mesa'
realizar ≠ realize 'darse cuenta'
excitar ≠ excite 'emocionar'
polo ≠ pole 'poste'
suceder ≠ succeed 'tener éxito'
cuestión ≠ question 'pregunta'
respecto ≠ respect 'respeto, -ar'
signo ≠ sign 'señal, letrero, firma'
argumento ≠ argument 'rencilla, disputa'
tarifa ≠ tariff 'arancel'

Conversely, the usual English meaning may be a possible one in Spanish in some contexts, but the Spanish cognate has other common meanings that English speakers cannot anticipate (see Batchelor and Pountain 1992, 19–32):

extremo: (extreme), *end*
formación: (formation), *training*
gracia: (grace), *wit, humor*
pintura: (picture), *paint*
raro: (rare), *strange*
compromiso: (compromise), *commitment*
tipo: (type), *rate, guy*
globo: (globe), *balloon*

15.3 Dialect differences in vocabulary. Regional differences in Spanish phonology and grammar have been discussed elsewhere in this book. Lexically, there are many differences such as the following:

'car': auto, carro, coche
'grass': hierba, césped, pasto
'ticket': boleto, billete, tiquete
'refrigerator': refrigerador, nevera, frigorífico
'peas': guisantes, arvejas, chícharos
'bus': autobús, ómnibus, camión, guagua
'corn': maíz, choclo
'sidewalk': acera, banqueta, vereda
'throw away': tirar, botar
'stamp': estampilla, sello, timbre
'city block': manzana, cuadra
'kitchen sink': fregadero, pila, lavadero

Besides assigning different words to the same meaning, dialects may assign different meanings to the same word. *Provocar* means 'be appealing' in Colombia, 'provoke' in most other areas; *pararse, liviano, barranca* are respectively 'stop, lewd, ravine' in Spain but 'stand up, lightweight, cliff' to most Spanish Americans. And of course, *coger* is innocently 'catch' in Spain and the Caribbean but a synonym of *joder* in many other areas.

The so-called standard word or meaning often coexists with a regional one, sometimes as formal vs. colloquial. Other times the term that Spaniards, at least, take to be standard is known elsewhere just as a book word, if at all. Etymologically, local terms derive from a variety of sources (Kany 1951; Zamora Vicente 1967; Cotton and Sharp 1988):

Older terms now archaic or marginal in Spain: *frazada* for *manta, lindo* for *bonito, fundo* for *finca, recibirse* for *licenciarse, prieto* for *oscuro, agora* for *ahora, ñudo* for *nudo*

Nautical terms generalized by seafaring colonists: *jalar ~ halar* for *tirar de, arribar* for *llegar, amarrar* for *atar*

Local neologisms using native morphemes and patterns: *dar una caminata* for *dar un paseo, arriba de* for *encima de, carniar* for *matar reses, nomás* for *sólo*

Borrowings from Amerindian languages: (Nahuatl) *cacahuete, tamal*; (Pipil) *cipote* 'niño', *peche* 'delgado'; (Quechua) *poncho, alpaca*; (Arawak) *yuca, jején, cacique, ají, papagayo, caimán, colibrí*

Borrowings from immigrant languages: (Italian) *chao, pibe*; (African languages), *ñame, marimba, dengue, banana*

Anglicisms from "el coloso del norte," often matched by Gallicisms from Spain's own "coloso del norte": *suiche = interruptor, chequear = revisar, zípper = cremallera, computador(a) = ordenador, software = logicial*

As Marrone (1974) noted, many differences arose as new products diffused through different societies before academies could come up with a standard term that all might accept. She interviewed students from each Spanish-speaking country and compiled their answers for forty-three items, among them the following (for which just six countries' usages are reported here):

- 'ballpoint': (Arg.) *biro(me),* (Col.) *lapicero,* (Cuba) *bolígrafo,* (Mex.) *pluma,* (Peru) *estilográfica,* (Spain) *bolígrafo ~ párker*
- 'folder': (Arg., Cuba, Spain) *carpeta,* (Col.) *fólder,* (Mex. and Peru) *cartapacio*
- 'faucet' (Arg.) *canilla,* (Col., Cuba) *llave,* (Mex.) *bitoque ~ llave,* (Peru) *caño,* (Spain) *grifo ~ pila*
- 'lightbulb': (Arg.) *lamparita,* (Col.) *bombilla ~ foco,* (Mex.) *foco,* (Cuba, Peru, Spain) *bombilla*
- 'closet': (Arg.) *placar(d),* (Col., Cuba, Mex., Peru) *clóset,* (Spain) *armario*
- 'pickup truck': (Arg., Peru) *picap ~ camioneta,* (Col., Mex.) *camioneta,* (Cuba) *pisicorre,* (Spain) *camioneta ~ furgoneta*

For 'bra', she found almost a dozen terms, and for 'panties', sixteen.

The degree of dialect divergence in Spanish is disputed. Those who assert their cultural autonomy may emphasize and exaggerate differences; those who look to international *hispanidad* interpret diversity as a communal wealth of resources available to all; those with strong beliefs about *casticidad* condemn local terms as *vulgarismos* that the "educated" avoid. But it must be borne in mind that the overwhelming bulk of Spanish vocabulary is held in common; unless the topic is uniquely one of local color, Spanish speakers from different countries or provinces really have little trouble understanding one another. Moreover, many regionalisms soon achieve broader currency through international communications, so that the dialectalness of a term becomes a matter of more-or-less rather than of here-but-never-there.

English dialects vary lexically too, between the United States and the United Kingdom (*elevator/lift, wrench/spanner, can/tin,* etc.) as well as inside the United States (*faucet/spigot, pail/bucket, quarter till/of/to*; see Kurath 1949), so students should not be surprised by similar variation in Spanish. Yet they often demand to know which term is "proper" Spanish, or (more to the point) which term they are expected to learn. Textbook writers confront the same problem; some try to adhere to one major country's usage (particularly Mexico's or Spain's), while others mix and match the equivalents: *coche carro, papa patata, computadora ordenador*. Spanish and English are international languages used by diverse societies and cultures and, unlike French, they are not defined by the cultural dominance of any one center; it is unreasonable to expect lexical uniformity in either, although pedagogy would certainly be simpler if that condition existed.

15.4 Different lexicons, different meanings. L2 learners expect to encounter different phonologies and grammars, but they tend to assume the same lexical organization. This is because a word denotes a concept, and monolinguals have had little experience with other conceptualizations; they assume that the things they see in the world are the same ones seen in other cultures, merely papered over with different labels. Foreign language materials generally do little to dispel this notion, introducing L2 words with L1 glosses as if they matched exactly. If one gloss is given, as in *la cena: dinner,* students proceed to adopt *cena* in all contexts where they have used *dinner,* just exchanging one name for another for the same Anglophone concept. If several glosses are given, as in the following dictionary entry,

GRADE: el grado; la clase; la calidad; la pendiente; la nota; a nivel

students construe the multiple equivalents as synonyms and arbitrarily choose one of them in translating their English thoughts; as one student wrote in an essay, *La maestra me dio la pendiente "A"*. Even if students realize that *grade* is a polyseme with several distinct senses (*grade* of an incline ≠ *grade* for class work), many dictionaries fail to clarify which Spanish word renders which meaning or to offer examples that would let users infer this for themselves.

15.4.1 Differences in denotation and connotation. Exact matches exist for relatively few concepts, such as common everyday objects, universally perceived characteristics, and international measurements and technical terms: *broom = escoba, hand = mano, red = rojo, kilometer = kilómetro, electricity = electricidad, lithium = litio.* Even if two languages agree on the basic senses or DENOTATIONS of such words, however, they may differ in their CONNOTATIONS, the subjective nuances carried by them. Some connotations are universal because of common psychological, biological, and ecological elements shared by all human beings; 'mother', for example, conjures up warm associations throughout the world (Osgood 1963). Others depend on the culture of a society. For instance, the denotations of *bargaining* and *regateo* are close enough, but the affect and situational appropriateness evoked by the two are quite different. Likewise, *church* and *home* may not evoke quite the same images as *iglesia* and *hogar,* and *honor* and *pull* may not be seen the same way as Hispanic *honor* and *enchufe/palanca*. In fact, returning to our one-to-one matches, we could say that *kilómetro* cannot be what a kilometer is in a society that still regards it as an alien conversion from miles.

In order to explore the cultural implications of connotation, Díaz Guerrero and Szalay (1991) gave Americans, Mexicans, and Colombians selected cue words and had them write other words that occurred to them by free association. Following is a small sampling of the most common responses of English-speaking Americans vs. Spanish-speaking Mexicans (the Colombians generally sided with the Mexicans):

1. father: dad, family, children, mother . . .
   padre: respeto, autoridad, amor, comprensión, trabajo, amigo, apoyo . . .
2. wife: woman, sex, companion, friend, marriage, mother, cook, house, love . . .
   esposa: mujer, compañera, amiga, matrimonio, madre, casa, amor, comprensión, fiel . . .
3. help: aid, assist, cry, trouble, emergency, need . . .
   ayudar: apoyo, gente, cooperar, compartir, entender . . .
4. security: police, guard, money, safe, lock, family . . .
   seguridad: estabilidad, familia, tranquilidad, bienestar . . .
5. government: politics, country, democracy, bureaucracy, laws, taxes . . .
   gobierno: política, país, presidente, pueblo, poder, corrupto, injusto . . .
6. power: electricity, energy, strength, control . . .
   poder: fuerza, potencia, autoridad, dinero, mandar, explotación . . .

Some of the associations (e.g., *wife—woman, esposa—mujer*) are denotative and held in common by the two groups, but others do seem to support the cultural contrasts the authors point out.

Yet not even denotations match in much of the Spanish and English lexicons. Some linguists and philosophers have considered thought to be essentially amorphous and unstructured in itself; by demarcating word-sized "concepts," it is language that imposes cognitive structuring on this amorphous "substance" (to use Saussure's terminology, [1915] 1959, 111). To the extent that their lexical setups differ, speakers of different languages might be led to think, perceive, relate, and reason differently (Whorf 1956).

One graphic way of contrasting lexical structure is with series of linear correspondences (Stockwell, Bowen, and Martin 1965, 274). Whereas some words match up rather well, as shown in (a) of figure 15.2, others correspond to a LEXICAL GAP remedied by a phrase or

Figure 15.2. Types of lexical correspondences

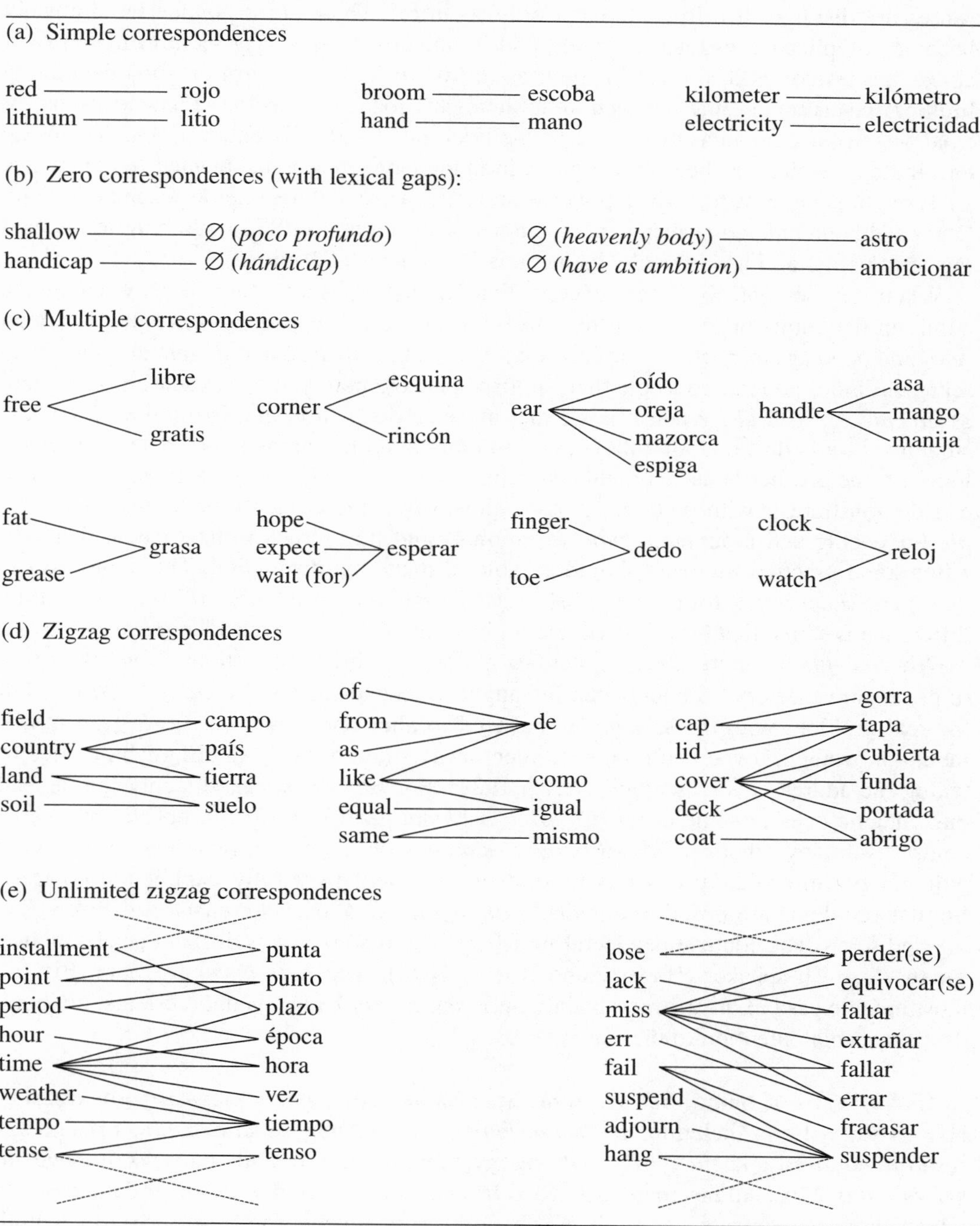

borrowing, as in (b). More often, there are multiple correspondences in which different senses are distinguished by different words, as in (c). These correspondences ultimately become complicated zigzags, as in (d), and in numerous cases they seem to march right across the lexicon with no end in sight, as in (e). To impose control on such dauntingly limitless vistas, many linguists and anthropologists focus on specific SEMANTIC FIELDS (or WORD FIELDS), lexical areas that are fairly well delimited and self-contained. One is kinship terminology, which has been investigated in many languages and subjected to contrastive analysis; in pedagogy, too, kinship words are often presented together as a semantic field. Other fields include color terms, prepositions of location (v. 10.3.3), clothing terms, and the adult/young and male/female distinctions for humans and animals.

When L2 uses one word for concepts that L1 distinguishes, students may perceive a common denominator that is the real meaning of the L2 word.[6] For example, although *reloj* and *dedo* are respectively divided into *clocks* and *watches,* and *fingers* and *toes,* they represent more general concepts that English speakers may know (but seldom verbalize) as *timepiece* and *digit.* When it is L2 that makes a distinction that is missing in L1, the students' task is different, and they might initially assume synonymy, as noted earlier for *grade*. If the distinction is clear and concrete, as with *rincón/esquina* or *pie/pata,* teachers can demonstrate it with pictures, glosses ('inside/outside corner'), or injunctions ("use *pie* for people and mountains, *pata* for animals and furniture—in most cases, that is"). After some practice, students should be able to make the distinction. This is not to say that they accept it yet, for their English-based "common sense" may still suggest that the difference is semantically picky, a useless nicety required by a weird language.

When distinctions are abstract, neither glosses nor brief injunctions (much less pictures) ensure mastery.[7] Students can be taught to amend their *I'm coming* to *Ya voy,* but the real problem with *ir* vs. *venir* is the need to alter one's own perspective on movement—movement toward self vs. movement away—and to avoid the English practice of taking the addressee's viewpoint (Jensen 1982). For *saber/conocer,* students can depend on syntactic cues in some cases (*Conozco a Elena,* not **Sé a Elena*), but the two verbs contrast in many others (*¿Sabes/Conoces esta canción?*), and the two kinds of knowing will not be immediately obvious to students, nor will they fully exploit the contrast. Similar problems are posed by *tomar/llevar, dejar/salir/irse, igual/mismo, pedir/preguntar,* and so on. The contrast between English *make* and *do* is just as difficult an abstraction for the Spanish speaker (Hagerty and Bowen 1973), who uses *hacer* for both. But the most notable case of an abstract distinction is *ser* vs. *estar,* and even the briefest textbook devotes special attention to these two verbs.

15.4.2 Verbs of being: *Ser* vs. *estar*. Spanish actually has a variety of verbs translatable as English *be*, including *ser, estar, haber, hacer, tener, quedar, sentar, verse, salir, resultar, hallarse,* and *encontrarse*. Pedagogy, however, traditionally narrows the focus to *ser* vs. *estar*. Most studies thereof proceed from an analysis of three sorts of data: cases in which only *ser* appears, those in which only *estar* appears, and those in which both appear in contrast. Examples of each case follow.[8]

Set 1: *ser* only

1a. Ya es tarde: son las cinco.

1b. Hoy es lunes. Ella es abogada. Ese es el vagón de primera clase. Tres más cuatro son siete.

1c. Es de España, es español. Es de María, es suyo. Es de plástico. Es de mucho interés.

1d. ¿Cuál es la fecha? Es el doce.

1e. Es que no lo saben. Puede ser que estén equivocados. ¡Esto no será!

Set 2: *estar* only

2a. Está corriendo.

2b. La finca está al norte (a 10 km. de aquí, cerca del río, en otra parte).

2c. Ella está sin empleo (en su tercer año).

2d. La ley está en vigor. El semáforo está en rojo.

2e. Está de prisa (de acuerdo, de luto, de vacaciones, de moda, de viaje, de cónsul, de turno).

2f. ¿A cuánto estamos? Estamos a doce.

2g. ¿Está el gerente? No, no está.

Set 3: *ser* vs. *estar*

3a. Son/Están para verlo mejor.

3b. La casa fue/estuvo destruida.

3c. El banquete (La sinfonía) es/está en otro cuarto.

3d. Mi casa es/está en Almería. Allí es/está Caracas.

3e. ¿Cómo es/está? Es/está malo, loco, listo, vivo, seguro, limpio, pobre, antipático, caro, bajo, sabroso, agrio, ciego, enfermo, borracho . . .

There is little dispute about the first two sets. *Estar* forms progressives (2a) and locates, literally (2b) or figuratively (2c). More precisely, *estar* locates definite NPs and *haber* handles indefinite ones (Bull 1965, 174): *¿Están ahí los médicos?* vs. *¿Hay ahí médicos/un médico?*[9] *Ser* is used with most other Predicate Attributes (PAs) to give the time (1a), identify or equate (1b), state origin/possession/purpose/makeup (1c), and so on. In a few cases such as (2d)–(e), the reason for copula selection seems obscure; perhaps these are extensions of location, or perhaps idioms. The expression of dates allows either copula, but in different constructions; this can be explained as alternative strategies (equation in (1d), location in a series in (2f)) for the same message. Except with *estar* 'be in, present' (2g) and with *ser* as a verb of existence (1e), there is usually some kind of PA determining selection, so that the two copulas are almost in complementary distribution (Stockwell, Bowen, and Martin 1965, 170), like allophones of one phoneme (v. 1.2).

But this is not true in set 3, where they occur with the same PA and contrast in meaning. The contrast in (3a) is perhaps just a superficial convergence of *ser para* for purpose and the (idiom?) *estar para* 'be about to'. Item (3b) contrasts a passivized event with the state resulting therefrom (v. 12.3). For (3c) one bears in mind that certain nouns represent either things or events; as things, they are located with *estar,* and as events, with *ser* ('take place'). Item (3d) also permits options: the speaker can either equate the noun with the place (*Caracas es allí*) or locate it there (*Caracas está allí*). It is when the PA is an Adj (3e), or its interrogative (*cómo*), that disagreements have arisen. We will examine below two main positions, one that can be called "traditional" and the other that is based on the converging views of Navas Ruiz (1963) and Bull (1965).[10]

The traditional explanation was laid down by the earlier grammars of the RAE (1924, 172), although it should probably be traced back to a comment from Bello ([1847] 1958, 200). With Adj, *ser* supposedly denotes permanent qualities while *estar* indicates transitory or accidental conditions. As worked out in many U.S. textbooks, this dichotomy has blossomed into the following five-part treatment:

- *ser*: permanence, inherence, characteristic or innate quality, natural state, essence
- *estar*: temporariness, accidental condition, transience, semblance of being
- exceptions to the above
- memorizable combinations: *ser* + nationality, *ser* + affiliation, and so on
- adjectives that "change meaning" according to the copula:[11]

es/está alto 'is tall/high'
es/está bueno 'is good/well'
es/está callado 'is taciturn/quiet'
es/está cierto 'is true/assured'
es/está listo 'is clever/ready'
es/está verde 'is green/unripe'
es/está malo 'is bad/sick'
es/está seguro 'is reliable/protected'

This approach persists today, and after many generations of confused students and of critical linguists and teachers, its durability through several revolutions in teaching methodology is a tribute to inertia in matters of pedagogical substance. The criticisms are directed at three serious inadequacies. First, the notions offered as criteria for copula selection are too vague for students to apply because they are questions of metaphysics, not of communication (Navas Ruiz 1963). Is a judgment of width natural or subjective? Are paper's whiteness, nature's variety, and humans' goodness essential or accidental? Are wealth, poverty, age, and psychological disposition temporary or permanent? What *are* essences, conditions, qualities, and semblances in the first place? As Bull (1965, 295) observed, "modern science cannot, with certainty, determine what is an inherent characteristic, and the difference between a quality and a condition becomes, in many instances, a subject for philosophical debate." Of course, there is nothing wrong with a debate on essences in a philosophy class, but few Spanish classes have the time to indulge in one just to practice two verbs for an activity on description.

Second, it wrongly depicts copula selection as automatically cued by the referent (the thing being referred to): snow must be described as *es blanca,* a citizen as *es francés,* and a person as either *es lista* if clever or *está lista* if ready. Yet Gili Gaya (1973, 60–65) noted that one can say both *el chico es alto* and *el chico está alto* for tallness rather than height, and both *la nieve es blanca* and *la nieve está blanca* for snow's whiteness. Bull (1965, 293) added that a person's cleverness can be expressed as either *es lista* or *está lista*;

Navas Ruiz (1963, 165–66) pointed out many other counterexamples, including *está muy francesa.* Thus, with adjectives the choice of copula is not automatic, but depends on what the speaker chooses to convey.

Third, to the extent that the traditional approach's notions are clear at all, they work in a few cases, seem forced in others, and are flatly contradicted by many others (Gili Gaya 1973). Virtually any generalization about human behavior has exceptions, but those that this approach must concede are glaring. Some of Navas Ruiz's observations are pertinent in this respect:

- *Ella es protestante,* yet religious affiliation is neither innate nor necessarily permanent
- *La casa es azul,* yet blueness is not inherent when the house must be painted that color
- *Es español,* although having Spanish citizenship is not a "quality"
- *¡Qué fría está la nieve!* although snow's coldness is an inherent quality by definition
- *Está muerto,* although death is permanent, and a natural state to boot

Bull (1965, 295) added that "there are few states more temporary than being young and none more permanent than being old, yet the Spaniard expresses both with either *ser* or *estar*." It is the theory with such holes in it that is anomalous, not its accumulating exceptions; and to continue using it, in Bull's words, is "to perpetuate a fraud on the students" (ibid.).

For Bull, the key to *ser* vs. *estar* is NORM. Attributes that the speaker takes to be normal for an entity are expressed with *ser,* while deviations or changes from the norm are shown by *estar. Estar* accompanies *muerto* because death is a change from the original condition in which one is remembered; its permanence, innateness, or semblance of being are beside the point. *Es viejo* indicates how one generally visualizes a certain individual; *está viejo* indicates a change in how the person strikes the speaker after an interval. The grass of a region *es verde* or *está verde* regardless of "ripeness"; it may be normally green, or greened up by a post-drought shower. With *es triste/enfermo/borracho*, the speaker regards a person as typically gloomy, prone to sickness, given to drunkenness; *está triste/enfermo/borracho* implies that these are aberrations from the person's usual or expected behavior or condition.

Four points are crucial for applying Bull's theory. First, "change" can simply be a greater degree of the attribute than usual, not necessarily a switch to the opposite. In *¡Qué altas están aquellas montañas!* and *Luisa no sabe lo bonita que está,* the speaker is suggesting that the observed mountains seem especially high for him/her (in comparison with others) and that Louise is especially good-looking today, rather than implying that a lot of mountain-building occurred overnight or that Louise has been ugly. Second, norms are subjective and relative to the individual's own perceptions, expectations, and generalization from prior experience. One person may describe carrots as *son ricas,* whereas another who hated them until trying them with a special marinade might say *están ricas.* In fact, a single individual can choose between different perspectives on the same observation. On being introduced to new software, he/she could form a norm from the evidence of this first contact and declare *Este programa es ingenioso,* or compare it to his/her existing norm for computer programs that seemed awkward and say *Este programa está ingenioso.* Third, norms can be revised and adjusted, as when one describes a heavy friend who lost weight as *está flaco,* and then later—with the friend's new weight stabilizing and seeming normal now—as *es flaco* (Bull 1972). And fourth, sometimes change is so constant, two opposing states so equally likely, and conditions so variable, that there is no real norm at all, as in *está cerrada* for a door or *está despejado* for a changing sky.

Although Bull's theory works to a large extent, sometimes the norm/deviation distinction becomes fuzzy.[12] Gili Gaya (1973, 63) observed that the contrast blurs when the aspectual force of the preterite or present perfect imposes a termination of a state and therefore a change: "toda persona de lengua española siente de un modo más o menos confuso que una frase como *esta señora ha sido elegante en otro tiempo* presenta muy atenuado el matiz que la separa de *esta señora ha estado elegante en otro tiempo.* Entre *la reunión fue muy lucida* y *la reunión estuvo muy lucida* apenas si notamos la diferencia." For Gili Gaya, then, any theory of *ser/estar* must eventually be tied to verbal aspect.

One of the fullest treatments was that of Navas Ruiz (1963). He compared *ser* and *estar* with other copulas (*ir, ponerse, resultar, parecer, quedar,* etc.), examined contrasts with all kinds of adjectives, and surveyed almost two dozen theories, discarding all of them. He agreed that *estar* implies change, and that copula selection depends on the speaker's point of view rather than on laws of grammar or metaphysics (p. 148). He rejected, though, the description of *ser* + Adj as "norm" because some uses of *estar* portray seemingly normal states: *la nieve de allí siempre está blanquísima, las camas de este hotel están limpias, la biblioteca está llena de libros.* His own generalization was as follows. *Ser* sets up a neutral relationship between an entity and an attribute; it is "un verbo enteramente gramaticalizado cuya función atributiva es señalar la mera relación" (p. 147). It does little else but "aportar unos caracteres verbales" to the PA, allowing a VP to be formed around it. Depending on the specific attribute and entity, one infers a relationship of classification, definition, identification, or expression of norm, but *ser* does not denote any of these in and of itself; the only sense it contributes is abstraction from the vicissitudes of time and duration—it is *atemporal*, timeless (pp. 171, 193). *Estar,* on the other hand, never imposes identity between Subj and PA, but establishes the possession of the attribute for a period of time; it is therefore *temporal* ('contingent on time', not 'temporary'). Since relating a Subj to a PA in time brings up possible cessation, result, intermittence, interruption, or a shift in viewpoint, *estar* implies mutability, similar to Bull's change or deviation:

> Cuando un individuo afirma: *la nieve es blanca,* no se trata de que objetivamente la nieve no pueda ponerse sucia, sino que subjetivamente, en aquel momento de su aserto, la ve así, blanca y sin posibilidad de no serlo. . . . Cuando

un individuo, por el contrario, afirma: *la nieve está blanca,* la ve como susceptible de cambio desde su punto de mira subjetivo, bien porque pueda ensuciarse o bien porque pueda estar menos blanca. (p. 147)

It is likely that the *ser/estar* contrast causes problems for the English speaker not because it is so much harder than other distinctions based on the speaker's viewpoint, but because many textbook writers fail to present it and practice it in terms that are clear, applicable, and accurate.

15.5 Idioms. Economy is gained in language by expressing special meanings through combinations of old words instead of neologisms. These are IDIOMS, phrases whose meaning is not the sum of the meanings of their parts. For example, although *meter la pata* and *tomarle el pelo* can mean literally 'stick in the paw' and 'take someone's hair', in many contexts they bear the special meanings of 'blow it' and 'pull one's leg'; the same observation applies to these two English expressions, which also have both literal and idiomatic meanings. Like *meter la pata* and *tomarle el pelo,* many idioms are fossilized metaphors:

dar en el clavo	echar sapos y culebras	estar en la luna
estirar la pata	poner por las nubes	no tener pelos en la lengua
meter la nariz	pedirle peras al olmo	dar gato por liebre
contra viento o marea	por si las moscas	entre la espada y la pared

Word formation can be based on metaphor too: *empantanado* and *bogged down* refer literally to being in a *pantano/bog,* but both also carry the meaning 'stuck, unable to proceed'.

Like proverbs (v. 16.2), metaphorical idioms evolve from the collective cultural experiences of a people, some of which are shared with other cultures. Thus, English speakers recognize some Spanish idioms as similar to their own: *dar en el clavo* should be clear to those who also regard 'hitting the nail on the head' as a measure of accuracy. Other idioms make sense in a suitable context, although they will seem unusual when their metaphor is not a salient image in English speakers' culture or a familiar vehicle of meaning in their linguistic experience; such is the case with *pedirle peras al olmo.* Still other idioms are deeply embedded in their respective cultures: *echar sapos y culebras* may seem bizarre to someone whose culture associated obscenity with blueness (*swear a blue streak*) rather than with medievally demonic toads and snakes. We can also cite the vivid contrast of the following Venezuelan substitutes for *nunca* (Gómez de Ivashevsky 1969, 227) with the English speaker's *when hell freezes over*:

cuando la rana eche pelos	cuando el gallo ponga
cuando el chato eche nariz	cuando San Juan agache el dedo

Some expressions are treated as idioms merely because their construction is fixed. In *Lo mató a sangre fría* there is no particular semantic or syntactic reason for the use of *a*; it does not have its literal meaning(s), is not required by the transitivity of *matar* or the nature of *sangre,* and does not reflect the speaker's choice of this Prep over *de, con, hacia,* and so on for a PP with a distinct message. *A sangre fría* is a set expression and *a* is an integral part of it (v. 10.4.1), just like the *in* of the corresponding English *in cold blood.*

Other expressions seem idiomatic not because their meaning or construction is totally arbitrary but because their usual sense is more specific than grammar alone might predict. For example, in both languages the combining of 'give' with 'hand' in a sentence opens up a wide range of potential meanings, including the literal (if unlikely) one of presenting a disconnected limb. But English has specifically narrowed down *give a hand* to assistance or applause, whereas Spanish has settled on handshaking for *dar la mano* and a manual application of paint for *dar una mano.* The narrowed senses are both logical in their own way and might be inferred from context, but they are not predictable from 'give' + 'hand' alone, nor do they match.

In pedagogy, IDIOM is misapplied to locutions whose meaning is clear to native speakers. Thus, English *housebroken* and *housewarming* are so semantically specialized (no connection to cracked homes or domestic heating) that they can be regarded as true idioms, as opposed to *housekeeper* and *house keys,* whose meanings are transparent to English speakers; using the same patterns, they can say *storekeeper* and *store keys,* whereas **storebroken* is odd. Yet to the Spanish speaker, any such compounds could be puzzling. Likewise, *get* + particle (*in, out, down, through, over, under*) makes sense to an English speaker, for whom *get* is an all-purpose verb of attainment, whether of things or of states, postures, and locations; but for the Spanish speaker, who uses *obtener* or *conseguir* for the attainment of things but verbs of movement or becoming otherwise, any two-word verb (v. 10.5) with *get* seems strange and therefore idiomatic.

Conversely, many Spanish expressions are labeled as idioms just because they strike English speakers as odd when analyzed in terms of English equivalents. As Kirshner (1951, 88) put it, students approach language learning with the premise that "Spanish is crazy and unpredictable whereas English is a model of clarity"; any Spanish expression that is different is weird and is relegated to the idiom list of the vocabulary. Yet many such collocations belong to systematic, productive patterns, and they make perfect sense to one who exploits them regularly. *Hacer* in *hace frío/viento/falta/tiempo que . . .* is impersonal, but otherwise not far off its basic meaning of 'producir, causar, componer' (RAE 1956, 693); to those who have grown up using different verbs in such contexts, however, it will seem more idiomatic than it is. Likewise, the vast series of collocations with *tener* (*frío, calor, razón, gracia, cuidado, ganas, miedo, hambre, sed, prisa, __ años*) is systematic in that the V relates one N to another in an attributive, nonclassificatory manner. *Tiene veinte años* is no idiom; this is how Spanish *normally* expresses measurements (*tiene ___ metros de largo*); nor is *tiene miedo/sed/calor/ganas* idiomatic when *dar* just as systematically expresses the onset of these conditions (*me da miedo/sed/calor/ganas*). Indeed,

English uses its *have* in the same way: *have a suspicion, a fever, a dread, a mind to, a hankering, a grudge, patience,* and so on. But English speakers happen not to choose this *have* pattern when an NP strikes them as cold, humorous, careful, or of a certain age or size. Hence, *tener paciencia* never appears in idiom lists for English speakers while *tener __ años* and *tener cuidado* always do, even though they are all cast out of the same mold and are definitely not idiomatic for Spanish speakers. As DiPietro (1971, 130) said, "a student is not likely to notice that *tener años* is an idiom in Spanish, meaning 'to be X years of age', if he speaks a language with a comparable expression, such as Italian *aver anni.*" Idioms do exist, but some are less idiomatic than others.

Notes for chapter 15

1. I have seen estimates of adult vocabulary size ranging from twenty-six thousand words to one hundred thousand; I choose sixty thousand here as the approximate midpoint of this range. But all such figures are conjectures, and if we were to attempt the daunting task of counting how many words an adult knows, several problems would arise. One is that the lexicon is not static, but keeps changing with continued education and new experiences. Another problem is the lack of agreement on the "words" to be counted. Should the hosts of proper names and their derivatives be included? Do *más allá* 'beyond', *irse* 'leave', and *año luz* 'light year' count as single terms or as phrases? Are *ella* and *la, amar* and *amante*, *mal* and *malísimo* six distinct words or variants of three? Do pairs such as *el frente* 'front' and *la frente* 'forehead', *gracioso* 'witty' and *gracioso* 'comic character', *cuándo* 'when?' and *cuando* 'when', and *auto* and *automóvil* 'car' constitute single or separate lexical entries? Many thousands of items would be affected by one's answer to such questions.

2. Spanish affixes deriving N and Adj from V are preceded by a form of the theme vowel (v. 6.1): *observ**a**ción/repet**i**ción, observ**a**torio/dorm**i**torio, cant**a**nte/crec**i**ente, cas**a**miento/crec**i**miento, resbal**a**dizo/beb**e**dizo*. For V infinitives that have become nouns (*el poder, el parecer, el lejano susurrar del viento*), see Díaz 1989.

3. See Gootch 1970 and Cruzado 1982 for fuller analyses of Spanish diminutives and augmentatives.

4. The suffixes *-ismo* and *-ista* have broadened their meaning and function. *Nerviosismo* is just a noun equivalent of *nervioso,* 'condition of being *nervioso*', not a doctrine, and people who, because of their work, are called *socorristas, oficinistas, electricistas,* and *futbolistas* have no defining *-isms* as groups.

5. In an experiment with native Spanish speakers, Eddington (1995) showed that they do perceive relatedness between words, but that it is on the basis of semantic and superficial phonetic similarity. Thus, his subjects related *carrera* to *correr* and *llanto* to *llorar*, pairs that have no morphophonemic or etymological connection.

6. This is not to imply that when L2 has one word corresponding to two or three in L1, L2 necessarily has "one concept" for these. Nobody can really define the concepts in anyone's mind, and it is debatable whether the Spanish speaker has only one concept in *esperar* where the English speaker sees the distinct ones of *waiting, hoping,* and *expecting.* After all, there is a Spanish distinction in the noun derivatives *la esperanza* vs. *la espera*. Vice versa, although *dull* covers the ground of both

deslustrado and *desfilado,* English distinguishes the two concepts or senses in the antonyms *shiny* for *dull* 'deslustrado' vs. *sharp* for *dull* 'desfilado' (Stockwell, Bowen, and Martin 1965, 273).

7. For a rich source for Spanish semantic and stylistic distinctions, see Batchelor and Pountain 1992, and more specifically Batchelor 1994.

8. It will be assumed in these contrasts that the structures are comparable. Thus, we ignore cases such as *¿Es el gerente?* vs. *¿Está el gerente?,* which resemble each other in surface structure but consist of copula + PA vs. copula + Subj.

9. According to Suñer (1982, 324), this *estar* = definite and *haber* = indefinite dichotomy works "95%" of the time and therefore has pedagogical value; but it is not foolproof. She studied counterexamples such as the following:

Allí había el diamante más grande del mundo.
Siempre hay la tendencia a la inercia, ¿no?
¿Hay el sistema ese en tu país?
—¿Cómo voy al centro? —Pues, hay el colectivo, y el subte . . .
Una pecera de cristal estaba sobre una mesita.

She concluded that *haber* asserts a NP's existence and presents it into discourse, while *estar* locates a NP whose existence is presupposed—which usually (but not always) implies definiteness.

10. Other contributions to the debate fall in between. DaSilva (1982, 141–47) conceded the inaccuracy of the traditional approach but tried to salvage it anyway, without success. Ramsey ([1894] 1956) started with a traditional classification but arrived at a conclusion similar to Bull's: "frequently the use of *estar* implies that the state is different from the normal or expected" (p. 310). Stockwell, Bowen, and Martin (1965, 171) began with 'classification' for *ser* vs. 'comment' for *estar* but then took a position similar to Bull's.

11. The list of putative meaning-changers with *ser* and *estar* varies according to the analyst; these come from Ramsey ([1894] 1956). Zierer (1974, 18–32) generated a long list of them distributed among eighteen different categories.

12. We do not always bear this fuzziness of semantic distinctions in mind when we expect either-or choices from students. In English, *up the street* contrasts with *down the street*—until we give directions on a level street, in which case we use either with no difference. Likewise, the *ser/estar* contrast is stronger in some contexts than in others.

Exercises for chapter 15

1. Error analysis: the following sentences are composites of real lexical problems from student writing. Explain each error and contrast its intended meaning with possible interpretations by a monolingual Spanish speaker.

(a) Tuvieron una cambia en su vivo estilo.
(b) Hay tormentos con trueno y aligeramiento.
(c) Tenemos que parar la raza del ratón.
(d) En este drama, al carácter principal le gustan chinches de rayo.
(e) Mi madre es una mujer belleza que vino de Europeo.
(f) Mi amiga perece muy joven; ejerce y juega muchos deportivos.
(g) Cuando escribes de un sujeto, debes soportarlo con evidencia.

2. Divide the following words into their morphemes using morpheme boundaries (+), bracketing, or trees (as in figure 15.1), as indicated by your instructor. For example (using +), *nerviosismo* = *nervi(o)+os(o)+ismo, aclarado* = *a+clar(o)+a+do.* As in these examples, show in parentheses sounds/letters that are morphophonemically dropped in derivation.

(a) incomodidad	(i) veintiseisavo	(q) apesadumbrado
(b) sentimental	(j) descompusieron	(r) limpiaparabrisas
(c) enojadizo	(k) avioncitos	(s) sobreviviente
(d) retención	(l) rítmicamente	(t) descuidadísimo
(e) enredaderas	(m) enloquecido	(u) ajusticiamiento
(f) lluviosa	(n) maniatados	(v) estadounidenses
(g) brillantez	(o) asociaciones	(w) desembarcadero
(h) invencible	(p) trabajadoras	(x) ininterrumpidamente

3. (a) To what extent is *-illo* really a diminutive suffix ('smaller version of'), given the specialized meanings of nouns such as the following?

ventanilla	planilla	tornillo	pasillo
camilla	vainilla	casilla	bocadillo
barbilla	tortilla	mantequilla	guerrilla
bombilla	cerilla	gatillo	bastardillas

(b) What is the semantic effect of the diminutive in *ahorita, calientito,* and *verdecito*?

4. The derivation *eléctrico* → *electricidad* shows two morphophonemic rules: the dropping of a final vowel (*eléctric**o***) before adding a vowel-initial suffix (*-idad*), and /k/ → /θ ~ s/ before a front vowel. Demonstrate the generality of both rules in the derivatives of *paso, casa, grande, joya, estúpido, suave, rojo, moda, grasa, opaco, sueco, místico*.

5. Many Latinate words in English do not have the cognates the student might expect in Spanish: **procrastinar, *expectar.* The reverse situation exists too, in Latinate Spanish words with no English counterparts. English may have the morphemes that make up such words, but not the words themselves. Following are some examples; can you think of others? To what extent would these give students trouble in comprehending them?

ambicionar	flexibilizar	tremendista	autoproclamación
colisionar	profundizar	posibilitar	problemática (noun)

6. The following list gives more "amigos falsos." Give (a) the English word(s) closest to each one for its usual meaning(s) and (b) the English word closest to it in appearance and a possible source of error. Model: *facultad = school, college, ≠faculty* 'profesorado'.

bombero	suceder, suceso	atender	asistir
intentar	desplazar(se)	contesta	renta, -able
manifestación	pretender	armar	quieto
recordar	jubilación	hacienda	sano
constipado	sujetar	pariente	retirar
sopa	ropa	librería	discutir

7. Explain the intended meaning of *integrar* and *resistir* in the following newspaper headlines, and the ways that English speakers might misunderstand them as cognates. Then try to find other examples of passages that English speakers might misinterpret because of "false friends."

Los jueces integraron el nuevo comité estatal.
España resistiría el cierre del estrecho de Ormuz.

8. Construct zigzag diagrams (as in figure 15.2) for denotative lexical correspondences between English and Spanish, using each of the following (or the ones assigned by your instructor) as a point of departure.

put (V)	smooth (Adj)	take	thick	add	hole
last (Adj)	soft	little	fit (V)	meet	agree

9. The question of how to present word meaning has been an enduring controversy in foreign language teaching. Consider the following techniques and discuss their pros and cons in view of the multiple aspects of meaning discussed in chapters 14 and 15. To make the question more concrete, consider specific examples and contexts, for example, 'grade' as illustrated in 15.4.

(I) Direct method: exclusively through L2, without recourse to L1
  (a) demonstration (pointing, showing, acting out, using visuals and realia)
  (b) contextual inference (teacher-talk with sufficient repetition and paraphrase of a new word to develop comprehension)
  (c) definition of the L2 word in L2 (as in monolingual dictionaries)

(II) Interlingual: explaining an L2 word via L1
  (a) simple glossing (matching to the one sense needed for the lesson)
  (b) multiple glosses (two or more senses)
  (c) multiple glosses with clarification and illustrative sentences for each

10. It was pointed out that idioms may or not seem idiomatic to native speakers. The following sets are often treated as idiomatic in textbooks; indicate whether you regard each as truly idiomatic in Spanish, and why or why not.

(a) trabar amistad, querer decir, hoy día, por si acaso, tal vez, por supuesto
(b) hacer +: mella en, aguas, caso, cola, falta, calor, -se con, juego (con), papel, hincapié
(c) dar +: a la calle, a conocer, ganas, a luz, una vuelta, contra (una pared), una ojeada
(d) echar +: al correo, la llave, la culpa, de menos, rayos, mano a, a perder
(e) llevar +: a cabo, libros, la cuenta, dos años de casado, el compás, -se bien con

11. Many Spanish nouns have adjectival equivalents (often derivatives of the same stem) that their English counterparts lack. In fact, at least in technical styles, such adjectives are freely created. Determine the affixes used for deriving adjectives that can substitute for each italicized PP below, and contrast the English equivalents. Example: una emisión *por televisión* → una emisión *televis**iva*** (English uses the compound *a television broadcast*).

una crisis *de bancos*	una costumbre *de Navidad*
la producción *de carbón*	unos problemas *con el presupuesto*
el movimiento *de la labor*	una conversación *por teléfono*
archivos *de la policía*	unos conflictos *de/en la frontera*

12. Onomatopoeia differs from one language to another almost as much as normal lexical items. See how many English/Spanish contrasts in sound effects you can collect. (A good source is comic strips.) For example, *bang—pum, woof/bowwow—guau.*

13. (a) What criticisms have been leveled at the traditional presentation of *ser/estar*? Where are the two copulas almost in "complementary distribution," and where do they contrast? How would you explain and illustrate the distinction to students?

(b) Following the mode of argument we used for *ser/estar*—from data (examples sorted into groups) to analysis and generalization—determine the distinctions among the various verbs of becoming in Spanish (*ponerse, volverse, hacerse, convertirse, llegar a ser . . .*).

14. Take a writing sample from a first- or second-year student of Spanish, and analyze the lexical problems and errors. Classify the apparent source of each one: English (Spanglish) such as **improvar* for *mejorar*, apparent misuse of the dictionary (as in the 'grade' example in section 15.4), and incorrect creations within Spanish (e.g., **cincocientos* for *quinientos*).

15. (a) It was pointed out that words often form sets called "semantic fields." One such area is sensation (Lindstrom 1980), as mapped out in the chart in figure 15.3. Fill in the remaining entries and then determine what differences, if any, would appear in English. To what extent might such classifications or listings be useful to students, and at what level? To what extent do many textbook writers already make use of semantic fields in their vocabularies?

(b) Choose some other semantic field and organize its terms in similar fashion.

16. In oral proficiency testing, examinees may talk smoothly in describing or narrating until they come up against something whose Spanish name they do not know or have forgotten. One of three things then happens: (1) their communication comes to an awkward halt; (2) they pause, plug in an English word (perhaps Hispanizing it), and stumble on; or (3) they circumlocute in Spanish around the gap and continue their story without interruption. According to the Educational Testing Service (1982), a few lexical gaps are not necessarily damaging to the evaluation, and successful circumlocution is even a plus. Why would circumlocuting and paraphrasing be a valued skill for a high performance level? How could teachers promote it?

Figure 15.3. A semantic field: nouns, verbs, and adjectives of sensation

sense	*body part*	*action*	*perception*	*stimulus*	*modifiers*
la vista	ojos	mirar	ver	color, forma, apariencia . . .	claro, oscuro, rojo, brillante, feo, hermoso, chillón, centelleante . . .
el olfato	. . .	. . .	. . .	. . .	. . .
el oído	. . .	. . .	. . .	. . .	. . .
el tacto	. . .	. . .	. . .	. . .	. . .
el gusto	. . .	. . .	. . .	. . .	. . .

17. The automobile culture has developed since the importation of Spanish into the New World, and terminology varies today. See how many Spanish equivalents you can find for the following semantic field, perhaps by comparing native-speaking informants.

(a) 'drive'
(b) 'turn around; turn at an intersection; turn a curve'
(c) 'pass (overtake) another vehicle'
(d) major parts of a car (e.g., 'hood', 'trunk', 'steering wheel', 'tire')
(e) types of vehicles: 'car', 'truck', 'station wagon', 'pickup', 'truck', 'van', 'bus'

18. Both *-ar* (*manzanar*) and *-al* (*peral*) can mean 'place where something is grown'. Collect as many examples of each as you can and try to determine a general rule for where each is used. Note: for studying suffixes it is useful to consult an INVERSE DICTIONARY (e.g., Bosque and Pérez Fernández 1987), which alphabetizes words by the way they end.

19. The following checklist for lexical variation between Spain and America is based on Steel 1975. Ask some native speakers their normal word for the item (if they do not speak English, elicit it with a definition, picture, or description), and check their usage against Steel's observations. After their first response, probe to see if they know the other term (and when and whether they might use it) or any other variants. You might add other items that occur to you, including other examples used in this chapter.

(a) 'sidewalk': America *vereda,* Spain *acera*
(b) 'pepper' (Capsicum): America *ají,* Spain *pimiento*
(c) 'tie': America *amarrar,* Spain *atar*
(d) 'pineapple': America *ananás,* Spain *piña*
(e) 'narrow': America *angosto,* Spain *estrecho*
(f) 'hurry up': America *apurarse,* Spain *darse prisa*
(g) 'peas': America *arvejas,* Spain *chícharos*
(h) 'bucket': America *balde,* Spain *cubo*
(i) 'ticket': America *boleto,* Spain *billete*
(j) 'throw away': America *botar,* Spain *tirar*
(k) 'earrings': America *caravanas ~ aretes,* Spain *pendientes*
(l) 'post office box': America *casilla,* Spain *apartado*
(m) 'ID card': America *cédula,* Spain *carné(t)*
(n) 'block': America *cuadra,* Spain *manzana*
(o) 'bedroom': America *recámara,* Spain *dormitorio*
(p) 'lock': America *chapa,* Spain *cerradura*
(q) 'peach': America *durazno,* Spain *melocotón*
(r) 'a stay (in a place)': America *estadía,* Spain *estancia*
(s) 'stamp': America *estampilla,* Spain *sello*
(t) 'money': America *plata,* Spain *dinero*
(u) 'lazy': America *flojo,* Spain *perezoso*
(v) 'drizzle': America *garúa,* Spain *llovizna*
(w) 'lightweight': America *liviano,* Spain *ligero*
(x) 'pretty': America *lindo,* Spain *bonito*
(y) 'peanut': America *maní,* Spain *cacahuete*
(z) 'socks': America *medias,* Spain *calcetines*

Chapter 16

Language knowledge and language use

16.0 Linguistic and communicative competence. Chomsky (1965) introduced the term COMPETENCE for the knowledge that native speakers have of their language: of its units, rules, and structures, and of what is grammatical and ungrammatical. This knowledge is generally unconscious; without training, one cannot easily describe question formation, vowel articulation, the use of determiners, or the placement of adverbs. In fact, to ask most Spanish speakers "¿Cómo se colocan las palabras en la oración?" would be about as fruitful as to ask "¿Cómo se resta?" or "¿Cómo se atan los cordones?" Yet they make skillful use of their language's units and rules for communicating, just as they quickly carry out subtractions or tie their shoelaces.

Although linguistic competence is fundamental and vast, speakers know and use much more in their communication. For one thing, they apply a knowledge of their world and culture that cannot always be separated from knowledge of language: to know the meanings of *entender, vaca* vs. *toro,* and *hostia* is to share with other speakers a certain understanding of practical epistemology, zoology, and religion (v. 14.1). Moreover, speakers constantly monitor how their message is being received, and their sentences reflect a tailoring to the situation as much as rules of grammar. Their speech is molded by their emotional states, premises, beliefs, cultural norms, and perception of consensus, and they follow certain linguistic routines prescribed by their societies. Expanding the scope still further, we observe that speakers accompany their verbal messages with nonverbal ones—eye contact, posture, facial expressions, body contact, and gestures (Coll, Gelabert, and Martinell 1990); these auxiliary modes, grouped together as PARALANGUAGE, can differ from one culture to another as much as morphemes and phonemes. Thus, it is hard to impose boundaries between language on the one hand and paralanguage, culture, and general world knowledge on the other. Linguistic competence is one part (a huge one, to be sure) of a broader COMMUNICATIVE COMPETENCE (Hymes 1972; Canale and Swain 1979).

Another part of communicative competence is PRAGMATICS (v. 0.1), the conventions for putting language to appropriate use. Specialists in pragmatics focus on two key factors:

The nature of the transaction, that is, the linguistic business that a speaker is trying to conduct in negotiation with the hearer(s). The word *pragmatics* derives from Greek *prâgma* 'matter, affair, business', with the related verb *pragmateúomai* 'carry out, do business'. If one's business is to give a persuasive scholarly presentation, for example, he/she does not adopt the same kind of language as when telling a joke or buying a drink.

The context, that is, situational information that speakers take into account when encoding a message and that hearers use in decoding it. "Context" includes a great deal, as summarized in figure 16.1, from the actual physical setting to the relevant information (called a SCHEMA) that speaker and hearer bring to bear on a topic and on what they say about it.

Throughout this book, we have noted that the units of language are used for carrying out certain functions; they do not exist by themselves in grammar books, but in the minds of speakers who use them to communicate meaning in context. Even phonology reflects pragmatics: intonation is part of the "key" of speech (Hymes 1974) and also conveys the speaker's beliefs and communication strategy, as shown by the following two versions of the same sentence (based on Lakoff 1971, 333; the numbers signal pitch, v. 4.2).

John called Mary a real lady, and then . . . (a) she in**SUL**ted him. (. . . 131↓)
(b) SHE insulted **HIM**. (. . . 314↓)

Version (a) presupposes that John paid Mary a compliment, whereupon she inexplicably turned on him; version (b) implies that *real lady* was taken as a sexist put-down, so that her response was understandable retaliation. This example shows that it is the whole background culture, and not just the physical microcontext, that affects interpretation; in a culture with different sensitivities, the thrust of (b) might be lost. At this point, then, linguists join up with sociologists and anthropologists in explaining communicative competence.

16.1 The pragmatics of the speaker-hearer relation. The most conspicuous figure in the social context of speech is the hearer, and the speaker makes certain assumptions about that hearer and about the EGO-ALTER ('I-other') relationship, as it is sometimes called. From those assumptions follow several linguistic decisions, among them the form of address, stylistic level, type of vocabulary to be used, and speaking strategies.

16.1.1 Address and reference, and *tú* vs. *usted*. In most textbooks, *tú* and *usted* are labeled respectively as "informal, intimate, familiar" vs. "formal, polite." Yet these labels have little meaning for someone who is unfamiliar with the norms of informality and politeness in Hispanic societies, and in specific situations they are unreliable. Any English speaker appreciates that speaking to one's spouse is intimate while speaking to royalty should be formal and polite. But what about speaking to an animal, a waiter, God,

Figure 16.1. The contexts of speech

Linguistic context	the surrounding discourse (CO-TEXT), into which each participant's contribution is expected to fit coherently
Physical context	the setting (place and time) of the interaction
Topical context	the range of topics that are currently out "on the table" for discussion
Social context	the participants' status, roles, and relationship as defined by their membership in a certain society
Emotional (affective) context	the participants' awareness of each other's state of mind and adaptations to that
Cultural context	customs and practices that are used or referred to during communication
Cognitive context	participants' background knowledge, and especially their schema for this kind of interaction on a subject

a seldom-seen young aunt, a beloved elderly aunt, a delivery person or secretary one sees periodically, a fellow student with whom there is no real intimacy, a favorite teacher, the dear old *señora* with whom one lodges, or someone who is called *don/doña* ____ with a *combination* of politeness and familiarity? How does one address audiences and exhort them to vote, to adopt modern farming methods, to buy a car, or to oppose insidious threats to the community? In such cases, it is unclear whether a "formal" or "familiar" pronoun is called for, and in fact these labels could cue exactly the wrong choice.

Older English had a similar distinction between *thou* and *you,* but *you* was eventually generalized (v. 9.2.1). In Modern English, the only comparable distinction is in VOCATIVES, the sentence tags for calling out to people and getting their attention.[1] In *Are you going, Jenny?* the vocative *Jenny* signals a *tú*-like relationship; in *Are you going, Ms. (Dr., President) Smith?,* the vocative suggests *usted.* In fact, a useful rule of thumb is to adopt *tú* if "you" would be addressed with a given name and *usted* if a title or title and last name would be used. This strategy is not infallible, however, given social differences between cultures. In the United States, a clergyman and adult parishioner, a professor and student, or a plumber and homeowner may proceed to reciprocal or nonreciprocal use of given names, whereas all three relationships tend toward *usted* in Spanish.

Brown and Gilman (1960) abandoned the undependable notions of familiarity and formality and took a fresh approach to describing "T/V" pronouns (named for French *tu/vous*) in European languages. After analyzing results from questionnaires that included a variety of DYADS (two-person relationships), they concluded that T/V usage is based on two distinct principles, power and solidarity (figure 16.2). With POWER, the person who is higher in rank, age, experience, position, or social advantage gives T and receives V, a nonreciprocal (asymmetric) usage. With SOLIDARITY, two people adopt reciprocal T for showing special bonding, mutual attraction, or commonality of background, goals, status, and affiliation; to maintain distance (nonsolidarity), they instead adopt mutual V. The

Figure 16.2. Brown and Gilman's analysis of T-forms (*tú*) and V-forms (*usted*)

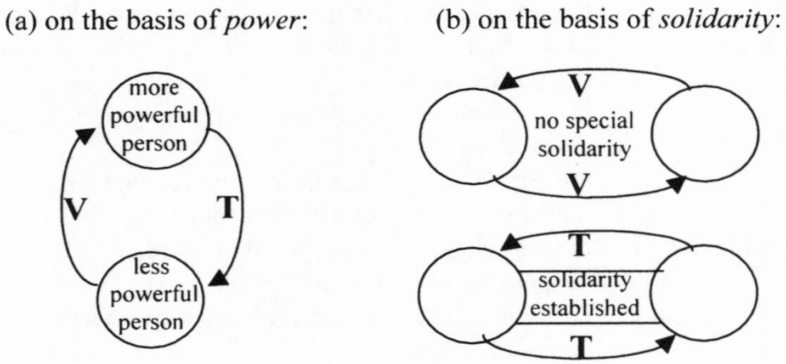

(a) on the basis of *power*:

(b) on the basis of *solidarity*:

power basis dominated in the social hierarchies of the Middle Ages, but more recently the trend has been toward solidarity vs. nonsolidarity. The main remnant of power in T/V today is that the person who is perceived as more powerful in the dyad is the one who gives DISPENSATION for the switch from V to T (*tuteo*) once sufficient solidarity has been recognized (as in English, "Just call me Jenny").

Brown and Gilman noted that the social relationships behind T/V are fluid, in that a mutual V ↔ V can shift to T ↔ T and vice versa, whether permanently or for transient attitudes. Thus, two drivers may change from a businesslike V to an angry shouting match with T; two acquaintances on T-terms may show estrangement or ironic detachment with V; and an employer and employee on V-terms for conducting office business may switch for a while to T while chatting about mutual acquaintances or community affairs.

Generalizations about T/V are tendencies, not absolute laws, since different societies and different individuals do not define "solidarity" in exactly the same way. Brown and Gilman observed differences between the French and Germans in the relevance of kinship to solidarity. Since Hispanic societies are even more diverse and heterogeneous than those of France and Germany, one would expect more variation there—which, in fact, is the case. At one extreme, Hispanics of the U.S. Southwest have generalized *tú* at the expense of *usted* (Sánchez 1982, 30; Jaramillo 1995); at the other, some Central and South Americans have generalized *usted* even for affectionate address (Kany 1951, 92; Carricaburo 1997), reserving *tú* or *vos* for special cases such as talking-down relationships (as a remnant of the power basis). In between lie countless variations. Lambert and Tucker (1976) found that Puerto Ricans apply power and solidarity according to their individual experiences, whereas children in Bogotá have more fixed norms: reciprocal T in the family, reciprocal V outside it (but nonreciprocal, power-based T ↔ V with much older people), and reciprocal T with peers (but V ↔ V among boys). Torrejón (1991) expanded the Brown and Gilman analysis to include Chilean *vos* and *sumerced*, and Carricaburo (1997) summarized a range of such studies for a country-by-country run-down, noting that in most areas, especially among younger generations, *tú* and *vos* are being extended today to relationships that were formerly marked with the *usted* of power or nonsolidarity.

The teacher grants that there is dialectal, social, and idiolectal variation in *tú/usted* (as there is also in English vocative usage), but in the classroom one needs to generalize, and the notions of "power" and "solidarity" are as useful generalizations as any. Nevertheless, students should be cautioned that the exact application of such principles will really become clear only through personal experience in particular societies.

16.1.2 Style, style shifting, stylistics. The relationship between two speakers is not defined in a sociolinguistic void; it also depends on their situation. In all the T/V languages, a judge and a lawyer might use mutual T at a soccer game or in a bar, but in the courtroom they switch to mutual V, regardless of their personal solidarity outside that context. But more than pronoun selection is affected by changes of situation; phonology, grammar, and lexicon also shift. Linguists describe these contextual levels of language as a scale of STYLES (or REGISTERS) that range from formal to casual (see figure 16.3). At the most formal extreme lies standard literary usage, with cultivated florid touches; at the most informal extreme is the level known in Spanish as *vulgar* (which translates not as 'vulgar' but as 'popular slang'). In between is a continuum of semiformal, colloquial, and semicasual levels. We shift among these styles of speech much as we change styles of clothing to reflect the occasion, and the ability to shift styles appropriately is a crucial marker of communicative competence.

We have already seen this stylistic differentiation in phonology: the application of variable rules increases or decreases according to the kind of speech used in a given setting (v. 3.0–2). Thus many Spanish speakers aspirate /s/ more when speaking casually (e.g., at home and about family concerns) than when delivering an address or broadcast to a large audience. In grammar, too, different speech levels appear in that the more formal the style, the longer and more complex the sentences and the more standardized the morphology. In the lexicon, words such as *proferir, perjudicial, acaecer* are more formal than the plainer *decir, dañino, pasar*, and *crisma, mamá, jorobar* are more colloquial than

Figure 16.3. Levels of style (register) and argot

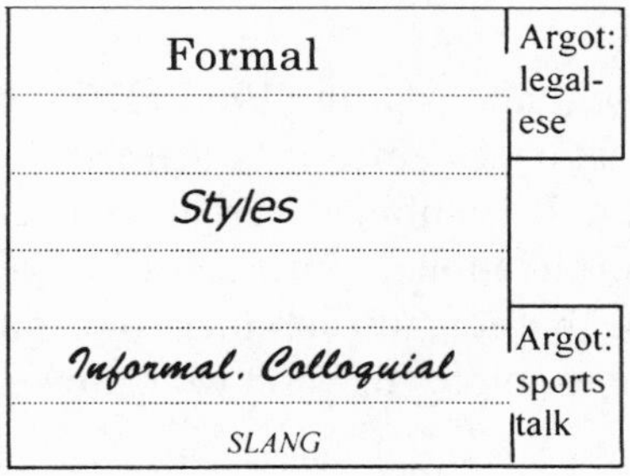

cabeza, madre, molestar.[2] Seizing on such differences, Lombardi and Peters (1981, 143) showed how sentences can be "translated" from style to style:

Formal:	*Colloquial:*	*"Vulgar":*
Tenga la bondad de callarse.	¡Cállate!	¡Cierra ese pico!
Está en estado interesante.	Está encinta.	Está preñada.
Pasó a mejor vida el rico.	Se murió el ricachón.	Estiró la pata el platudo.

The products of foreign language classes tend to be monostylistic, steeped in a formal, even literary, register. Proceeding abroad, they hear, and are expected to respond to, *¿Quiay?, 'Tá bravo, Pal reffriao nomá,* and so on for what they learned as *Buenos días, Está enojado,* and *(Es) solamente para el resfriado.* They may be unaware that a switch from *Buenos días* to *¿Quiay?* can be just as strong a sign of bonding as the change from *usted* to *tú.* In the same way, Hispanic students of English learn *Could you not find them?* and *I must leave* but instead hear *Couldncha findem?* and *Gotta go,* and they may fail to pick up on the social message of the style switch. Until students round out their repertoire of registers, their relentlessly formal language can project an interpersonal distance they do not intend, and may keep them from recognizing the friendly overtures being expressed by more casual speech.

The term *style* is also used in a second sense, namely for the special characteristics and conventions of cultivated exposition. This is the STYLISTICS of literary or journalistic writing, and Vásquez Ayora (1977) devoted a whole chapter to Spanish/English contrasts in this area. Some of his generalizations seem simplistic, for example, that English dwells on a plane of reality while Spanish prefers the level of intellect or analytical abstraction (pp. 82–83). Still, especially for would-be translators, he offered convincing evidence for his claim that English tends toward graphic "palabras imágenes" that are usually not conveyed in Spanish, as in the following cases:

(1a) The boss *waved* the messenger *to* a chair.
(1b) El jefe le indicó al mensajero que tomase asiento.
(2a) He lifted him *off his feet* and swung him *around and back through* the *swinging* doors and *into* the other man.
(2b) Lo levantó en alto y tomando impulso con un giro de atrás hacia adelante lo precipitó contra la puerta y contra el otro hombre. (p. 84)

However, as Stockwell, Bowen, and Martin (1965, 276) observed, useful generalizations are hard to lay down for stylistics since it is learned through absorption of native models, not by following rules. It combines verbal mannerism, a feel for rhythmic cadences, attention to precise formulation, a practice of lexical and syntactic refinement, and the native "mold of thought," but it is too complex to be pinned down by any of these notions. Some of the contrasting examples of Stockwell, Bowen, and Martin further illustrate the problem.

(3a) He saved himself in the nick of time by ducking behind a post.
(3b) Se salvó oportunamente al refugiarse detrás de una columna.
(4a) They spent the whole morning working without thought for themselves.
(4b) Estuvieron trabajando toda la mañana con abnegada y sacrificada labor.
(5a) The police had to fire several shots in order to stop the escapees.
(5b) Los policías tuvieron que realizar varios disparos para detener a los prófugos.

Even with English speakers' best efforts at style-shifting (and restraint with "palabras imágenes"), it would probably not occur to them to resort to a phrase like *con abnegada y sacrificada labor* as in (4b). Thinking in English and then attempting a Spanish translation, they might try *sin pensamiento para sí mismos,* which sounds odd. Correcting this to *sin pensar en sí mismos* improves it grammatically and semantically, but it still is not as "sofisticado" (as one native speaker put it) as the Spanish phrase. But until they assimilate this kind of stylistics to some extent, students' Spanish may sound wooden, plain, and hot off an electronic translator.

16.1.3 Words of group identity: Argot and slang. As noted earlier (v. 15.0), a large number of words recorded in dictionaries belong to the special jargon or ARGOT of particular fields and subcultures. Consequently, the average Spanish or English speaker is unlikely to use terms such as the following without some degree of experience in the indicated fields.

retorta/retort (chemistry)	médula oblonga/medulla oblongata (anatomy)
isobara/isobar (meteorology)	umbela/umbel (botany)
doble bemol/double flat (music)	escarificador/harrow (farming)
asíntotas/asymptotes (geometry)	positrón/positron (physics)
devolución de revés/backhand (tennis)	subrutina/subroutine (computers)
escoria/slag (mining)	amortizar/amortize (economics)
sobreseimiento/stay (law)	fonema/phoneme (linguistics)
estribor/starboard (sailing)	barrena/auger (carpentry)

As shown in figure 16.3, each such argot is a kind of sublexicon opening out onto a specific level of the general system. Sports talk, for example, is conducted with a colloquial grammar and pronunciation; legalese, on the other hand, is used with a very formal overall style. In a detailed study of samples of administrative, legal, journalistic, and political Spanish, Stewart (1999, 138–55) brought out just how dense and complex such registers can become.

The learning of argot is often regarded as just a matter of personal need: in most realms of life speakers can get along without knowing of legal stays, but if they ever study law or are affected by a stay, then they will pick up *sobreseimiento* and other legalese terms as needed. Yet there is another side to argot: just as speakers change their pronouns, vocatives, and styles in response to one another's status, they adopt vocabularies that identify shared experience in life. Therefore, argot not only provides terms for specialized senses, but has a social function in projecting one's identity as a member of a certain vocational or avocational group.

In this social respect, argot resembles slang. Slang is more colloquial than professional argot, but both are used to define solidarity within a group. Some expressions offered by Lombardi and Peters (1981, 156–64, 289–94) include the following:

student slang: *profe* 'profesor', *cole* 'colegio', *materia jodida* 'clase aburrida'
underworld *caló*: *afufar* 'escaparse', *birlar* 'robar', *tasquera* 'pelea'
the *lunfardo* of the Buenos Aires underclass: *morfar* 'comer', *cana* 'policía', *falluto* 'fanfarrón', *aceitar* 'sobornar', *macanear* 'mentir'

León (1988) compiled a dictionary of peninsular Spanish slang, including *gilipollas* 'majadero', *mona* 'borrachera', *tío* 'individuo', *súper* 'buenísimo', *ligue* 'relación sexual pasajera', and the prolific derivatives of *cojones, coño,* and *joder*. Many usages of Chicano dialect may also be considered slang: for example, *birria* 'cerveza', *gabachado* 'asimilado a los gringos', *migra* 'agente de inmigración', and the prolific derivatives of *chingar*.

Argot and slang generally receive low priority in foreign language classes for general audiences. Slang is useful, but since it is so localized and fast-changing, it is best acquired during stays in Hispanic societies. Argot occasionally appears in readings but is usually handled by glossing; otherwise it, too, is best acquired through experience with the group that uses it. On the other hand, foreign language specialists are finding a greater need for expanded professional lexicons in the growth of technical translation and interpreting and of specialized language courses such as *Español comercial, Español para médicos,* and *Español para policías*.

16.1.4 Speaking strategies: Politeness and genderlect. Another aspect of the ego-alter relationship is the notion of FACE as developed by Brown and Levinson (1978). Some acts of "linguistic business" (such as requests, proposals, advice, criticism, bad news, and potentially divisive topics) can be "face-threatening" to the addressee, and the default strategy in conversation is to show politeness to spare a loss of face. There are numerous politeness strategies: showing personal interest in the hearer, adopting in-group markers (vocatives, slang), avoiding disagreement, joking, using an impersonal expression or inclusive *we*, adopting less direct syntax (e.g., a question), and mitigation. Thus, an impersonal or passive *se*, as in *Esas faltas no se deben cometer,* has the effect of "defocalizing" the addressee's shortcomings—and potential loss of face—than the more direct *No cometa . . .* or even *Usted no debe cometer . . .* (Haverkate 1984). Similarly, hedges like *pues, bueno, yo que tú, en realidad, que yo sepa, hasta cierto punto, mirándolo bien, lo que pasa es . . .* soften the blow of assertion and lessen the risk of dissent.

Brown and Levinson believed politeness strategies to be universal but granted that the specific *norms* for what is considered to be polite vary culturally. In a discourse analysis of telephone conversations, Placencia (1995) discovered such differences between

Ecuadorians and Britons that seem to characterize Spanish and English speakers in general. In either language, a caller may respond to the routine *Hello?* or *¿Aló?* with either an extended request such as *Buenas tardes, si fuera tan amable, ¿se encuentra Patricia?* or a "reduced" (elliptical) one such as *Buenas tardes, el señor Augusto Flores, por favor*. For the most part, though, (British) English speakers are likelier to opt for the briefer version under the assumption that it is more polite to save the addressee's time, whereas (Ecuadorian) Spanish speakers assume that politeness requires at least token recognition of the addressee as a person. Her advice to English speakers was "Do not reduce where reduction leads to unclarity or where the addressee does not get the consideration he/she is due" (p. 138).

We have seen (v. chapter 3) that the two sexes often differ in their application of variable rules. They also differ in lexical preferences and favored topics for bonding. But one of the most consistent results of genderlect research in Anglophone and Hispanic societies is that women tend to use more politeness strategies than men in order to mitigate the force of statements and requests. According to Lozano Domingo (1995), this is because women see conversation as interpersonal in purpose and collaborative in nature, so that they tend to focus on shared experience; men, though, see it as primarily informational in purpose and competitive in nature, so that they vie to hold the floor in proposing solutions. Thus, in the following dialogue (p. 166), the woman wants the couple to go to a party but proposes it as a face-saving question; unfortunately, her partner responds to it as merely a question, not as an expression of her wish to go:

Ella: ¿Te apetece ir a la fiesta de María esta tarde?
Él: No.

The woman now regards him as inconsiderate for ignoring her real thrust, but her strategy again collides with the man's different interpretation:

Ella: Bueno, pues si tú no quieres ir, iré yo sola.
Él: Si querías ir a la fiesta de tu amiga sin mí, lo podías haber dicho claramente.

As Lozano Domingo noted, the argument predictably expands with "yo no he dicho que quisiera . . ." and "tú solo me has preguntado que si . . ." until both end up angry over what began as a mere misinterpretation. The same breakdown in male-female communication could occur in English too.

Clearly, we do not say all that we mean, but take it for granted that our hearers will infer missing connections from context and from assumed norms of polite expression. Azevedo (1992, 270) illustrated this point with the following exchanges, in which speaker B uses the same rejoinder to imply different reactions to what A has just said:

(1) A: Voy a darle aquel jersey verde a un mendigo.
B: ¡Pero si ha sido un regalo mío! (= 'Me ofendes')

(2) A: ¿Cuándo quieres que te devuelva aquel jersey verde?
B: ¡Pero si ha sido un regalo mío! (= '¿No te das cuenta que fue un regalo?')

Likewise, because of the indirectness of polite expression, an innocent-sounding question may be ambiguous, and the hearer has to rely on the situation (including personal knowledge of the speaker) in order to interpret the real intent:

¿Es éste el vestido que compraste ayer?
= Te lo pregunto por cortesía, pero me parece un trapo.
= Es que me parece haberlo visto en otra ocasión.
= Quiero que sepas que lo encuentro muy elegante. (ibid., 269)

In this basic principle of discourse, English speakers can be just as indirect with each other as their Spanish-speaking counterparts. Yet in their L2, they are often still processing what they hear literally, missing subtle paralinguistic clues and the thrust of different speaking strategies: thus, they understand the sentence but are confused about what the speaker means by it.

16.2 Proverbs and other cultural allusions.

> In our cosmopolitan-oriented culture, folk wisdom as expressed in the proverb has lost much of its meaning, and, even more, its prestige. Hispanic culture is still close to the land, its characteristic wisdom is still legal tender among the educated, and the proverb is a key to understanding the people. Tell students that they are going to learn some of the most common proverbs, first to learn more vocabulary and patterns, and second to get to understand Spanish-speaking people better. (LaMadrid, Bull, and Briscoe 1974b, 121)

This statement was too sweeping, since many English speakers (whether "close to the land" or not) likewise use proverbs and since equally "cosmopolitan" Hispanics are not necessarily walking *refraneros* like Sancho Panza.[3] It is true, however, that Spanish speakers as a whole seem to use more proverbs, and to use them more often, than most English speakers.

It is also true that proverbs can help students to understand Spanish speakers and their culture to some extent, because such sayings are verbal repositories of the collective experiences and traditions of a people. By appealing to proverbs, speakers do several things: they identify themselves with their society's values, they imply consensus in a given situation rather than ideological independence, and they economize on a fuller discussion by citing a time-tested generalization. For example, an allusion to *A bird in hand is worth two in the bush* or to *Más vale pájaro en mano que cien volando* relates an issue to conventional wisdom, assumes agreement and a shared perspective on life, and reduces a lengthy exposition on risk-taking to one short sentence. In this example, the two languages converge on the same hunting metaphor; in *A big frog in a small pond* vs. *En tierra de ciegos el tuerto es rey,* the images differ but they make the same point. But cultural outlooks can differ, and proverbial wisdom with them. English speakers are often exhorted to speak out and speak up, for *The squeaky wheel gets the grease*; Spanish speakers, however, learn that *Por la boca muere el pez* and *En boca cerrada no entran moscas.* Here, Spanish culture seems more akin to that of Japan, where one grows up on *Deru kugi wa utareru* ('the nail that sticks up gets hit'). Yet cultures are multifaceted and include opposing philosophies, so that no single proverb conveys the entire communal wisdom. The speaker who sighs in resignation after saying *Más vale pájaro en mano . . .* can be rebutted by the rejoinder *Pero quien no se aventura no pasa la mar.*

The sociocultural context of communication seeps into language in many other places. Foreign visitors attempting to use their second language with their hosts are hit with a barrage of allusions to folklore, history, literature, national heroes and antiheroes, current fads and trends, agencies, place-names (TOPONYMS), and sports teams. There are references to domestic products and the sociopolitical scene, jokes about local affairs, and in-group euphemisms and innuendos, and foreign visitors may fail to get the point. Their dictionaries will probably not explain allusions such as the following:

esos etarras de Euskadi	the Truman surprise in '48
Guadalupe me ha oído	the IRS ignores IRAs
¿Ganó el Real Madrid?	gimme a B.L.T. on wheat
es como otro *fujimorazo*	a meeting on M.L.K. Jr. Day

One may have an excellent command of general grammar and vocabulary but no familiarity with local terms for foods, drinks, flora and fauna, TV shows, medications, clothing sizes, landmarks, banking procedures, and so on; and knowing these for one country does not guarantee competence in the next. Thus the Spanish scholar Ramón Carnicer (1977, 99–120) related how, on his first trip to Mexico, he was struck not only by the expected dialect differences, but also by references to *la mordida* (bribe), *salaciones* (bad luck caused by salt), *balaceras* (gunfights in the streets), *loncherías* (fast-food restaurants), *licuados, mole, tequila, Zona Rosa,* and so on.

When course syllabi are already so full that final chapters cannot be covered, teachers may argue that it is one thing to introduce an occasional proverb or cultural capsule but quite another to cover soccer teams, political parties, commercial products, and the ephemeral "celebs" and fashions of the countries where the L2 is spoken. Knowing a language requires knowing something about its speakers' culture, but for the student some details of native speaker life can be regarded as relatively marginal. But it is harder to excuse ignorance of cultural norms that govern the structure of conversation itself, as in the cases discussed below.

16.3 Communicative functions in discourse. The emphasis on communicative competence has led to major changes in language teaching. One is that activities focus more on normal functions of language in typical situations. Asking students "¿Tienen hambre?" before lunch can initiate a real exchange of information, whereas showing them a pencil and asking "¿Es un lápiz?" is communicatively phony (Dulay, Burt, and Krashen 1982, 263). Another change is the realization that students internalize grammar through the process of using it to achieve a goal in negotiation with other speakers—which ought to be implicit in pragmatics as the "carrying out of business" with language.

A third consequence is a greater concern for discourse. A DISCOURSE is any coherent stretch of linguistic output, spoken or written: a conversation, story, speech, essay, poem, prayer, recipe, announcement, list of instructions, and so on. For these, we obviously do not communicate in single words or single sentences, but in larger monologues and dialogues. Hence, students should be exposed to realistic (authentic whenever possible) whole samples of speech and writing, and even drill-like practice should be given a context and thematic continuity (Omaggio 1993).

16.3.1 Grammar in discourse. Linguists such as Givón (1979a) have emphasized the functional (as opposed to purely structural) side of grammar and the need to study its role in overall discourse (as opposed to decontextualized sentences). Grammar provides numerous options, but the real purpose of machinery such as word-order permutations, tenses, determiners, adverbials, and noun clauses emerges only when one examines the functions that these carry out in what participants presuppose and assert in their overall interaction with each other.[4]

Figure 16.4 illustrates the discourse functions of selected grammatical items from previous chapters. Note that a given item does not carry out a function by itself, but does so in conjunction with others. Determiners function together with other NP modifiers to define *¿a quién me refiero?*, and the preposition *a*, which has little value in itself, joins with word order, clitics, and verb endings at a discourse level to help define *¿quién le hace qué a quién?*

Likewise, adverbials are not just optional add-ons (adjuncts) as they may seem in a purely syntactic analysis. Some of them (*antes, a la vez, en el acto* . . .) work with tense and aspect in specifying chronology in a narrative; others (*por consiguiente, además, en cambio* . . .) belong to a set of tools called COHESIVE DEVICES that serve to relate ideas and to give cohesion to the discourse. Note how the following grammatical options all serve as cohesive devices:

sentence adverbials: *Hizo explosión un coche bomba en la Calle Mayor.* ***Por consiguiente****, murieron ocho víctimas inocentes.*

subordinating conjunctions: *Hizo explosión un coche bomba en la Calle Mayor,* ***de modo que*** *murieron ocho víctimas inocentes.*

gerund phrases: *Hizo explosión un coche bomba en la Calle Mayor,* ***dejando*** *muertas ocho víctimas inocentes.*

nonrestrictive relatives: *Hizo explosión un coche bomba en la Calle Mayor,* ***por lo cual*** *murieron ocho víctimas inocentes.*

Pronominalization (v. 9.4.1) is another discourse-based process that, despite the claims of some theories of syntax, cannot be accounted for within sentence-level grammar alone (Blackwell 1998). For ANAPHORA, or reference to a previously mentioned NP, Spanish speakers may use a pronoun for DO, IO, and OP but Ø for Subj, reserving subject pronouns for emphasis, contrast, or SWITCH-REFERENCE (Cameron 1995), that is, for changing to a new Subj. There are other options for the same functions: demonstratives (*este*), nominalization (*el otro*), and RENAMING, the use of a new NP (e.g., *el tipo*) to refer back to the old one. What is seldom realized, however, is that pronominalization and its alternatives are not just grammatical substitutes for NP, but likewise constitute a cohesive device. Each time a speaker adopts these, he or she instructs the hearer to stay focused on the entity and gradually strings together a REFERENTIAL CHAIN of successive allusions to it: *Un cirujano viejo . . . lo . . . él . . . pero el tipo . . . se . . . Ø . . . . le . . . este médico . . . el cual . . . su . . . éste . . . lo . . . el muy imbécil . . .* Such chains are threads that hold discourse together and are what gives *text* its *texture* (Halliday and Hasan 1976, 2). Lack of these chains is one reason that the essays of lower-level L2 students sound odd: they tend to write loose independent sentences, without the transitions, chainings, and carryover of information that create the texture of genuine discourse.

16.3.2 Accuracy and function in proficiency development. Given the linkage of grammar to discourse, Givón (1979a, 89) saw a special challenge that young children face in acquiring their L1. Their input from adults reflects an intricate, elaborate system designed for all the functions (reference, cohesion, presupposition, and so on) of mature discourse, and this puts children under "communicative stress." Initially, then, they dispense with much of the language's machinery: they can *learn* it but not make meaningful

Figure 16.4. Items and functions

Grammatical items	Discourse functions
word order transformations (e.g., passive, clefting, Subj postposing, Obj preposing...)	to focus on a topic and to highlight assertions that the speaker judges as new or contrastive in context
determiners, adjectives, relative clauses	to define and distinguish referents being introduced into the discourse
tenses, aspect, adverbials	to sequence events, to define their distance from the present point or recalled point, to advance the action in the narrative foreground against a background of anterior or concurrent actions
mood, modal verbs, noun clauses (full or reduced), adverbials of speaker attitude	to signal differences such as reported statement vs. reported command, and to convey assumptions about reality or evaluation thereof

use of it until achieving greater overall competence. It should go without saying (although Givón said it well, p. 227) that L2 learners likewise feel communicative stress. Their stress is even more acute because they are used to enjoying full competence but find themselves reduced to toddler talk ("Es un *lápiz*"), severely restricted in what they can say, and unable to converse naturally, to narrate, to joke, to argue—in short, to "discourse" (the noun has been verbed)—as they are accustomed to doing in their L1. The L2 ability they seek is going to develop much more slowly and laboriously than they probably expected.

There are many theories of learning in general, and of L2 acquisition in particular, two sets of which are considered in section 16.4. Here, we are more concerned with the impact of L1 on the development of overall communicative competence. It will be recalled (v. 0.3) that student interlanguage combines L1 transfer with general acquisitional strategies of L2 items.[5] As Anderson (1983) put it in his "Transfer to Somewhere" principle:

> A grammatical form or structure will occur consistently and to a significant extent in the interlanguage as a result of transfer if and only if (1) natural acquisitional principles are consistent with the L1 structure or (2) there already exists within the L2 input the potential for (mis-)generalization from the input to produce the same form or structure. Furthermore, in such transfer preference is given in the resulting interlanguage to free, invariant, and functionally simple morphemes which are congruent with the L1 and L2 (or there is congruence between the L1 and natural acquisitional processes) and the morphemes occur frequently in the L1 and/or the L2. (p. 182)

This principle has had a strong influence in SLA, and its corollary—that when two or more forces support a given interlanguage usage, that usage will resist restructuring—has helped explain why some errors are particularly persistent.

In partial verification of Anderson's principle, VanPatten (1985) taped interviews with students at various points during a Spanish course to discover tendencies in the development of the *ser/estar* contrast, and he found evidence for four acquisitional stages. First, students seize on one Spanish copula, *ser,* that seems "functionally simple" and "congruent" with their *be,* and they proceed to generalize it to all contexts where they use *be*; at this stage direct L1 transfer is strongest. Second, *estar* emerges, but just for progressives; third, *estar* is extended to locatives, and fourth, to adjectives of condition.

By using oral interviews, VanPatten tapped into students' real proficiency in the language instead of the short-term knowledge that they cram for a quiz and then forget. PROFICIENCY (Omaggio 1993) is one's ability to "do business" with the language in a spontaneous (unrehearsed) way, and it is used as a measure of communicative competence. Proficiency testing (Educational Testing Service 1982) has determined that there are several discrete levels of L2 development, as summarized in figure 16.5, each one requiring successively longer experience with the language and its culture.[6] At each such

Figure 16.5. Levels of proficiency

Proficiency level	Functions and content	Grammar, lexicon, pronunciation
0. Novice	counting, listing, naming, answering with memorized material; no discourse; no real communicative ability.	asyntactic (tends to speak in single words); little accuracy in inflection; handful of active vocabulary; nonfluent; L1 phonology.
1. Intermediate	can create with L2, especially in two-part exchanges (e.g. question-and-answer); can satisfy basic survival needs but communication breaks down easily beyond immediate here-and-now issues; sociocultural competence based on L1.	combines words but with little or no complexity or modification; constant errors in morphology and functors; little use of tense besides present; larger vocabulary but centered onpersonal needs; gaps that can bring conversation to a halt; fluency uneven, L2 phonemic distinctions emerging but with continued L1 interference.
2. Advanced	true discourse; describes, narrates, predicts, converses without breakdown, especially in areas of personal experience; discusses current events; could live in L2 society.	good use of past/future forms, pronouns, transitions; sentences are linked, sometimes embedded; mastery of basic grammar but with entrenched error patterns; large lexicon but with verbal groping at times; possible accent but speech is intelligible to native speakers.
3, 4, 5. Superior	L2 frame of reference in presenting message, evidently thinking in L2; extensive organization of material; hypothesizes, conjectures, supports opinion, negotiates, persuades, argues; seldom comes undone in any situation even outside of personal experience; emerging ability to tailor speech to the situation by using different registers.	no error patterns with any usage; varied sentence structure; control of contrary-to-fact structure and other devices for showing presupposition and attitude; extensive vocabulary (concrete and abstract), precise word choice, comfortable circumlocution around gaps; native-like pronunciation and fluency; uses L2 fillers (uh, in other words...) naturally instead of halting or stumbling.

level, there is a consolidation of the learner's simultaneous command of *functions* (e.g., describing, introducing, purchasing, narrating), of *content* (the range of topics or notions that can now be handled), and of *accuracy* (precise use of the requisite grammatical and lexical tools for these functions and notions); the three therefore develop synergistically, with growth in one of them drawing on and reinforcing advances in the others.

Some SLA researchers wonder if the acquisitional sequences postulated in short-term experiments like VanPatten's should not be reinterpreted in terms of overall proficiency development. Thus, Gunterman (1992a, b) looked beyond the introductory year of Spanish and found that both *ser/estar* and *por/para* show a more complex, long-term development tied to diversification of content and function at each level, without full acquisition until Level 3. Nor is L1 transfer limited to just one stage, since nonnative speakers who have mostly acquired *por* and *para* continue using Anglicisms like **buscar para* even at advanced levels.

Whether because of natural acquisitional order or because of long-term stages in overall proficiency growth, it is clear that some grammatical items cannot be acquired before their time. At stages where students' competence limits them to single phrases and sentences with a concrete "here-and-now" perspective, they are unable to make real use of tense and aspect distinctions, subordinated clauses with mood contrasts, and pronominalization in referential chains. All of these only become functionally important, or communicatively useful, once the student is finally narrating (Level 2) or even hypothesizing (Level 3) in L2. Hence, no matter how much the teacher dwells on the past perfect subjunctive (*Si hubiera tenido más tiempo en el colegio, habría jugado al béisbol*), and no matter how well students regurgitate it on a quiz, neither the form nor the construction is permanently acquired until higher levels at which students are carrying out advanced functions such as expressing wishful thinking in a narrative. It is communicative need, not merely input or practice, that drives L2 acquisition.[7]

16.3.3 Discourse organization. Certain sociolinguistic routines (v. 16.4.3) are so structured that they seem to follow a preset script; the term SCRIPT is in fact used for these routines. Recipes are also highly structured: a list of ingredients to prepare followed by command forms in chronological sequence. In genres such as storytelling, on the other hand, the script is looser: the speaker is expected to be more creative while still following certain conventions. In this light, Price (1987) brought out the framework of Ecuadorian women's "illness stories": an initial orientation, a chronological unfolding of the events, and an evaluative coda, with speaker-hearer consensus throughout on characters' roles, background procedures and relationships, typical causes and effects, and above all the scoring of the rhetorical point "I did the right thing."

A discourse genre especially prized in education is exposition. Aside from already acknowledged differences in stylistics (v. 16.1.2), to what extent do Spanish and English speakers use grammar for similar expository functions? Many composition textbooks assume considerable similarity and therefore positive transfer value. Thus, in practicing Spanish composition of various types, Valdés, Dvorak, and Hannum (1999) review the same notions that students have studied in their (L1) English classes: prewriting, citation, topic sentences, supporting a position, tailoring the writing to the reader, proofreading, peer editing, selected grammar checking, studying models, and so on. For the most part, the only *new* knowledge students are assumed to need for writing Spanish is special vocabulary such as transition words and typical expository verbs such as *consiste en, se*

Figure 16.6. Discourse tendencies in five languages or language groups (Kaplan 1966, 15)

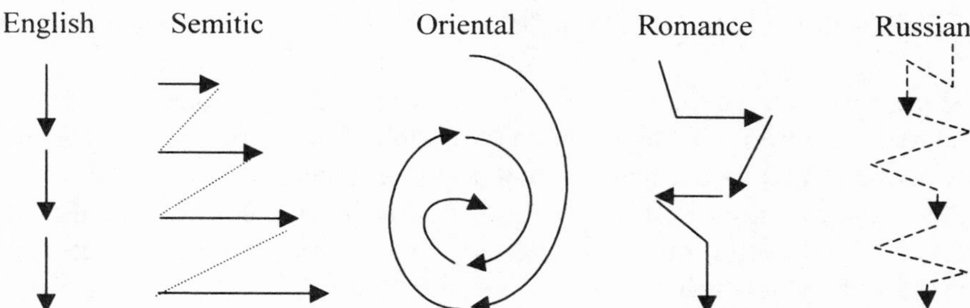

basa en, se trata de, and *opinan que.* L2 composition, then, is regarded as essentially the same as L1 composition.

Yet some analysts believe that discourse strategies cannot always be transferred to L2. As a first step toward what he called "contrastive rhetoric," Kaplan (1966) compared samples of writing from various L1 backgrounds and concluded that their discourse strategies differed strikingly in the ways shown in figure 16.6. According to Kaplan, English-speaking writers (and therefore readers) tend to be "linear," tolerating little deviation from one main path of expository development. Writers of Semitic languages (Arabic and Hebrew) learn to use parallel restatements of an idea to develop it. East Asian writers tend to spiral in around a thesis, avoiding a head-on attack as too direct. Writers of Romance languages such as Spanish proceed to a point via digressive zigzags that, to English speakers, seem extraneous and confusing, while Russian speakers do likewise but in complex megasentences.

In developing a theory of translation or *traductología*, Vásquez Ayora (1977, 196) likewise undertook contrastive discourse analysis. He suggested that a major difference between Spanish and English is the way that ideas are commonly joined to form sentences and paragraphs. English speakers tend to state a point directly and then develop it with PARATAXIS, that is, loose joining of simple clauses with coordinating conjunctions and sentence adverbials. Spanish speakers, however, tend toward a less abrupt start and prefer to link ideas through HYPOTAXIS, that is, embedded clauses with subordinating conjunctions. Compare, for instance, his examples below: sentence (2) is a fully grammatical Spanish translation of (1), but in retaining English parataxis it sounds less typical than version (3) with hypotaxis:

1. We must quickly find means of coordination and cooperation in trade policy, or many countries will face new, insurmountable difficulties.
2. Debemos encontrar pronto medios de coordinación y cooperación en políticas de intercambio, o muchos países enfrentarán nuevas e insuperables dificultades.

3. Si no encontramos pronto medios de coordinación y cooperación en lo que a políticas de intercambio se refiere, muchos países enfrentarán nuevas e insuperables dificultades. (pp. 200–201)

Spanish/English contrasts in discourse were confirmed by Montaño Harmon (1991), who compared the writing of Mexican and (Anglophone) American ninth graders. On the one hand, both groups adopted features such as topic sentences and referential chains, but even at this age they showed differences in the expository styles they were assimilating. She found a significantly higher preference among the Mexicans than among the Americans for the following:

- long sentences, often run-on
- reexpression by synonyms and hyperbole for a buildup effect
- more formal, literary choices of words and word-order transformations
- frequent deviations from the main idea

Furthermore, the Mexicans developed an idea through additive or explicative comments, whereas English speakers made heavy use of ordinal listing of points ("First . . . Second . . . Next . . . Finally . . ."). Montaño Harmon therefore summarized her two groups as "fancy, flowery, formal, complicated" vs. "linear, deductive, enumerative" (p. 423) and predicted intercultural problems when writers transfer their L1 discourse strategies to L2 and collide with the expectations of native readers.

16.3.4 Speech acts and their verbal lubricants. Speakers use special verbal rituals and procedures to conduct SPEECH ACTS, that is, linguistic transactions such as requests, proposals, and introductions. As with discourse functions, there is no one-to-one match between speech acts and grammatical items. For the speech act of *request* (or *directive*), one does not necessarily use the imperative but chooses from a range of options according to contextual appropriateness, as illustrated in figure 16.7. (See Bustamante López and Niño-Murcia 1995 for further options, classified by degrees of politeness and power in Brown and Gilman's sense.)

As noted earlier, many speech acts conform to a rather fixed sociolinguistic routine or SCRIPT (Omaggio 1993, 134). Certain words and phrases are then intended, and understood, as having a special meaning cuing a certain behavior in that situation. An example from English is *Can you pass the salt?,* which in an appropriate dining context does not inquire into the addressee's salt-passing ability but instead implies (1) 'there's a salt shaker near you', (2) 'I want it', and (3) 'pass it to me'. Note that the response to this ostensible yes/no question is not the usual "yes" or "no" but the carrying out of the implicit command, often with the verbal accompaniment of *Here you are* (which is also pragmatically specialized, ≠ 'You are here').

As another example, the short phrase *Cash or charge?* in a shopping script is pragmatically interesting in three ways. First, it presupposes familiarity with the prevailing pur-

Figure 16.7. Speech acts and grammar: how to get someone to shut a window.

direct command	Ciérrala.
elaborate command	Hazme el favor de cerrar esa ventana.
mitigated yes/no question	¿Quisieras cerrar esa ventana? *or* ¿Podrías cerrar esa ventana?
yes/no question	¿Quieres cerrar esa ventana? *or* ¿Puedes cerrar esa ventana?
information question	¿Por qué no cierras esa ventana?
declarative	Mejor la cierras. *or* Prefiero/Deseo que la cierres. or La calefacción no funciona bien con la ventana abierta.
phrase or word	¡Qué frío!
nonverbal but still vocal	¡Ejem! (with glance at open window)
nonvocal	(grimace, point at window, mime shutting)

chasing options in a culture; *charge,* even when defined in a bilingual dictionary, may have little meaning for a traveler from a society that prefers cash. Second, this phrase is ELLIPTICAL, whittled down from the fuller version *Are you going to pay with cash, or are you going to charge your purchase?* By ellipsis, a sentence is shortened to a formula that is understandable only because native speakers fill in the missing information from their schema (v. 14.1) for what customarily transpires in the situation. Third, this seems to be a choice question, grammatically akin to *Coffee or tea?* (= *Would you prefer coffee, or tea?*), but in this situation the cashier is not giving an either/or choice but is merely asking how the customer wishes to pay. An unmentioned option such as *Check* or *Debit card* is therefore an acceptable response, *in this situation.* Otherwise, choice questions exclude unmentioned options; if a hostess offers *Coffee or tea?* the answer *A margarita with a twist of lemon* would be humorous or a social gaffe. Formulas such as *Cash or charge?* are part of a linguistic etiquette that encodes a vast knowledge about expected behavior in a situation, and they lubricate and expedite our interpersonal transactions.

Comparable PRAGMATIC FORMULAS are, of course, used in Spanish. A native speaker may begin an encounter with *Hola, ¿qué hay?* The student who is unfamiliar with this script may interpret the opener as a strange question—*¿Qué hay DÓNDE?* But it has the force of a greeting, like English *How's it going?* or *How are you?* (both of which are also pragmatically specialized for this meaning). If one asks *¿Sabe Ud. la fecha?* this is meant as a request for the date (and presupposed but not stated, *today's* date), not an inquiry into the hearer's mastery of calendar systems. If the addressee does not know, he/she may answer *Lo siento, no sé,* with the *lo siento* signifying merely the inability to comply with the request, not (in this situation) regret, commiseration, or an apology. Likewise, in most situations the phrases *A sus órdenes* and *A la orden* are polite ways of signaling 'yes sir/ma'am' and 'not at all, you're welcome', respectively; they certainly are not an invitation to start issuing orders, and could cause offense if interpreted in that way. And on being introduced to a new person, one conventionally replies with *Mucho gusto* (*encantado, para servirle . . .*), regardless of how much pleasure is felt. These formulas supplant responses such as *Me alegro de que nuestro amigo nos haya presentado,* which makes sense but departs from the expected script.

Some speech acts are two-part exchanges called ADJACENCY PAIRS: greetings and farewells are mutual, a question is followed by an answer, a *gracias* cues an immediate *de nada* or *no hay de qué*. Sometimes the adjacency pair is only partly formulaic: both English and Spanish have pragmatic formulas for invitation + acceptance (the expected or default response), but the cultural etiquette of both speech communities requires some linguistic creativity to decline the invitation in a face-saving way or to demur (stall)—and many Hispanic societies then add a second adjacency pair of insistence + response (García 1992).

These examples are but the tip of the iceberg. Among the communicative functions in which linguists have discovered specialized usages are the following:[8]

requesting (and complying or declining)
excusing, apologizing, thanking (and responding to these)
sympathizing, complimenting, congratulating (and acknowledging these)
narrating, expounding
arguing, criticizing, debating, objecting, counseling
initiating and concluding conversation, interrupting, turn-taking
hesitating, hedging, qualifying
expressing affect (anger, shock, dismay, relief, etc.)
promising (bets, contracts, commitments, etc.)
rituals (parliamentary procedure, ceremonies, introducing guest speakers, prayers)
transacting business (telephone calls, purchases, bartering)
phatic communion (speech for establishing or maintaining contact, as in chitchat about the weather or about each other's families)

The cultural expectations embedded in the situational scripts for these functions can and do confuse nonnative speakers and cause them to misinterpret native speakers' attitudes and intentions (García 1996).

We learn the verbal procedures for speech acts through long experience in a variety of sociocultural settings. Hence it is debatable how much can be taken up in a sterile classroom that is psychologically and physically distant from the culture and the people being studied. One traditional solution has been to present common situational exchanges in minidialogues that students memorize as communicative shortcuts. As prefabricated *frases hechas,* the formulas can boost the performance of beginning students who still lack the proficiency to create fuller utterances of their own. In this regard, Krashen and Scarcella (1978) distinguished whole-utterance ROUTINES (*No comprendo, ¿Cuánto cuesta?, Lo siento mucho*) from partial fill-in PATTERNS (*Me llamo* ___, *¿Cómo se dice* ___*? Yo quisiera* ___). But although such "automatic speech" does seem to be learned as wholes, Krashen and Scarcella doubted that it enters into true language acquisition. In addition, problems arise later when students proceed to analyze these wholes in creating their own sentences: this is when the teacher hears errors such as **Me llamo es* ___ (analyzed on the basis of L1) or **Yo quisiero* ___ (overgeneralization of Spanish present-tense inflection to a form that has not been explained as past subjunctive).

A related issue is pedagogical selection: which formulas, for which speech acts? All textbooks introduce basic *fórmulas de cortesía* such as *gracias, hola, por favor,* and *adiós,* but there is little consensus on what else should be included. The National Foreign Language Standards movement (Lafayette 1996) promotes concrete goals of communication, culture, connections, comparison, and communities, and scholars such as Klee (1998) have mapped out the tools that students need for communicative competence, but there are few resources that teachers and textbook writers can consult for deciding what to focus on and how to present and practice it. As one step in the right direction, Lindstrom (1980) advocated changing vocabulary presentation so as to focus more on the pragmatic functions of words such as *bueno, ahora, nomás, a ver, o sea,* and *pues*, which serve as conversational FILLER WORDS with the meaning of 'keeping the lines of communication open'. Far from being mere colloquial touches, they also act as discourse markers delimiting blocks of speech for hearers (Brizuela, Anderson, and Stallings 1999) and as GAMBITS for facilitating the flow of conversation (Taylor 2002). Instead of acquiring these naturally from input alone, students often misconstrue them, as Lindstrom (1980) learned when a student "deciphered the repetitive *o sea's* of her professor as appeals to the prophet Hosea" (p. 719); and when they fail to adopt such markers in their own Spanish, they miscue their interlocutors, making for awkward conversations that may fail.

Some formulas in L1 have ready equivalents in L2, and they are equated in teaching: *oye/oiga = hey, eh(ste) = uh, ¿y (qué)? = so (what)?, eso es = that's right, felicitaciones = congratulations.* Others may match in most situations, but certain cases call for more florid variants in either or both languages. Thus, students are taught that *thanks, I'm sorry,* and *please* are, respectively, *gracias, lo siento,* and *por favor*; yet Spanish speakers sometimes prefer *es favor que me hace* (e.g., 'thank you' in response to a compliment), *dispense Ud.* (e.g., 'I'm sorry' in apology for lateness), and *sírvase* (*tenga la bondad de, me hace el favor de . . .*).

There may be a difference in emotive content or forcefulness too: *¡Dios mío!* and other invocations of holy figures are not as strong in Spanish as their literal equivalents tend to be in much of the Anglophone world. The phrase *te mato* (*Si no vienes a mi fiesta, te mato*) is a conventionalized exaggeration between friends, devoid of the serious threat conveyed by its English counterpart. Likewise, taboo words (Steel 1985, 53; Stewart 1999, 156) and their euphemisms (e.g., *mecacho*) are mild imprecations in one lect but shocking in another. As Azevedo (1992, 268) expressed this point,

> Para los hispanohablantes que viajan de un país a otro—y aun más para los que han aprendido el español como lengua extranjera—los tabúes lingüísticos reservan muchas sorpresas, puesto que lo que es una expresión normal e inocente en un lugar de pronto se convierte en vulgaridad soez en otro. No hay nada que hacer, además de pedir excusas y aprender que lo que no se dice puede ser tan importante como lo que se dice—o aun mas.

In other cases, comparable verbal conventions in two languages cue different behaviors. The English speaker's *excuse me* covers at least three situations that Spanish distinguishes with *¿cómo?* (failure to comprehend), *perdón/perdone* (after committing a social offense), and *con permiso* (in anticipation of inconvenience). It would be boorish to say *con permiso* after stepping on another's foot. Sometimes, too, a literal translation of pragmatic formulas can be quite misleading. Travelers approaching a shopkeeper's open door may hear *¡Pasen!* or *¡Sigan!* and wrongly infer that they are unwelcome and have been told to pass on by without entering. Often a verbal convention will seem mysterious to the nonnative because it entails a special local schema for what to do in this situation. For example, on showing a postal clerk a package to be mailed, the tourist may be told *Hay que revisarlo* and be dismissed; to the foreigner, this seems a brusque non sequitur (even when he/she knows that *revisar* is 'check', not 'revise'); yet to locals it entails 'así que suba la escalera y siga a la aduana'.

Gorden (1974) studied the cultural conflicts that ensued when American students stayed with Colombian host families. As a sociologist, his main interest was not linguistic, but he found copious cases in which misuse of linguistic rituals led to misunderstanding, estrangement, and reinforcement of negative stereotypes. Some of his examples are summarized below:

1. The American grits his teeth and endures a cold shower before retiring. Amazed, the *señora* asks if he prefers cold showers at night. The student misunderstands and says yes. Actually, his hostess was using a question, valued in Colombia as a politeness strategy, to imply that *warm* showers were available in the morning when one normally bathes (in Colombia), but that the water heater could be turned on specially for him if he wanted that (p. 41).
2. The *criada* pours concentrated Colombian coffee into the cup before adding warm milk, expecting the drinker to say "when." The American says *Bastante* but she keeps on pouring. It turns out that *bastante* is elliptical for *quiero bastante,* not *es bastante*; the correct signal is of course *Ya* (p. 41).
3. Americans acknowledge some favors with a simple *thanks*—if at all (silence or a nod is sometimes more tactful). Colombians accept *gracias* for a simple favor like lending a match but expect more verbal profusion for larger favors. Several families were therefore upset when an expensive excursion they had set up for their lodgers was acknowledged by a mere *gracias.* Those few lodgers who waxed on and on in appreciation—excessively, by U.S. standards—were praised as *bien educados* (p. 107).
4. Americans thought they were polite in greetings, but that Colombians gave mixed signals as to coming or going. The Colombians felt the same way about Americans. The Americans did not know that Colombians (a) expect frequent greetings, (b) expect personal touches to be added to greetings (*¿Qué tal está la familia?*) and to farewells (*Saludos en tu casa*), (c) acknowledge each other in passing with *adiós* (vs. *hi* among Americans), and (d) use *buenos días* and *buenas noches* for both greetings and farewells (compare English *good morning* and *good evening* for greetings vs. *good day* and *good night* for leave-taking) (pp. 107–9).

It is easy for students to get the idea that they still do not know the language when, despite their studies and best efforts, they keep on saying the wrong thing. Their hosts may share this impression with them, and the escalating misunderstandings can give the students a sense of personal rejection and failure. At this point, it takes a receptive attitude and strong motivation to keep trying.

16.4 Aptitude and attitude in language learning and use. The road to communicative competence in L2 is fraught with a constant correcting of errors and a never-ending flood of new words and new usages, and many students give up long before encountering major pragmatic hurdles. Even those who continue onward may regress and, to the frustration of their teachers, seem to forget usages after demonstrating apparent mastery of them in drills or on tests. The teacher can present the facts of the language and practice them intensively, but knowledge alone does not ensure nativelike performance in the target language.

Part of the problem is that foreign languages are treated as content courses instead of skill courses; many students still approach Spanish and French as they do history or biology. As a corrective, textbooks have emphasized the "four skills," "communication," "functions," and other aspects of the conversion of knowledge-about to proficiency-in. There is a greater awareness that knowledge of, say, tense and mood must evolve into unthinking, automatic use of these in active communication. Consequently, students should be given as much contact as possible with the language in a variety of situations. Many educators have in fact promoted total immersion in L2, reasoning that foreign language learners (adults) need the same continuous stimulation available to first language learners (children), in all contexts and for all their needs.

But although total immersion has enjoyed success—after all, everyone agrees that more contact helps—its underlying analogy between children and adults (or adolescents) is not entirely valid. Children internalize a language effortlessly and rapidly, and through it they build their personalities and cognitive systems. Adults, on the other hand, tend to be more plodding and analytical, and they are already set in their ways culturally and linguistically. Moreover, children can acquire a second or third language with the same ease and maintain them as distinct systems, whereas adults pass through a long period of interlanguage that draws on their L1 and shows constant interference. It seems to be a common experience, when families spend an extended period abroad, for the children to pick up the new language in months by just playing with peers while their parents show more limited (and laborious) progress with the L2 and retain L1 features (allophones, intonation, rhythm, lexical usage, favored syntax and pragmatic strategies) that betray them as foreigners.

Two theories have attempted to explain this difference between children and adults. The first, which we will call the "Ability" or "Aptitude" Theory, is based on rationalist traditions and postulates that children are born with a special inductive and deductive capacity for figuring out rules (grammar) from raw data or input (speech). Adults retain only an attenuated degree of this aptitude. Studies suggest that the cutoff point is around puberty, so that the first decade or so of life is the CRITICAL AGE for language learning.

Afterward, speakers make additions to their lexicons and stylistic repertoires, but these are mere accretions on an already congealed system; they can no longer start from scratch as children can. According to Chomsky (1959 and subsequent writings), who has been one of the foremost exponents of an Ability Theory, this developmental pattern is genetically programmed into human development. (See Strozer 1991 for a defense of this theory and its implications for teaching Spanish.)

The opposing theory, or cluster of theories, proposes that the difference between children and adults has less to do with innate ability than with sociocultural conditioning of attitudes; this will be called the "Motivation" or "Attitude" Theory. Many of its supporters drew their tenets and terms from behaviorism, a psychological theory that posits that children do not figure out rules but form habits in imitation of their parents, with the latter directing this habit formation by teaching, reinforcement, and control of input. The older the children become, the stronger their habits become and the harder they are to modify, though modification is not altogether impossible. The critical age is explained in terms of external influences such as socialization; increasingly, children's self-image becomes fixed, they are motivated by their peer group values, they are inured to one kind of behavior, and their approach to new information is less flexible. In short, postpuberty language learners have less motivation to adopt completely new behavior, although in principle new behavior can be acquired under conditions that favor different habits.

Other adherents to a Motivation Theory agree with Chomsky that language is based on rules and principles for creating speech, not merely habits, but they insist that the ability to acquire those rules and to reset underlying parameters continues after puberty. Dulay, Burt, and Krashen (1982, 78–93), for example, believed that adults' difficulties are not due to any loss of natural ability (they may even have an advantage for some aspects of grammatical and lexical development) but rather are due to excessive self-monitoring and affective factors such as anxiety. This is one reason that VanPatten (1997, 106) emphasized that adult L2 acquisition proceeds on the basis of *intake,* not merely *input,* necessitating a different pedagogical approach.

As with the larger Nature versus Nurture debate, the truth here may lie between the extremes, for each side can marshal evidence from developmental studies. On the side of the Ability Theory are facts such as the following, which resist explanation unless some special basis for language acquisition during childhood is recognized.

1. Parents do not overtly teach, drill, or explain linguistic structure as language teachers do; most, in fact, would have no idea how to describe pronunciation, tense systems, sentence structure, or the morphology and meanings of copulas. Nevertheless, their children somehow determine complex rules and patterns with amazing efficiency and rapidity.
2. Parents do not specifically reinforce mastery of each unit, rule, and construction; they actually reinforce *errors* by remarking on their cuteness and by adopting them in their own speech with children. Without direct reinforce-

ment—or in spite of it—children still learn, and the only reinforcement they seem to need for language is interactive use of it.

3. Although children are certainly imitative, from the start they take building blocks of their parents' language and spontaneously recombine them to create sentences they have never heard before. Evidently, they do not imitate their parents' speech directly, but extract rules for producing their own sentences. They learn morphological rules as well, as shown by their ignoring adult models and producing forms they have not heard from any adult input. Resnick (1981) illustrated this point as follows:

   > Oímos a un niño de dos o tres años decir, por ejemplo, **yo cabo*. Si el niño aprendiera principalmente por imitación, entonces diría *yo quepo,* como lo dicen los adultos que lo rodean. Sin embargo, el niño dice **cabo* por la abrumadora evidencia de otras formas verbales. . . . El niño formula su hipótesis en base a los datos que oye y a la necesidad humana de buscar orden y estructura en el aparente caos de la producción verbal de sus interlocutores. . . . Y no importa cuántas veces la gente le corrija su palabra juvenil, el niño no la suelta hasta que se convence de que su hipótesis está al menos parcialmente errónea y de que tiene que formular una o más reglas aparte para producir la forma anómala *quepo.* (p. 116)

4. Regardless of the language, the culture, the conditions of upbringing, and even differences in intelligence, children follow parallel paths through clear-cut stages that seem predetermined. Comparative studies have shown that the uniformity in phonological, grammatical, and lexico-semantic development across different languages is quite striking. In phonology, intonation comes early, /t/ comes before /r/ (any kind of /r/), /n/ before /l/, and /s/ before /θ/; and lest this be attributed to mere ease of articulation, it should be recalled that /s/, for instance, is articulatorily more complex than /θ/ (v. 2.1.4.2). In their syntactic development (see González 1978 for Spanish in particular), all children pass through single-word (holophrastic) and then two-word stages, and then break out to longer sentences, establishing basic phrase structures before tackling most transformed patterns, with no linguist present to point out PSRs and transformations to them and with no teacher to plan this sequence for them.
5. The reason for adults' difficulties with language acquisition is not merely entrenched habits that interfere with new ones. It turns out that even with *no* prior linguistic experience, older learners undertake language learning differently from children. In a famous case, Fromkin et al. (1981) reported on Genie, an adolescent of normal intelligence who was rescued from a home where she had been kept from hearing or using language; she soon began learning some English, but haltingly, with errors and problems that children

do not have, and without ever gaining full competence. The critical age does seem to have a biological basis.

Before asking "¿Por qué nos esforzamos entonces?" we turn to those who focus on the effects of motivation, for they also have a point. Even if adults do not attain total native proficiency (Level 5) in a second language, they can make considerable headway with determination and a favorable attitude. In this regard, Lambert et al. (1963) distinguished two kinds of motivation in L2 study and explored their consequences. With INSTRUMENTAL motivation, learners study L2 as a means to an end, for example, to get ahead or for access to information; they may have no intention of becoming part of the target group or even talking with it. If they do communicate with L2 speakers, it is to satisfy routine personal needs (*Necesito una habitación. ¿Cuánto cuesta?*), in which case they require basic active skills, expressive and receptive, but need not assimilate to those speakers. With INTEGRATIVE motivation, on the other hand, learners identify with the target people and their culture and seek to join them through their language; they want to be part of and act like that group, and to be accepted by it. Some examples of the two types:

Instrumental: the student who studies Spanish to sing Hispanic folk songs or to read Mexican anthropological journals; or, moving toward real communication, the nurse who learns enough Spanish to treat occasional Hispanic patients, or the tourist or visiting scientist who wants to learn enough to "get around" during a trip to Costa Rica.

Integrative: the student who studies Spanish because he or she likes Spain (Mexico, etc.) and wants to live there among its people.

Instrumental motivation is SELF-LIMITING because the learner does not require the full system of L2: basic pronunciation alone might suffice for the singer, the reader of Mexican journals will not have to speak the language, and the nurse with Hispanic clients does not need a range of registers, a flawless pronunciation, or a complete lexicon. Since tourists and visitors are outsiders who may not wish to pass for natives anyway, their messages can be of a rather simple type; despite a strong accent or fractured grammar, they are satisfied if they can make themselves understood in the limited exchanges they anticipate. With instrumental motivation, lifelong attitudes and modes of behavior do not have to be greatly altered.

With integrative motivation, learners open up to the changes needed for full adaptation. They seek to become at one with the target group and to adopt the ways it talks and acts. Eventually, they may become bicultural bilinguals at home in both societies. But although this motivation seems to lead to greater proficiency, it incurs a special risk. Many well-motivated students have been observed to make steady progress up to a point and then stagnate on a plateau: instead of continuing to adapt to target norms, their interlanguage begins to show hardened or FOSSILIZED errors as though learning had ceased. For Lambert (1972), this condition results from learners' realization that they are midway between leaving the security of their native society and attaining the foreign norms; they have left one niche but are not yet secure in the next one, with doubts about continuing further. Exacerbating their situation is the fact that they have now learned enough to get into trouble by seeming more culturally and linguistically competent than they are. Native speakers make allowances for a foreign tourist or nurse with whom they will have limited dealings but have higher expectations of someone with a better command of the language and with ambitions to live with them; they naturally assume that one who uses the allophones, colloquial idioms, and past subjunctives of a native can behave like a native too (Gorden 1974, 169). Moreover, since successful integration requires a readjustment of personality and self-image, students hold back from what is turning into a sociopsychological metamorphosis. Lambert and his followers called this syndrome ANOMIE and predicted two outcomes: learners back off and retreat to the security of their native identity, or they emerge determined to take the final steps to join the target culture, with a more realistic acceptance of the extent to which that is possible for them.

As with other classifications of humans, this one oversimplifies.[9] Students' motivations can change, and they make progress with other goals too: to get good grades, to pass a requirement, for purely academic study, for verbal pats on the head by an admired teacher. In addition, attitude is distinct from motivation, for one can have a strong instrumental motivation and yet feel positive, negative, or neutral toward L2 and its speakers. Moreover, as shown by García Gutiérrez (1993), fossilization also appears in favorably inclined, well-integrated learners who feel satisfied with a communicative level they have attained through L1 transfer, for example, an Italian ("Franca") living in Spain:

> Las conclusiones a las que hemos llegado apuntan casi siempre a un mismo factor explicativo de todo el proceso en Franca: la transferencia lingüística desde su competencia en L1, el italiano, hacia su IL [interlengua] orientada a la L2, el español. A nuestro modo de ver esta estrategia ha operado activamente en la adquisición de L2, y, el éxito obtenido con la misma, si bien es un éxito relativo, como veremos, creemos que ha sido uno de los factores que más ha podido influir en el hecho de que el sujeto, una vez alcanzado un nivel de conocimientos en L2 considerable, haya detenido inconscientemente las exigencias en el avance adquisitivo y en su perfeccionamiento, fosilizando los errores que caracterizasen en este punto a su IL. (p. 85)

Nevertheless, granting the problems with an Attitude (or Motivation) Theory, it makes the points that some individuals can attain near-native proficiency in a foreign language (for example, at Level 3) despite a late start, and success in mastery (or resistance to further mastery) is affected by nonlinguistic factors such as personality, attitude, and personal goals. The more positive and receptive these factors are, the greater the command achieved; the more negative, the sooner that L2 acquisition grinds to a halt. Indeed, some students are *unmotivated* or even hostile from the start; they see no personal need for the language (aside from satisfying a requirement they do not accept), and they resist at every step of the way a teacher's attempt to change they way that they think and communicate.

The intrinsic motivation of individual learners is a point that we teachers, in our own enthusiasm for Spanish, do not always take into account. In asking students to change their articulation (/d/ → [ð], /a/ must not → [ə]), to reset the parameters of what they regard as natural word order, to narrate in terms of beginning/middle/end and real/unreal, to show subjects by verb endings alone, to change customary strategies for everyday speech acts, to adopt the perspective of another people, and to relexify the entire universe, we are challenging them to remake themselves into new persons. This was the argument of Stevick (1976), who maintained that every linguistic unit and pattern is a meaningful part of oneself. Even pronunciation has meaning in this sense, for if students attain any more than an approximate (or "gross") phonemic accuracy, they sound funny to themselves and to their peers. He also pointed out that some advice only worsens this problem, as when students are told that Spanish /r̄/ is an imitation of a motor or that French /ʀ/ is a dry gargle, sounds that they may then disdain even more as ridiculous for normal speech. Failure to adopt and use an L2 element is a meaningful act in itself—a rejection of assimilation and a way of keeping foreignness at arm's length.

We began this final chapter with a discussion of what else speakers bring to the task of communicating besides knowledge of phonology, grammar, and lexicon. However much this communicative competence includes, an infant born to a native Spanish-speaking family will acquire it in a different way from a teenaged or adult English speaker who labors over it in a classroom with a textbook and restricted input. To the extent that the difference is determined by innate developmental programming, there is nothing to do but reassert the need for starting foreign language study earlier in elementary school; but to the extent that it depends on psychological and sociocultural factors, we teachers can try to facilitate a long process that can be painful even for the well motivated. And to keep reminding ourselves of just how hard that process can be, we can become students again ourselves by sitting in a desk to learn an L3—or L4, or L5.

SLA specialists have espoused numerous methods and techniques to ease students' fear and anxiety and to lessen the tension between teachers and students who have different expectations of what is to happen, but there are no magic solutions for eliminating these hurdles entirely. L2 study does require the acquisition of a new phonology, grammar, lexicon, and pragmatic system, and these can differ from their L1 counterparts in many ways; the teacher who is aware of these systemic differences can be ready for likely errors and give students a precise diagnosis of their problem. Yet knowledge alone of these components does not ensure nativelike use of them, for second language acquisition involves the appreciation of—and assimilation to—new ways of thinking, new norms for behaving, and new strategies for interacting with others. Unlike surface-level adjustments such as the contraction of *de* and *el* or the accents on interrogatives, these eventually reach down into one's very identity.

Notes for chapter 16

1. Hispanic culture is particularly rich in vocatives, as in *Ven acá paisano (joven, m'hijita, tripón, tío, compadre, guapa, cuate, maestro . . .)*, including regional markers such as *che* in Argentina and its neighbors. See Carricaburo 1997 and Gómez de Ivashevsky 1969 (who gathered about two hundred vocatives for Venezuela alone).

2. See Batchelor and Pountain 1992 for an especially useful resource on lexical differences in register in contemporary Spanish, from slang and obscenity to cultivated literary usage.

3. As one urbanite from Buenos Aires put it when she taught from the LaMadrid book, "I've never heard those *refranes* and feel awkward pretending they're natural for me."

4. It should be clear that not only can discourse clarify the function of grammar, but grammar informs our understanding of discourse. As an example, see Lunn and Albrecht (1997), who applied linguistic descriptions of aspect (v. 7.1.3) to the distribution of preterites and imperfects in a story by Cortázar to shed light on its structure and interpretation.

5. For a summary of studies on L2 acquisition order and L1 effects on it, see Larsen-Freeman and Long (1991, 88–107).

6. Note that proficiency levels (e.g., Intermediate, or Level 1) are defined differently from high school and college course levels (e.g., second year, or intermediate), which are based merely on year of study. Even at the Foreign Service Institute, which is more intensive (and selective) than high school or college courses, it takes about 240 hours of training just to reach proficiency Level 1 in Spanish, and *three* times as long, 720 hours, to reach the next level (Omaggio 1993, 28).

7. This is not to say that teachers and textbooks should *avoid* such structures altogether until higher levels. Small children likewise do not produce contrary-to-fact conditionals with the past perfect subjunctive, but they are still exposed to them in adult speech, and early exposure and input is arguably necessary for later emergence of the structure.

8. For coverage of some of these categories, see Gómez de Ivashevsky 1969 for Venezuelan Spanish and Steel 1985 for peninsular Spanish.

9. See Larsen-Freeman and Long 1991 for a fuller critique of SLA theories, including the ones we are calling "Ability" and "Motivation."

Exercises for chapter 16

1. Error analysis: the following sentences (all real) from student writing include errors of all sorts, including phonological ones to judge from misspellings. Locate each error and explain its source and impact on communication.

   (a) *Un hombre injurié su rodilla pero la enfermedadera se ayuda.

   (b) *Mi y mis amigos tuvieron un vez bueno.

(c) *El criminal hace seis anos sin liebre en un prisón.
(d) *Recibí un llama por teléfono y estaba sorpresado.
(e) *Todos quieren el medico le dar un receta, posible las pustillas.
(f) *Quierido mis padres: Hola! Como estás? Yo soy bien.

2. What is paralanguage? Why would its effective use be part of communicative competence? What differences between English and Spanish speakers are you aware of in this regard? Do any of the differences tend to be sex-linked?

3. Many textbooks and readers include Hispanic political cartoons and comic strips. What advantages do these have? On the other hand, what problems might they give to students?

4. L2 learners are often petrified by having to use the telephone in the foreign country. In view of the points discussed in this chapter, why should telephone calls seem difficult?

5. English *okay* is used as a "filler" cue in a variety of situations, and some Spanish speakers have adopted it too. Aside from the borrowed *oquey,* how might Spanish speakers convey each of the following? (Add other examples that occur to you.)
(a) "*Okay,* now turn to page 32."
(b) "I think I'll leave now, *okay?*"
(c) "Let's meet for dinner tomorrow, *okay?*"

6. Contrast Y's answers in these exchanges with how an English speaker might respond.
(a) X: ¿Me hace Ud. el favor de pasarme ese horario?
Y: Tome Ud.
(b) X: ¿Me hace Ud. el favor de abrir esa maleta?
Y: Ya está.

7. Three situations discussed in Handelsman, Heflin, and Hernández (1981, 122) are the following:
(a) X tells Y any of the following:
Quisiera que Ud. escriba el informe ahora.
¿Una entrevista? Pues, reunámonos mañana.
Nos vemos esta noche a los ocho. ¿Conviene?
(b) X meets Y for some item of business. They do not *ir al grano* right away, but instead digress to chat about a current festival or to inquire about each other's family.
(c) X proposes to Y, "Vamos a tomar un cafecito."
Now, consider how Y might construe the time references in (a), the chitchat in (b), and the proposal in (c) (hint: who pays?), depending on whether Y is Hispanic or "Anglo." Can you think of other cases in which English and Spanish speakers might misunderstand one another because of a different cultural schema behind speech?

8. Study the following list of words and phrases; then (a) suggest English equivalents, where possible, and (b) pinpoint the communicative function each item carries out in speech acts or discourse. Also, (c) identify any regional variants you know of in these formulas.

allá él (ella, tú)	¡chócala!	hasta luego	se me ocurre . . .
a ver	de todos modos	lo siento	total
claro	dime/dígame	no hay de qué	¿vale?
¿cómo?	eh, este	o sea	ya lo creo
¿cómo no?	en cambio	pues	¿y qué?

9. Repeat the above instructions for these interjections (and for others that occur to you):

ay	caramba/caray	huy	dale
Jesús	bah	vaya	ojo
qué va	mecachis	epa	uf

10. The following is a tiny sample of Spanish proverbs. Contrast them with equivalent English proverbs you may know for similarity of metaphor and of meaning. Even if English has no ready equivalent familiar to you, would the cultural values behind the Spanish proverb reflect those of English speakers too? What other common Spanish proverbs would you add to this list?

(a) Donde una puerta se cierra, otra se abre.
(b) Cuando a Roma fueres, haz como vieres.
(c) Agua pasada no muele molinos.
(d) A quien madruga, Dios le ayuda.
(e) Aunque la mona se vista de seda, mona se queda.
(f) Antes que decidas nada, consúltalo con la almohada.
(g) No hay mal que dure cien años, ni cuerpo que lo resista.
(h) A caballo regalado no se le mira el diente.
(i) A mal tiempo, buena cara.
(j) Cría cuervos y te sacarán los ojos.
(k) De la mano a la boca se pierde la sopa.
(l) Cada cabeza es un mundo.
(m) La vida no es senda de rosas.
(n) Quien siembra vientos recoge tempestades.
(o) No se ganó Zamora en una hora.
(p) Padre mercader, hijo caballero, nieto limosnero.
(q) Dijo la sartén a la caldera, "quítate de allá, que me tiznas."

11. Contrast the connotations of each of the following Spanish/English pairs, and offer an explanation of how they might derive from cultural differences.

(a) *perra*, bitch
(b) *profesor*, professor
(c) *arroyo*, creek
(d) *siesta*, nap
(e) *novia*, girlfriend
(f) *piropos*, compliments
(g) *azotea*, flat roof
(h) *tertulia*, bull session

12. Construct a questionnaire on the use of second-person pronouns in Spanish. (You might bear in mind not only *tú* and *usted,* but variants such as *vos*, v. 9.2.) The basic format might be the following (see Jaramillo 1995 for an example of a more complete questionnaire); try to include as broad a range of dyads as possible. Elicit responses from a native speaker and then compare your results with those of your classmates.

¿Qué pronombre suele usar Ud. en las siguientes situaciones?
(a) hablando con su esposo o novio (esposa o novia)?
(b) hablando con una prima menor/mayor?
(c) quejándose de algo en un almacén?
(d) diciéndole a un perro que se vaya?
(e) insultando a un chofer que acaba de abollarle el carro (coche)?
(f) conversando con otra persona de su edad que acaba de conocer?
(g) en una rencilla con su papá? (etc.)

13. Reread *Don Quijote* and study the second-person pronoun usage. Determine (a) the forms Don Quijote and Sancho Panza normally use with one another, (b) those with which they address other characters, and (c) cases in which their usual T/V relationship is temporarily inverted. Explain your observations in terms of Brown and Gilman's (1960) theory.

14. You have been asked by your employer, church, or other community agency to set up a three-week course for a group interested in learning just enough Spanish to "get by" in dealing with Hispanics in the area. How do you evaluate this proposal, and why? How do you respond?

15. The Educational Testing Service (1982) developed its criteria for oral proficiency testing in conjunction with ACTFL (the American Council on the Teaching of Foreign Languages) and the U.S. Defense Language Institute. At Levels 0, 1, and 2 or Novice, Intermediate, and Advanced (figure 16.4), grammatical variables and functional variables weigh about equally, but for the Superior levels, grammatical and lexical accuracy are taken for granted and the interviewee is expected to carry out functions such as the following:

(a) conjecture and argue on abstract issues
(b) negotiate, persuade
(c) tailor language to the situation (e.g., introduce a distinguished guest)
(d) use appropriate references to nativelike experiences

Why would these tasks require a special kind of communicative competence?

16. In what ways does attitude toward a foreign language and its speakers affect mastery of it? Which attitudes and personality characteristics might promote greater fluency and proficiency? What preconceived ideas and what emotional states can get in the way of L2 acquisition? What can a teacher do to ease these problems?

17. Collect examples of argot (v. 16.1.3) in a subject that interests you, whether professionally or as a hobby. Assume that this is for introducing students to the vocabulary needed for a reading on, and discussion of, that topic. (You might examine such an article in a magazine or journal or on the Web.) Indicate which words in your glossary would be for active mastery and which ones would be for passive recognition, and explain why. One criterion might be the difference between words that educated native speakers outside the area might know and use (in your judgment), as opposed to words that only serious specialists might employ.

18. In addressing linguistic diversity, many U.S. agencies and businesses are having their signs, brochures, ads, and forms translated into Spanish, often by employees without professional

training in translation. Such agencies tend to be unaware of the jargon and culture-specific references that fill their literature. A case in point is BUREAUCRATESE, an argot characterized by acronyms, euphemisms, a dense, imposing style, and local office-defined phrasings. The following sample is just one sentence from such a brochure to be translated for local Hispanic residents: "ADETS (Alcohol and Drug Education Traffic School) is a 10 hour diversionary course for individuals convicted of DWI and found NOT to have a substance abuse handicap." Assume that you have been asked to translate such a document into Spanish. How would you respond? What would you suggest? Why?

19. Following is a sample of pragmatic formulas for indicated functions. Brainstorm to add other formulas that would be possible, distinguishing them according to context, stylistic level, and regional affiliation, and marking any that might be brusque or offensive. Also, for any speech acts that are adjacency pairs, indicate the usual response. In which cases do the Spanish formulas differ most strongly from their English counterparts?

(a) to greet: all-purpose: *Hola, ¿qué tal?* . . .
special occasions: *Feliz Navidad* . . .
in passing: *Adiós* . . .
a phone caller: *Aló* . . .
in letters: *Estimado* . . .
(b) to ask permission to leave or intrude: *con permiso* . . .
(c) to thank: *Mil gracias por* . . .
(d) to change the subject: *a propósito* . . .
(e) to apologize or excuse oneself: *Disculpe Ud.* . . .
(f) to express sorrow: *Mi más sentido pésame* . . .
(g) to silence someone: *chis* . . .
(h) when starting to eat: *buen provecho* . . .
(i) when starting to drink, or to toast: *salud y pesetas* . . .
(j) to invite comment and continue the dialogue: *y tú ¿qué piensas?* . . .
(k) to comment on misfortune: *qué lástima* . . .
(l) to correct foolishness: *¡qué va!, no faltaba más* . . .
(m) to encourage: *ánimo* . . .
(n) to insult or put down: *imbécil, bestia* . . .

Appendix 1

English/Spanish glossary of linguistic terminology

The following glossary is offered in order to facilitate class discussion of the material in Spanish. Although it is not exhaustive, it covers the major linguistic terms used in this book. While the author has verified all the Spanish terms in native writings, some might prefer a different equivalent in some cases. For names of verb categories (tenses, moods, forms), see chapter 6 (figure 6.1).

Gender of nouns can be assumed to be masculine if ending in *-n, -o, -r, -s, -e, -l* and feminine if ending in *-a, -d,* or *-ción/sión,* unless otherwise indicated by (M) or (F). Adjectives used as nouns—(los) *adverbiales* for 'adverbials'—are usually masculine except for phonetic labels, which tend to be feminine as nouns: *las fricativas, una vocal alta*.

absolute (gerund): (gerundio) absoluto
absorption (of yod): absorción (de yod)
accent: acento; acentuar; accented: acentuado, tónico; accent mark: acento ortográfico, tilde (F)
acquire (a language): adquirir (ie), aprender; acquisition: adquisición, aprendizaje
address: tratamiento; tratar; addressee: interlocutor
adjective: adjetivo; adjective phrase: frase adjetival (F), sintagma adjetival (M)
adverb: adverbio; adverbial: adverbial; adverbial phrase: frase adverbial (F), sintagma adverbial (M), complemento circunstancial
affix: afijo
affricate: africado
agree: concordar (ue); agreement: concordancia
allomorph: alomorfo
allophone: alófono
alternate (V): alternar; alternation: alternancia
alveolar: alveolar; alveopalatal: alveopalatal; alveolar ridge: alvéolos
antecedent: antecedente
antonym: antónimo
apex: ápice, punta (de la lengua)
apocope: apócope (F); apocopate: apocopar
appositive: apositivo
argot: lenguaje profesional, jerga
article: artículo
articulate: articular; articulation, articulación; articulatory: articulatorio; manner/place of articulation: modo/punto de articulación

aspect: aspecto; beginning, middle, end: iniciativo, imperfectivo, terminativo
aspirate: aspirar; aspiration: aspiración
assibilate: asibilar
assimilate: asimilar; assimilation: asimilación
auxiliary: (verbo) auxiliar

back (vowel): (vocal) posterior, velar
beginning (aspect): iniciativo
bilabial: bilabial
bilingual: bilingüe; bilingualism: bilingüismo
boundary (#, +, ., ||): lindero, linde (F)
branching (diagram): (diagrama) ramificado

case: caso (nominativo, dativo, acusativo, preposicional)
category: categoría; categorization: categorización
circumlocution: circunlocución
clause: subordinada (relativa, nominal, adverbial), cláusula
clitic: clítico
clefted sentence: oración hendida (*or* escindida)
cluster: grupo (consonántico)
coda: coda
cognate: cognado
collocation: locución
colloquial: coloquial
command: mandato; mandar
comparison: comparación; (of adjectives) gradación; comparative: comparativo
competence: competencia
complement: complemento; complementary: complementario; complementizer: complementante
complex: complejo, compuesto
compound: compuesto; compounding: composición
conjugate: conjugar; conjugation: conjugación
conjunction: conjunción; coordinating/subordinating conjunction: conjunción coordinante/subordinante
connotation: connotación
consonant: consonante (F); consonantal: consonántico
constituent: constituyente
contrast: contraste, oposición; contrastar; contrasting: contrastante; contrastive analysis: análisis contrastivo
copula: cópula, (verbo) copulativo
count (noun): (nombre) contable

declarative: aseverativo
deep (structure): (estructura) profunda
definite: definido, determinado
degree word: palabra de grado
deictic: deíctico
delete, drop: suprimir, elidir; deletion: supresión, elisión
demonstrative: demostrativo
dental: dental
derive: derivar; derivative: derivativo; derivation: derivación
determiner: determinante
devoice: ensordecer; devoicing: ensordecimiento
dialect: dialecto; dialectal: dialectal
digraph: digrama (M), dígrafo
diphthong: diptongo; diphthongal: diptongal; diphthongize: diptongar; falling/rising diphthong: diptongo creciente/decreciente
direct object: complemento (*or* objeto) directo
discourse: discurso

ellipsis: elipsis (F); elliptical: elíptico
embed: incrustar, incorporar
emphasis: énfasis; emphatic: enfático
end (aspect): terminativo
ending (inflectional): desinencia
environment (of a rule): entorno
epenthesis: epéntesis (F)
epicene: epiceno
Equi-NP: equivalencia de FN (Frases Nominales), correferencia
etymology: etimología
extraposition: extraposición

feature (grammatical or phonological): rasgo
feminine: femenino

flap: vibrante simple (F)
focus: enfoque, foco
form: forma; formar; formation: formación
fricative: fricativo; friction: fricación, (of /j/ in particular) rehilamiento
front (vowel): (vocal) anterior, palatal
functor: palabra gramatical

gender: género
generate: generar: generative: generativo
Germanic: germánico
gerund: gerundio
glide: semivocal (F), paravocal (F), deslizada
glottal: glotal; glottal stop: golpe de glotis
govern: regir (i)
grammar: gramática; grammarian; gramático; grammatical: gramatical

head (of phrase): núcleo
hearer: oyente
height (of vowels): altura
hiatus: hiato
high (vowel): (vocal) alta, cerrada
homonym, homophone: homónimo, homófono

idiolect: idiolecto
idiom: modismo, giro; idiomatic: idiomático
impersonal: impersonal; unipersonal (verb such as *haber* or *llover* that is 3sg.)
indefinite: indefinido, indeterminado
indirect object: complemento (*or* objeto) indirecto
Indo-European: indoeuropeo
infinitive: infinitivo
inflection: flexión, inflexión; inflectional: flexivo
interlanguage: interlengua
interrogative: interrogativo
intonation: entonación; intonational: entonacional
intransitive: intransitivo

join: unir, enlazar

language: lengua, idioma (M); (speech, way of talking) lenguaje
larynx: laringe (F)
lateral: lateral
lax: laxo, lenis, relajado
length: duración; lengthen: alargar
lexicon: léxico; lexical: léxico
liaison: enlace
linguist: lingüista; linguistic: lingüístico; linguistics: lingüística
link, linking (between words): unir, enlazar; enlace; linking (verb): (verbo) copulativo
liquid: líquido
loanword: préstamo, extranjerismo; loan translation: calco
low (vowel): (vocal) baja, abierta

main (clause): matriz (F), (cláusula) principal
masculine: masculino
mass (noun): (nombre) de masa
matrix: matriz (F), (cláusula) principal
mean: significar; meaning: significado, sentido
mid (vowel): (vocal) media
middle (aspect): imperfectivo
minimal pair: par mínimo
modal: modal
modify: modificar; modifier: modificador
mood: modo
morpheme: morfema (M); morphology: morfología; morphological: morfológico
morphophonemic: mor(fo)fonológico; morphophonemics: mor(fo)fonología
move (a constituent): desplazar, mover; movement: desplazamiento

nasal: nasal
negate: negar (ie); negative: negativo; negation: negación
neuter: neutro (*lo, esto,* etc.), asexuado (*el libro,* etc.)
neutralize: neutralizar; neutralization: neutralización
node (in a phrase marker): nódulo, nudo
nominalize (an NP): sustantivar (una FN); nominalization: sustantivación

nonfinite: infinito, (forma) infinita, no finita
noun: sustantivo, nombre; noun phrase: frase nominal (F), sintagma nominal (M); noun clause: cláusula nominal
nucleus: núcleo
number: número

object: complemento, objeto; object of a preposition: término de preposición
oblique object: complemento (*or* objeto) oblicuo
obstruent: obstruyente
onset: cabeza (de sílaba)

palate: paladar; palatal: palatal
paradigm: paradigma (M)
part of speech: parte (F) de la oración, categoría
participle: participio
particle: partícula
passive: pasivo; passivization: pasivización
pattern: pauta, patrón
periphrasis: perífrasis; periphrastic: perifrástico
person (1, 2, 3): (primera, segunda, tercera) persona
phone: fono; phonetic: fonético; phonetics: fonética
phoneme: fonema (M); phonemic: fonemático; phonology: fonología; phonological: fonológico
phonotactics: fonotaxis (F)
phrase: frase (F), sintagma (M); phrase structure rule: regla de estructura de frase, regla ahormacional; set phrase: frase hecha; phrase marker: marcador de frase
pitch: tono
place, put: colocar, poner; place in front: anteponer; place after: posponer; place next to: yuxtaponer; place in between: interponer; placement: colocación
plural: plural
polyseme: palabra polisémica; polysemy: polisemia
possession: posesión; possessive: posesivo
postpose: posponer; postposition: posposición
pragmatics: pragmática
predicate: predicado; predicate attribute, PA: atributo predicativo
prefix: prefijo
prepose: anteponer; pre-position: anteposición
preposition: preposición; prepositional phrase: frase (F) preposicional, sintagma (M) preposicional
progressive: progresivo
pronoun: pronombre; pronominal: pronominal; pronominalize: pronominalizar
pro-verb: proverbo, sustituto verbal
proverb: refrán, proverbio, dicho
pseudoreflexive: seudorreflejo
put. *See* place, put

quantifier: cuantificativo, cuantificador
question: interrogativa, pregunta; information (Wh-) question: interrogativa parcial; tag question: interrogativa dubitativa; yes/no question: interrogativa general

raising: (of vowels) cerrazón; (of embedded subject to object) elevación
reciprocal: recíproco
reduce: reducir; reduction: reducción
reflexive: reflejo (for all morphological reflexives), reflexivo (for true reflexives); reflexive verb: verbo pronominal
related: relacionado; (in etymology): emparentado; relation: relación
relative: relativo; headless relative: relativo libre; relator: nexo
restrict: restringir; restriction: restricción; restrictive: restrictivo
retroflex: retroflejo; retroflexion: retroflexión
rheme: rema (M)
rhyme: rima
rhythm: ritmo
Romance: románico, romance
rounded: redondeado, labializado; rounding: redondeamiento
r-sound: rótico
rule: regla

schwa: schwa, vocal reducida
scope (of negation): abarque, alcance (de la negación)
semantic: semántico; semantics semántica, semiología
sentence: oración; sentential: oracional
sibilant: sibilante
singular: singular
slang: argot, caló, habla vulgar
sonorant: sonante, sonorante
speaker: hablante
speech: habla; speech act: acto de elocución
spelling: deletreo (de una palabra), grafía (de un sonido), ortografía (en general); spelling change: cambio ortográfico
spirantization: espirantización, lenición
standard: estándar, normativo
stem: raíz (F), radical; stem change: cambio radical
stop: oclusivo, plosivo
strengthen: reforzar (ue); strengthening: refuerzo
stress: acento (de intensidad); stressed: tónico, acentuado; stress-timing: isocronía acentual
strong (verb): (verbo) fuerte, pretérito fuerte
structure: estructura; structural: estructural
style: estilo; stylistic: estilístico
subject: (grammatical) sujeto (de la oración o del verbo); (= topic) tema (M)
subordinate: subordinar; subordinating: subordinante
suffix: sufijo
suppletion: supletivismo
suprasegmental: suprasegmental, prosodia, prosodema (M)
surface (structure): (estructura) superficial, patente
syllable: sílaba; syllabic: silábico; syllable-timing: isocronía silábica; syllabication: silabeo
syncope: síncopa
syncretism: sincretismo
syneresis: sinéresis (F) (inside words), sinalefa (between words)
synonym: sinónimo; synonymy: sinonimia
syntax: sintaxis (F); syntactic: sintáctico

tap: vibrante simple (F)
target language: lengua objeto
tense: (vowel) tenso, fortis; (of verb) tiempo
terminal (of intonation): cadencia; falling/rising: descendente/ascendente, cadencia/anticadencia
theme: tema (M); theme vowel: vocal temática
theory: teoría; theoretical: teórico
Tough-movement: elevación de complemento
transform: transformar; transformation: transformación
transitive: transitivo
tree (for representing structure): diagrama arbóreo
trill: vibrante múltiple (F)

underlying: subyacente
ungrammatical: agramatical
unstressed: átono, inacentuado
utterance: enunciado

vary: variar (í); variable: variable; variant: variante (F); variation: variación
velar: velar; velum: velo (del paladar)
verb: verbo; verb phrase: frase verbal (F), sintagma verbal (M)
vocabulary: vocabulario
vocal cords: cuerdas vocales
vocative: vocativo
voice: voz (F), sonoridad; sonorizar; voiced: sonoro
vowel: vocal (F)

word: palabra, voz (F), vocablo; word order: orden de palabras

Appendix 2

Phonological index

For more direct access, most phonological terms and symbols have been placed here instead of in the index. Phonemes (/ /) are listed alphabetically for each language, with descriptions of their main allophones ([ ]) and references to sections on their articulation or behavior. Alternative symbols used by some linguists (often with conflicting values) are shown in parentheses following the symbols used in this book, which are those of the International Phonetic Alphabet except [r̄ ř ɹ̆] for IPA [r ɾ ɹ]. Other formalisms are listed in the last two sections.

Spanish phonemes and their major allophones (twenty-three to twenty-five total; see figures 2.1 and 2.7 in chapter 2)

/a/ low central or low front unrounded vowel: 1.1.4, 2.2.1
/b/ voiced bilabial stop: 3.1.6
  [β] (ƀ) voiced bilabial fricative: 3.1.6, 3.1.7
/d/ voiced dental stop, [d̪]: 2.1.2, 3.1.6
  [ð] (đ, δ) voiced dental fricative: 1.2, 3.1.6, 3.1.7
/e/ mid front unrounded vowel: 2.2.1
/f/ voiceless labiodental fricative: 3.1.8
  [ɸ] voiceless bilabial fricative (in some dialects): 3.1.8
/g/ voiced velar stop: 3.1.6
  [ɣ] (ǥ) voiced velar fricative: 3.1.6, 3.1.7
/i/ high front unrounded vowel: 2.2.1
/j/ = [i̯] (y) voiced palatal glide, yod: 2.1.4.1, 2.2.3, 3.1.10
  [ʝ] (y, ǰ) voiced palatal fricative: 3.1.1
  [ɟ] (ŷ) voiced palatal stop: 3.1.1
  [ʒ] (ž) voiced alveopalatal fricative (in some dialects): 3.1.1
  [dʒ] (ǰ) voiced alveopalatal affricate (in some dialects): 3.1.1
/k/ voiceless velar stop: 2.1.1
/l/ voiced alveolar lateral, "clear" [l̥]: 3.2.5
  [l̪] voiced dental lateral: 3.1.3
  [ɺ] voiced alveolar lateral flap (in some dialects): 3.1.8
/ʎ/ (ƛ, l̰) voiced palatal lateral (in *lleísta* dialects): 2.1.4.1
/m/ voiced bilabial nasal: 3.1.2
/n/ voiced alveolar nasal: 3.1.2
  [ɱ] voiced labiodental nasal: 3.1.2
  [n̪] voiced dental nasal: 3.1.2
  [ŋ] voiced velar nasal: 3.1.2, 3.1.8
/ɲ/ (ñ, n̰) voiced palatal nasal, the *eñe*: 2.1.3.1, 3.1.2
/o/ mid back rounded vowel: 2.2.1

/p/ voiceless bilabial stop: 3.2.1
/r/ voiced alveolar flap, [ɾ]: 2.1.3.3
[ɹ̌] assibilated apicoalveolar fricative: 3.1.8
/r̄/ voiced alveolar trill: 2.1.3.3
[ř] assibilated alveolar trill: 3.1.8
[ʀ] uvular trill (in some dialects): 3.1.8
[x] voiceless velar fricative (in some dialects): 3.1.8
/s/ voiceless alveolar fricative, sibilant (grooved), usually laminal [s̻]: 2.1.4.2, 3.1.4
[s̺] (ś) apicoalveolar fricative, sibilant (in some dialects): 2.1.4.2
[s̪] dentalized apicoalveolar fricative, sibilant (in some dialects): 2.1.4.2
[z] voiced alveolar fricative, sibilant: 3.1.4
[h] voiceless glottal fricative, aspirate (in some dialects), variably dropped: 2.1.2
/t/ voiceless dental stop, [t̪]: 2.1.2
/tʃ/ (č ĉ, ŝ) voiceless alveopalatal affricate, sibilant: 1.1.3
[ʃ] (š) voiceless alveopalatal fricative, sibilant (in some dialects): 1.1.3
/θ/ voiceless dental fricative (in some dialects): 2.1.4.2
/u/ high back rounded vowel: 2.2.1
/w/ = [u̯] rounded voiced labiovelar glide: 2.2.3, 3.1.1
[ɣw] rounded voiced velar fricative: 3.1.3
/x/ voiceless velar fricative, the *jota* sound: 2.1.3.2
[χ] voiceless uvular fricative (the *jota* of some dialects): 2.1.3.2
[ç] (x̂) voiceless palatal fricative (in some dialects): 3.1.8
[h] voiceless glottal fricative, aspirate (in some dialects): 2.1.3.2

English phonemes and their major allophones (forty total; see figures 2.2 and 2.7 in chapter 2)

/ɑ/ (a) low back unrounded vowel: 2.2.1 (rounded British variant /ɒ/: 2.2)
/æ/ low front unrounded vowel: 2.2.1
/aj/ = [ai] (ay) rising front unrounded diphthong: 1.1.4, 2.2.2
/aw/ = [au] rising back rounded diphthong: 1.1.4, 2.2.2
/b/ voiced bilabial stop: 2.1.1
/d/ voiced alveolar stop: 2.1.2
[ɾ] (ᴅ) voiced alveolar flap: 2.1.3.3, 3.2.3
/dʒ/ (ǰ) voiced alveopalatal affricate, sibilant: 3.1.1
/ð/ voiced dental fricative: 1.2
/e/ mid front unrounded tense vowel, usually diphthongal [ej] (ey, ei): 2.2.1, 3.2.6
/ɛ/ mid front unrounded lax vowel: 1.1.3
/ə/ mid central reduced vowel, schwa: 1.1.4, 2.2, 3.2.7, 3.2.8
/ər/ mid central retroflex vowel, [ɚ]: 2.2, 3.2.8
[ɜ] tensed (but non-retroflex) mid central (in British English): 2.2
/f/ voiceless labiodental fricative: 2.1.1
/g/ voiced velar stop: 2.1.1
/h/ voiceless glottal fricative, aspirate: 1.1.3
/i/ high front unrounded tense vowel, sometimes diphthongal [ij] (iy): 2.2.1, 3.2.6
/ɪ/ (ɩ) high front unrounded lax vowel: 1.1.3
/j/ (y) voiced palatal glide, yod: 1.1.1, 1.1.3, 3.1.1
/k/ voiceless velar stop: 3.2.1
[kʰ] aspirated: 3.2.1
[ʔk] preglottalized: 3.2.2
/l/ voiced alveolar lateral, generally "dark" (velarized) [ɫ]: 3.2.5
/m/ voiced bilabial nasal: 2.1.1
/n/ voiced alveolar nasal: 2.1.1
/ŋ/ voiced velar nasal: 3.1.8
/o/ mid back rounded tense vowel, usually diphthongal [ow] (ou, əu): 2.2.1, 3.2.6
/ɔ/ mid back rounded lax vowel (in most dialects): 1.1.3
/ɔj/ = [ɔi] (oy) rising-fronting diphthong: 1.1.4, 2.2.2
/p/ voiceless bilabial stop: 3.2.1
[pʰ] aspirated: 3.2.1
[ʔp] preglottalized: 3.2.2

/r/ voiced retroflex ([ɻ]) or alveolar ([ɹ]) approximant: 2.1.3.3
[ɻ^{w}] or [ɹ^{w}] rounded: 1.2, 2.1.3.3
/s/ voiceless alveolar fricative, sibilant: 2.1.4.2
/ʃ/ (š) voiceless alveopalatal fricative, sibilant: 1.1.3
/t/ voiceless alveolar stop: 2.1.2, 3.2.1
[t^{h}] aspirated: 3.2.1
[ʔt], [ʔ] preglottalized or replaced by glottal stop: 3.2.2
[ɾ] (D) voiced alveolar flap: 2.1.3.3, 3.2.3
/tʃ/ (č) voiceless alveopalatal affricate: 1.1.
[tʃ^{h}] aspirated: 3.2.1
[ʔtʃ] preglottalized: 3.2.2
/θ/ voiceless dental fricative: 2.1.4.2
/u/ high back or central rounded tense vowel, usually diphthongal [ʉw]: 2.2.1, 3.2.6
/ʊ/ high back rounded lax vowel: 1.1.3
/ʌ/ mid back unrounded lax vowel: 2.2
/v/ voiced labiodental fricative: 2.1.1
/w/ voiced labiovelar glide, rounded: 3.1.1
/z/ voiced alveolar fricative, sibilant: 2.1.1
/ʒ/ (ž) voiced alveopalatal fricative, sibilant: 3.1.1

Diacritics and other symbols
(*C* = consonant, *V* = vowel)

ˈCV = CV́ primary stressed syllable
ˌCV = CV̀ secondary stressed syllable
CV̆ unstressed syllable (but usually left unmarked)
Vː lengthened
Ṽ nasalized
C̥V̥ devoiced
C̟ advanced, more forward in the mouth
C̩ syllabic consonant
→ becomes, changes to
< from (historical linguistics)
> became (historical linguistics)
~ varying with
Ø null, zero, deleted
{ } or
/ / phonemic representation
[ ] phonetic representation; features; constituents
/ in the environment of
+ morpheme boundary
# word boundary
| foot boundary
|| phrase boundary, pause
. or $ syllable boundary
σ syllable
↑ or ↗ rising intonation
↓ or ↘ falling intonation
* impossible, incorrect, ungrammatical

Reference list of phonological features (with selected phones of Spanish and English)

	t	tʰ	d	ʔ	p	k	x	tʃ	ɹ	ɾ	r̄	l	n	ɲ	s	θ	a	o	i	ɪ	j	w
[consonantal]	+	+	+	+	+	+	+	+	+	+	+	+	+	+	+	+	-	-	-	-	-	-
[syllabic]	-	-	-	-	-	-	-	-	-	-	-	-	-	-	-	-	+	+	+	+	-	-
[sonorant]	-	-	-	-	-	-	-	-	+	+	+	+	+	+	-	-	+	+	+	+	+	+
[voice]	-	-	+	-	-	-	-	-	+	+	+	+	+	+	-	-	+	+	+	+	+	+
[spread glottis]	-	+	-	-	-	-	-	-	-	-	-	-	-	-	-	-	-	-	-	-	-	-
[constricted glottis]	-	-	-	+	-	-	-	-	-	-	-	-	-	-	-	-	-	-	-	-	-	-
[labial]	-	-	-	-	+	-	-	-	-	-	-	-	-	-	-	-	-	+	-	-	-	+
[round]	-	-	-	-	-	-	-	-	-	-	-	-	-	-	-	-	-	+	-	-	-	+
[coronal]	+	+	+	-	-	-	-	+	+	+	+	+	+	-	+	+	-	-	-	-	-	-
[anterior]	+	+	+	-	+	-	-	-	-	+	+	+	+	-	+	+	-	-	-	-	-	-
[dorsal]	-	-	-	-	-	+	+	-	-	-	-	-	-	+	-	-	-	-	-	-	-	+
[high]	-	-	-	-	-	+	+	-	-	-	-	-	-	+	-	-	-	-	+	+	+	+
[back]	-	-	-	-	-	+	+	-	-	-	-	-	-	-	-	-	-	+	-	-	-	+
[low]	-	-	-	-	-	-	-	-	-	-	-	-	-	-	-	-	+	-	-	-	-	-
[tense]	-	-	-	-	-	-	-	-	-	-	-	-	-	-	-	-	+	+	+	-	-	-
[long]	-	-	-	-	-	-	-	-	-	-	+	-	-	-	-	-	-	-	-	-	-	-
[nasal]	-	-	-	-	-	-	-	-	-	-	-	-	+	+	-	-	-	-	-	-	-	-
[lateral]	-	-	-	-	-	-	-	-	-	-	-	+	-	-	-	-	-	-	-	-	-	-
[continuant]	-	-	-	-	-	-	+	-	+	-	-	+	-	-	+	+	+	+	+	+	+	+
[strident]	-	-	-	-	-	-	-	+	-	-	-	-	-	-	+	-	-	-	-	-	-	-
[delayed release]	-	-	-	-	-	-	-	+	-	-	-	-	-	-	-	-	-	-	-	-	-	-
[distributed]	-	-	-	-	+	+	+	+	-	-	-	-	-	+	+	-	-	-	-	-	-	-

References

Agard, Frederick B. 1984. *A course in Romance linguistics.* Vol. 1: *A synchronic view.* Washington, D.C.: Georgetown University Press.

Aid, Frances. 1973. *Semantic structures in Spanish: A proposal for instructional materials.* Washington, D.C.: Georgetown University Press.

Alarcos Llorach, Emilio. 1999. *Gramática de la lengua española.* Colección Nebrija y Bello / Real Academia Española. Madrid: Espasa Calpe.

Alonso, Amado. 1967. *Estudios lingüísticos: temas hispanoamericanos.* Madrid: Editorial Gredos.

———. 1974. Estilística y gramática del artículo en español. In *Estudios lingüísticos: temas españoles.* Madrid: Editorial Gredos.

Alonso, Dámaso. 1950. Vocales andaluzas. *Nueva revista de filología hispana* 4:209–30.

Alvar, Manuel, A. Llorente, and G. Salvador, eds. 1964. *Atlas lingüístico y etnográfico de Andalucía.* Granada: Universidad de Granada.

Amastae, Jon. 1995. Variable spirantization: Constraint weighing in three dialects. *Hispanic Linguistics* 6/7:265–85.

Amastae, Jon, and Lucía Elías-Olivares, eds. 1982. *Spanish in the United States: Sociolinguistic aspects.* Cambridge: Cambridge University Press.

Anderson, Roger W. 1983. Transfer to somewhere. In *Language transfer in language learning,* ed. Susan M. Gass and Larry Selinker, 177–201. Rowley, Mass: Newbury House Publishers.

Atlas lingüístico de la península ibérica. 1962. Madrid: Consejo Superior de Investigaciones Científicas.

Azevedo, Milton. 1992. *Introducción a la lingüística española.* Englewood Cliffs, N.J.: Prentice Hall.

Babcock, Sandra. 1970. *The syntax of Spanish reflexive verbs.* The Hague: Mouton.

Barrutia, Richard, and Armin Schwegler. 1994. *Fonética y fonología españolas: teoría y práctica.* New York: Wiley & Sons.

Batchelor, R. E. 1994. *Using Spanish synonyms.* Cambridge: Cambridge University Press.

Batchelor, R. E., and C. J. Pountain. 1992. *Using Spanish: A guide to contemporary usage.* Cambridge: Cambridge University Press.

Bell, Anthony. 1980. Mood in Spanish: A discussion of some recent proposals. *Hispania* 63:377–89.

Bello, Andrés (with Rufino Cuervo). [1847] 1958. *Gramática de la lengua castellana.* Edited by Niceto Alcalá-Zamora y Torres. Buenos Aires: Editorial Sopena Argentina.

Benrabah, M. 1997. Word stress: A source of unintelligibility in English. *International Review of Applied Linguistics* 35/3:157–65.

Bergen, John. 1978a. One rule for the Spanish subjunctive. *Hispania* 61:218–34.

———. 1978b. A simplified approach for teaching the gender of Spanish nouns. *Hispania* 61:865–76.

———. 1980. The semantics of gender contrasts in Spanish. *Hispania* 63:48–57.

Bjarkman, Peter, and Robert Hammond, eds. 1989. *American Spanish pronunciation.* Washington, D.C.: Georgetown University Press.

Blackwell, Sarah. 1998. Constraints on Spanish NP anaphora: The syntactic vs. pragmatic domain. *Hispania* 81:606–18.

Bolinger, Dwight. 1954. English prosodic stress and Spanish sentence order. *Hispania* 37:152–56.

———. 1972. Adjective position again. *Hispania* 55:91–94.

———. 1974. One subjunctive or two? *Hispania* 57:462–71.

———. 1976. Again—one subjunctive or two? *Hispania* 59:41–49.

Bond, Z. S., and Joann Fokes. 1985. Non-native patterns of English syllable timing. *Journal of Phonetics* 13:407–20.

Bordelois, Ivonne. 1978. Animacy or subjecthood: Clitic movement and Romance causatives. In *Contemporary studies in Romance linguistics*, ed. Margarita Suñer, 18–40. Washington, D.C.: Georgetown University Press.

Bosque, Ignacio, and Manuel Pérez Fernández. 1987. *Diccionario inverso de la lengua española.* Madrid: Editorial Gredos.

Bowen, J. Donald, and Robert Stockwell. 1955. The phonemic interpretation of semivowels in Spanish. *Language* 31:236–40.

Boyd-Bowman, Peter. 1960. *El habla de Guanajuato.* México: Imprenta Universitaria de la Universidad Nacional Autónoma.

Briscoe, Laurel, and Enrique LaMadrid. 1978. *Lectura y lengua: curso intermedio.* Boston: Houghton Mifflin.

Brizuela, Maquela, Elaine Anderson, and Lynne Stallings. 1999. Discourse markers as indicators of register. *Hispania* 82:128–41.

Brown, Penelope, and Stephen Levinson. 1978. Universals in language usage: Politeness phenomena. In *Questions and politeness,* ed. Esther Goody, 56–310. Cambridge: Cambridge University Press.

Brown, Roger, and A. Gilman. 1960. The pronouns of power and solidarity. In *Style in language,* ed. T. A. Sebeok, 253–76. Cambridge, Mass.: MIT Press.

Bull, William. 1947. Modern Spanish verb-form frequencies. *Hispania* 30:451–66.

———. 1965. *Spanish for teachers: Applied linguistics.* New York: Ronald Press.

———. 1972. *The visual grammar of Spanish.* University of California and Houghton Mifflin.

Bustamante López, Isabel, and Mercedes Niño-Murcia. 1995. Impositive speech acts in northern Andean Spanish: A pragmatic approach. *Hispania* 78:885–97.

Butler, Christopher. 1992. A corpus-based approach to relative clauses in the spoken Spanish of Madrid. *Hispanic Linguistics* 5:1–42.

Butt, John, and Carmen Benjamin. 1988. *A new reference grammar of modern Spanish.* London: Edward Arnold.

Cameron, Richard. 1995. The scope and limits of Switch Reference as a constraint on pronominal subject expression. *Hispanic Linguistics* 6/7:1–27.

Campbell, Joe, Mark Goldin, and Mary Wang, eds. 1974. *Linguistic studies in Romance languages.* Washington, D.C.: Georgetown University Press.

Campos, Héctor. 1993. *De la oración simple a la oración compuesta: Curso superior de gramática española*. Washington, D.C.: Georgetown University Press.

Campos, Héctor, and Fernando Martínez Gil, eds. 1991. *Current studies in Spanish linguistics*. Washington, D.C.: Georgetown University Press.

Canale, Michael, and Merrill Swain. 1979. *Communicative approaches to second language teaching and testing*. Toronto: Ontario Ministry of Education.

Canfield, D. Lincoln. 1981. *Spanish pronunciation in the Americas*. Chicago: University of Chicago Press.

Cárdenas, Daniel. 1967. *El español de Jalisco*. Madrid: Consejo Superior de Investigaciones Científicas, *Revista de filología española*, anejo 85.

Carnicer, Ramón. 1977. *Tradición y evolución en el lenguaje actual*. Madrid: Editorial Prensa Española.

Carratalá, Ernesto. 1980. *Morfosintaxis del castellano actual*. Barcelona: Editorial Labor.

Carreira, María. 1991. The alternating diphthongs of Spanish: A paradox revisited. In *Current studies in Spanish linguistics*, ed. Héctor Campos and Fernando Martínez Gil, 407–45. Washington, D.C.: Georgetown University Press.

Carricaburo, Norma. 1997. *Las fórmulas de tratamiento en el español actual*. Madrid: Arco/Libros.

Casagrande, Jean, and Bohdan Saciuk, eds. 1972. *Generative studies in Romance languages*. Rowley, Mass.: Newbury House.

Cepeda, Gladys. 1995. Retention and deletion of word-final /s/ in Valdivian Spanish (Chile). *Hispanic Linguistics* 6/7:329–53.

Champion, James. 1979. Derivatives of irregular verbs. *Hispania* 62:317–20.

Chomsky, Noam. 1957. *Syntactic structures*. The Hague: Mouton.

———. 1959. Review of *Verbal behavior* by B. F. Skinner. *Language* 35:26–58.

———. 1965. *Aspects of the theory of syntax*. Cambridge, Mass.: MIT Press.

———. 1981. On binding. In *Binding and filtering*, ed. F. W. Heny, 47–103. Cambridge, Mass.: MIT Press.

———. 1982. *Some concepts and consequences of the theory of government and binding*. Cambridge, Mass.: MIT Press.

Coll Mestre, Josep, María José Gelabert, and Emma Martinell Gifre. 1990. *Diccionario de gestos con sus giros más usuales*. Madrid: Edelsa.

Contreras, Heles. 1974. *Indeterminate subject sentences in Spanish*. Bloomington: Indiana University Linguistics Club.

———. 1979. Clause reduction, the saturation constraint, and clitic promotion in Spanish. *Linguistic Analysis* 5:161–82.

Cook, Walter, S.J. 1969. *Introduction to tagmemic analysis*. Washington, D.C.: Georgetown University Press.

Corder, S. P. 1967. The significance of learners' errors. *International Review of Applied Linguistics* 5:161–69.

Cotton, Eleanor Greet, and John M. Sharp. 1988. *Spanish in the Americas*. Washington, D.C.: Georgetown University Press.

Cressey, William. 1969. Teaching the position of Spanish adjectives: A transformational approach. *Hispania* 52:878–81.

Cruzado, Anna. 1982. Diminutive, augmentative, and pejorative suffixes in English and Spanish. In *Readings in Spanish-English contrastive linguistics III*, ed. Rose Nash and Domitila Belaval, 66–92. San Juan: Inter American University Press.

Cuervo, Rufino José. [1886–93] 1953. *Diccionario de construcción de la lengua castellana*. Bogotá: Instituto Caro y Cuervo.

———. 1948. *Disquisiciones sobre filología castellana*. Buenos Aires: Ateneo.

Curme, George C. 1947. *Principles and practice of English grammar*. New York: Barnes and Noble.

Dalbor, John. 1980. Observations on present-day *seseo* and *ceceo* in southern Spain. *Hispania* 63:5–19.

———. 1997. *Spanish pronunciation: Theory and practice*. 3rd ed. New York: Holt, Rinehart and Winston.

Danesi, Marcel. 1982. The description of Spanish /b d g/ revisited. *Hispania* 65:252–8.

DaSilva, Zenia Sacks. 1982. *On with Spanish*. New York: Harper and Row.

DaSilva, Zenia Sacks, and Gabriel Lovett. 1965. *A concept approach to Spanish*. New York: Harper and Row.

Davies, Mark. 1995. Analyzing syntactic variation with computer-based corpora: The case of modern Spanish clitic climbing. *Hispania* 78:370–80.

Davis, J. Carey. 1969. The IO of possession in Spanish. *University of Southern Florida Language Quarterly* 7:2–6.

De Granda, Germán. 1998. Replanteamiento de un tema controvertido: génesis y retención del doble posesivo en el español andino. *Revista de filología española* 77:139–47.

De Mello, George. 1990. Denotation of female sex in Spanish occupational nouns: The DRAE revisited. *Hispania* 73:392–400.

———. 1993. *-Ra* vs. *-se* subjunctive: A new look at an old topic. *Hispania* 76:235–44.

———. 1995a. El dequeísmo en el español hablado contemporáneo: ¿un caso de independencia semántica? *Hispanic Linguistics* 6/7:117–52.

———. 1995b. Preposición + sujeto + infinitivo: "para yo hacerlo". *Hispania* 78:825–36.

De Miguel, Elena. 1993. Construcciones ergativas e inversión en la lengua y la interlengua española. In *La lingüística y el análisis de los sistemas no nativos*, ed. Juana Liceras, 178–95. Ottawa Hispanic Studies 12. Ottawa: Dovehouse Editions Canada.

Demonte, Violeta. 1991. Temporal and aspectual constraints on predicative adjective phrases. In *Current studies in Spanish linguistics*, ed. Héctor Campos and Fernando Martínez Gil, 165–200. Washington, D.C.: Georgetown University Press.

Devney, Dorothy M. 1992. *Guide to Spanish suffixes*. Chicago: Passport Books (NTC).

Díaz, Enrique. 1989. The analysis of NP's with infinitival heads in Spanish. *Hispanic Linguistics* 3:1–25.

Díaz Guerrero, Rogelio, and Lorand B. Szalay. 1991. *Understanding Mexicans and Americans: Cultural perspectives in conflict*. New York: Plenum Press.

Dinnsen, Daniel. 1972. Additional constraints on clitic order in Spanish. In *Generative studies in Romance languages*, ed. Jean Casagrande and Bohdan Saciuk, 176–83. Rowley, Mass.: Newbury House.

D'Introno, Francesco. 1990. *Sintaxis transformacional del español*. 3rd ed. Madrid: Cátedra.

DiPietro, Robert. 1971. *Language structures in contrast*. Rowley, Mass.: Newbury House.

Dowdle, Harold. 1967. Observations on the uses of *a* and *de* in Spanish. *Hispania* 50:329–34.

Dowty, David. 1991. Thematic proto-roles and argument selection. *Language* 67:547–619.

Drake, Dana, Manuel Ascarza, and Oralia Preble. 1982. The use and non-use of a preposition or other word between a noun and the following infinitive. *Hispania* 65:79–85.

Dulay, Heidi, and Marina Burt. 1974. Goofing: An indicator of children's second language learning strategies. In *Error analysis: Perspectives on second language acquisition*, ed. Jack C. Richards, 54–68. London: Longman.

Dulay, Heidi, Marina Burt, and Stephen Krashen. 1982. *Language two*. New York: Oxford University Press.

Eckman, Fred. 1977. Markedness and the Contrastive Analysis Hypothesis. *Language Learning* 27:315–30.

Eddington, David. 1995. The psychological relevance of phonological generalizations in Spanish: An experiment. *Hispania* 78:875–84.

Educational Testing Service. 1982. *ETS oral proficiency testing manual*. Princeton, N.J.: Educational Testing Service.

Escandell Vidal, M. Victoria, and Manuel Leonetti Jungl. 1989. Notas sobre la aposición nominal. *Revista de filología española* 69:163–78.

Fasold, Ralph, and Roger Shuy, eds. 1977. *Studies in language variation*. Washington, D.C.: Georgetown University Press.

Fernández-Ordóñez, Inés. 1994. Isoglosas internas del castellano: el sistema referencial del pronombre átono de tercera persona. *Revista de filología española* 74:71–125.

Fernández Sevilla, Julio. 2000. Los fonemas implosivos en español. In *Panorama de la fonología española actual*, ed. Juana Gil Fernández, 207–34. Madrid: Arco/Libros.

Fidelholz, James. 1975. Word frequency and vowel reduction in English. *Chicago Linguistic Society regional meeting: Papers* 11:200–213.

Fillmore, Charles. 1968. *The case for case*. In *Universals in linguistic theory,* ed. Emmon Bach and Robert T. Harms, 1–88. New York: Holt, Rinehart and Winston.

Fish, Gorden. 1961. Adjectives fore and aft: Position and function in Spanish. *Hispania* 44:700–708.

———. 1967. *A* with a Spanish direct object. *Hispania* 50:80–85.

Flórez, Luis. 1951. *La pronunciación del español en Bogotá*. Bogotá: Instituto Caro y Cuervo.

Fontanella de Weinberg, María Beatriz. 1974. *Un aspecto sociolingüístico del español bonaerense*. Bahía Blanca: Cuadernos de lingüística.

Fromkin, Victoria, Stephen Krashen, Susan Curtiss, David Rigler, and Marilyn Rigler. [1974] 1981. The development of language in Genie: A case of language acquisition beyond the "critical period." In *Language: Introductory readings,* ed. Virginia Clark, Paul Eschholz, and Alfred Rosa, 142–69. New York: St. Martin's Press.

Fromkin, Victoria, and Robert Rodman. 1998. *An introduction to language*. 6th ed. Fort Worth: Harcourt Brace.

Garcés, María Pilar. 1997. *Las formas verbales en español: Valores y usos*. Madrid: Editorial Verbum.

García, Carmen. 1992. Refusing an invitation: A case study of Peruvian style. *Hispanic Linguistics* 5:207–43.

———. 1996. Teaching speech act performance: Declining an invitation. *Hispania* 79:267–77.

García, Erica. 1975. *The role of theory in linguistic analysis: The Spanish pronoun system*. Amsterdam: North-Holland.

García, Erica, and Ricardo Otheguy. 1977. Dialect differences in *leísmo*: A semantic approach. In *Studies in language variation*, ed. Ralph Fasold and Roger Shuy, 65–87. Washington, D.C.: Georgetown University Press.

García, MaryEllen. 1995. *En los sábados, en la mañana, en veces*: A look at *en* in the Spanish of San Antonio. In *Spanish in four continents: Studies in language contact and bilingualism,* ed. Carmen Silva-Corvalán, 196–213. Washington, D.C.: Georgetown University Press.

García Gutiérrez, Marta. 1993. El español como lengua segunda de un italiano. In *La lingüística y el análisis de los sistemas no nativos*, ed. Juana Liceras, 81–123. Ottawa Hispanic Studies 12. Ottawa: Dovehouse Editions Canada.

García Miguel, José M. 1995. *Transitividad y complementación preposicional en español.* Santiago de Compostela: Universidade de Santiago de Compostela.

García-Pelayo y Gross, Ramón. 1983. *Pequeño Larousse ilustrado*. Vitoria: Larousse.

Gass, Susan M., and Larry Selinker, eds. 1983. *Language transfer in language learning*. Rowley, Mass: Newbury House Publishers.

Gil Fernández, Juana, ed. 2000. *Panorama de la fonología española actual*. Madrid: Arco/Libros.

Gili Gaya, Samuel. 1973. *Vox curso superior de sintaxis española*. Barcelona: Bibliograf.

Givón, Talmy. 1979a. *On understanding grammar.* New York: Academic Press.

———, ed. 1979b. *Syntax and semantics.* Vol. 12: *Discourse and syntax.* New York: Academic Press.

Goldin, Mark. 1972. Indirect objects in Spanish and English. In *Generative studies in Romance languages*, ed. Jean Casagrande and Bohdan Saciuk, 376–83. Rowley, Mass.: Newbury House.

———. 1974. A psychological perspective of the Spanish subjunctive. *Hispania* 57:295–301.

Gómez de Ivashevsky, Aura. 1969. *Lenguaje coloquial venezolano*. Caracas: Instituto de Filología Andrés Bello, Facultad de Humanidades y Educación, Universidad Central de Venezuela.

Gonzales, Patrick. 1995. Progressive and nonprogressive imperfects in Spanish discourse. *Hispanic Linguistics* 6/7:61–92.

González Bueno, Manuela. 1993. Variaciones en el tratamiento de las sibilantes: inconsistencia en el seseo sevillano. *Hispania* 76:392–98.

———. 1997. The effect of formal instruction on the acquisition of Spanish stop consonants. In *Contemporary perspectives on the acquisition of Spanish*, ed. Ana Teresa Pérez-Leroux and William Glass, 2:57–75. Somerville, Mass.: Cascadilla Press.

González, Gustavo. 1978. *The acquisition of Spanish grammar by native Spanish-speaking children*. Rosslyn, Va.: National Clearinghouse for Bilingual Education.

González, Luis, and M. Stanley Whitley. 1999. *Lo es*: un clítico anómalo en la teoría de roles. *Hispania* 82:298–308.

González, Nora. 1997. A parametric study of Spanish L2 acquisition: Interpretation of Spanish word order. In *Contemporary perspectives on the acquisition of Spanish*, ed. Ana Teresa Pérez-Leroux and William Glass, 1:133–48. Somerville, Mass.: Cascadilla Press.

Gootch, Anthony. 1970. *Diminutive, augmentative, and pejorative suffixes in modern Spanish: A guide to their use and meaning*. Oxford: Pergamon Press.

Gorden, Raymond. 1974. *Living in Latin America: A case-study in cross-cultural communication.* Skokie, Ill.: National Textbook Co. and the American Council on the Teaching of Foreign Languages.

Graham, Carol. 1978. *Jazz chants*. New York: Oxford University Press.

Greenberg, Joseph. 1963a. Some universals of grammar with particular reference to the order of meaningful elements. In *Universals of language*, ed. Joseph Greenberg, 73–113. Cambridge, Mass.: MIT Press.

———, ed. 1963b. *Universals of language*. Cambridge, Mass.: MIT Press.

Guitart, Jorge. 1978. Aspects of Spanish aspect: A new look at the preterite/imperfect distinction. In *Contemporary studies in Romance linguistics*, ed. Margarita Suñer, 132–68. Washington, D.C.: Georgetown University Press.

Gunterman, Gail. 1992a. An analysis of interlanguage development over time: Part I, *por* and *para*. *Hispania* 75:177–87.

———. 1992b. An analysis of interlanguage development over time: Part II, *ser* and *estar*. *Hispania* 75:1294–1303.

Hadlich, Roger. 1971. *A transformational grammar of Spanish.* Englewood Cliffs, N.J.: Prentice-Hall.

Hagerty, Timothy, and J. Donald Bowen. 1973. *A contrastive analysis of a lexical split*. In *Readings in Spanish-English contrastive linguistics*, ed. Rose Nash, 1–71. San Juan, P.R.: Inter American University Press.

Haiman, John. 1983. Iconic and economic motivation. *Language* 59:781–819.

Halliday, M. A. K., and R. Hasan. 1976. *Cohesion in English*. London: Longman.

Hammond, Robert. 1980. Las realizaciones fonéticas del fonema /s/ en el español cubano rápido de Miami. In *Dialectología hispanoamericana: estudios actuales*, ed. Gary Scavnicky, 8–15. Washington, D.C.: Georgetown University Press.

———. 1989. American Spanish dialectology and phonology from current theoretical perspectives. In *American Spanish pronunciation*, ed. Peter Bjarkman and Robert Hammond, 137–50. Washington, D.C.: Georgetown University Press.

Handelsman, Michale, William Heflin, and Rafael Hernández. 1981. *La cultura hispana: dentro y fuera de los Estados Unidos*. New York: Random House.

Harris, David P. 1971. The intonation of English "yes-no" questions: Two studies compared and synthesized. *TESOL Quarterly* 5:123–27.

Harris, James. 1969. *Spanish phonology*. Cambridge, Mass.: MIT Press.

———. 1983. *Syllable structure and stress in Spanish*. Cambridge, Mass.: MIT Press.

———. 1989. Our present understanding of Spanish syllable structure. In *American Spanish pronunciation*, ed. Peter Bjarkman and Robert Hammond, 151–69. Washington, D.C.: Georgetown University Press.

Haverkate, Henk. 1984. *Speech acts, speakers, and hearers: Reference and referential strategies in Spanish*. Amsterdam: John Benjamins Company.

Hernán, Laura. 1994. VIPI, visualización del pretérito y del imperfecto. *Hispania* 77:280–86.

Holton, James. 1960. Placement of object pronouns. *Hispania* 43:584–85.

Hooper, Joan B. 1976. *An introduction to natural generative phonology.* New York: Academic Press.

Hualde, José. 1989. Silabeo y estructura morfémica en español. *Hispania* 72:821–31.

Hurley, Joni Kay. 1995. The impact of Quichua on verb forms used in Spanish requests in Otavalo, Ecuador. In *Spanish in four continents: Studies in language contact and bilingualism,* ed. Carmen Silva-Corvalán, 39–51. Washington, D.C.: Georgetown University Press.

Hurst, Dorothy. 1951. Spanish case: Influence of subject and connotation of force. *Hispania* 34:74–78.

Hymes, Dell. 1972. On communicative competence. In *Sociolinguistics: Selected Readings,* ed. J. B. Pride and Janet Holmes, 269–93. Middlesex, U.K.: Penguin.

———. 1974. Ways of speaking. In *Explorations in the ethnography of speaking,* ed. R. Bauman and J. Sherzer, 433–510. Cambridge: Cambridge University Press.

International Phonetic Association. 1999. *Handbook of the International Phonetic Association.* Cambridge: Cambridge University Press.

Jacobs, Roderick, and Peter Rosenbaum. 1968. *English transformational grammar.* Waltham, Mass.: Xerox College Publishing.

Jaeggli, Osvaldo, and Kenneth J. Safir, eds. 1989. *The Null Subject parameter.* Dordrecht: Kluwer Academic Publishers.

James, Carl. 1980. *Contrastive analysis.* London: Longman.

———. 1998. *Errors in language learning and use: Exploring error analysis.* New York: Longman.

Jaramillo, June. 1995. Social variation in personal address etiquette. *Hispanic Linguistics* 6/7:191–224.

Jelinski, Jack. 1977. A new look at teaching the Spanish subjunctive. *Hispania* 60:320–26.

Jensen, John B. 1982. Coming and going in English and Spanish. In *Readings in Spanish-English contrastive linguistics III,* ed. Rose Nash and Domitila Belaval, 37–65. San Juan: Inter American University Press.

Jorge Morel, Elercia. 1974. *Estudio lingüístico de Santo Domingo.* Santo Domingo: Editora Taller.

Kany, Charles. 1951. *American-Spanish syntax.* Chicago: University of Chicago Press.

Kaplan, Robert. 1966. Cultural thought patterns in inter-cultural education. *Language Learning* 16:1–20.

Kelm, Orlando. 1995. Acoustic measurement of Spanish and English pitch contours: Native and non-native speakers. *Hispanic Linguistics* 6/7:435–48.

Kempchinsky, Paula. 1992. Syntactic constraints on the expression of pronouns in Spanish. *Hispania* 75:697–704.

Kendris, Christopher. 1963. *201 Spanish verbs fully conjugated in all tenses.* Woodbury, N.Y.: Baffon's Educational Series.

Keniston, Hayward. 1937. *Spanish syntax list: A statistical study of grammatical usage.* New York: Holt.

King, Larry, and Margarita Suñer. 1980. The meaning of the progressive in Spanish and Portuguese. *Bilingual Review* 7:222–38.

Kirshner, Robert. 1951. Let's do away with idioms. *Hispania* 34:87.

Klee, Carol. 1998. Communication as an organizing principle in the National Standards: Sociolinguistic aspects of Spanish language teaching. *Hispania* 81:339–51.

Klein, Philip. 1984. Apparent correspondences in Spanish to English infinitival *to. Hispania* 67:416–19.

Kliffer, Mike. 1979. Levanto la mano/me lavo las manos/me levanto la mano. *Canadian Modern Language Review* 35:217–26.

Krashen, Stephen, and Robin Scarcella. 1978. On routines and patterns in language acquisition and performance. *Language Learning* 28:283–300.

Kurath, Hans. 1949. *Word geography of the eastern United States.* Ann Arbor: University of Michigan Press.

Kurath, Hans, and Raven McDavid Jr. 1961. *The pronunciation of English in the Atlantic states.* Ann Arbor: University of Michigan Press.

Kvavik, Karen. 1980. Las unidades melódicas en el español mexicano. In *Dialectología hispanoamericana: estudios actuales*, ed. Gary Scavnicky, 48–57. Washington, D.C.: Georgetown University Press.

Ladefoged, Peter. 1982. *A course in phonetics.* 2nd ed. New York: Harcourt, Brace, Jovanovich.

Lado, Robert. 1957. *Language across cultures.* Ann Arbor: University of Michigan Press.

Lafayette, Robert C., ed. 1996. *National Standards: A catalyst for reform.* Lincolnwood, Ill.: National Textbook Company and ACTFL.

Lafford, Barbara. 1989. Is functionalism a fact? Data from the Caribbean. *Hispanic Linguistics* 3:49–74.

———. 2000. Spanish applied linguistics in the twentieth century: A retrospective and bibliography (1900–99). *Hispania* 83:711–32.

Lakoff, George. 1971. Presupposition and relative well-formedness. In *Semantics: An interdisciplinary reader,* ed. Danny Steinberg and Leon Jakobovits, 329–40. Cambridge: Cambridge University Press.

LaMadrid, Enrique, William Bull, and Laurel Briscoe. 1974a. *Communicating in Spanish.* Boston: Houghton Mifflin.

———. 1974b. *Communicating in Spanish: Instructor's guide.* Boston: Houghton Mifflin.

Lambert, W. E. 1972. A study of the roles of attitudes and motivation in second-language learning. In *Readings in the sociology of language,* ed. Joshua Fishman, 473–91. The Hague: Mouton.

Lambert, W. E., and G. Richard Tucker. 1976. Tu, vous, usted: *A social psychological study of address patterns.* Rowley, Mass.: Newbury House.

Lambert, W. E., et al. 1963. Attitudinal and cognitive aspects of intensive study of a second language. *Journal of Abnormal and Social Psychology* 66:358–68.

Lang, M. F. 1990. *Spanish word formation: Productive derivational morphology in the modern lexis.* London: Routledge.

Lantolf, James P. 1978. The variable constraints on mood in Puerto-Rican American Spanish. In *Contemporary studies in Romance linguistics*, ed. Margarita Suñer, 193–217. Washington, D.C.: Georgetown University Press.

Larsen-Freeman, Diane, and Michael H. Long. 1991. *An introduction to Second Language Acquisition research.* London: Longman.

León, Víctor. 1988. *Diccionario de argot español.* Madrid: Alianza Editorial.

Liceras, Juana. 1993a. Los principios de la gramática universal. In *La lingüística y el análisis de los sistemas no nativos*, ed. Juana Liceras, 24–58. Ottawa Hispanic Studies 12. Ottawa: Dovehouse Editions Canada.

———, ed. 1993b. *La lingüística y el análisis de los sistemas no nativos.* Ottawa Hispanic Studies 12. Ottawa: Dovehouse Editions Canada.

Liceras, Juana, B. Soloaga, and A. Carballo. 1992. Los conceptos de tema y rema: problemas sintácticos y estilísticos de la adquisición del español. *Hispanic Linguistics* 5:43–88.

Lindstrom, Naomi. 1980. Making the bilingual dictionary safer for students. *Hispania* 63: 718–22.

Lipski, John. 1978. Subjunctive as fact? *Hispania* 61:931–34.

———. 1989. Beyond the isogloss: Trends in Hispanic dialectology. *Hispania* 72:801–9.

———. 1994. *Latin American Spanish.* London: Longman.

———. 1998. Spanish linguistics, the past 100 years: Retrospective and bibliography. *Hispania* 81:248–60.

Liskin-Gasparro, Judith. 2000. The use of tense-aspect morphology in Spanish oral narratives: Exploring the perceptions of advanced learners. *Hispania* 83:829–44.

Lombardi, Ronald, and Amalia Boero de Peters. 1981. *Modern spoken Spanish: An interdisciplinary perspective*. Washington, D.C.: University Press of America.

Long, Donna Reseigh. 1999. Methodology and the teaching of Spanish in the twentieth century: A retrospective and bibliography (1900–99). *Hispania* 83: 711–32.

Lope Blanch, Juan. 1963. En torno a las vocales caedizas del español mexicano. *Nueva revista de filología hispana* 17:1–19.

———. 1992. La falsa imagen del español americano. *Revista de filología española*: 72:313–35.

López Ortega, Nuria. 2000. Tense, aspect, and narrative structure in Spanish as a second language. *Hispania* 83:488–502.

Lozano, Anthony. 1970. Non-reflexivity of the indefinite *se* in Spanish. *Hispania* 53:452–57.

———. 1972. Subjunctives, transformations, and features in Spanish. *Hispania* 55:76–90.

———. 1975. In defense of two subjunctives. *Hispania* 58:277–83.

———. 1995. Cognitive development, deontic and epistemic subjunctives. *Hispanic Linguistics* 6/7:93–115.

———. 1997. Spanish reflexives: A critique of pedagogical descriptions. *Hispania* 80:549–55.

Lozano Domingo, Irene. 1995. *Lenguaje femenino, lenguaje masculino: ¿condiciona nuestro sexo la forma de hablar?* Madrid: Minerva Ediciones.

Lunn, Patricia, and Jane Albrecht. 1997. The grammar of technique: Inside *Continuidad de los parques*. *Hispania* 80:227–33.

MacDonald, Marguerite. 1989. The influence of Spanish phonology on the English spoken by United States Hispanics. In *American Spanish pronunciation*, ed. Peter Bjarkman and Robert Hammond, 215–36. Washington, D.C.: Georgetown University Press.

Mackenzie, Ian. 1995. The supposed imperfectivity of the Latin American present perfect. *Hispanic Linguistics* 6/7:29–60.

Marcos, Marcelino. 1993. La inversión del sujeto en las construcciones interrogativas del español no nativo. In *La lingüística y el análisis de los sistemas no nativos*, ed. Juana Liceras, 196–217. Ottawa Hispanic Studies 12. Ottawa: Dovehouse Editions Canada.

Marrero, Victoria. 1990. Estudio acústico de la aspiración en español. *Revista de filología española* 70:346–97.

Marrone, Nila. 1974. Investigación sobre variaciones léxicas en el mundo hispano. *Bilingual Review/Revista Bilingüe* 1:152–68.

Medina Rivera, Antonio. 1999. Variación fonológica y estilística en el español de Puerto Rico. *Hispania* 82:529–41.

Mejías Bikandi, Errapel. 1994. Assertion and speaker's intention: A pragmatically based account of mood in Spanish. *Hispania* 77:892–902.

———. 1998. Pragmatic presupposition and old information in the use of the subjunctive mood in Spanish. *Hispania* 81:941–48.

Meyer, Paula. 1972. Some observations on constituent order in Spanish. In *Generative studies in Romance languages*, ed. Jean Casagrande and Bohdan Saciuk, 184–95. Rowley, Mass.: Newbury House.

Michalson, Dorothy, and Charlotte Aires. 1981. *Spanish grammar: Un buen repaso*. Englewood Cliffs, N.J.: Prentice Hall.

Miles, Cecil, and Romelia Arciniegas. 1983. *Tener a*—a Spanish myth. *Hispania* 66:84–87.

Monroy Casas, Rafael. 1980. *Aspectos fonéticos de las vocales españolas*. Madrid: Sociedad General Española de Librería.

Montaño Harmon, María Rosario. 1991. Discourse features of written Mexican Spanish: Current research in contrastive rhetoric and its implications. *Hispania* 74:417–25.

Moody, Raymond. 1971. More on teaching Spanish adjective position. *Hispania* 54:315–21.

Moreno de Alba, José. 1978. *Valores de las formas verbales en el español de México*. México: Universidad Autónoma de México.

Moulton, William G. 1970. *A linguistic guide to language learning*. Menasha, Wisc.: Modern Language Association.

Mujica, Barbara. 1982. *Entrevista*. New York: Holt, Rinehart and Winston.

Nash, Rose, ed. 1973. *Readings in Spanish-English contrastive linguistics*. San Juan, P.R.: Inter American University Press.

Nash, Rose, and Domitila Belaval, eds. 1982. *Readings in Spanish-English contrastive linguistics III*. San Juan: Inter American University Press.

Navarro Tomás, Tomás. 1948. *El español en Puerto Rico: contribución a la geografía lingüística hispanoamericana*. Río Piedras, P.R.: Universidad de Puerto Rico.

———. 1967. *Manual de pronunciación española*. 6th ed. New York: Hafner.

———. 1975. *Capítulos de geografía lingüística de la península ibérica*. Bogotá: Instituto Caro y Cuervo.

Navas Ruiz, Ricardo. 1963. Ser y estar: *estudio sobre el sistema atributivo del español*. Acta Salmanticensia: Serie de Filosofía y Letras, vol. 17, no. 3. Salamanca: Talleres Gráficos Cervantes.

Núñez Cedeño, Rafael. 1991. Headship assignment resolution in Spanish compounds. In *Current studies in Spanish linguistics*, ed. Héctor Campos and Fernando Martínez Gil, 573–98. Washington, D.C.: Georgetown University Press.

Núñez Cedeño, Rafael, and Alfonso Morales Front. 1999. *Fonología generativa contemporánea de la lengua española*. Washington, D.C.: Georgetown University Press.

Obaid, Antonio. 1973. The vagaries of the Spanish *S*. *Hispania* 56: 60–67.

Ocampo, Francisco. 1991. Word order in constructions with a one-valency verb, a subject NP, and a PP in spoken Rioplatense Spanish. *Hispania* 74:409–16.

O'Grady, William, John Archibald, Mark Aronoff, and Janie Rees-Miller. 2001. *Contemporary linguistics: An introduction*. 4th ed. Boston: Bedford/St. Martin's.

Olbertz, Hella. 1998. *Verbal periphrases in a functional grammar of Spanish*. Berlin: Mouton de Gruyter.

Omaggio Hadley, Alice. 1993. *Teaching language in context*. 2nd ed. Boston: Heinle & Heinle.

Oroz, Rodolfo. 1966. *La lengua castellana en Chile*. Santiago: Facultad de Filosofía y Educación, Universidad de Chile.

Osgood, Charles E. 1963. Linguistic universals and psycholinguistics. In *Universals of language*, ed. Joseph Greenberg, 299–322. Cambridge, Mass.: MIT Press.

Otaola Olano, Concepción. 1988. La modalidad (con especial referencia a la lengua española). *Revista de filología española* 78:97–117.

Otheguy, Ricardo. 1978. A semantic analysis of the difference between *el/la* and *lo*. In *Contemporary studies in Romance linguistics*, ed. Margarita Suñer, 241–57. Washington, D.C.: Georgetown University Press.

Ozete, Oscar. 1981. Current usage of relative pronouns in Spanish. *Hispania* 64:85–91.

———. 1983. On the so-called Spanish gerund/participle. *Hispania* 66:75–83.

Pennington, Martha C. 1998. The teachability of phonology in adulthood: A re-examination. *International Review of Applied Linguistics* 36/4:323–41.

Penny, Ralph. 2000. *Variation and change in Spanish*. Cambridge: Cambridge University Press.

Pensado, Carmen. 1995. *El complemento directo preposicional*. Madrid: Visor Libros.

Pérez-Leroux, Ana Teresa, and William Glass, eds. 1997. *Contemporary perspectives on the acquisition of Spanish*. 2 vols. Somerville, Mass.: Cascadilla Press.

Perissinotto, Giorgio. 1975. *Fonología del español hablado en la ciudad de México: ensayo de un método sociolingüístico*. Translated by Raúl Ávila. México: Colegio de México.

Perlmutter, David. 1971. *Deep and surface structure constraints in syntax*. New York: Holt, Rinehart and Winston.

Pike, Kenneth. 1954, 1955, 1960. *Language in relation to a unified theory of the structure of human behavior.* Glendale, Calif.: Summer Institute of Linguistics.

Pilleux, Mauricio, and Hernán Urrutia. 1982. *Gramática transformacional del español*. Madrid: Ediciones Alcalá.

Placencia, María. 1995. Explicitness and ellipsis as features of conversational style in British English and Ecuadorian Spanish. *International Review of Applied Linguistics* 33/2:129–41.

Poplack, Shana. 1980. Deletion and disambiguation in Puerto-Rican Spanish. *Language* 56:371–85.

Prado, Marcial. 1982. El género español y la teoría de la marcadez. *Hispania* 65:258–66.

———. 1989. Aspectos semánticos de la pluralización. *Hispanic Linguistics* 3:163–83.

Price, Laurie. 1987. Ecuadorian illness stories: Cultural knowledge in natural discourse. In *Cultural models in language and thought,* ed. Dorothy Holland and Naomi Quinn, 313–42. Cambridge: Cambridge University Press.

Quilis, Antonio, and Joseph A. Fernández. 1975. *Curso de fonética y fonología españolas para estudiantes anglo-americanos*. 8th ed. Madrid: Instituto Cervantes, Consejo Superior de Investigaciones Científicas.

Quilis, Antonio, and Matilde Graell Stanziola. 1992. La lengua española en Panamá. *Revista de filología española* 72:583–638.

Quilis-Sanz, María José. 1998. Las consonantes [-r] y [-l] implosivas en Andalucía. *Revista de filología española* 78:125–56.

Quirk, Randolph, Sidney Greenbaum, Geoffrey Leach, and Jan Svartvik. 1972. *A grammar of contemporary English*. London: Longman.

Ramsey, Marathon. [1894] 1956, revised by Robert Spaulding. *A textbook of modern Spanish*. New York: Holt, Rinehart and Winston.

Ranson, Diana. 1993. The interaction of linguistic and contextual number markers in Andalusian Spanish. *Hispania* 76:919–30.

Real Academia Española. 1924. *Gramática de la lengua española*. Madrid: Perlado, Páez.

———. 1956. *Diccionario de la lengua española.* 19th ed. Madrid: Espasa Calpe.

———. 1979. *Esbozo de una nueva gramática de la lengua española*. Madrid: Espasa Calpe.

———. 1992. *Diccionario de la lengua española.* 21st ed. Madrid: Espasa Calpe.

Reider, Michael. 1989. Clitic promotion, the evaluated proposition constraint, and mood in Spanish verbal complements. *Hispania* 72:283–94.

———. 1990. Neg-transportation, Neg-trace, and the choice of mood in Spanish. *Hispania* 73:212–22.

Resnick, Melvyn C. 1975. *Phonological variants and dialect identification in Latin American Spanish*. The Hague: Mouton.

———. 1981. *Introducción a la historia de la lengua española*. Washington, D.C.: Georgetown University Press.

———. 1984. Spanish verb tenses: Their names and meanings. *Hispania* 67:92–99.

Richards, Jack C., ed. 1974. *Error analysis: Perspectives on second language acquisition*. London: Longman.

Rivero, María-Luisa. 1971. Una restricción de la estructura superficial sobre la negación en español. In *Los fundamentos de la gramática transformacional,* ed. Heles Contreras. México: Siglo Veintiuno.

Rivers, Wilga. 1981. *Teaching foreign-language skills.* 2nd ed. Chicago: University of Chicago Press.

Rivers, Wilga, Milton Azevedo, and William Heflin Jr. 1988. *Teaching Spanish: A practical guide*. Chicago: National Textbook Company.

Roldán, Mercedes. 1971a. The double object constructions of Spanish. *Language Sciences* 1971, no. 15: 8–14.

———. 1971b. Spanish constructions with *se*. *Language Sciences* 1971, no. 18: 15–29.

———. 1973. Reflexivization in Spanish. In *Readings in Spanish-English contrastive linguistics*, ed. Rose Nash, 197–219. San Juan, P.R.: Inter American University Press.

———. 1974. Constraints on clitic insertion in Spanish. In *Linguistic studies in Romance languages*, ed. Joe Campbell, Mark Goldin, and Mary Wang, 124–38. Washington, D.C.: Georgetown University Press.

Saciuk, Bohdan. 1980. Estudio comparativo de las realizaciones fonéticas de /y/ en dos dialectos del Caribe hispánico. In *Dialectología hispanoamericana: estudios actuales*, ed. Gary Scavnicky, 16–31. Washington, D.C.: Georgetown University Press.

Salaberry, M. Rafael. 1999. The development of past tense verbal morphology in classroom L2 Spanish. *Applied Linguistics* 20/2:151–78.

Sallese, Nicholas, and Oscar Fernández de la Vega. 1968. *Repaso: gramática moderna.* New York: Van Nostrand.

Sánchez, Rosaura. 1982. Our linguistic and social context. In *Spanish in the United States: Sociolinguistic aspects*, ed. Jon Amastae and Lucía Elías Olivares, 9–46. Cambridge: Cambridge University Press.

Saporta, Sol. 1956. A note on Spanish semivowels. *Language* 32:287–90.

———. 1959. Morpheme alternants in Spanish. In *Structural studies on Spanish themes,* ed. Henry Kahane and Angelina Pietrangeli. Acta Salmanticensia: Serie de Filosofía y Letras, vol. 12, no. 3. Salamanca: Universidad de Salamanca.

Saussure, Ferdinand de. [1915] 1959. *Course in general linguistics*. Compiled by Charles Bally and Albert Sechehaye. Translated by Wade Baskin. New York: McGraw-Hill.

Scavnicky, Gary, ed. 1980. *Dialectología hispanoamericana: estudios actuales*. Washington, D.C.: Georgetown University Press.

Selinker, Larry. 1972. Interlanguage. *International Review of Applied Linguistics* 10:209–30.

———. 1992. *Rediscovering interlanguage*. New York: Longman.

Serrano, María-José. 1998. Estudio sociolingüístico de una variante sintáctica: el fenómeno dequeísmo en el español canario. *Hispania* 81:392–405.

Sheen, Ronald. 1996. The advantage of exploiting contrastive analysis in teaching and learning a foreign language. *International Review of Applied Linguistics* 34/3:183–97.

Silva-Corvalán, Carmen. 1982. Subject expression and placement in Mexican-American Spanish. In *Spanish in the United States: Sociolinguistic aspects*, ed. Jon Amastae and Lucía Elías Olivares, 93–120. Cambridge: Cambridge University Press.

———. 1983. Tense and aspect in oral Spanish narrative. *Language* 59:760–80.

———, ed. 1995. *Spanish in four continents: Studies in language contact and bilingualism*. Washington, D.C.: Georgetown University Press.

Silva-Corvalán, Carmen, and Tracy D. Terrell. 1989. Notas sobre la expresión de futuridad en el español del Caribe. *Hispanic Linguistics* 2:191–208.

Smead, Robert. 1994. En torno al modo en oraciones seudo-escendidas y exclamativas: patrones entre monolingües y bilingües. *Hispania* 77:842–54.

Spann, Susan. 1984. To translate the English gerund into Spanish, don't use the infinitive. *Hispania* 67:232–9.

Steel, Brian. 1975. Checklists of basic "americanismos" and "castellanismos." *Hispania* 58:910–20.

———. 1985. *A textbook of colloquial Spanish*. Madrid: Sociedad General Española de Librería.

Stevick, Earl. 1976. *Memory, meaning, and method*. Rowley, Mass.: Newbury House.

Stewart, Miranda. 1999. *The Spanish language today*. London: Routledge.

Stiehm, Bruce. 1978. Teaching Spanish word order. *Hispania* 61:410–34.

Stockwell, Robert P., and J. Donald Bowen. 1965. *The sounds of English and Spanish*. Chicago: University of Chicago Press.

Stockwell, Robert P., J. Donald Bowen, and John Martin. 1965. *The grammatical structures of English and Spanish*. Chicago: University of Chicago Press.

Strozer, Judith. 1991. Non-native language acquisition from a Principles and Parameters perspective. In *Current studies in Spanish linguistics*, ed. Héctor Campos and Fernando Martínez Gil, 71–113. Washington, D.C.: Georgetown University Press.

Studerus, Lenard. 1979. A model of temporal reference for Spanish verbs. *Hispania* 62:332–36.

———. 1989. On the role of Spanish meaning-changing preterites. *Hispanic Linguistics* 3:131–45.

———. 1995. Some unresolved issues in Spanish mood use. *Hispania* 79:94–104.

Suñer, Margarita. 1974. Where does the impersonal *se* come from? In *Linguistic studies in Romance languages*, ed. Joe Campbell, Mark Goldin, and Mary Wang, 146–57. Washington, D.C.: Georgetown University Press.

———. 1981. *Por* vs. *de*: Agential prepositions? *Hispania* 64:278–83.

———. 1982. *Syntax and semantics of Spanish presentational sentence-types*. Washington, D.C.: Georgetown University Press.

———. 1989. Spanish syntax and semantics in the eighties: The Principles-and-Parameters approach. *Hispania* 72:832–47.

———. 2000. Some thoughts on *que*: Description, theory, and L2. *Hispania* 83:867–76.

———, ed. 1978. *Contemporary studies in Romance linguistics*. Washington, D.C.: Georgetown University Press.

Szabo, Robert. 1974. Deep and surface order of the Spanish clitics. In *Linguistic studies in Romance languages*, ed. Joe Campbell, Mark Goldin, and Mary Wang, 139–45. Washington, D.C.: Georgetown University Press.

Takagaki, Toshihiro. 1984. Subjunctive as the marker of subordination. *Hispania* 67:248–56.

Taylor, Gregory. 2002. Teaching gambits: The effect of instruction and task variation on the use of conversation strategies by intermediate Spanish students. *Foreign Language Annals* 35:172–89.

Terker, Andrew. 1985. On Spanish adjective position. *Hispania* 68:502–9.

Terrell, Tracy. 1989. Teaching Spanish pronunciation in a communicative approach. In *American Spanish pronunciation*, ed. Peter Bjarkman and Robert Hammond, 196–214. Washington, D.C.: Georgetown University Press.

Terrell, Tracy, and Joan Hooper. 1974. A semantically based analysis of mood in Spanish. *Hispania* 57:484–94.

Terrell, Tracy, and Maruxa Salgués de Cargill. 1979. *Lingüística aplicada a la enseñanza del español a anglohablantes*. New York: John Wiley and Sons.

Teschner, Richard V. 2000a. *Camino oral*. 2nd ed. Boston: McGraw Hill.

———. 2000b. *CUBRE: Curso breve de gramática española*. 3rd ed. Boston: McGraw-Hill.

Teschner, Richard V., and Jennifer Flemming. 1996. Special report: Conflicting data on Spanish intransitive verbs in two leading dictionaries. *Hispania* 79:477–90.

Tesnière, Lucien. 1959. *Éléments de syntaxe structurelle*. Paris: Klinksieck.

Toledo, Guillermo Andrés. 1988. *El ritmo del español: estudio fonético con base computacional*. Madrid: Editorial Gredos.

———. 1989. Organización temporal del español I: compresión silábica en la palabra. *Hispanic Linguistics* 2:209–28.

Torreblanca, Maximiliano. 1978. El fonema /s/ en la lengua española. *Hispania* 61:498–503.

———. 1980. Factores condicionadores de la distribución de los alófonos consonánticos españoles. *Hispania* 63:730–6.

Torrejón, Alfredo.1991. Fórmulas de tratamiento de segunda persona singular en el español de Chile. *Hispania* 74:1068–76.

Uber, Diana Ringer. 1985. The dual function of *usted*: Forms of address in Bogotá, Colombia. *Hispania* 68:388–92.

———. 1989. Noun phrase pluralization in the Spanish of Cuban Mariel Entrants. *Hispanic Linguistics* 3:75–88.

Valdés, Guadalupe, Trisha Dvorak, and Thomasina Hannum. 1999. *Composición: proceso y síntesis*. 3rd ed. Boston: McGraw-Hill.

Van Els, Theo, with Theo Bongaerts, Guus Extra, Charles van Os, and Anne-Mieke Janssen-van Dieten. 1984. *Applied linguistics and the learning and teaching of foreign languages*. Translated by R. R. van Oirsouw. Baltimore: Edward Arnold.

VanPatten, Bill. 1985. The acquisition of *ser* and *estar* by adult learners of Spanish: A preliminary investigation of transitional stages of competence. *Hispania* 68:399–411.

———. 1987. On babies and bathwater: Input in foreign language learning. *Modern Language Journal* 71:156–64.

———. 1997. The relevance of input processing to second language theory and teaching. In *Contemporary perspectives on the acquisition of Spanish*, ed. Ana Teresa Pérez-Leroux and William Glass, 2:93–108. Somerville, Mass.: Cascadilla Press.

Varela Ortega, Soledad. 1990. *Fundamentos de morfología*. Madrid: Editorial Síntesis.

Vásquez Ayora, Gerardo. 1977. *Introducción a la traductología.* Washington, D.C.: Georgetown University Press.

Weissenrieder, Maureen. 1991. A functional approach to the accusative *a*. *Hispania* 74:146–56.

———. 1995. Indirect object doubling: Saying things twice in Spanish. *Hispania* 78:169–77.

Wells, J. C. 1982. *Accents of English.* Cambridge: Cambridge University Press.

Whitley, M. Stanley. 1978. Person and number in the use of *we, you, they*. *American Speech* 53:18–39.

———. 1986a. *How*—the missing interrogative in Spanish. *Hispania* 69:82–96.

———. 1986b. Cláusula e infinitivo tras verbos y preposiciones. *Hispania* 69:669–76.

———. 1990. Pronombres que no lo son: aspectos descriptivos y pedagógicos. *Hispania* 73:1106–17.

———. 1995a. *Gustar* and other psych verbs: A problem in transitivity. *Hispania* 78:573–85.

———. 1995b. Spanish glides, hiatus, and conjunction lowering. *Hispanic Linguistics* 6/7:355–85.

———. 1999. Psych verbs: Transitivity adrift. *Hispanic Linguistics* 10:115–53.

Whitley, M. Stanley, and Luis González. 2000. *Gramática para la composición.* Washington, D.C.: Georgetown University Press.

Whorf, Benjamin Lee. 1956. *Language, thought, and reality.* Cambridge, Mass.: MIT Press.

Wonder, John. 1981. The determiner + adjective phrase in Spanish. *Hispania* 64:348–59.

Zagona, Karen. 1991. Perfective *haber* and the theory of tenses. In *Current studies in Spanish linguistics*, ed. Héctor Campos and Fernando Martínez Gil, 379–403. Washington, D.C.: Georgetown University Press.

Zamora Vicente, Alonso. 1967. *Dialectología española.* Madrid: Editorial Gredos.

Zampini, Mary. 1994. The role of native language transfer and task formality in the acquisition of Spanish spirantization. *Hispania* 77:470–81.

———. 1998. L2 Spanish spirantization: A prosodic analysis and pedagogical implications. *Hispanic Linguistics* 10/1:154–88.

Zierer, Ernesto. 1974. *The qualifying adjective in Spanish.* The Hague: Mouton.

Zlotchew, Clark. 1977. The Spanish subjunctive: Non-experience or emotion. *Hispania* 60:938–9.

General index

The following index refers to section numbers and includes topics, terms, and abbreviations (**bolded**) featured in this book. For phonetic symbols, phonemes, and allophones, see the separate Phonological Index (appendix 2).